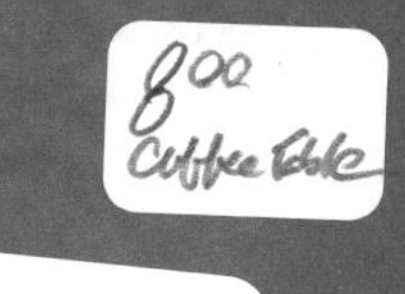

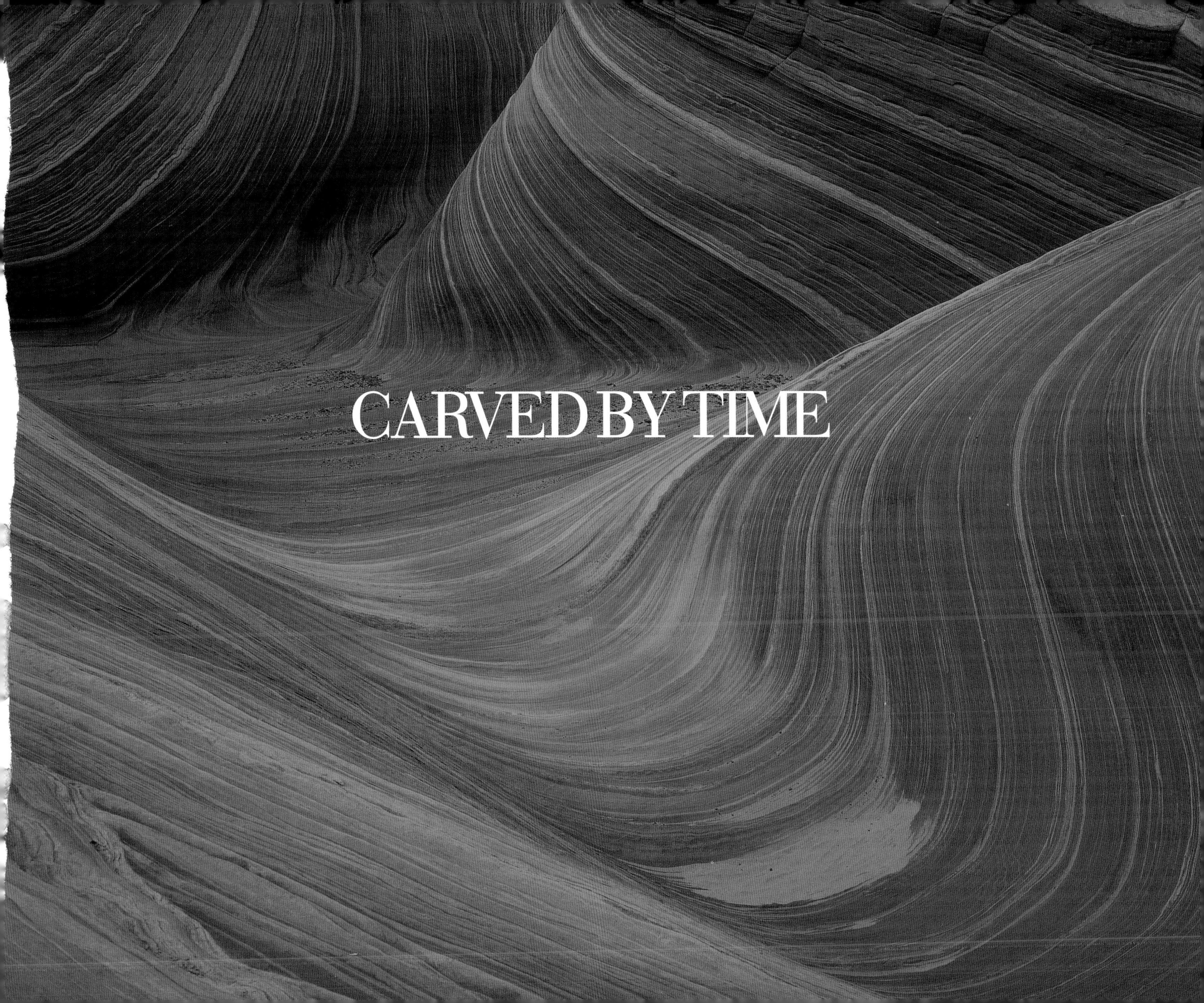
CARVED BY TIME

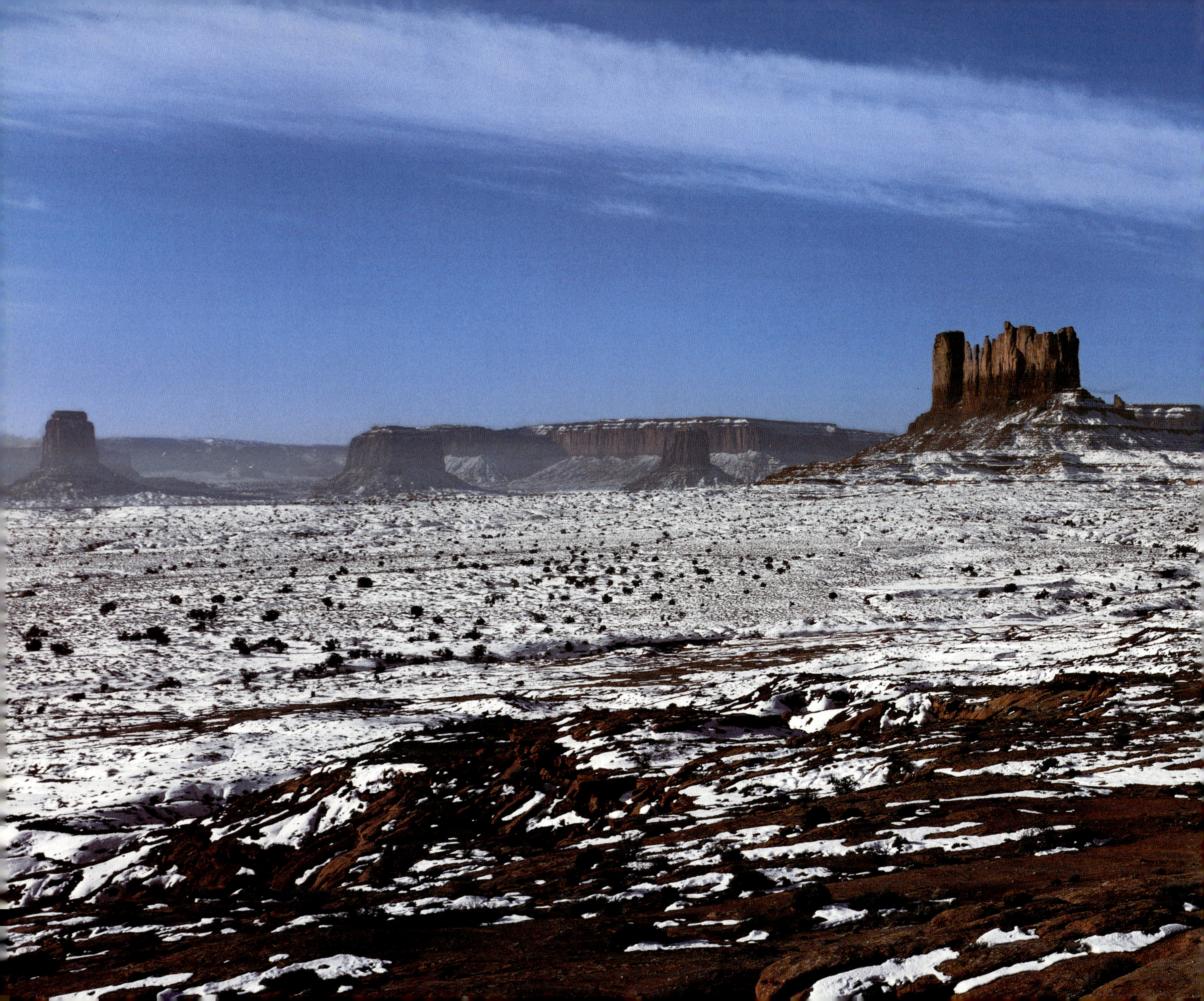

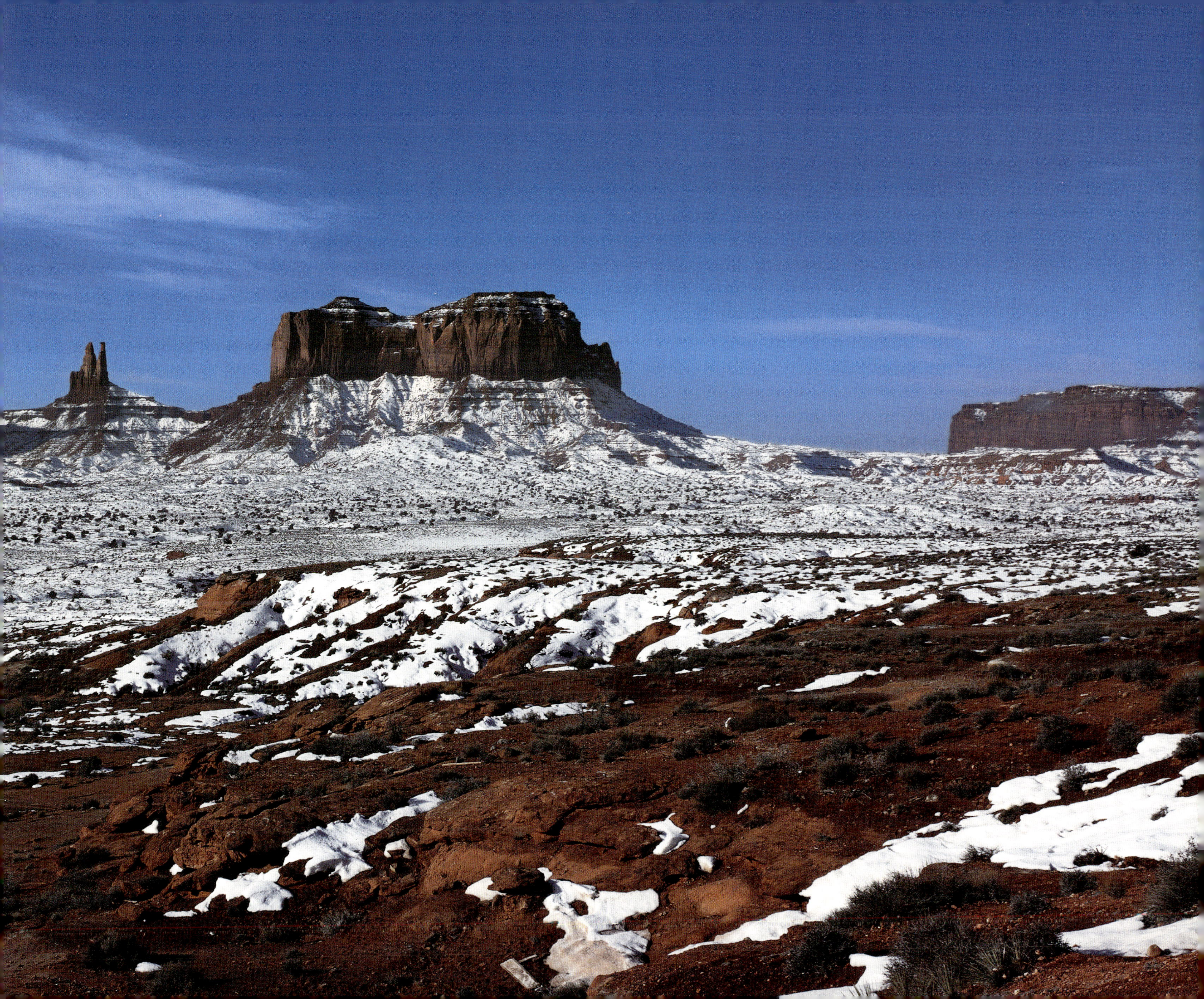

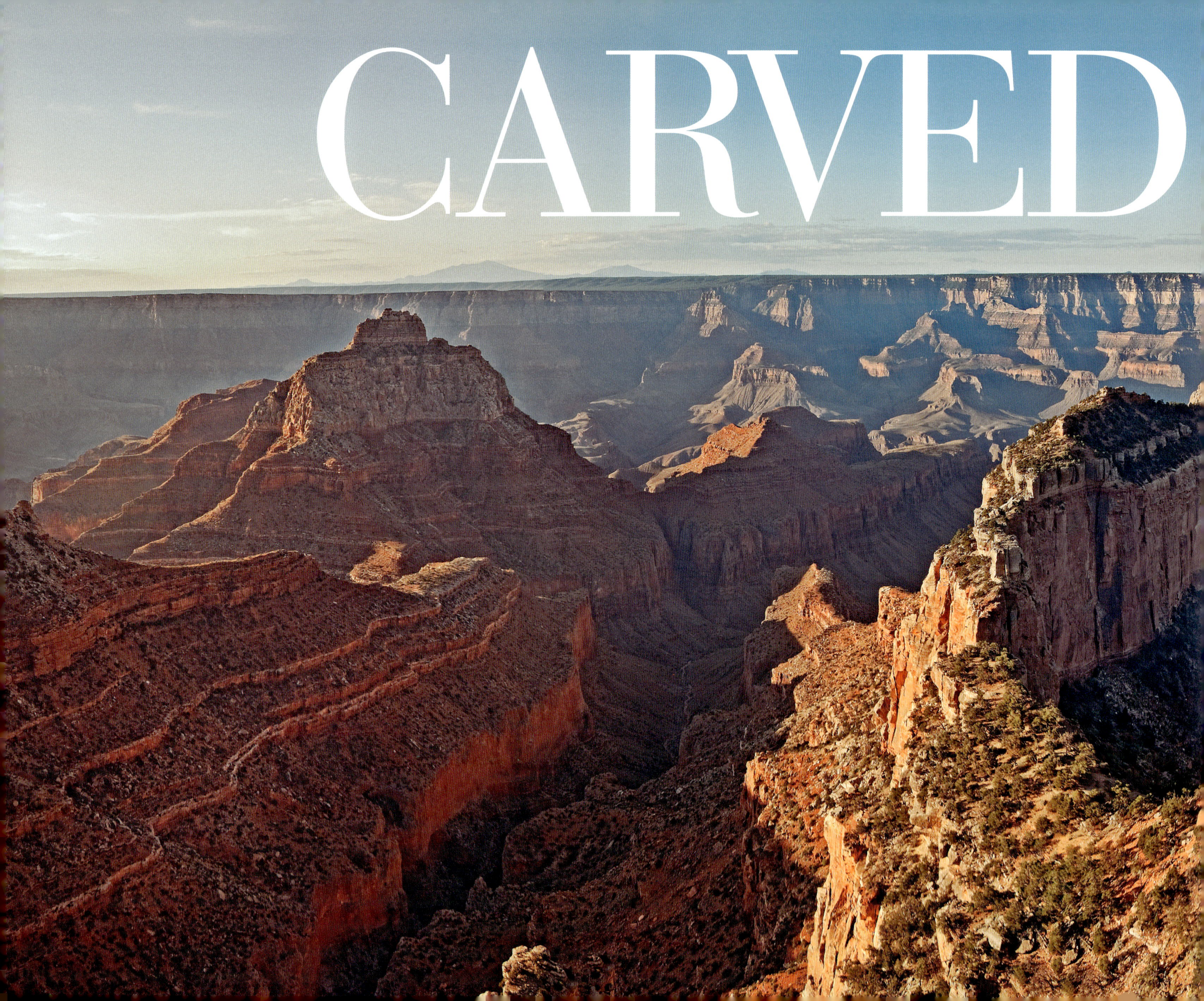
CARVED

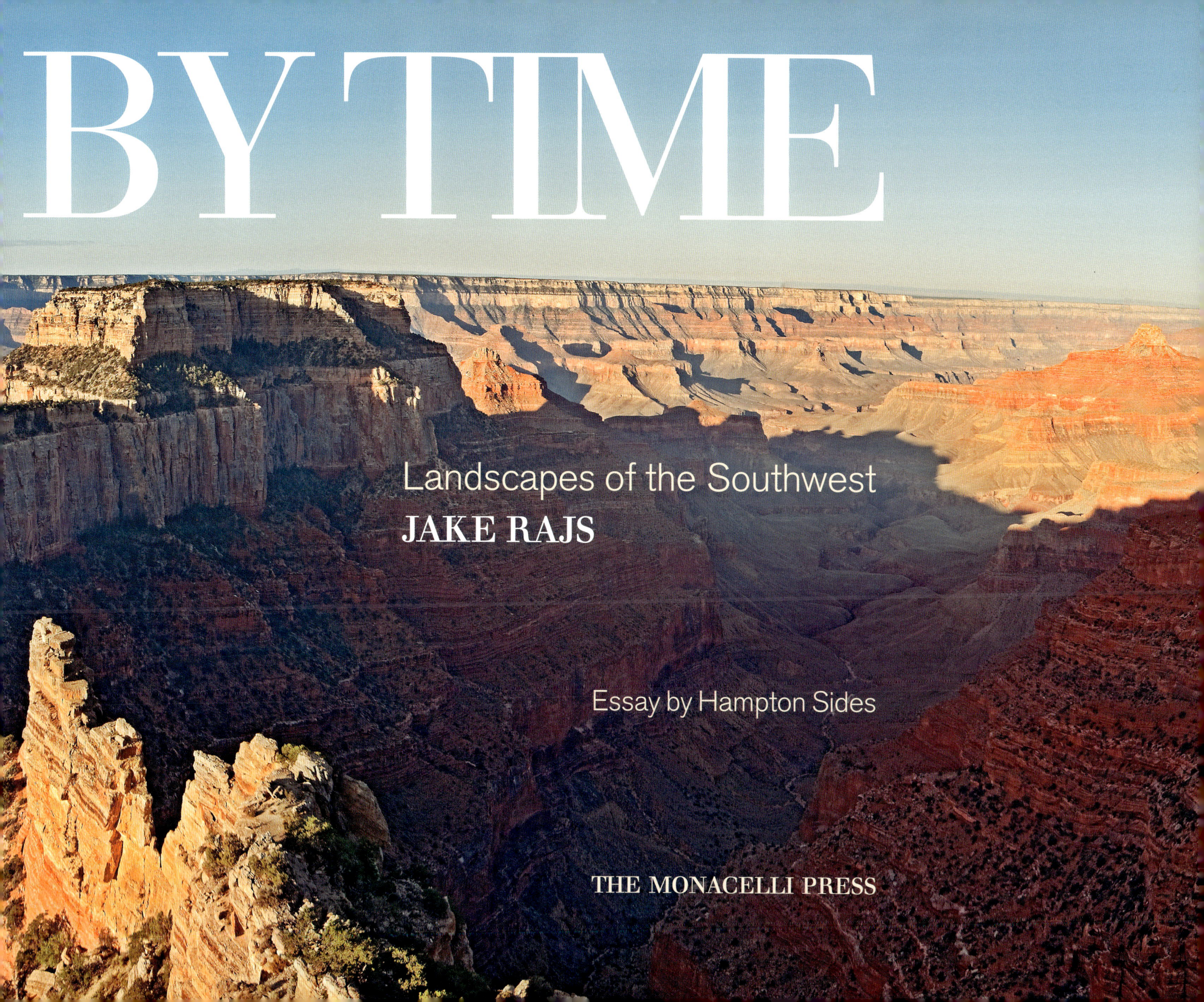
BY TIME
Landscapes of the Southwest
JAKE RAJS
Essay by Hampton Sides
THE MONACELLI PRESS

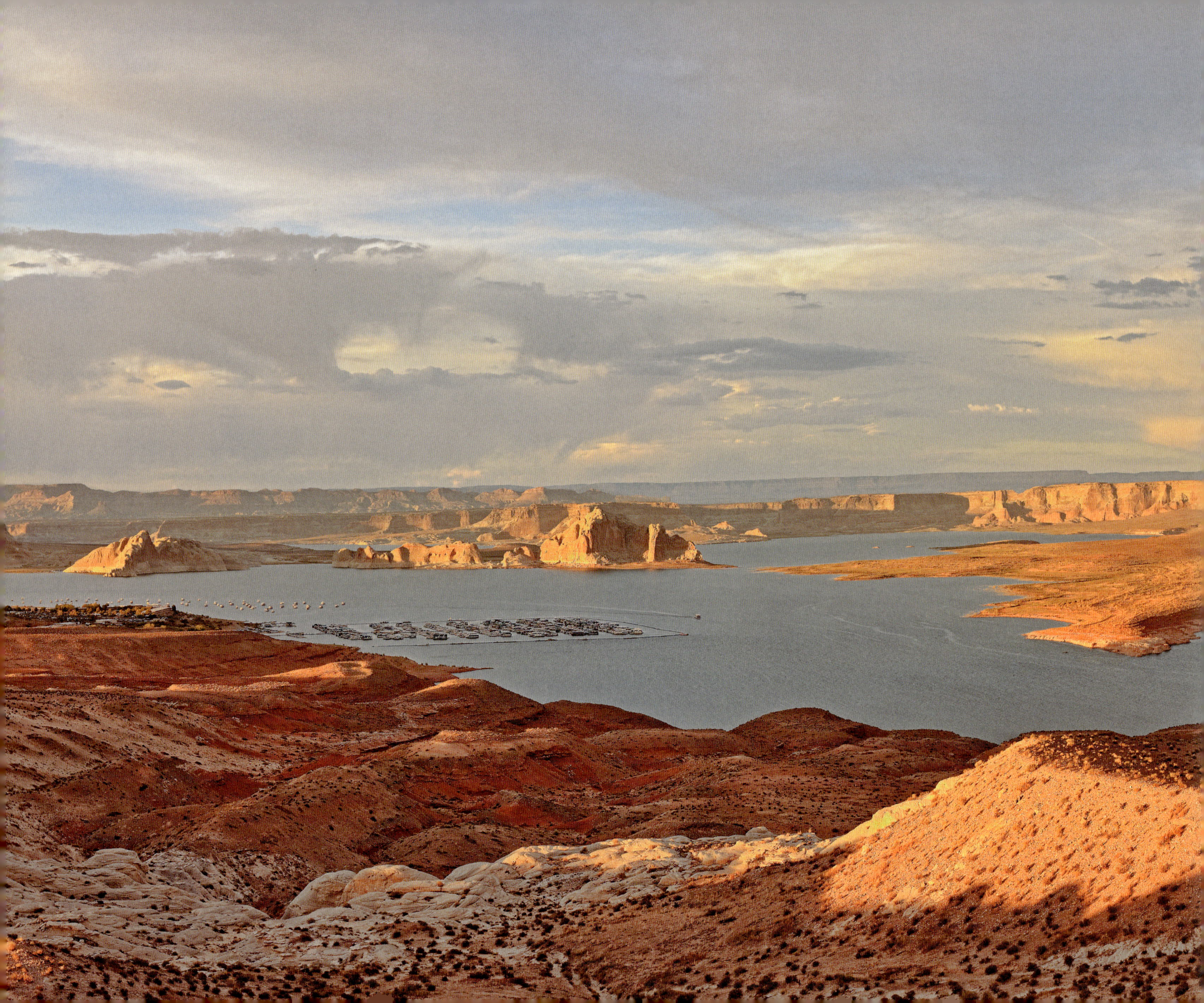

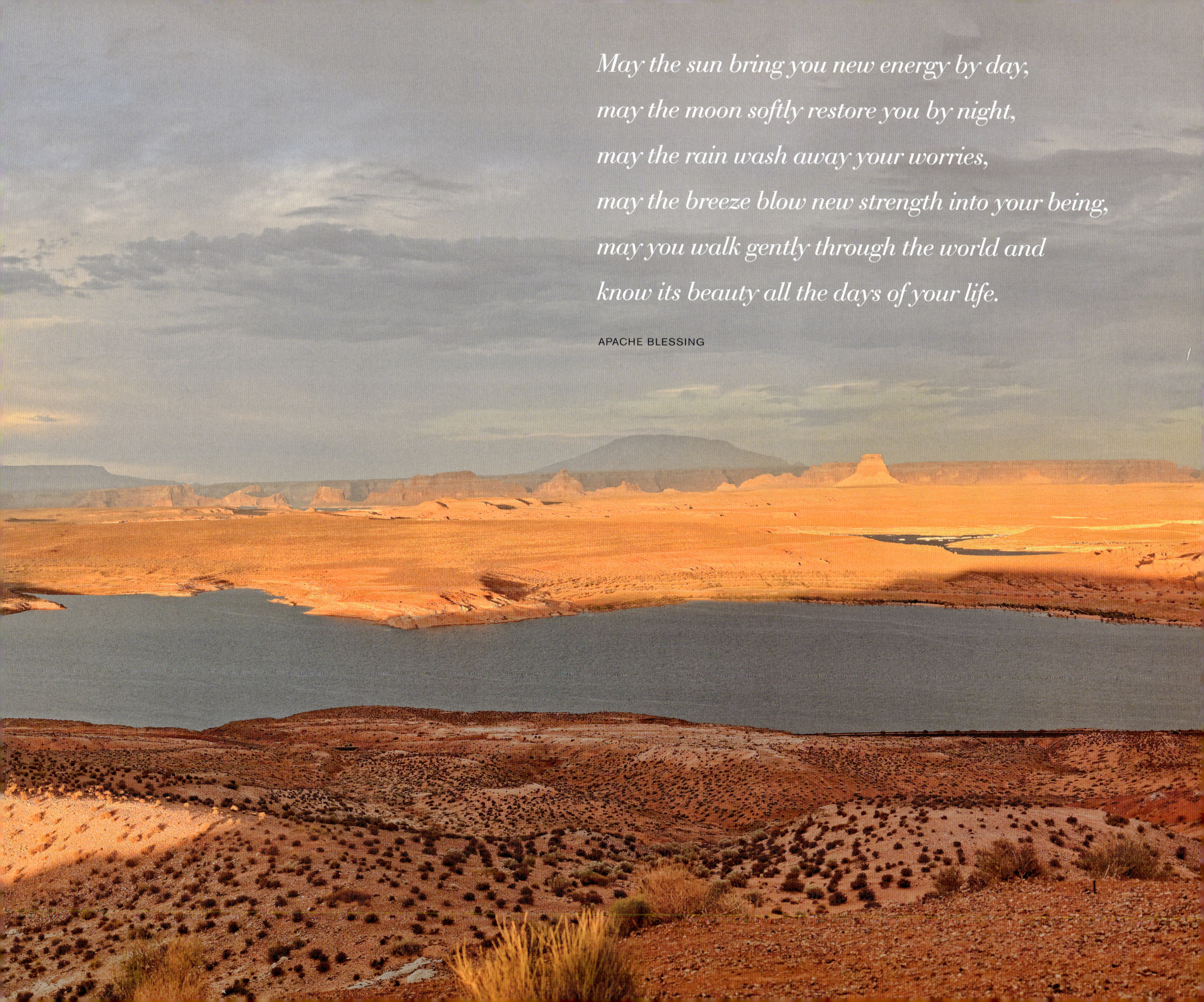

May the sun bring you new energy by day,
may the moon softly restore you by night,
may the rain wash away your worries,
may the breeze blow new strength into your being,
may you walk gently through the world and
know its beauty all the days of your life.

APACHE BLESSING

Published in the United States by
The Monacelli Press, a division of
Random House, New York.

The Monacelli Press and the M design
are registered trademarks of
Random House, Inc.

ISBN: 978-158093-218-9
Library of Congress Control Number:
2010921724

Designed by Joseph Guglietti
Printed in China

www. monacellipress.com

10 9 8 7 6 5 4 3 2 1

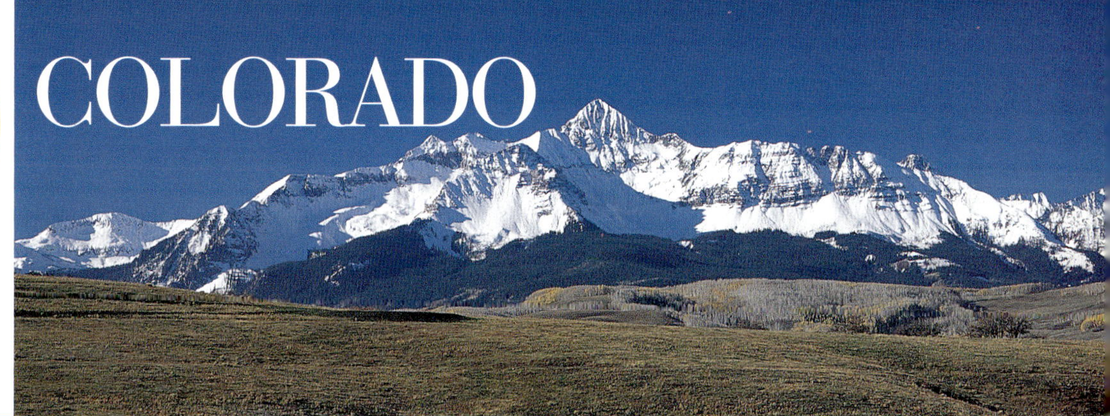

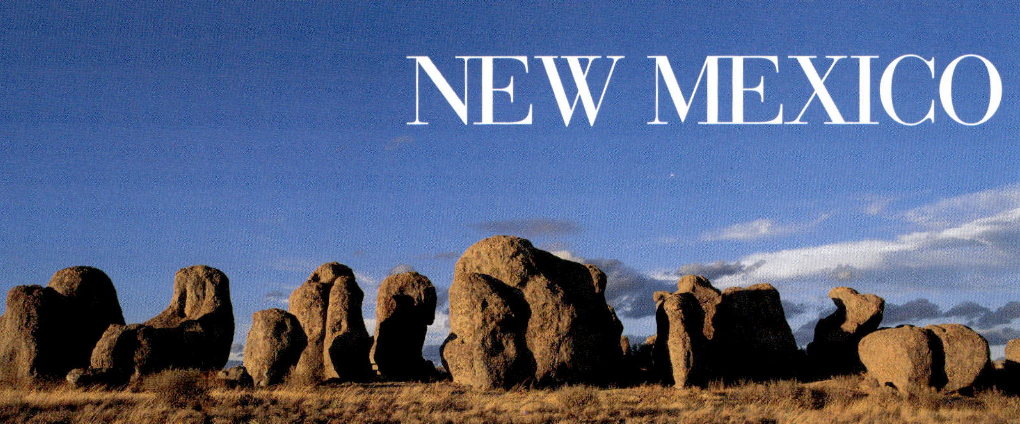

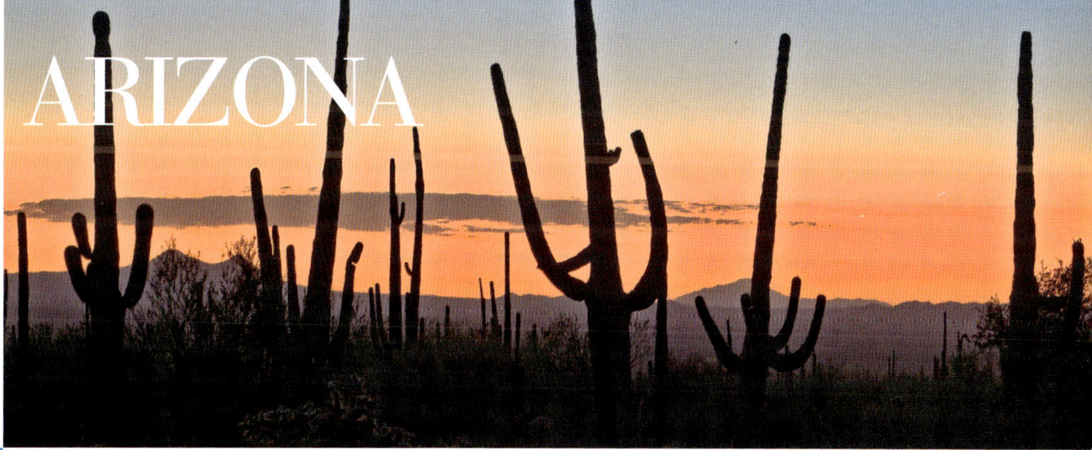

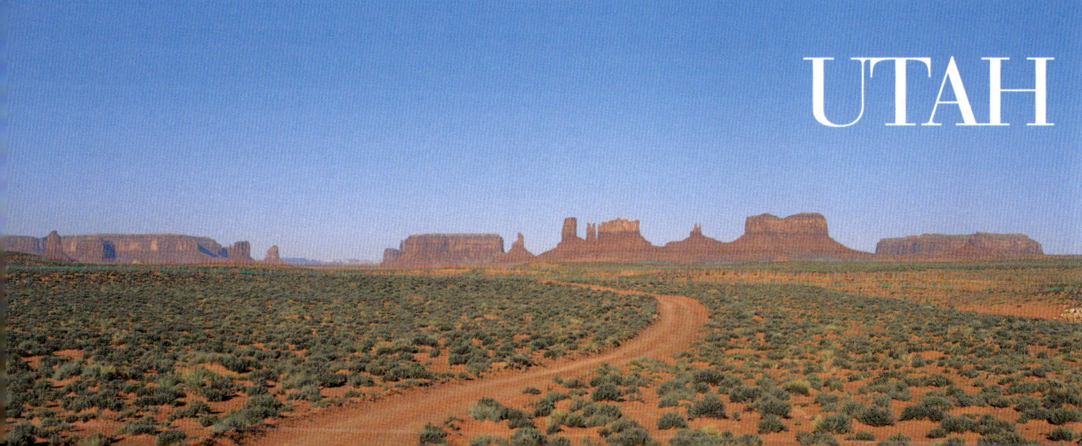

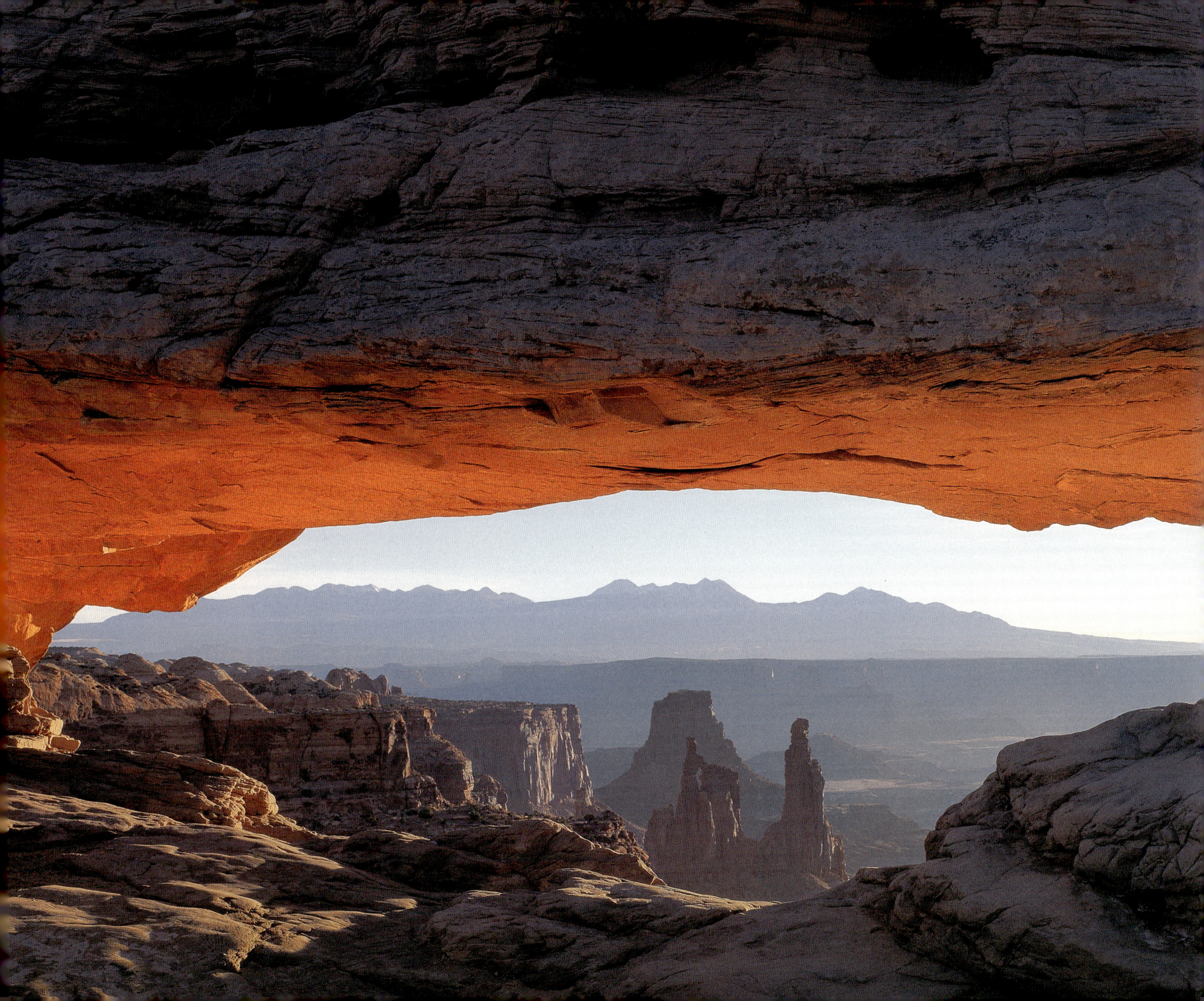

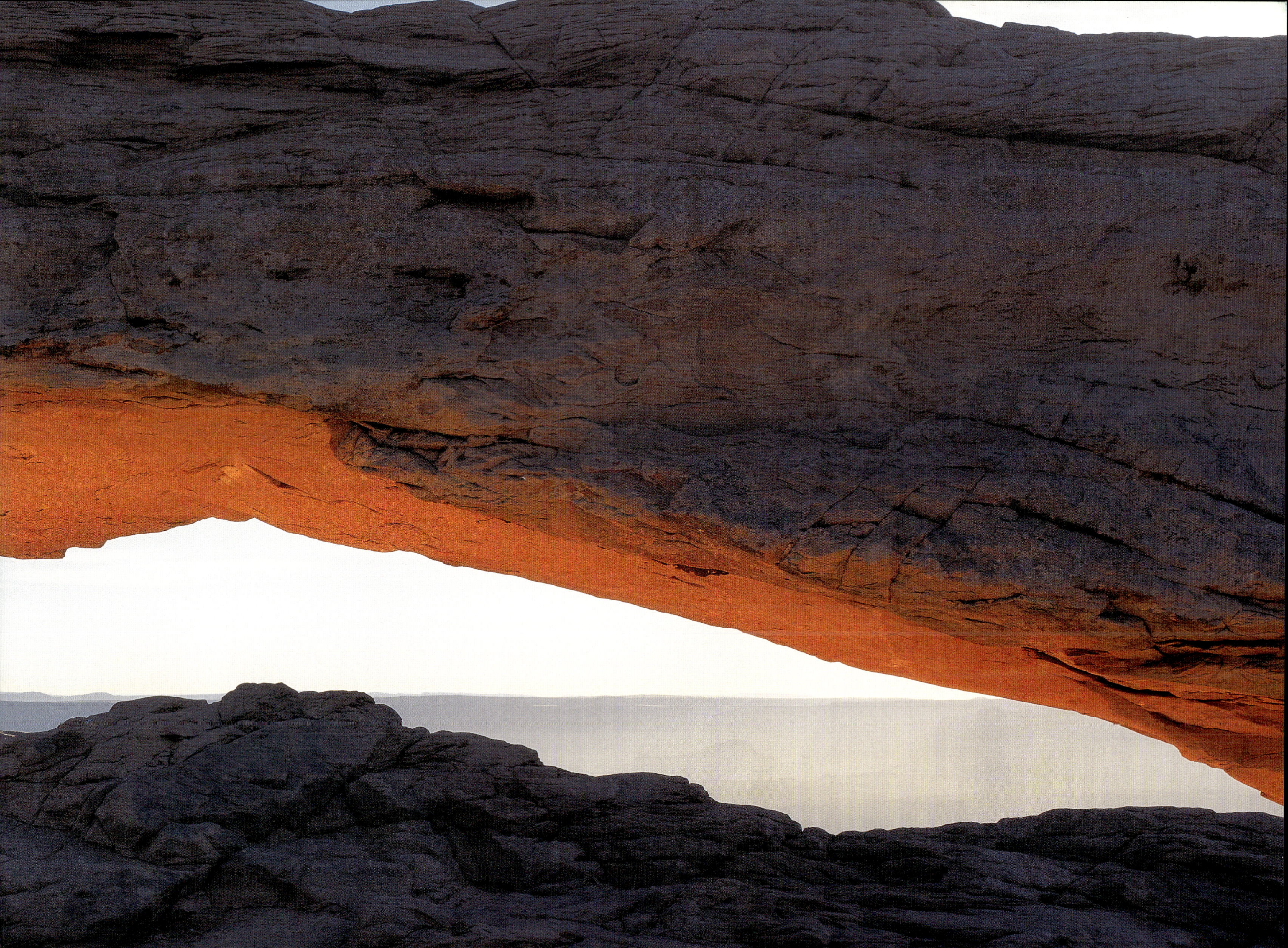

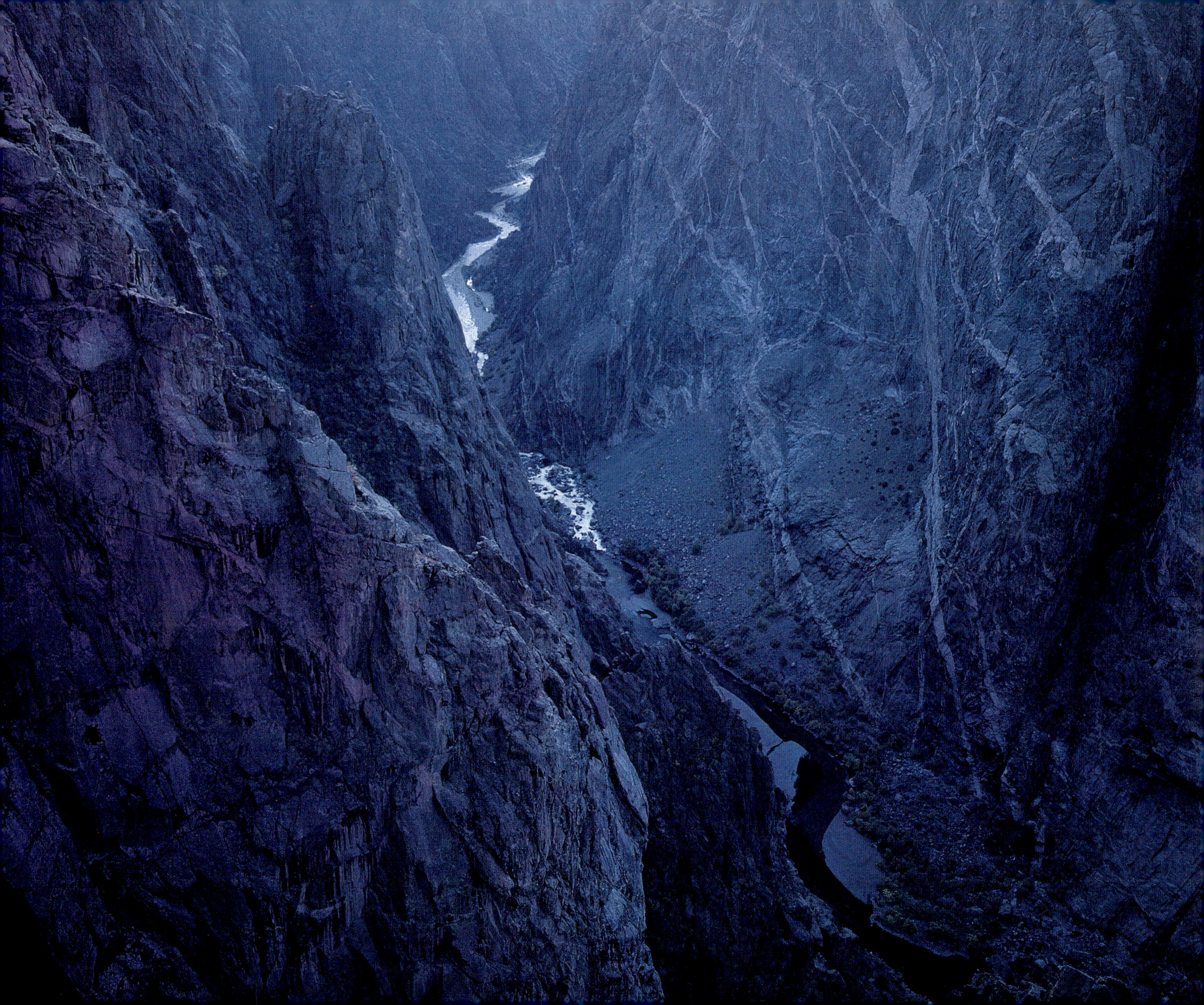

NATURE, EXPOSED

Hampton Sides

FOR THOSE OF US who are drawn to the Desert Southwest, and especially for those of us who're lucky enough to live in its abiding magnificence, this book is not only a work of art—it's a reaffirmation of a love affair, a kind of renewal of vows. When I first came to live in New Mexico, fifteen years ago, I went around for months with a dumbfounded expression on my face. I couldn't believe I lived here, amongst all this surreal and spectral beauty. I couldn't shake my enchantment with this high and dry landscape—a landscape so different from the South where I was raised, or from the East where I'd lived most of my young adulthood. There was something about it, some delicate combination of the light, the latitude, the altitude, and the bone-dryness of the air, that was ineffably powerful. I really felt I'd landed in a part of heaven. Nearly every day, I saw dramas of geology and meteorology, dramas of wind and erosion, that slayed me.

My stupefaction eventually wore off, of course. New Mexico became my home, and its strange and dynamic beauty became—not ho-hum, by any means—but part of the daily panorama of my life.

The places that Jake Rajs has captured with such power and grace in these pages take me back to that first feeling of being utterly smitten with a landscape. There's no place like the Desert Southwest. It is real estate without peer, without comparison, *sui generis*. It's a land of parched canyons, bleached solitudes, and bulwarks of intoxicating rock. A land of sky islands, cinder cones, and mesas the size of battleships, crisscrossed by two great river drainages, the Colorado and the Rio Grande. It's the country made famous by Edward Abbey,

Black Canyon of the Gunnison National Park, Colorado

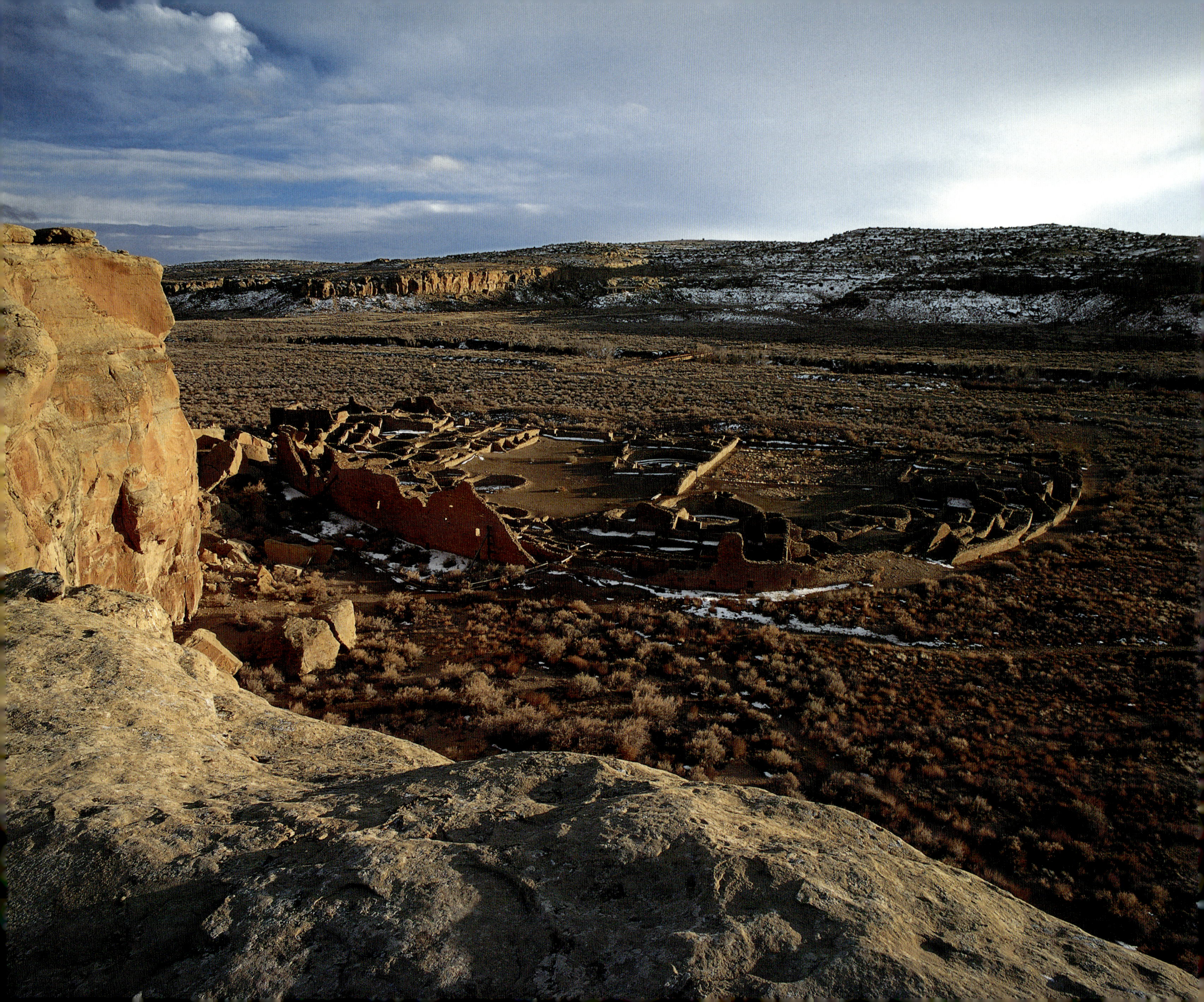

Wallace Stegner, and Georgia O'Keeffe, a queer world of upheaval and stark finality cooked in an unforgiving forge. The scale of it dwarfs human beings, not only spatially but also chronologically, suggesting chasms of time that mock our relevance in the story of creation. Walking over it, rafting through it, camping amongst it, we feel squishably insignificant—a feeling that I find paradoxically uplifting. To me, it's a source of solace to know that we're nothing, that nature always wins, and that, in the end, we homo not so sapiens are mere spore-specks in the record of time.

People didn't always regard this country as beautiful or uplifting—at least not Americans coming from the "civilized" East. When the Southwest became part of the United States, shortly after the Mexican War and the 1849 Treaty of Guadalupe Hidalgo, most visitors from the East found the place ugly, scary, and vaguely threatening: an alien slagheap. Early expeditions of the U.S. topographical corps found little to recommend, declaring it a "cursed land" and a "broken country." Senators in Washington seriously proposed giving it all back to Mexico. What was the point of it? You couldn't farm it, you couldn't settle it, and the land looked just plain weird. It was, they said, a *dead place*—geology without biology. People from greener, wetter climes seemed to lack the retinal nerve allowing them to see, and appreciate, the aesthetic of this high, arid world. It would take several generations before artists, poets, painters, photographers, and scientists (people like Edward Curtis, John Wesley Powell, Aldo Leopold, Ansel Adams, as well as O'Keeffe) began to put this strange country in proper perspective—and, finally, to call it beautiful.

Pueblo Bonito, Chaco Culture National Historical Park, New Mexico

JAKE RAJS has been coming out to the Southwest, and renewing his vows with the landscape, since 1976. His first visit took him to Monument Valley, that iconic place that over the decades has inspired John Ford films, Roadrunner cartoons, and countless artists. Monument Valley changed him forever, and helped shape him to become what he is today—one of America's preeminent landscape photographers. "In Monument Valley, I was transported," he says. "The light was clear and crisp, and had a vibrancy you don't get anywhere else. It was a landscape that took me out of myself."

Jake, who was born in Poland, lived as boy in Israel, and came to America on an immigrant ship, carries a bit of the outsider's perspective everywhere he goes. I see in these pages a freshness of wonder, a sense of the visitor forever encountering something new. I see glimmerings of that same dumbfoundedness I felt when I first moved here. In Chaco Canyon, in Arches and Mesa Verde and Zion—places that are no strangers to the lenses of great photographers—Jake manages to find fresh perspective and a note of hushed splendor. He sees life in rocks and ruins; he comes upon ancient things as though they were something entirely new. On some level, he's still an immigrant kid, enchanted by the novel spectacle in his viewfinder. "Beauty, when you stumble upon it, is the most powerful emotion," he says.

Jake has organized these photographs along the forthright theme of Colorado, New Mexico, Arizona, and Utah, the states that form the famous Four Corners, the only spot in the U.S. where four states meet at a single point. On a map, the region looks tidy, clean-lined,

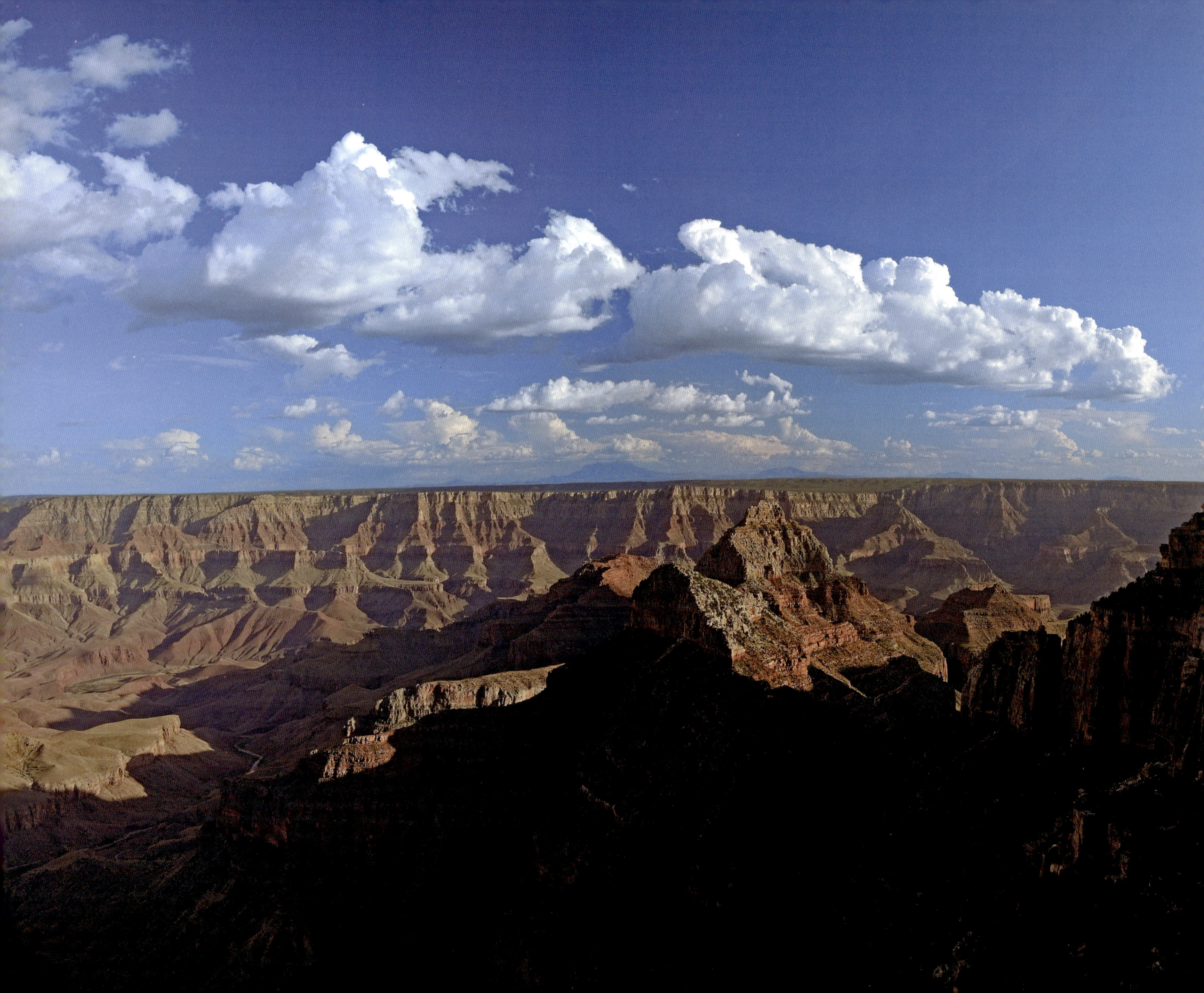

rigidly rectilinear, but nothing could be further from the truth on the ground. The country radiating outward from the Four Corners is perhaps the most wrinkled, most gnarled, and most dazzlingly convoluted wilderness in these United States, and any attempt to frame it in ruler-straight lines is of course a gross abstraction.

This is not only a topographical fact, but an anthropological one as well. Though the Desert Southwest is sparsely populated, it has been populated by multiple competing cultures for millennia, a crazy-quilt of warring and overlapping civilizations. Evidence of these civilizations can be found everywhere. Etched with petroglyphs and studded with ruins, the Four Corners is a wonderland of North American archaeology, having long attracted the lions of the field—people like Earl Morris and A.V. Kidder. Although New Mexico, Utah, and Arizona were among the last states in the Lower 48 to join the Union, they are also among the most ancient places in our country. Taos Pueblo, for example, is widely considered to be the oldest continuously inhabited spot in North America, and the Southwest's Spanish culture predates Jamestown or Plymouth Rock. Make no mistake, the Desert Southwest, sometimes touted by boosters and boomers as the sparkling "New Sunbelt," is *old, old, old*—and thoroughly suffused with the ghosts of antiquity.

ONE OF THE PLACES that Jake has photographed so lovingly in this book is Chaco Canyon, the most impressive prehistoric ruin in the American West. The Great Houses of Chaco are the remnants of a vanished Anasazi civilization that thrived aorund 950 A.D. The centerpiece of this maze of monuments is Pueblo Bonito, a vast apartment complex that once stood four stories high and had more than seven hundred rooms. It is a beautiful, and slightly spooky place that gives Jake a potent feeling of déjà vu. "I feel like I lived there before," he says. "It's such a powerful, mysterious place. You can *feel* the history." Chaco was abandoned around 1130 A.D.—most likely the result of an environmental apocalypse brought on by overfarming, overlogging, and a series of terrible droughts—but their culture lives on in the many smaller pueblos that still dot the landscape of New Mexico and Arizona: Hopi, Zuni, Acoma, Taos, and the many old settlements along the Rio Grande.

Perhaps my favorite place that Jake has captured in this book is Canyon de Chelly. The literal and metaphorical heartland of the Navajo Nation, Canyon de Chelly is a rock world with a human pulse, with peach orchards and cornfields planted along a sinuous sandy floor that's framed by massive luminous sandstone walls. The great mythologist and writer Joseph Campbell called Canyon de Chelly "the most sacred place on earth." I've spent many days hiking and climbing down in the canyon, hooked by its intrigues, exploring its myriad notches and alcoves. Marked by such marquee attractions as Fortress Rock, Spider Rock, and White House Ruin, the Canyon de Chelly complex is seventy serpentine miles of rock art and ancient artifacts interspersed

Walhalla Overlook, North Rim, Grand Canyon, Arizona

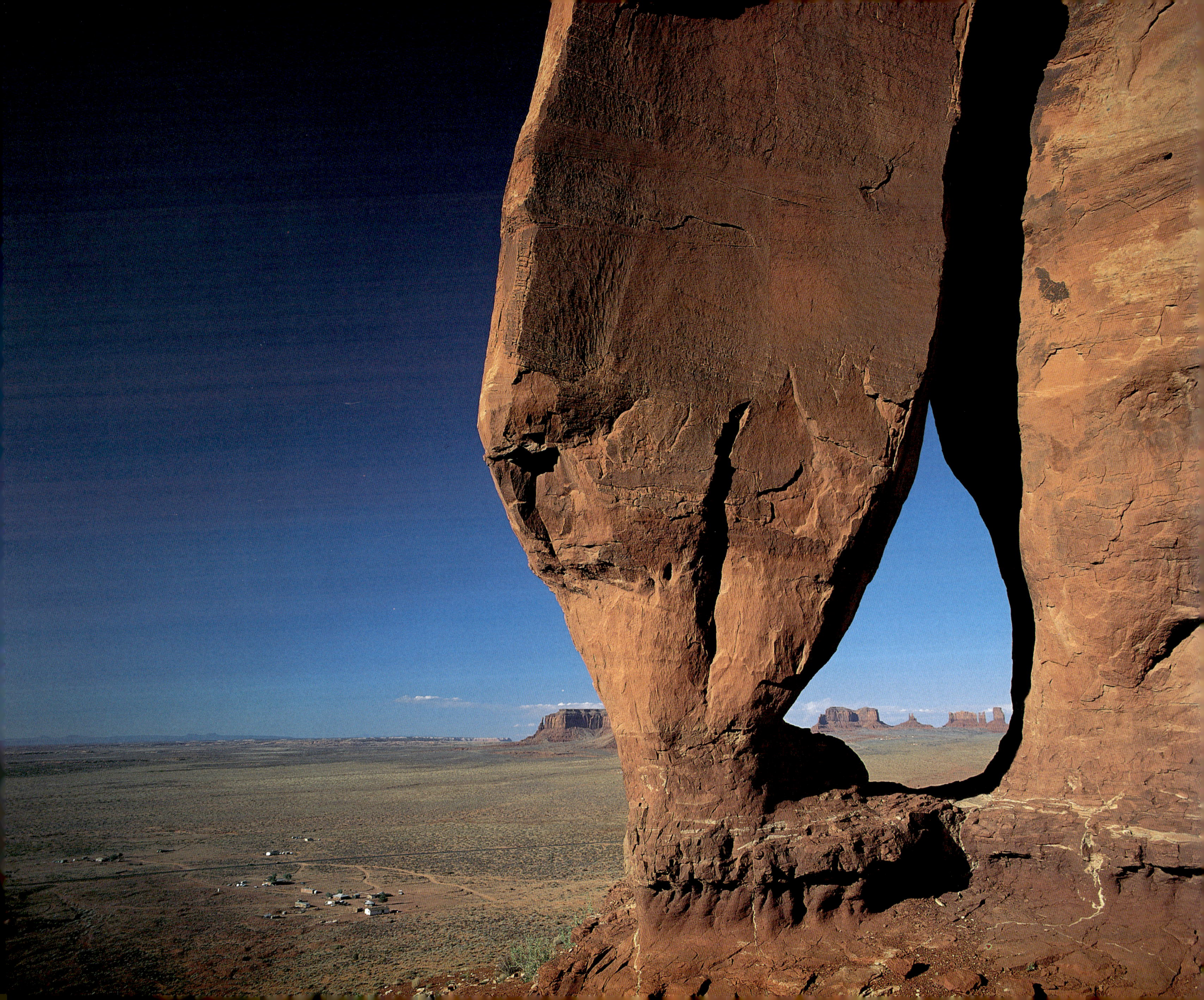

with contemporary Navajo civilization: People still *live* there. Carl Jung said Canyon de Chelly was "the essence of antiquity." By that, he meant not just the presence of the old, but the seamless cohabitation of the old with the modern. In Canyon de Chelly, it's all mixed up together, giving the visitor a sense of chronological vertigo that's confusing but also strangely pleasing. All those petroglyphs and pictographs on the walls remind us that humans have been at it a long, long time, scrawling our Kilroys, constructing our towns. We American moderns are just a passing thing, destined to be supplanted by other folks who're different, but not so different, from ourselves. Those figures up on the wall are us.

One of the early U.S. Army topographical explorers thought Canyon de Chelly's walls appeared to be "chiselled by the hand of art." The canyon seemed to him less a work of haphazard nature, and more like a temple, a spectacle of conscious human design. It's a trait that I find throughout the pages of this book—a strong sculptural, and even architectural, sensibility. This is no accident. For decades, Jake has made his living photographing landscapes of all kinds, but he is perhaps best known for his fine-art photographs of Manhattan skyscrapers. He's adept at making sense of objects erected on a huge scale, adept at finding the angles and catching the subtle plays of light on skins of steel, stone, and glass. It's a training that stands him in good stead when presented with the challenge of photographing the outsized spires and monoliths and chasms of the Southwest. "Scale is the hardest thing to master in the West," he says. "The size of the shapes, the boldness of the lines. It feels architectural."

I sense in these beautiful images Jake's acute appreciation not only for the landscapes themselves, but also for the natural processes that made them; or, to extend the architectural metaphor, he seems to love not only the buildings but the underlying whimsies and inspirations of the architects who designed them. Whether it's Monument Valley, the Black Canyon of the Gunnison, or, especially, the Grand Canyon, I can think of no region of the United States where one can see the raw processes of nature so brutally exposed—erosion, sedimentation, volcanism. The country Jake has photographed here has moved modern geologists, ordinarily a dry and understated lot, to employ a vocabulary of doom: On the maps, you'll find terms like Paradox Basin, Defiance Uplift, the Great Unconformity. It's beautiful terrrain, yes, but terrain stamped with terrific violence.

In these pictures, I see the hand of time and the patient but relentless creativity of nature. And I remain smitten in the face of these bold buildings of the Southwest—buildings conjured by God, masoned by the epochs, and kissed by clear desert light.

Tear Drop Arch, Monument Valley, Utah

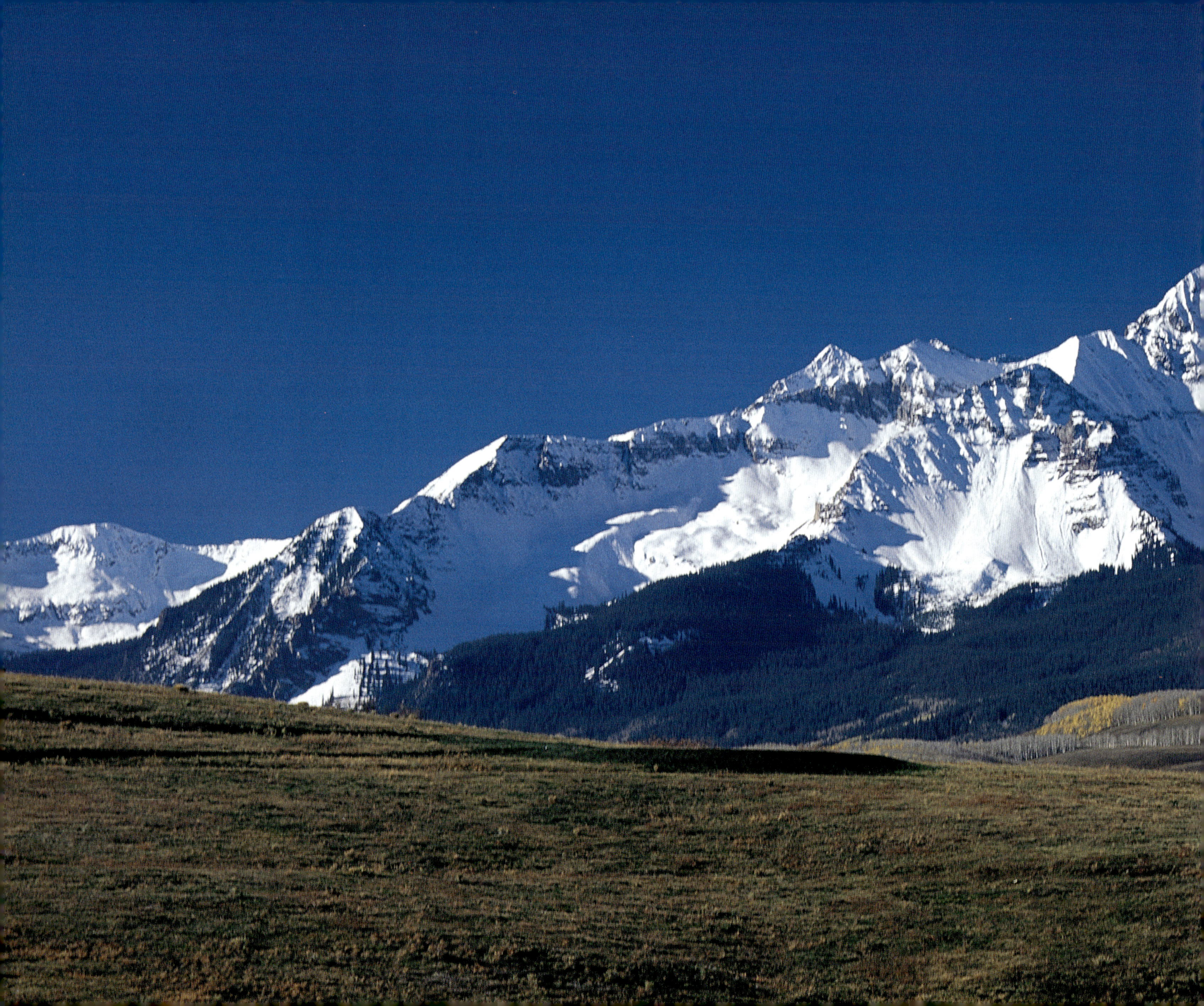

COLORADO

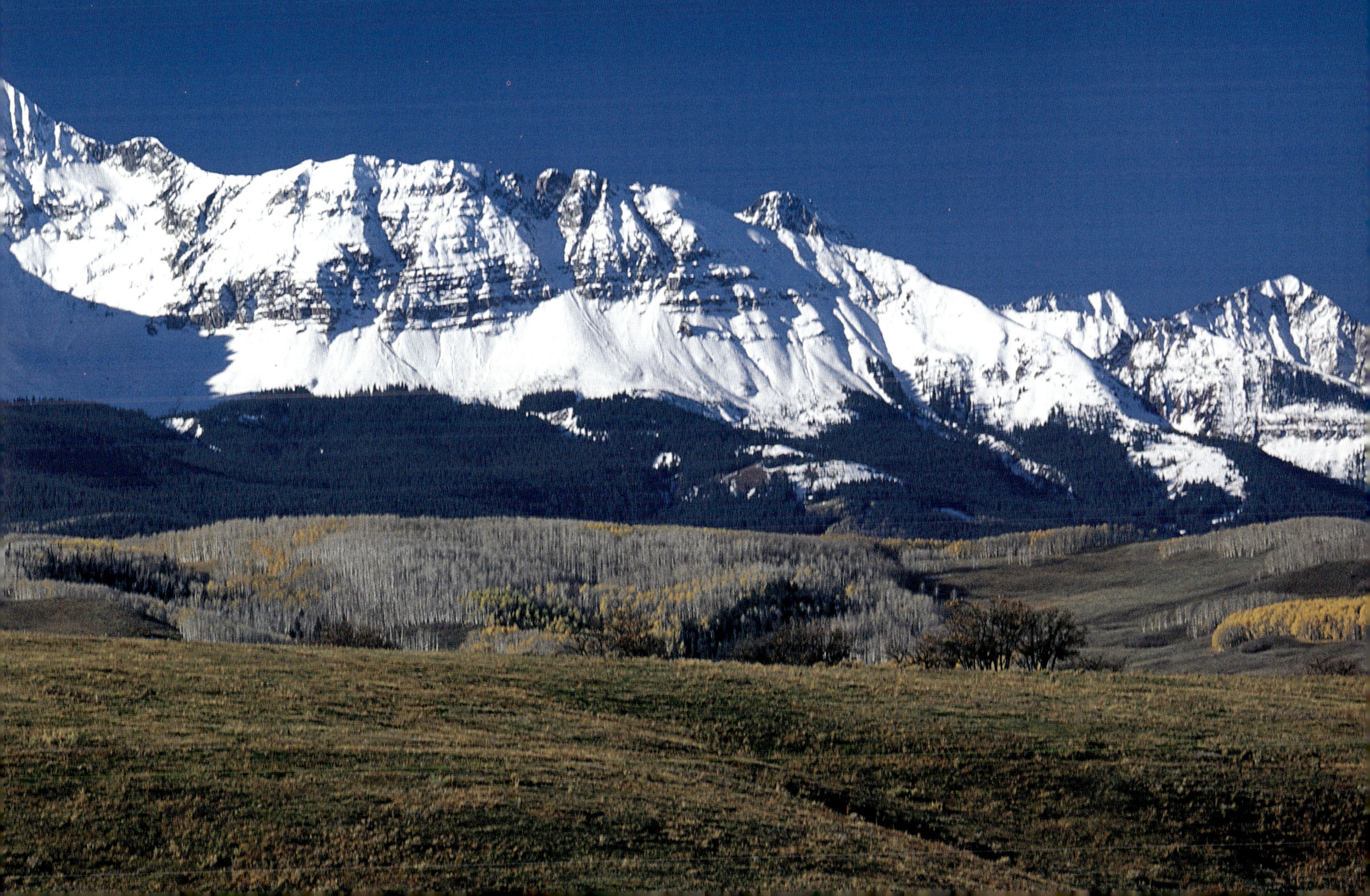

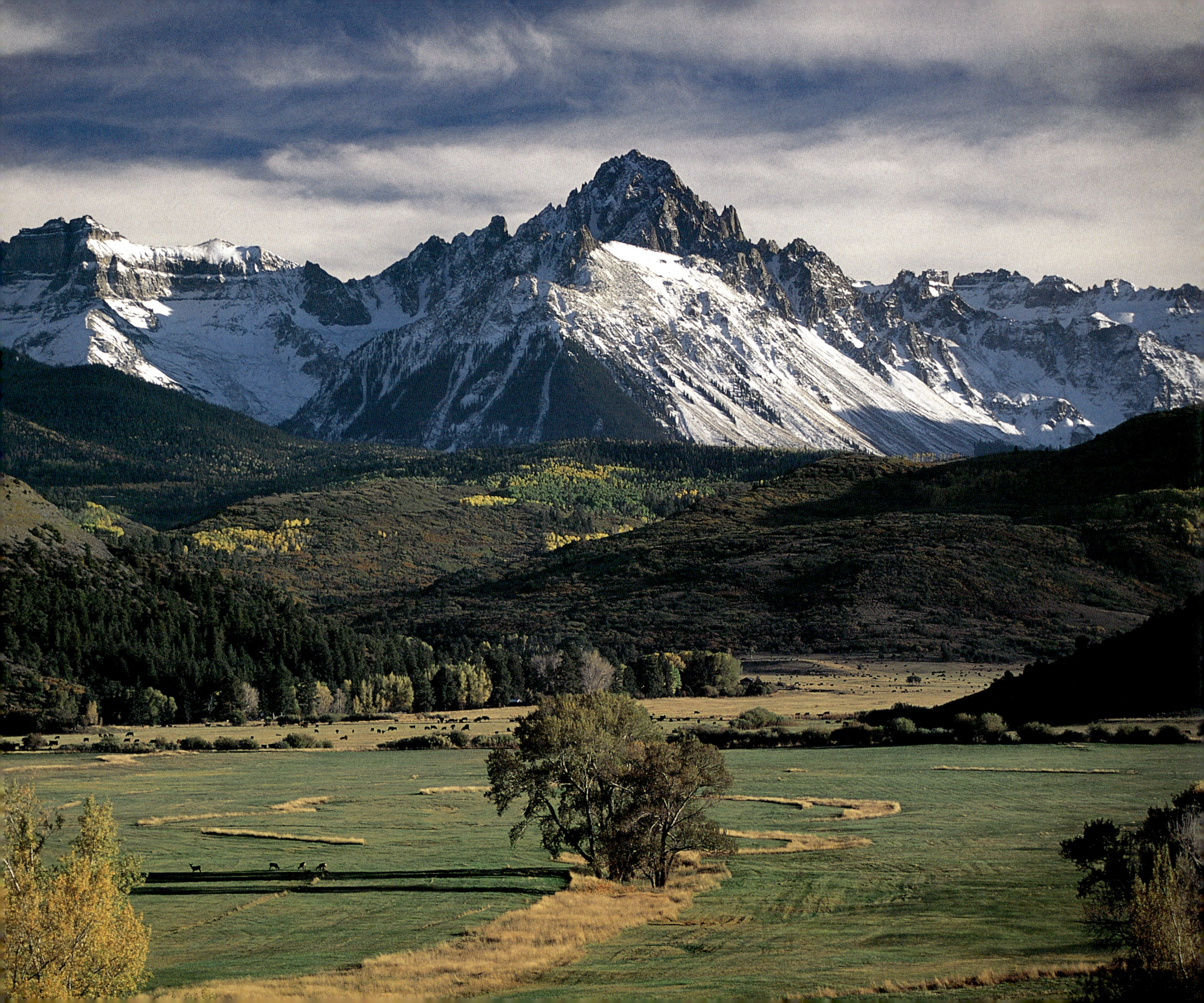

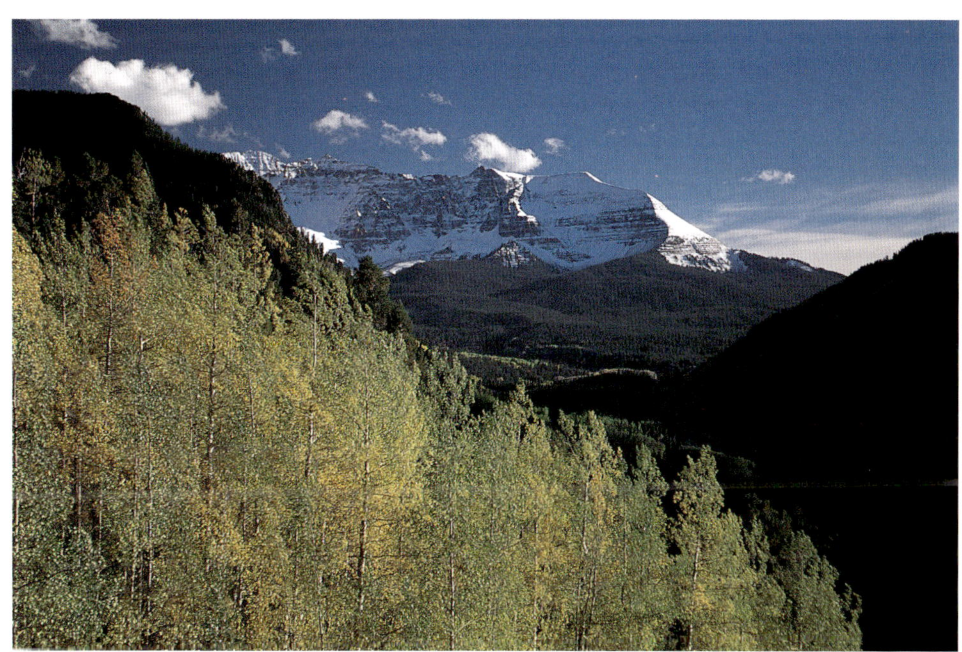

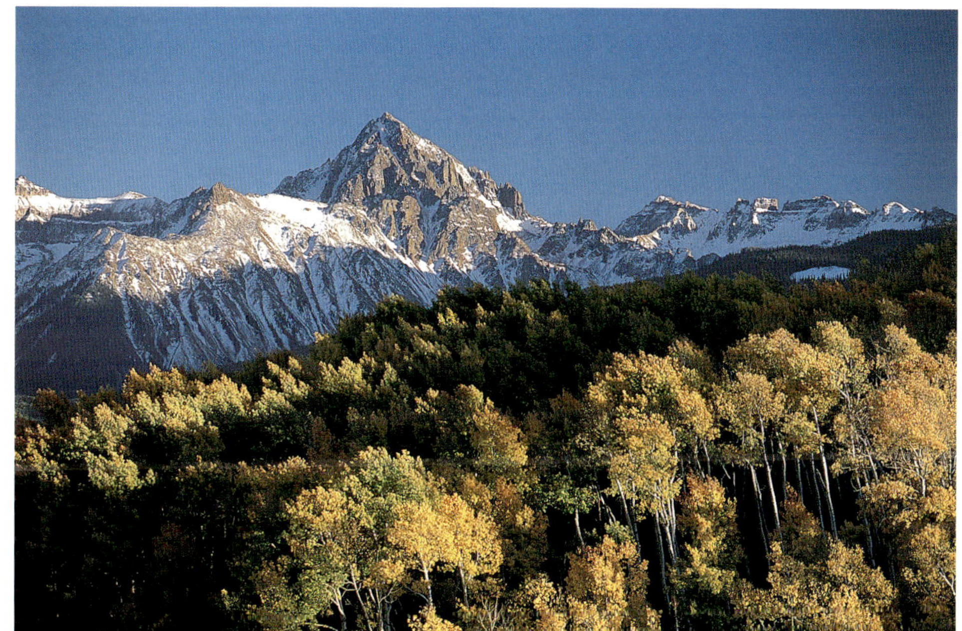

↑Mount Sneffels Wilderness ← Double RL Ranch, Telluride

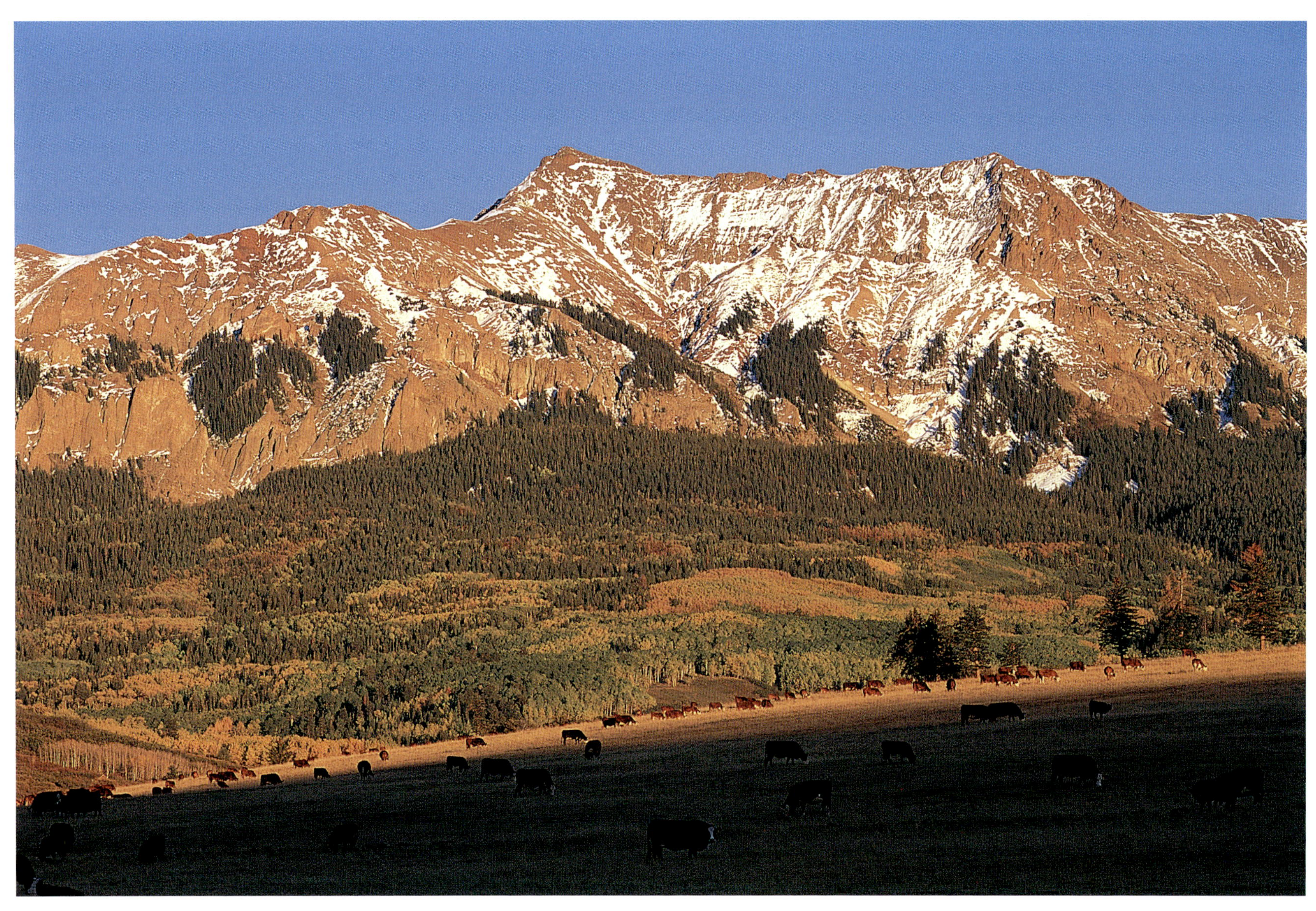

↑ View of Mount Sneffels from Last Dollar Road →Outside Telluride

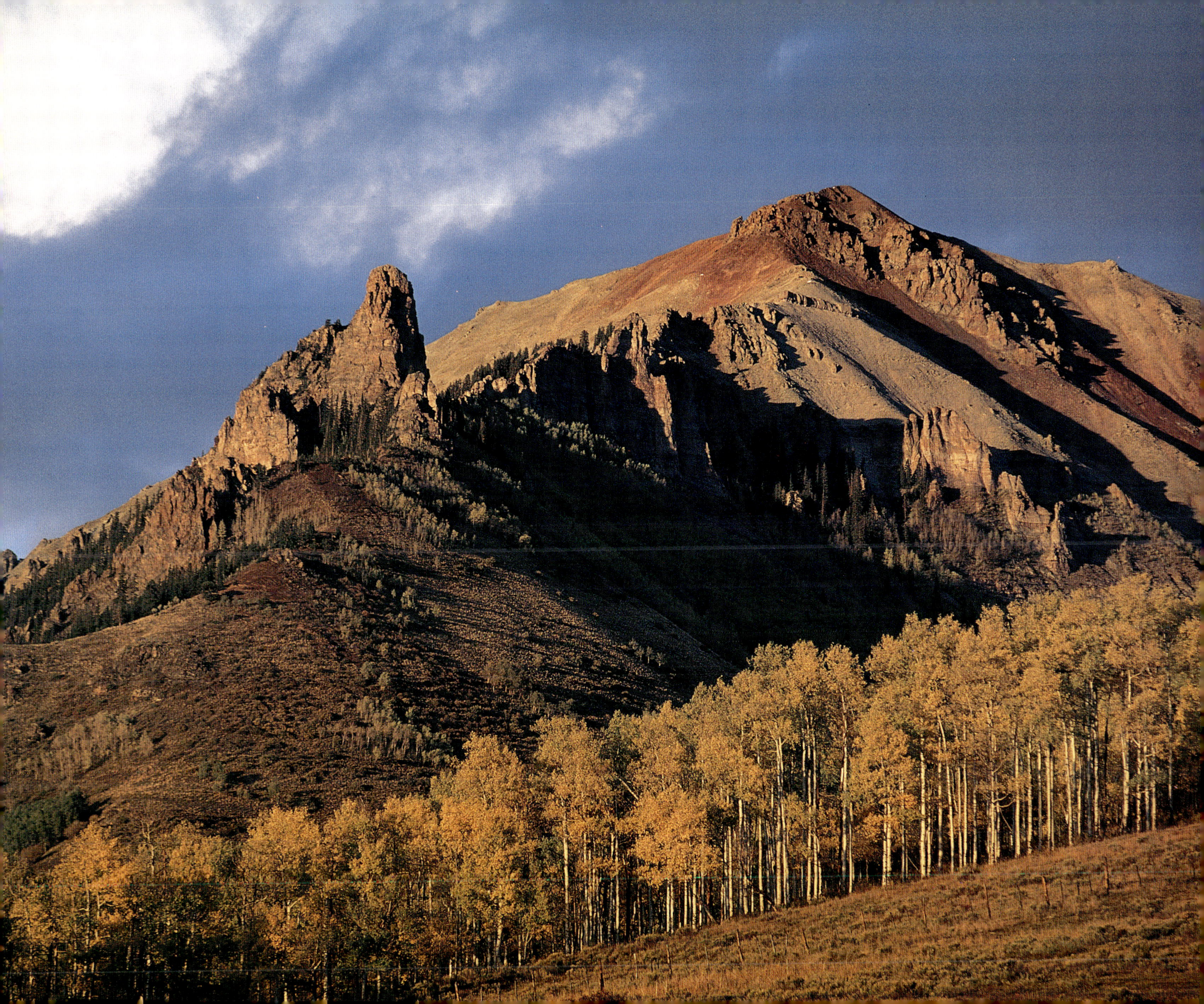

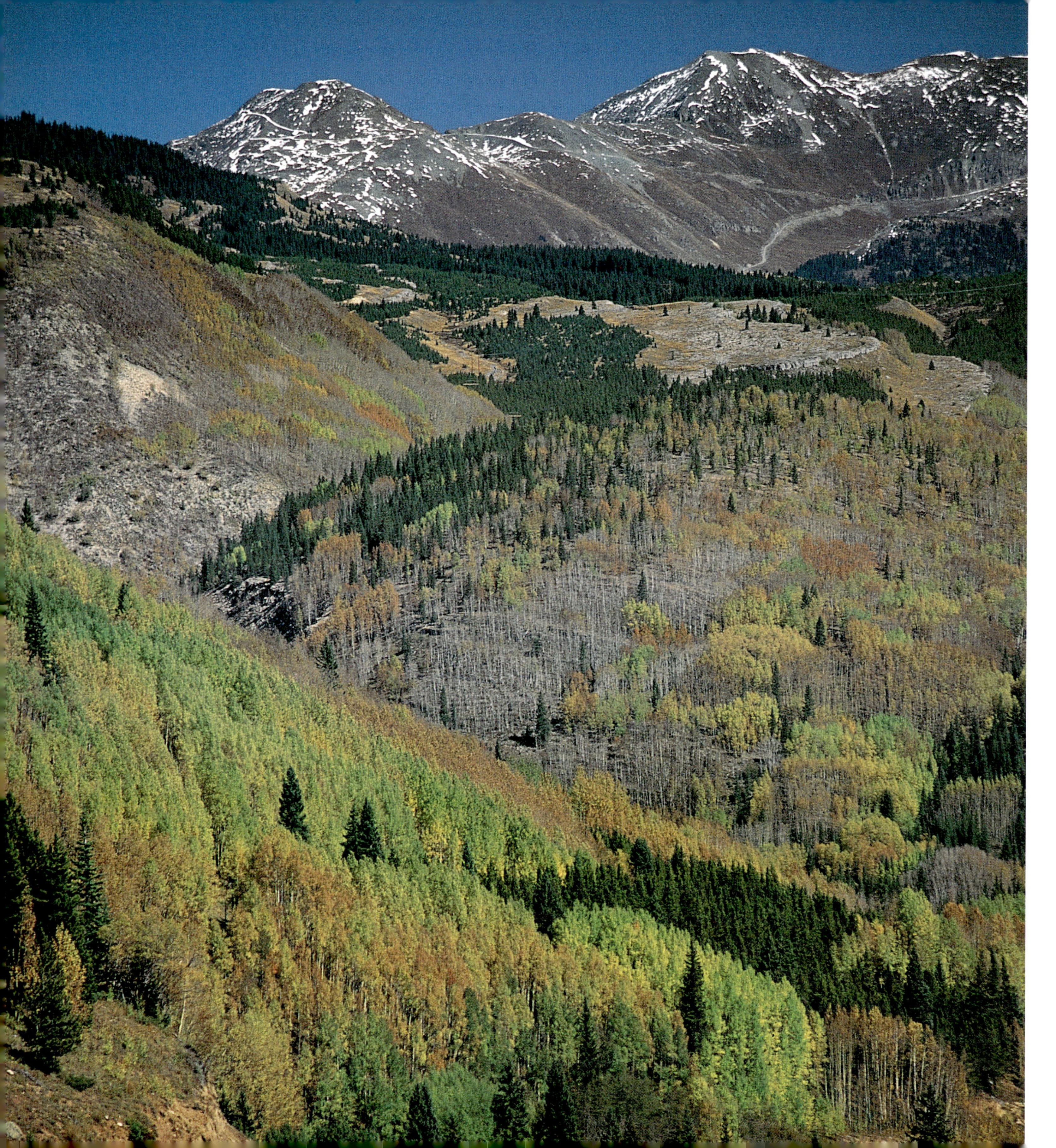

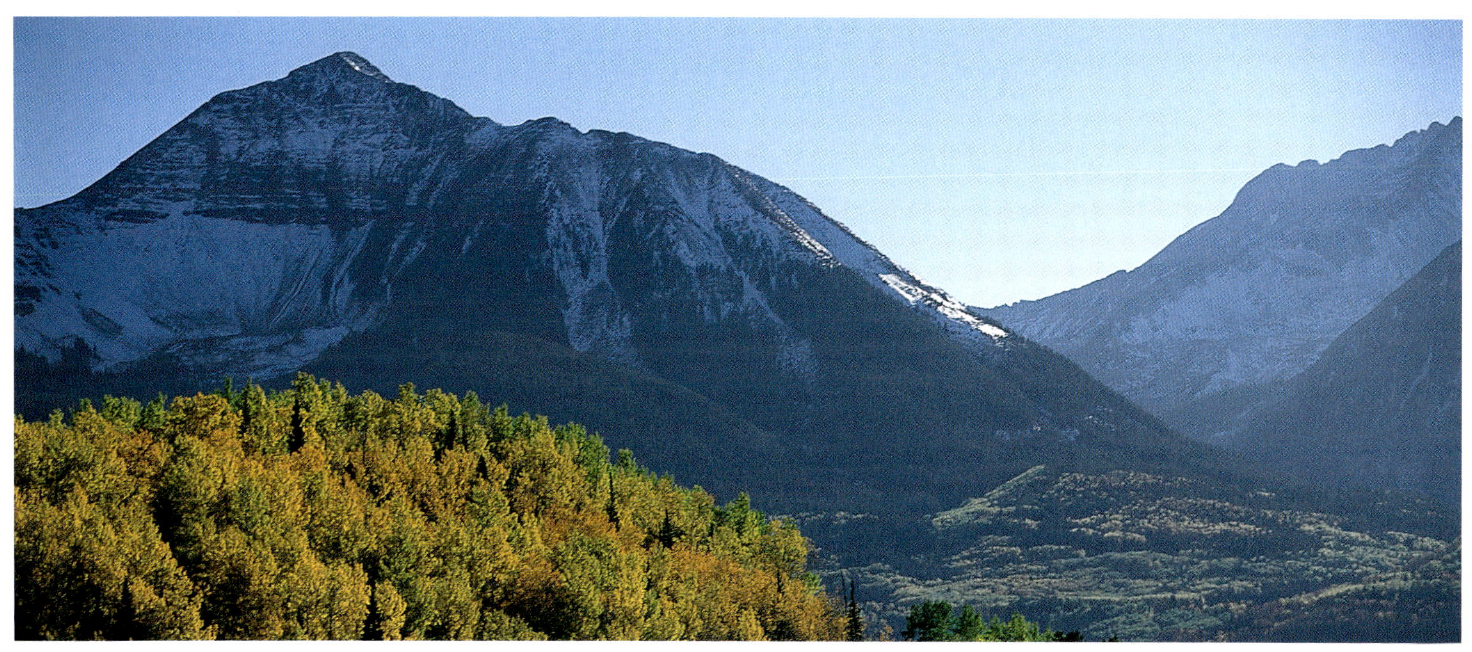

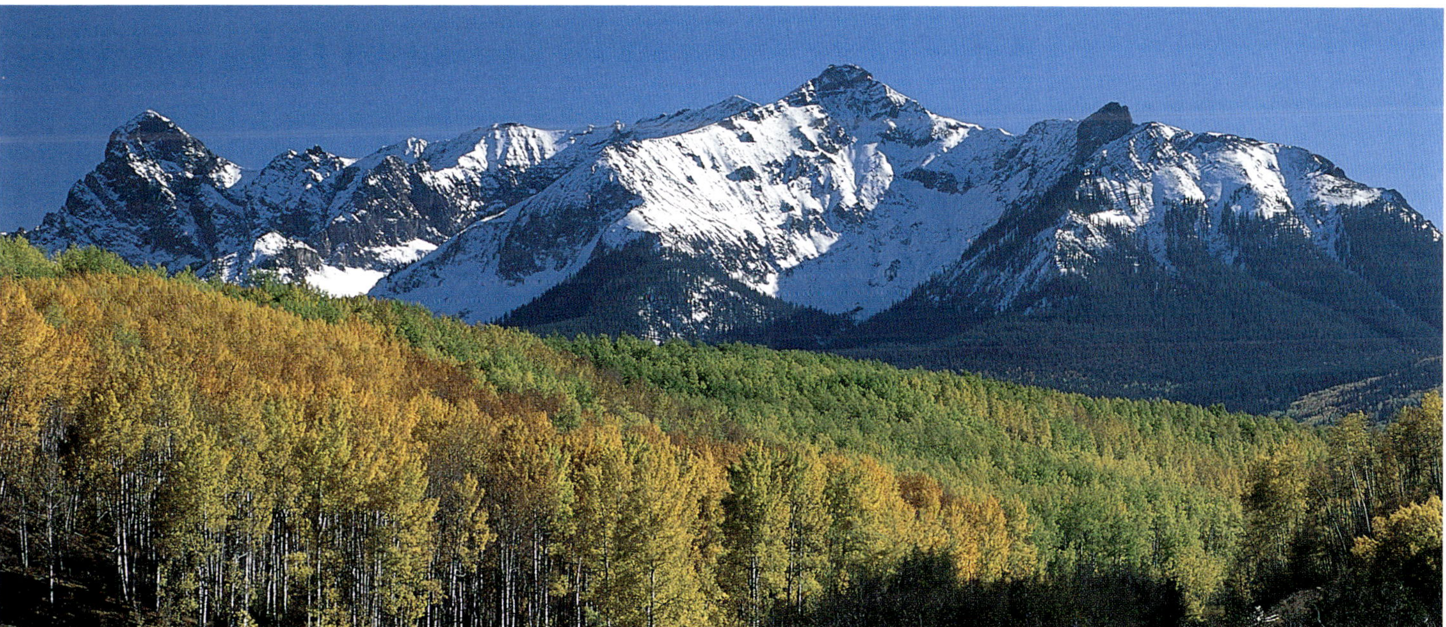

↑Sunshine Mountain, San Juan Scenic Skyway, San Juan National Forest ← Mount Sneffels Range

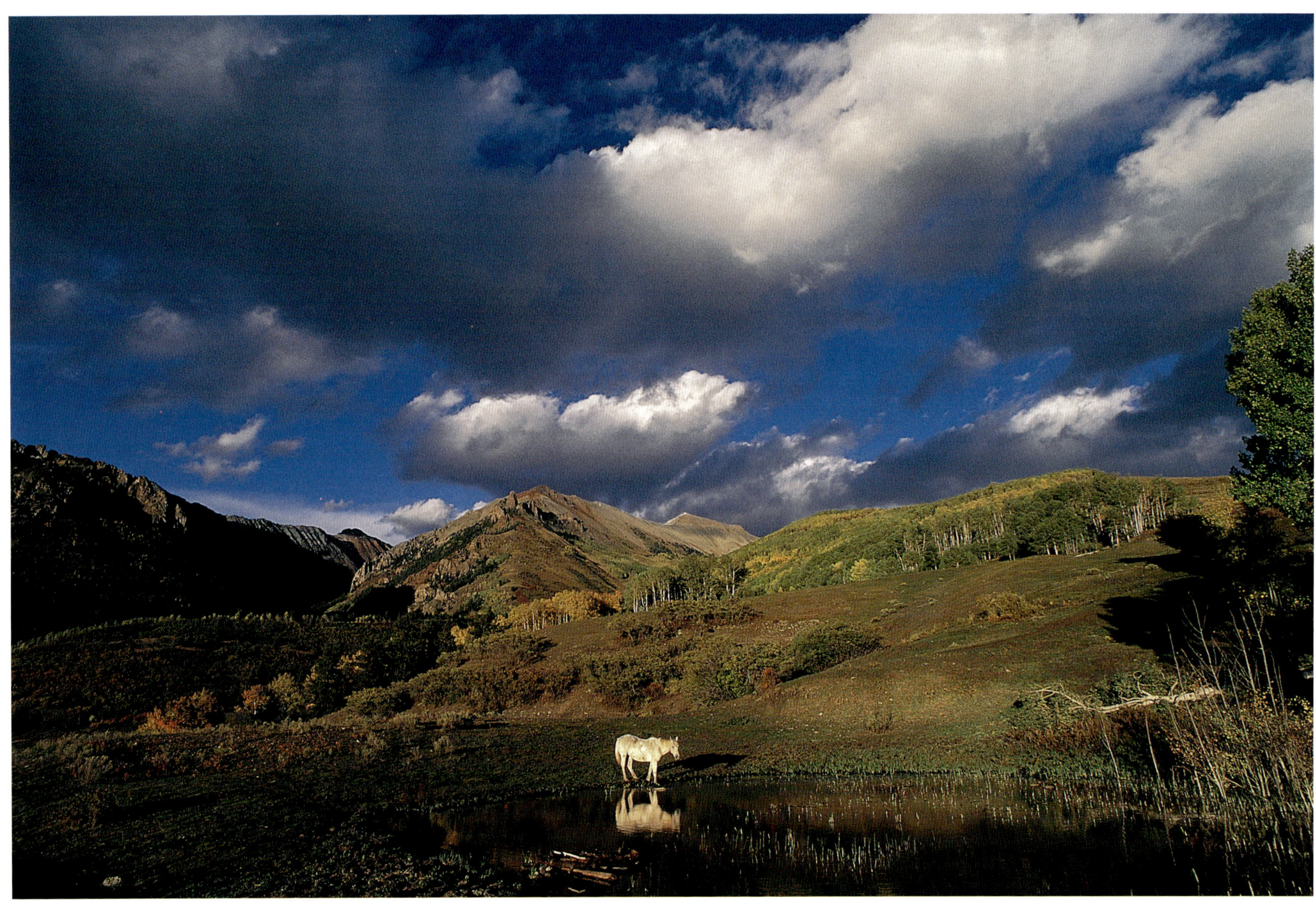

↑Outside Telluride →Gunnison National Forest ↓Birches in Kebler Pass, Gunnison National Forest

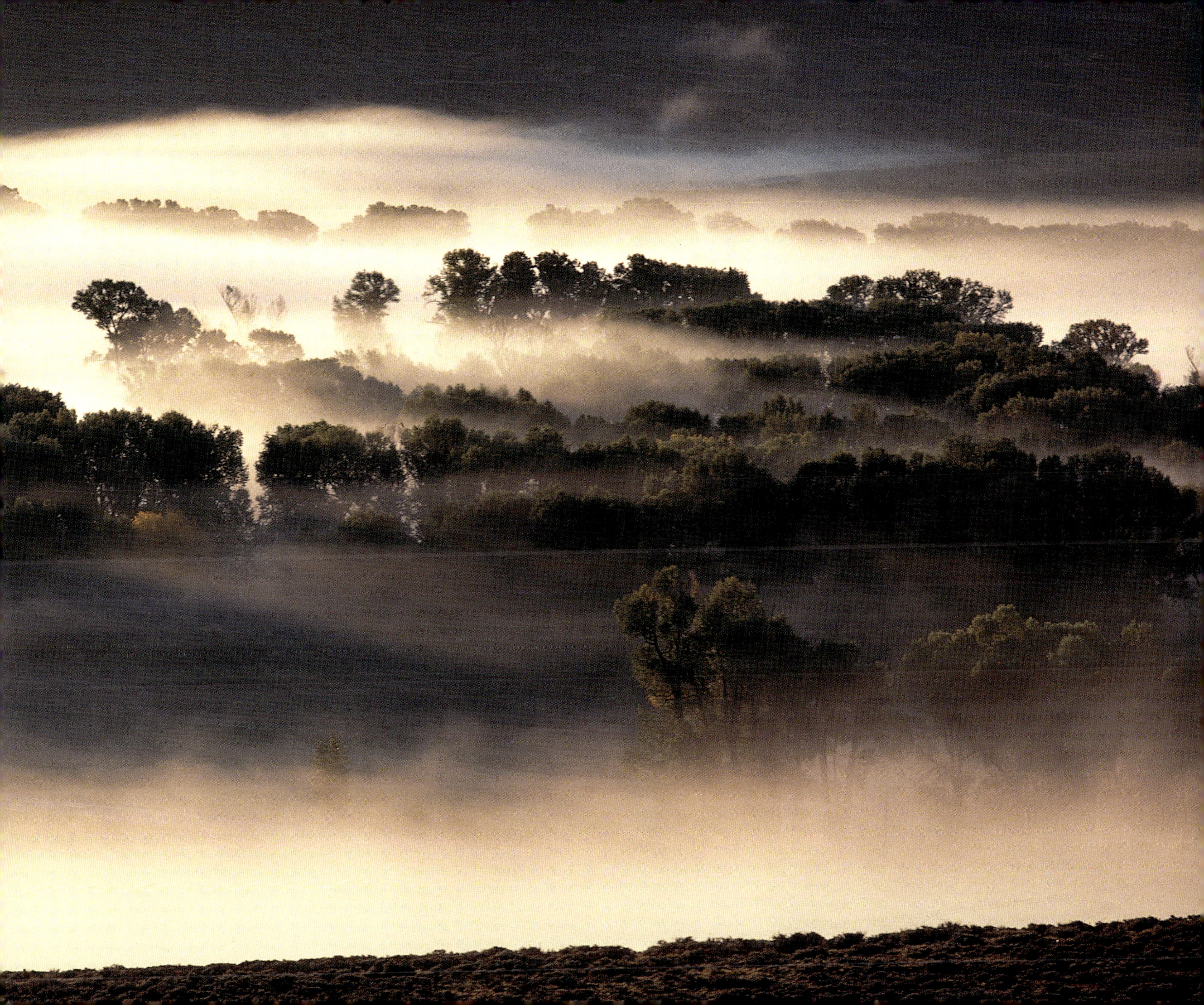

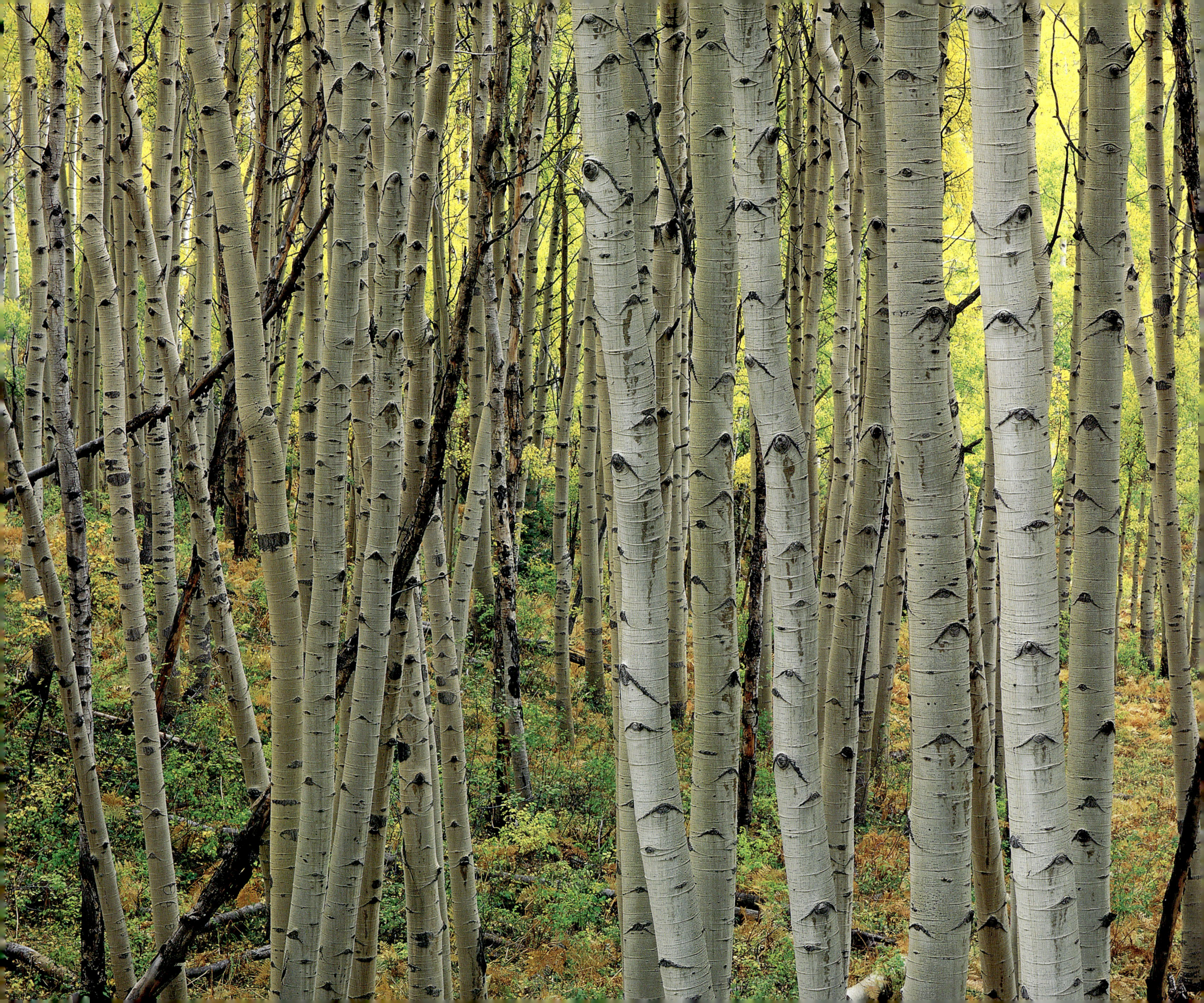

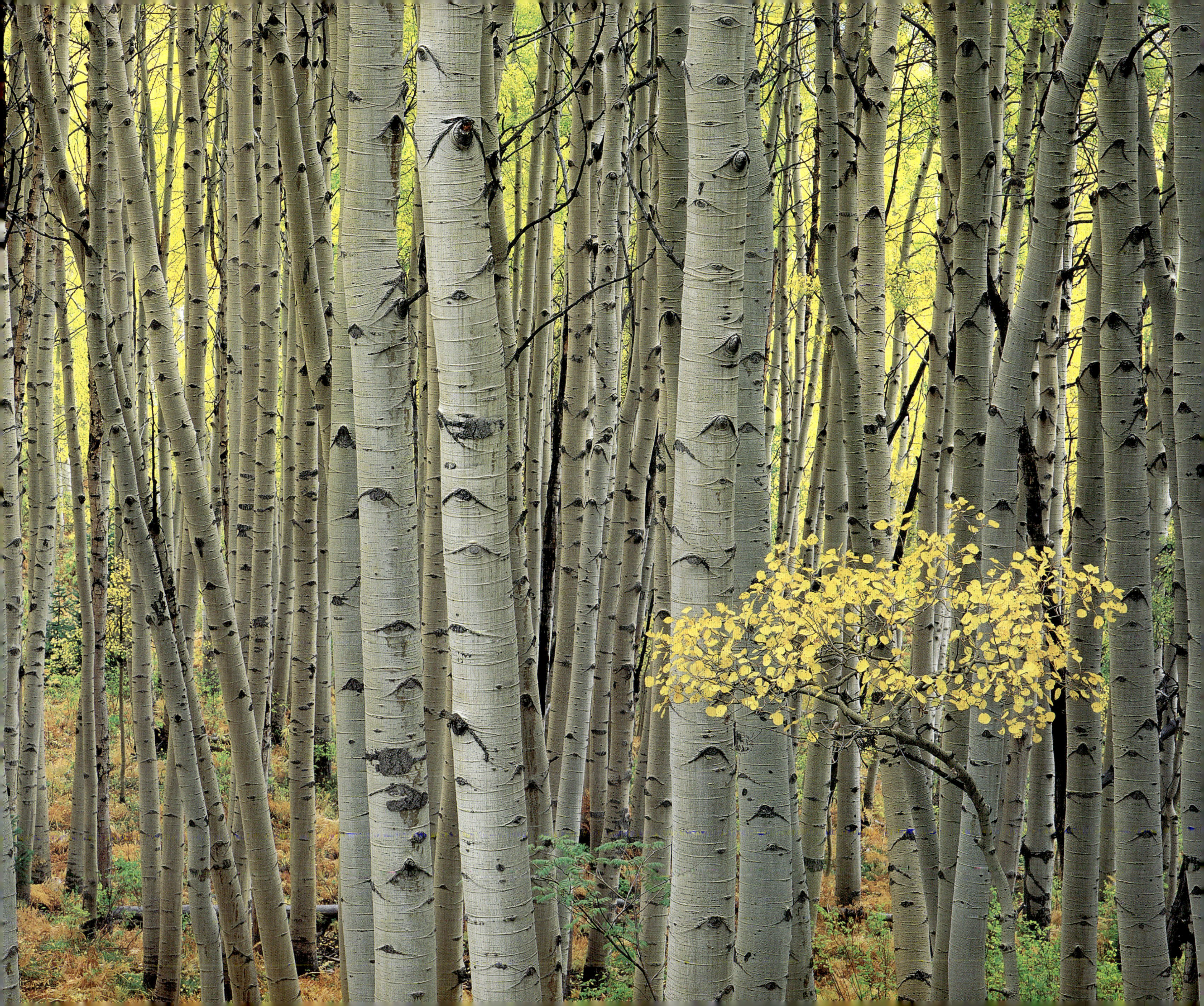

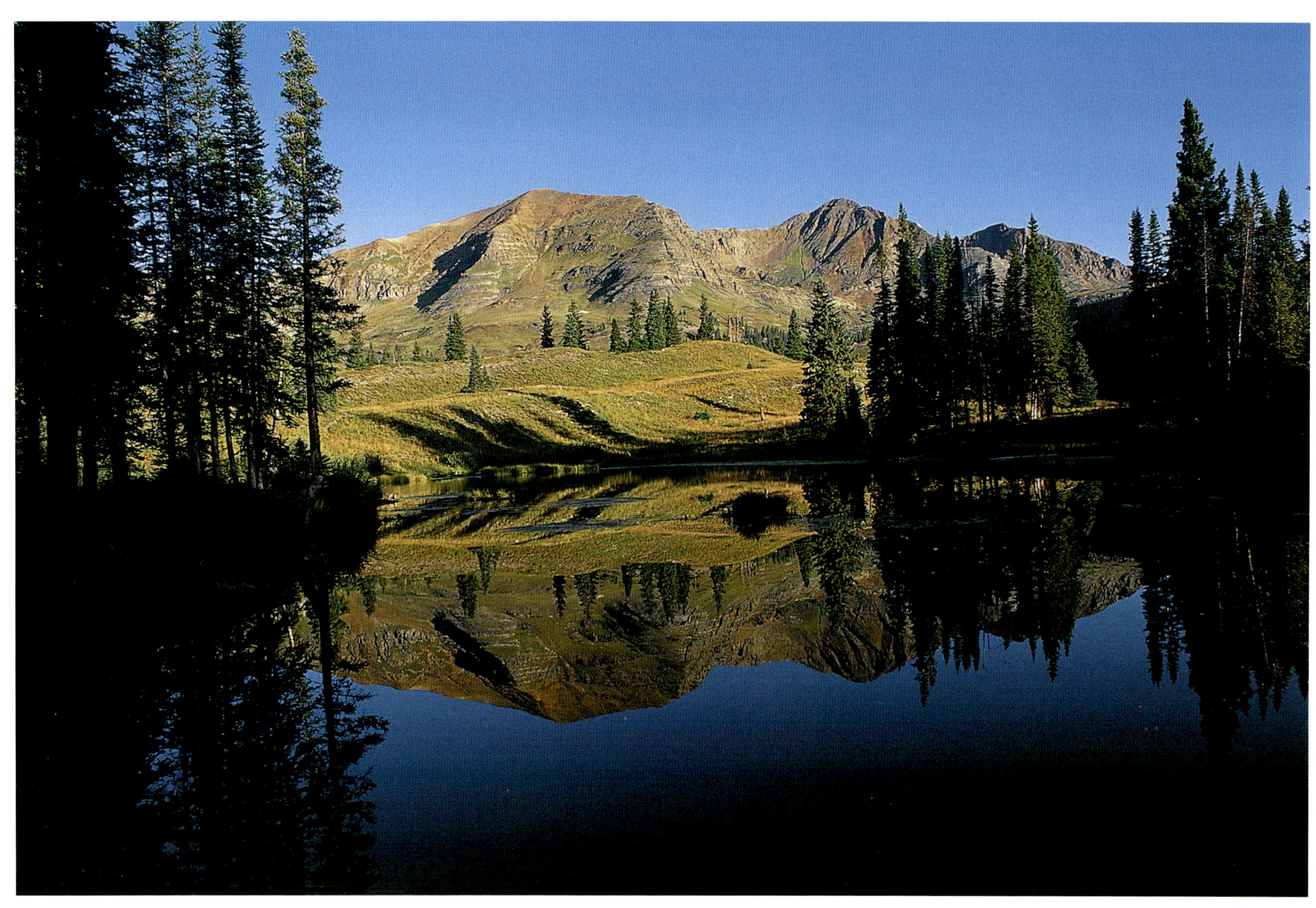

↑ Spruce Tree House, Mesa Verde National Park →Lost Lake, Gunnison National Forest

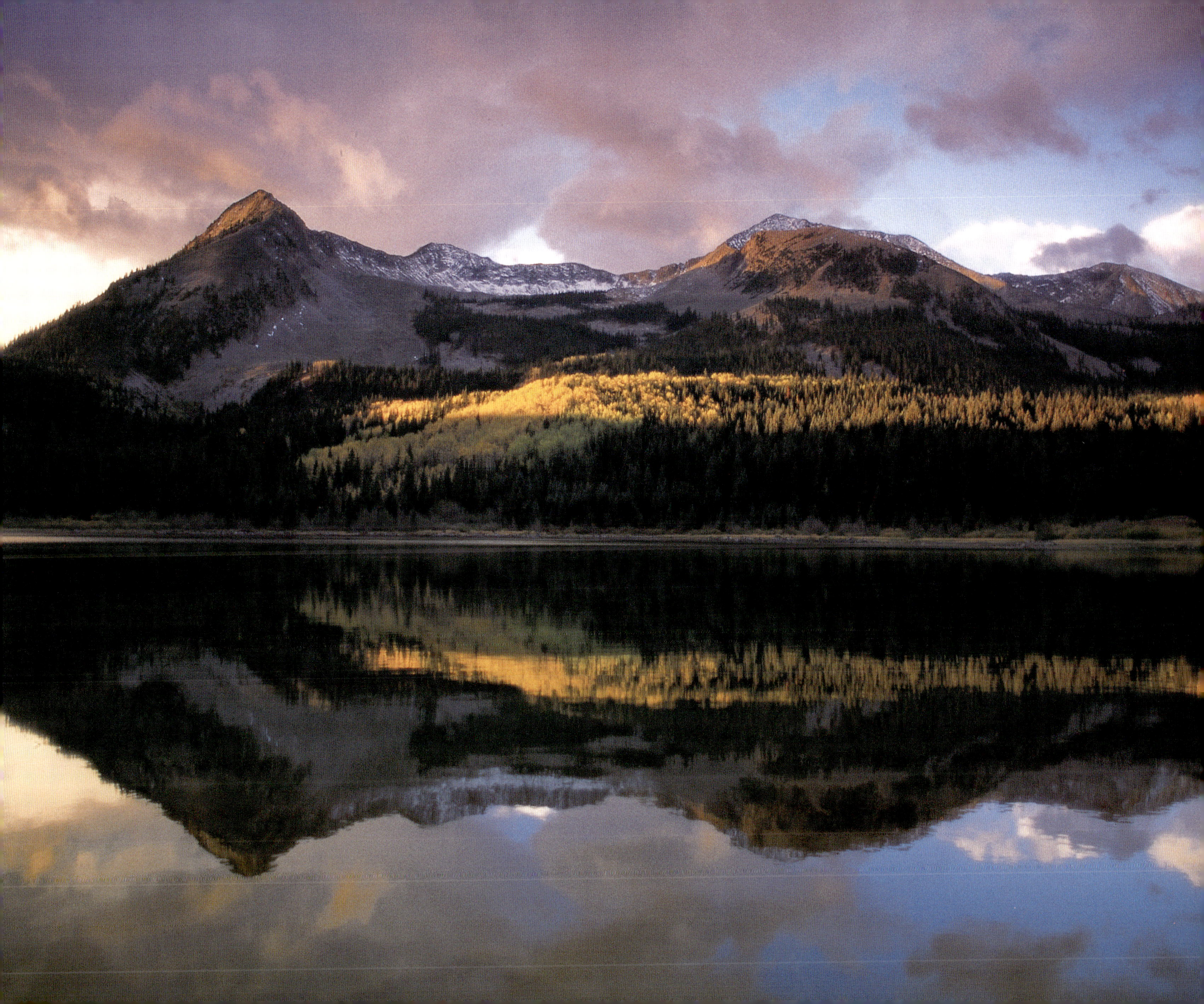

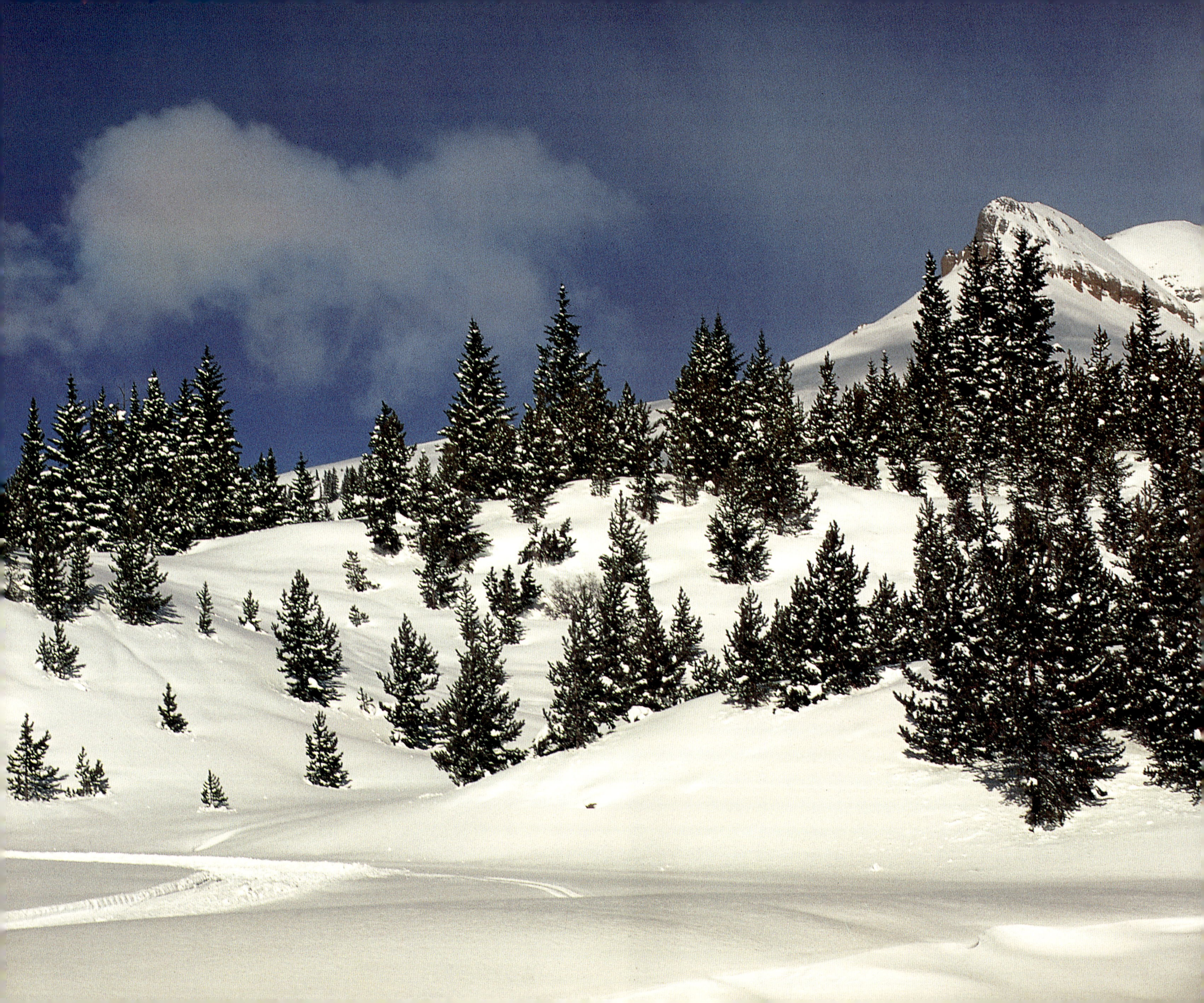

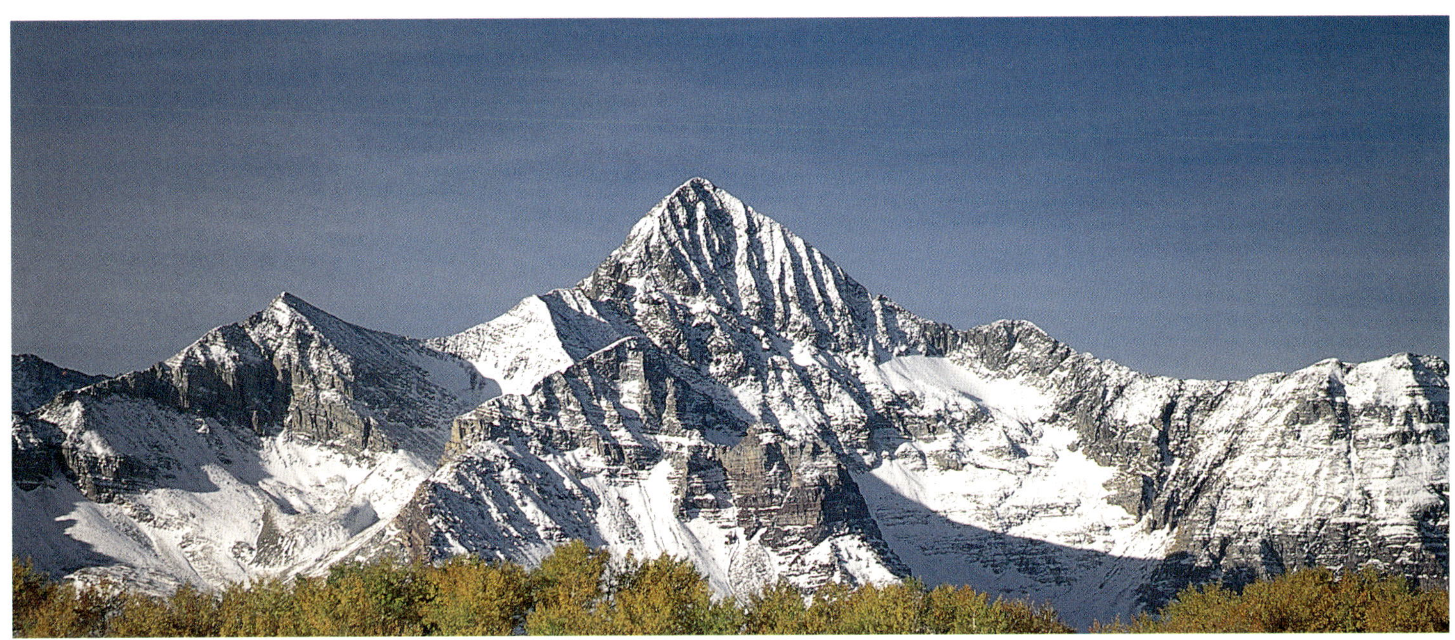

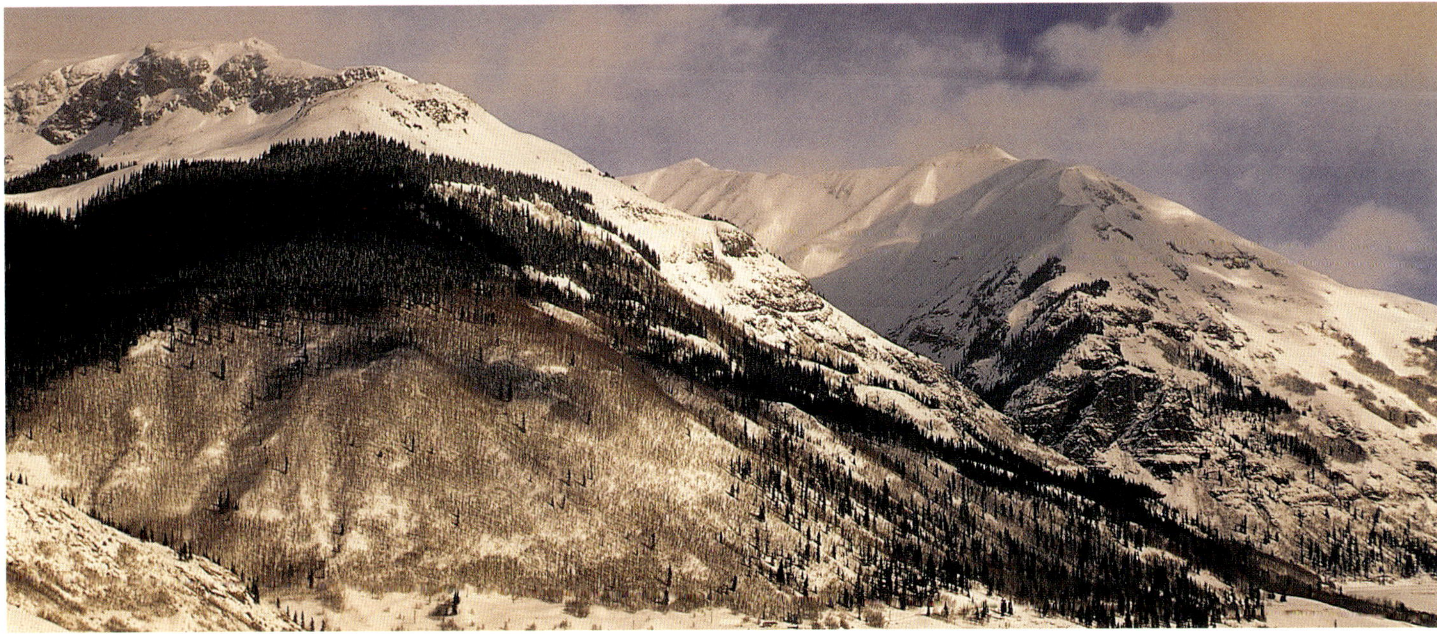

↑← San Juan Skyway, Scenic Byway ↑Mount Wilson

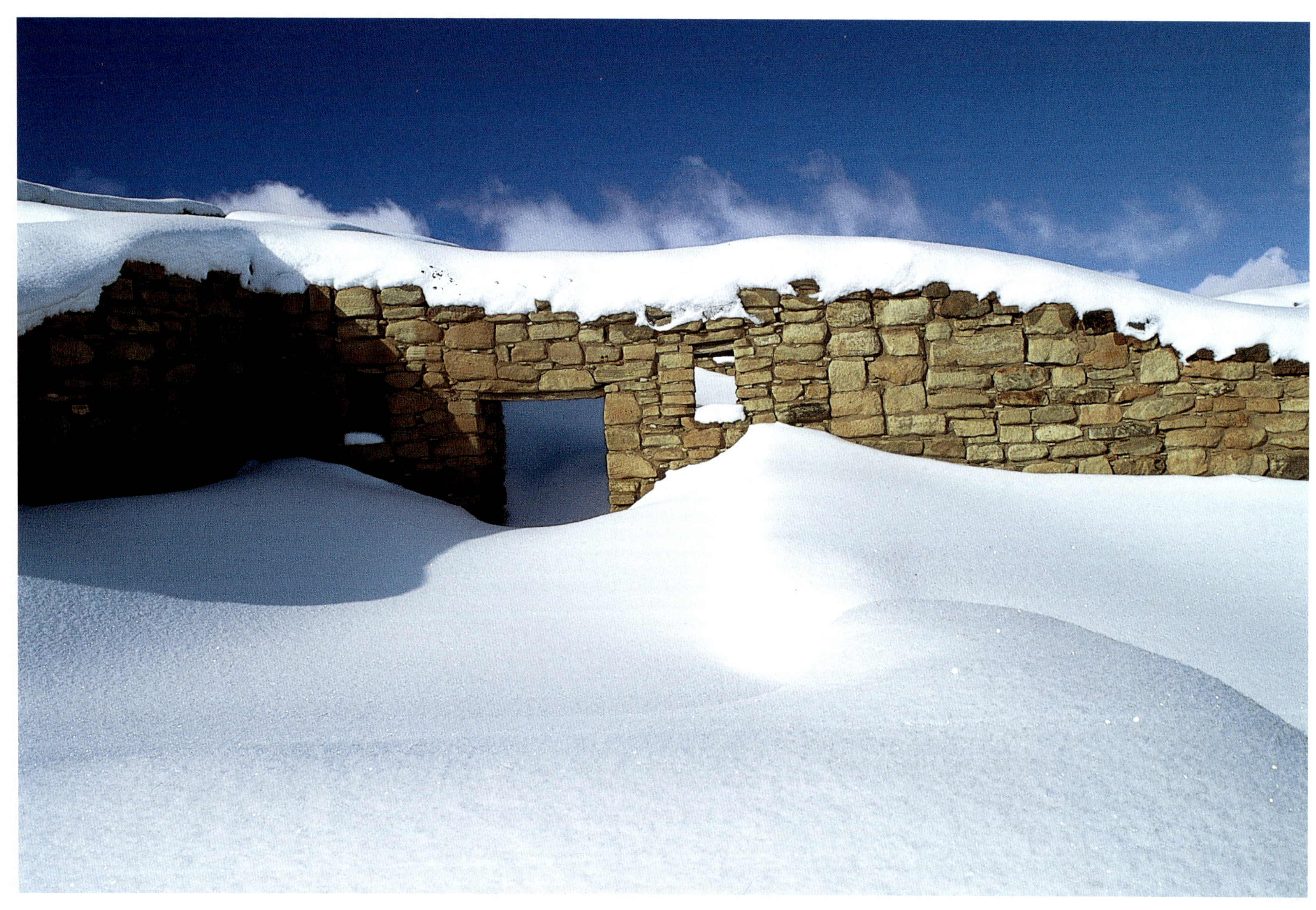

↰→Lowry Pueblo, Canyons of the Ancients National Monument ↓ Cliff Palace, Mesa Verde National Park

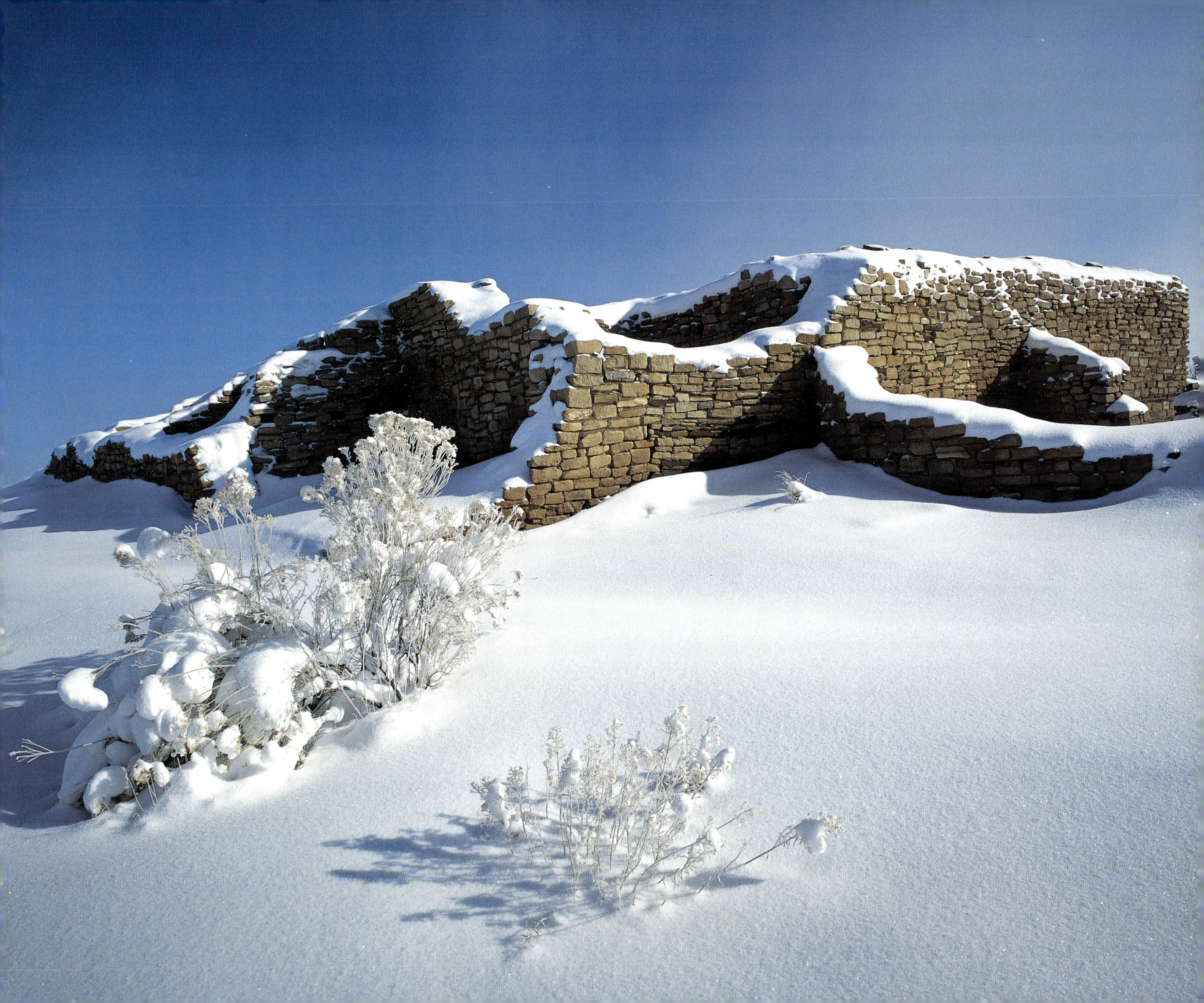

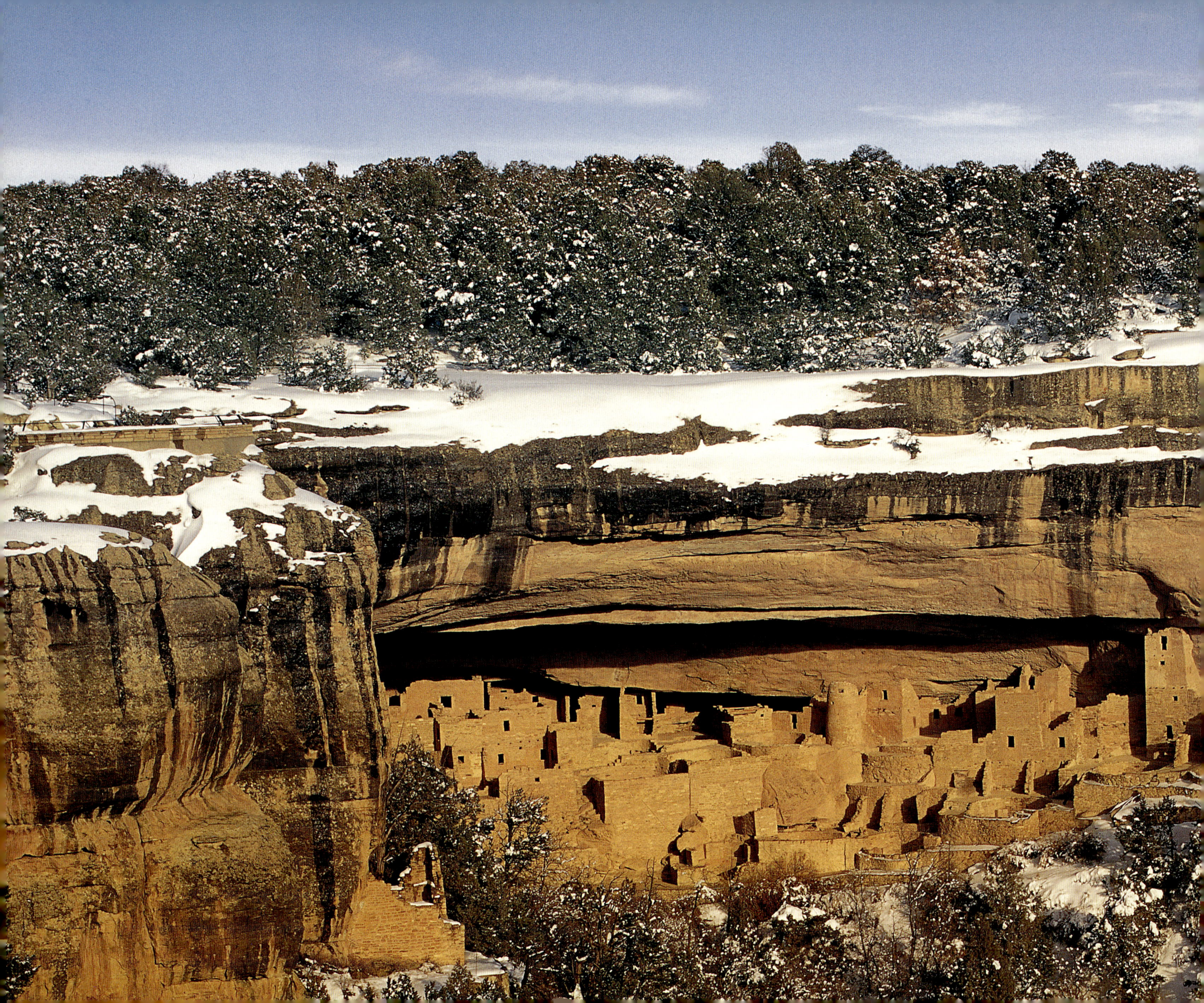

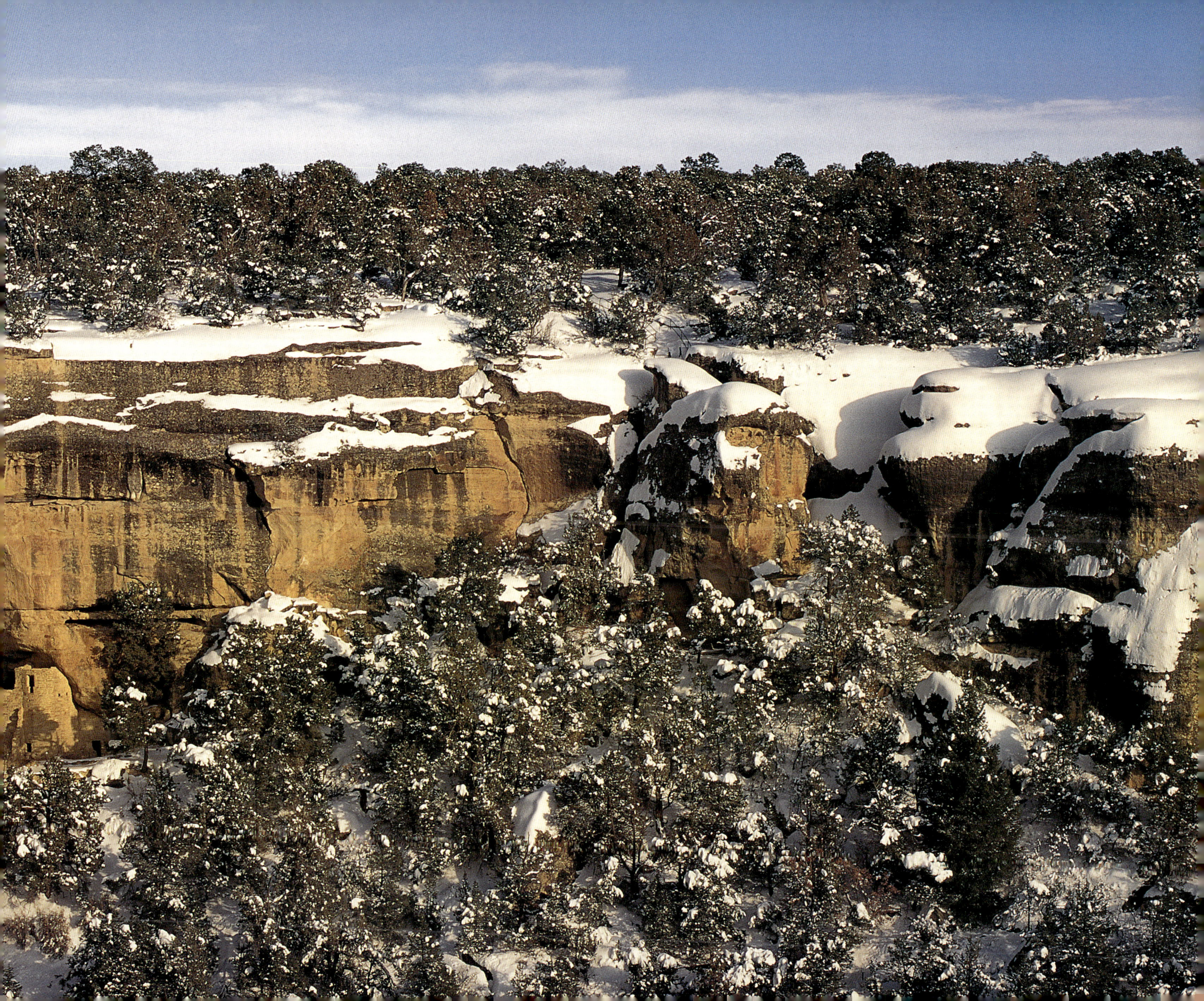

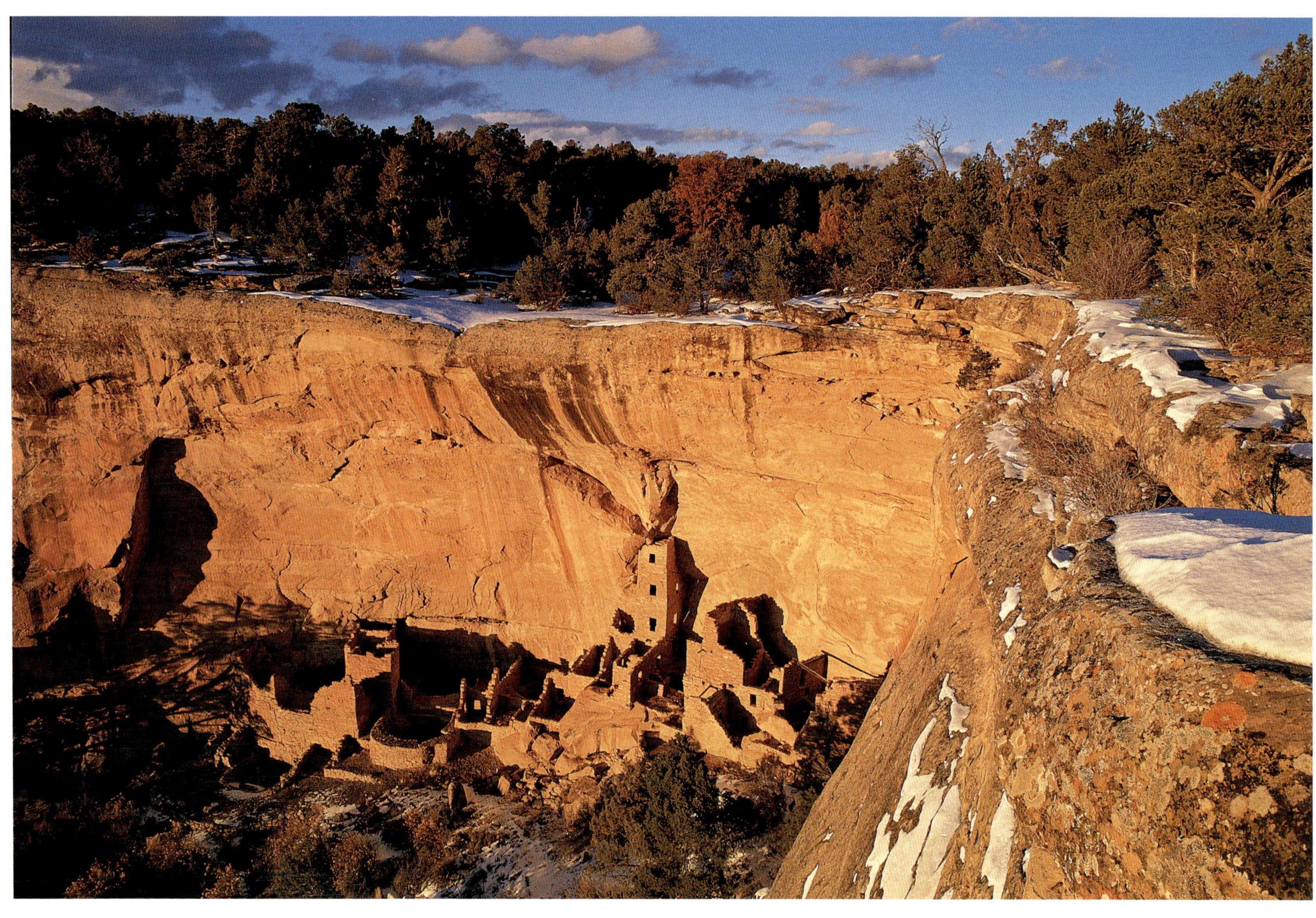

↑→ Square Tower House, Mesa Verde National Park

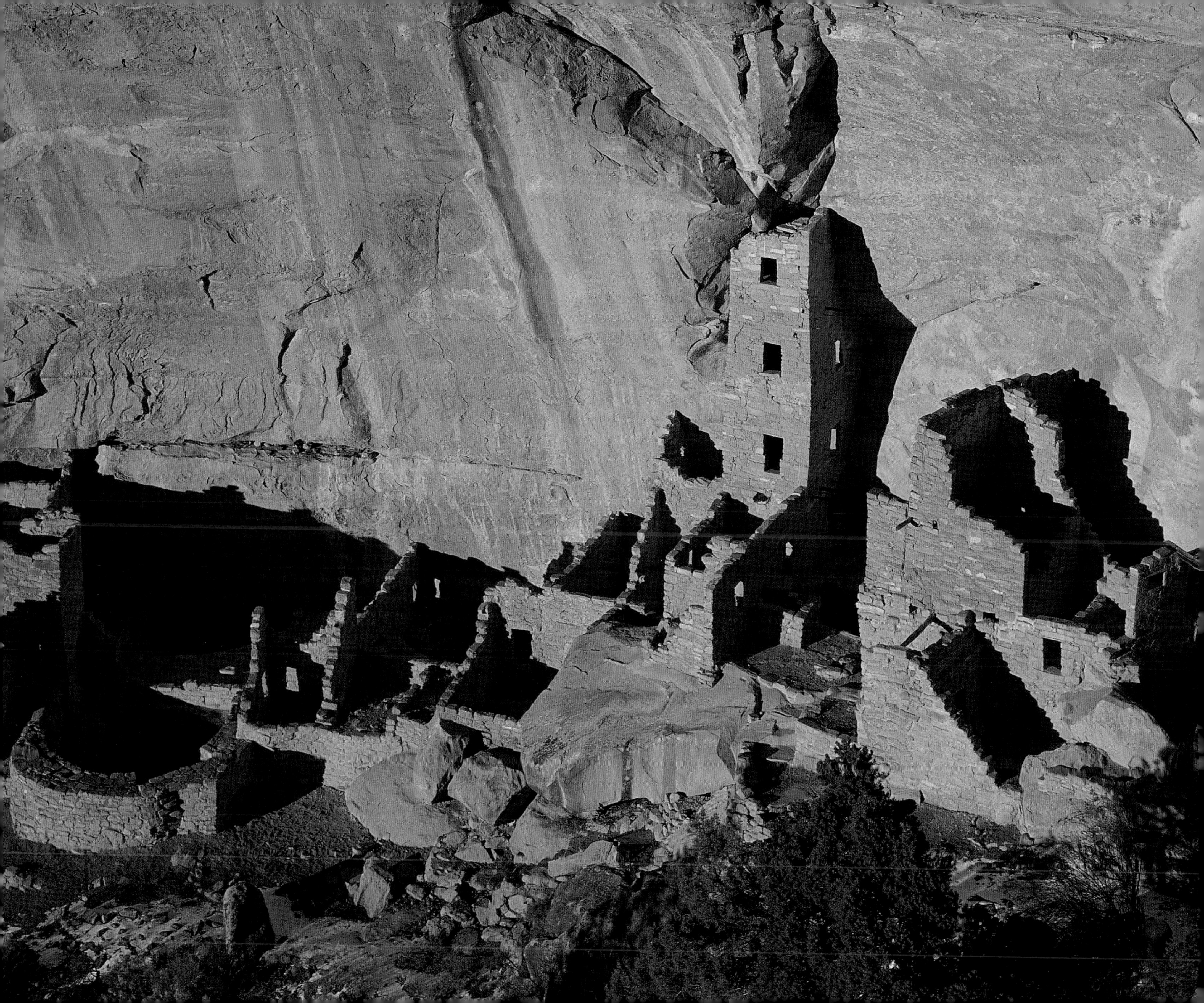

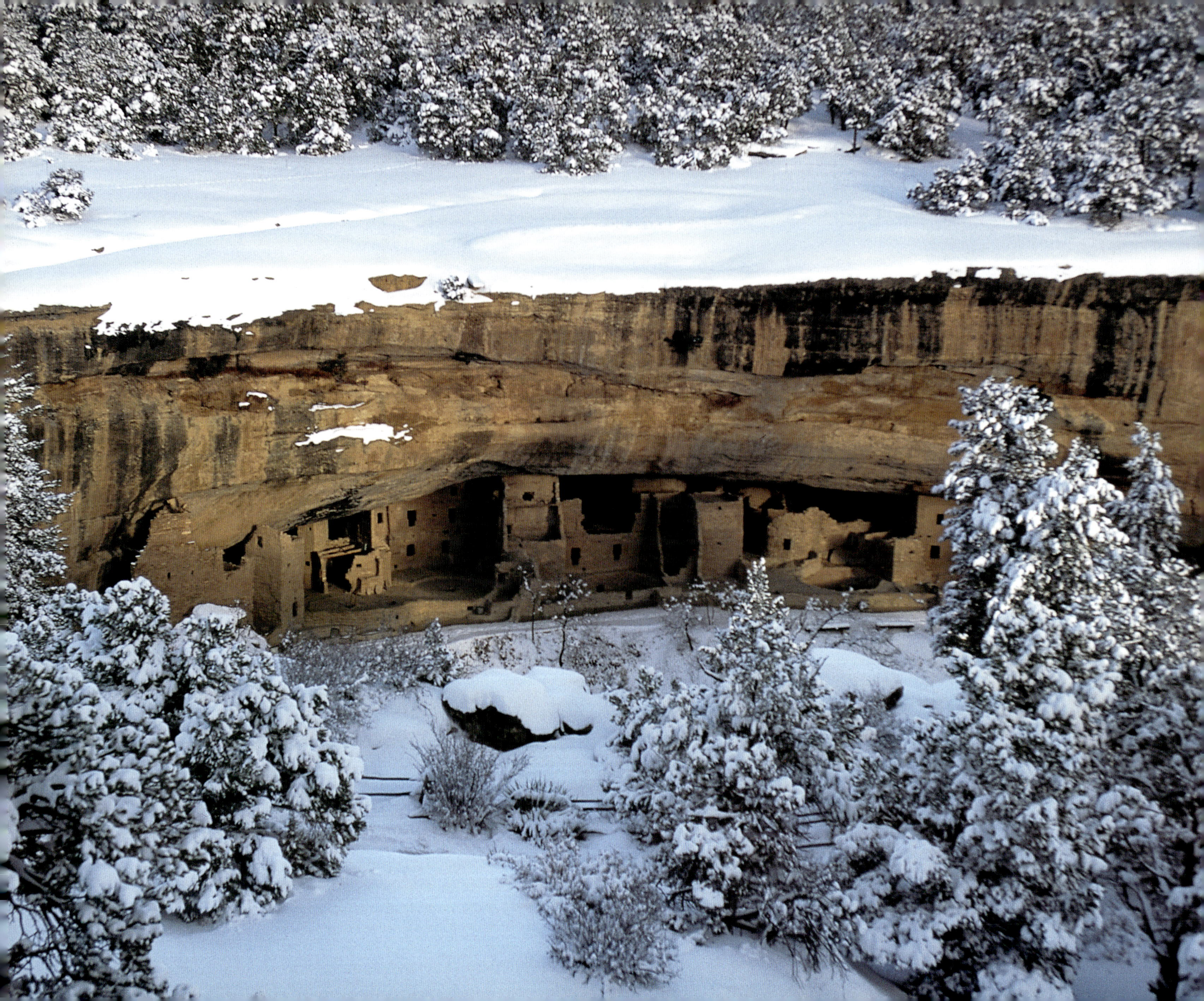

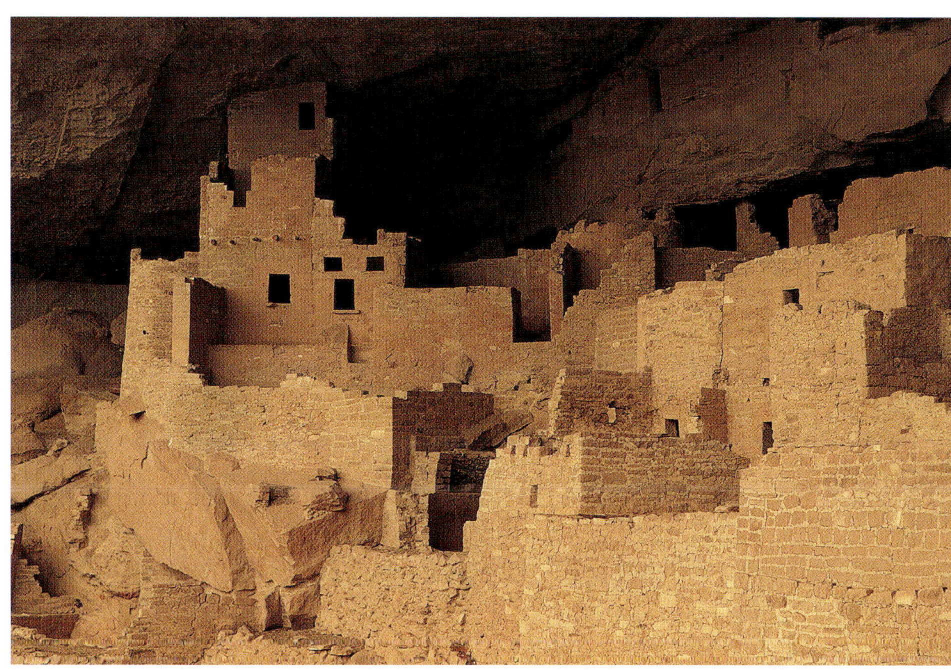

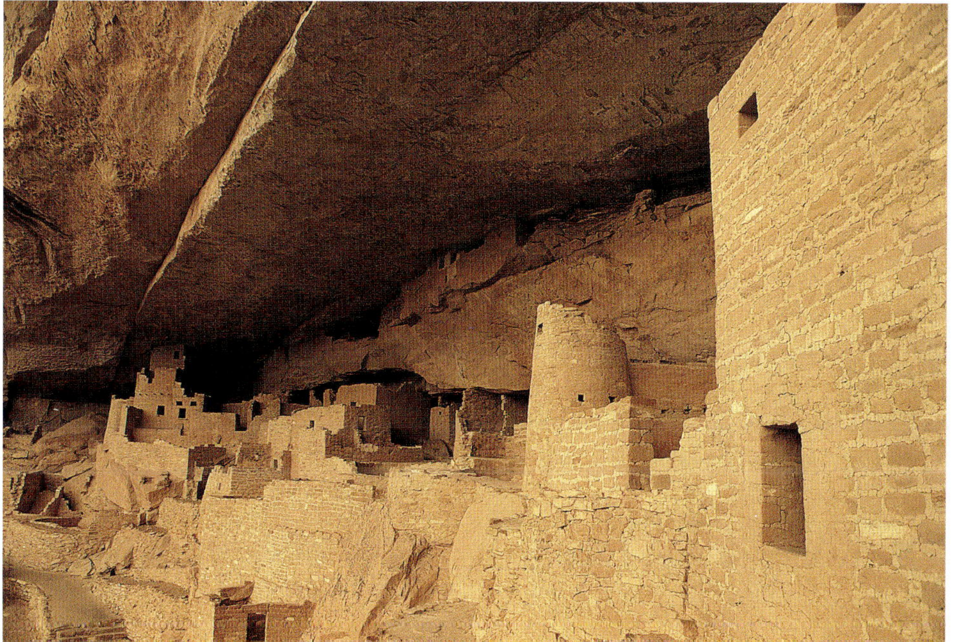

↑← Cliff Palace, Mesa Verde National Park

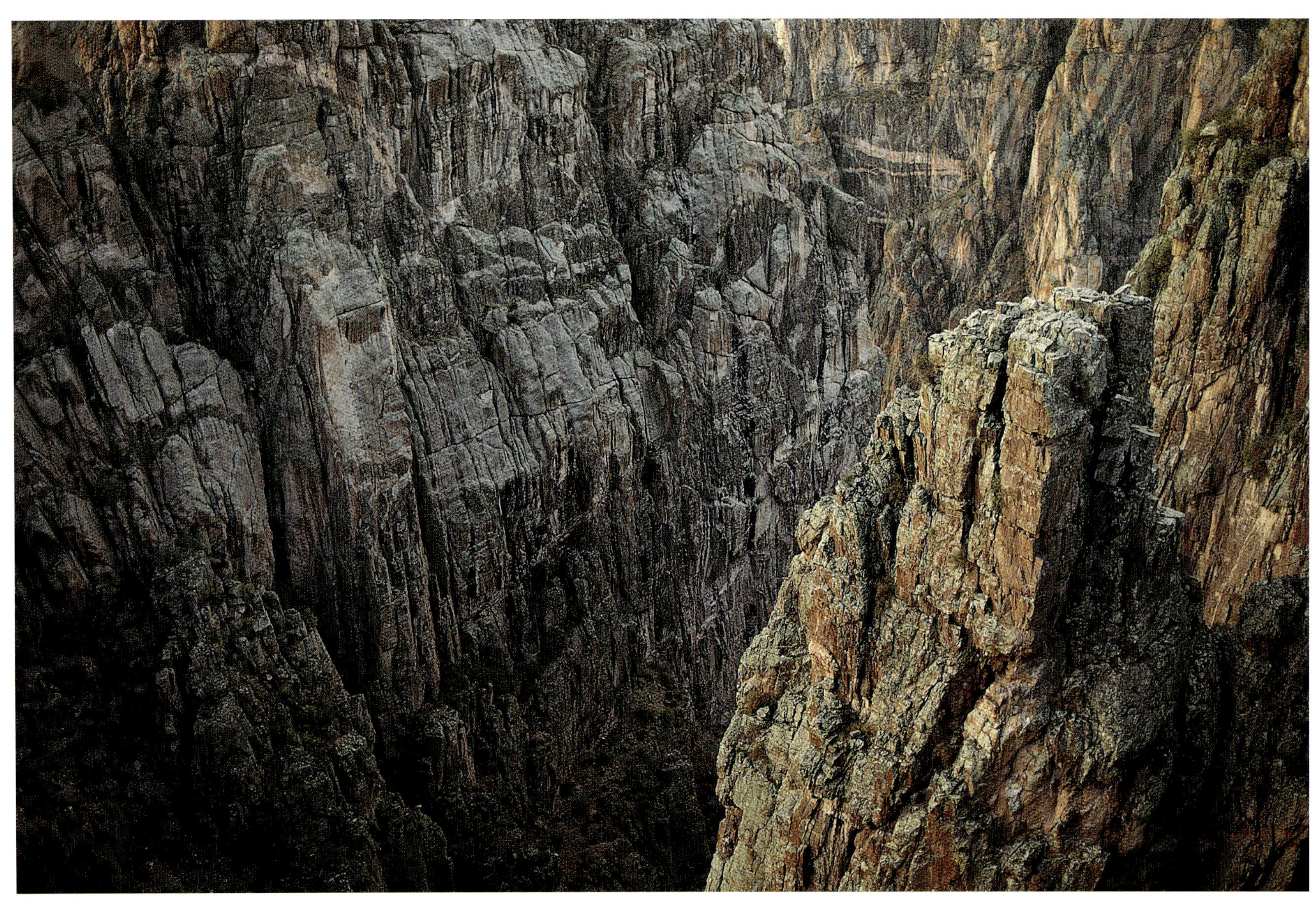

↑→ Black Canyon of the Gunnison National Park

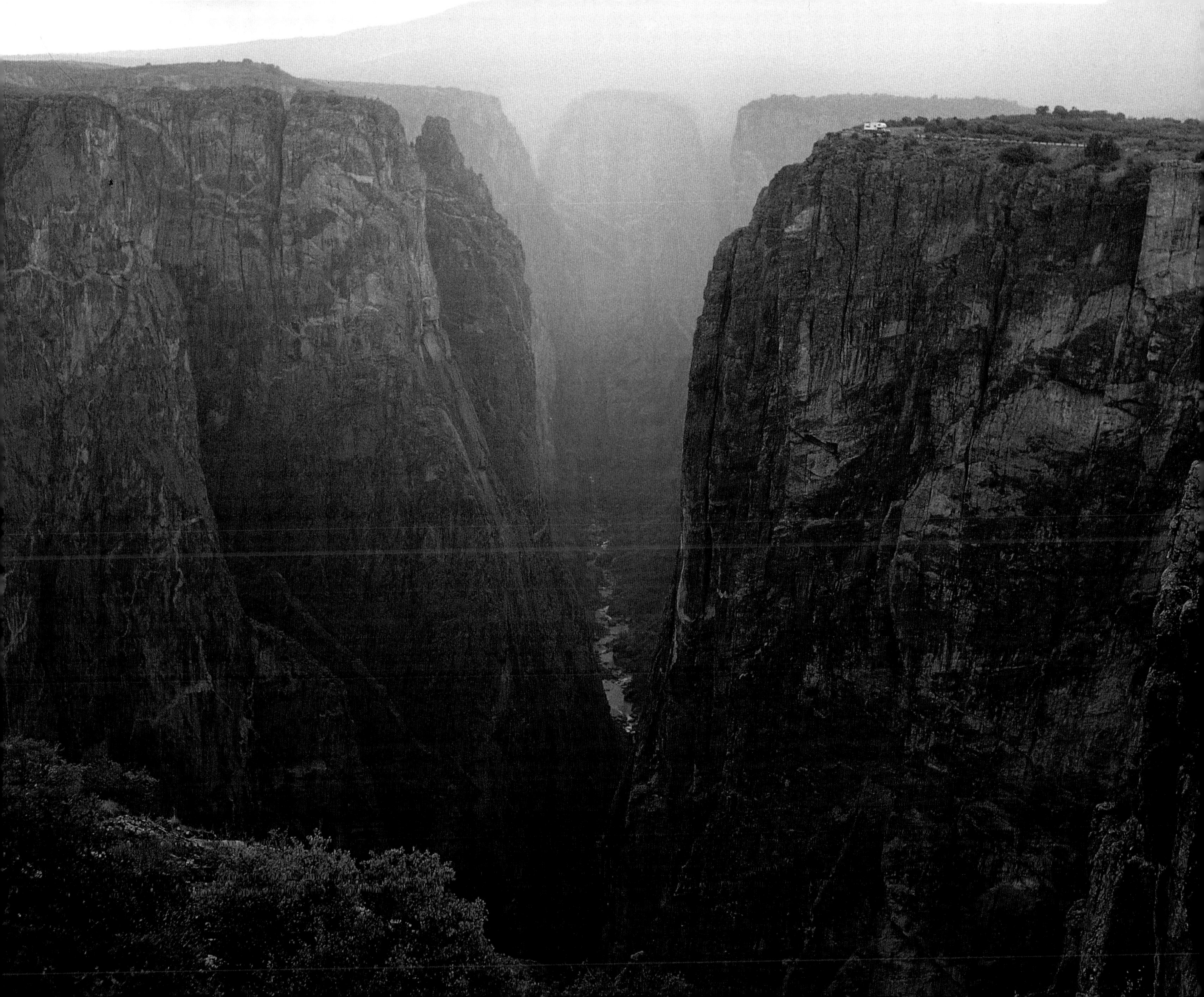

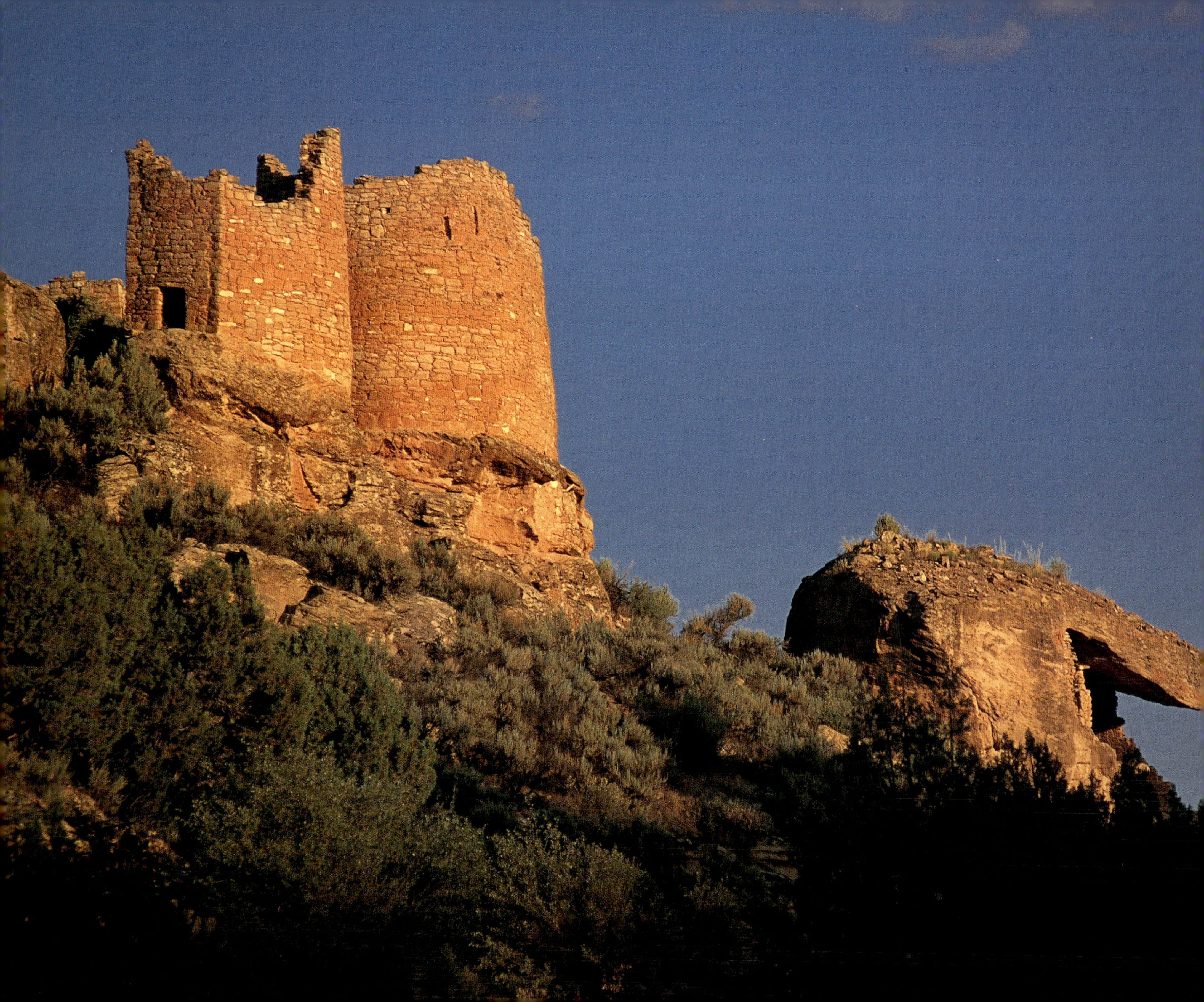

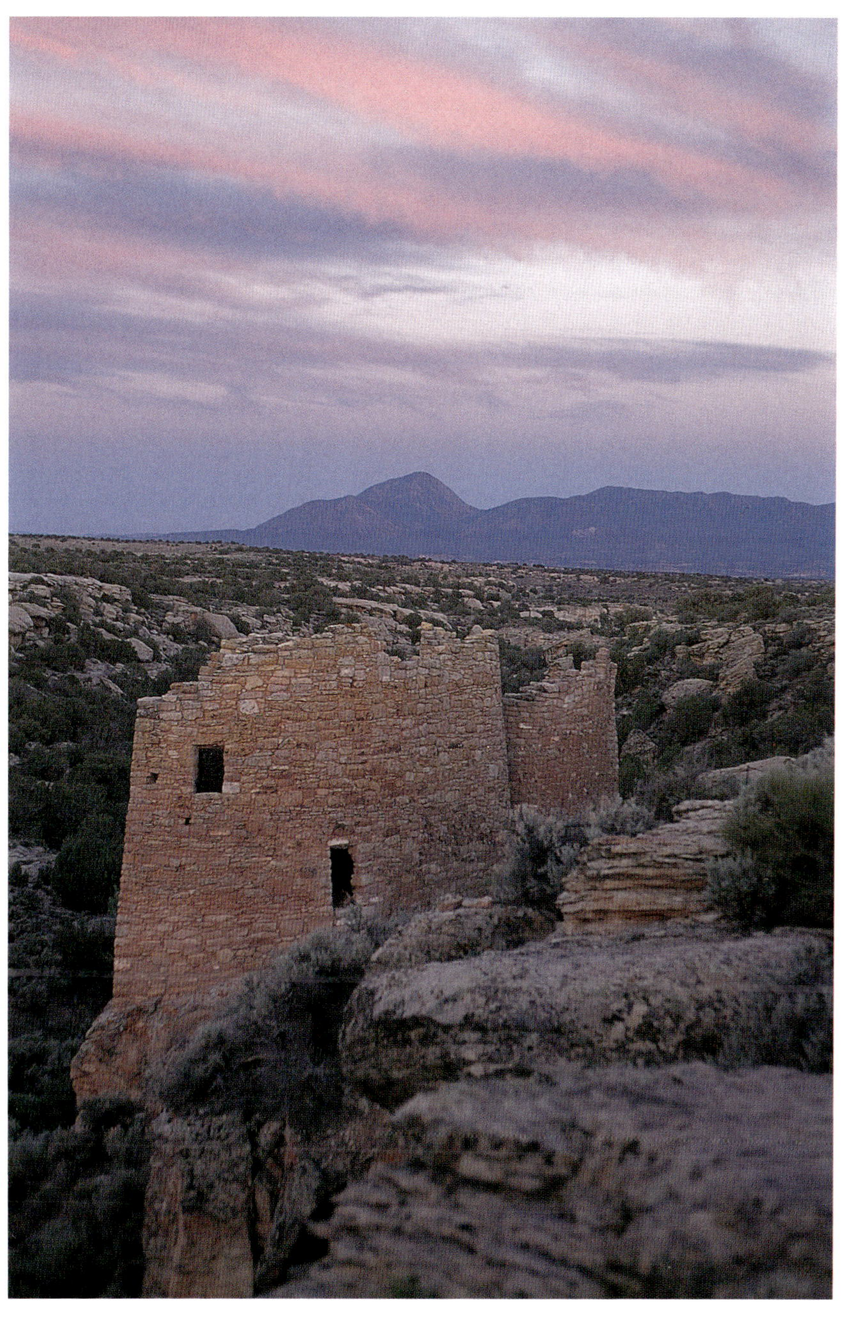

↑← Twin Towers, Hovenweep National Monument

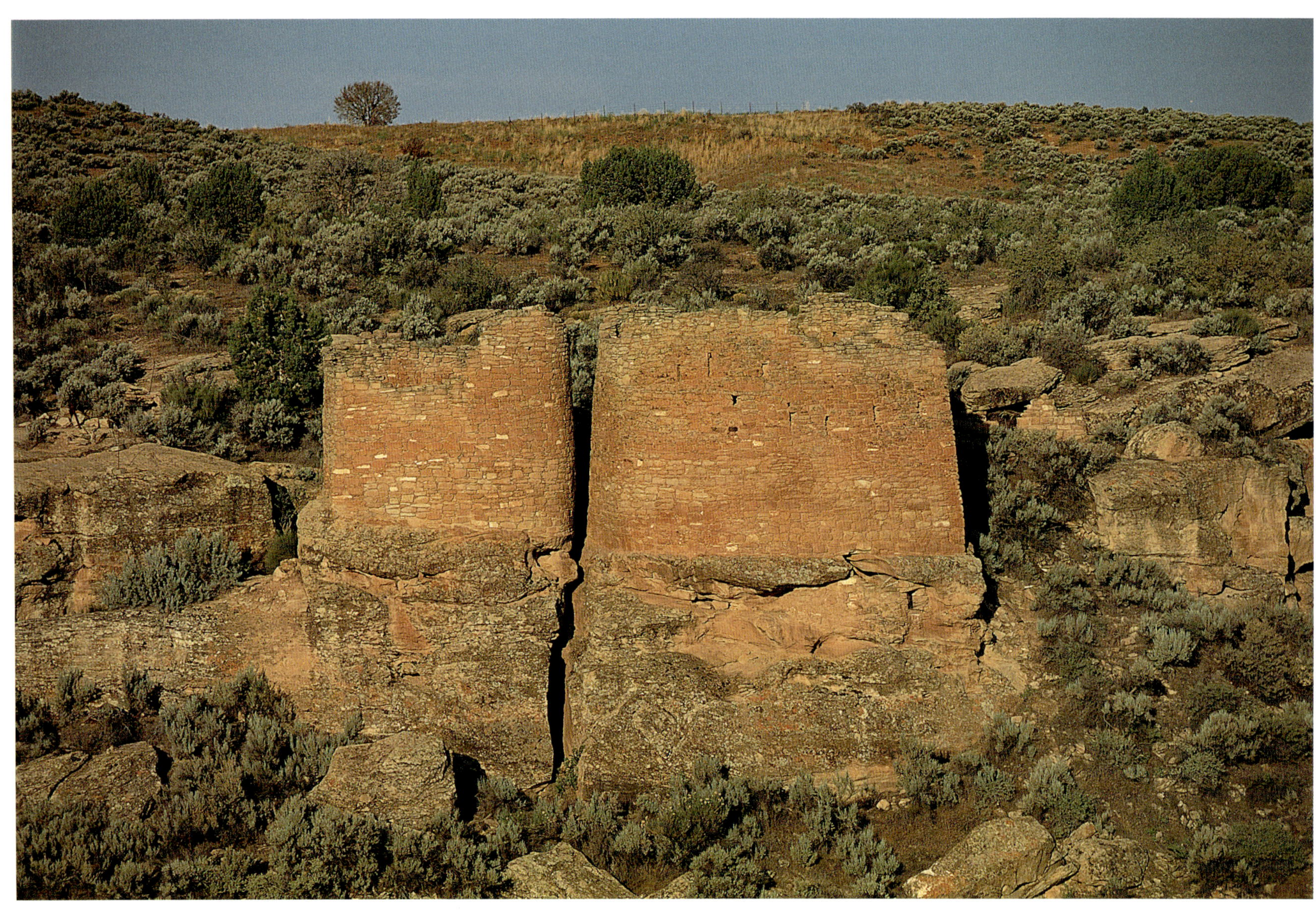

↑ Twin Towers, Hovenweep National Monument → Holly House in front, Great House in rear, Hovenweep National Monument

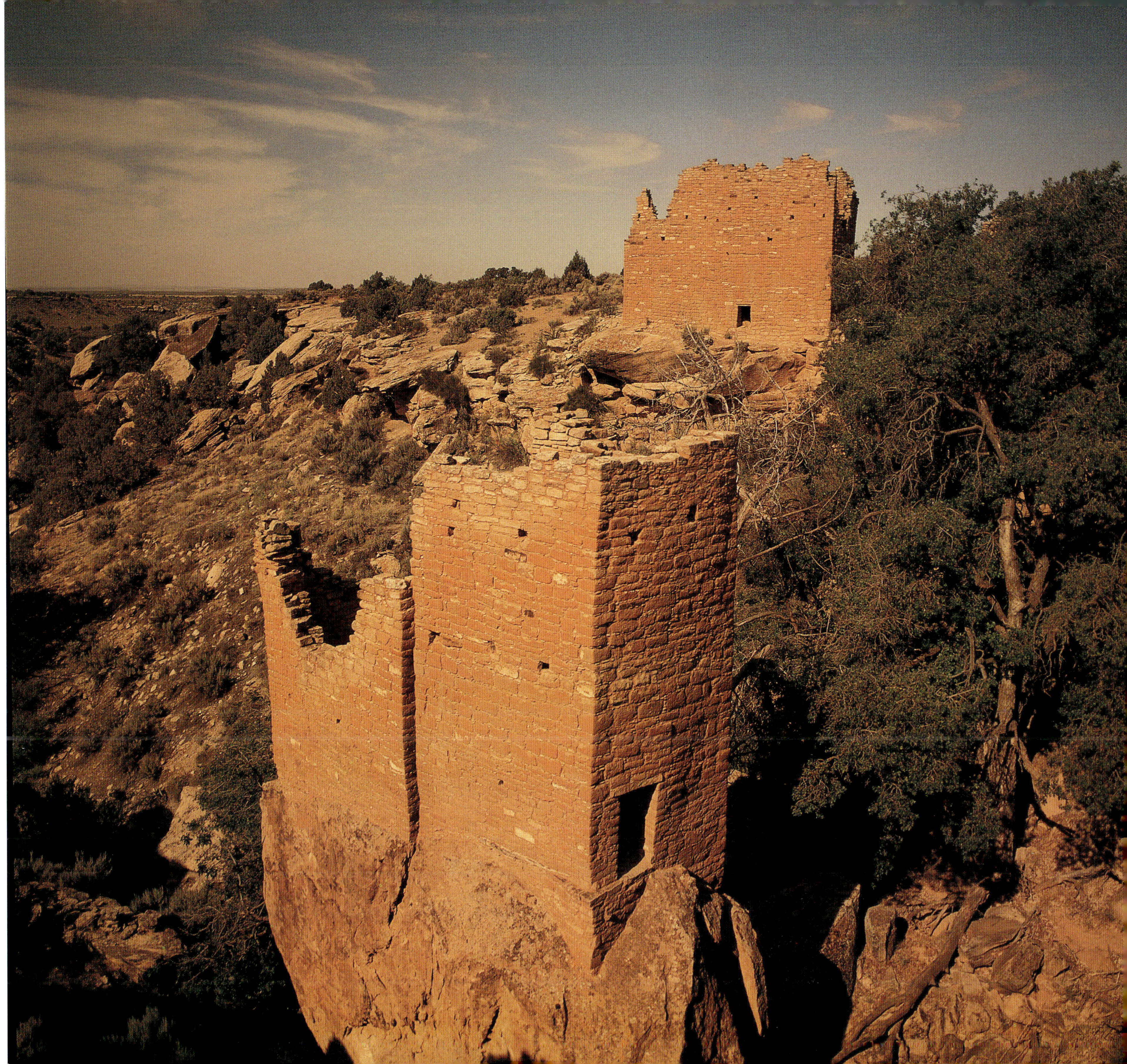

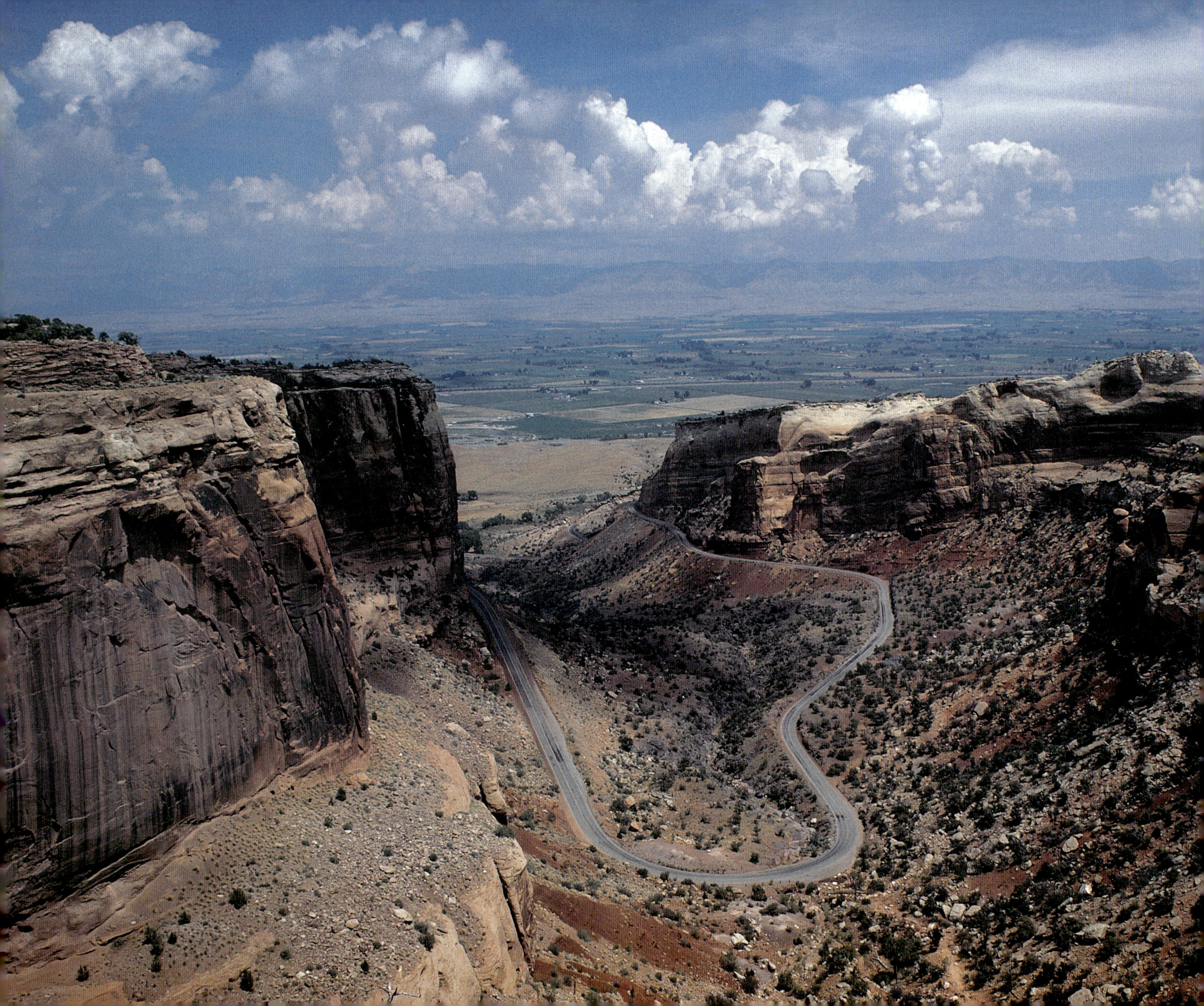

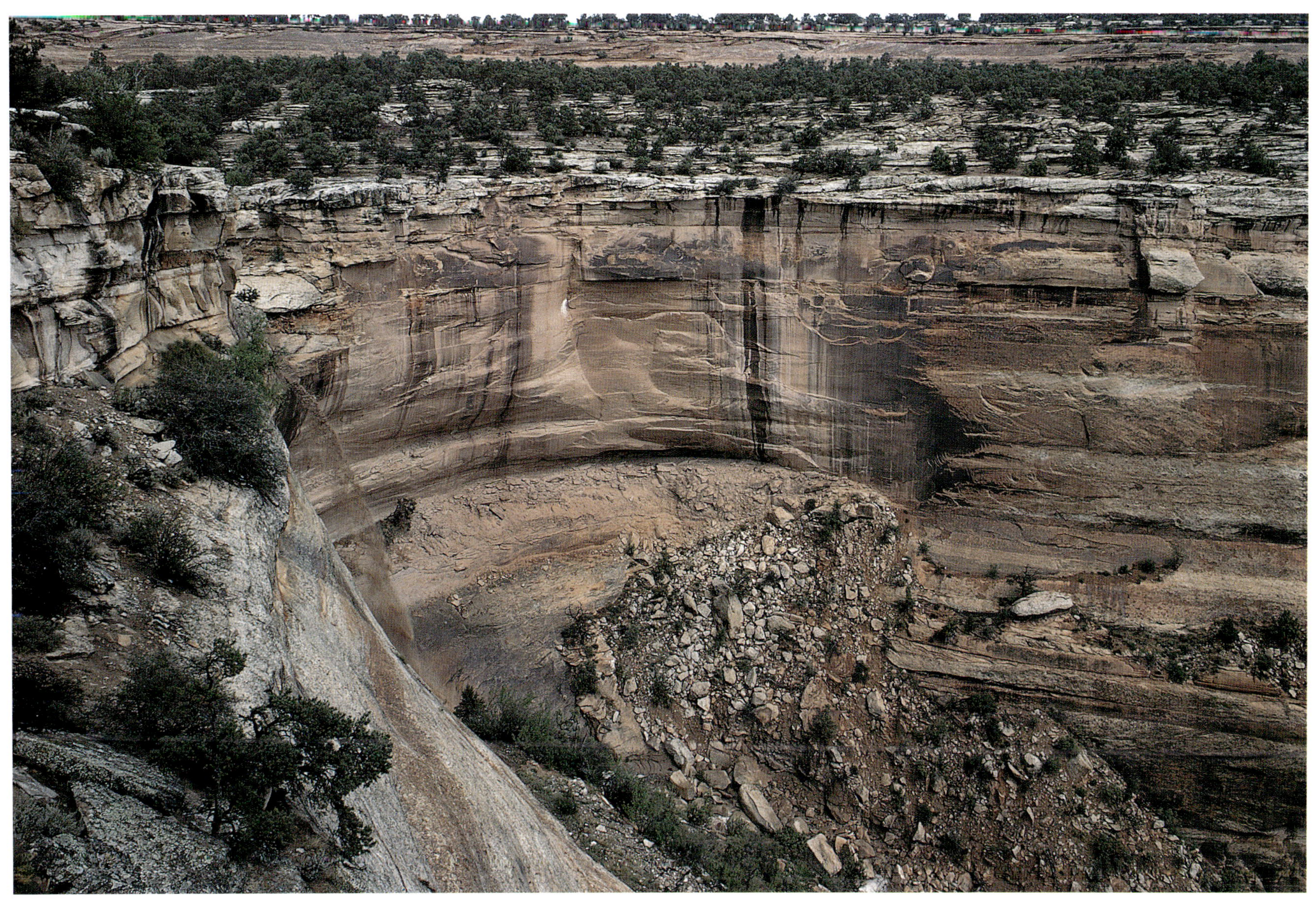

↑← Colorado National Monument

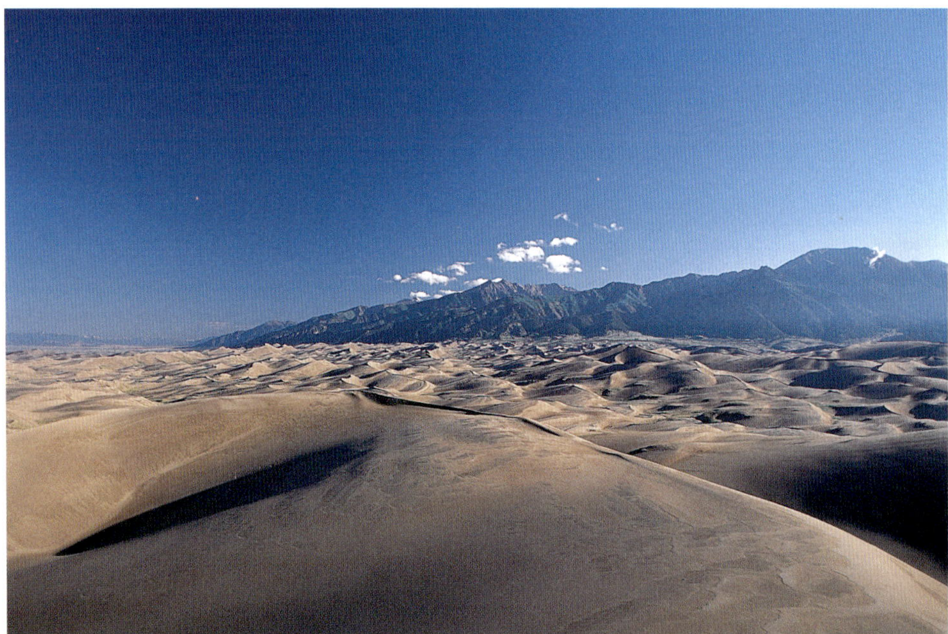

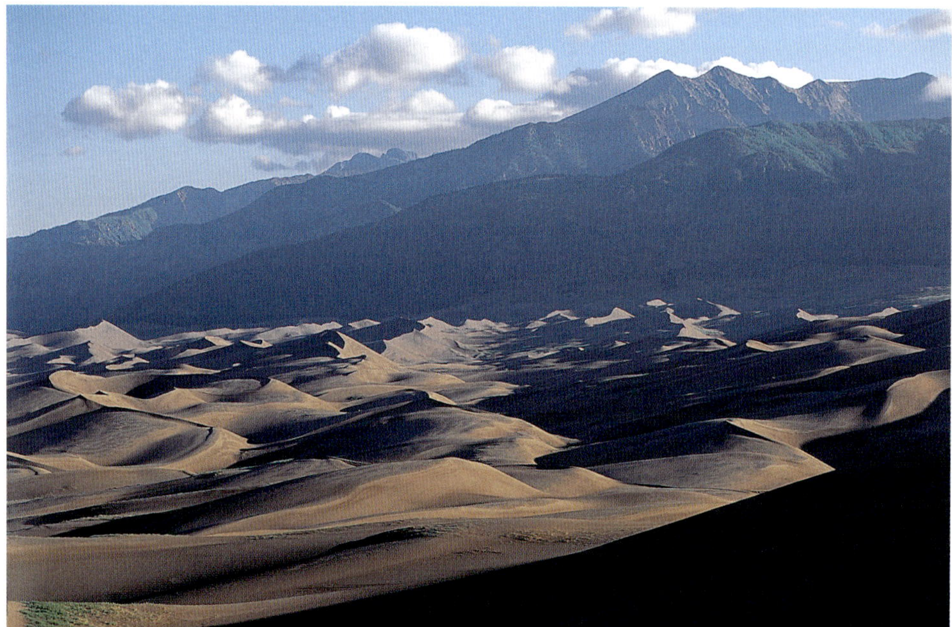

↑→ Great Sand Dunes National Park and Preserve

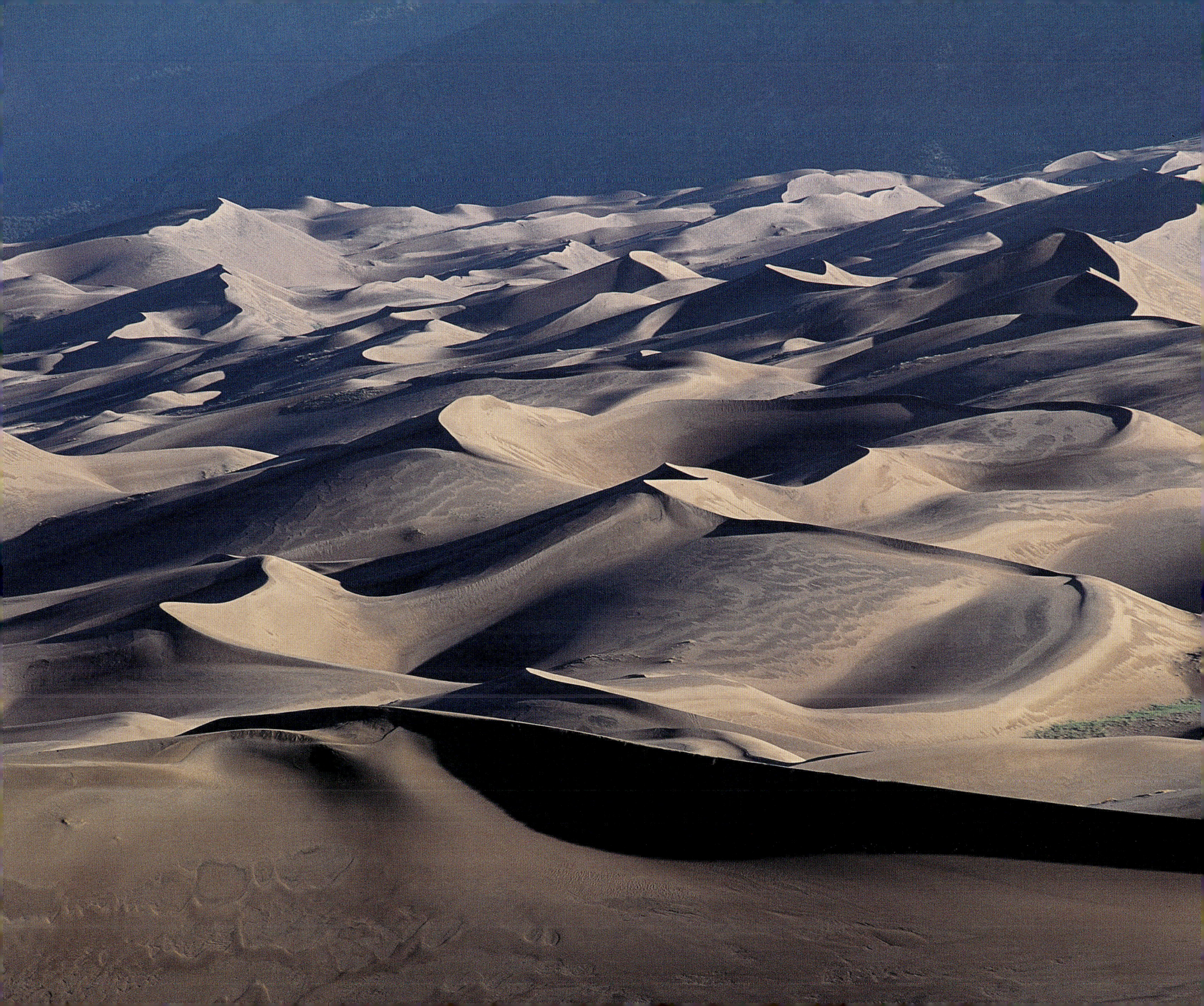

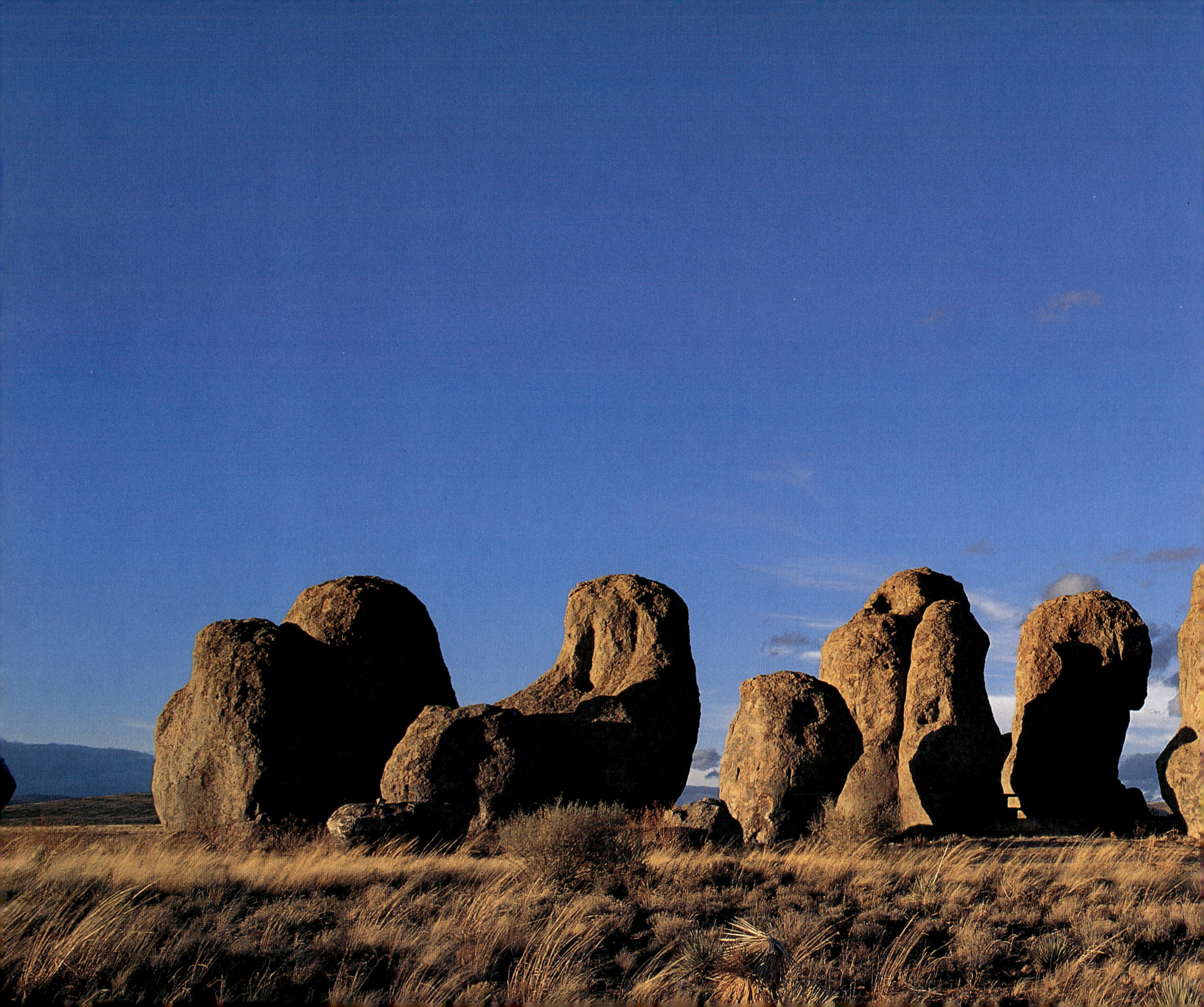

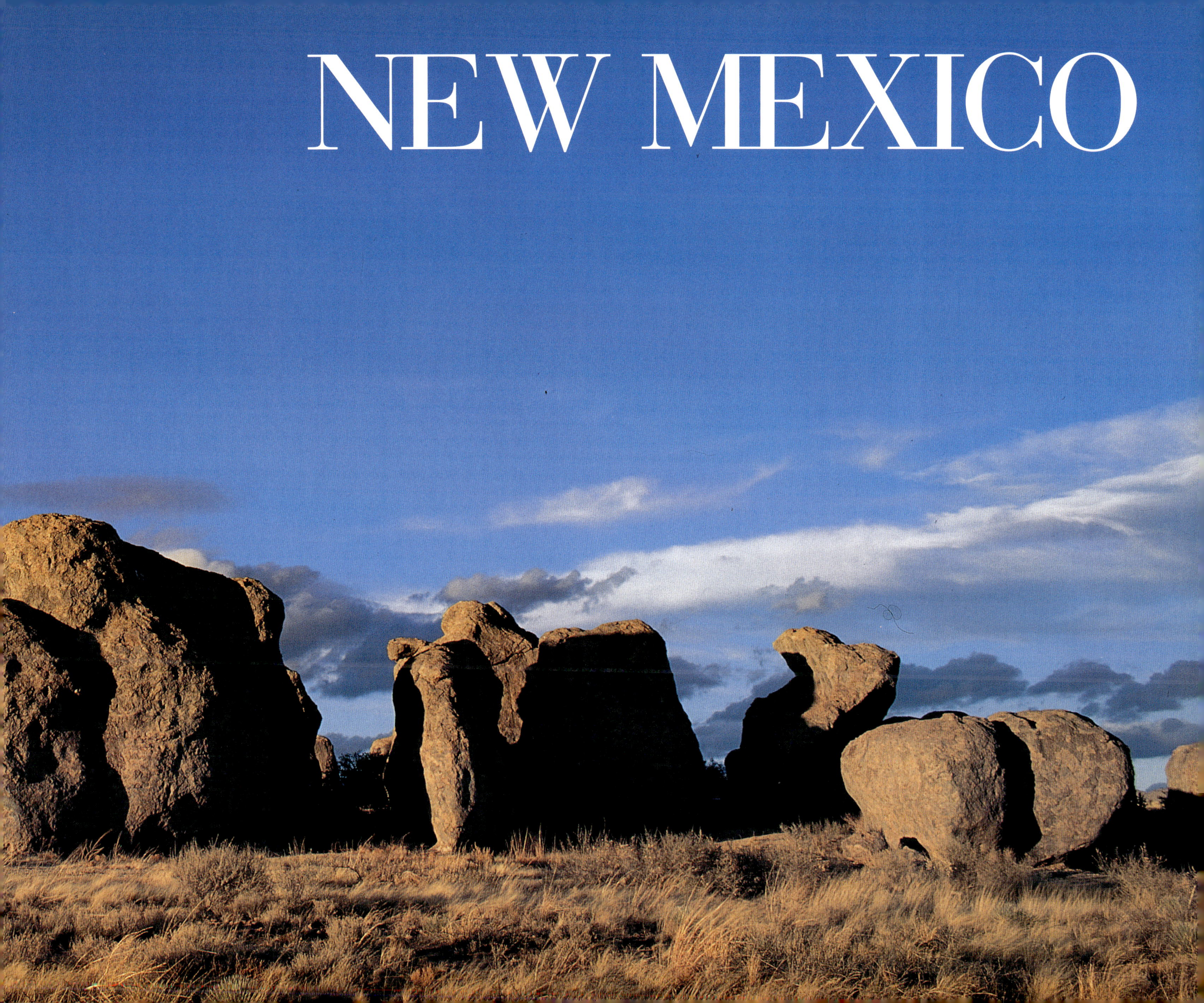
NEW MEXICO

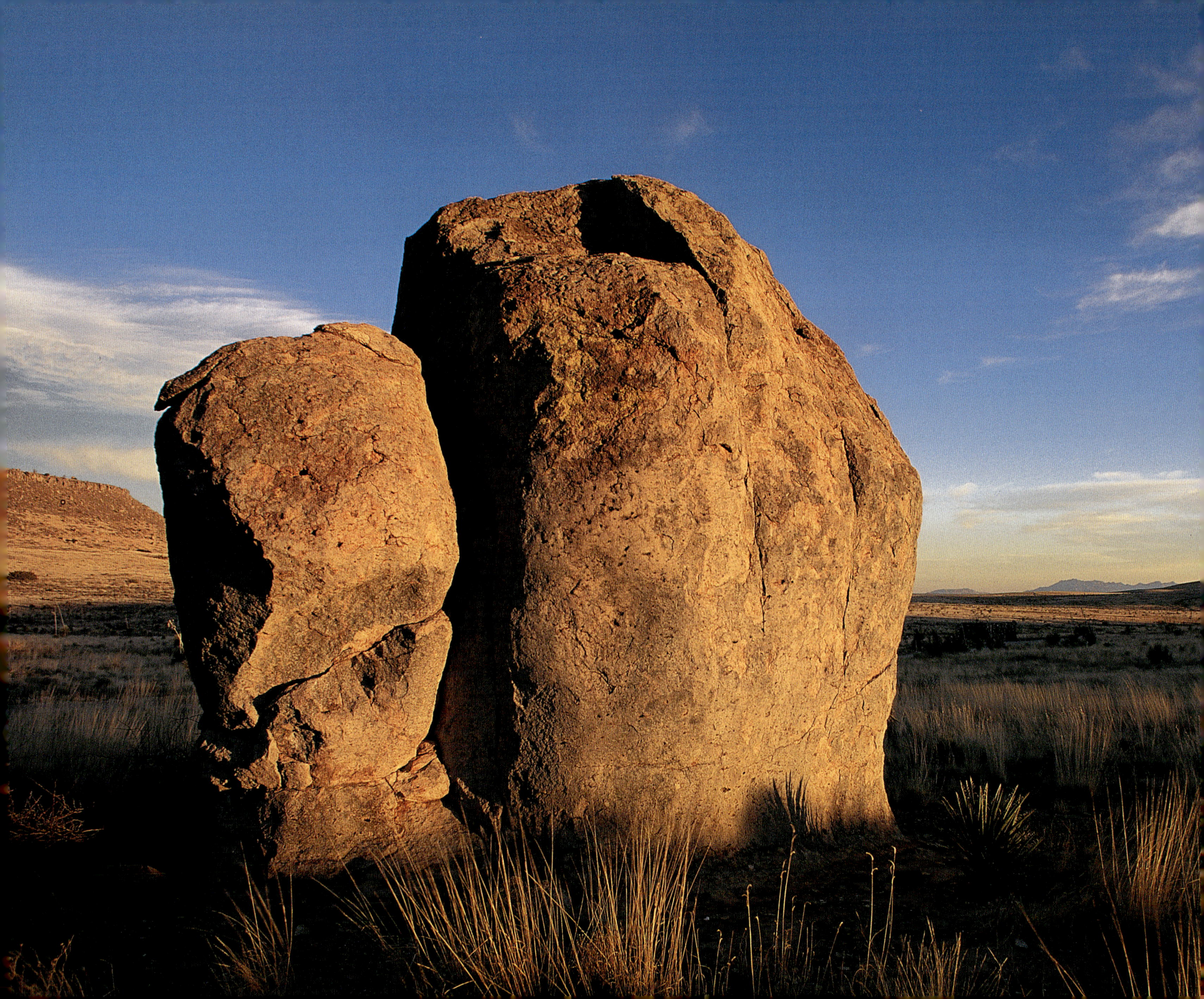

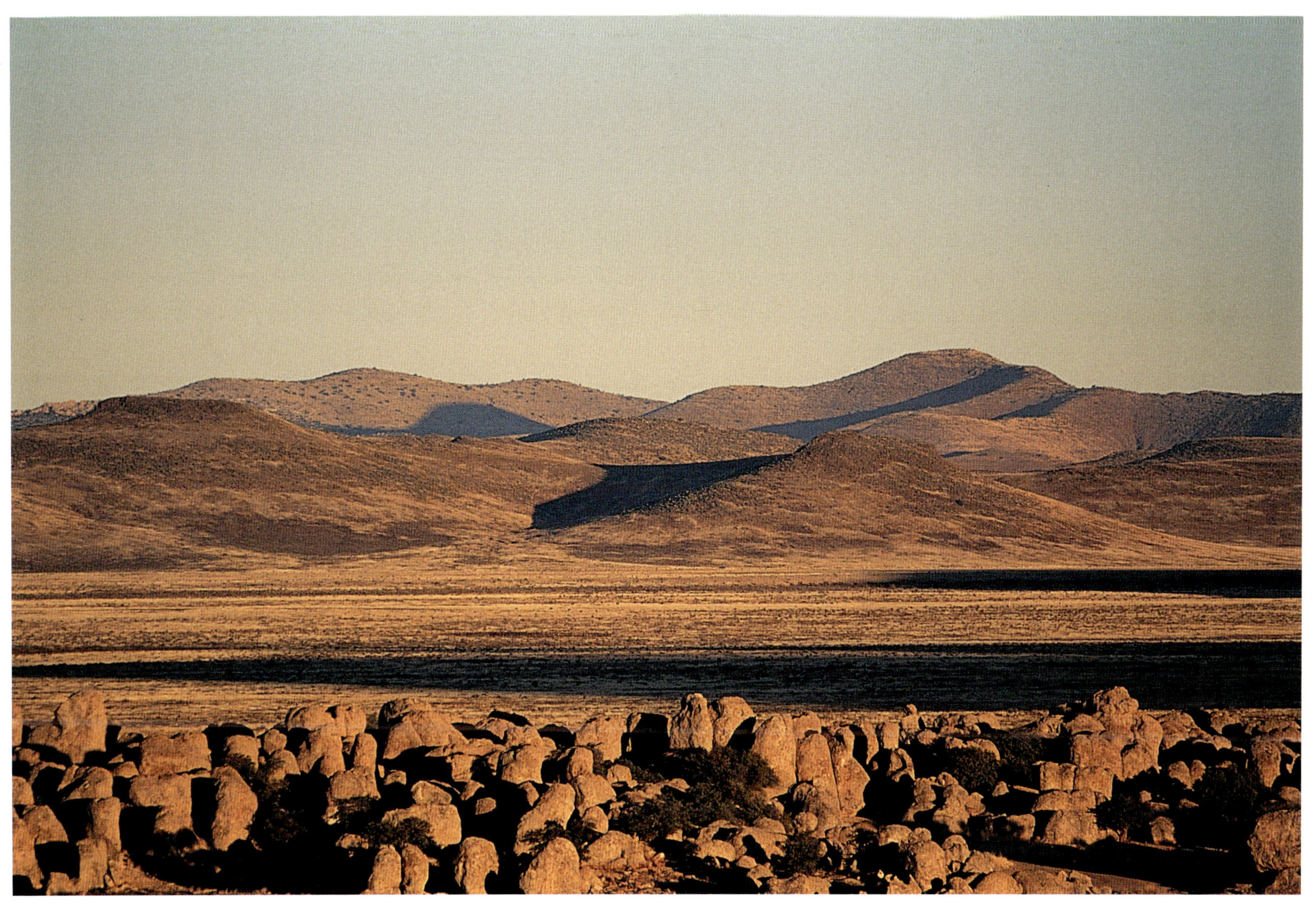

↑←City of Rocks State Park

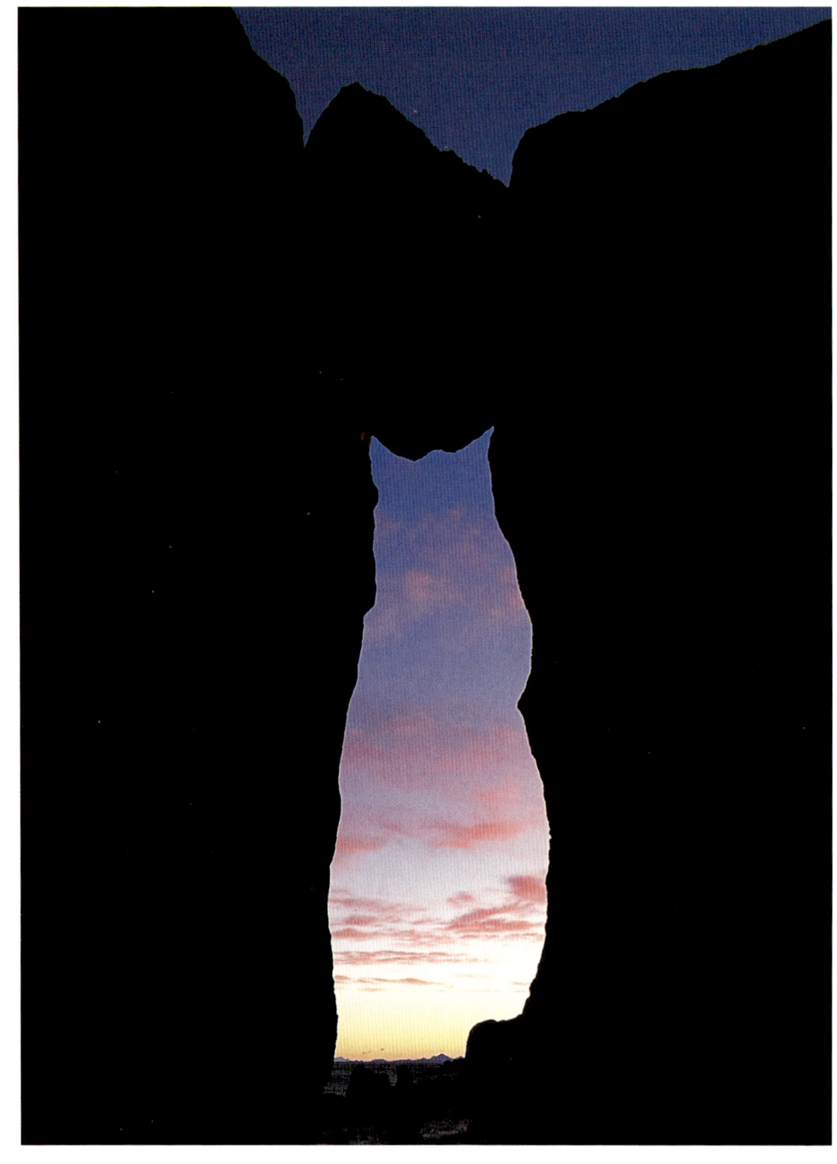

↰ City of Rocks State Park

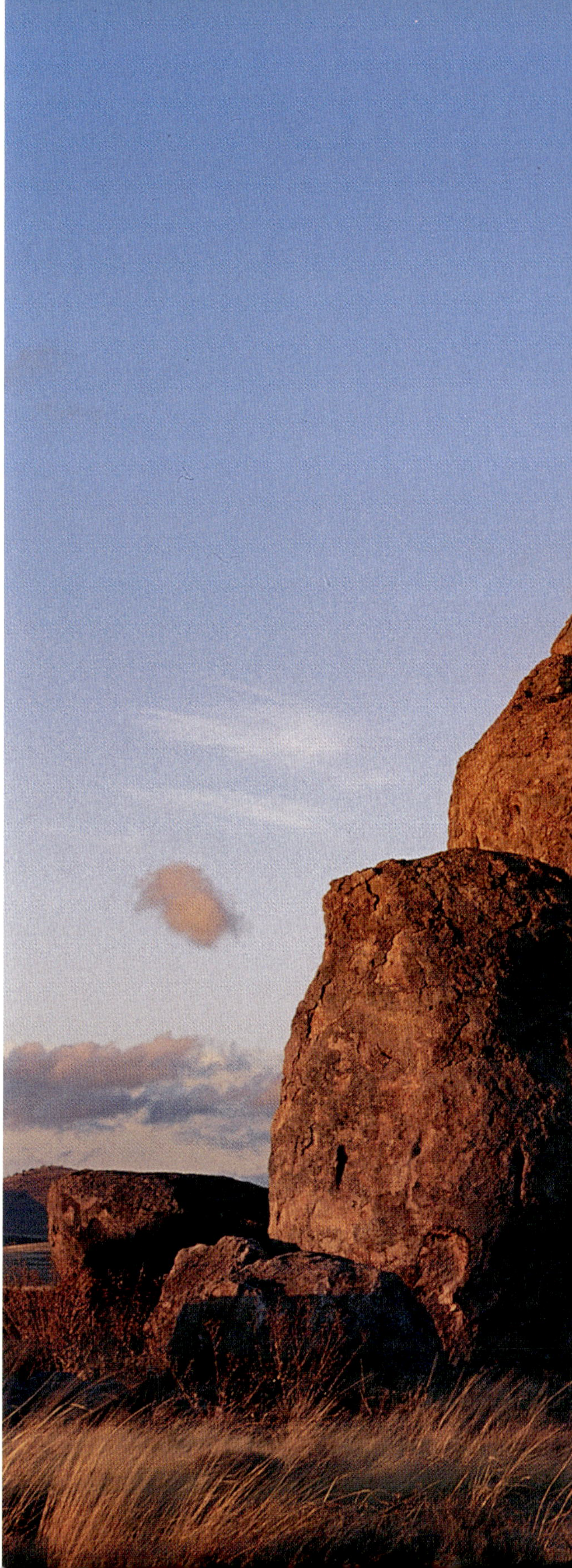

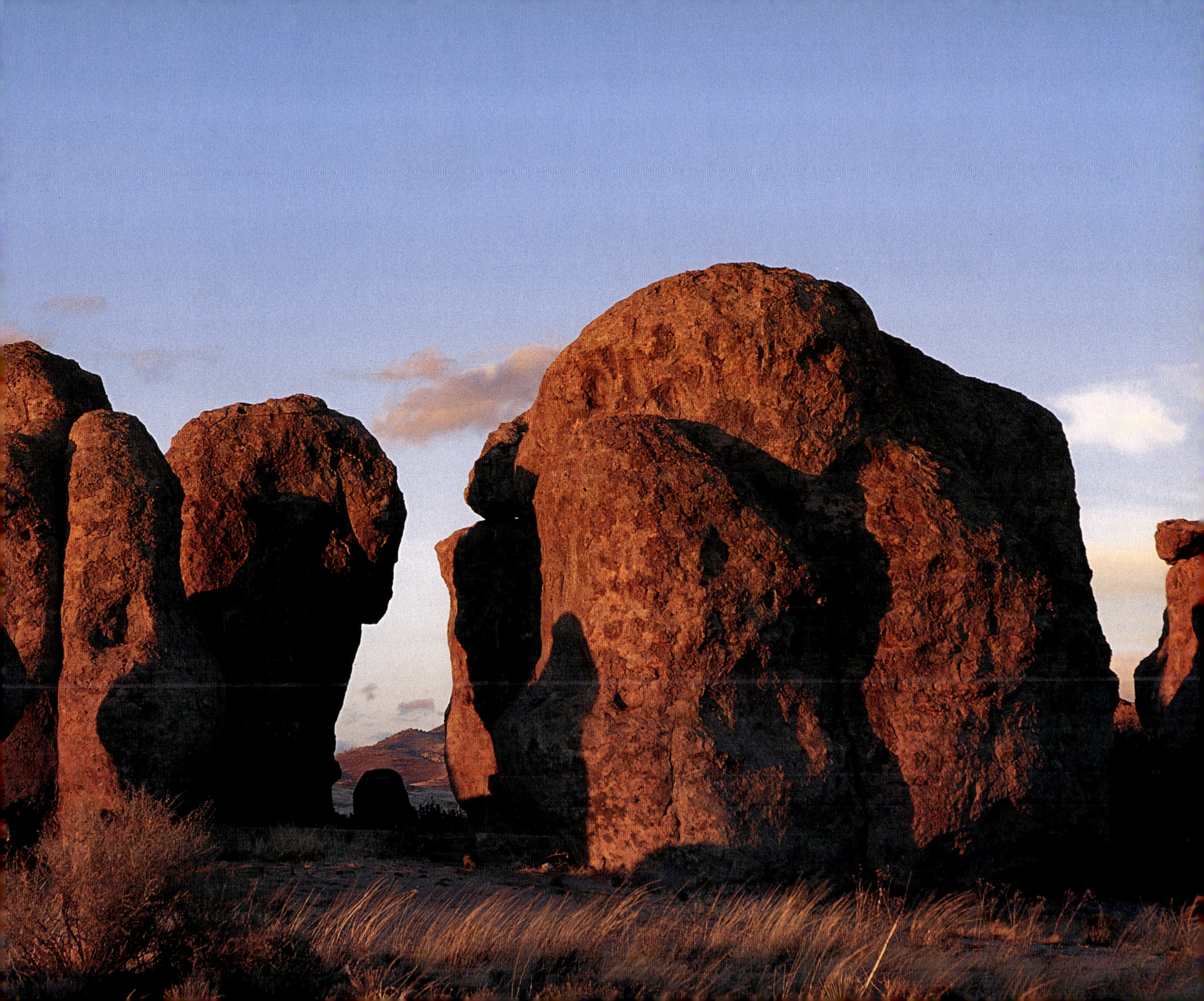

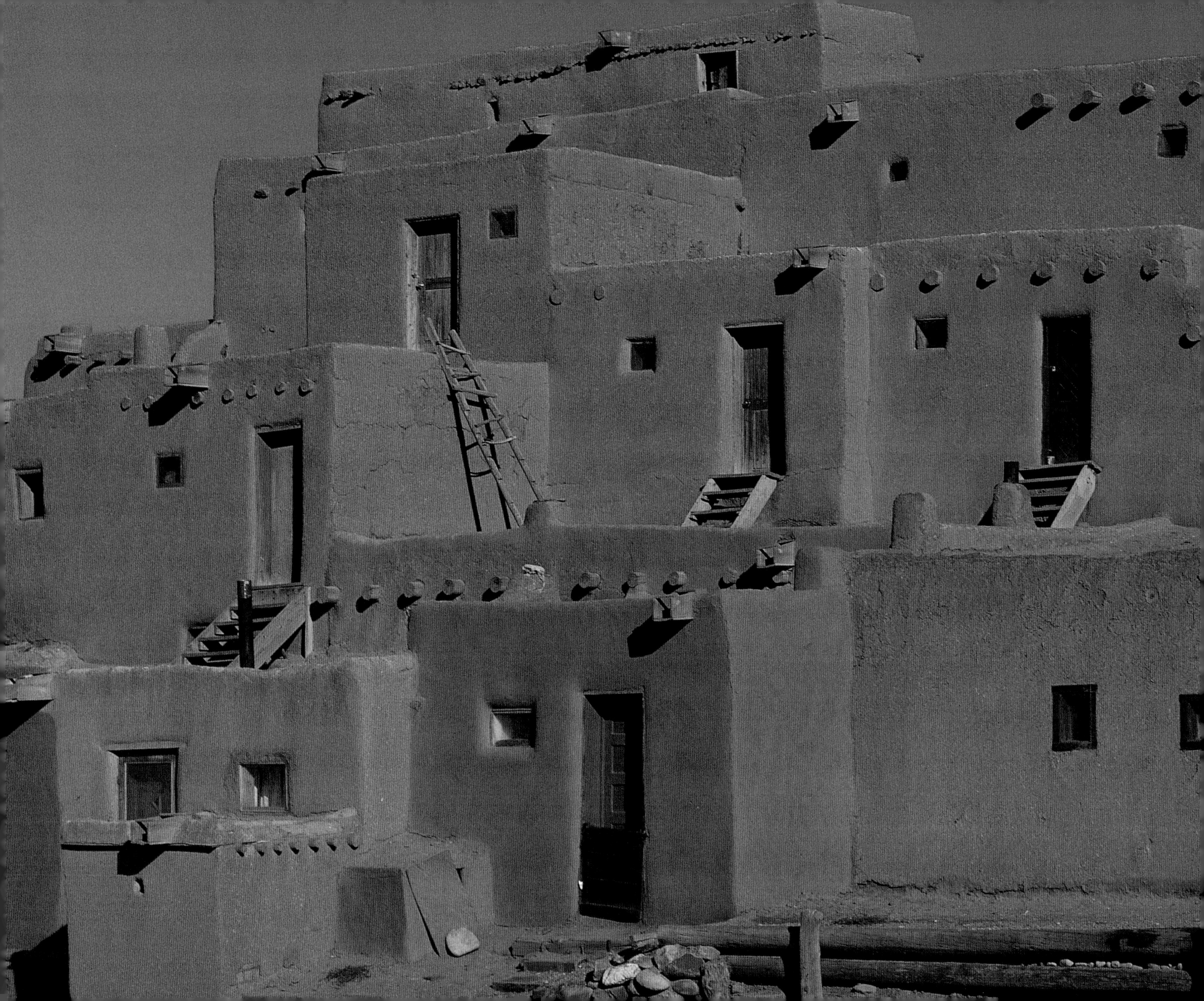

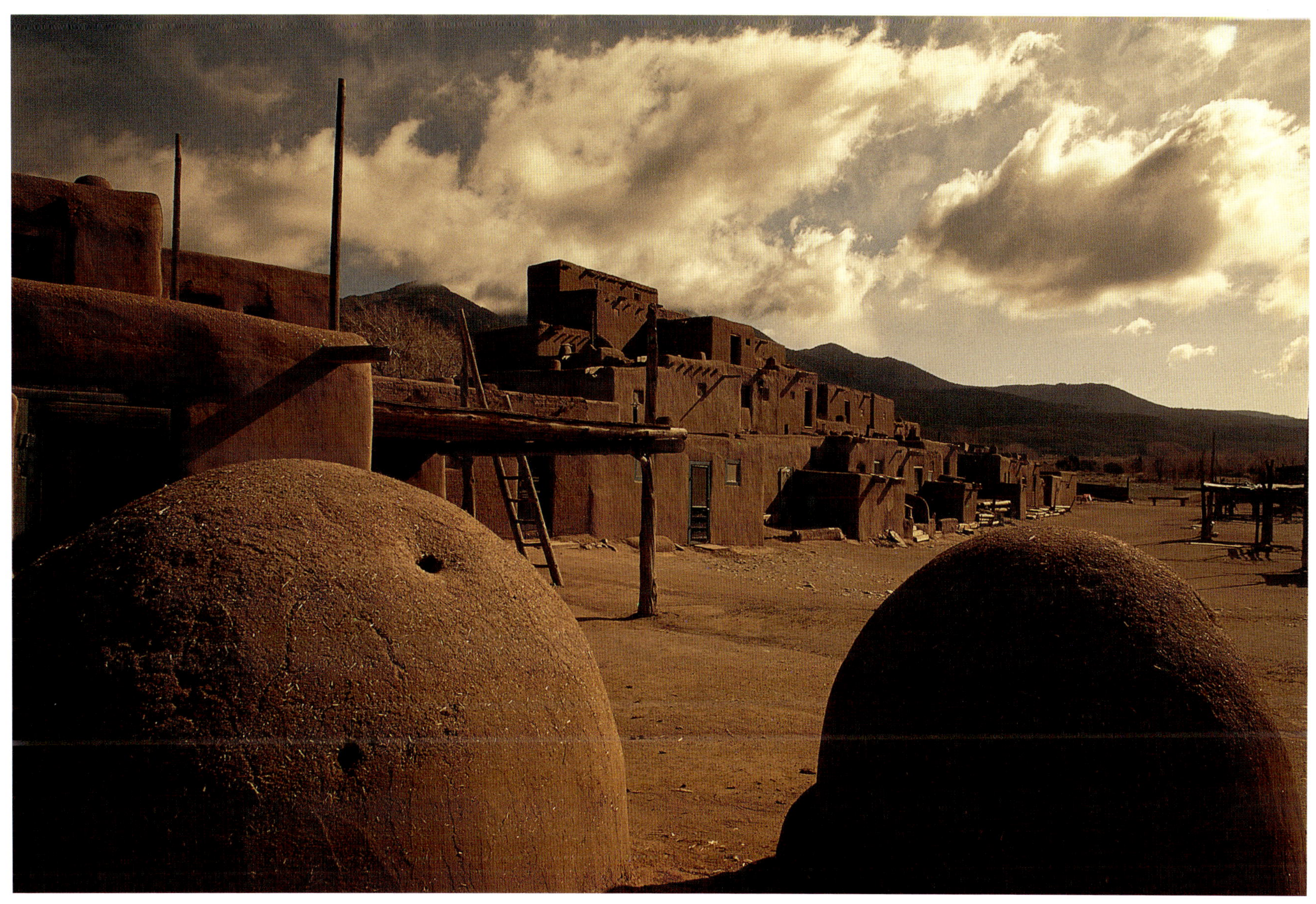

↑←Taos Pueblo ↓ Pueblo Bonito, Chaco Culture National Historic Park

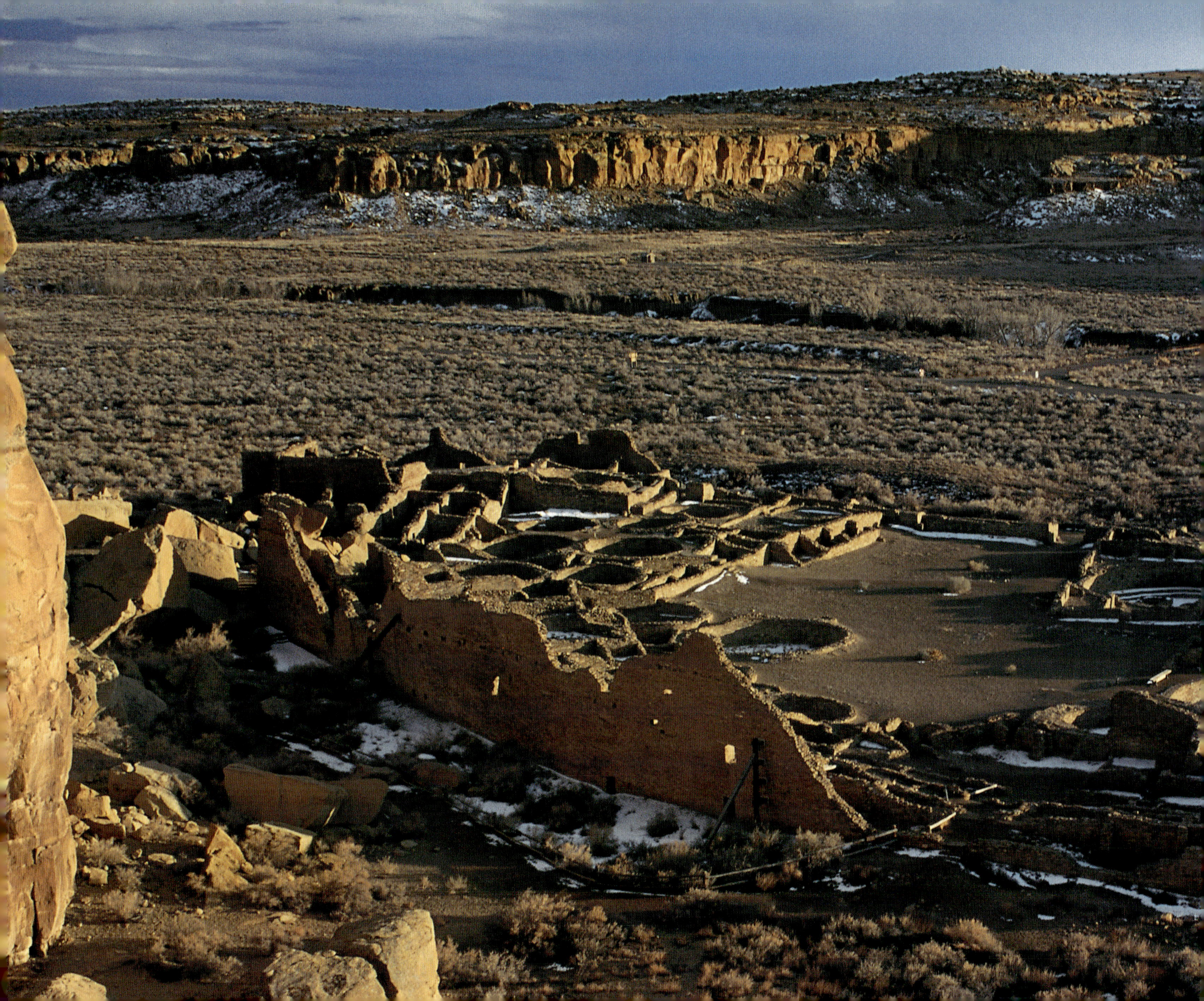

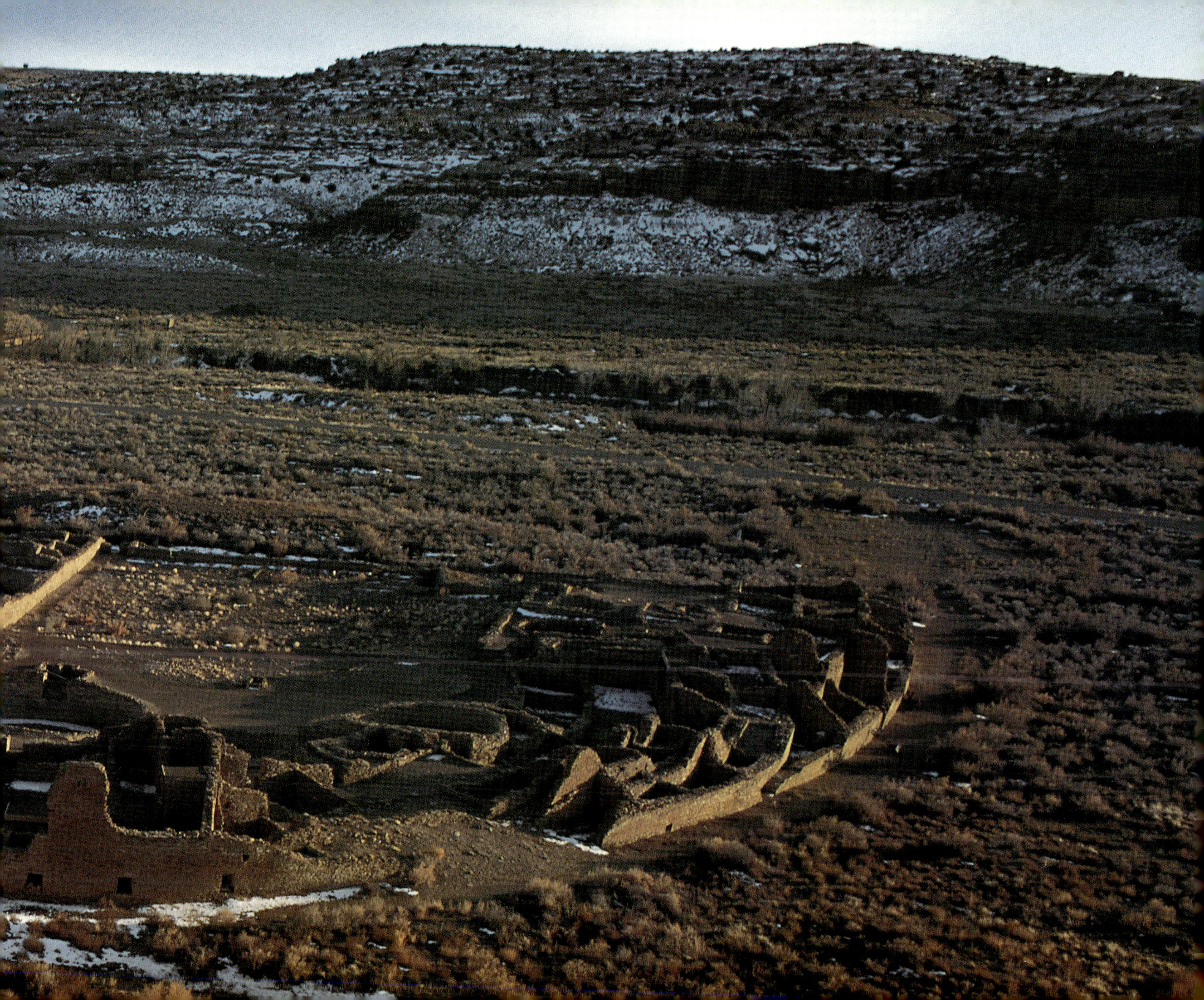

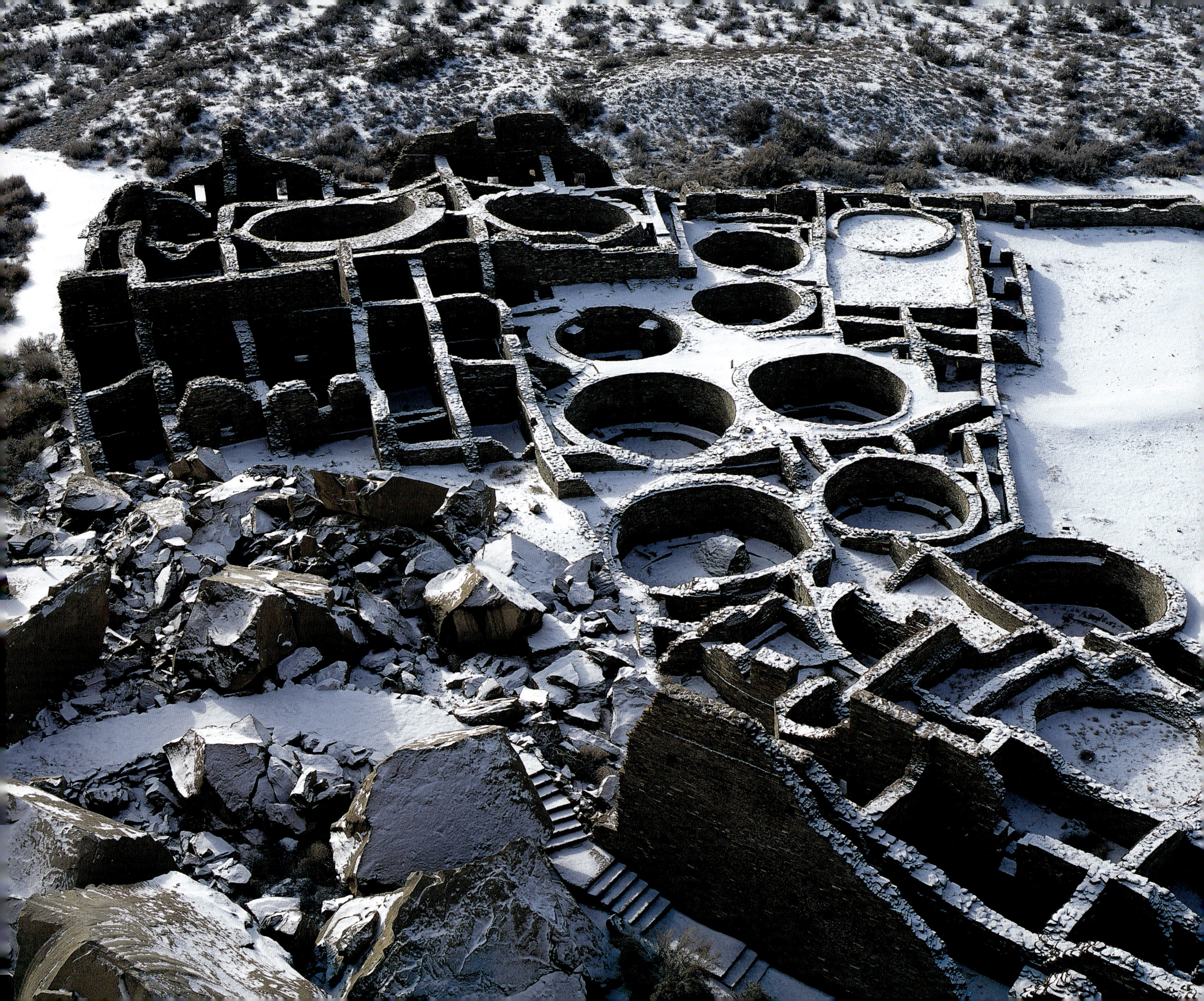

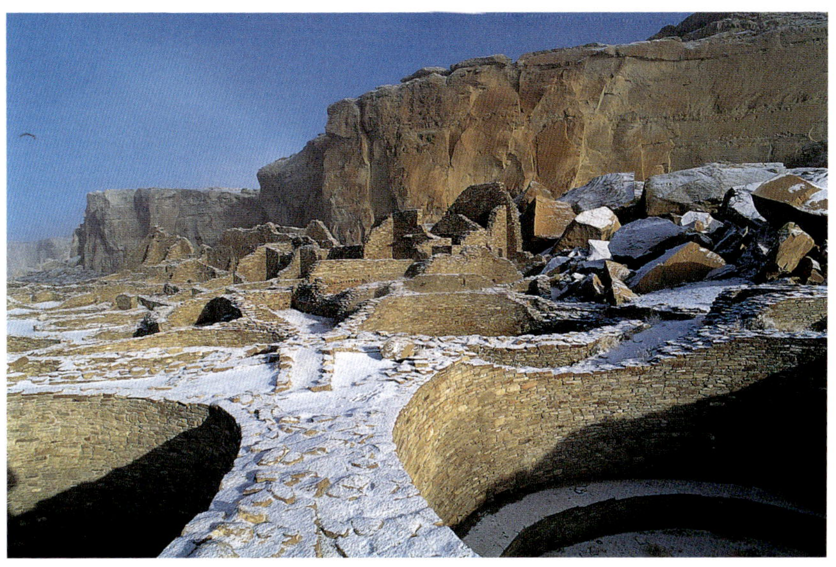

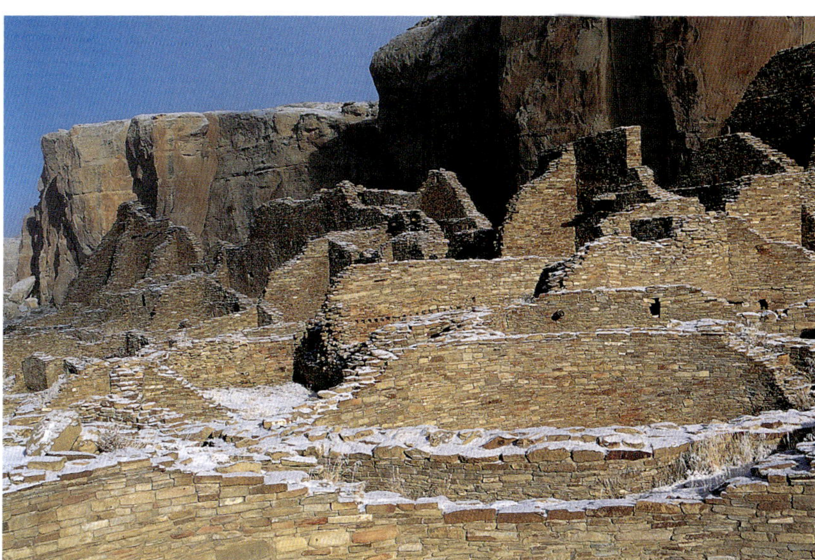

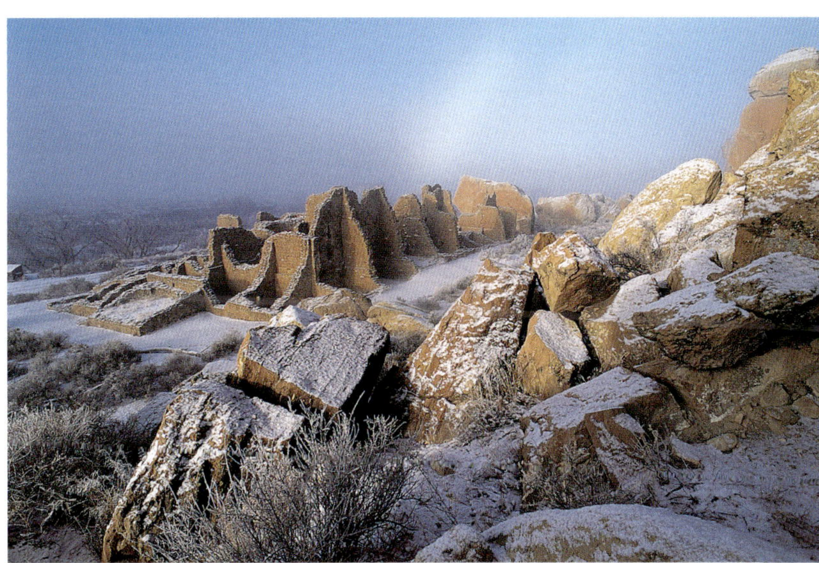

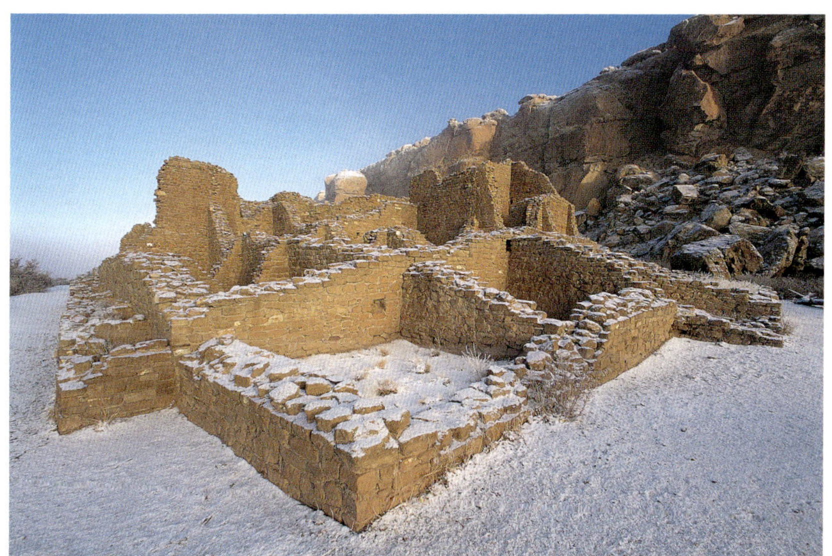

↑ ← Pueblo Bonito, Chaco Culture National Historical Park ↑ Kin Kletso, Chaco Canon National Historic Park

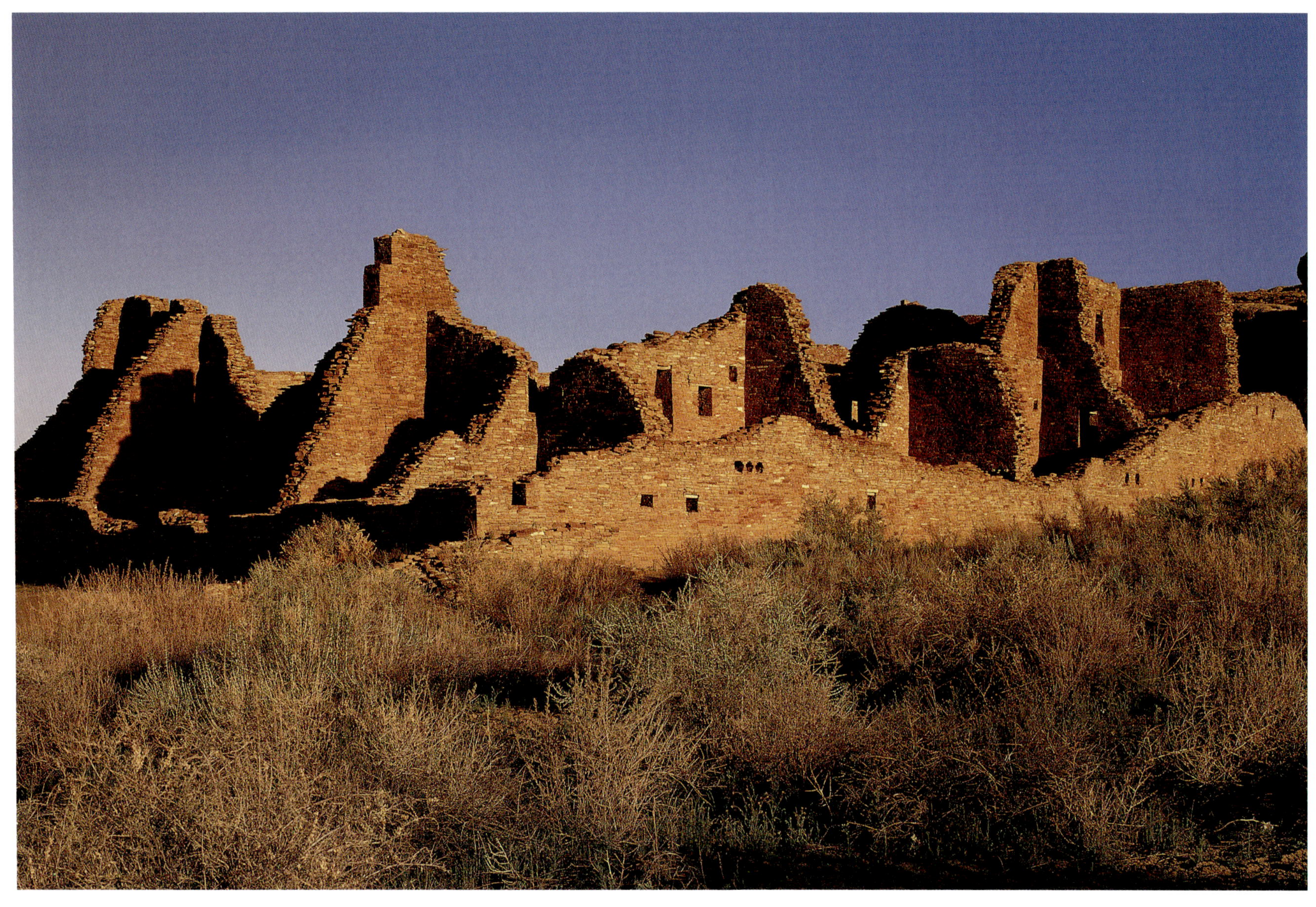

↑→ Pueblo Bonito, Chaco Culture National Historical Park

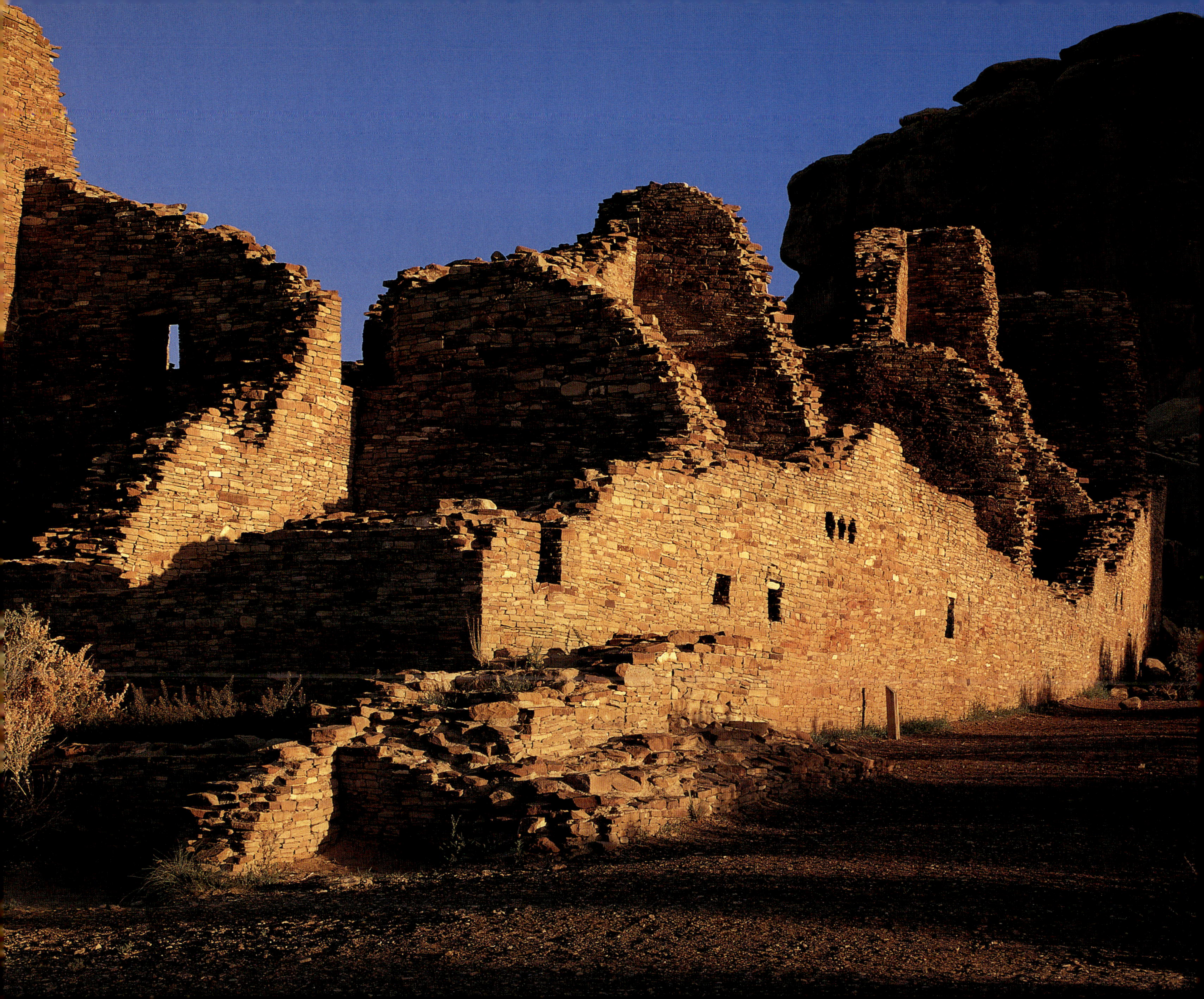

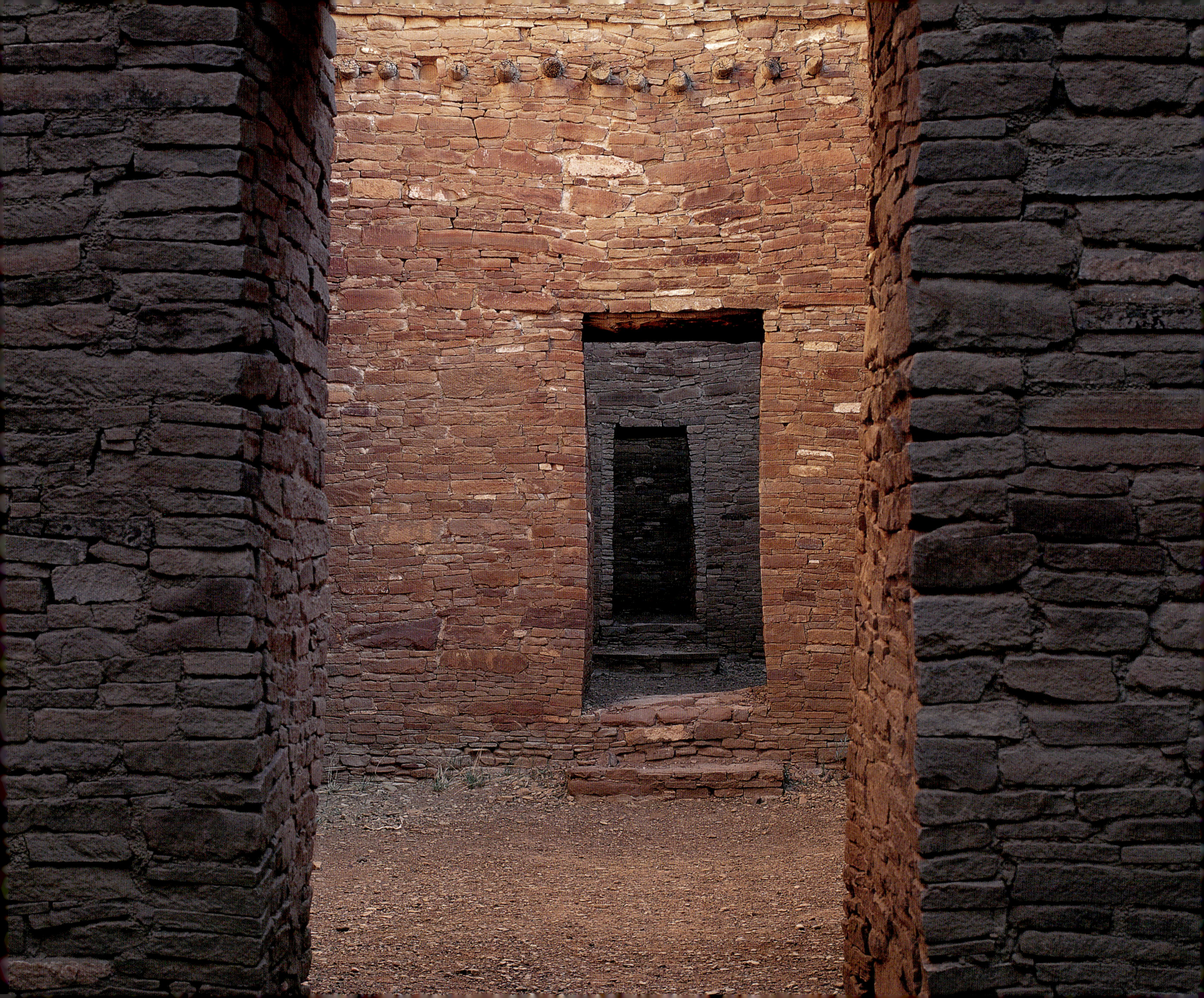

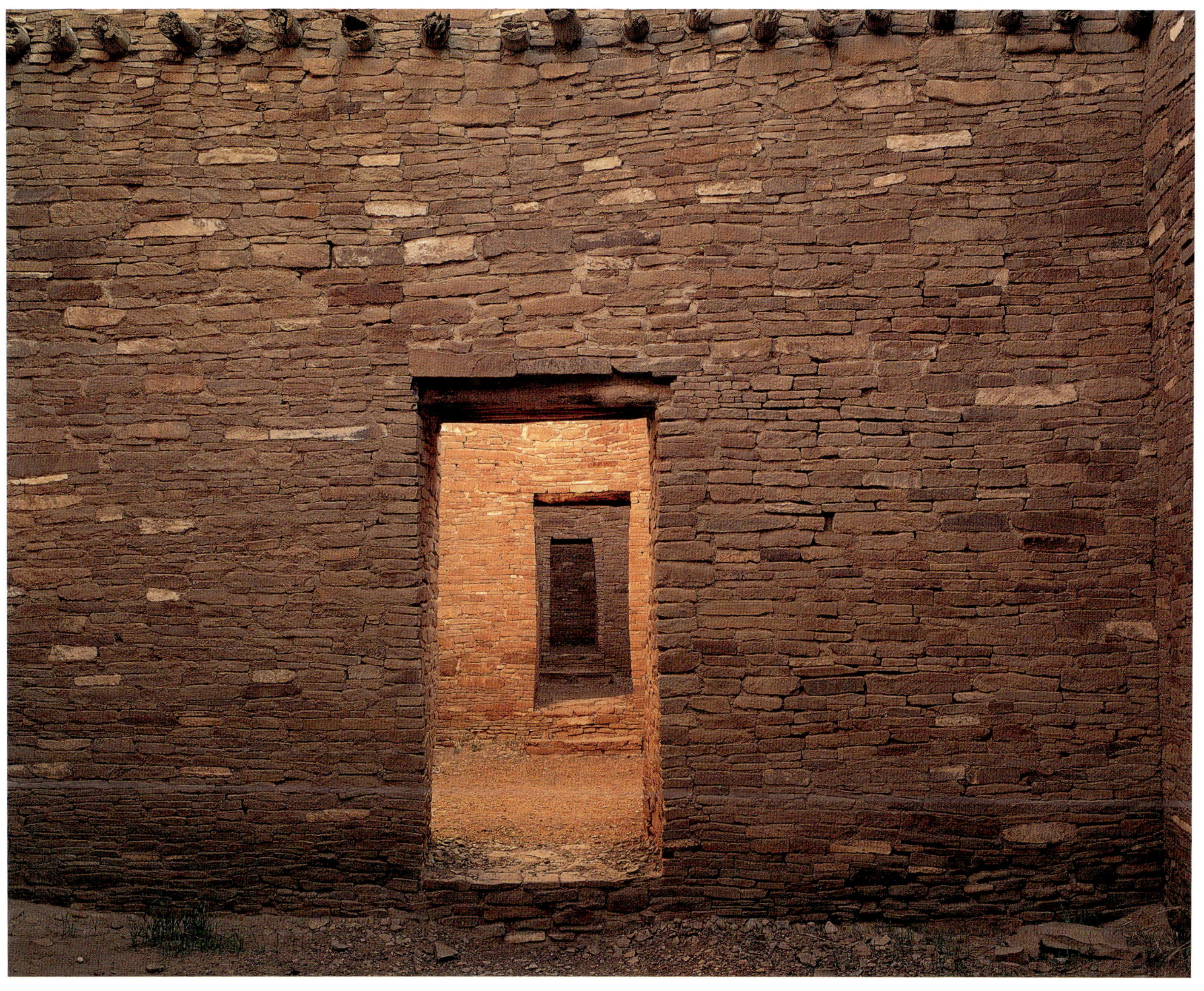

↑←↓ Pueblo Bonito, Chaco Culture National Historical Park

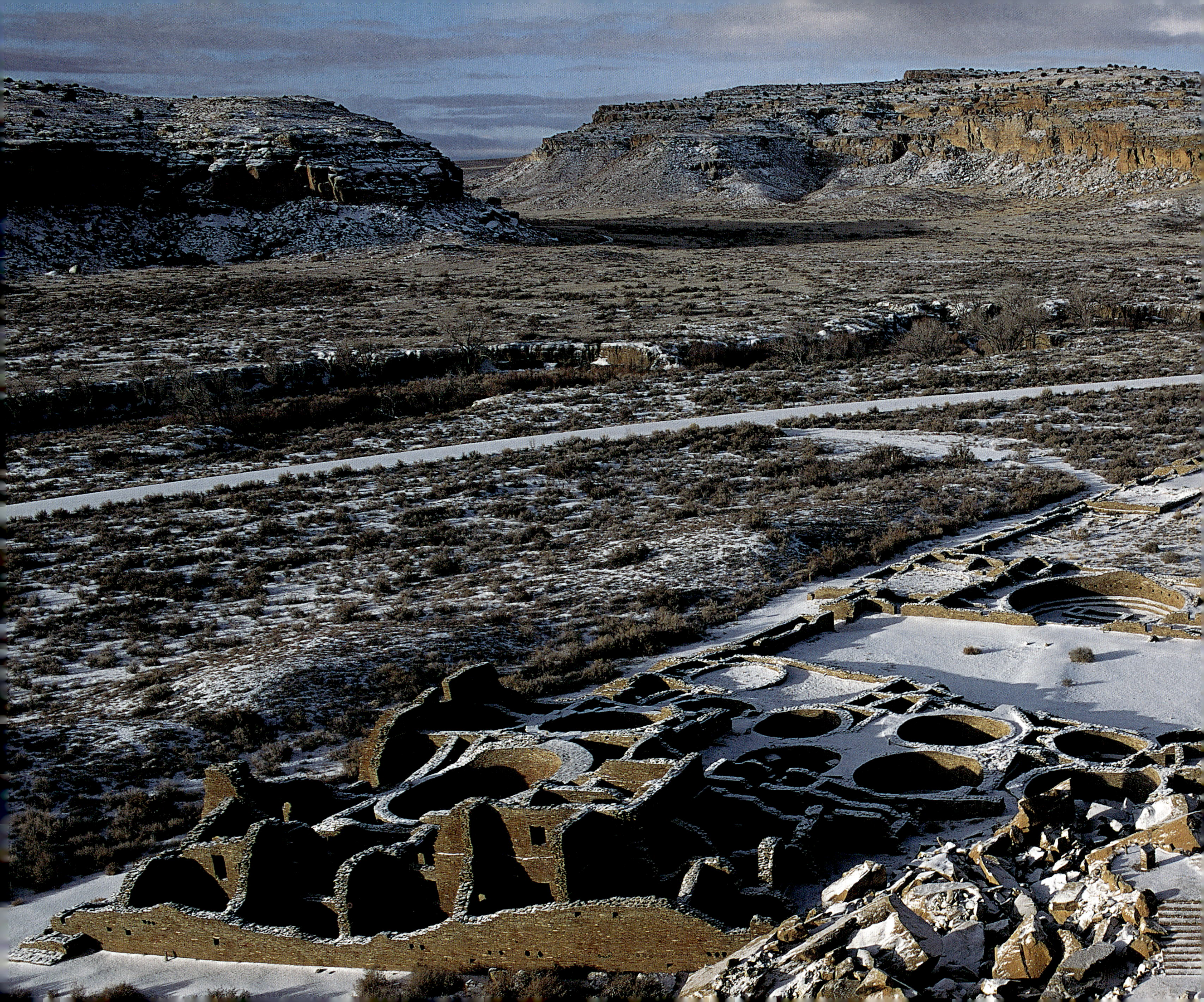

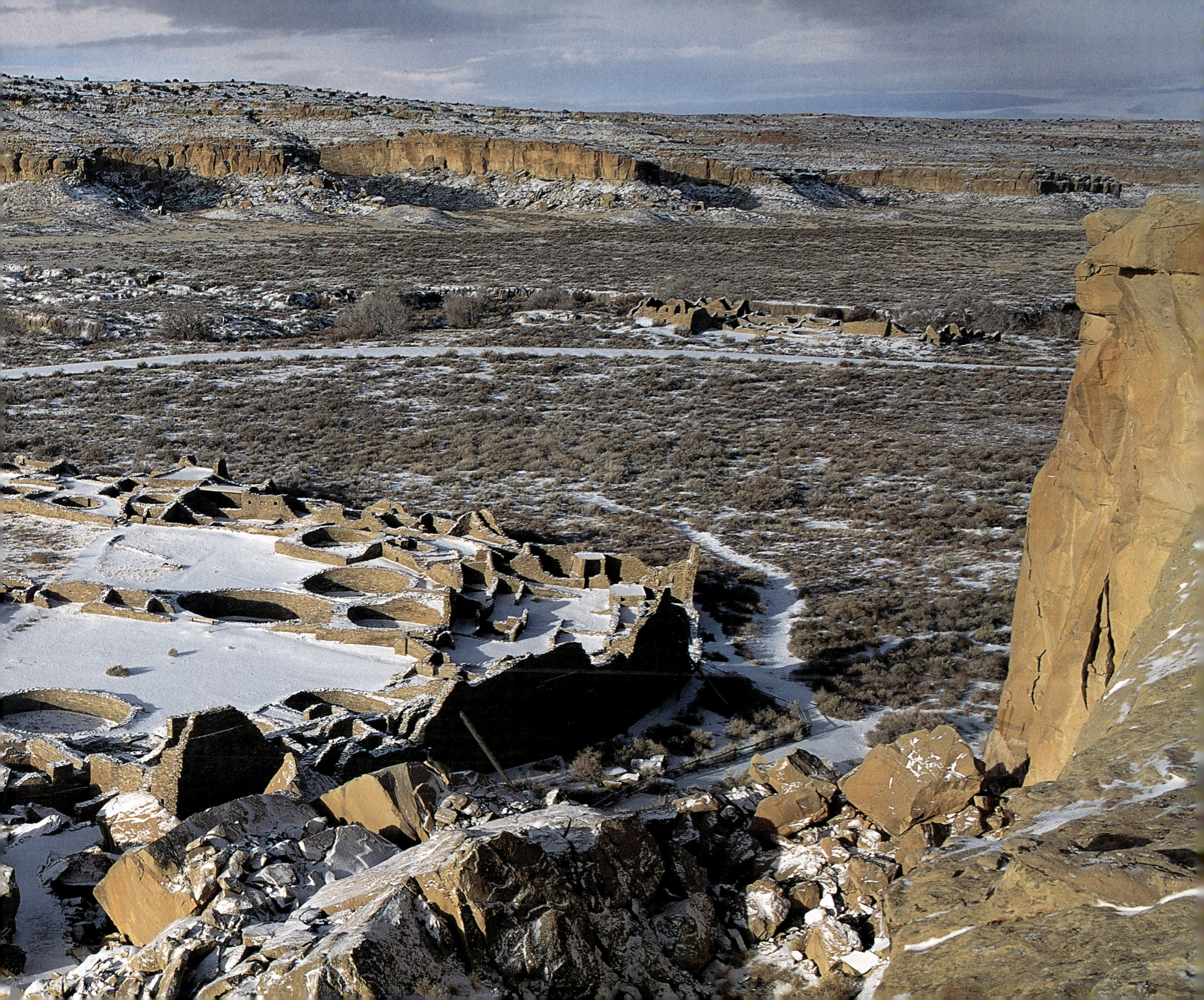

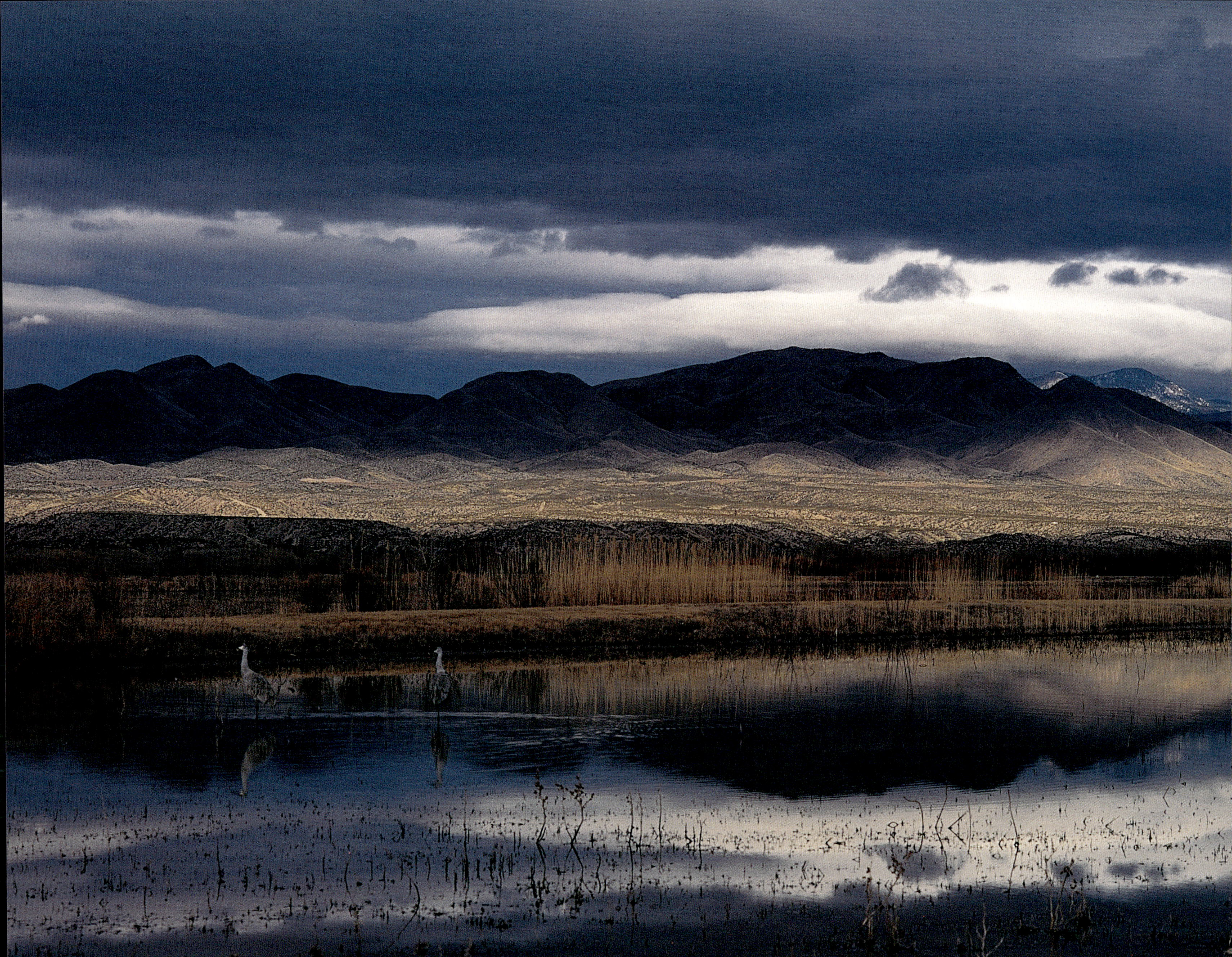

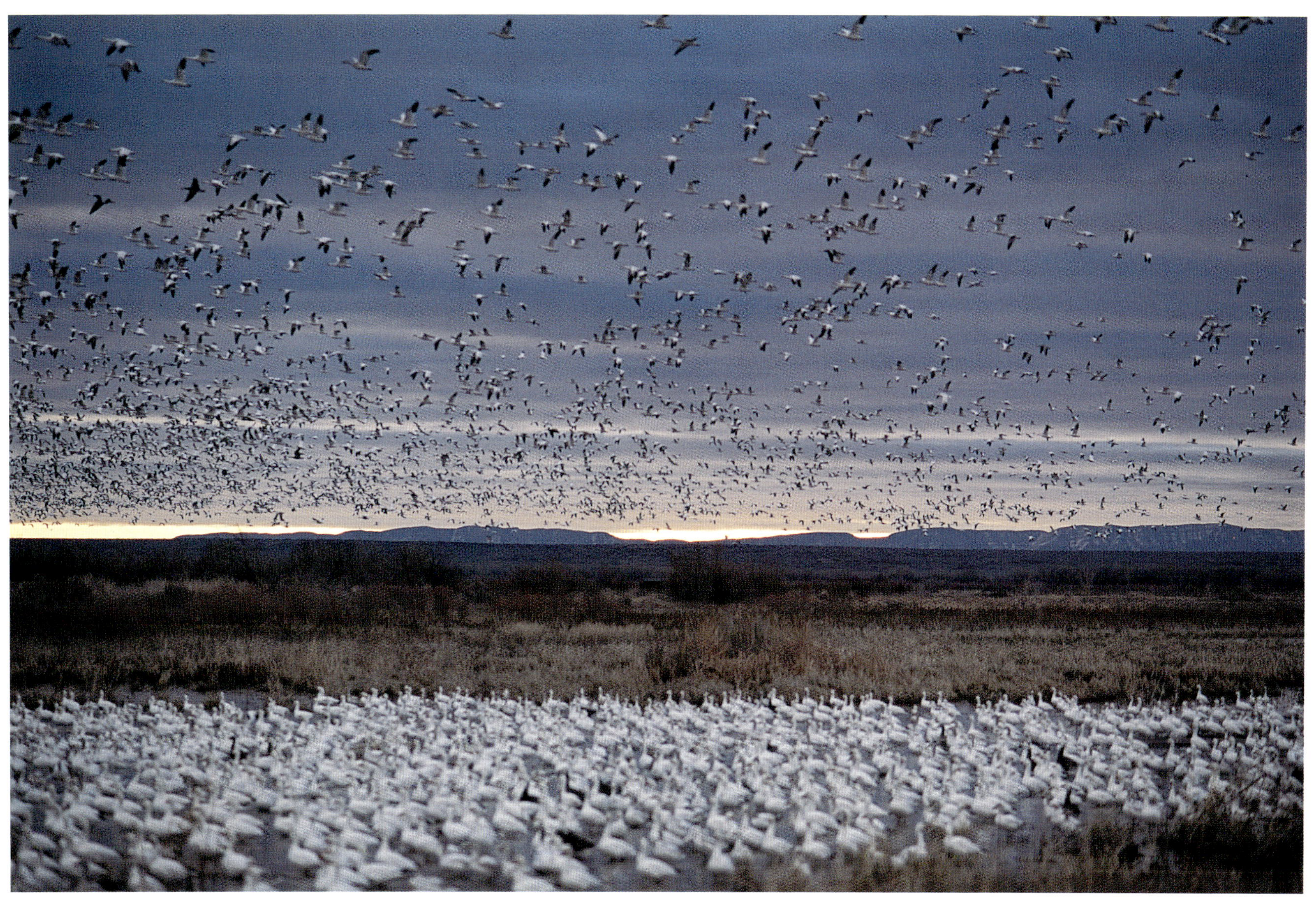

↑←Bosque del Apache National Wildlife Refuge

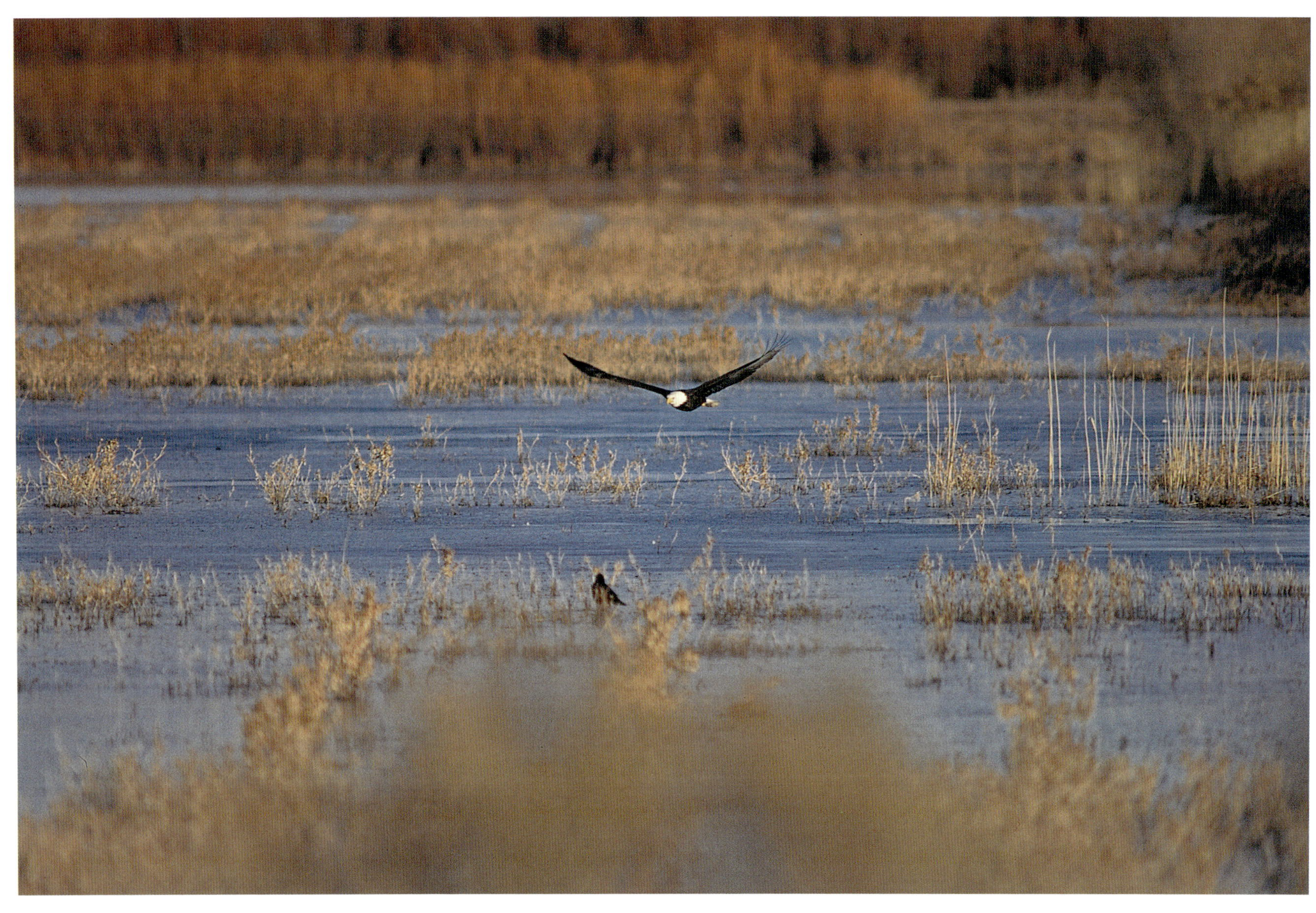

↱ Bosque del Apache National Wildlife Refuge ↓ Fort Union National Monument

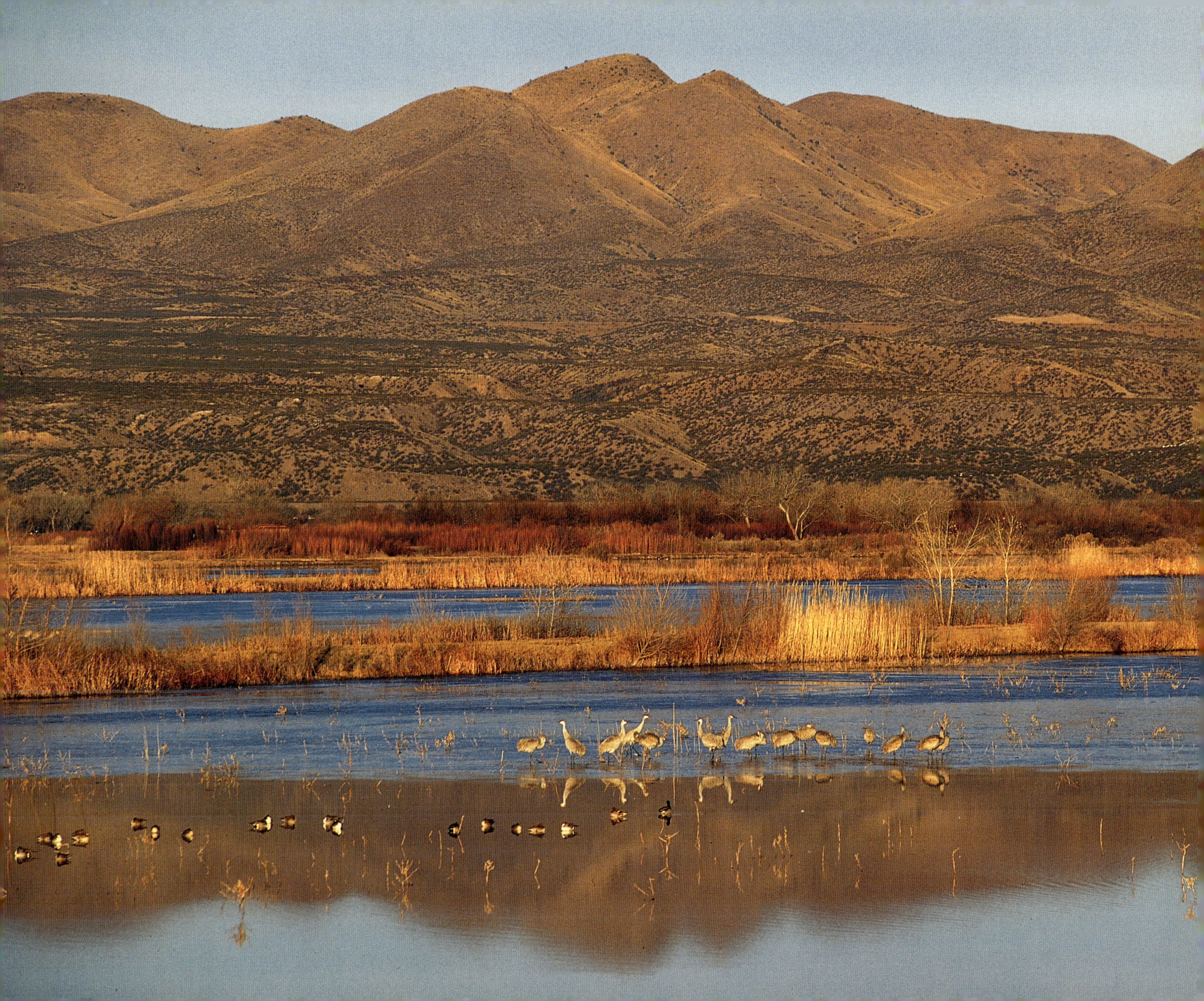

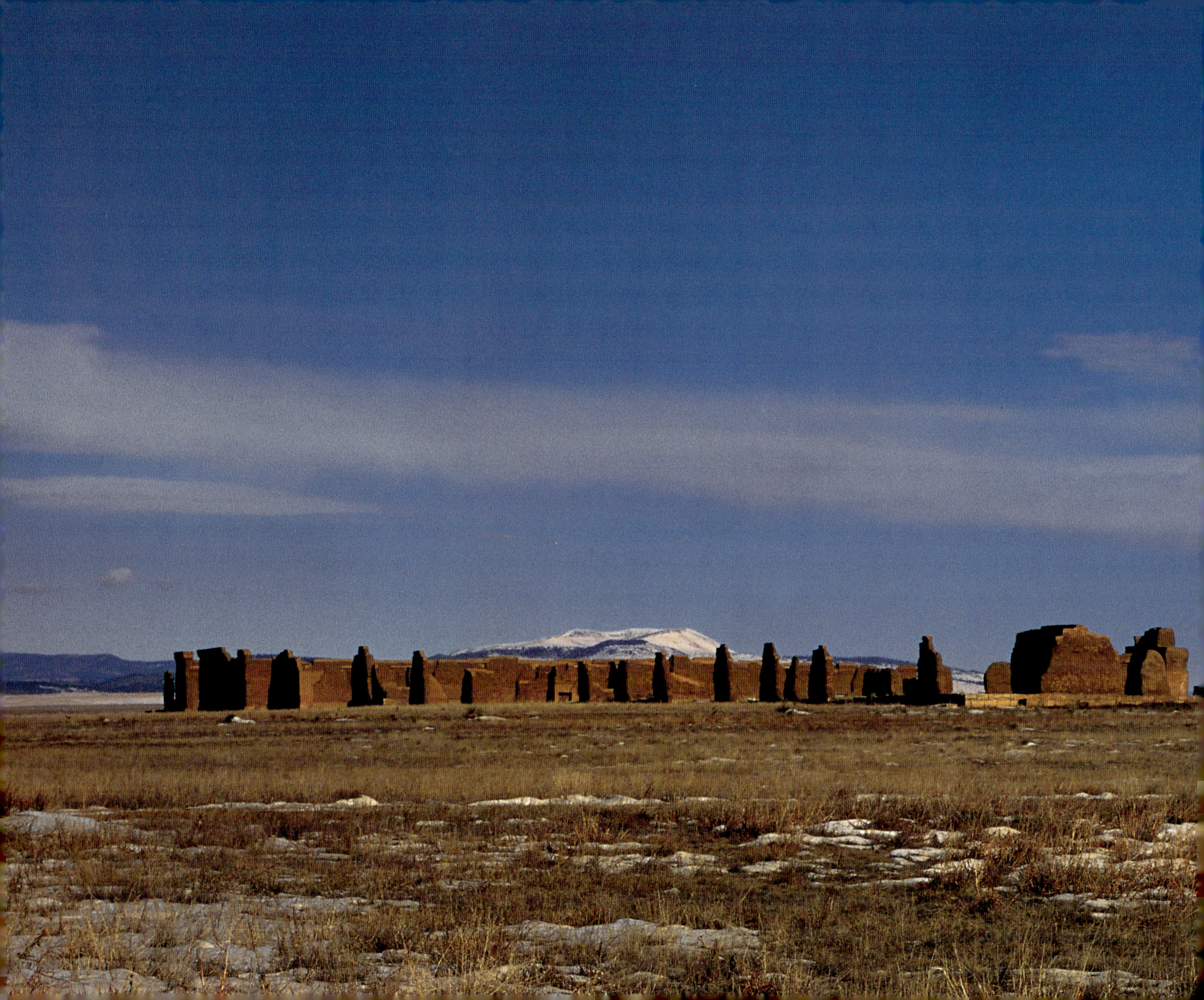

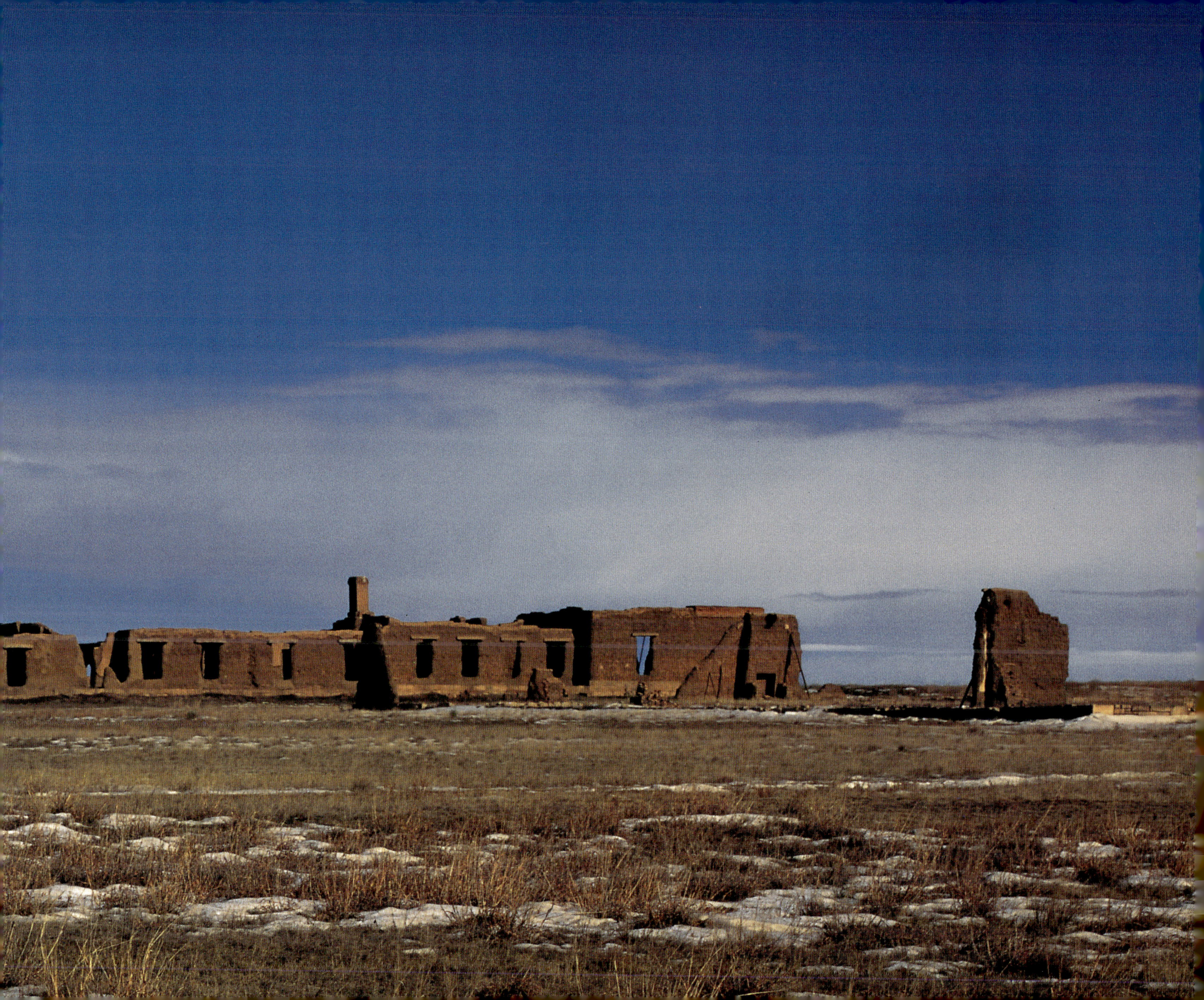

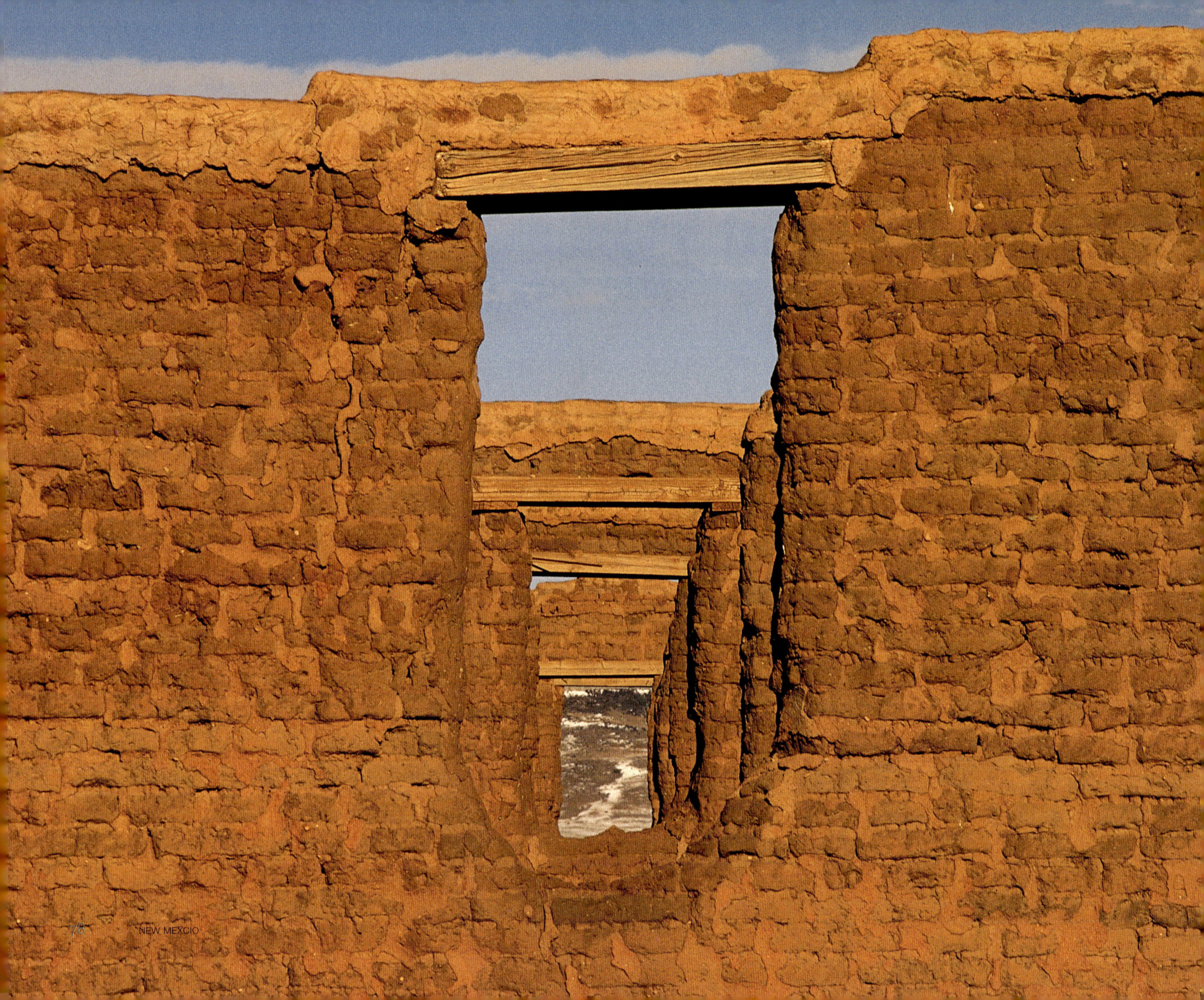

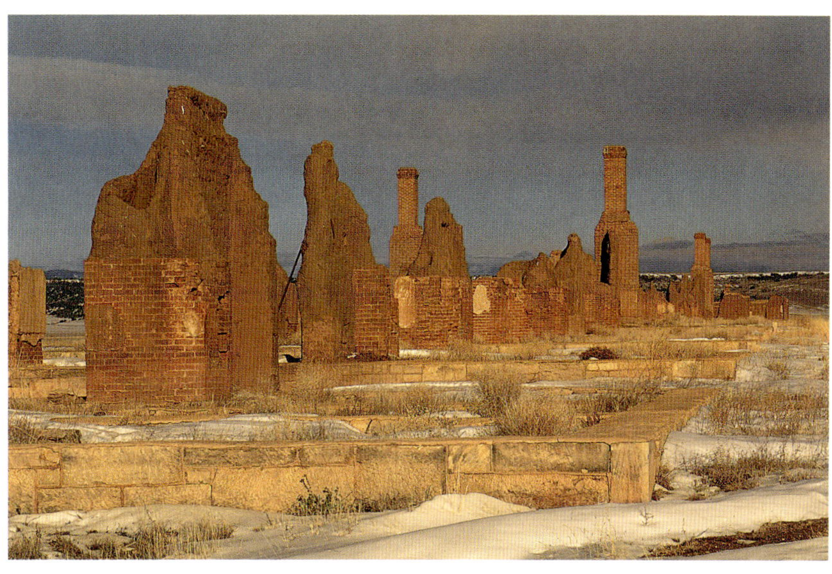

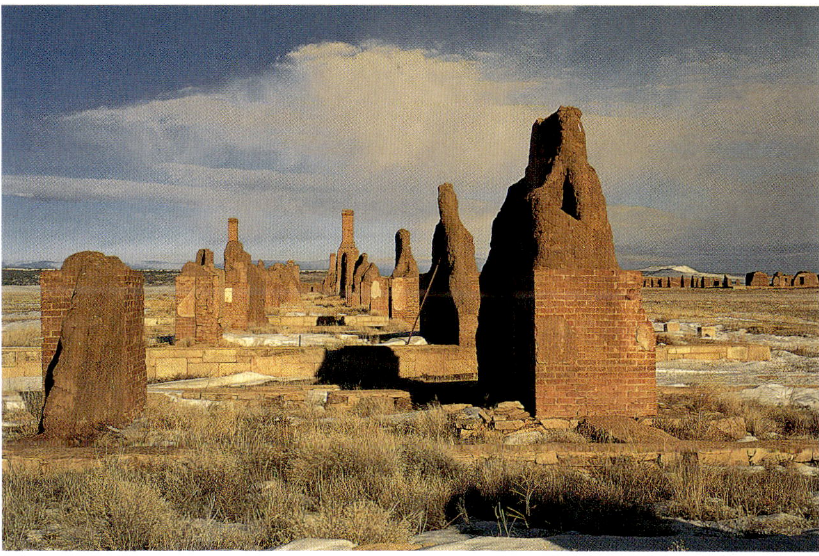

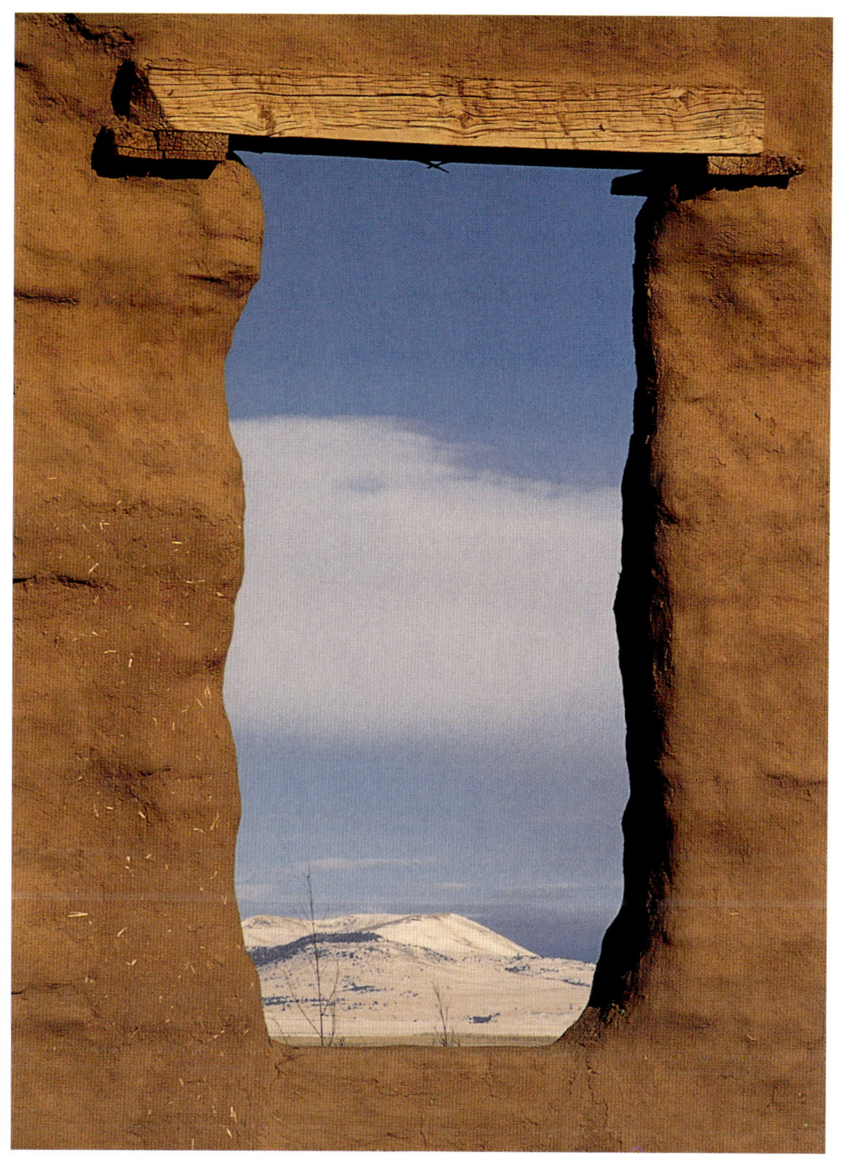

↑←Fort Union National Monument

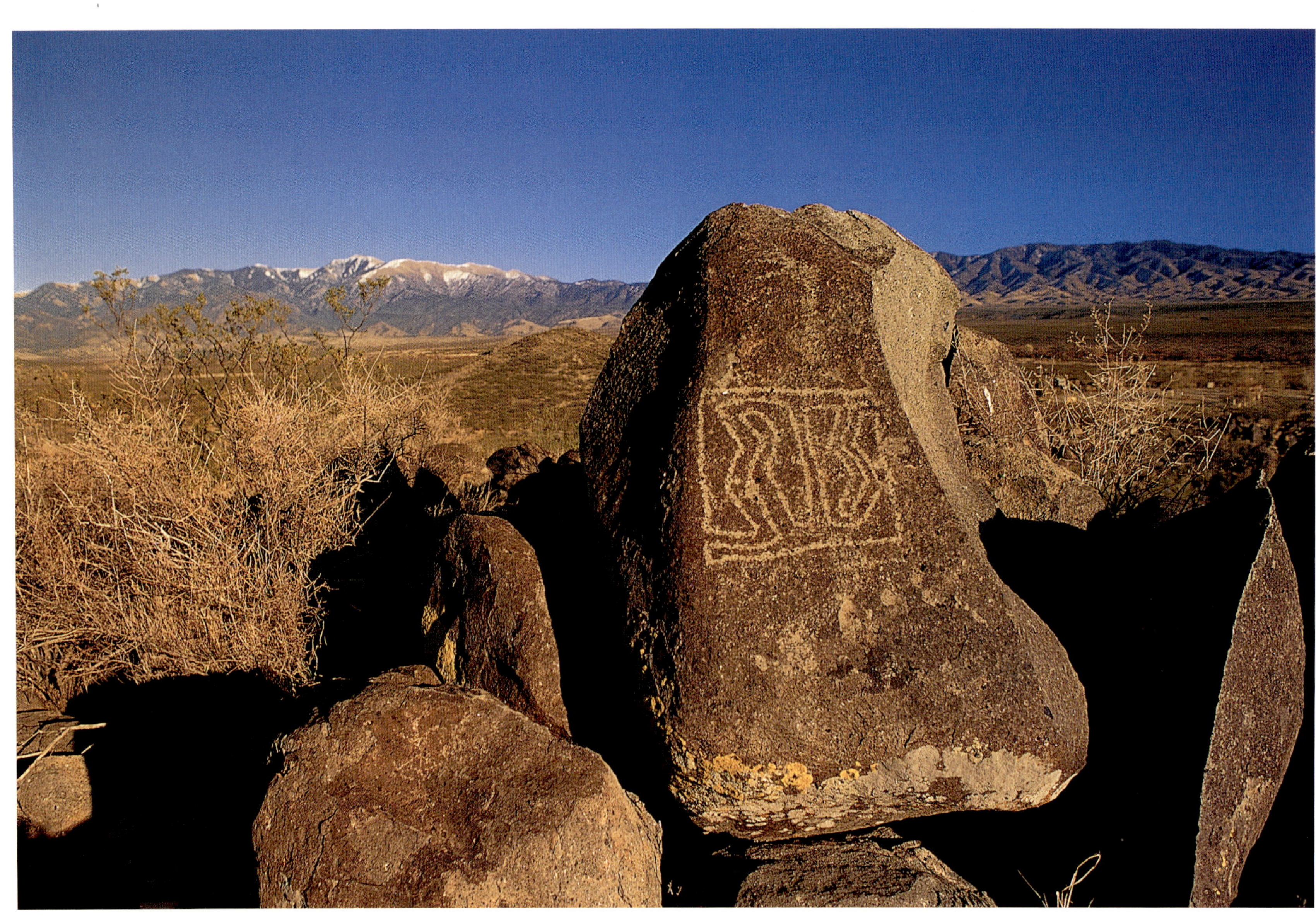

↪ Three Rivers Petroglyph Site

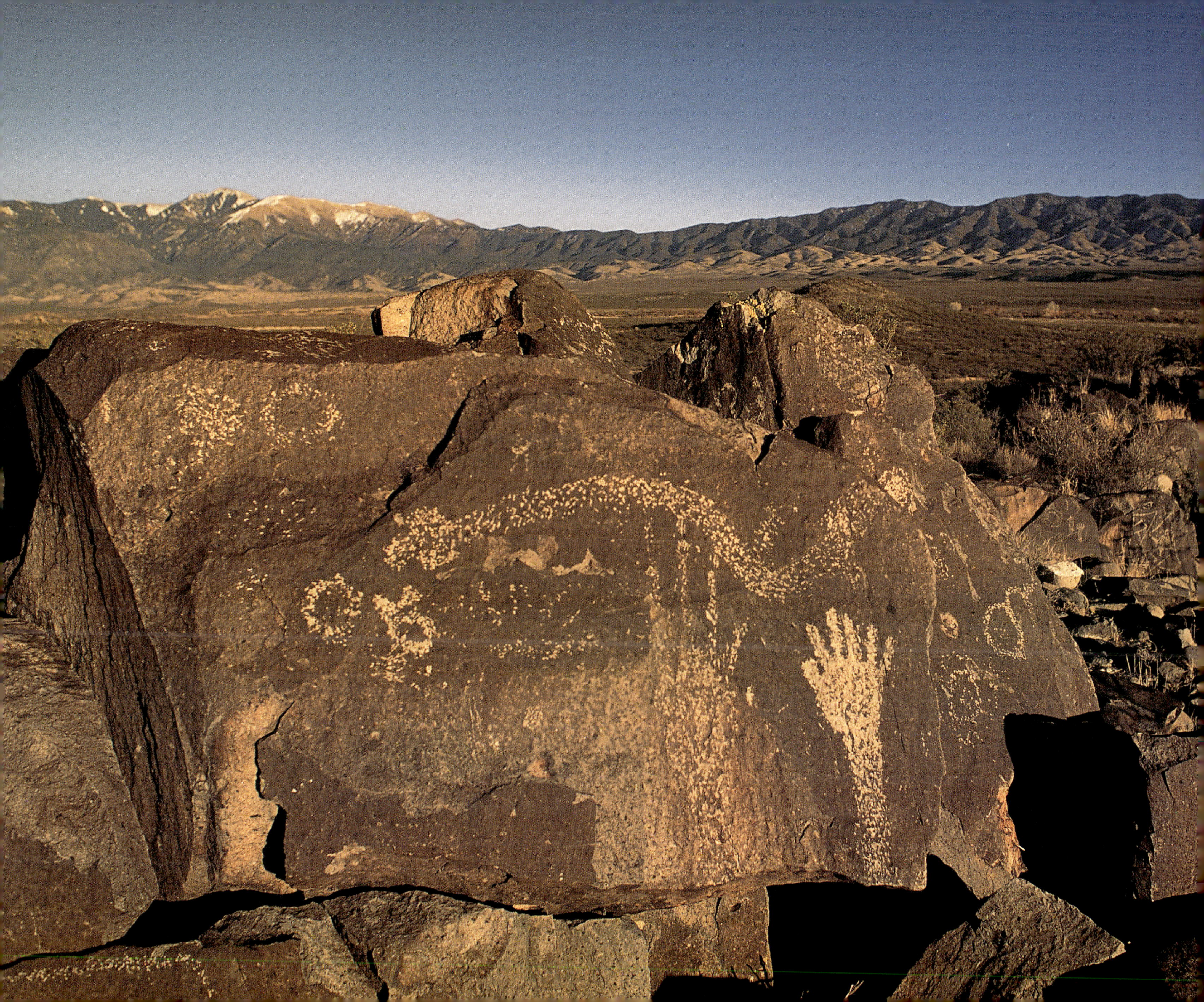

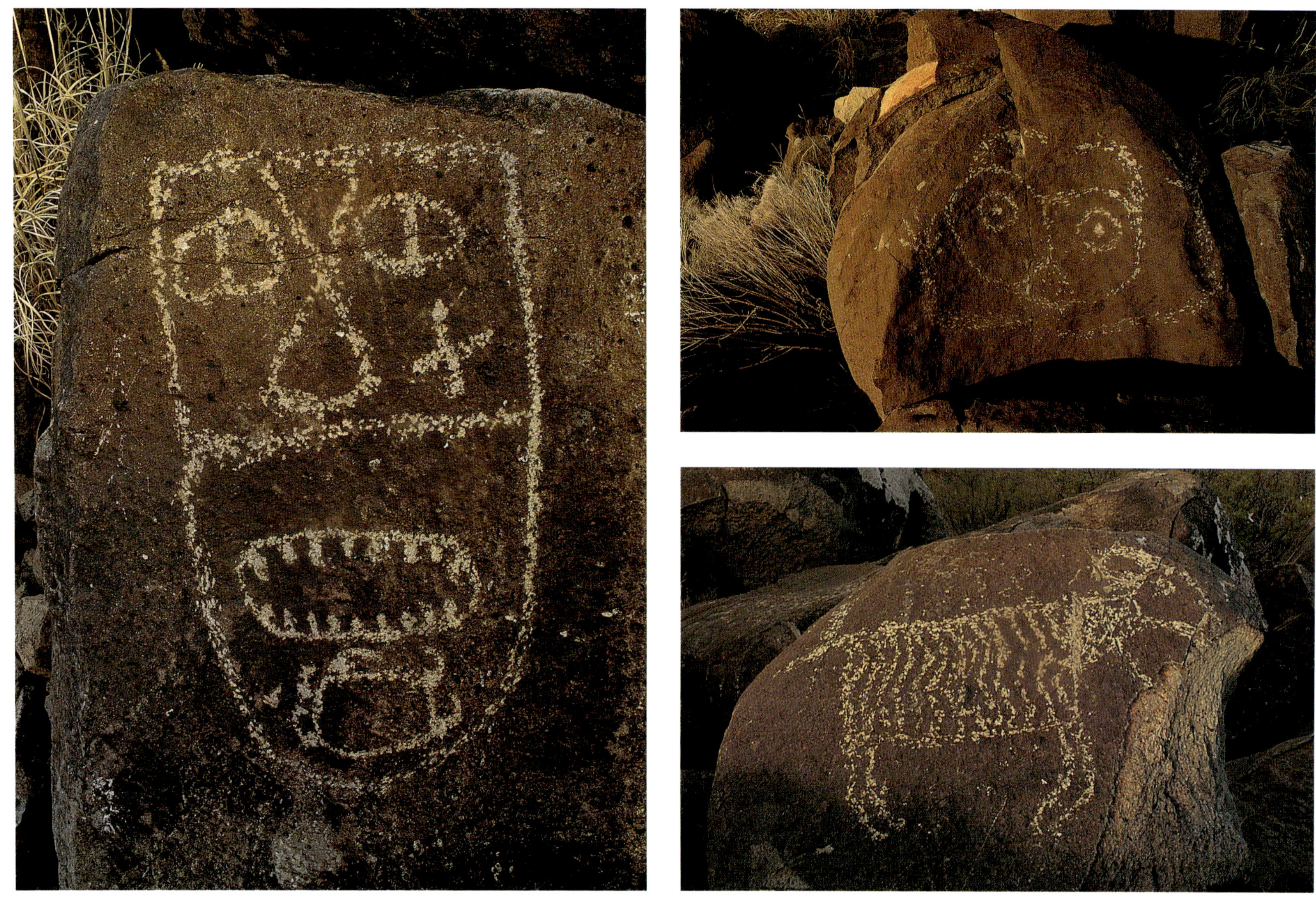

↪ Three Rivers Petroglyph Site

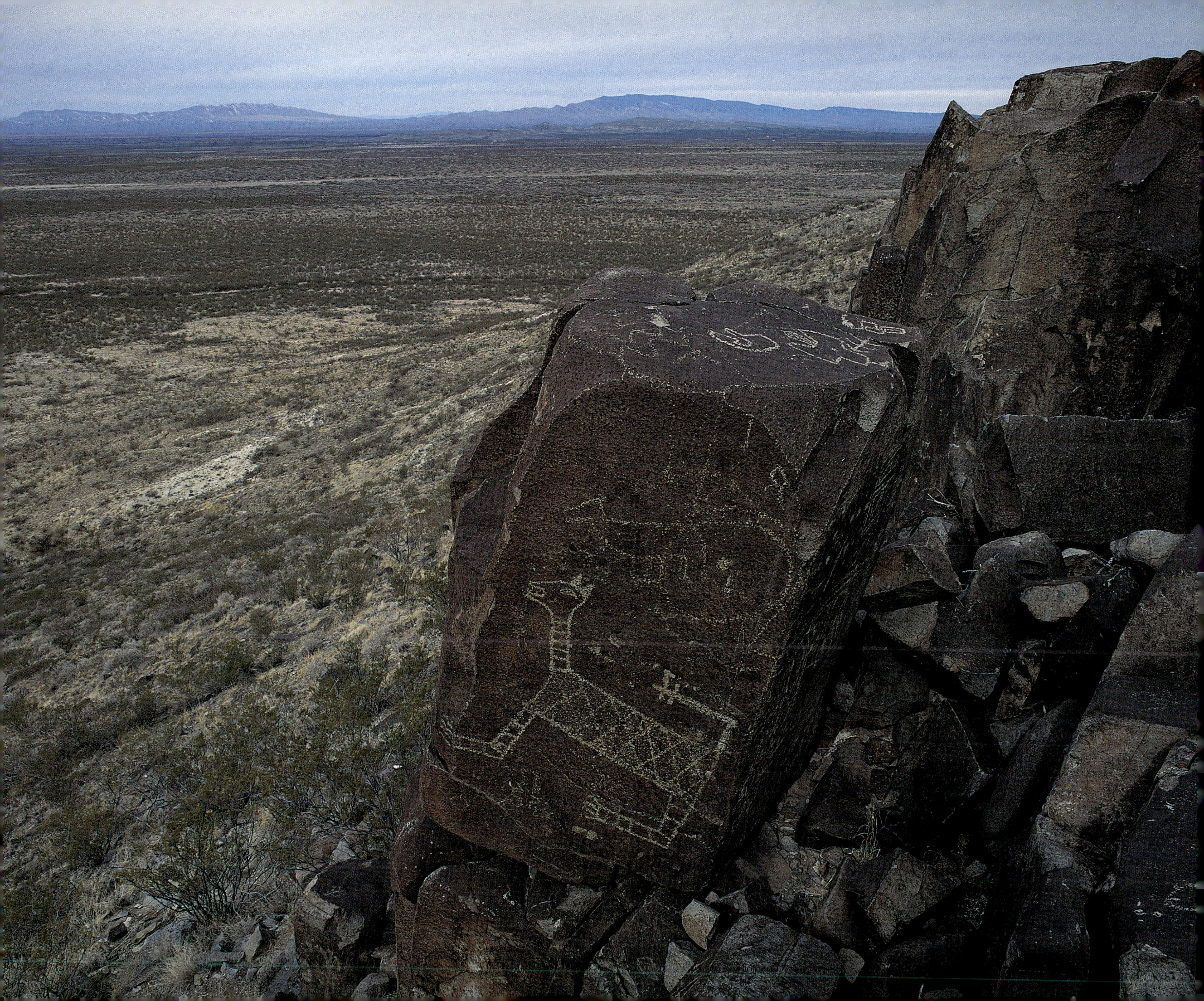

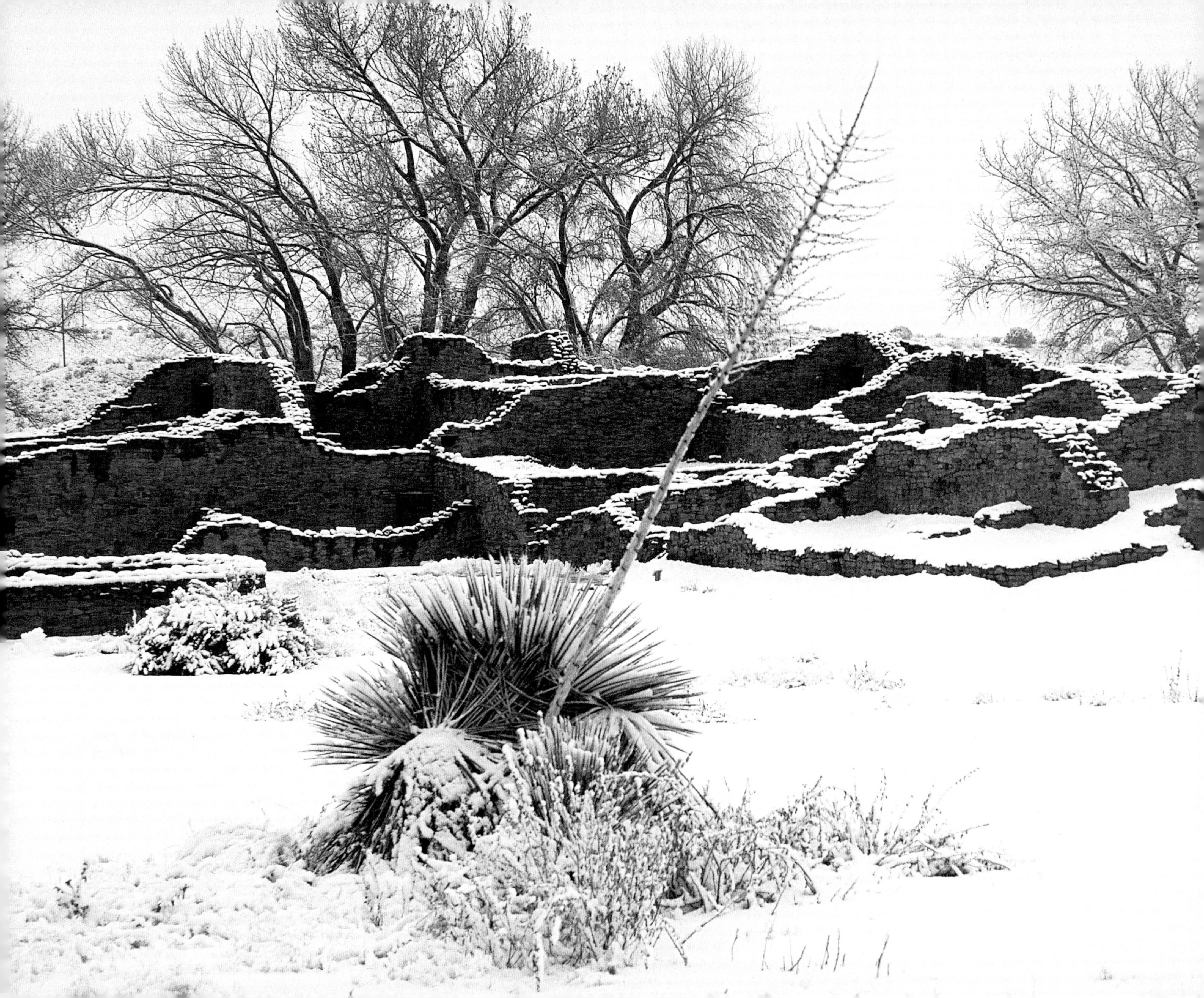

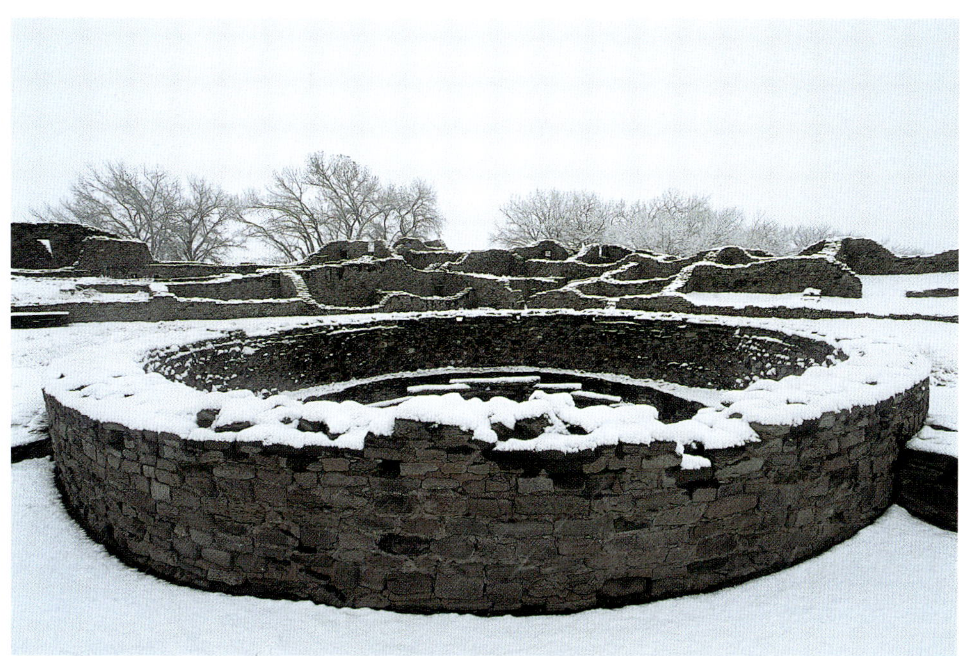

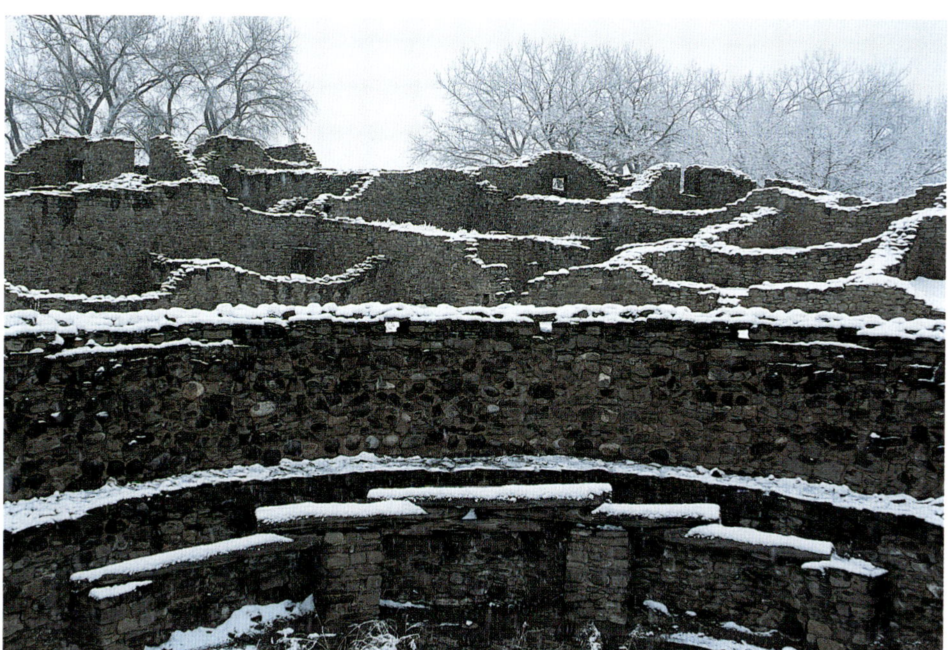

↑←Aztec Ruins National Monument

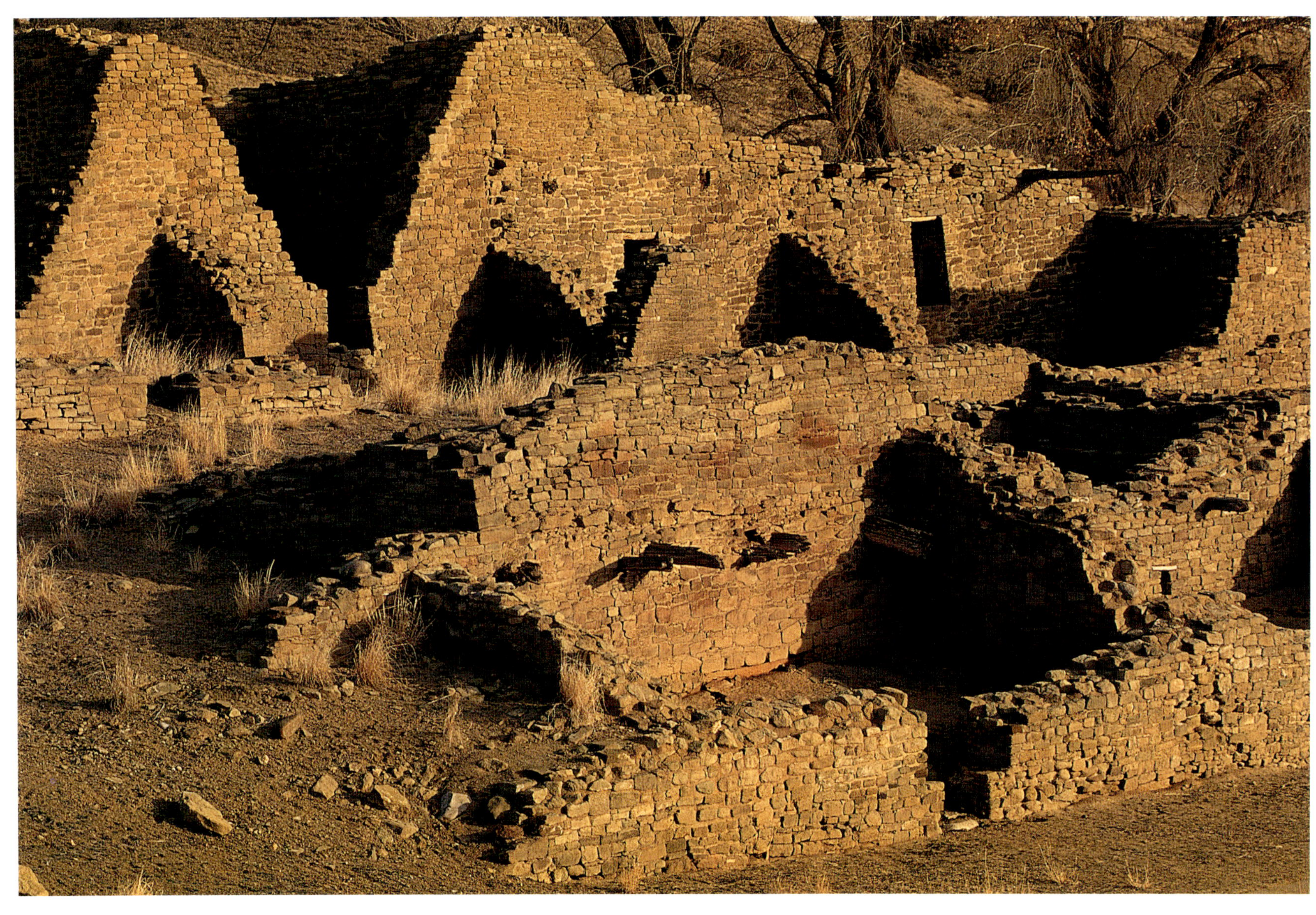

↑→Azteec Ruins National Monument ↓ White Sands National Monument

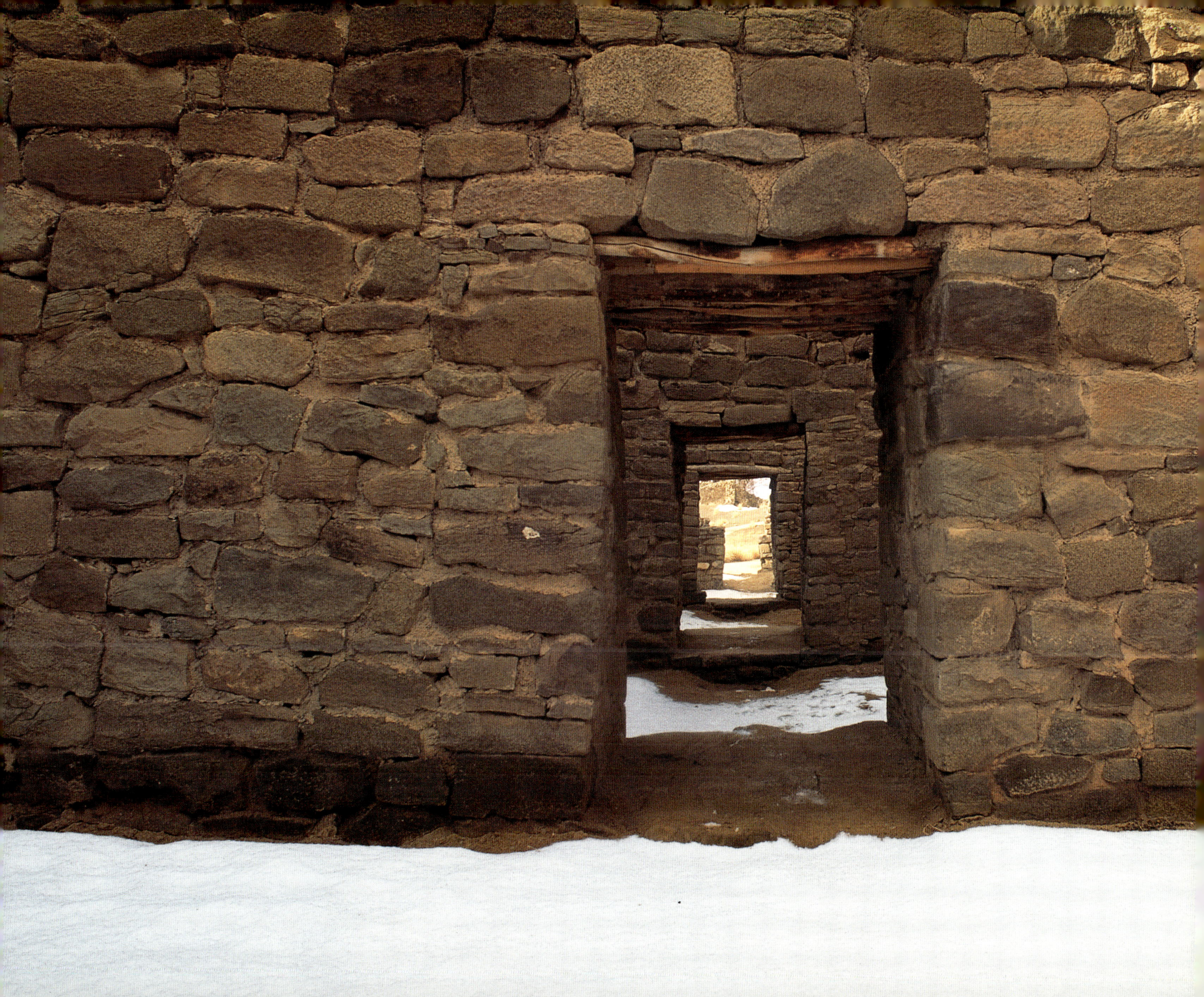

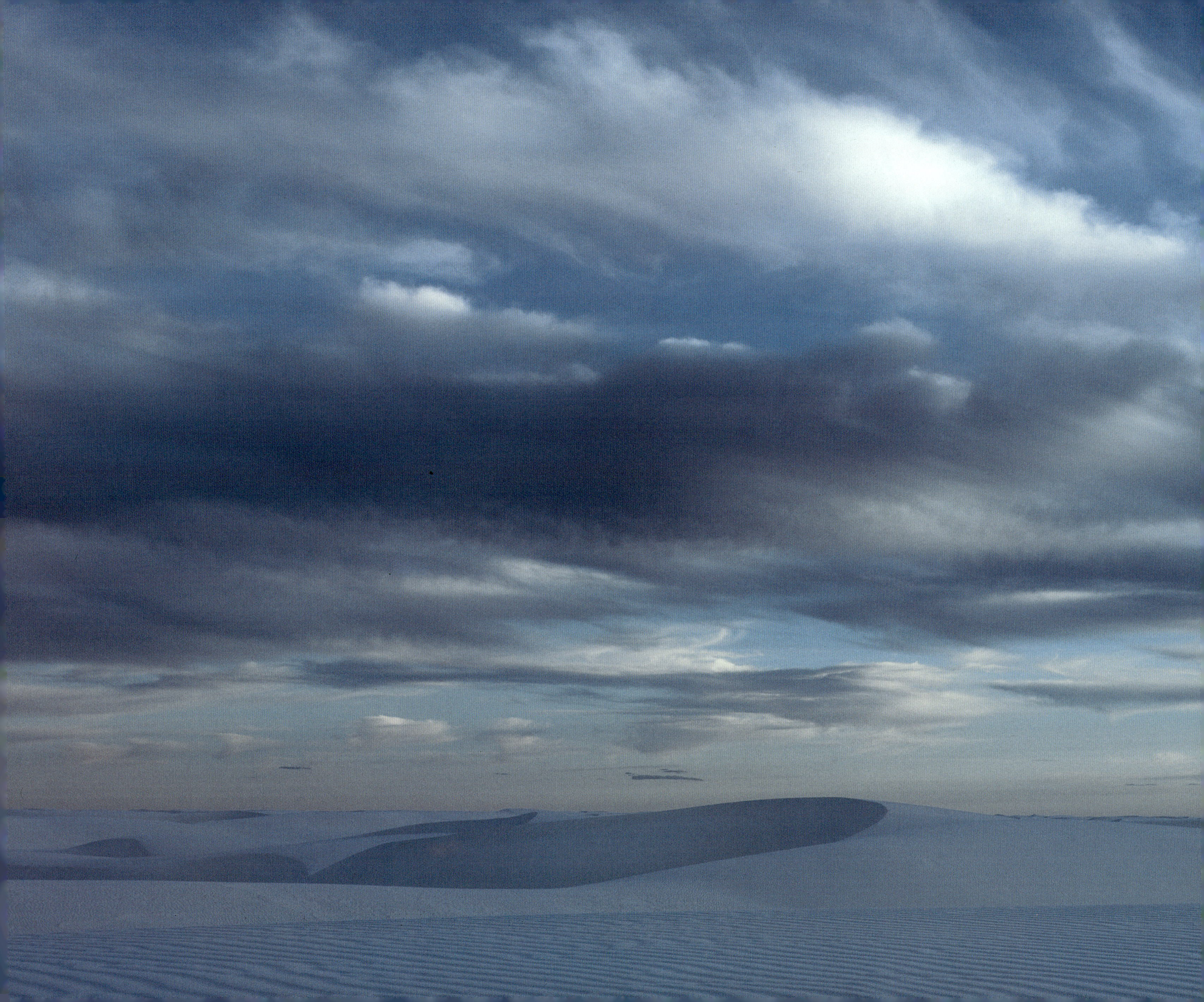

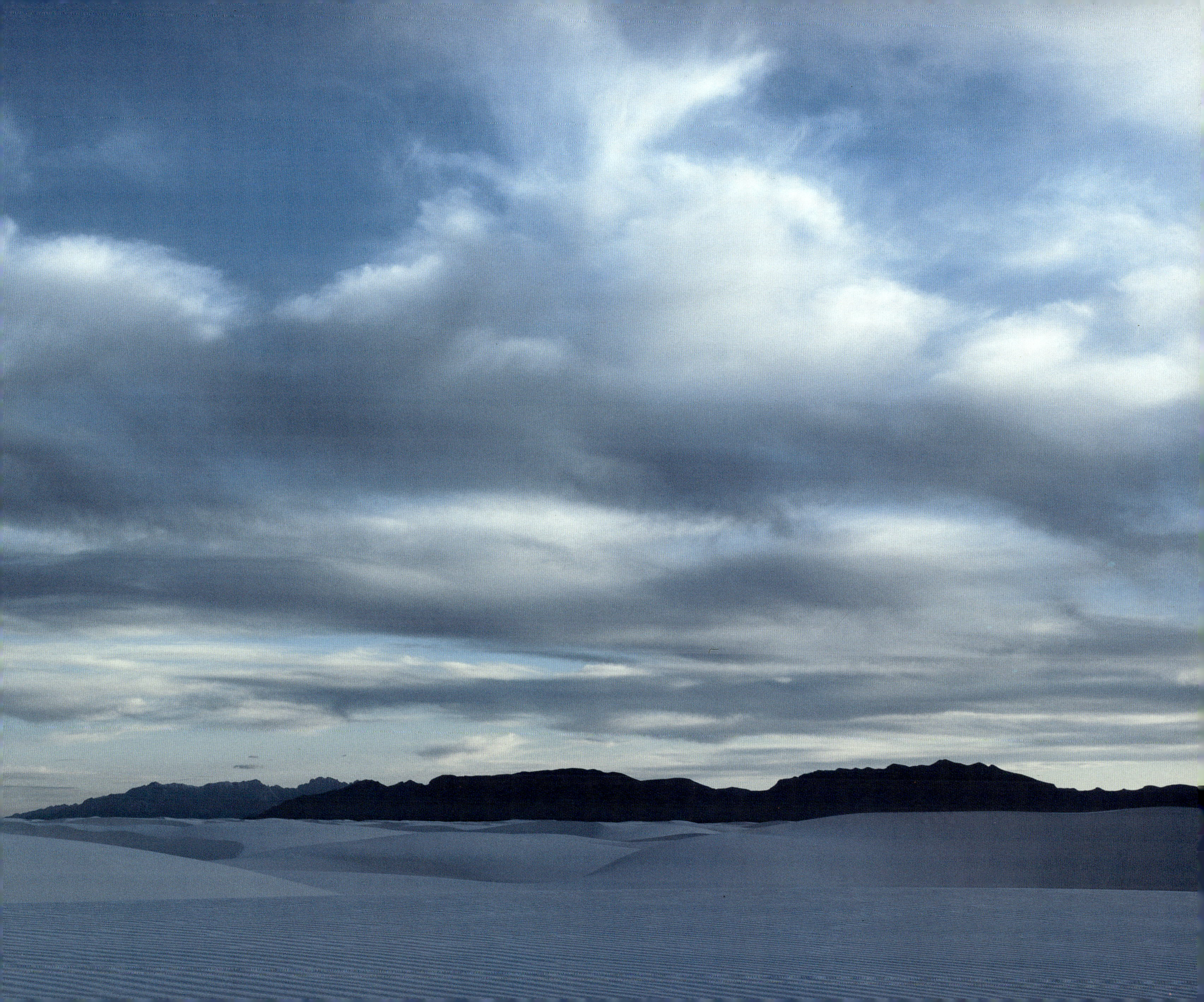

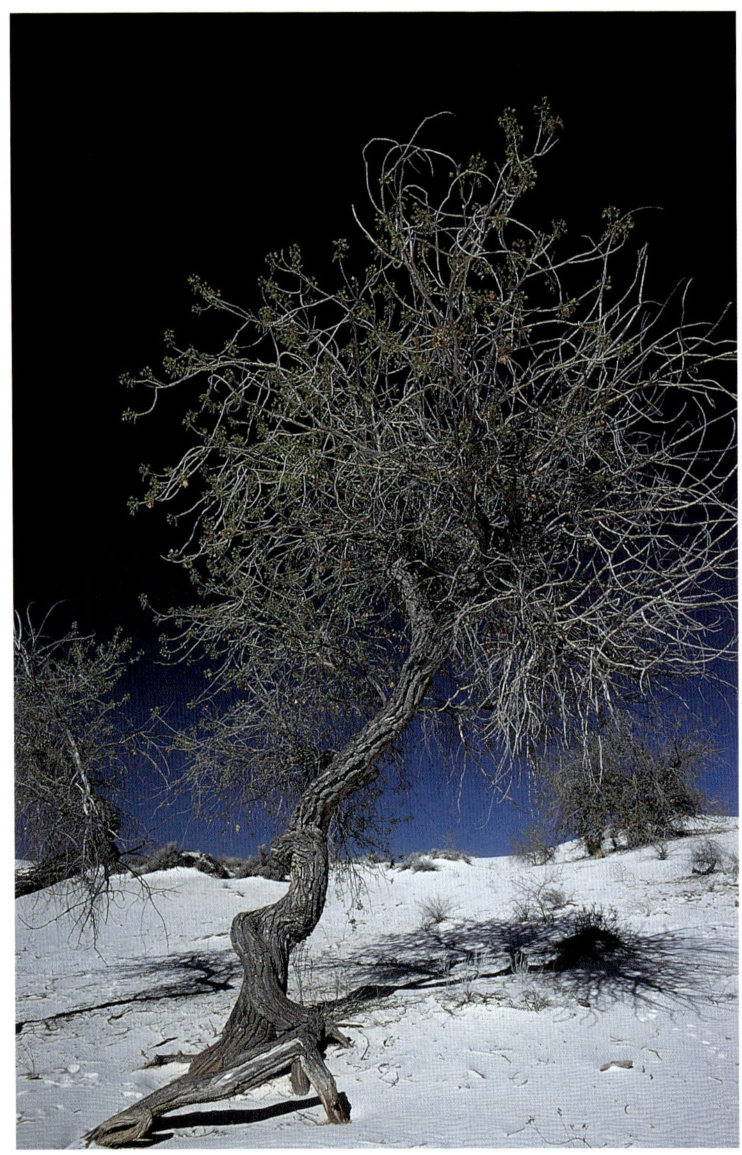

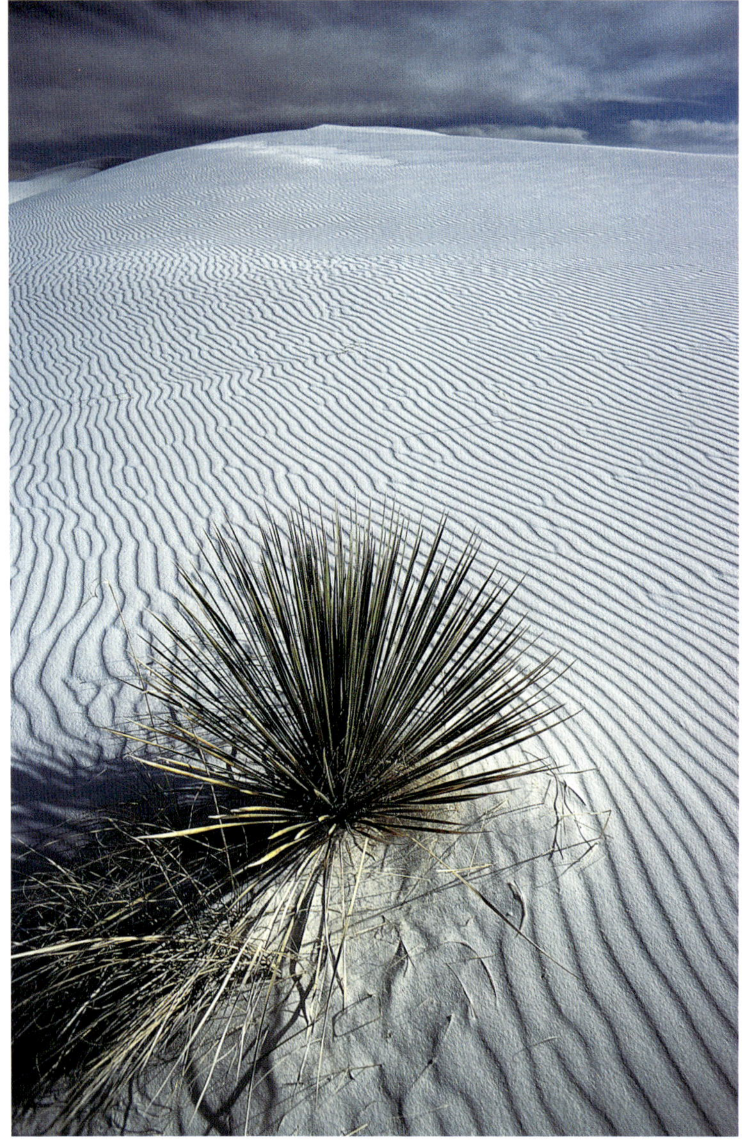

↬ White Sands National Monument

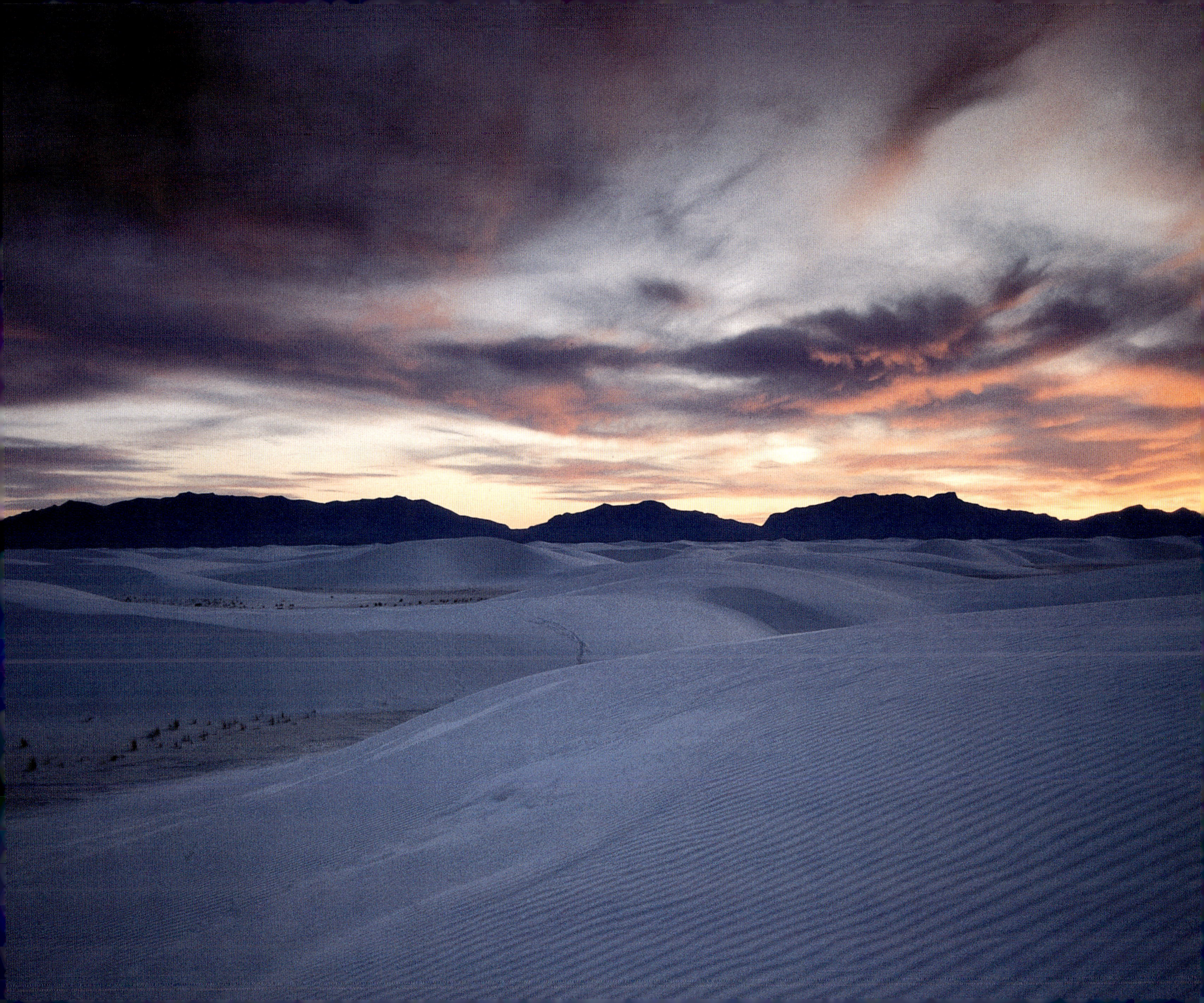

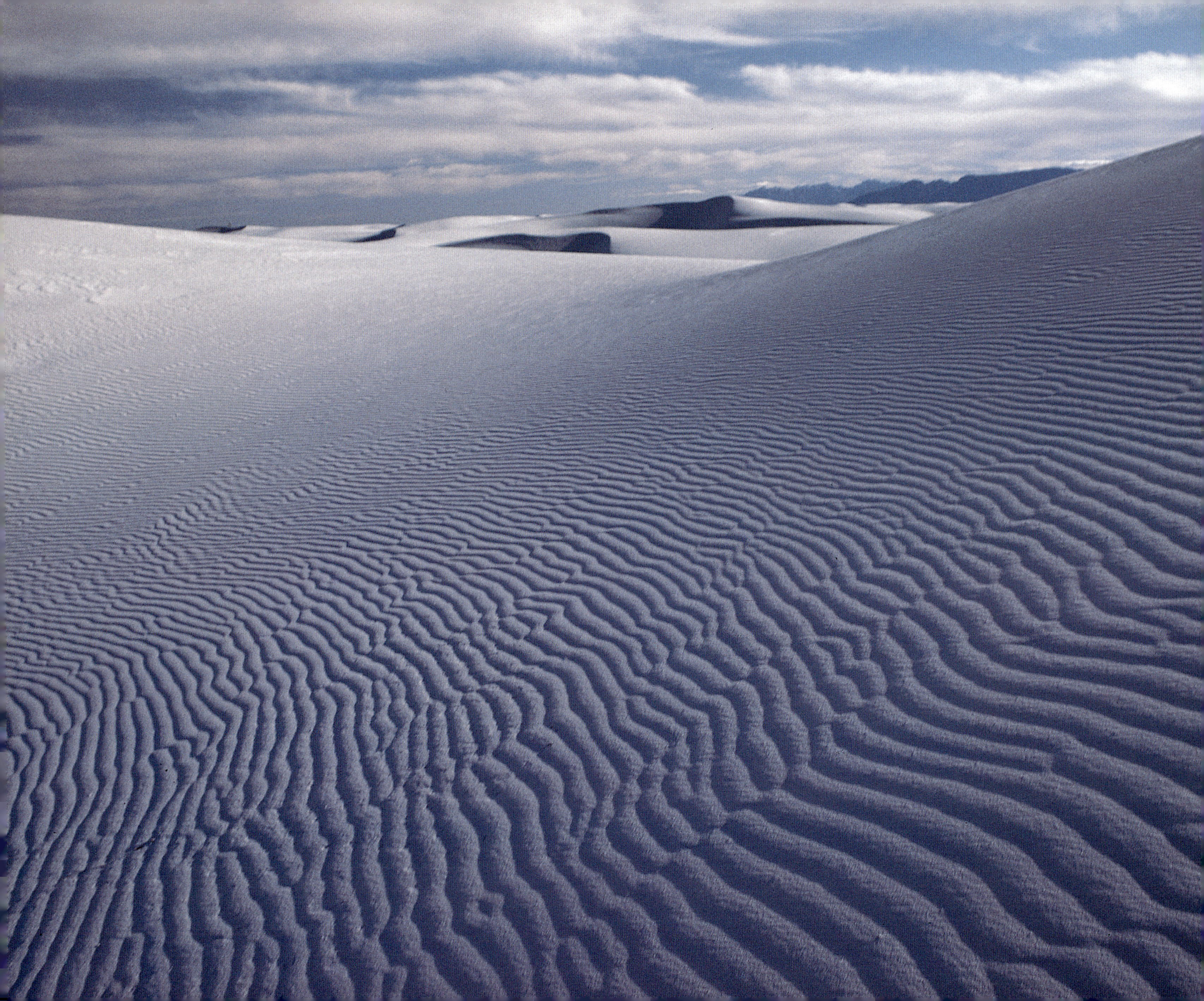

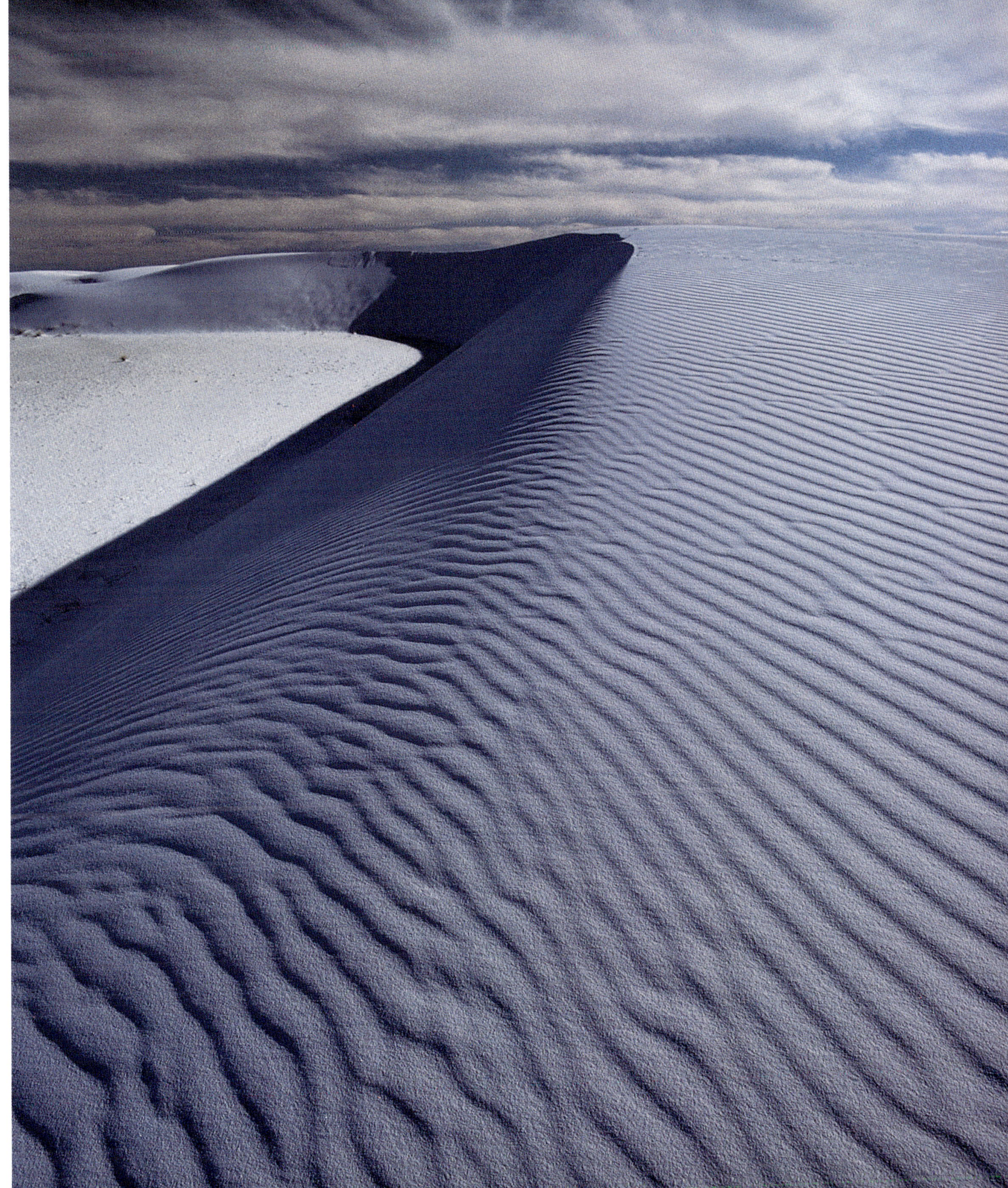

←→ White Sands National Monument

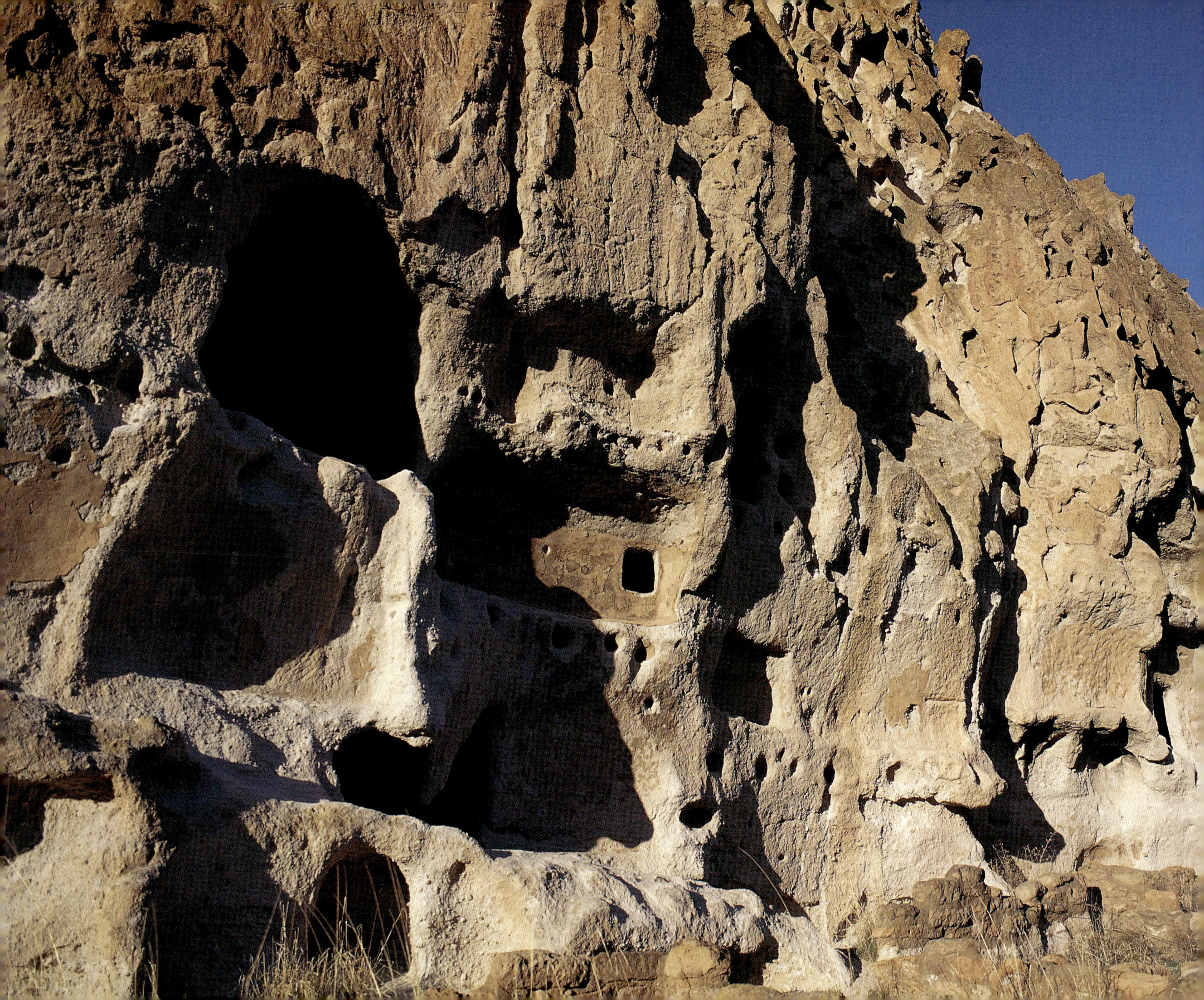

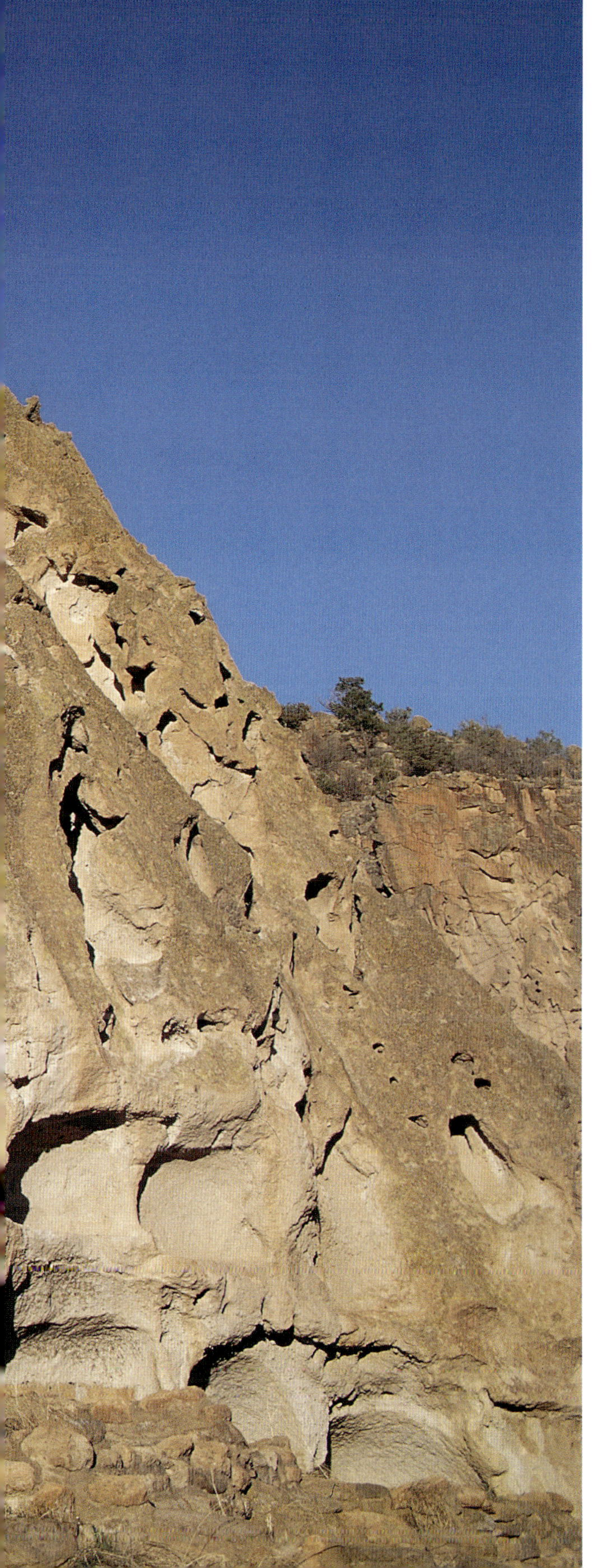

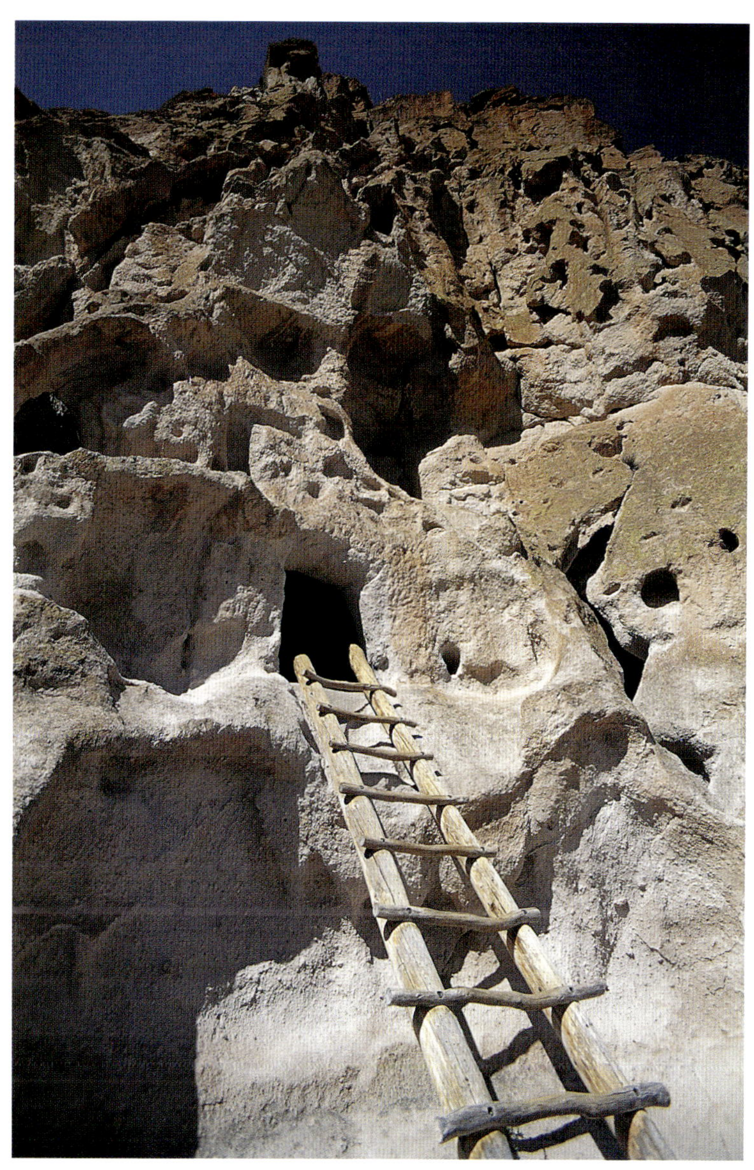

↑←Bandelier National Monument

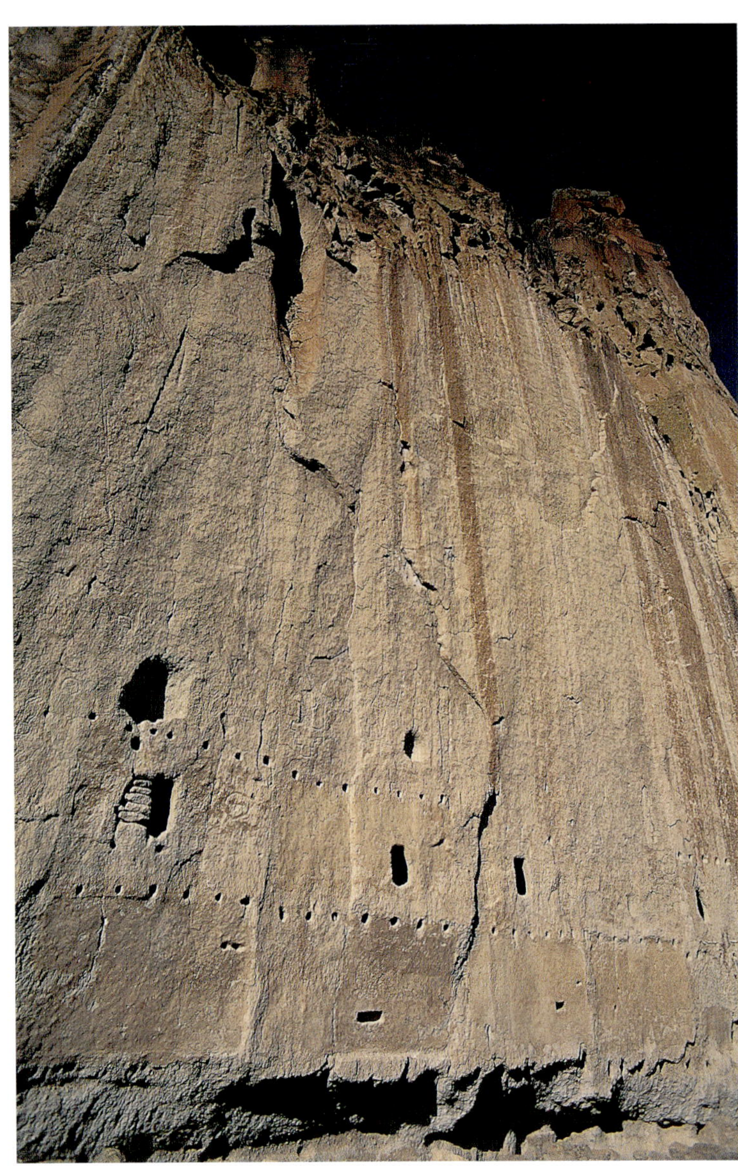

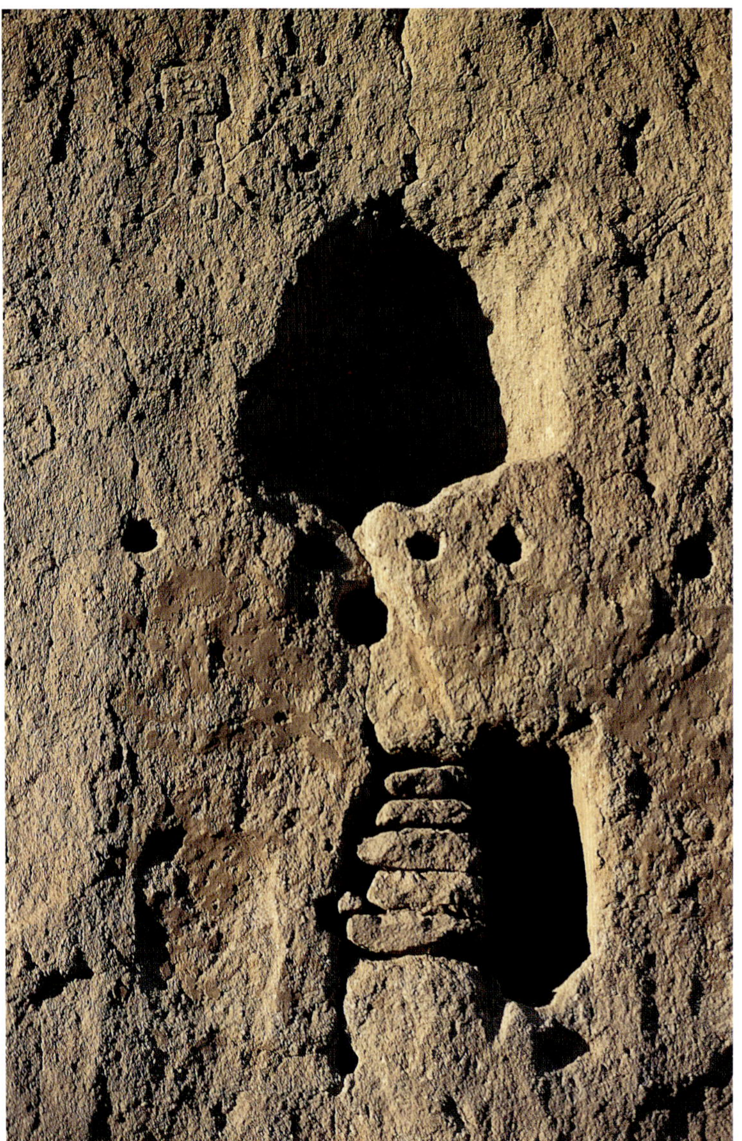

↑→ Bandelier National Monument ↓ Misión de la Purísima Concepción de Cuarac, Quarai, Salinas Pueblo Missions National Monument

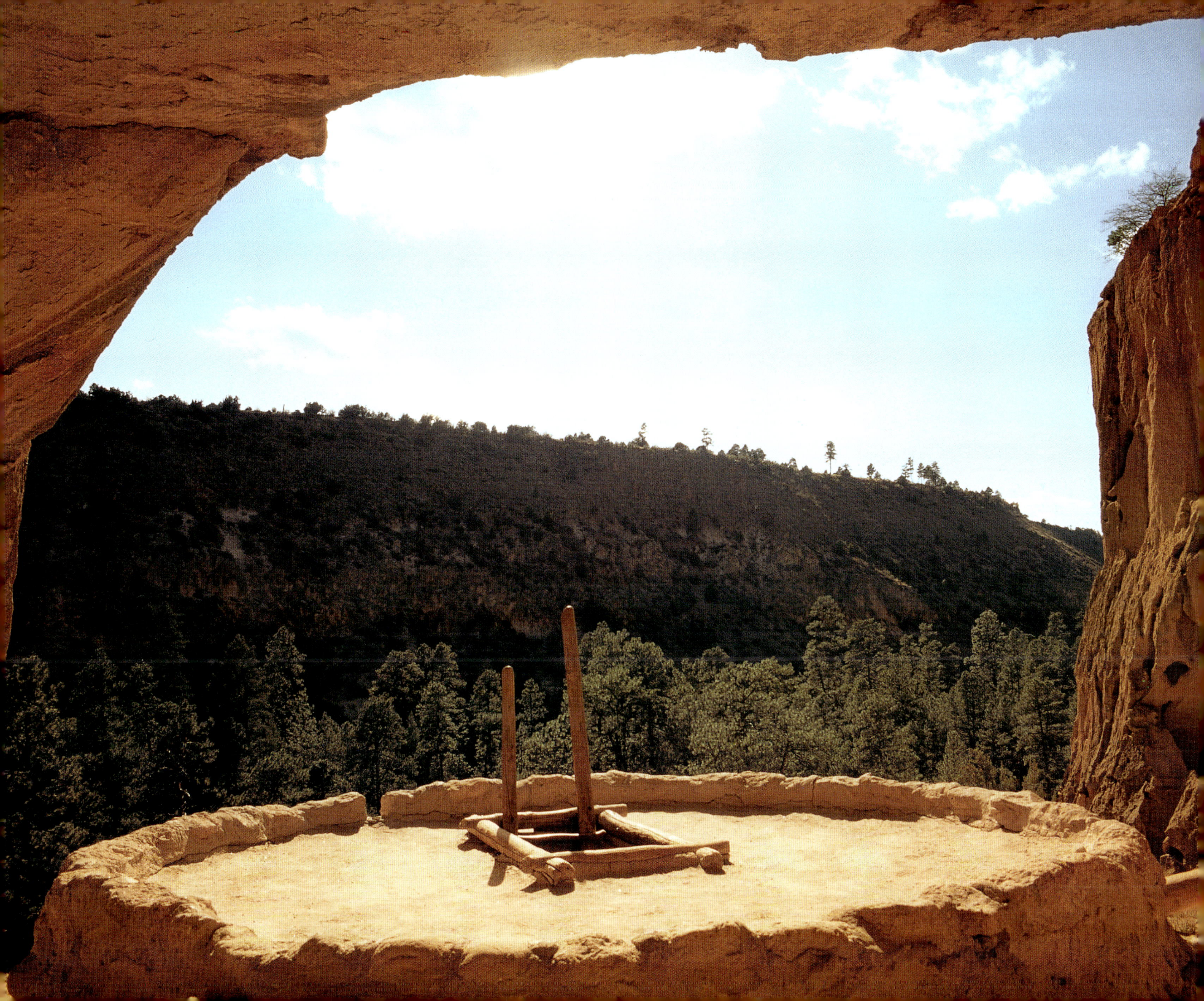

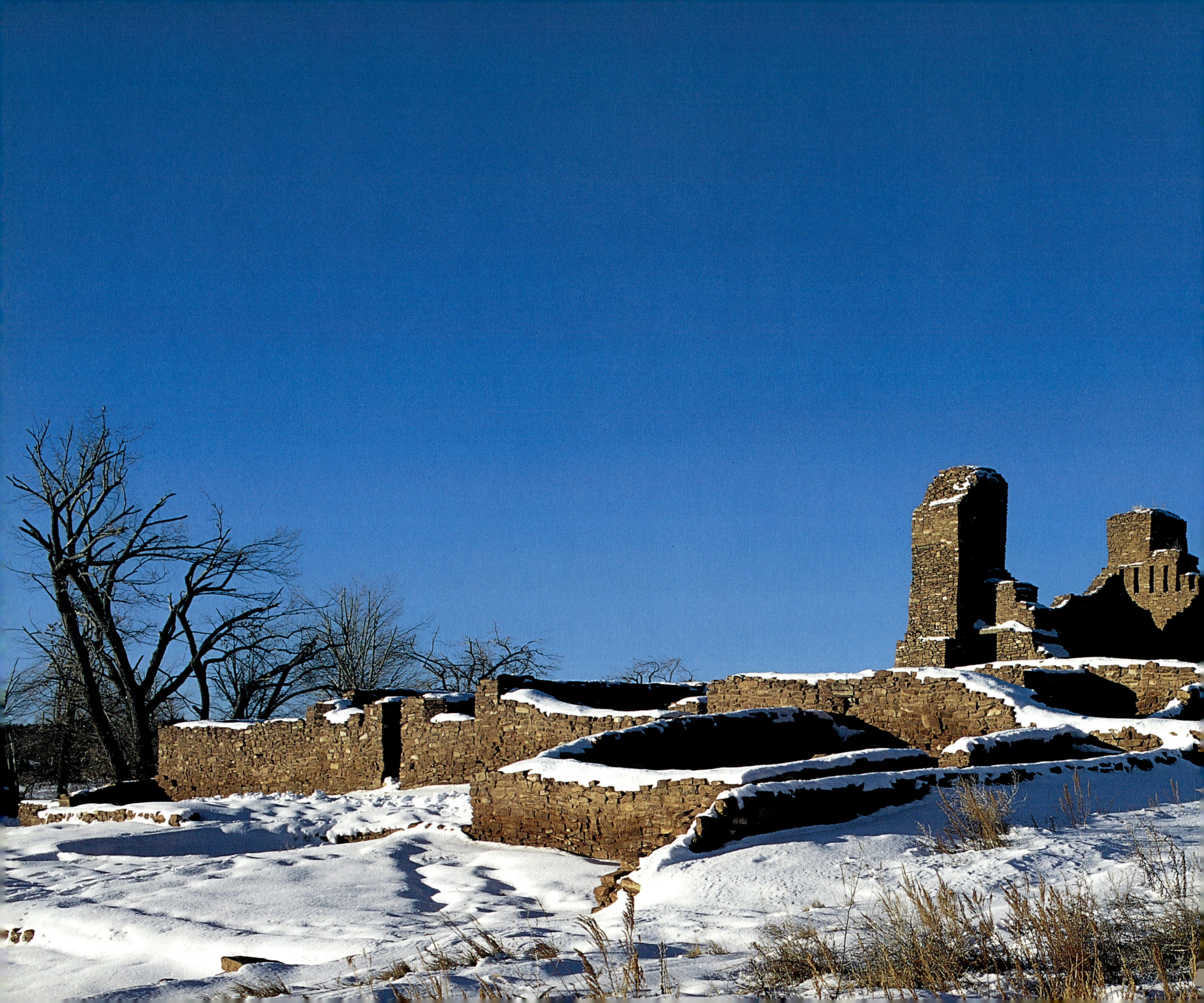

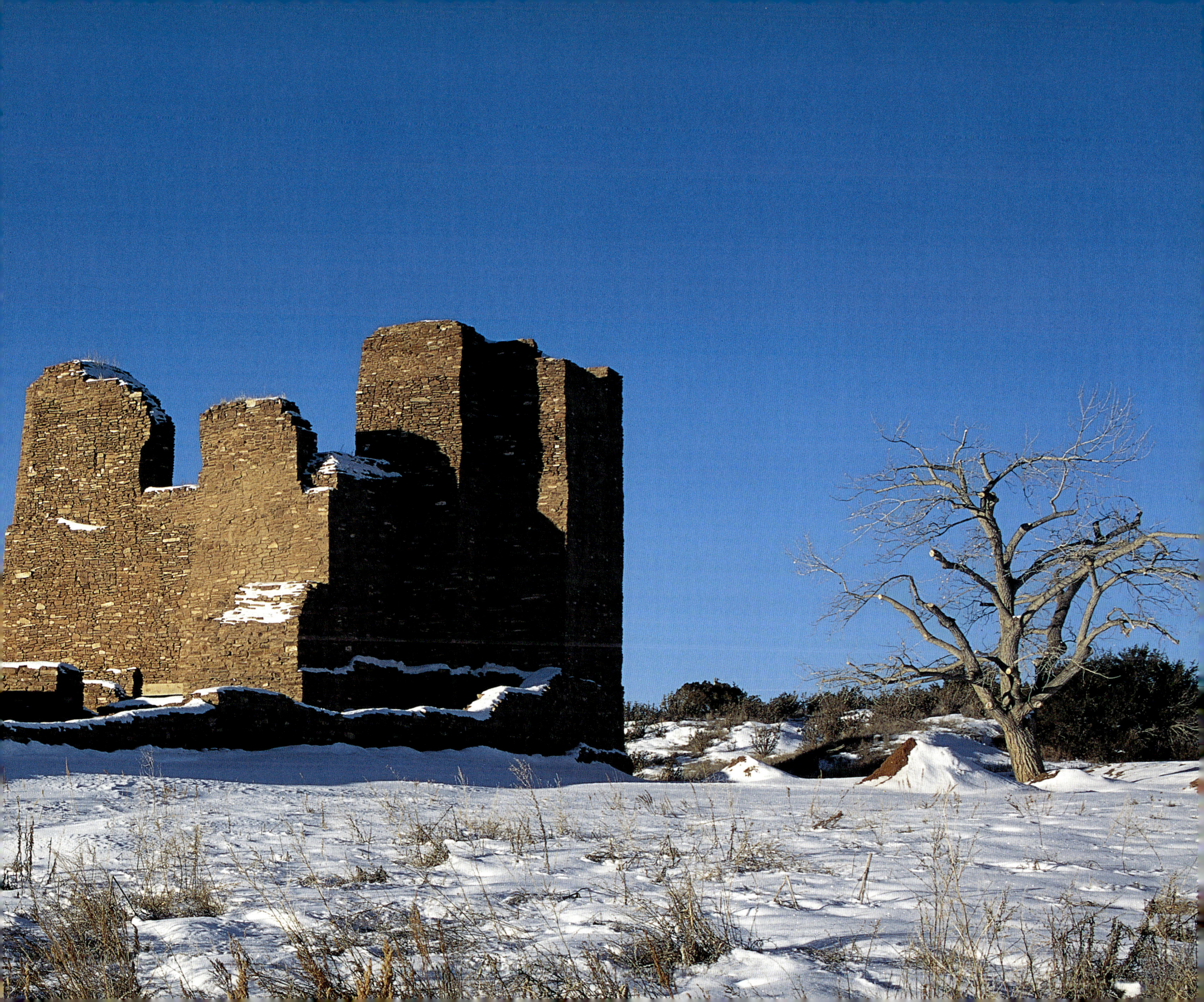

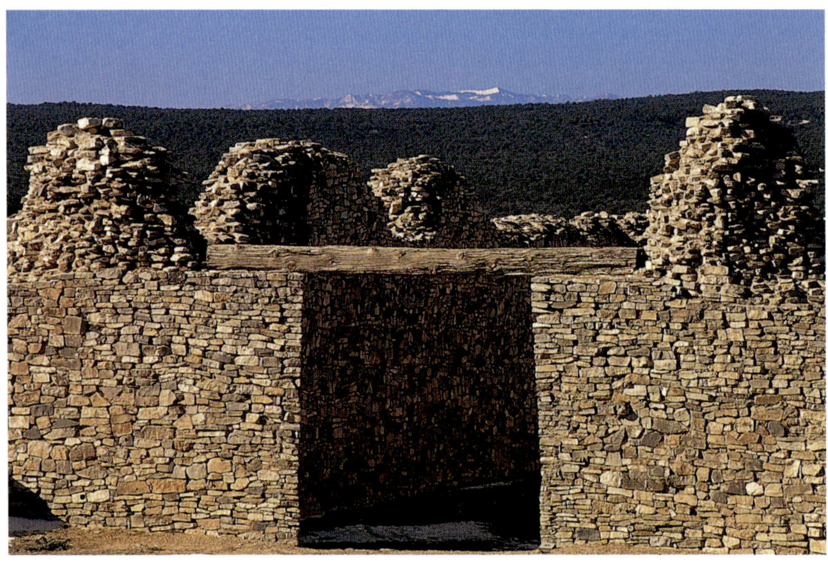

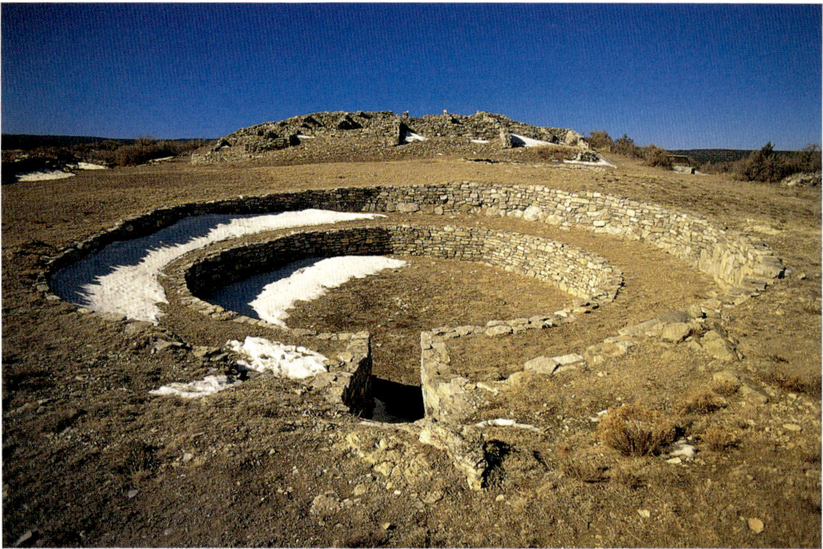

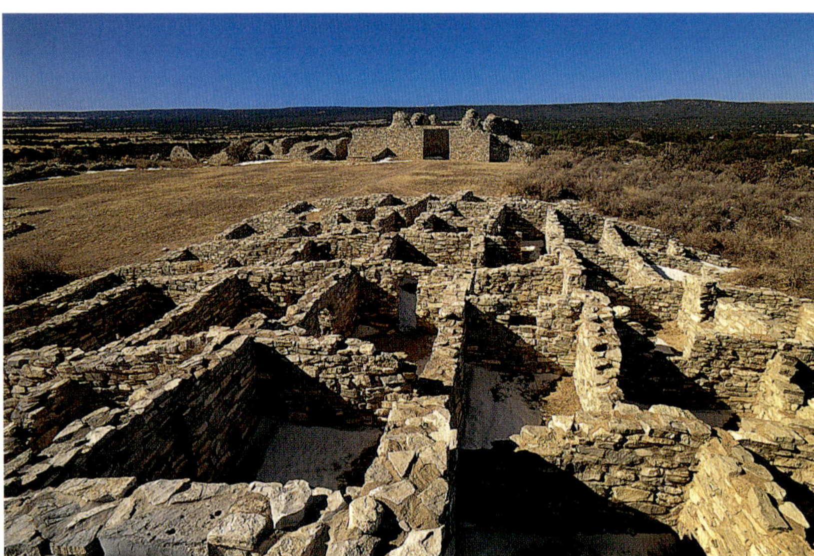

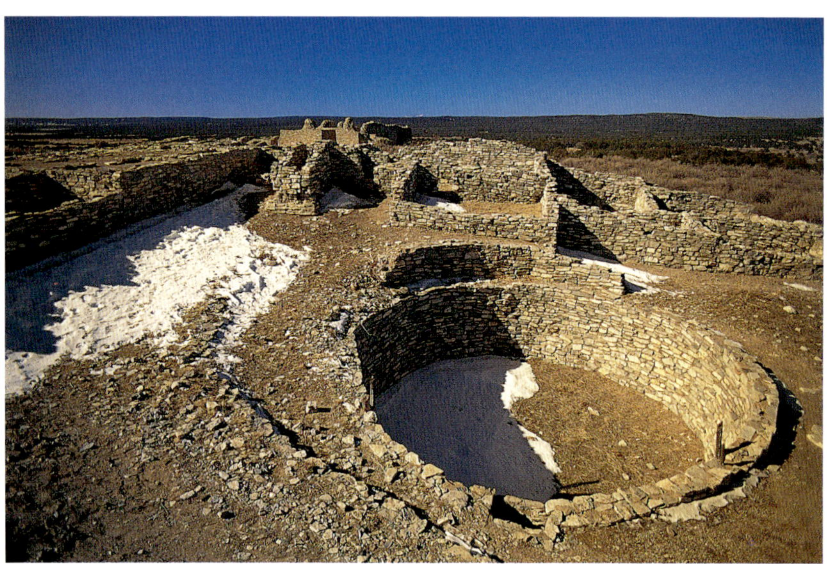

↑ Iglesia de San Buenaventura, Gran Quivira, Salinas Pueblo Missions National Monument
→ Misión de la Purísima Concepción de Cuarac, Quarai, Salinas Pueblo Missions National Monument

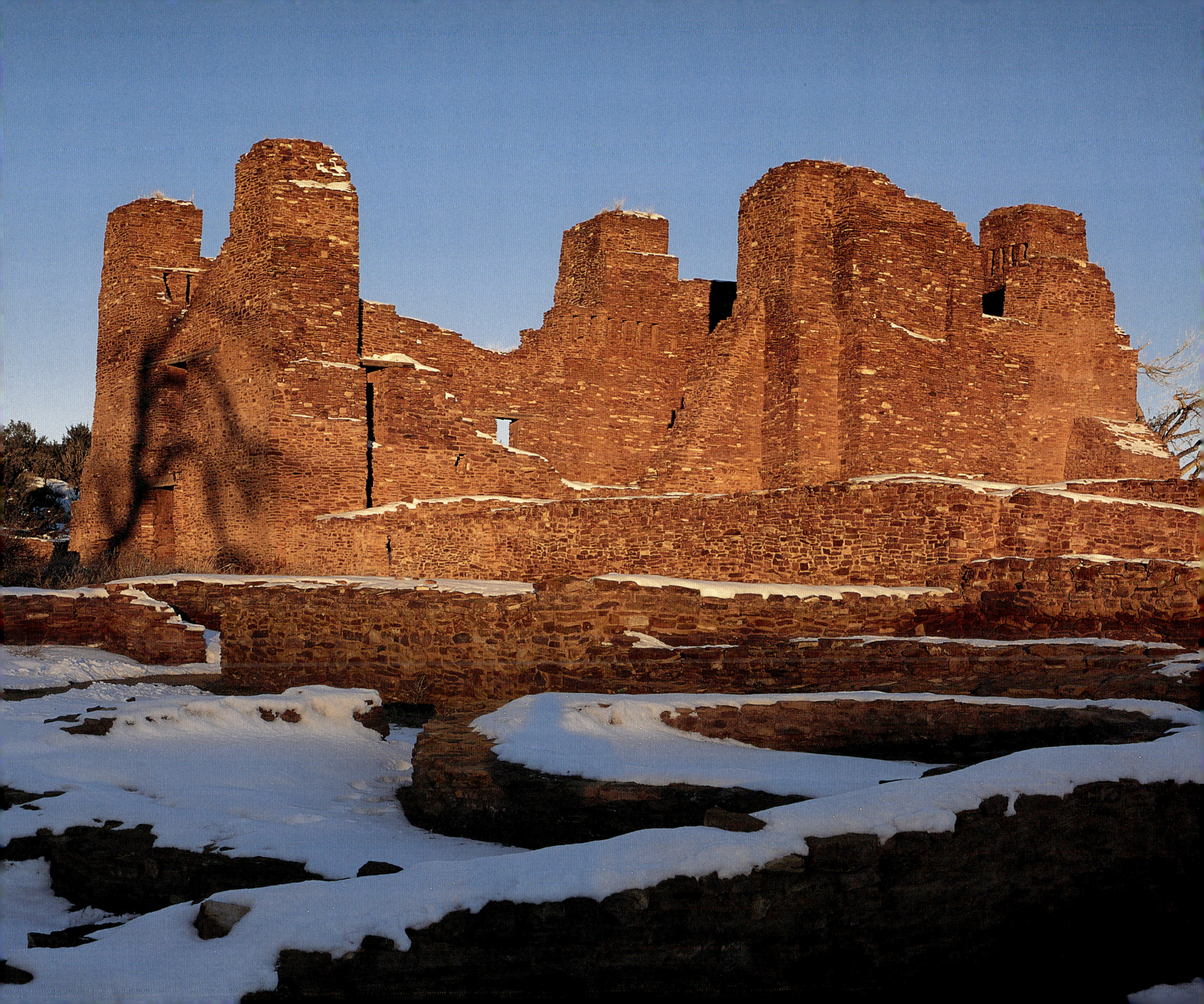

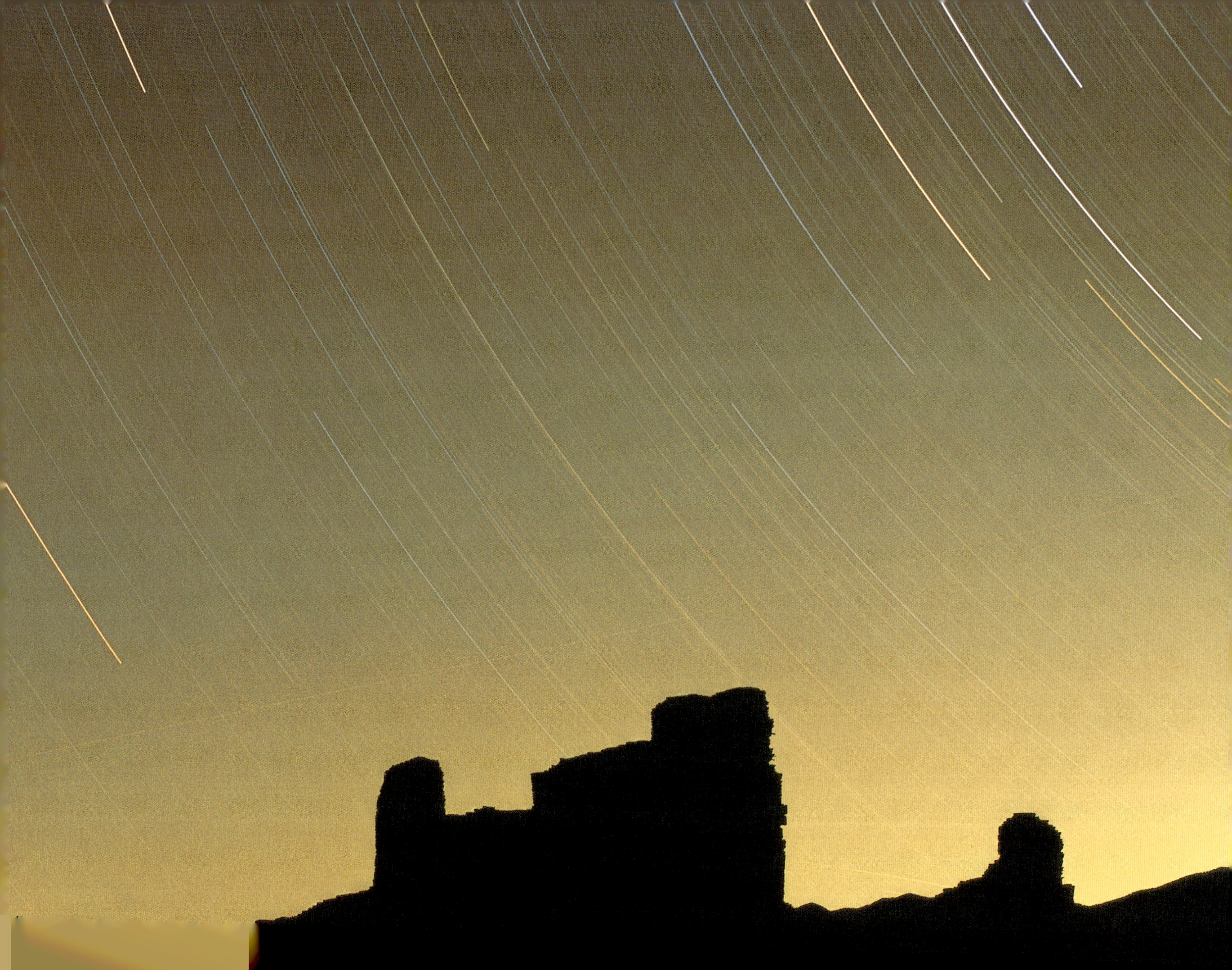

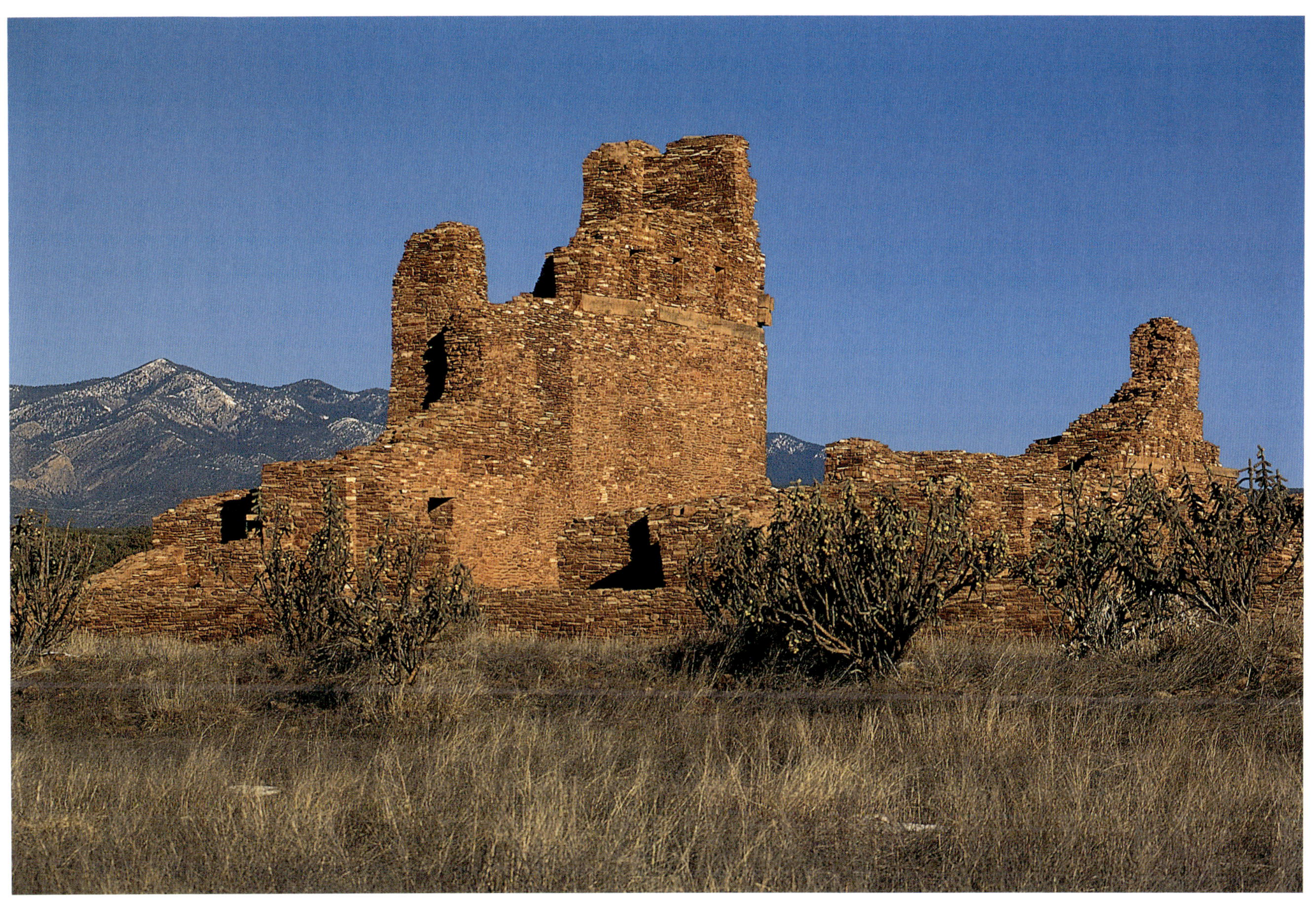

↑←Misión San Gregorio de Abo, Abo, Salinas Pueblo Missions National Monument

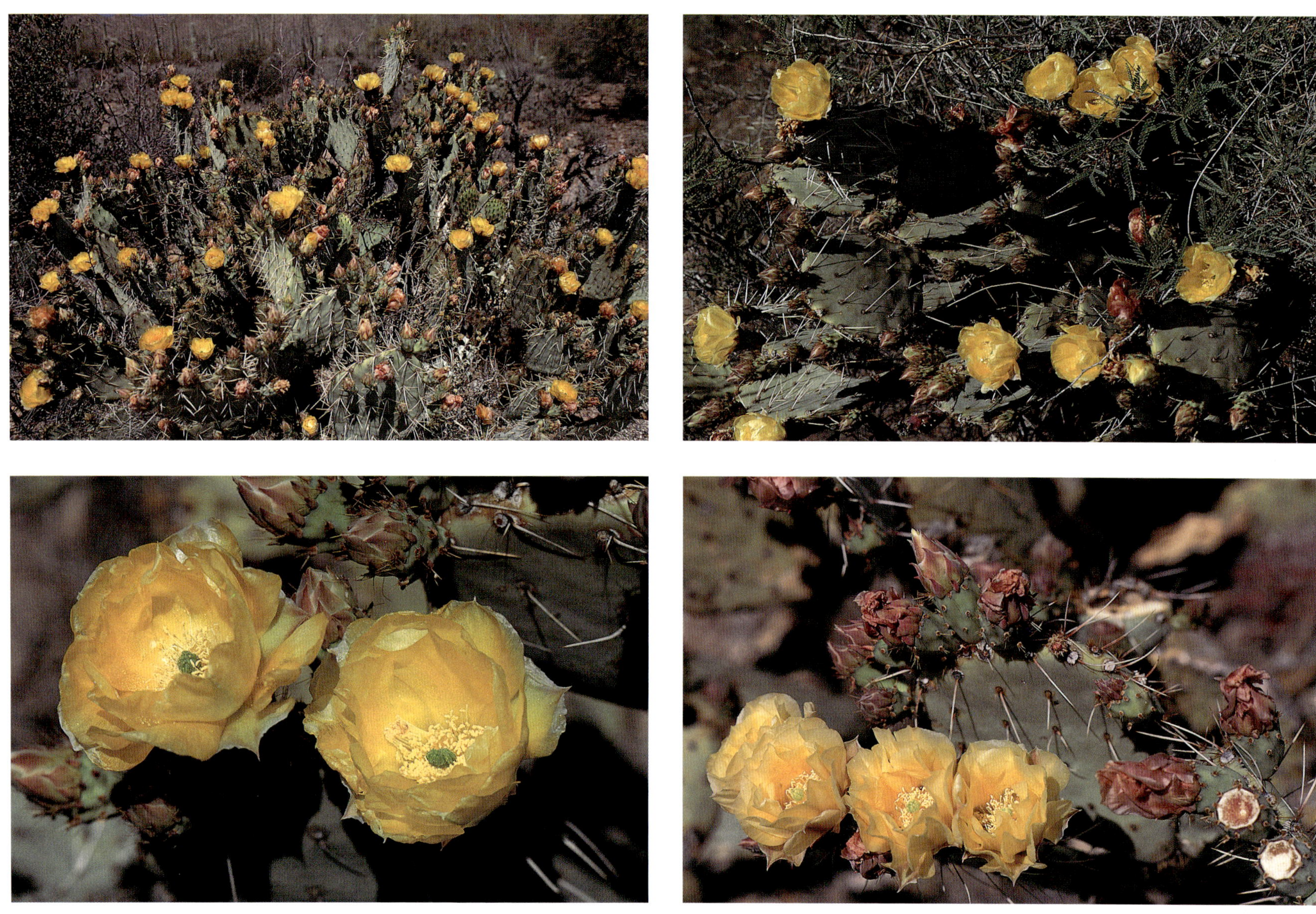

↰ Cactus

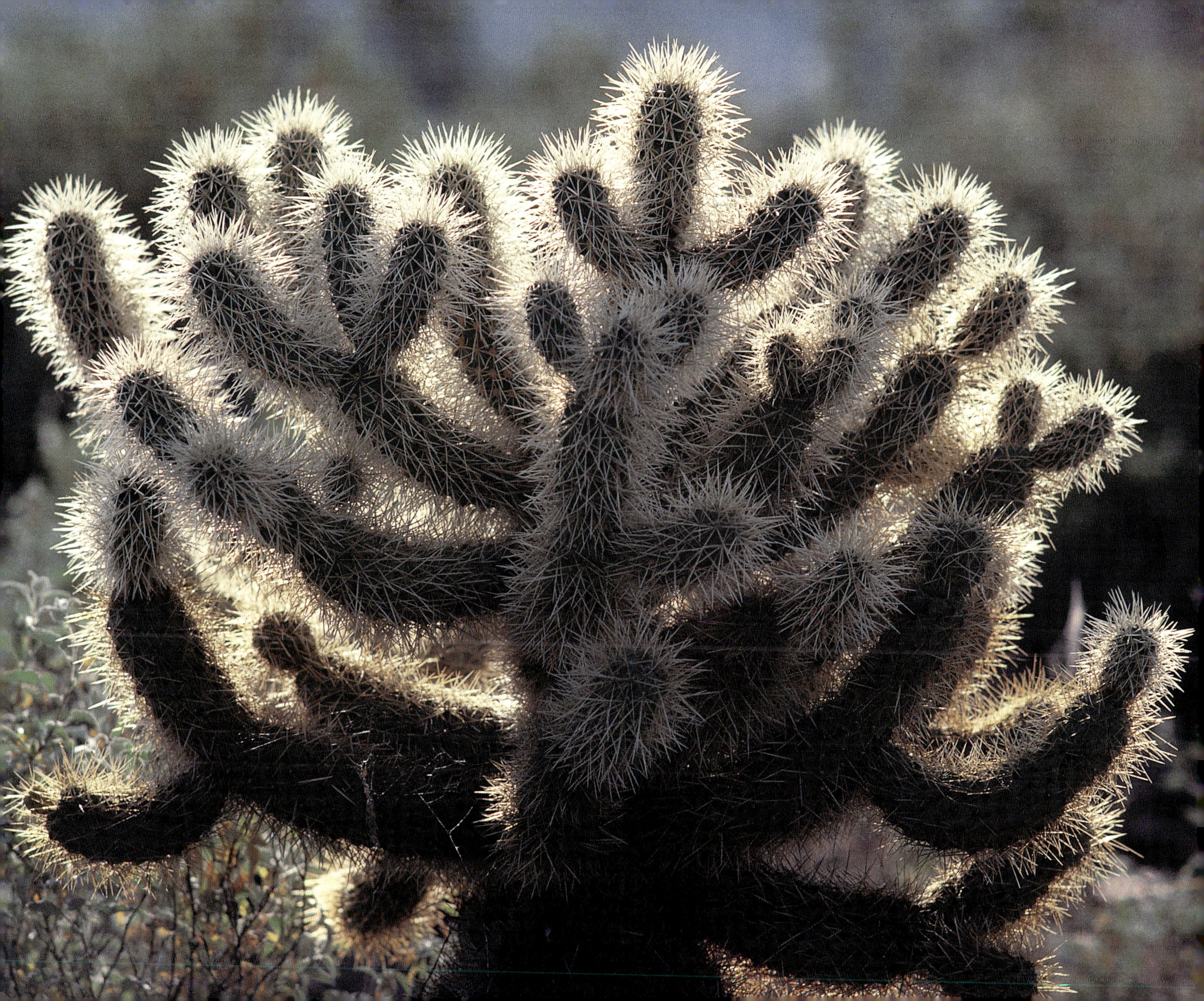

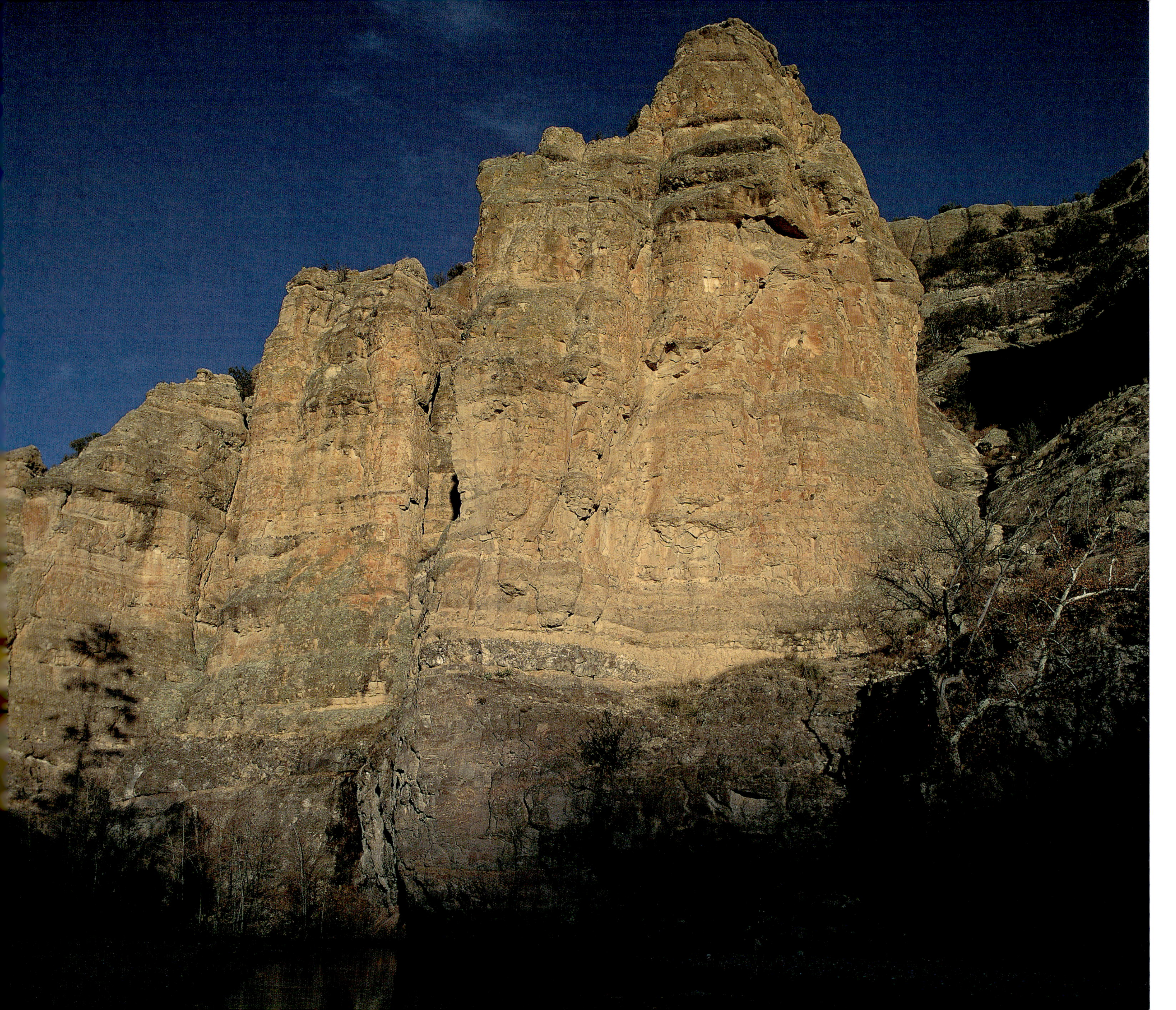

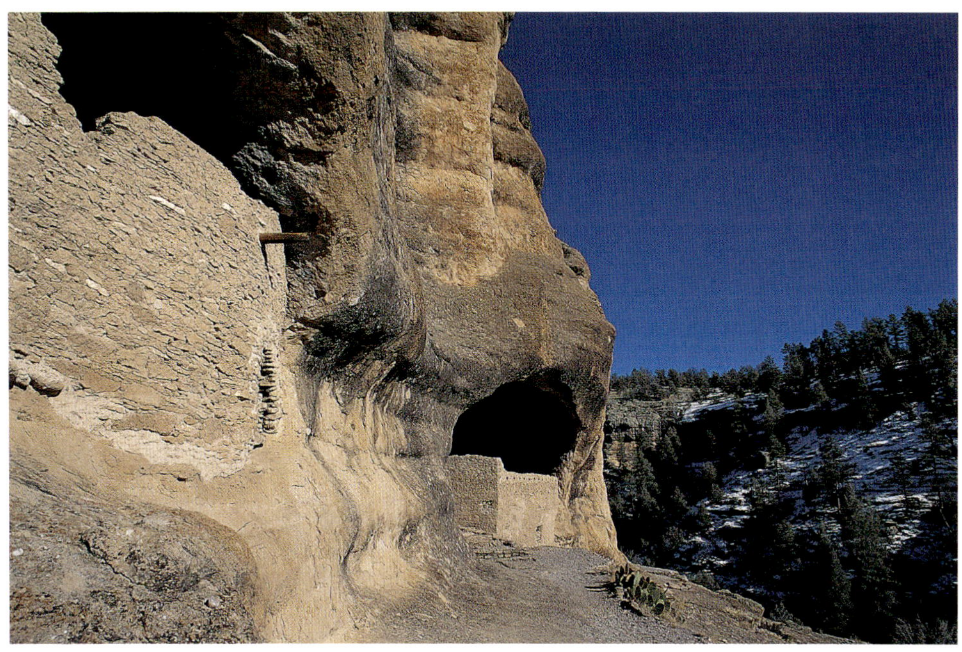

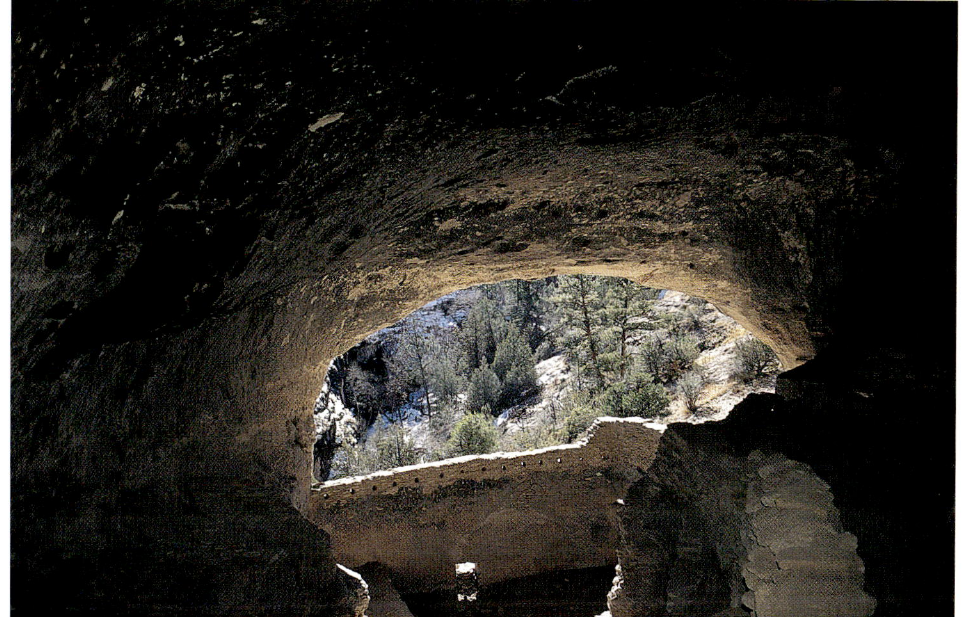

↑←Gila Cliff Dwellings National Monument

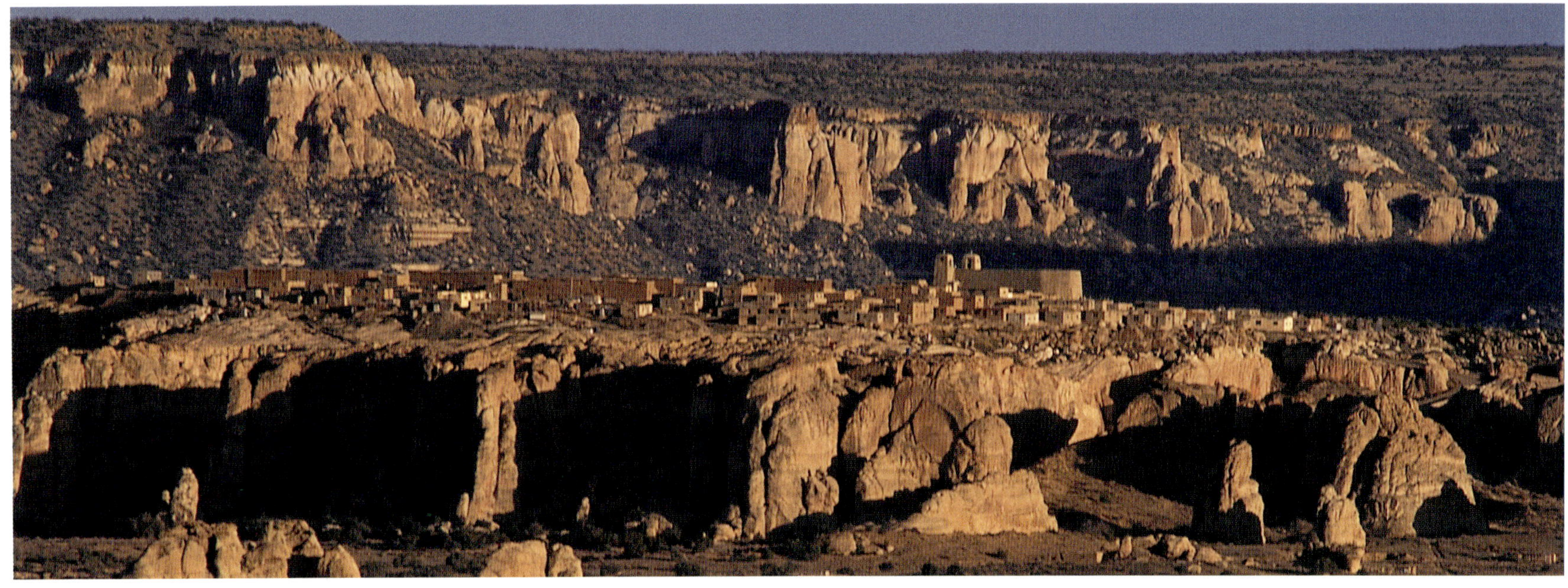

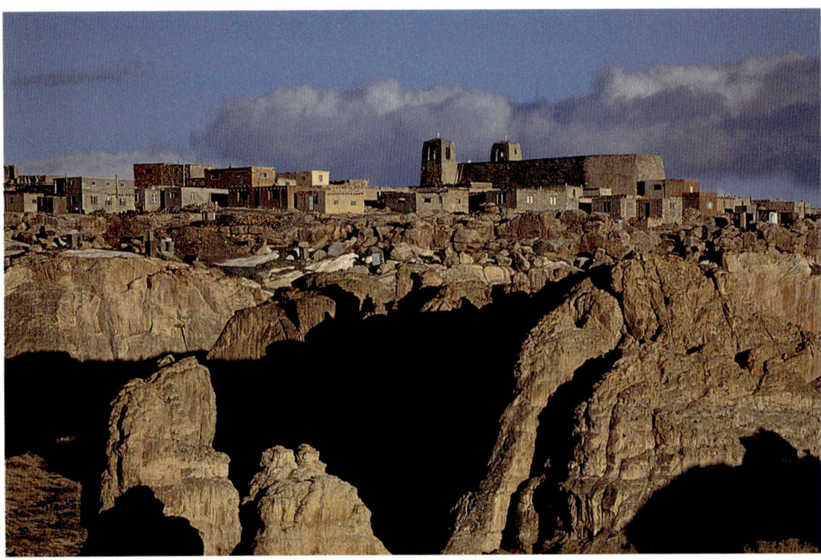

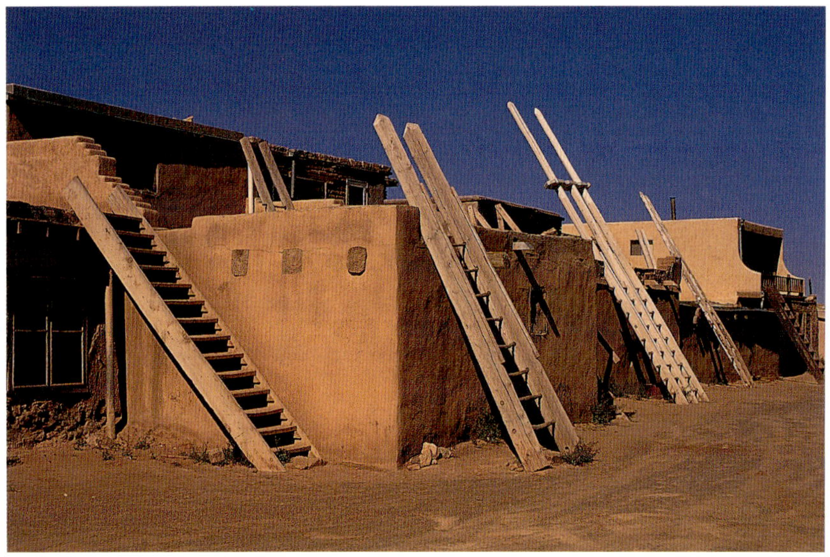

↑ Acoma Pueblo → Acoma, Enchanted Mesa

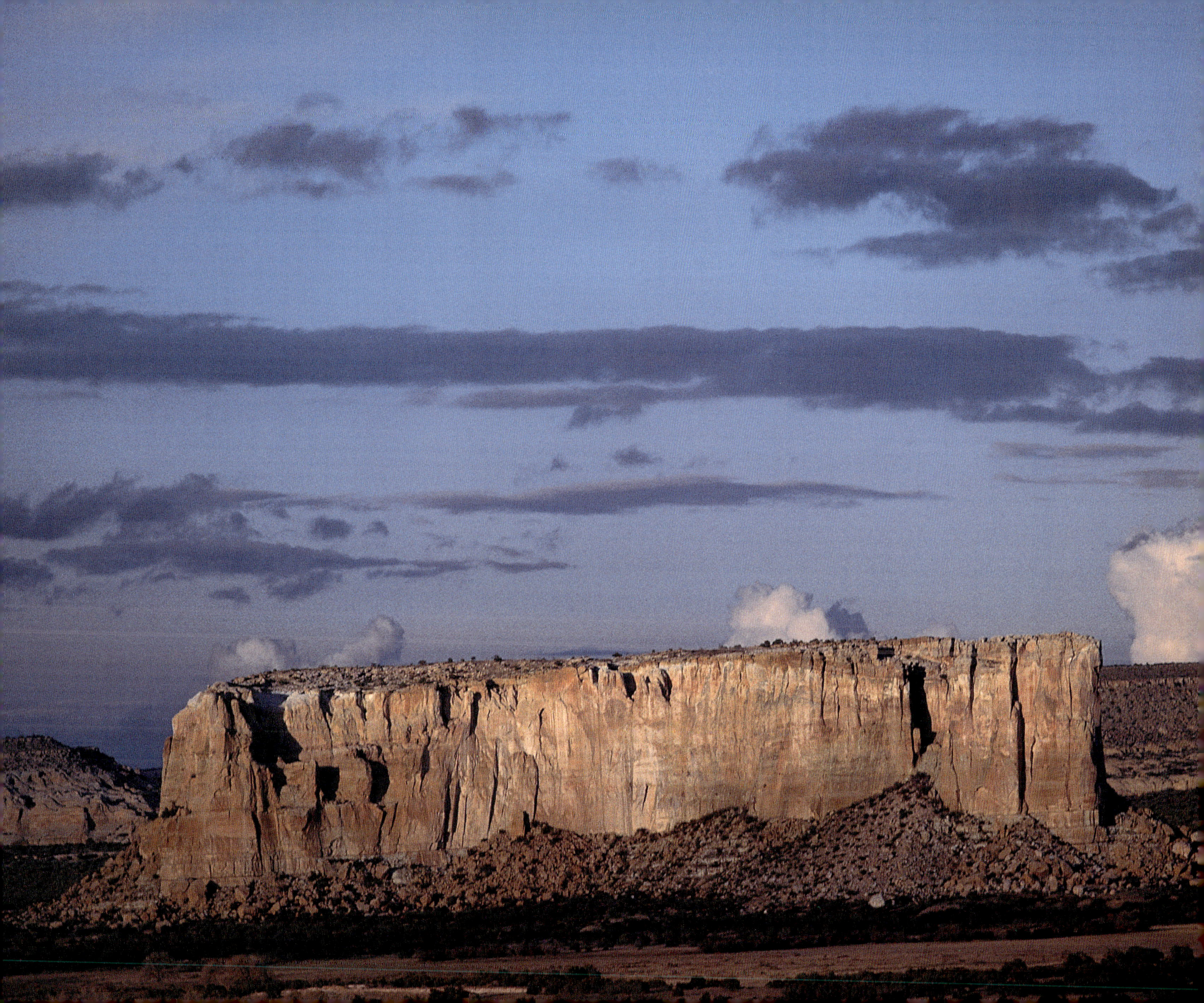

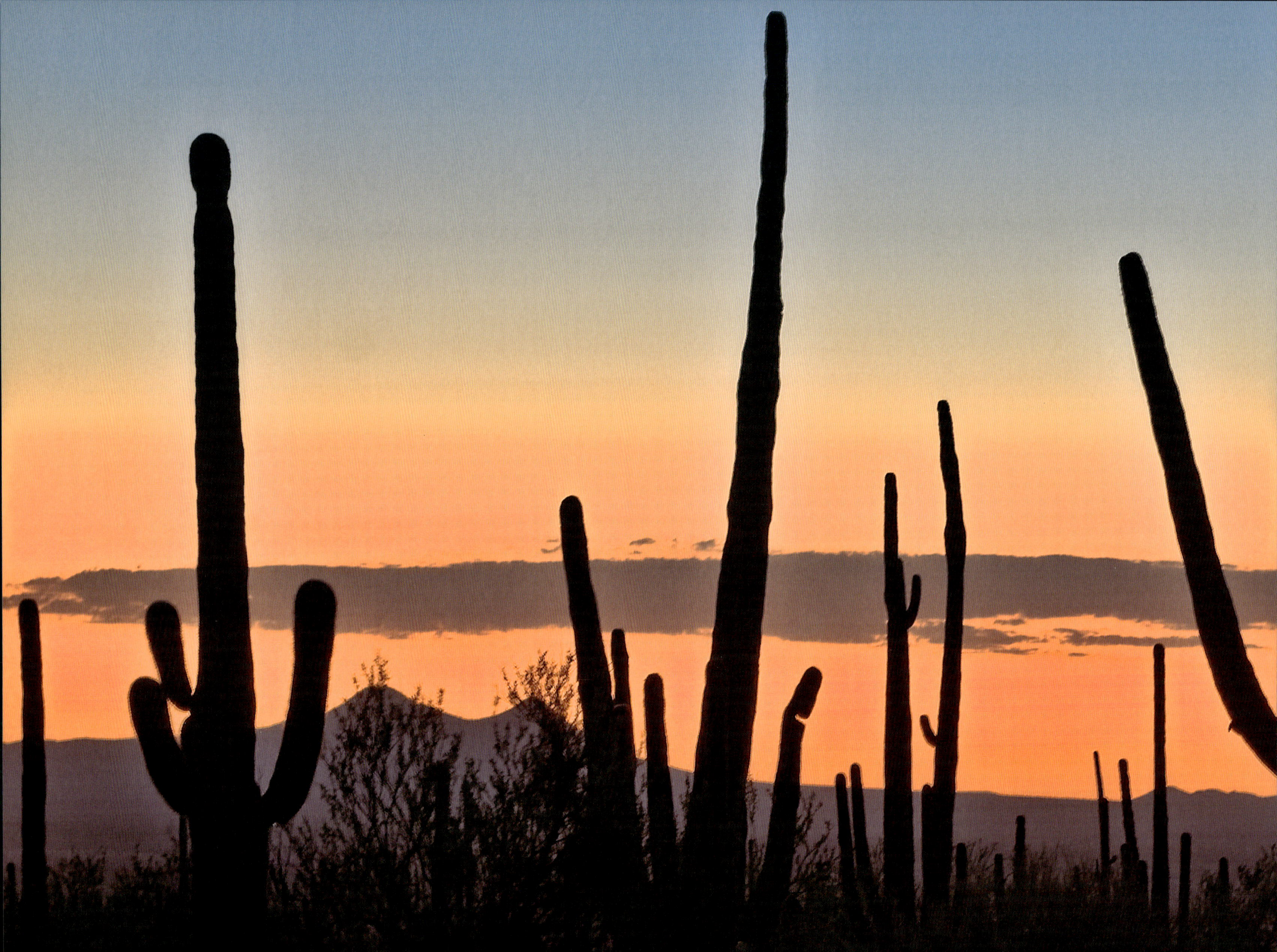

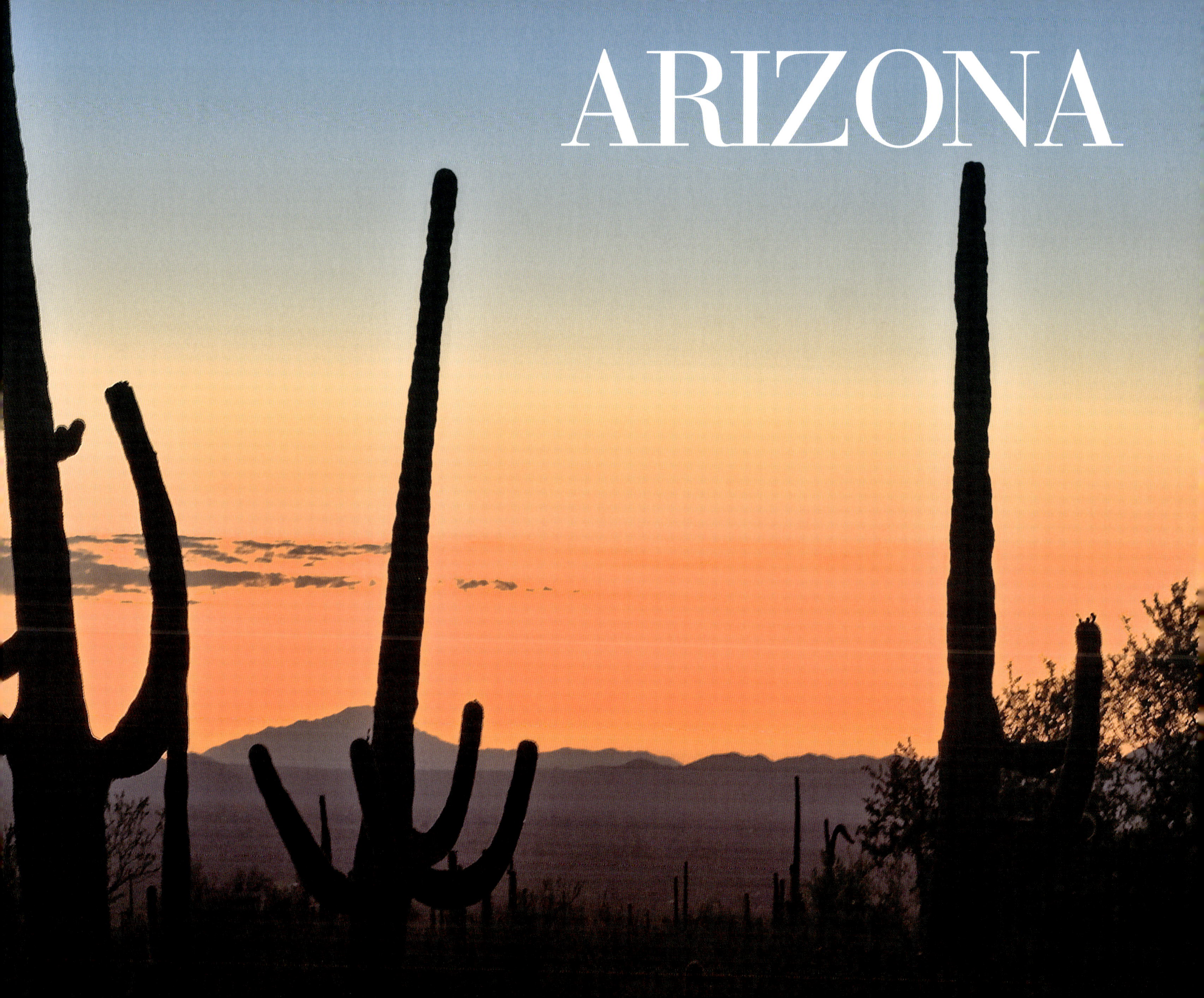
ARIZONA

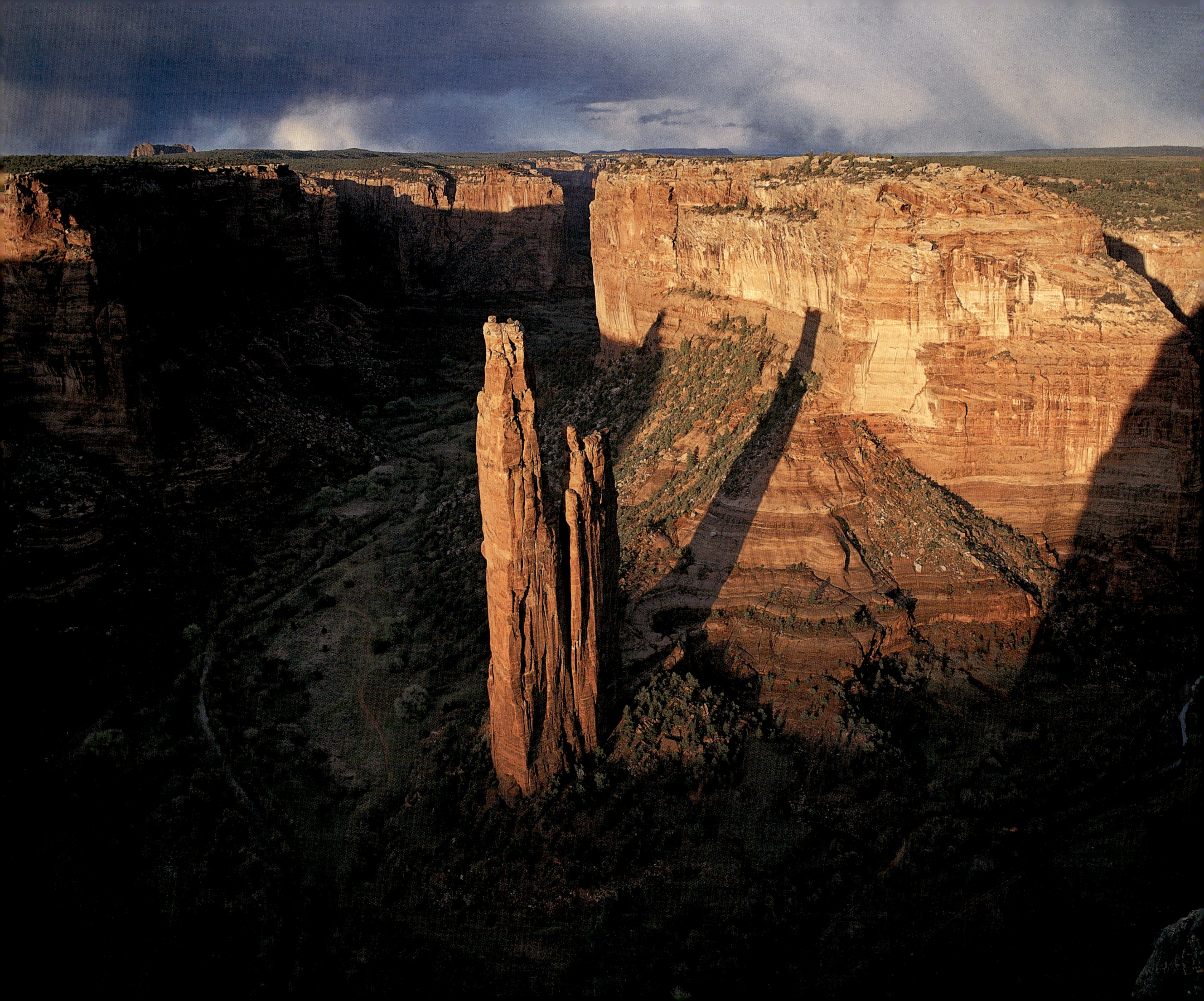

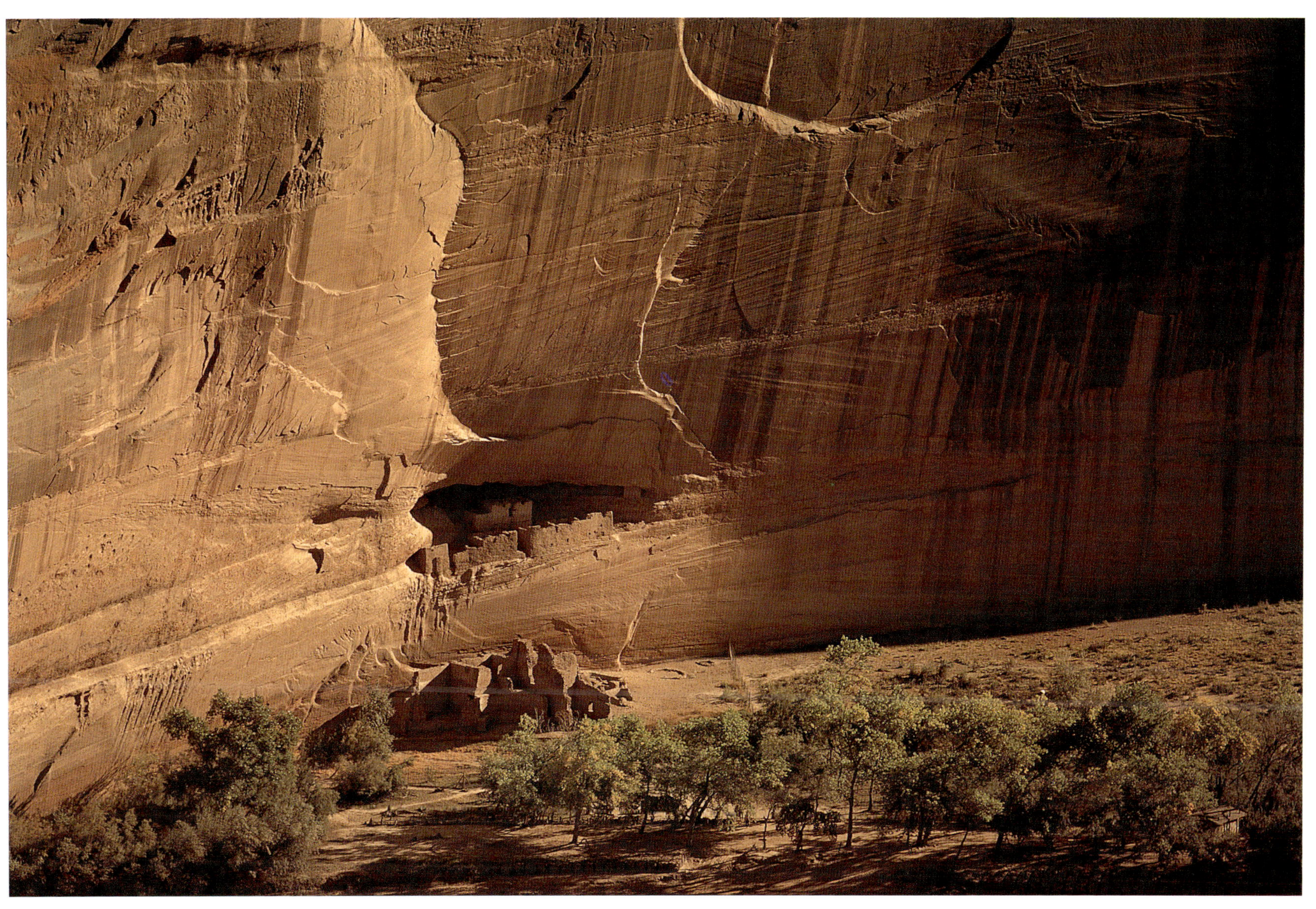

↑ White House Ruins, Canyon de Chelly National Monument ← Spider Rock, Canyon de Chelly National Monument ↓ Montezuma Castle National Monument

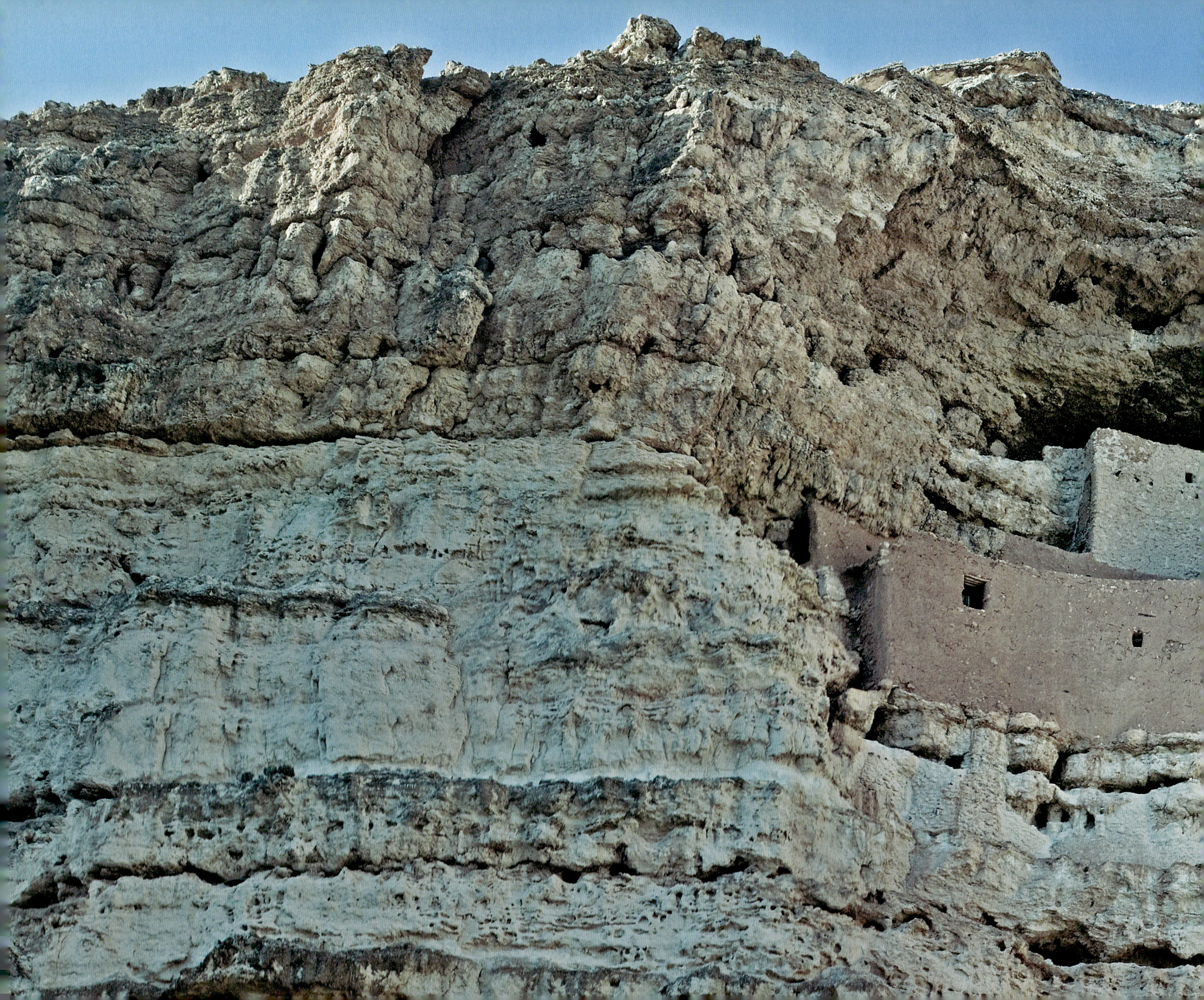

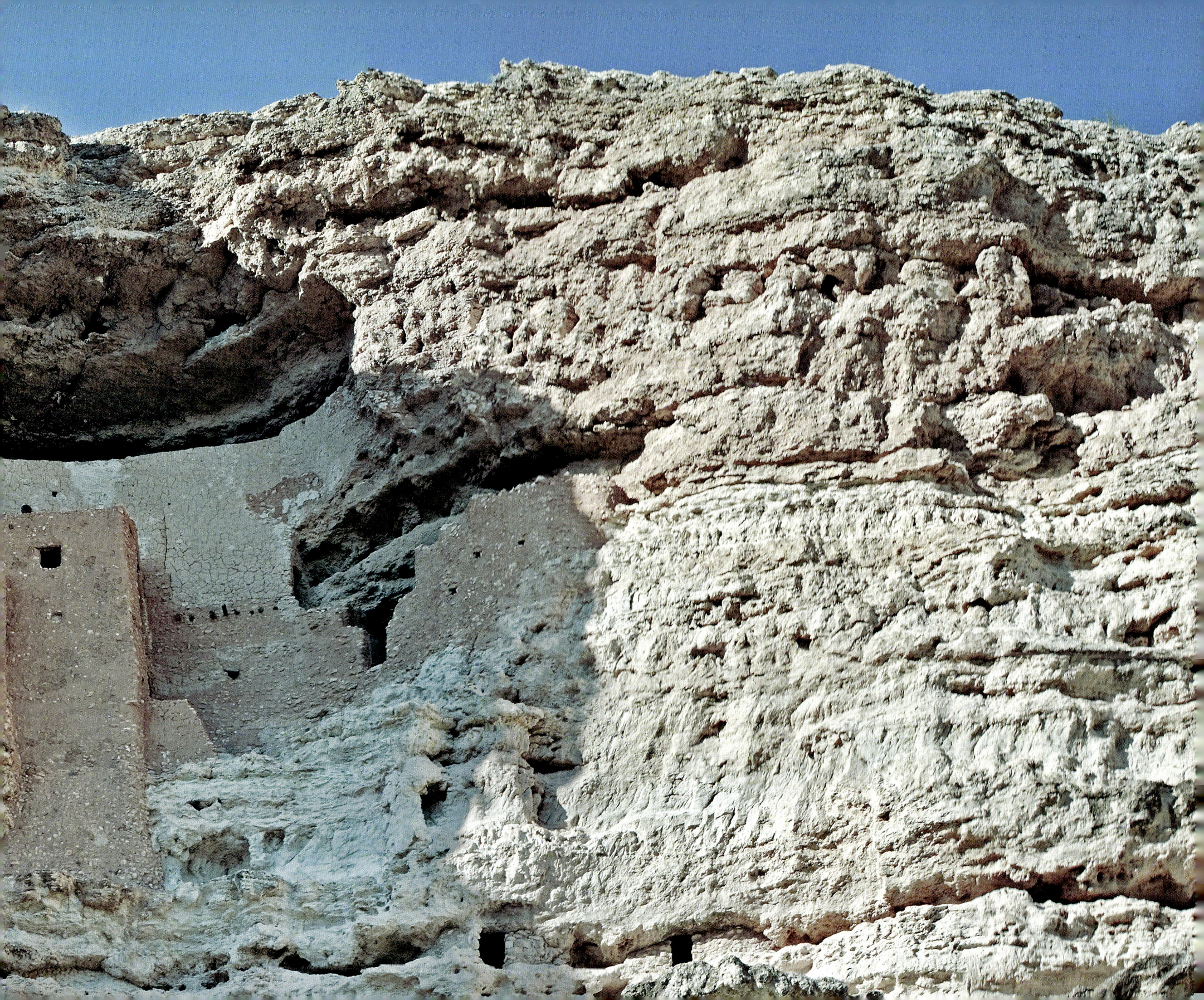

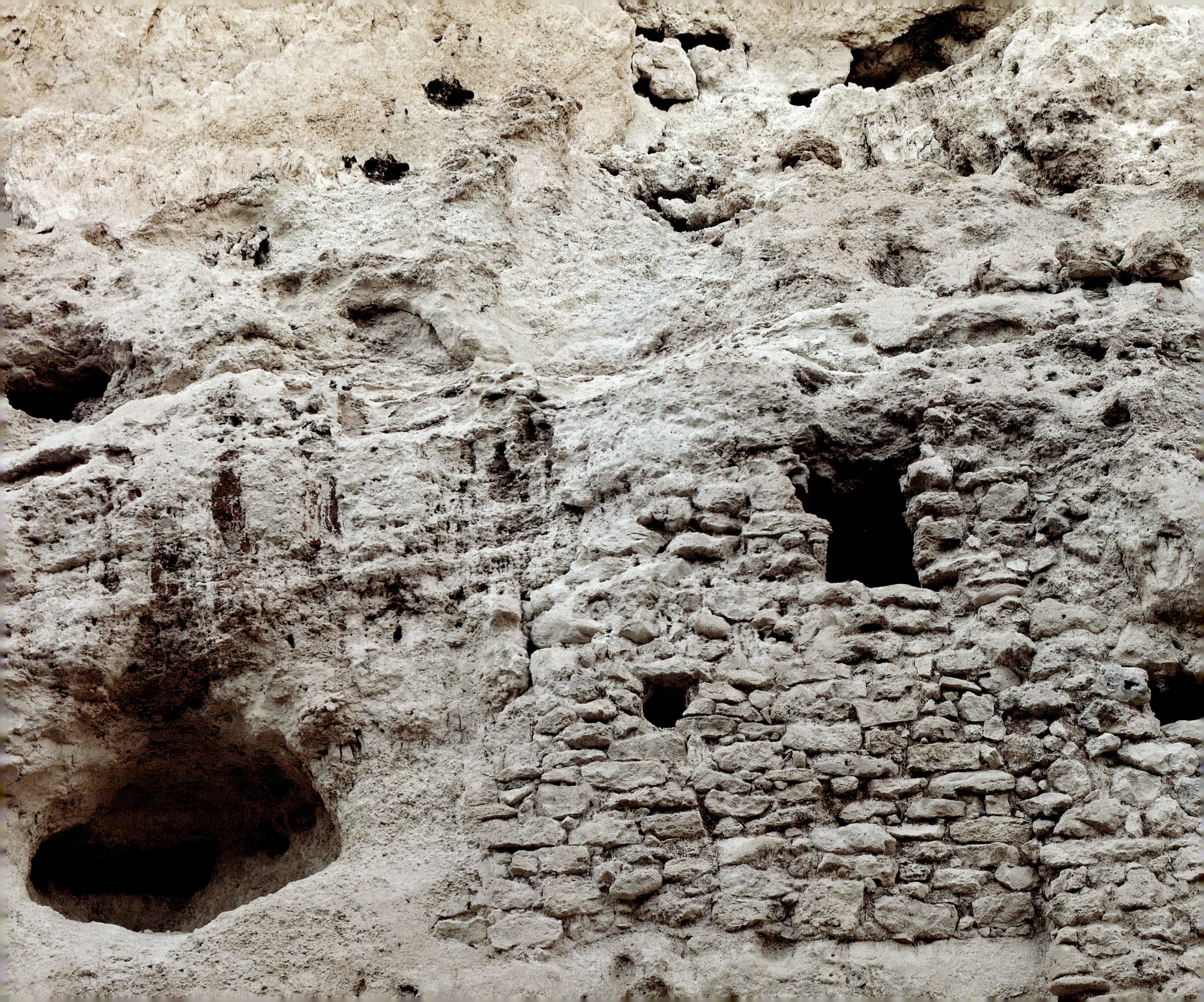

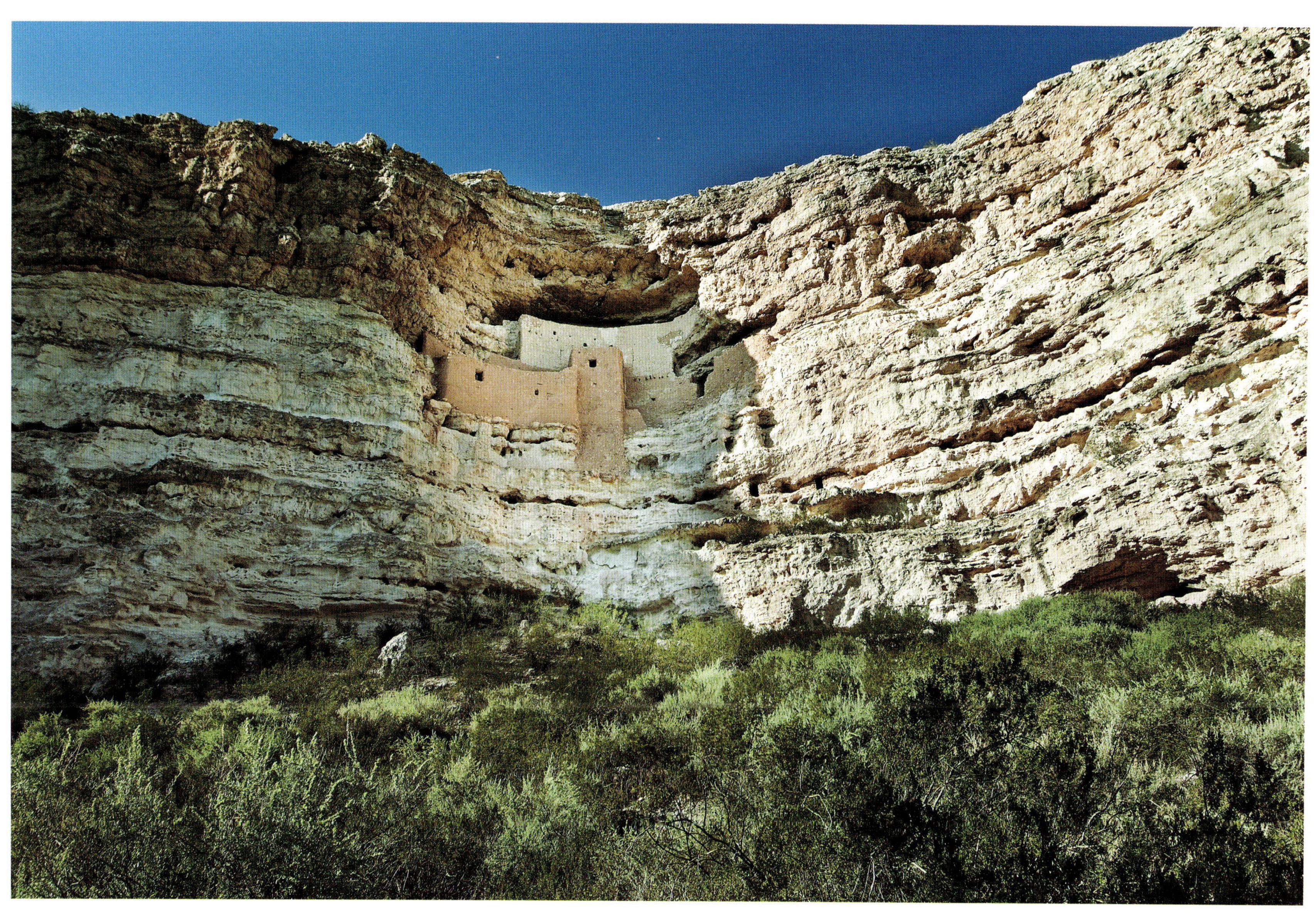

↩↑ Montezuma National Monument ↓Sunset Crater, Sunset Crater Volcano National Monument

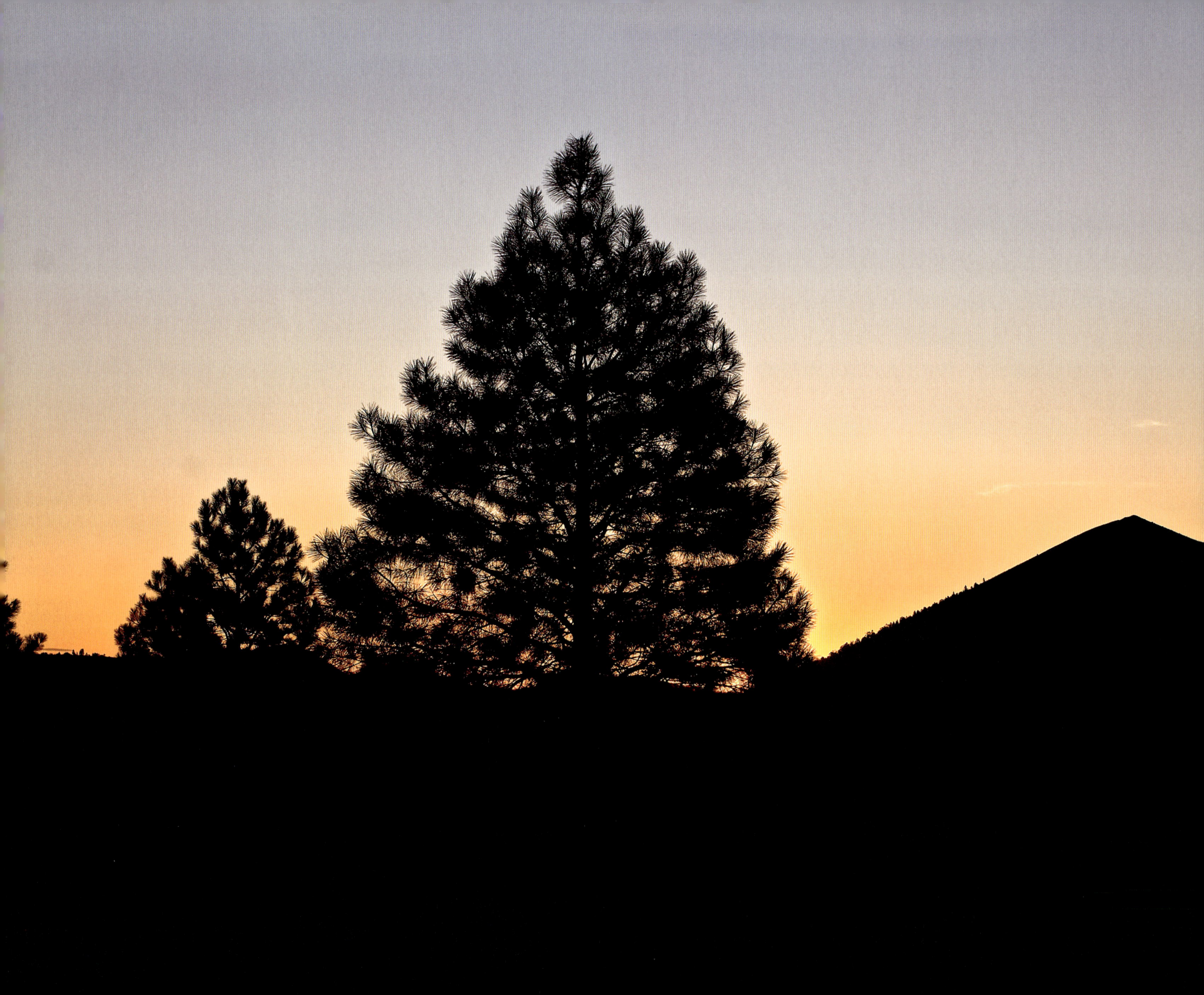

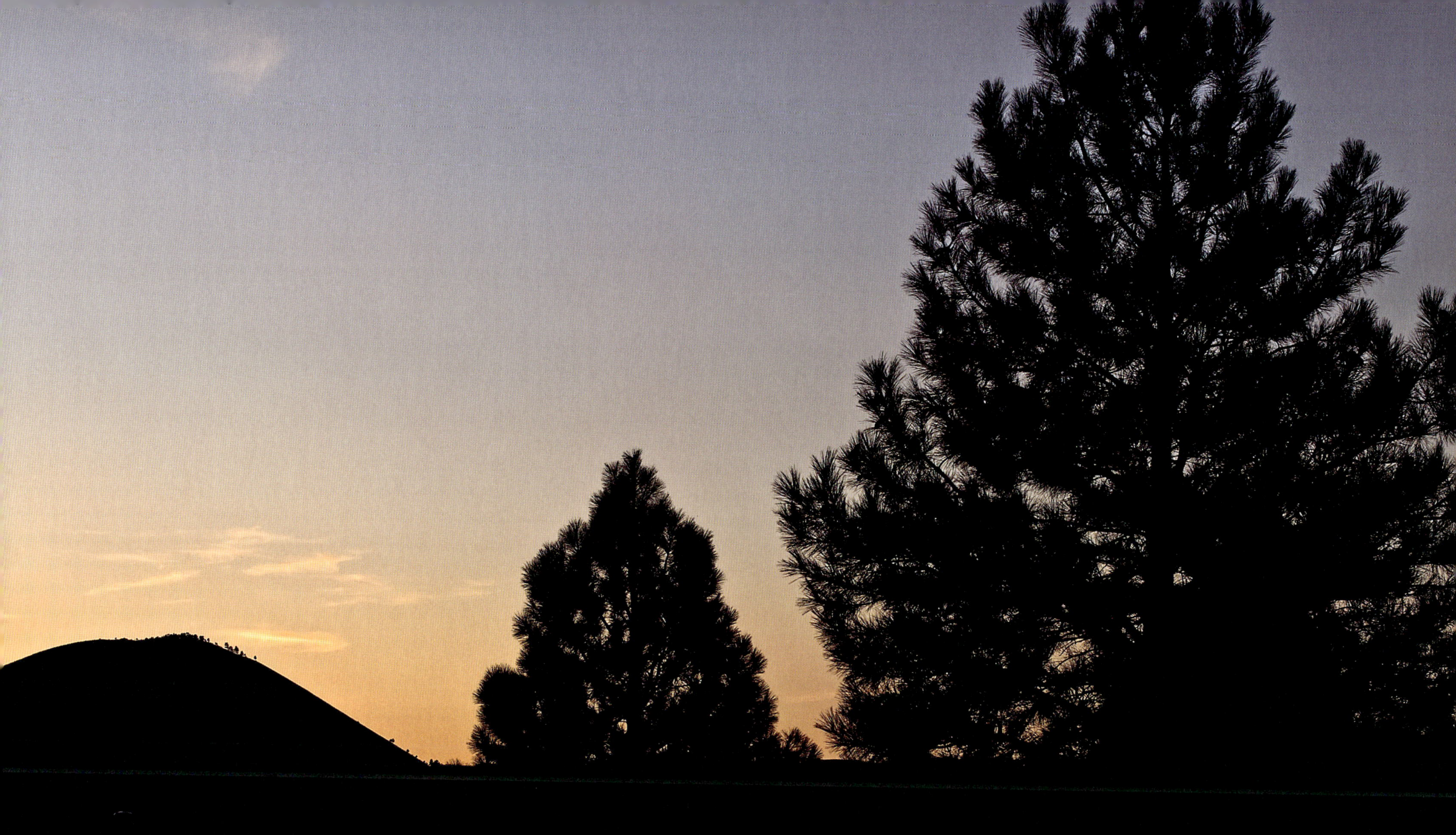

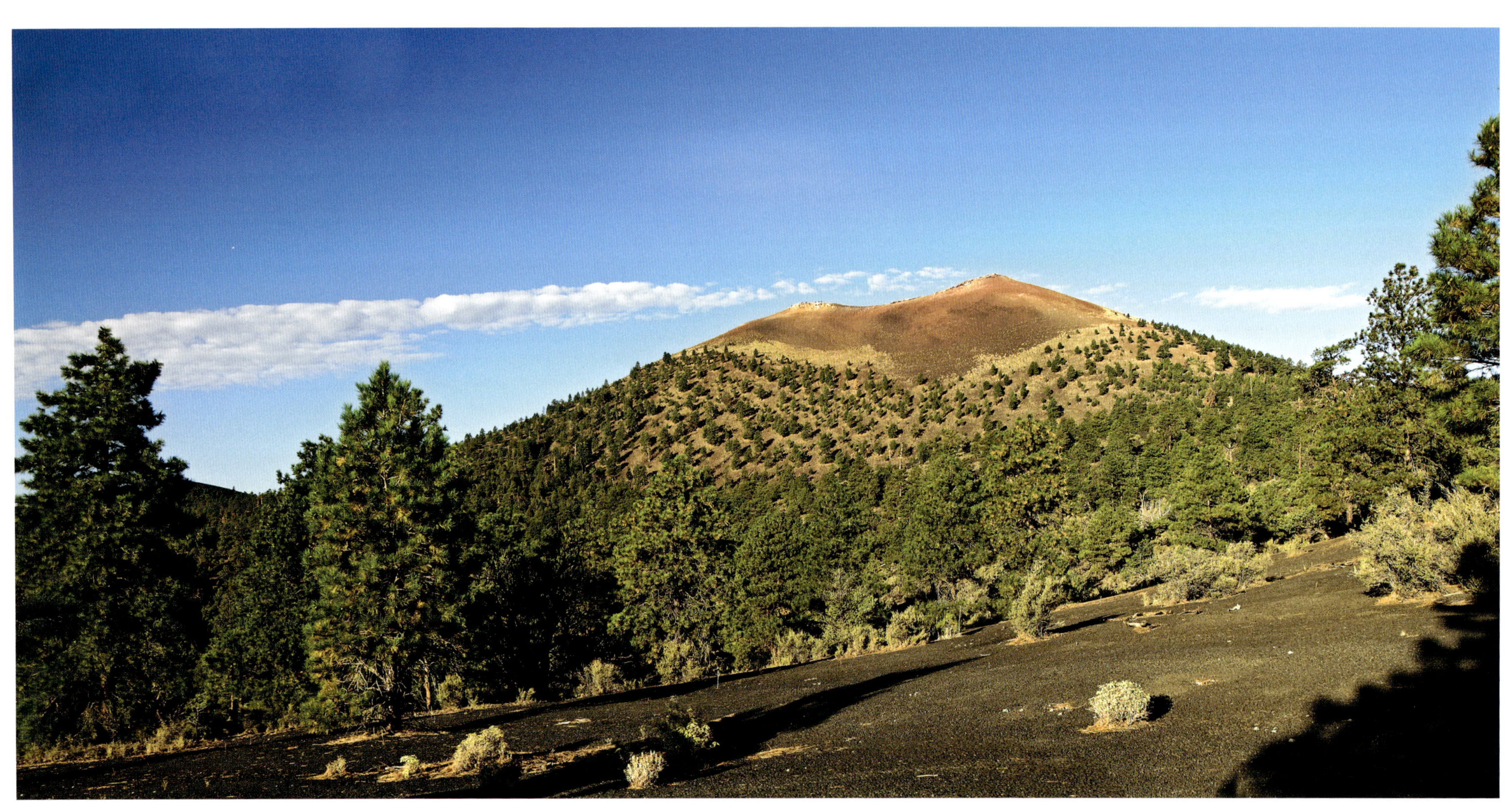

↑→ Sunset Crater Volcano National Monument ↓Vermilion Cliffs National Monument

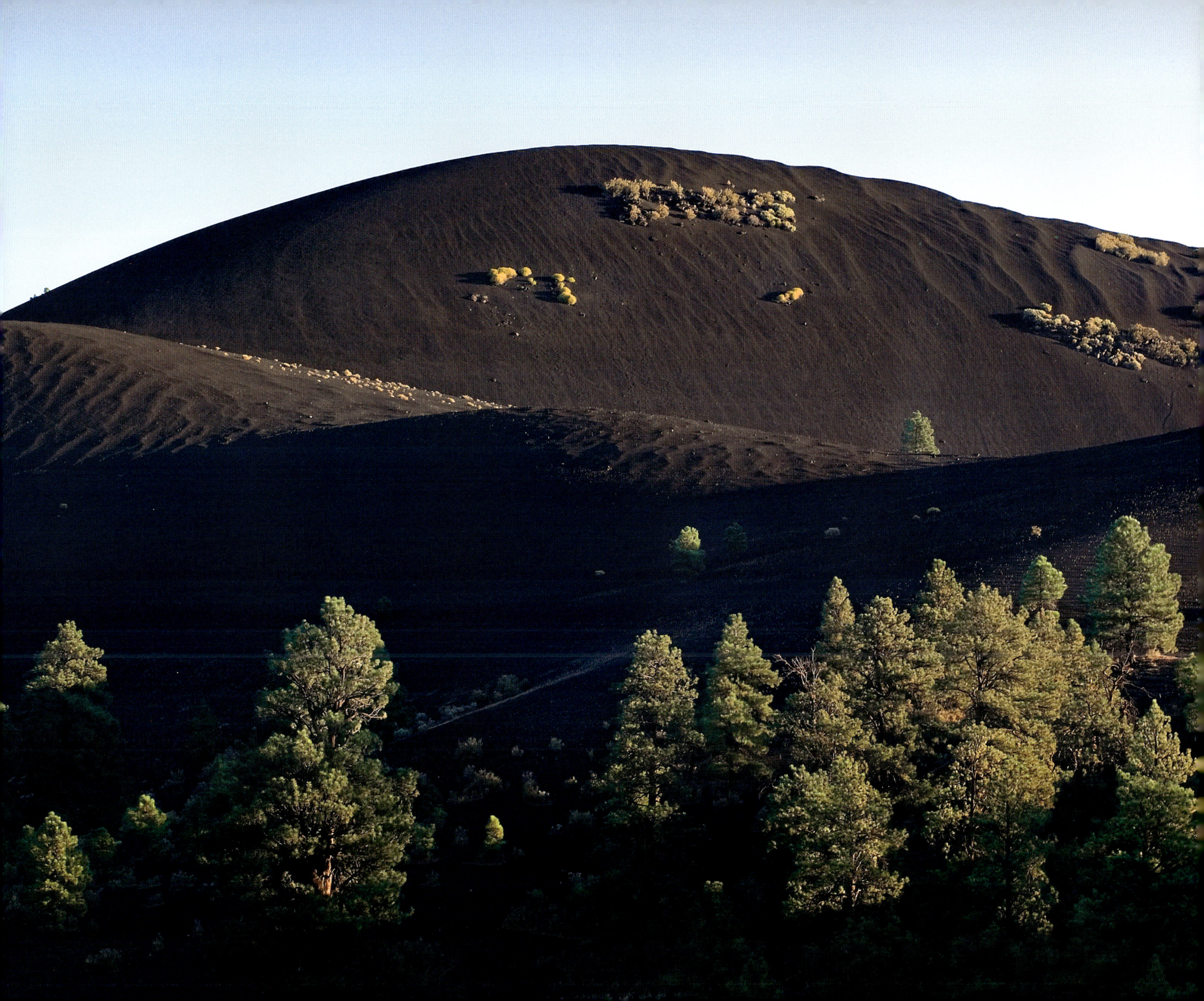

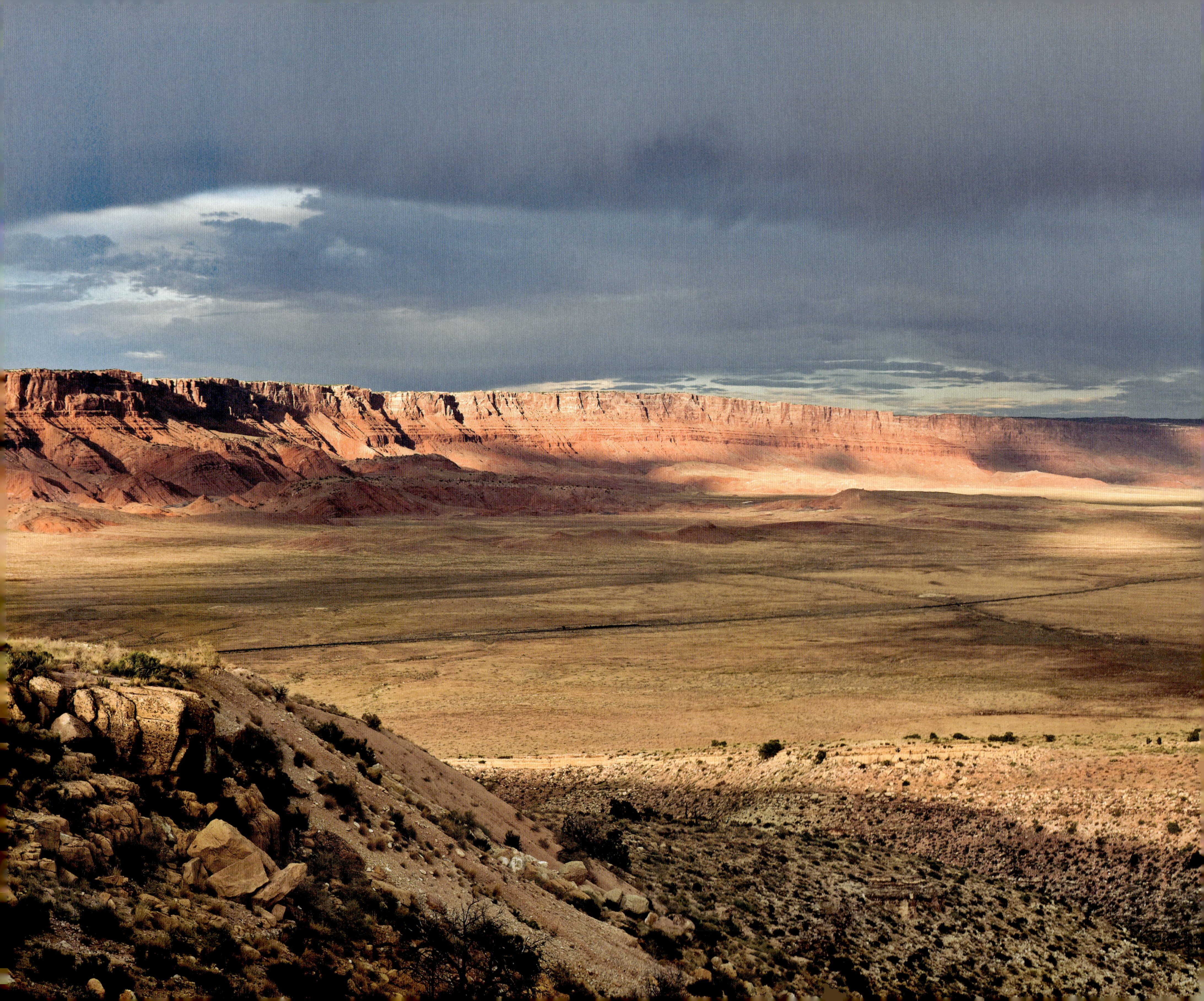

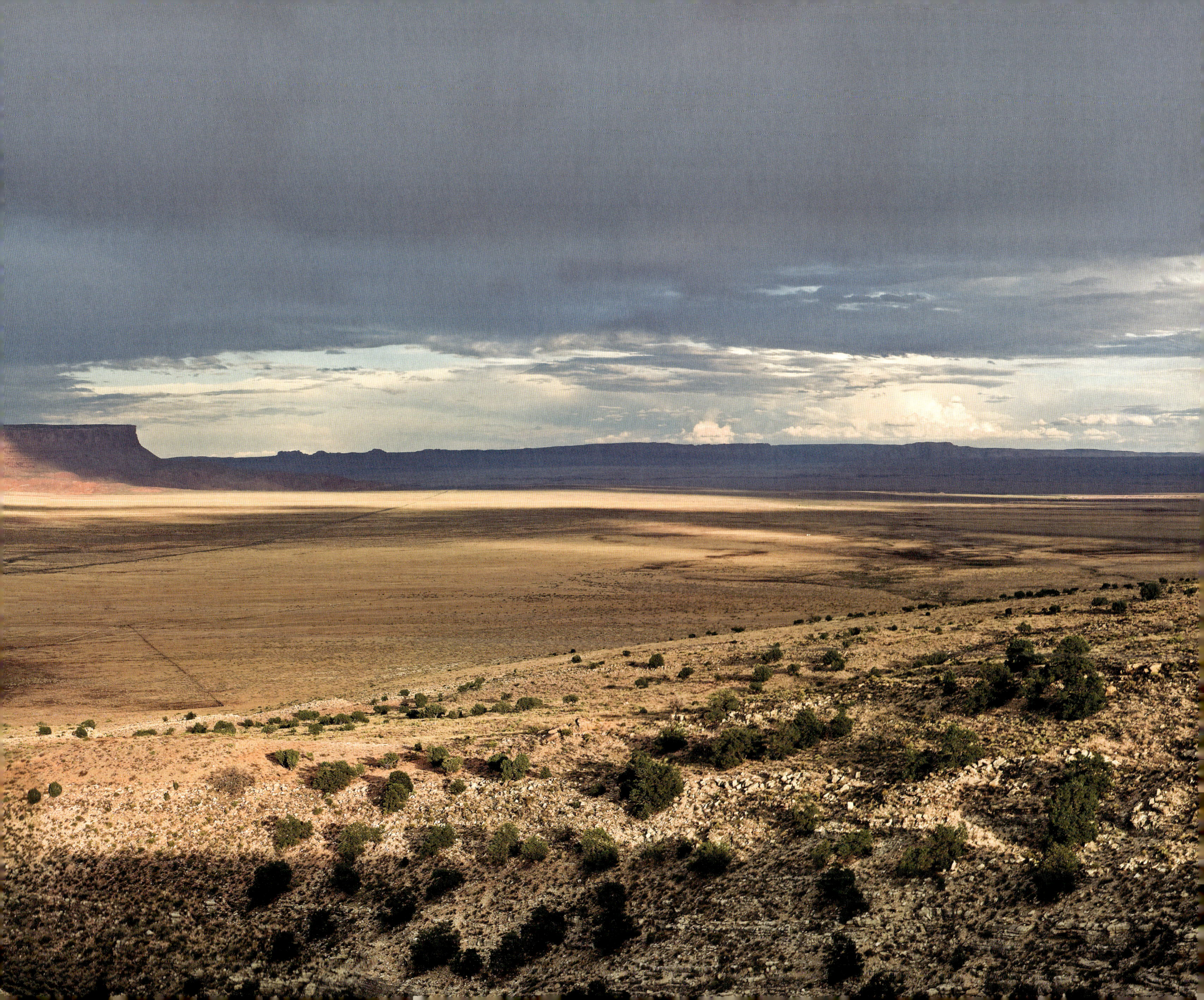

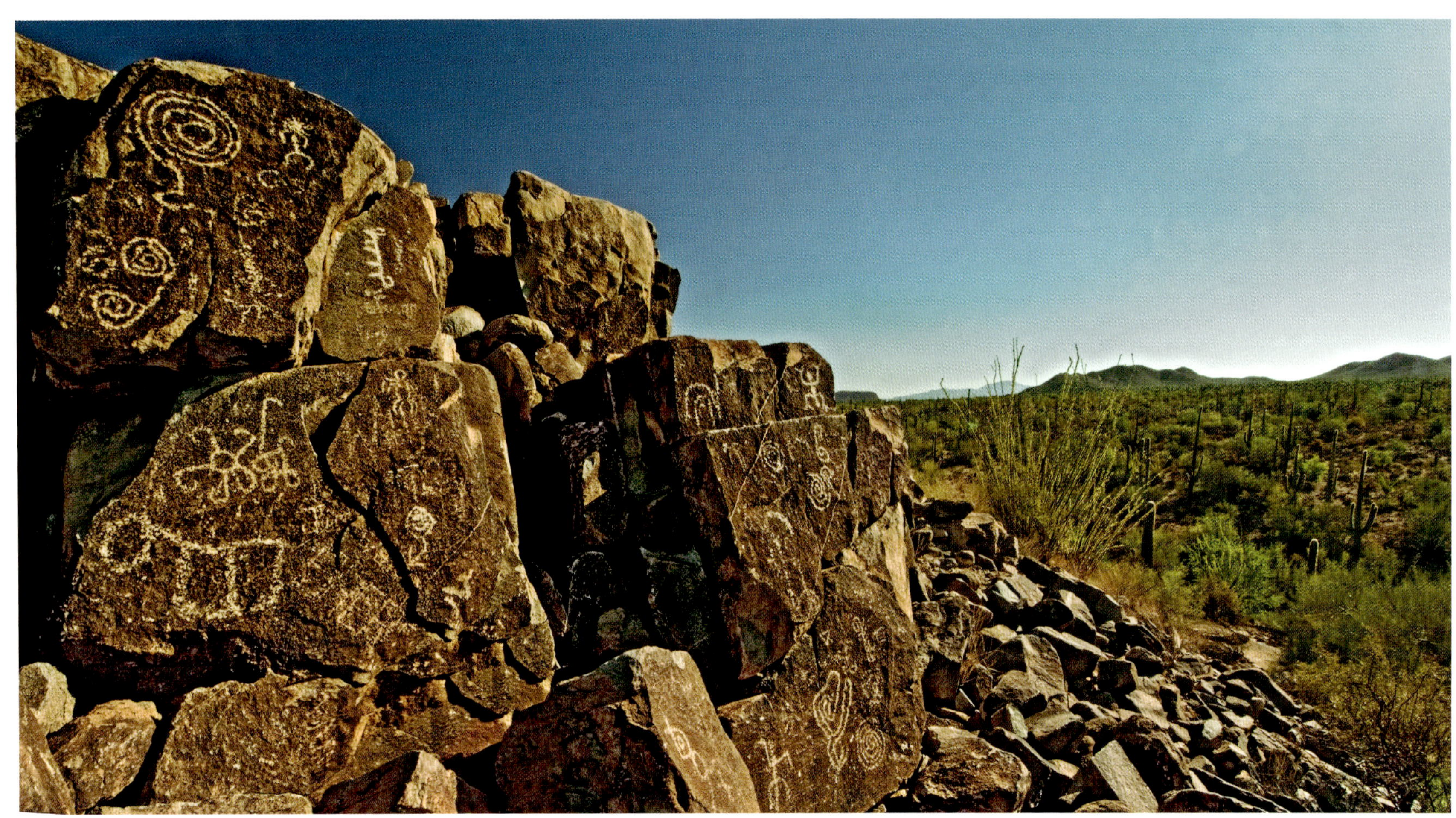

↑→ Signal Hill, Saguaro National Park ↓View from Highway 89 near Bitter Springs

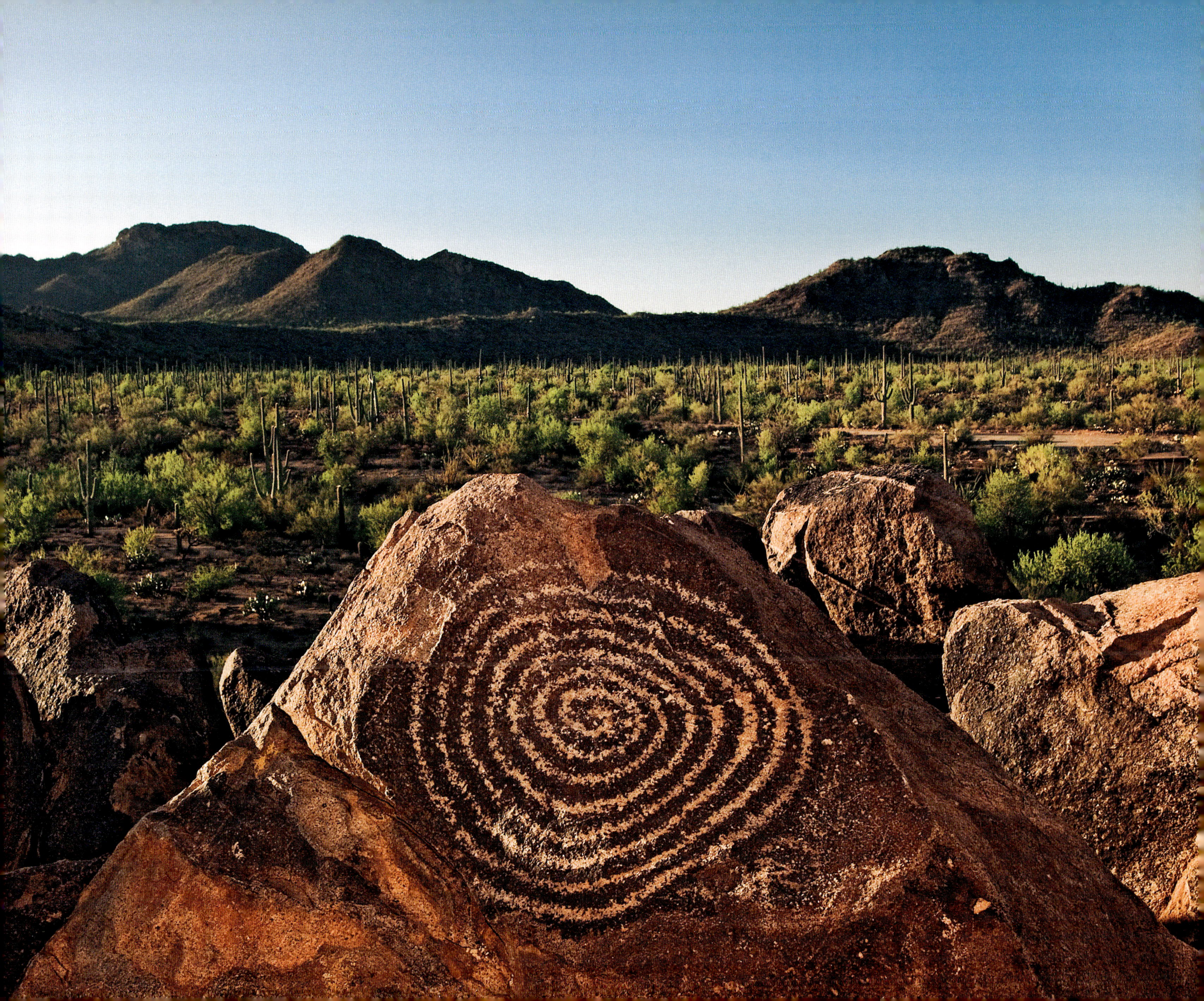

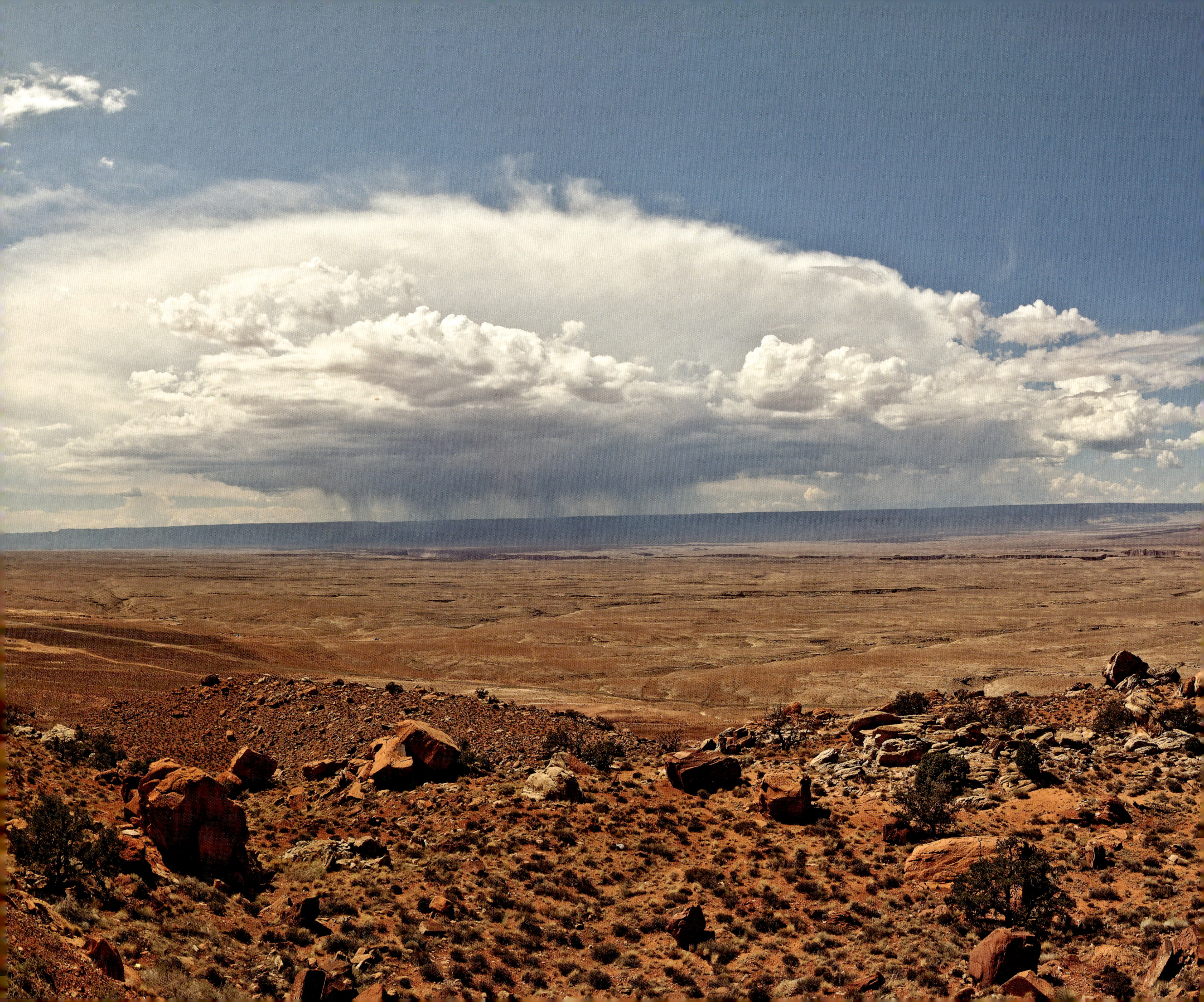

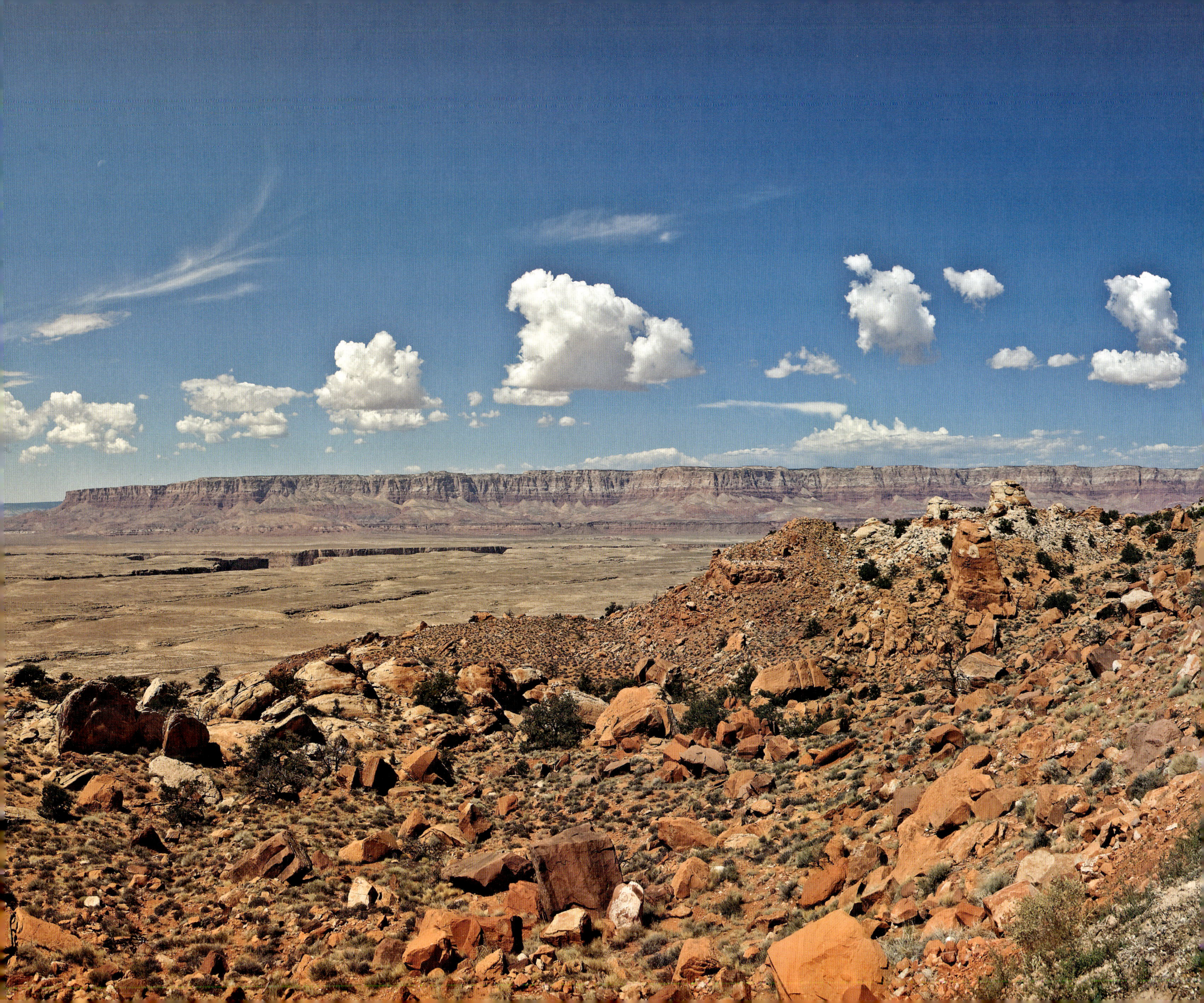

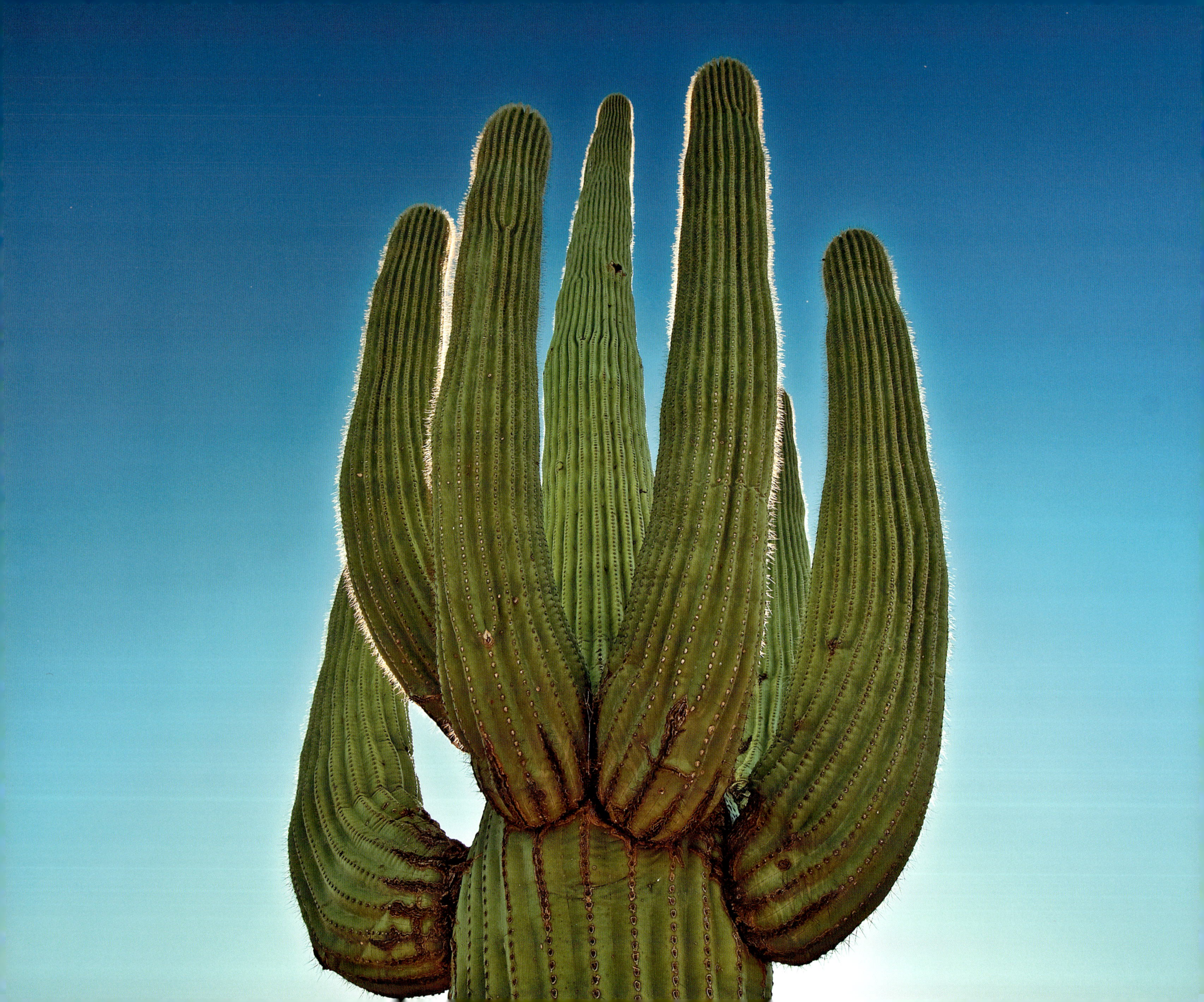

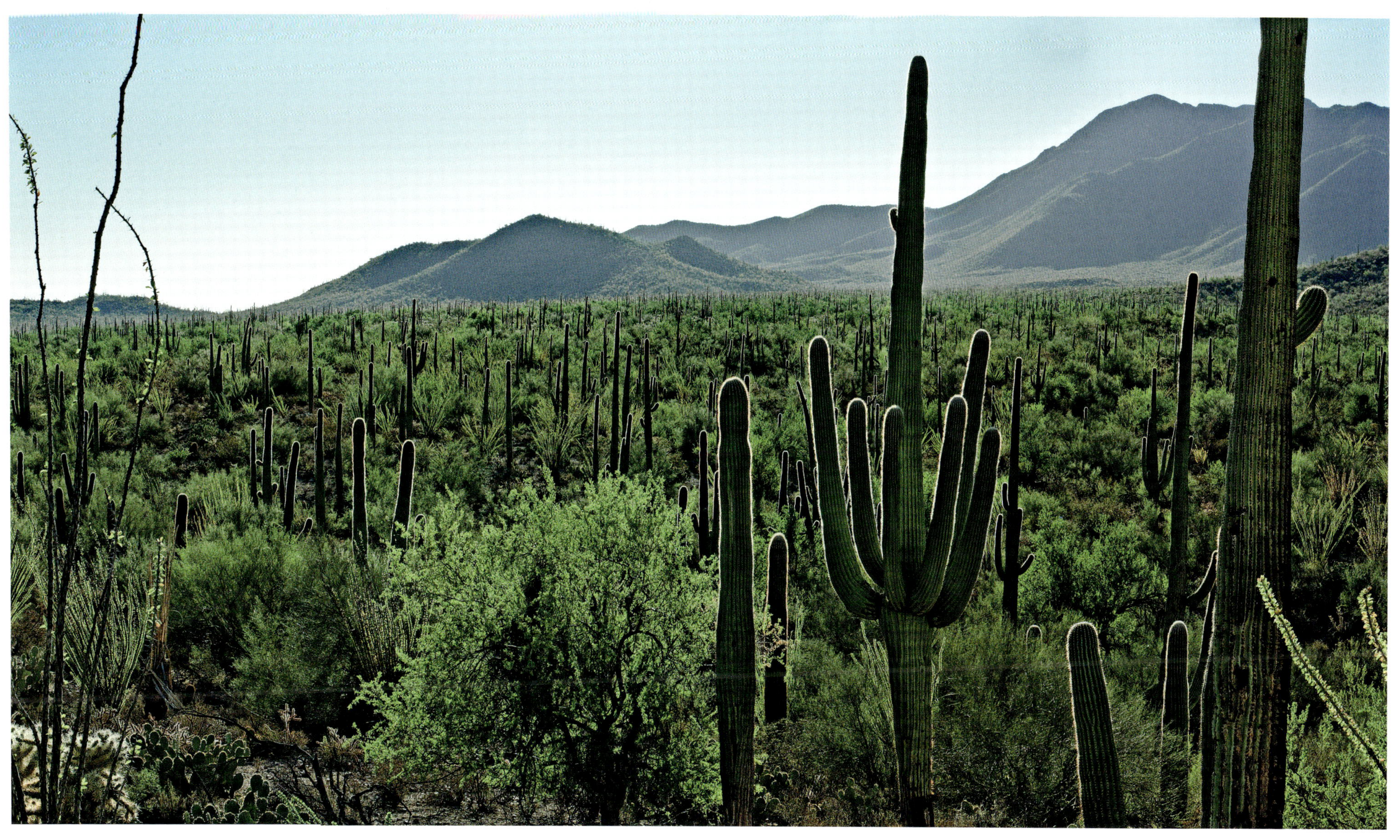

← ↑ ↓ Saguaro National Park

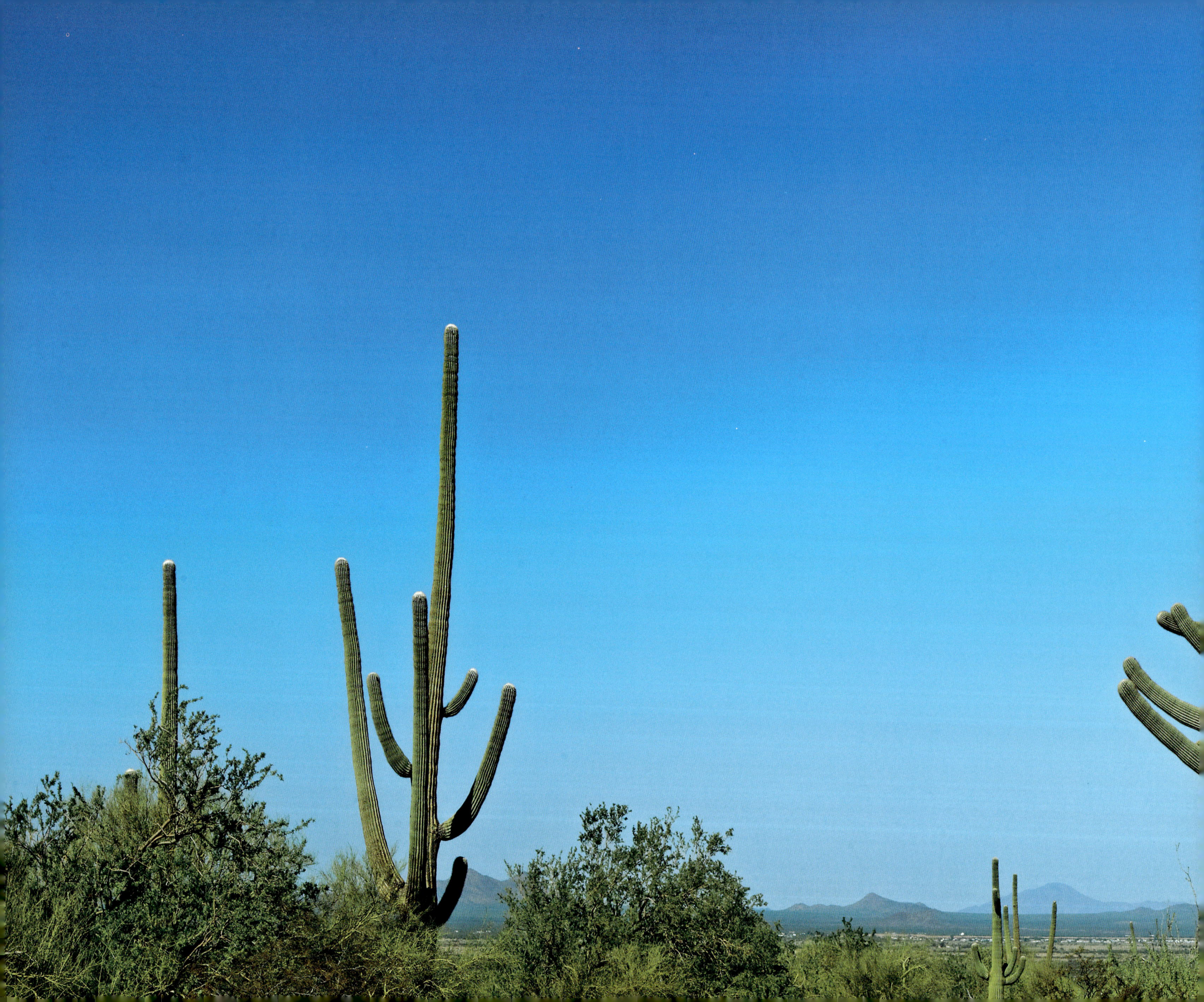

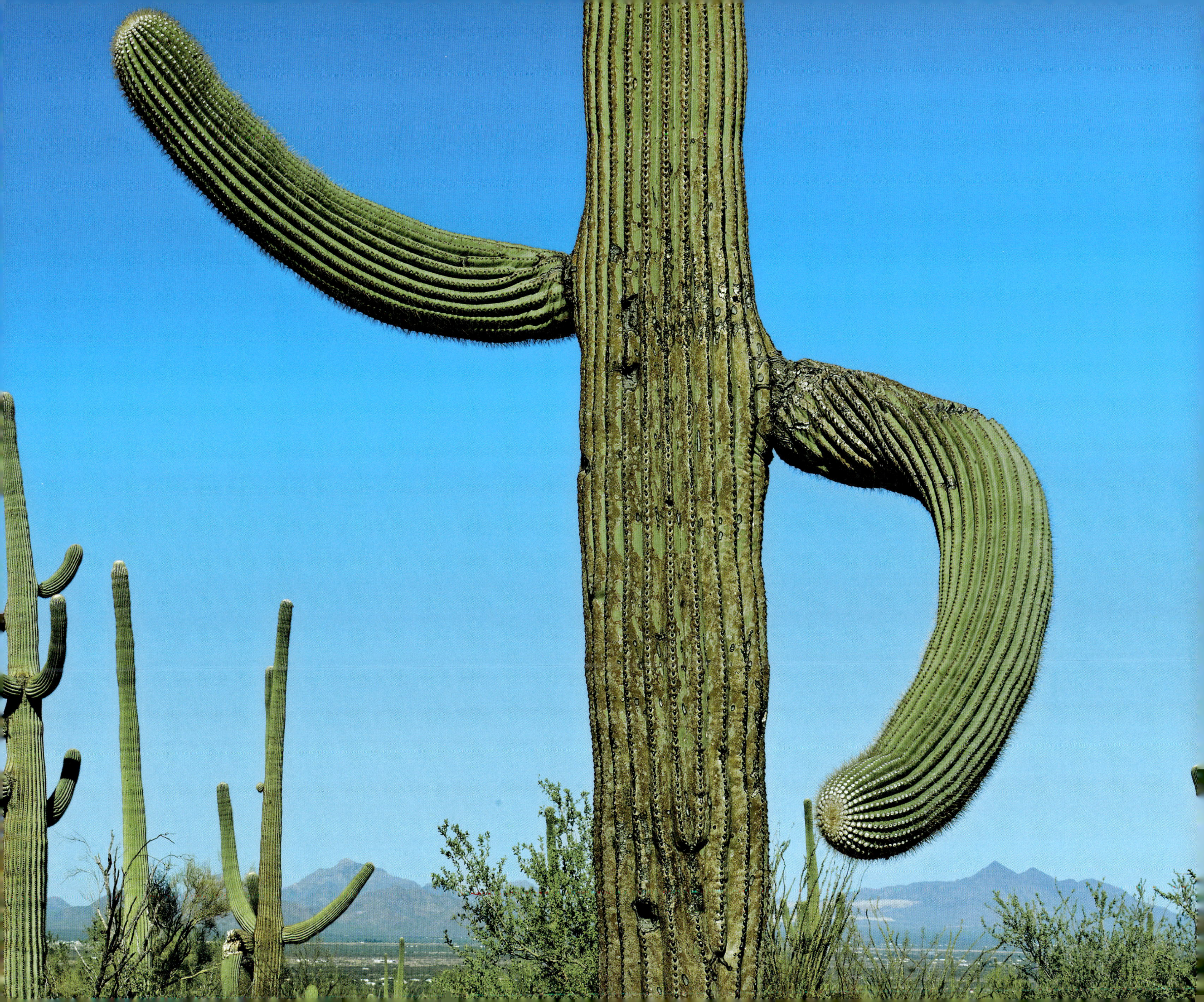

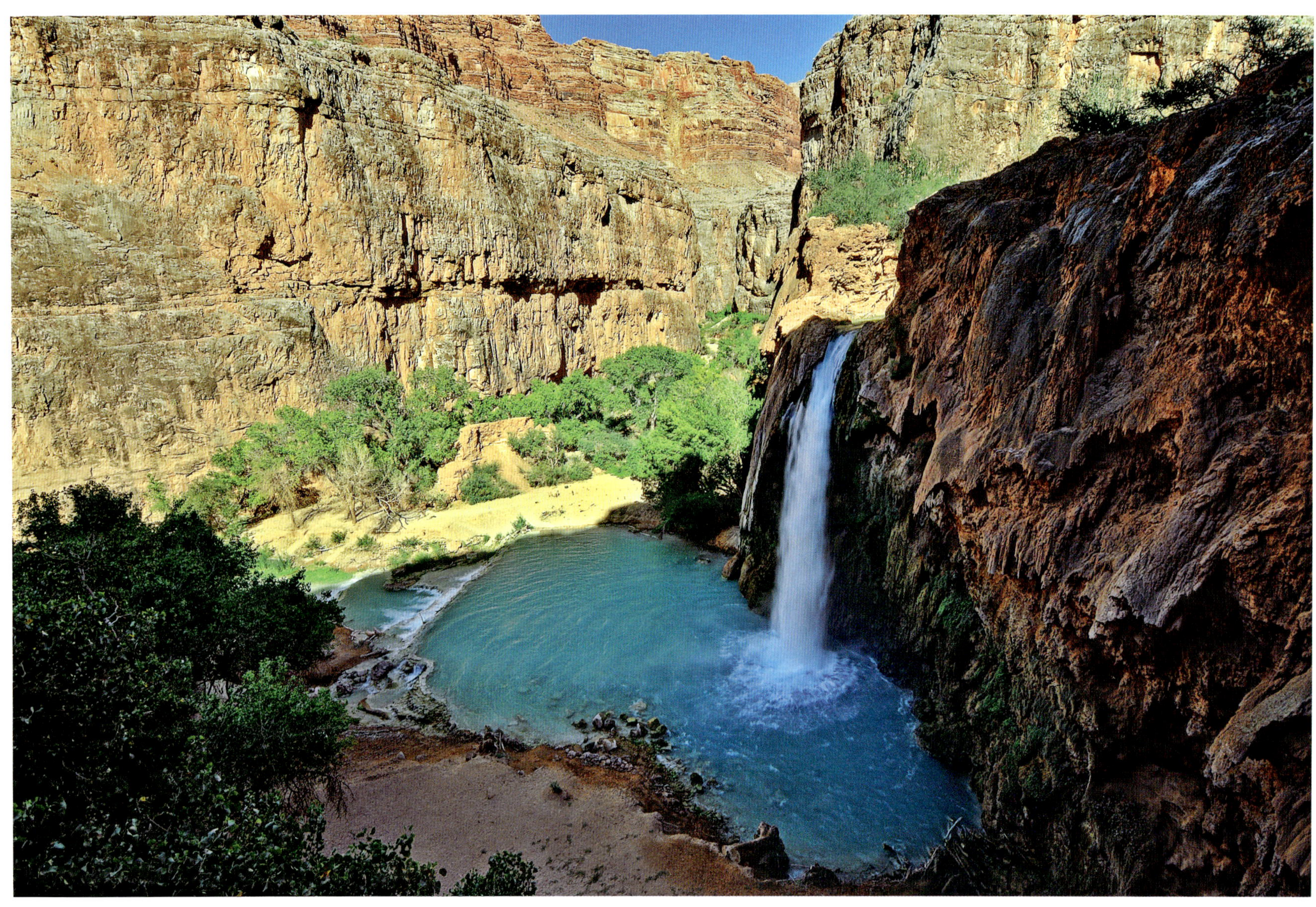

↑ Havasu Falls, Havasupai Indian Reservation, Havasu Canyon, Grand Canyon → Mooney Falls, Havasupai Indian Reservation, Havasu Canyon, Grand Canyon
↓ Waterfall, Havasupai Indian Reservation, Havasu Canyon, Grand Canyon

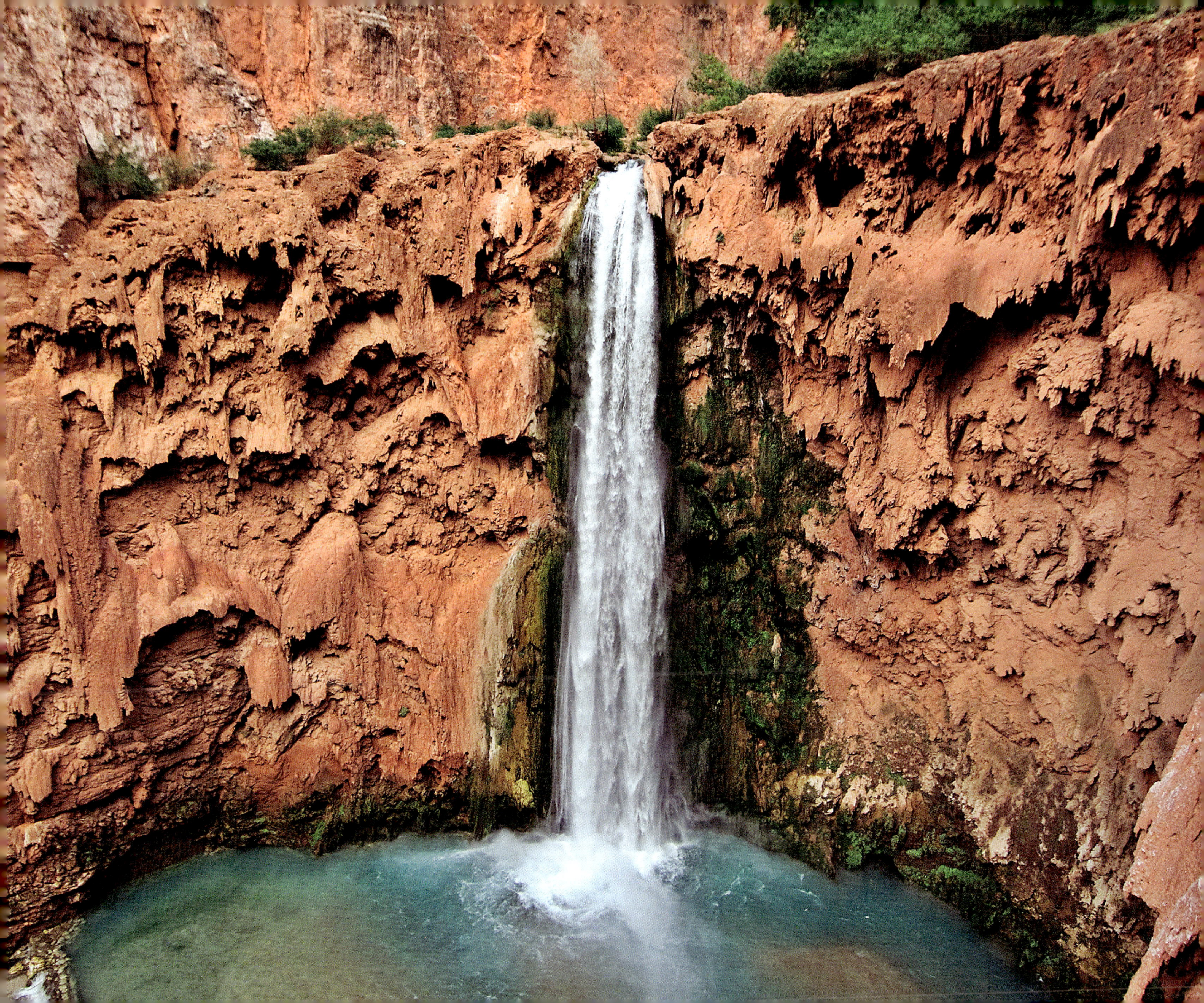

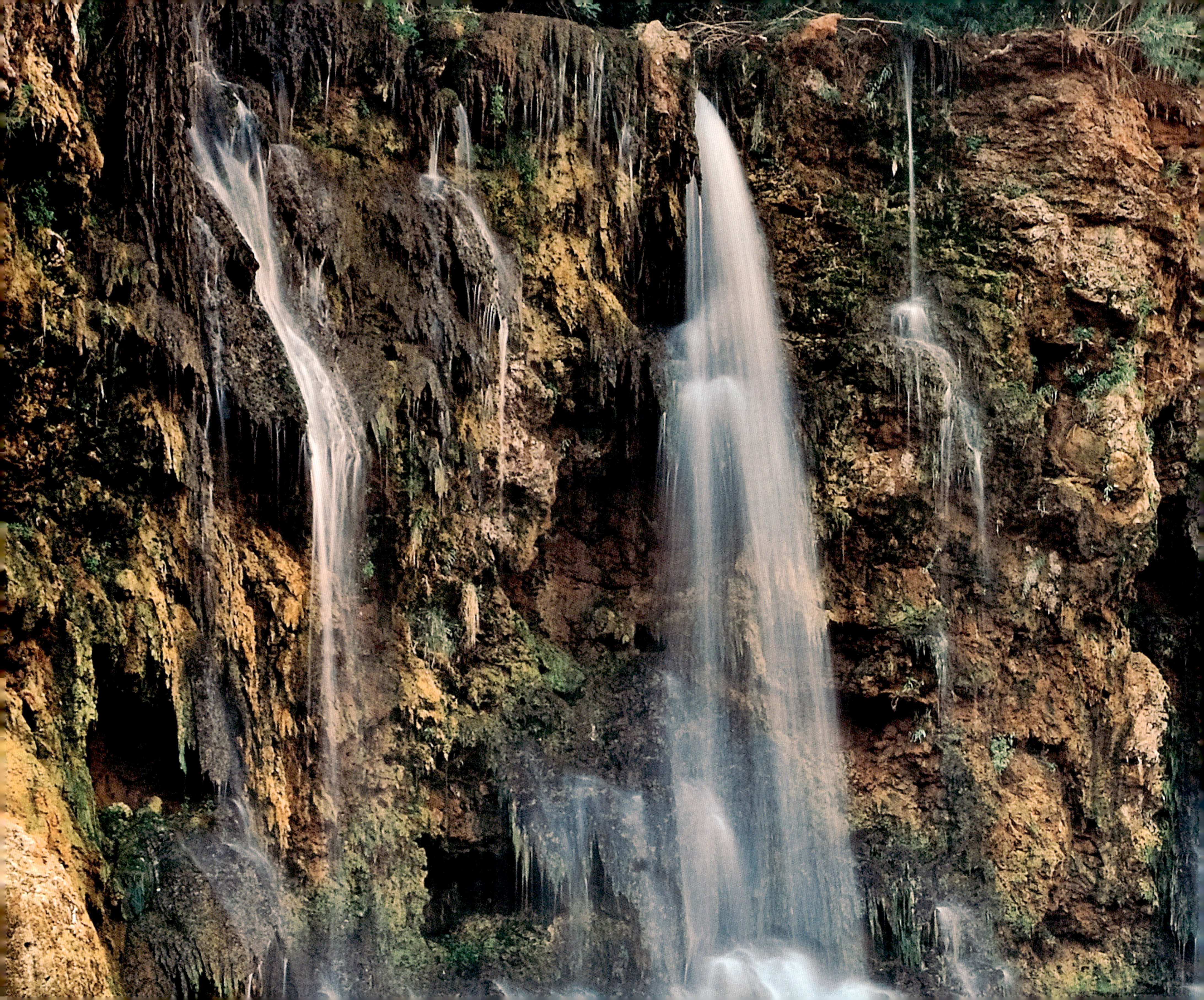

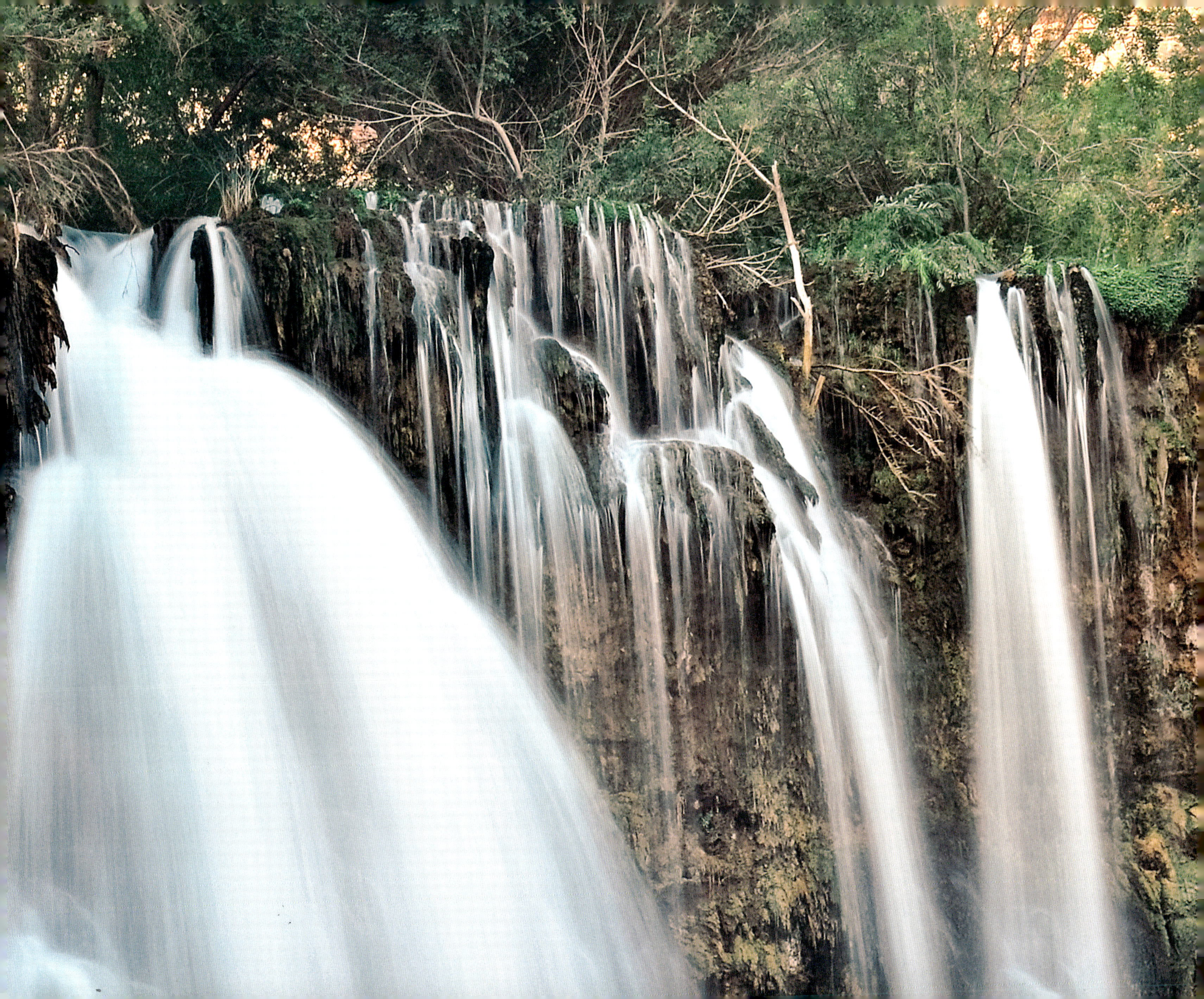

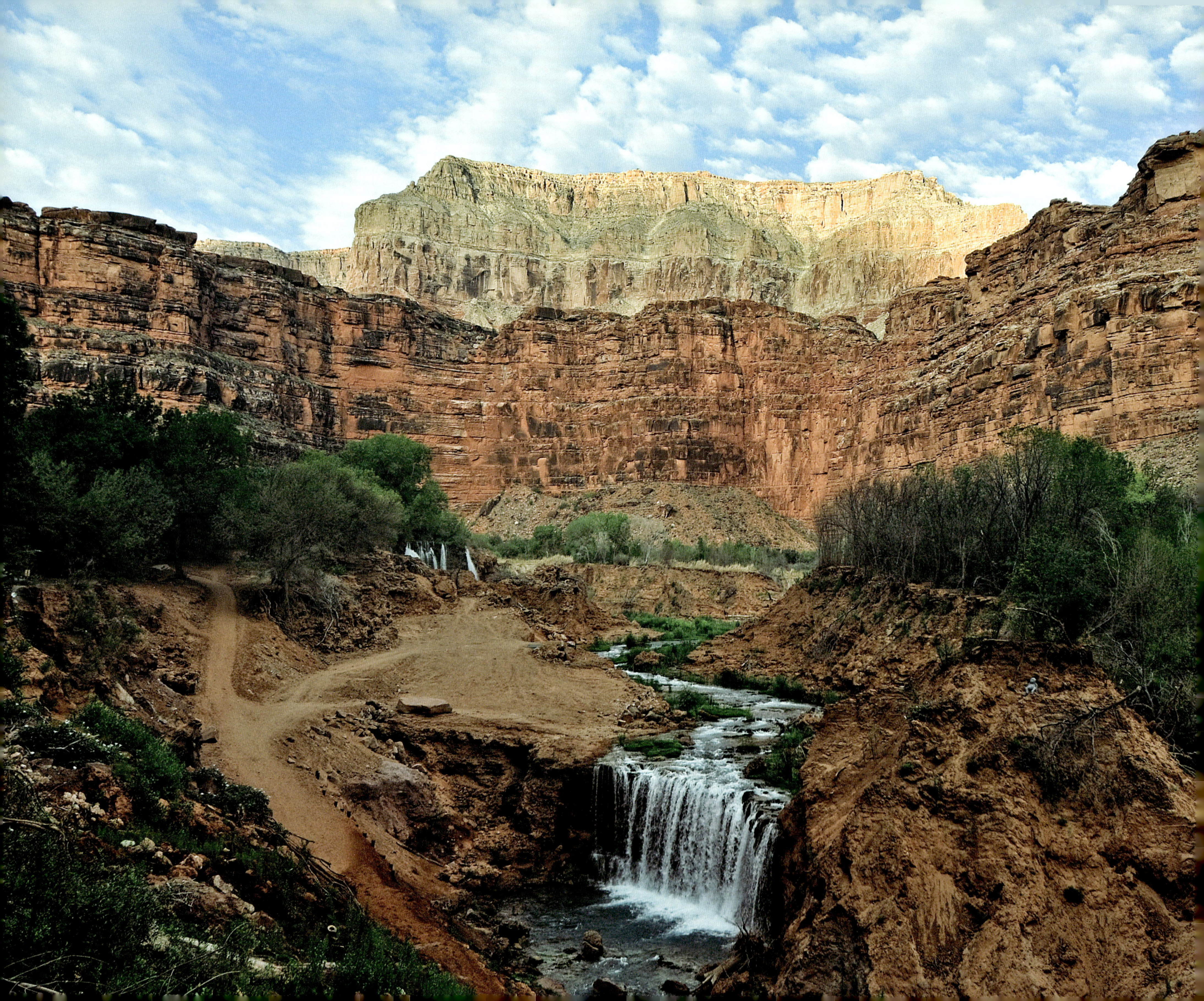

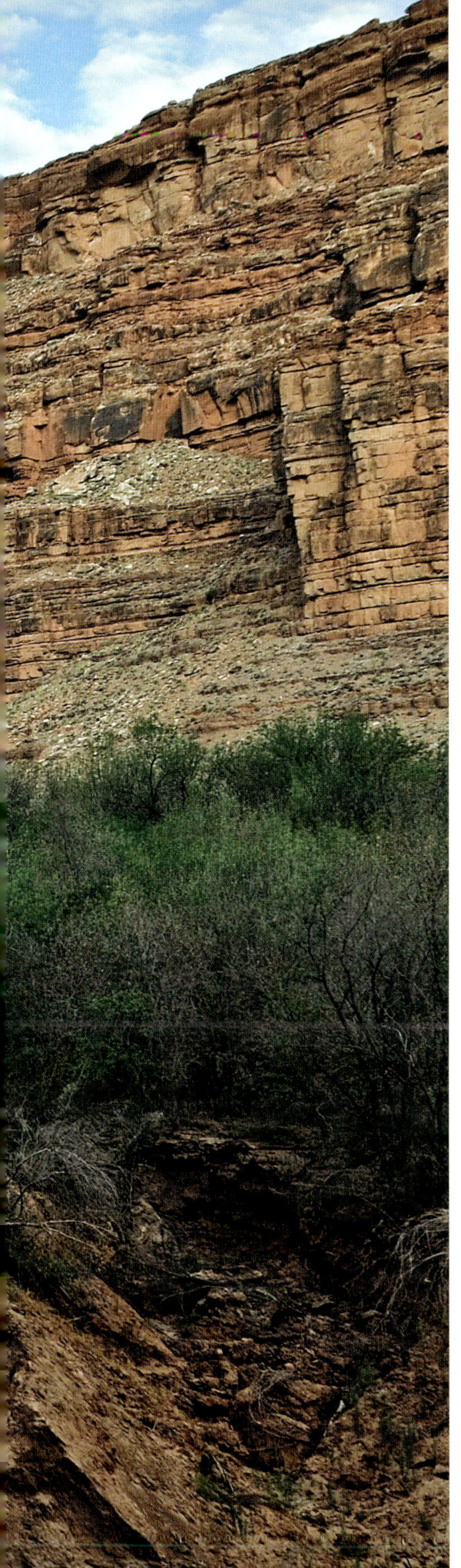

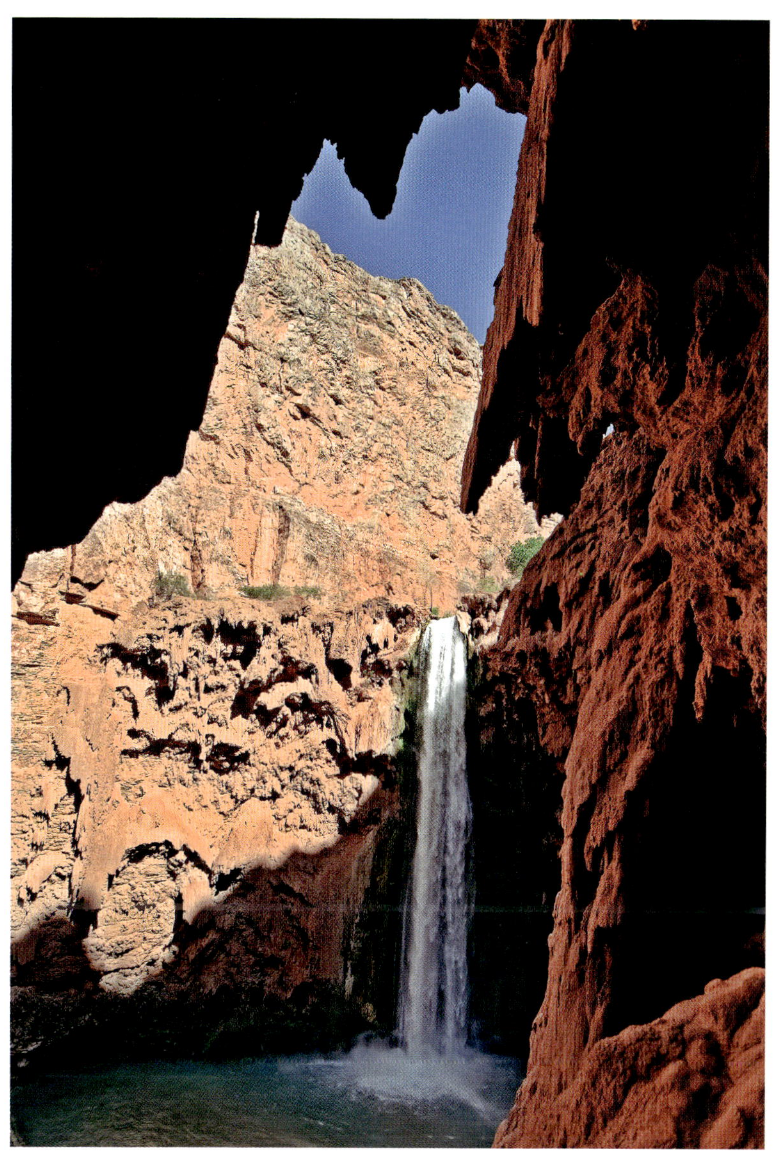

↑ Mooney Falls, Havasupai Indian Reservation, Havasu Canyon, Grand Canyon
← Waterfall, Havasu Creek, Havasupai Indian Reservation, Havasu Canyon, Grand Canyon ↓View from Scenic Highway 17 south of Munds Park, toward Sedona
↓Sinagua ruins, Walnut Canyon National Monument

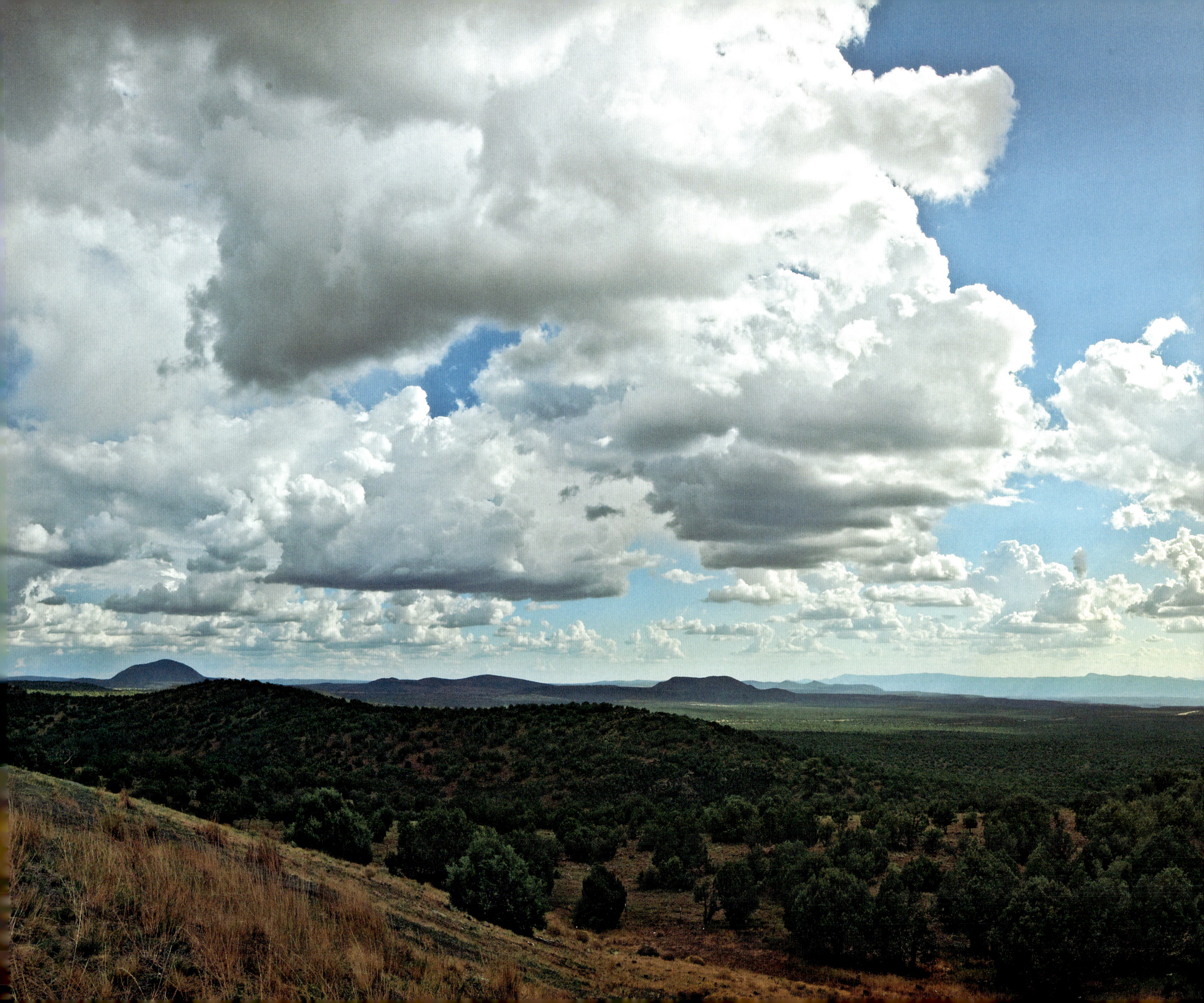

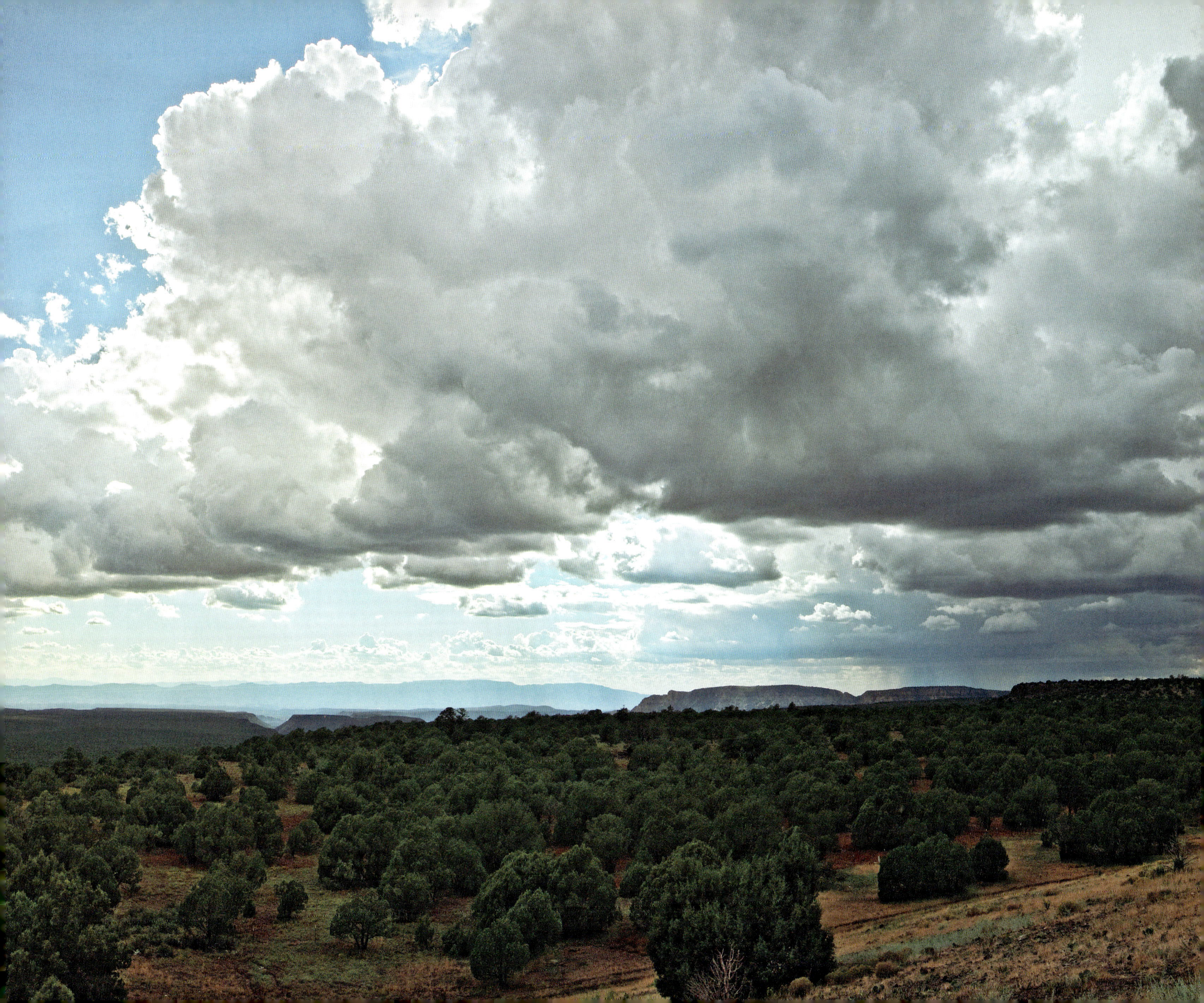

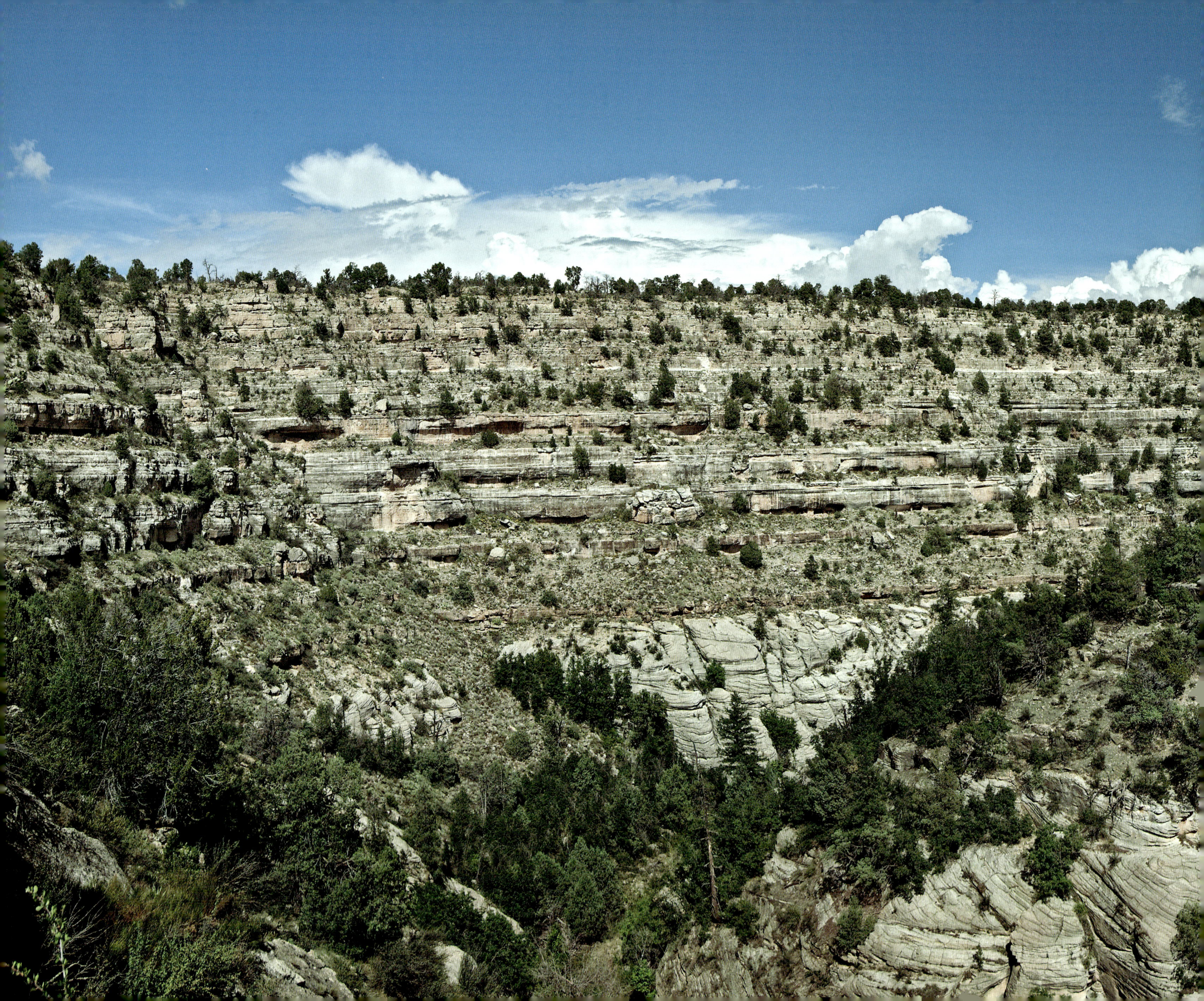

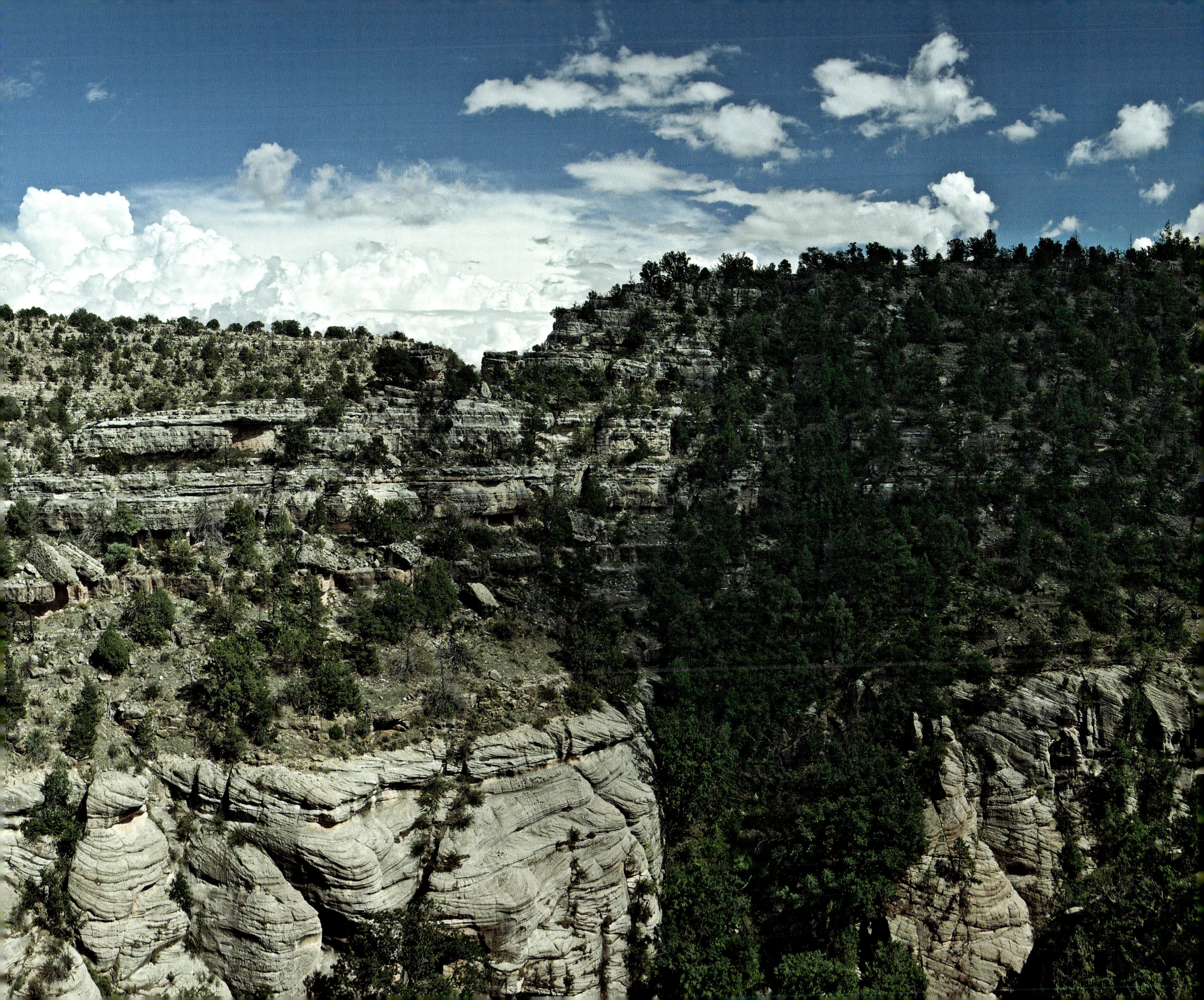

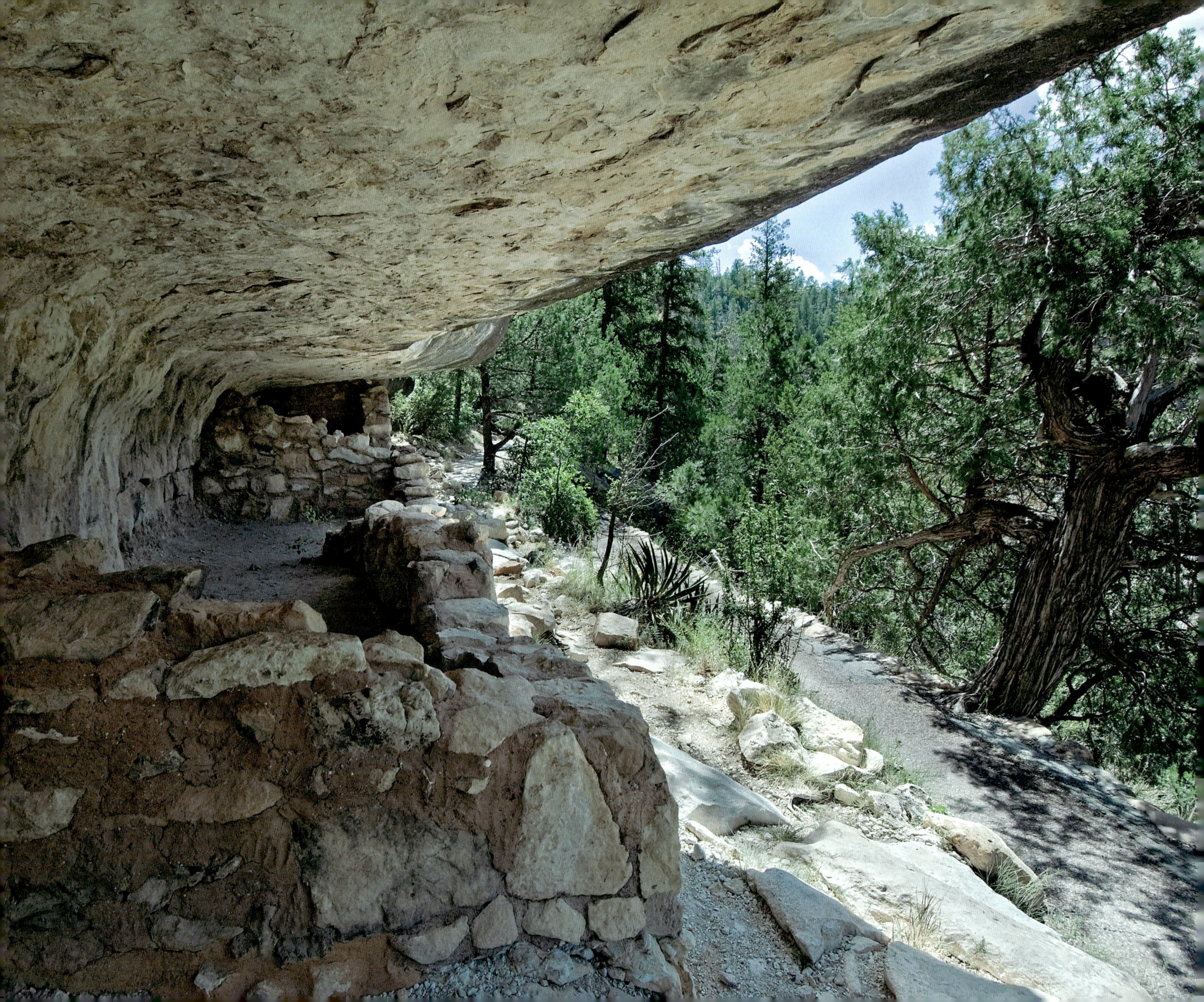

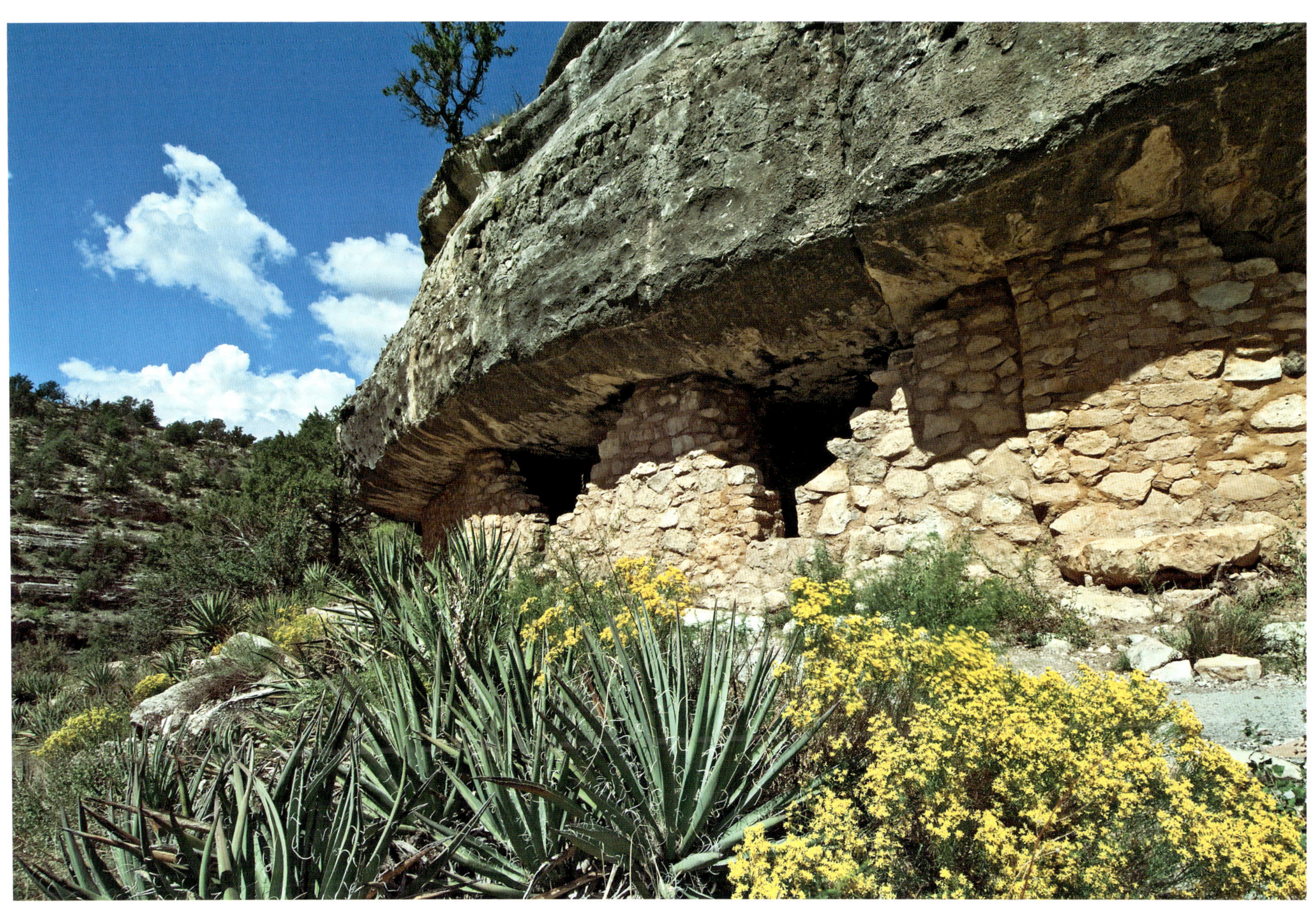

← ↑ ↓ Sinagua ruins, Walnut Canyon National Monument ↓ Red Rocks, Sedona

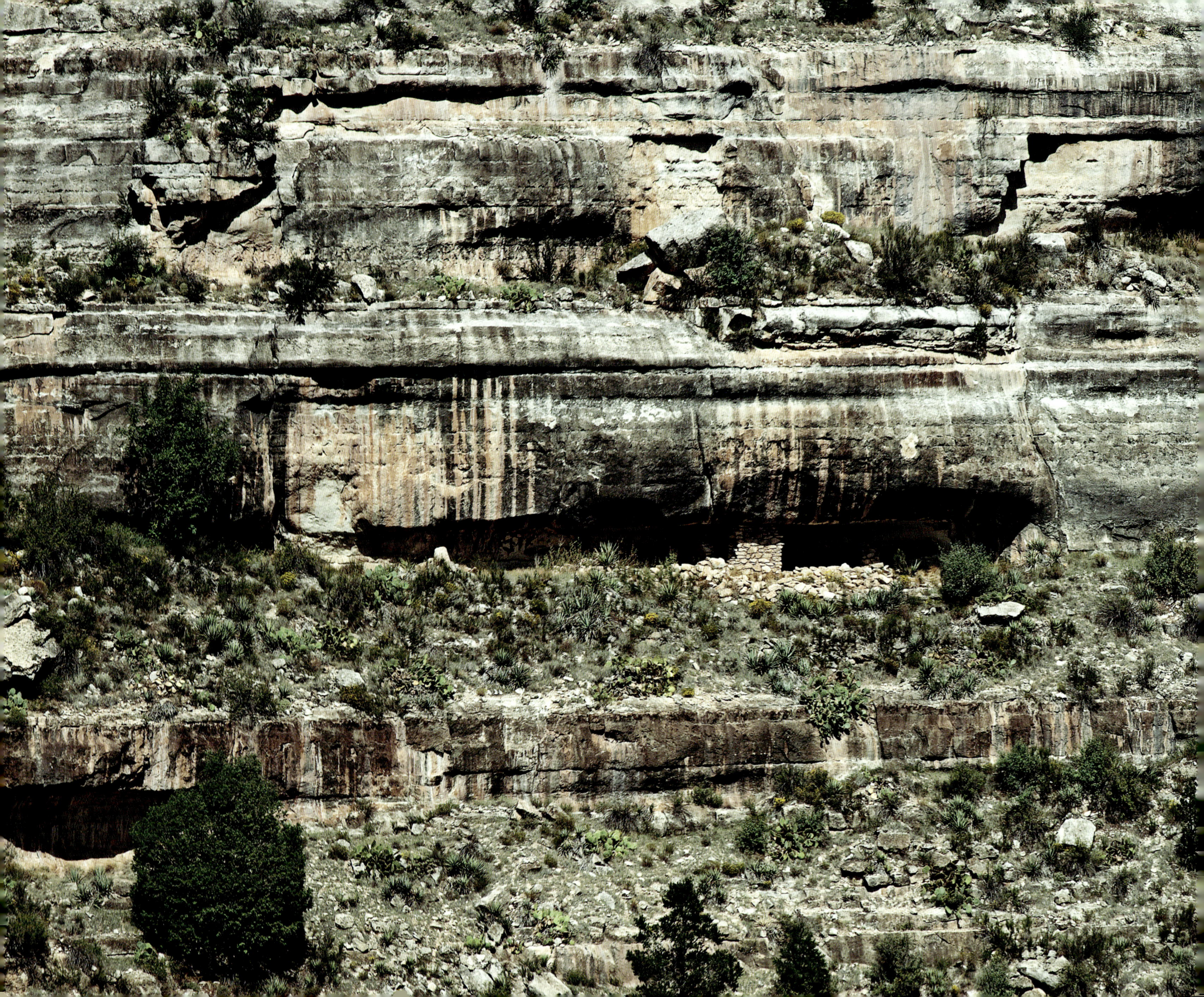

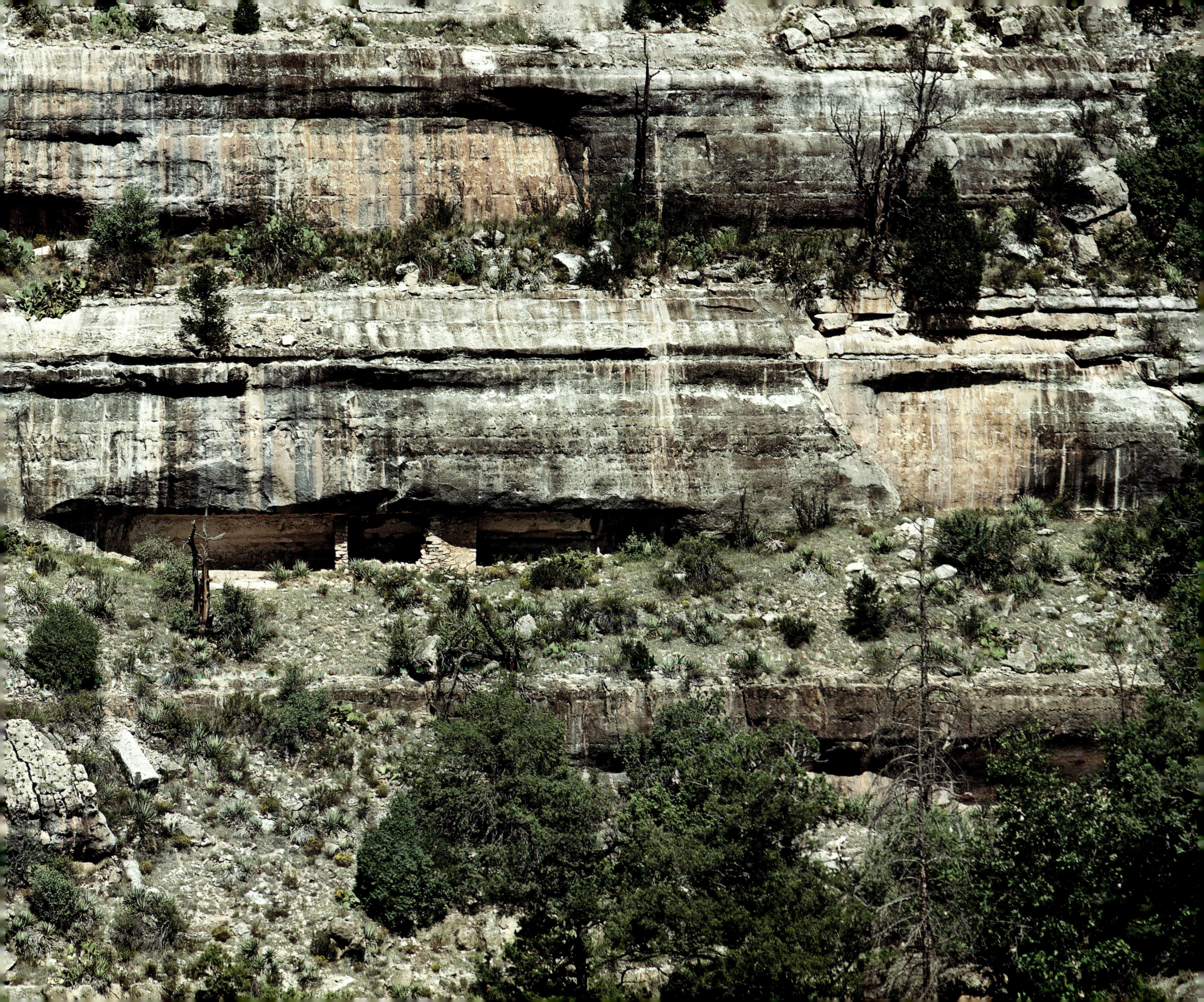

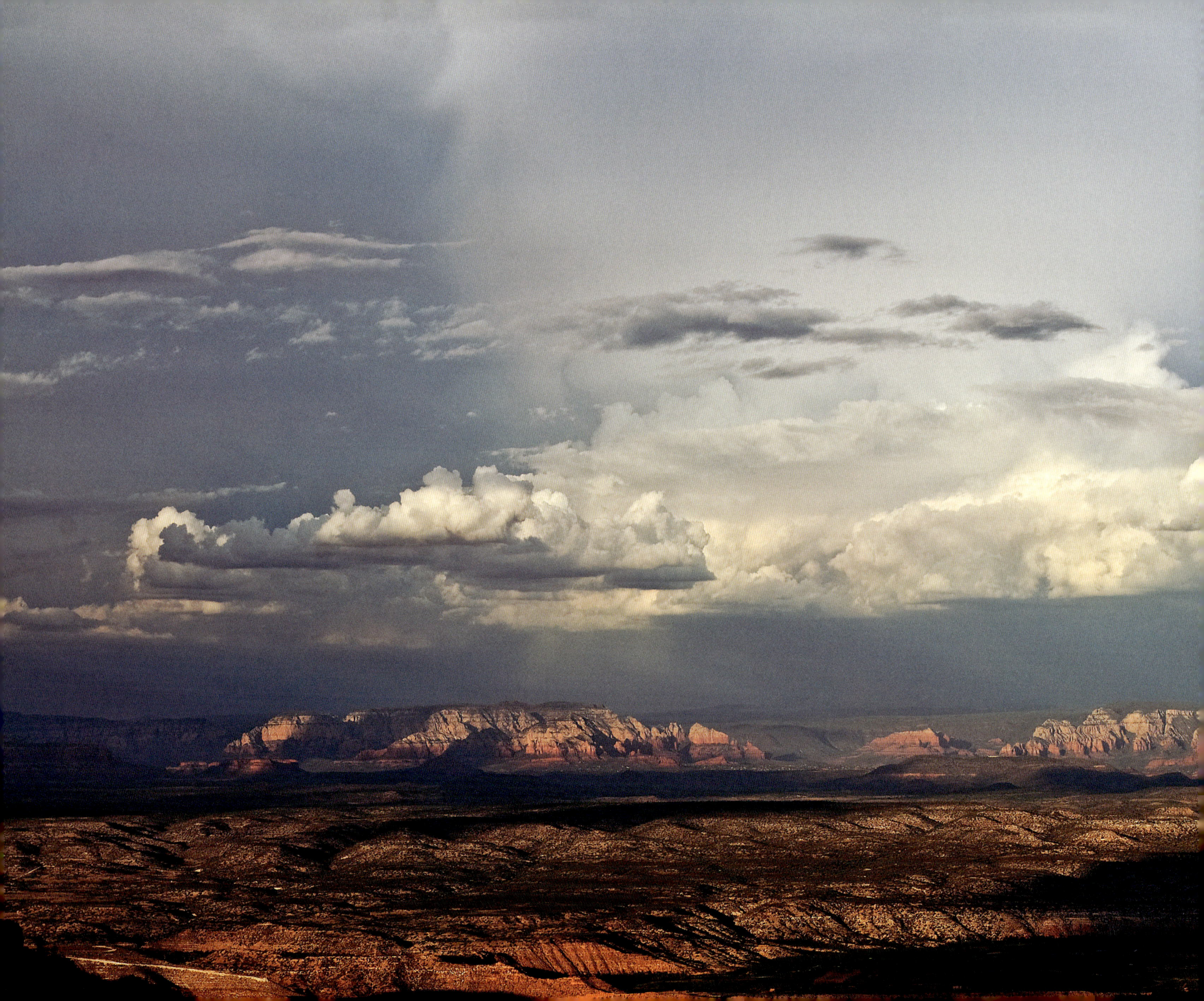

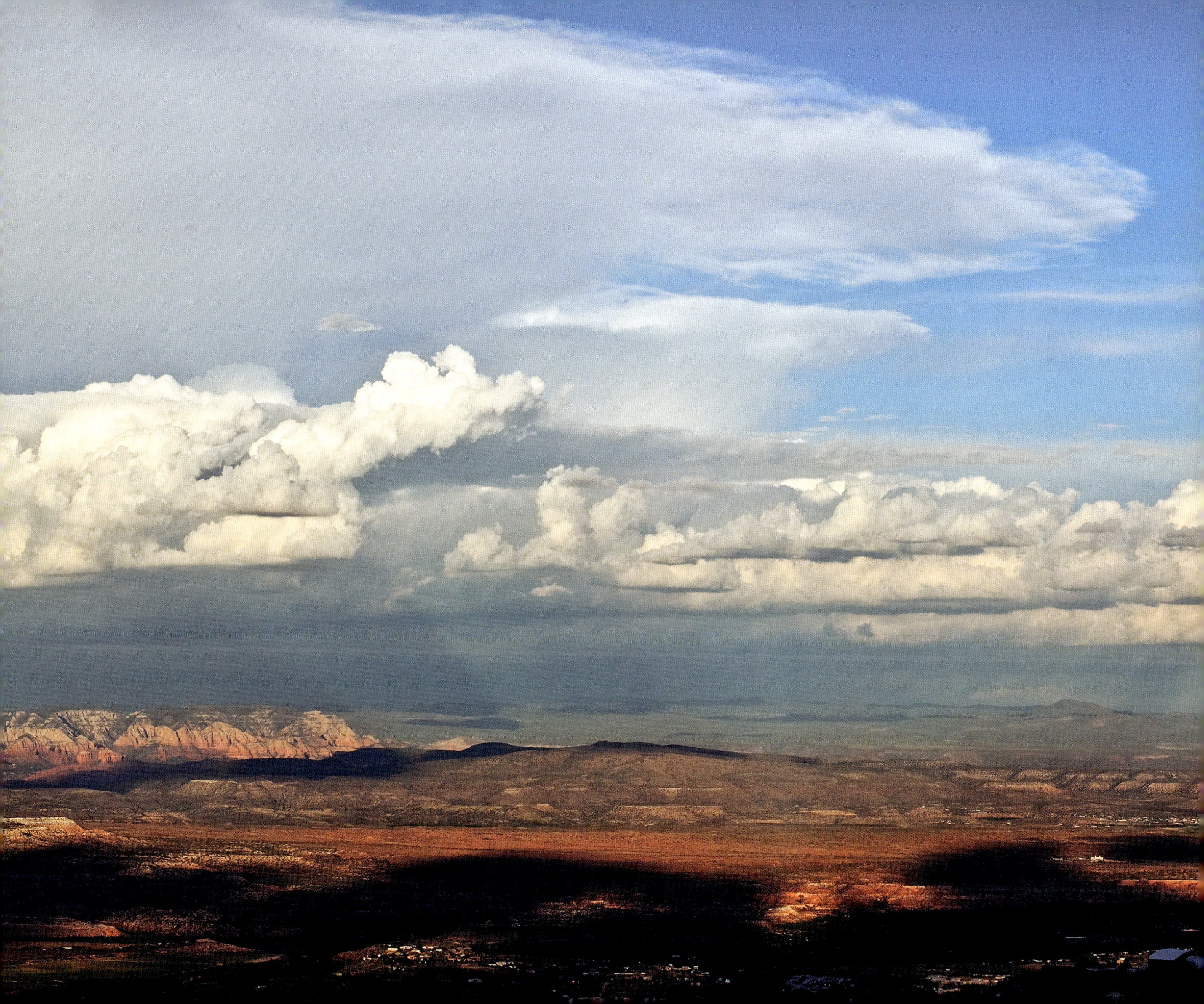

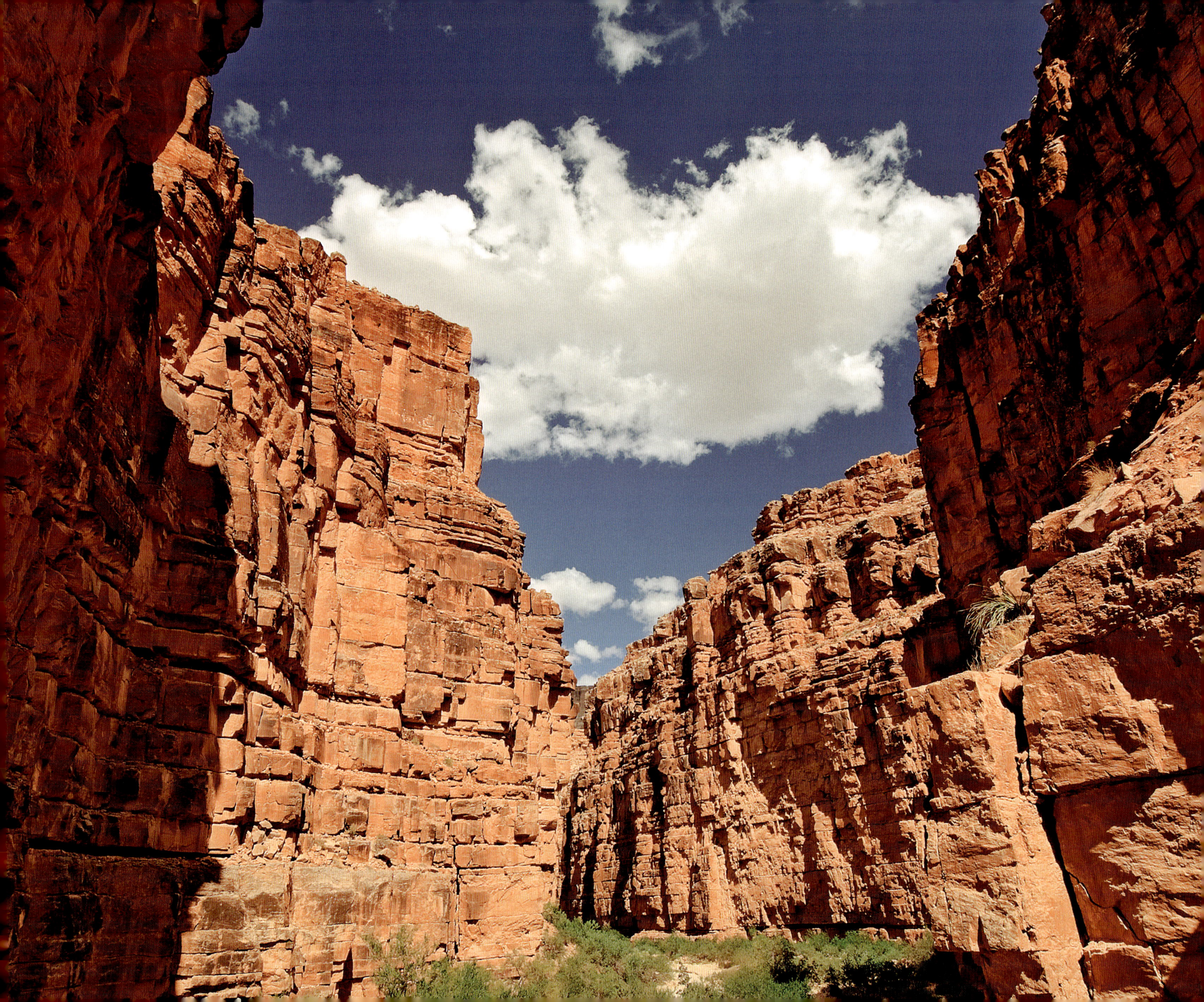

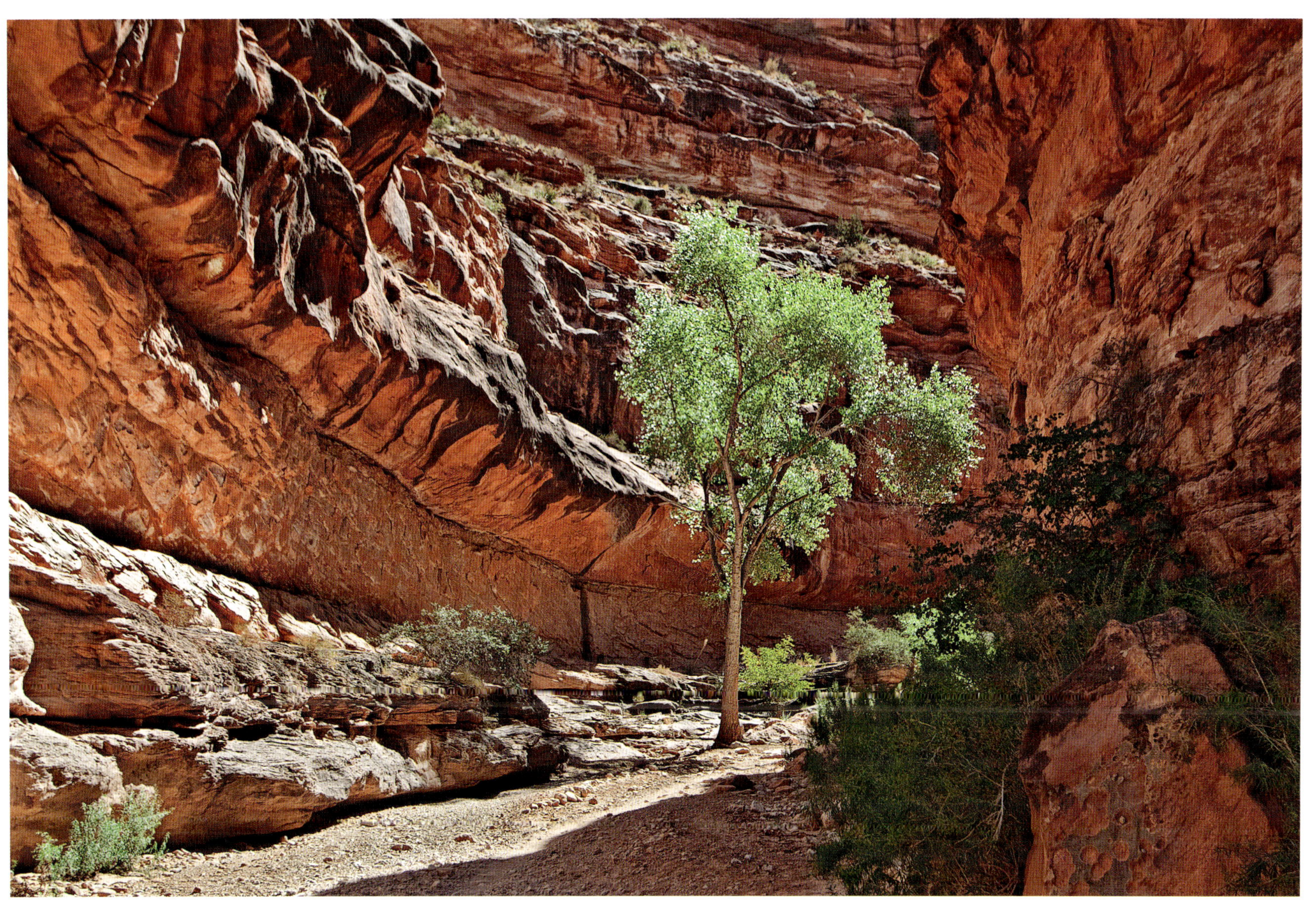

↑←↓ Hualapai Canyon, Havasupai Indian Reservation, Grand Canyon

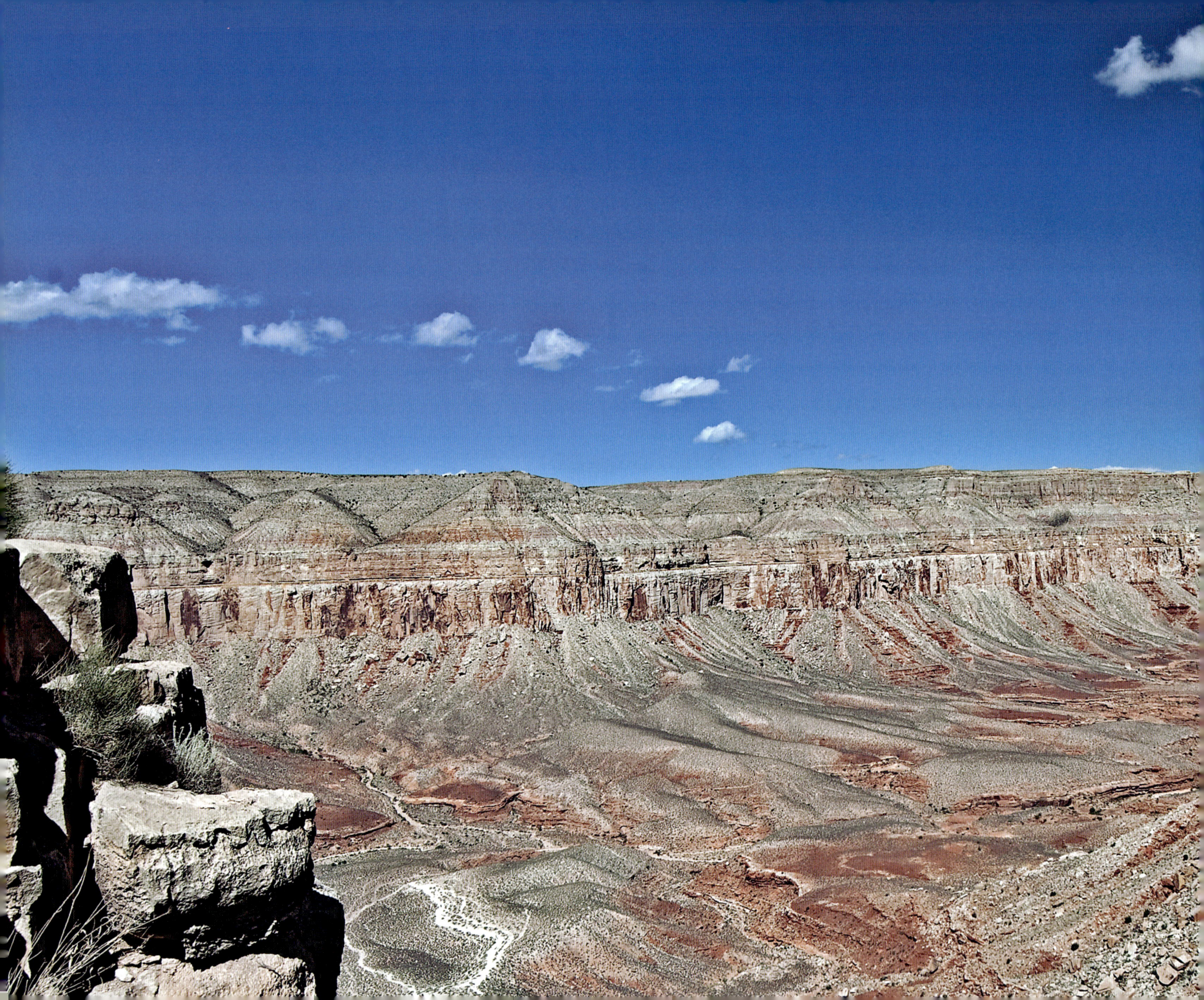

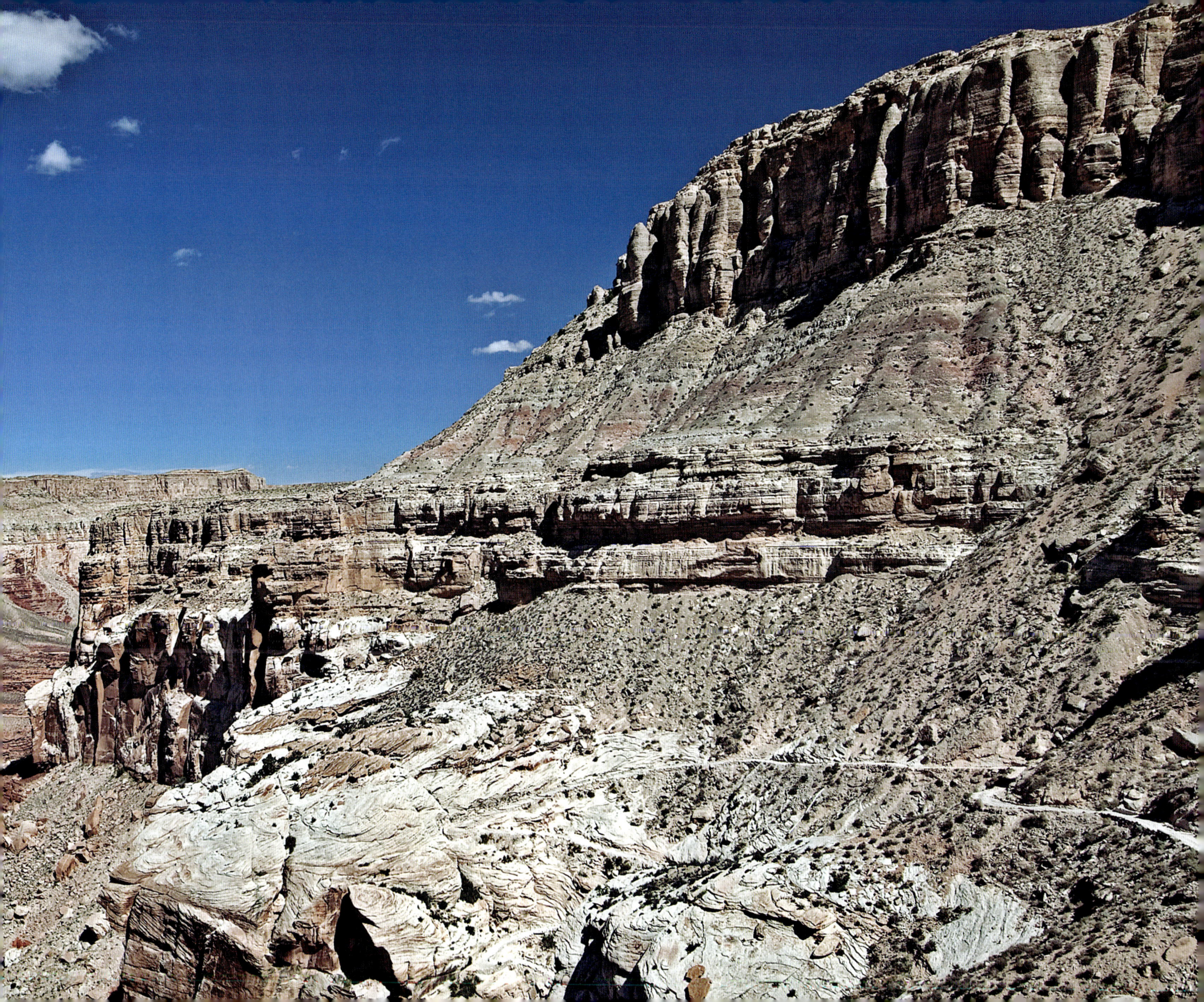

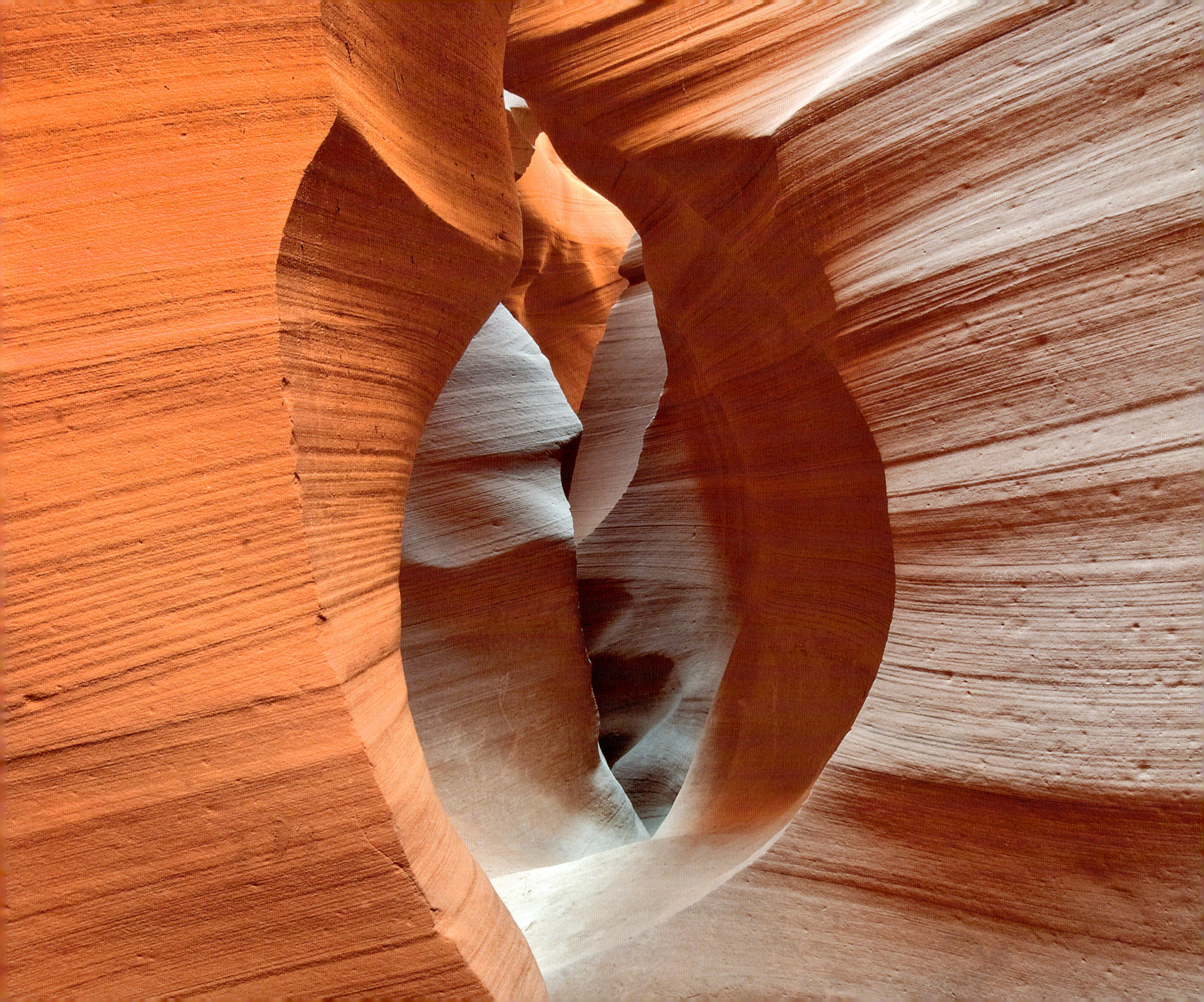

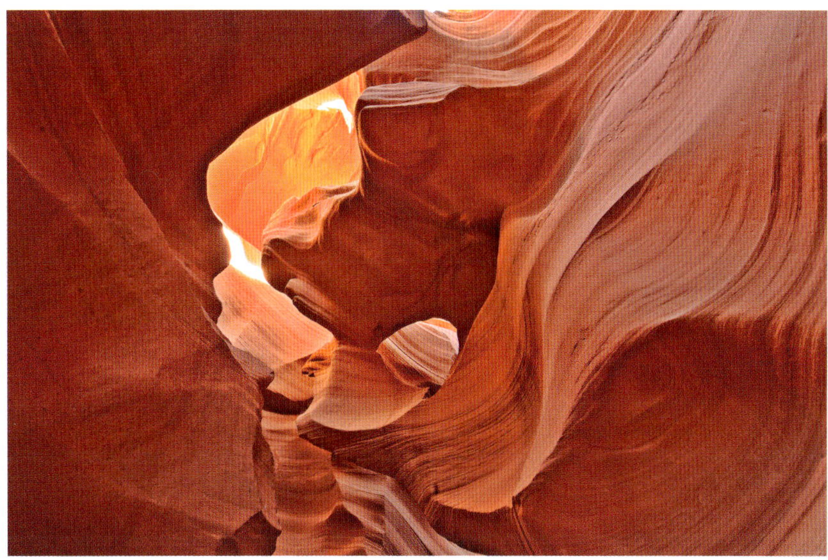

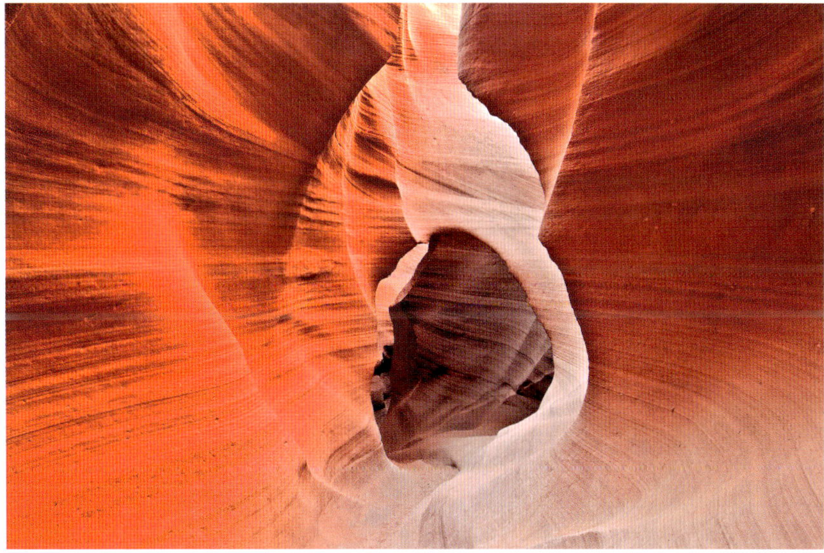

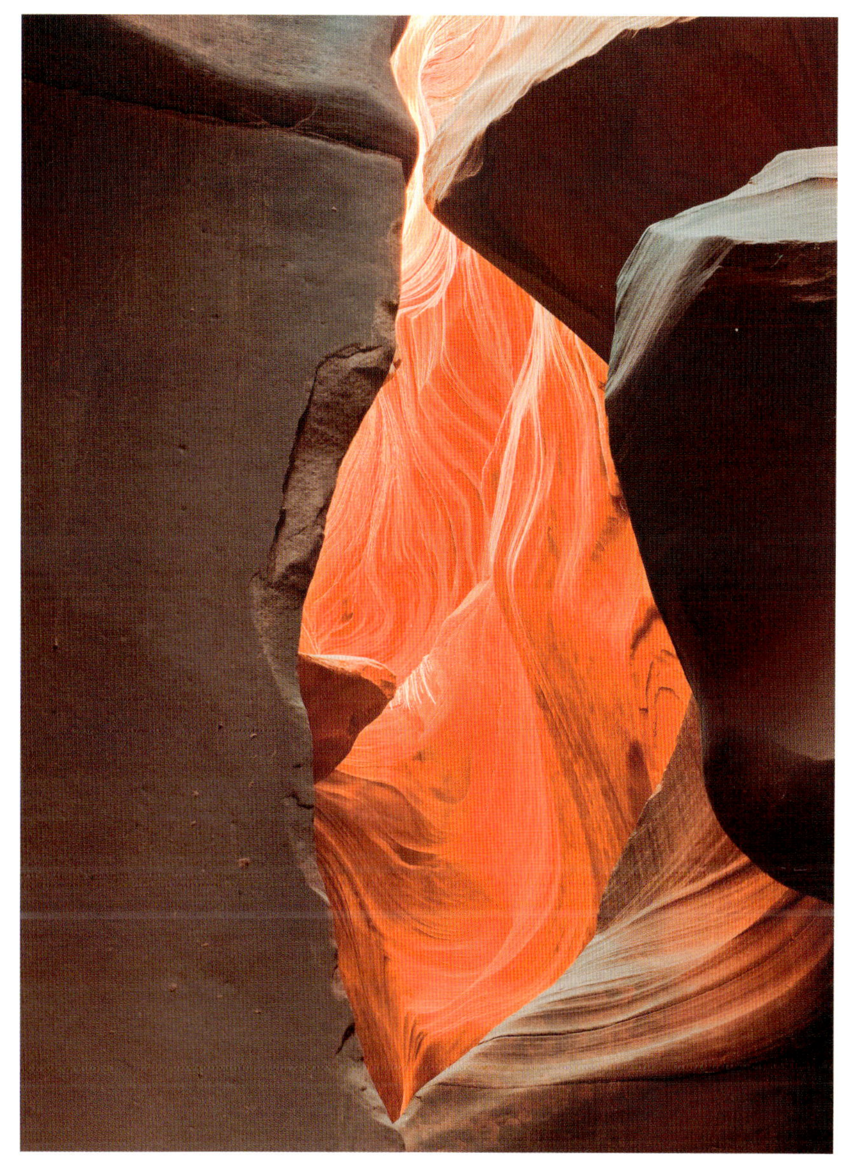

↑←Antelope Canyon, Navajo Tribal Park

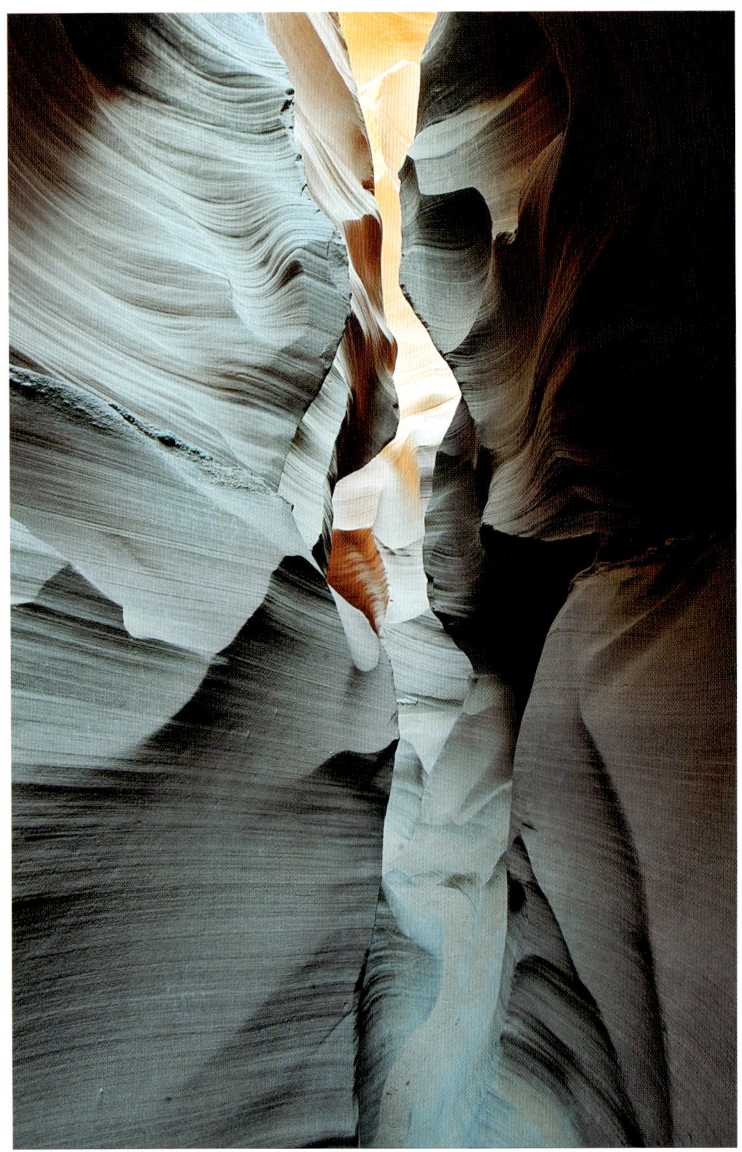

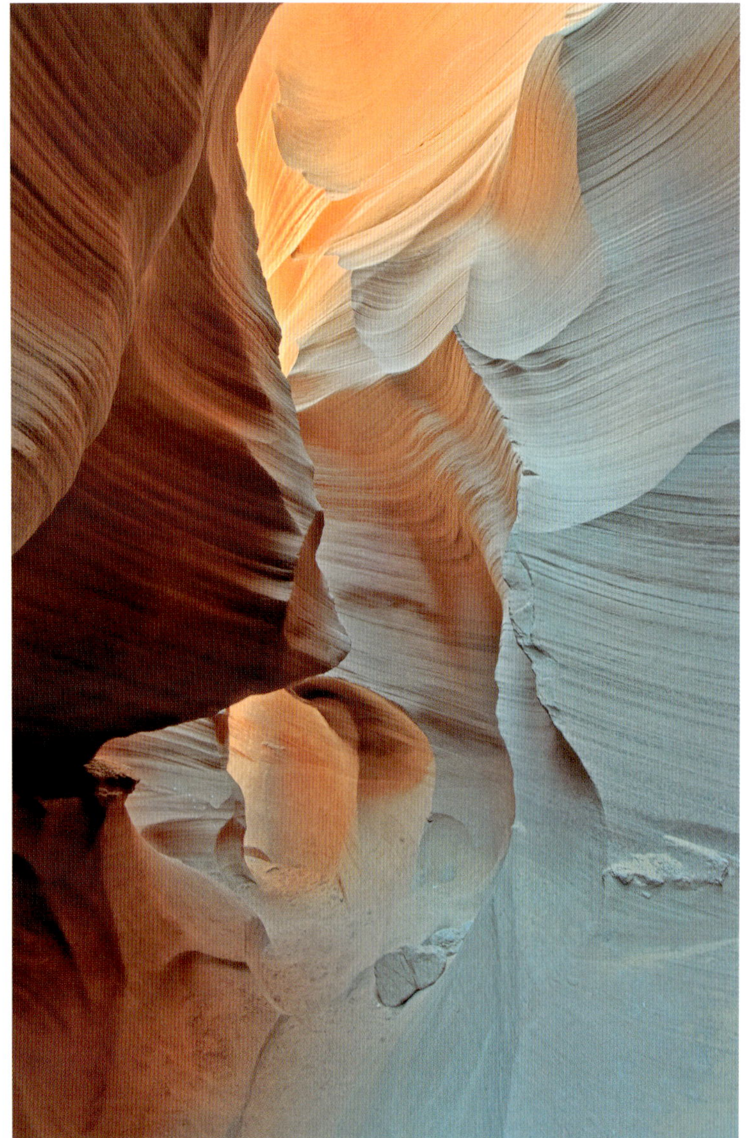

↑→ Antelope Canyon, Navajo Tribal Park ↓Grand Canyon National Park, North Rim, View from Point Imperial

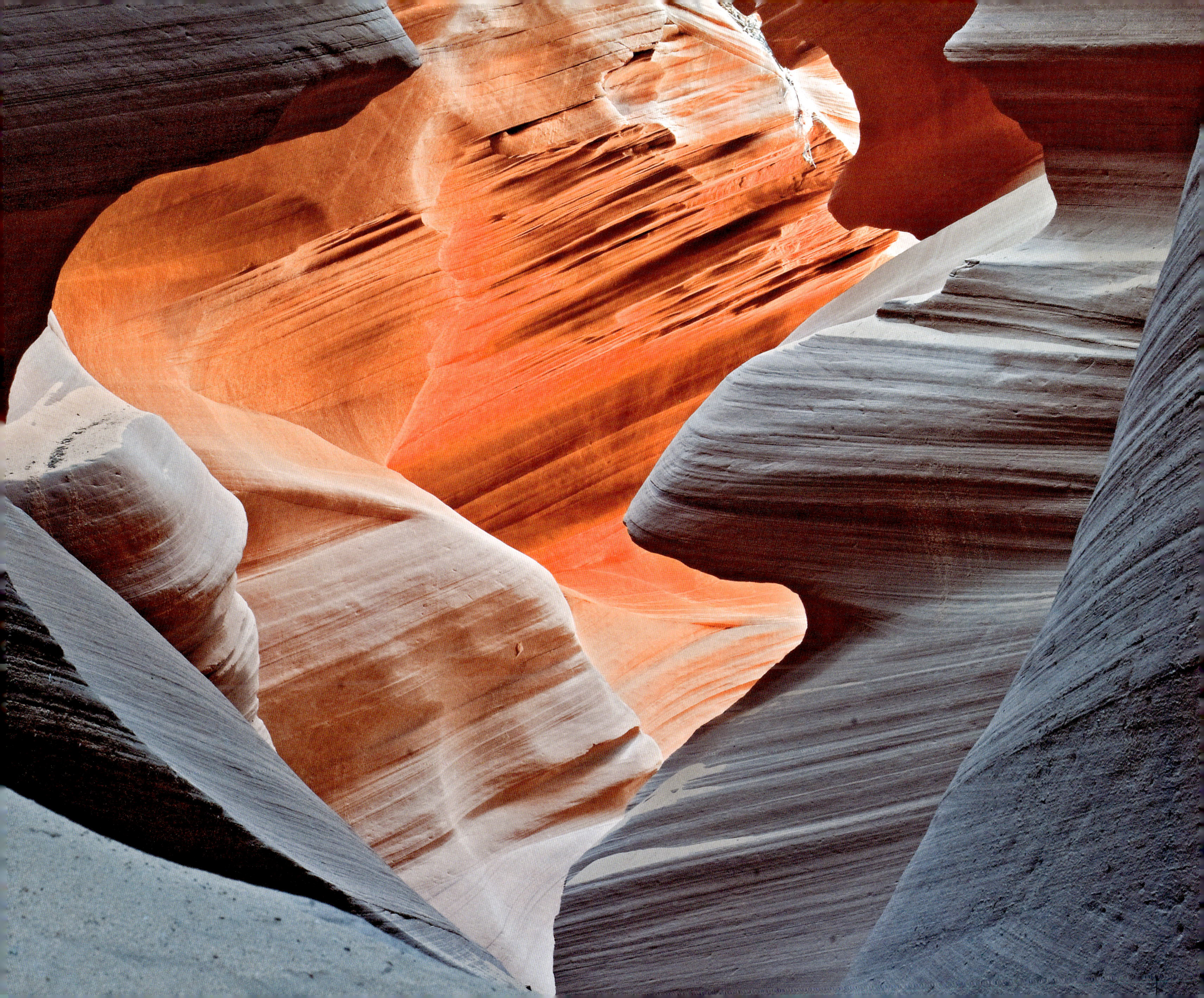

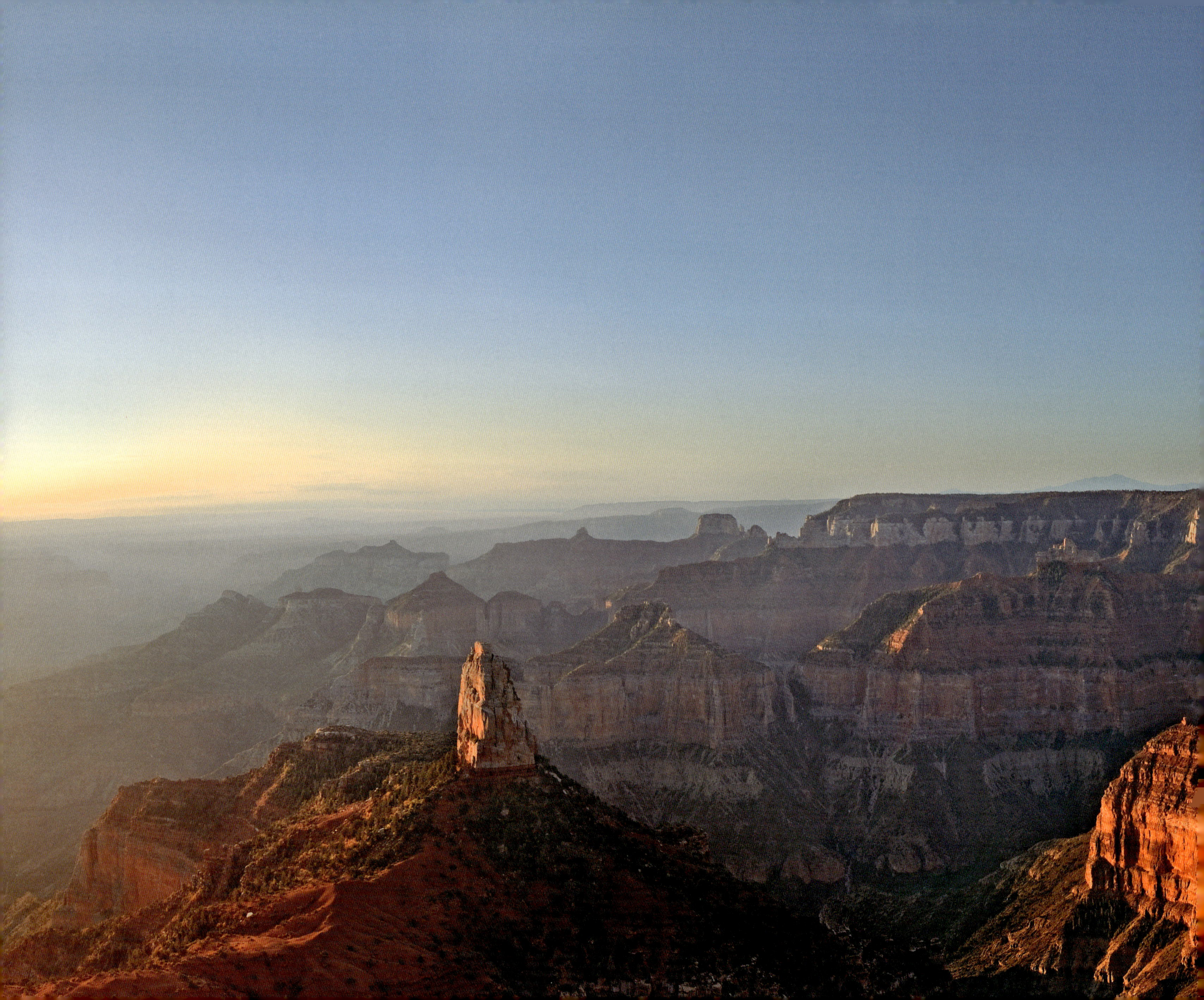

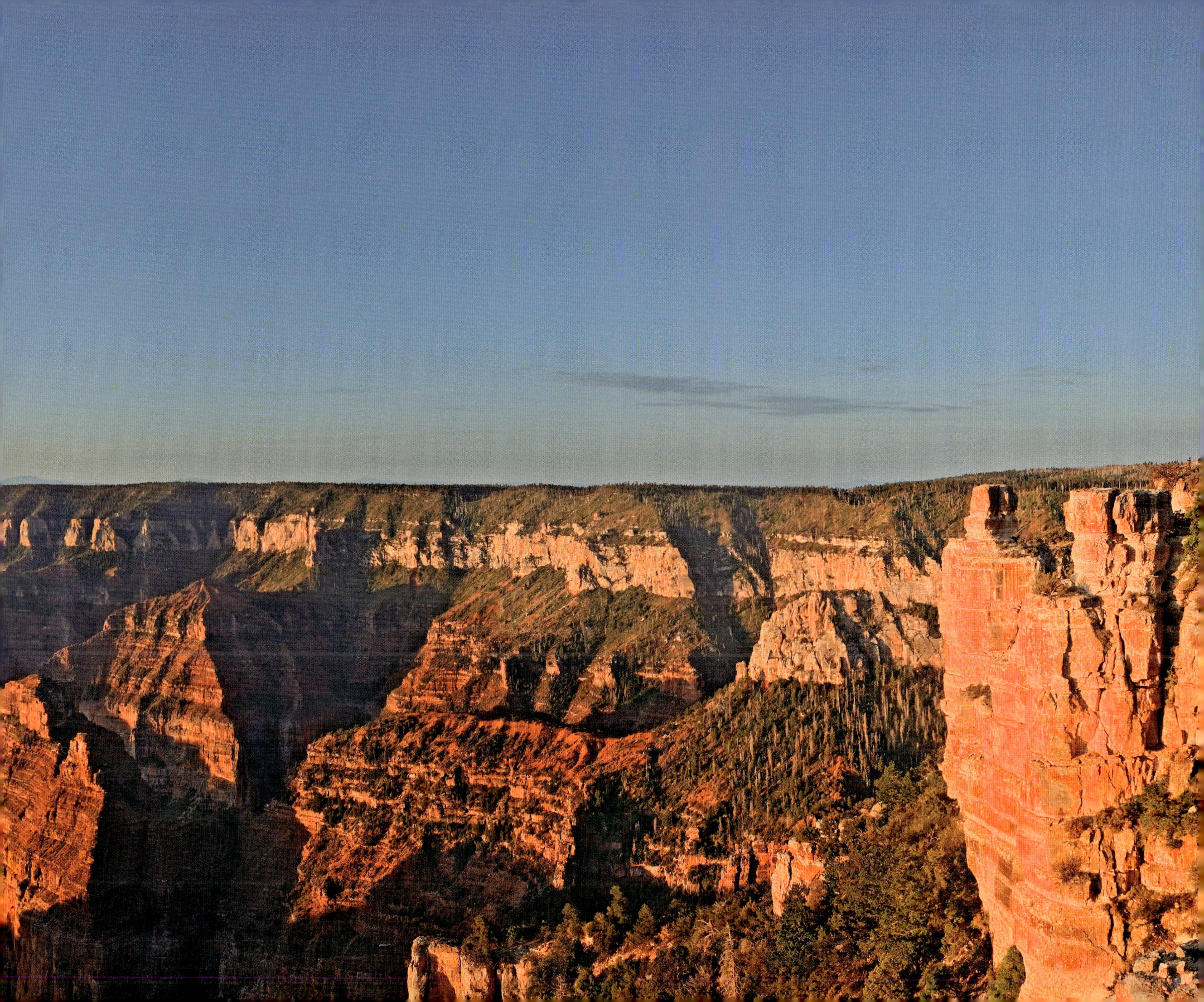

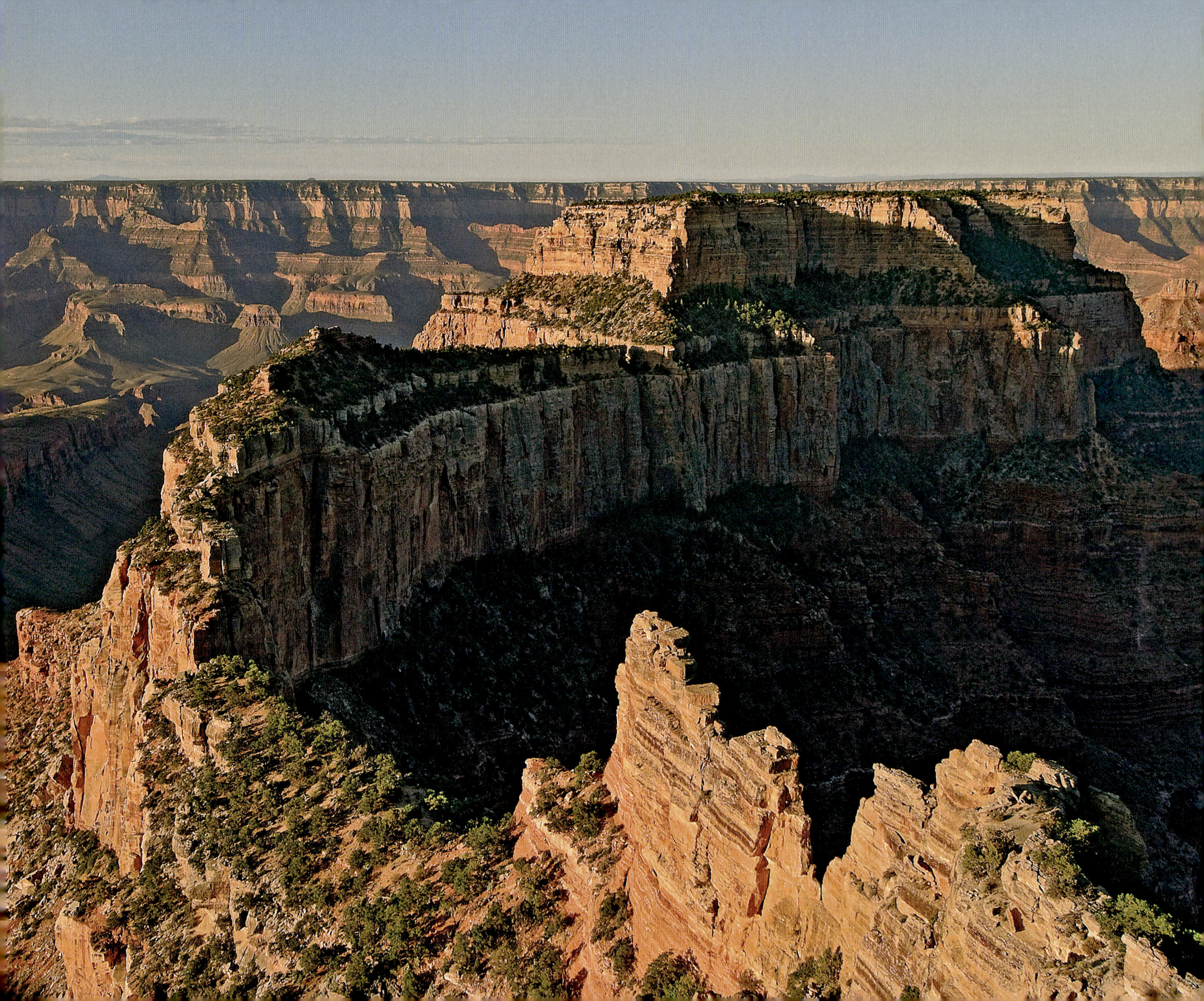

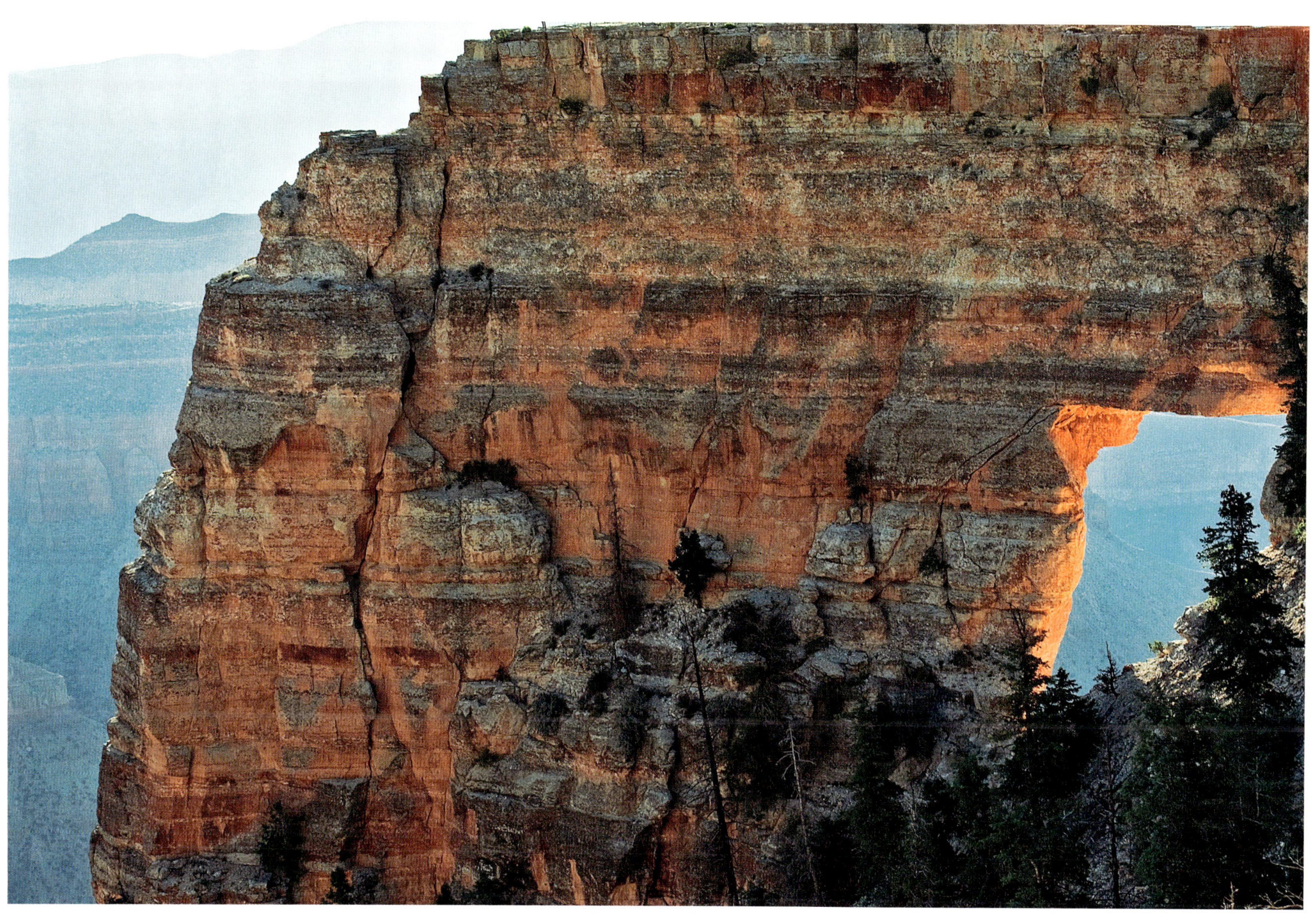

↑ Angels Window, view from Cape Royal, North Rim, Grand Canyon National Park ←↓ View from Cape Royal, North Rim, Grand Canyon National Park

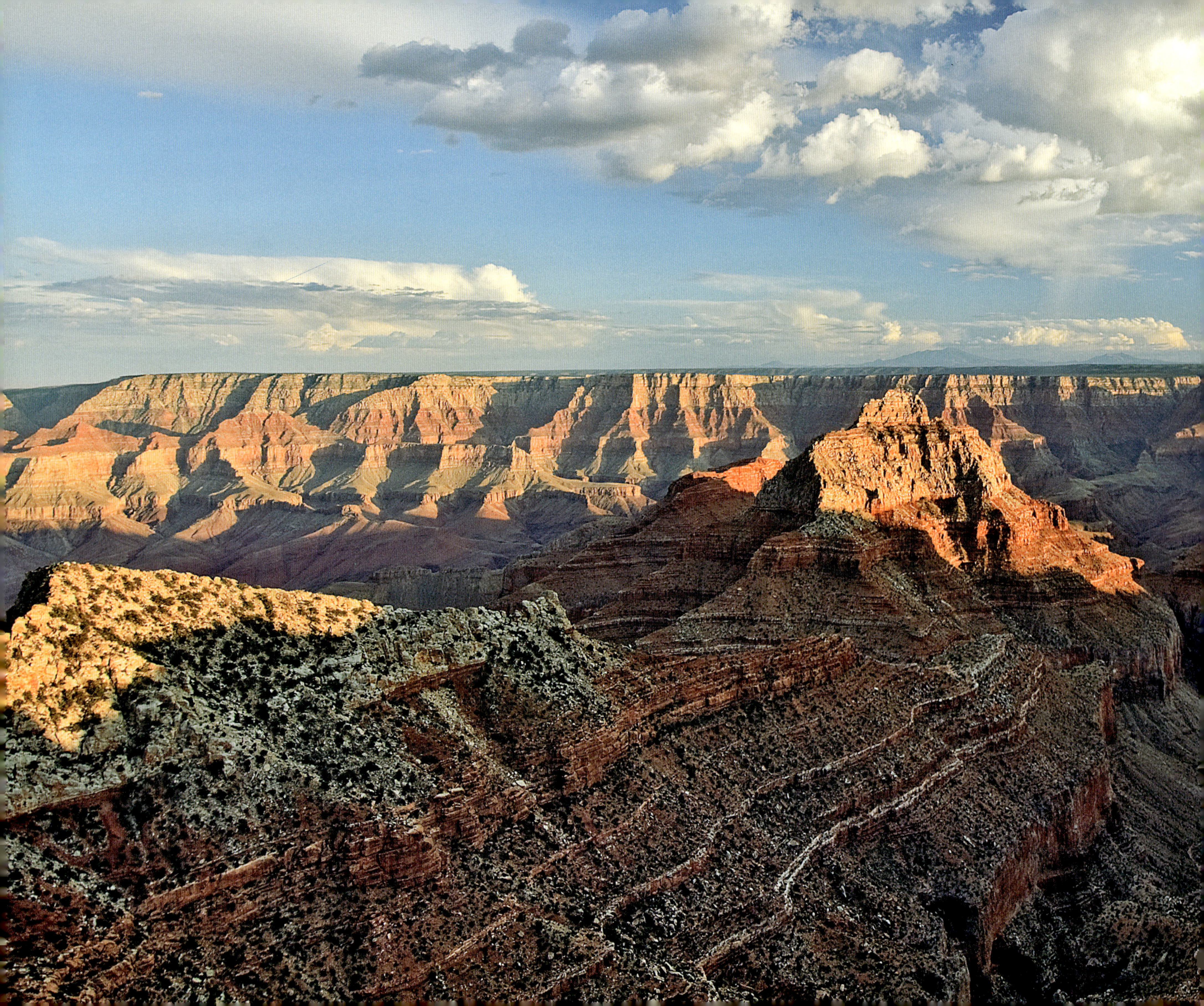

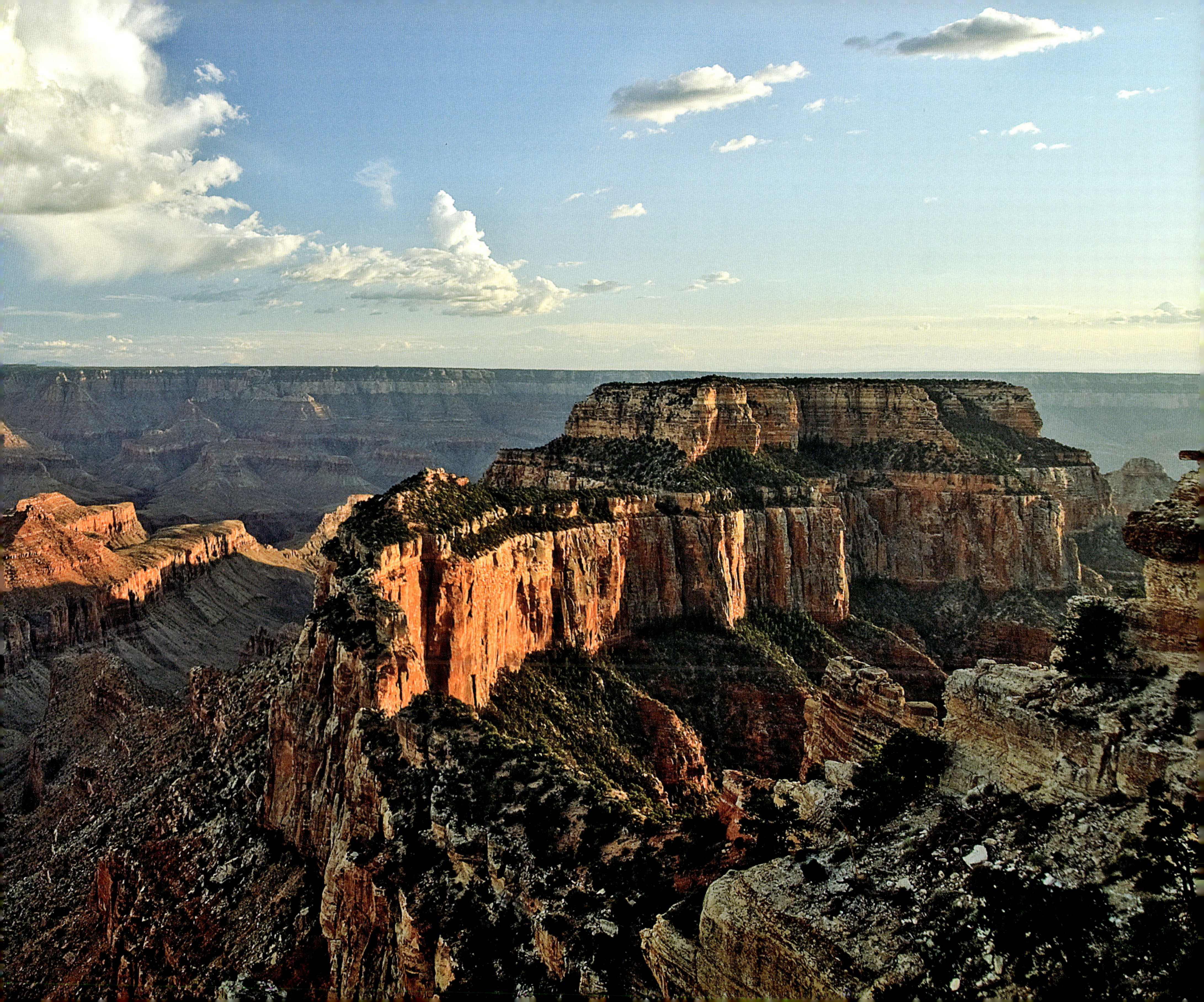

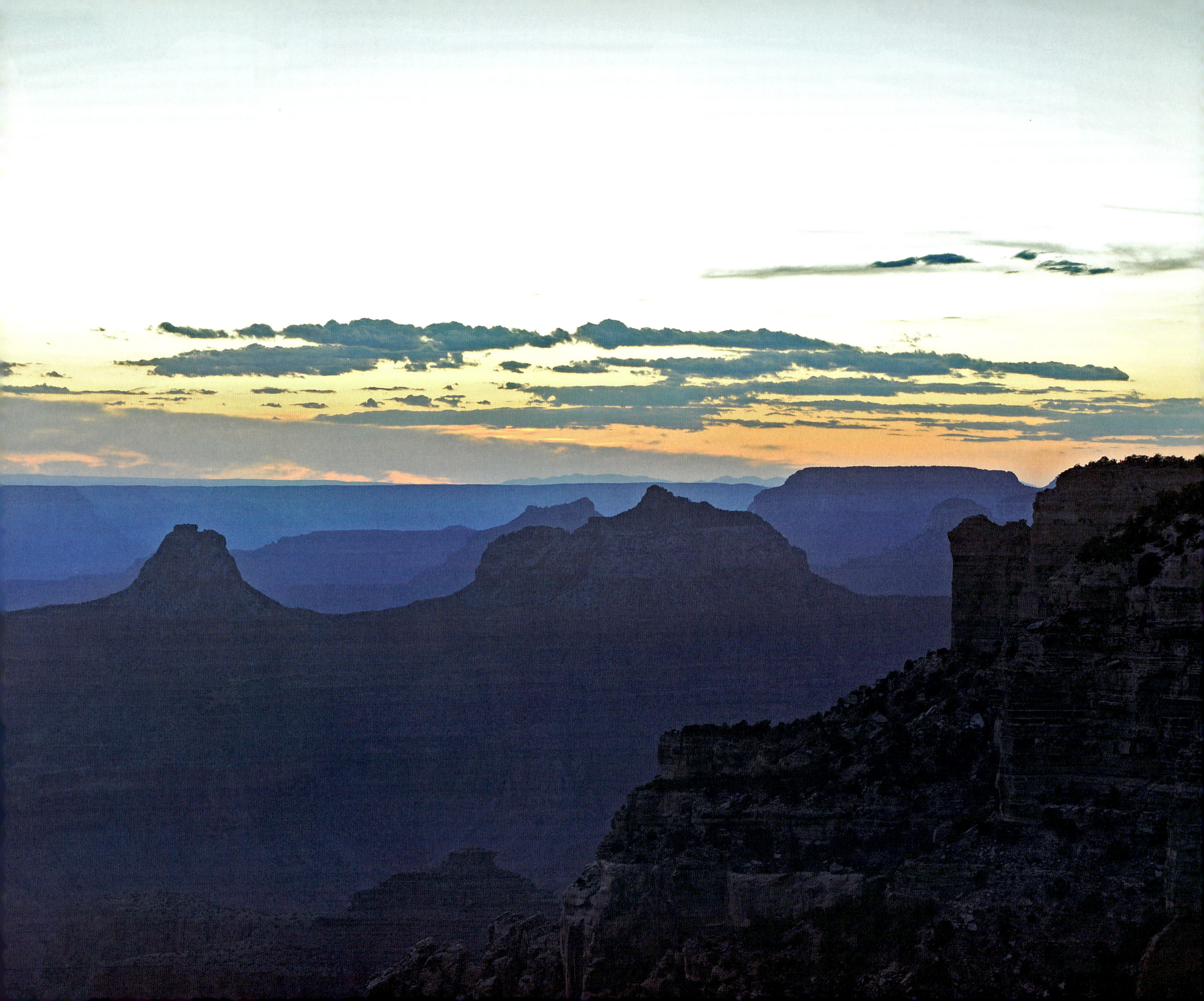

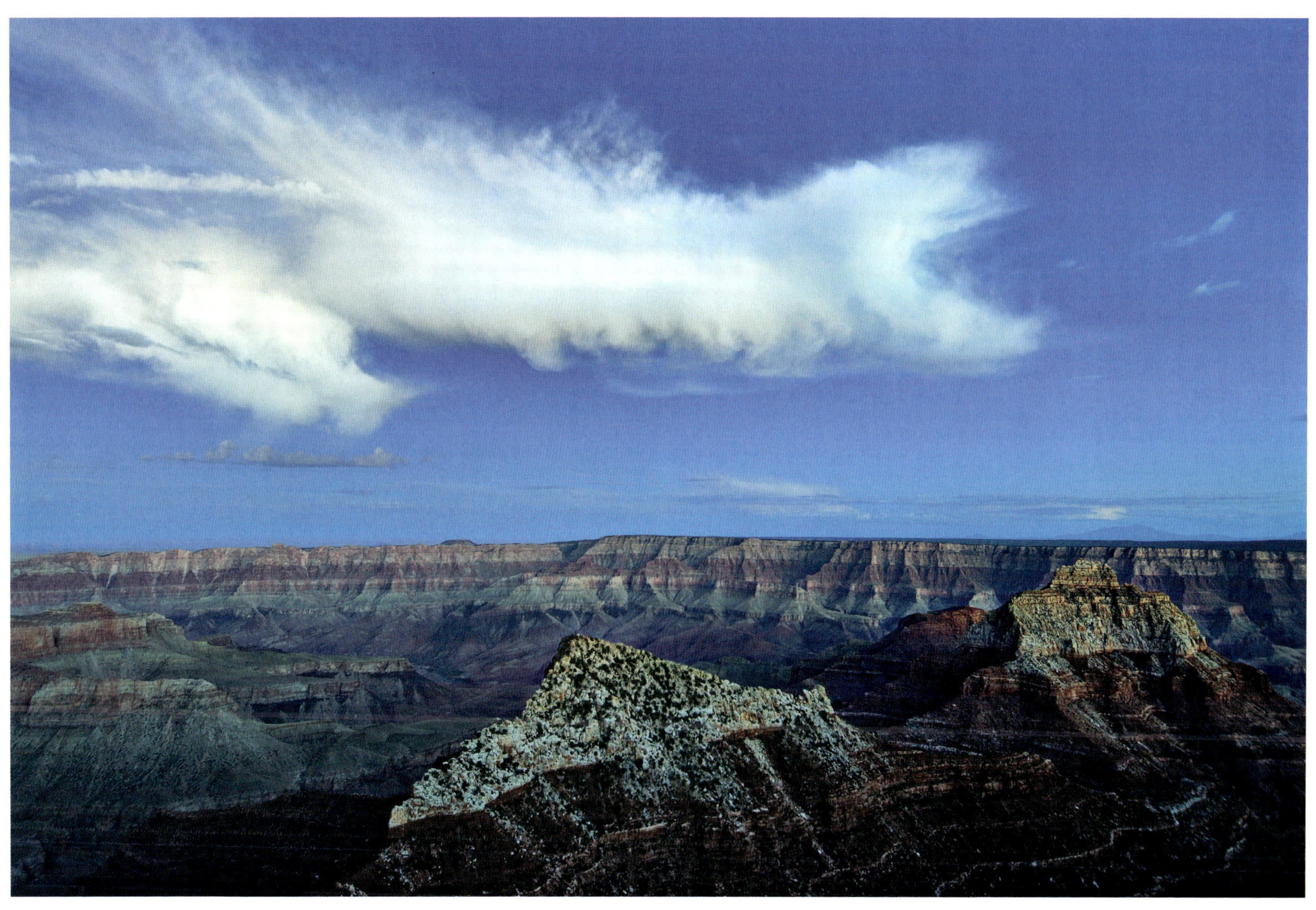

← ↑ View from Cape Royal, North Rim, Grand Canyon National Park ↓ Walhalla Overlook, North Rim, Grand Canyon National Park

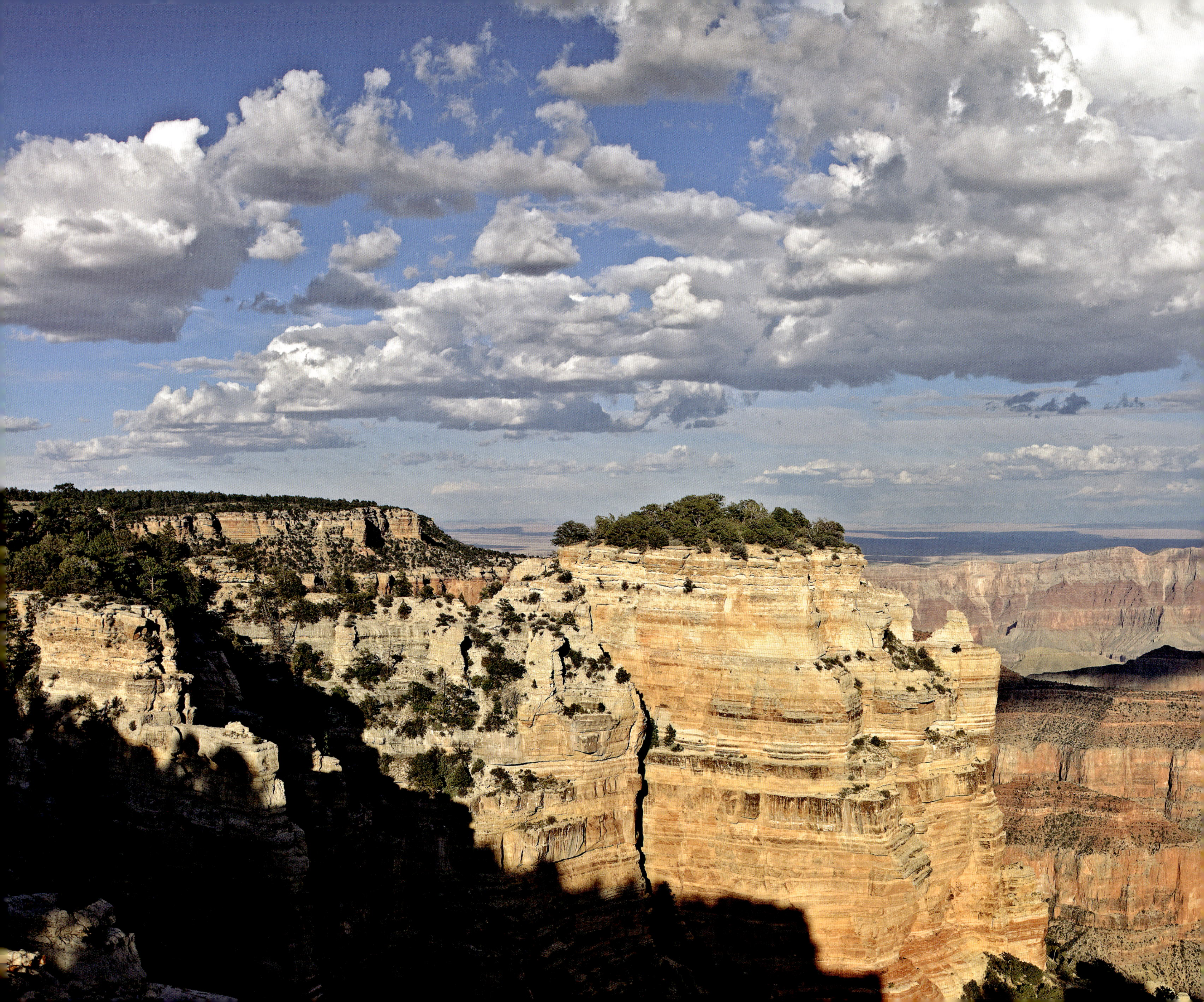

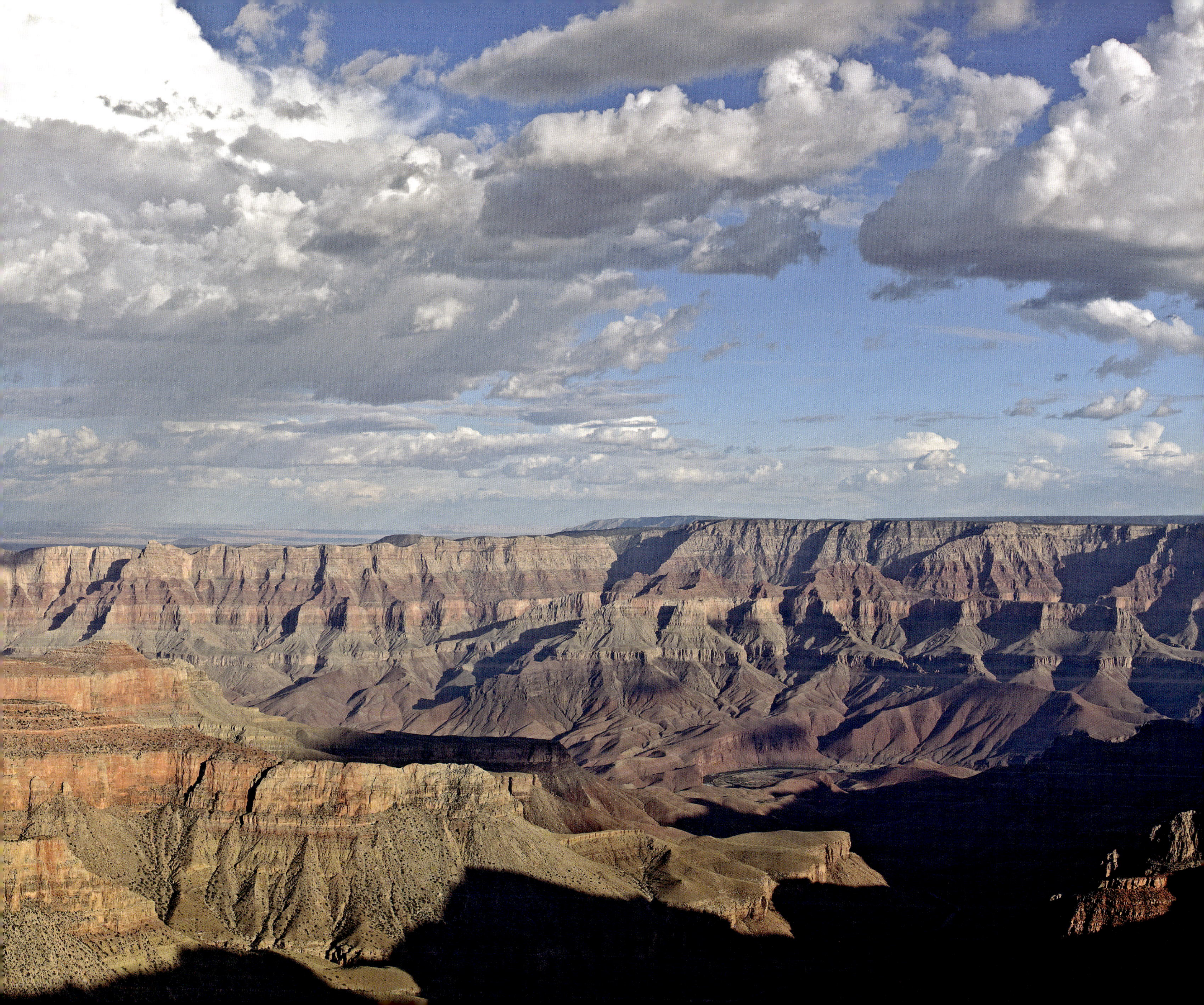

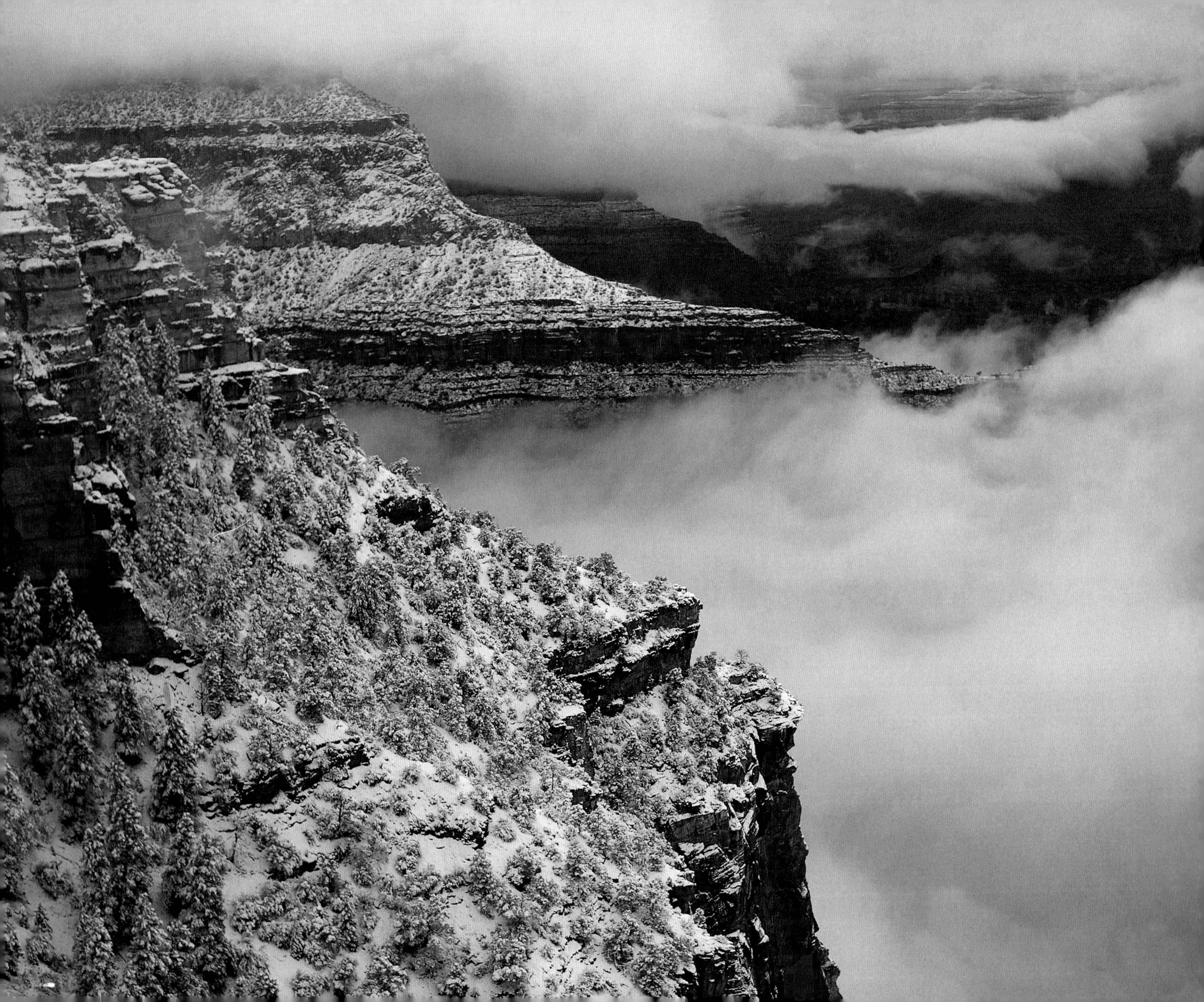

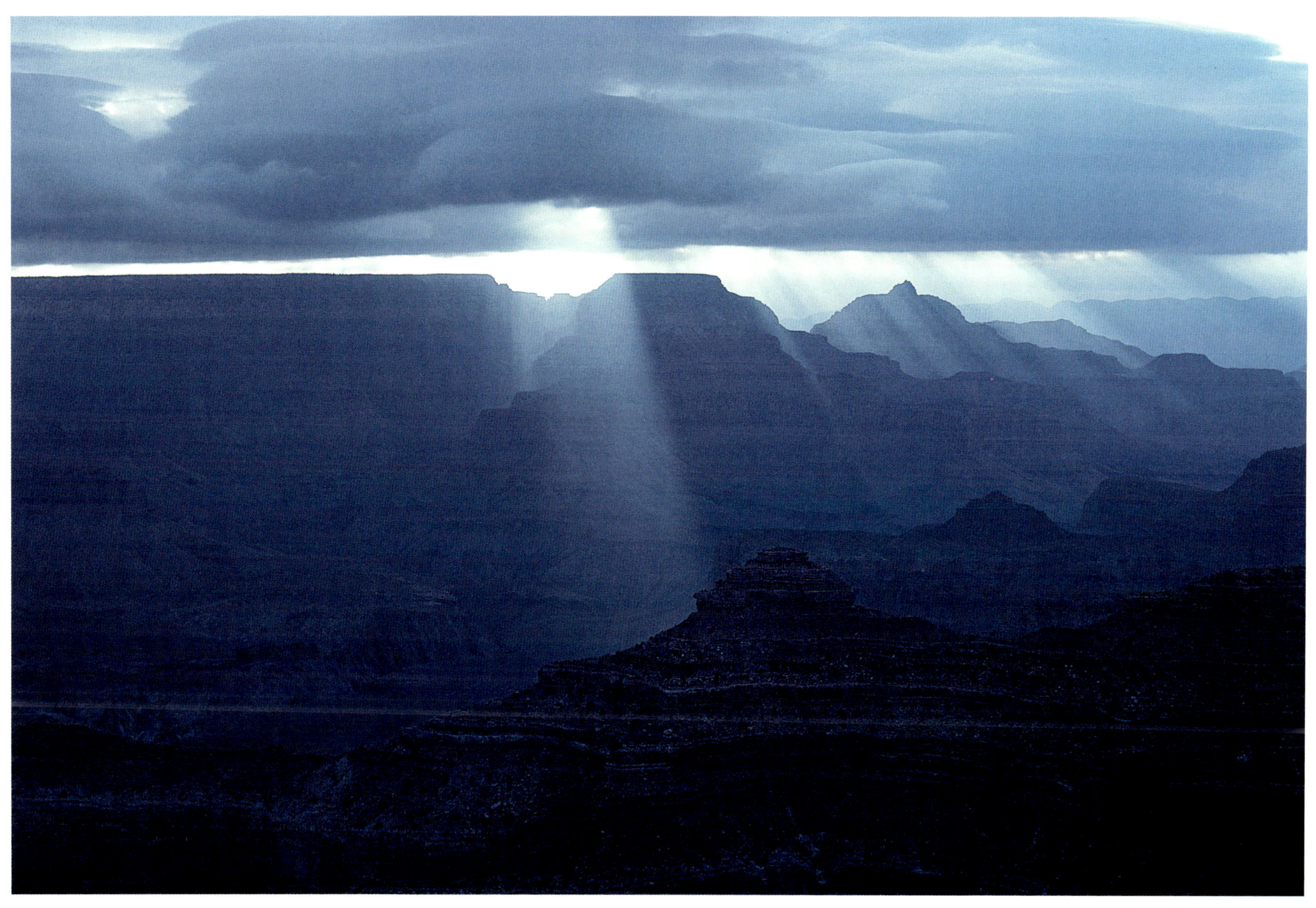

←↑ South Rim, Grand Canyon National Park

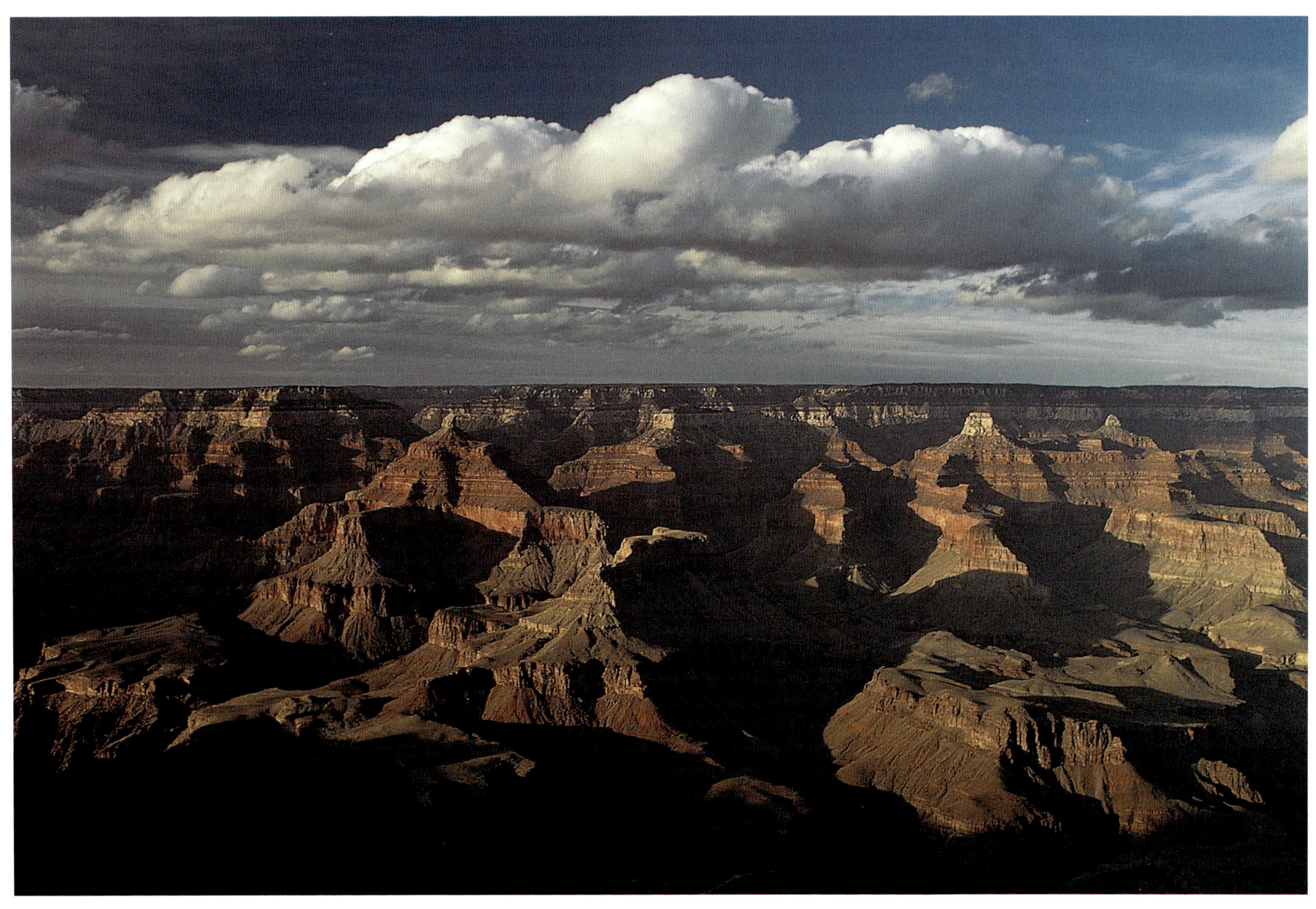

↑ South Rim, Grand Canyon National Park → Walhalla Overlook, North Rim, Grand Canyon National Park ↓ Vermilion Cliffs National Moument, Paria Canyon-Vermilion Cliffs Wilderness

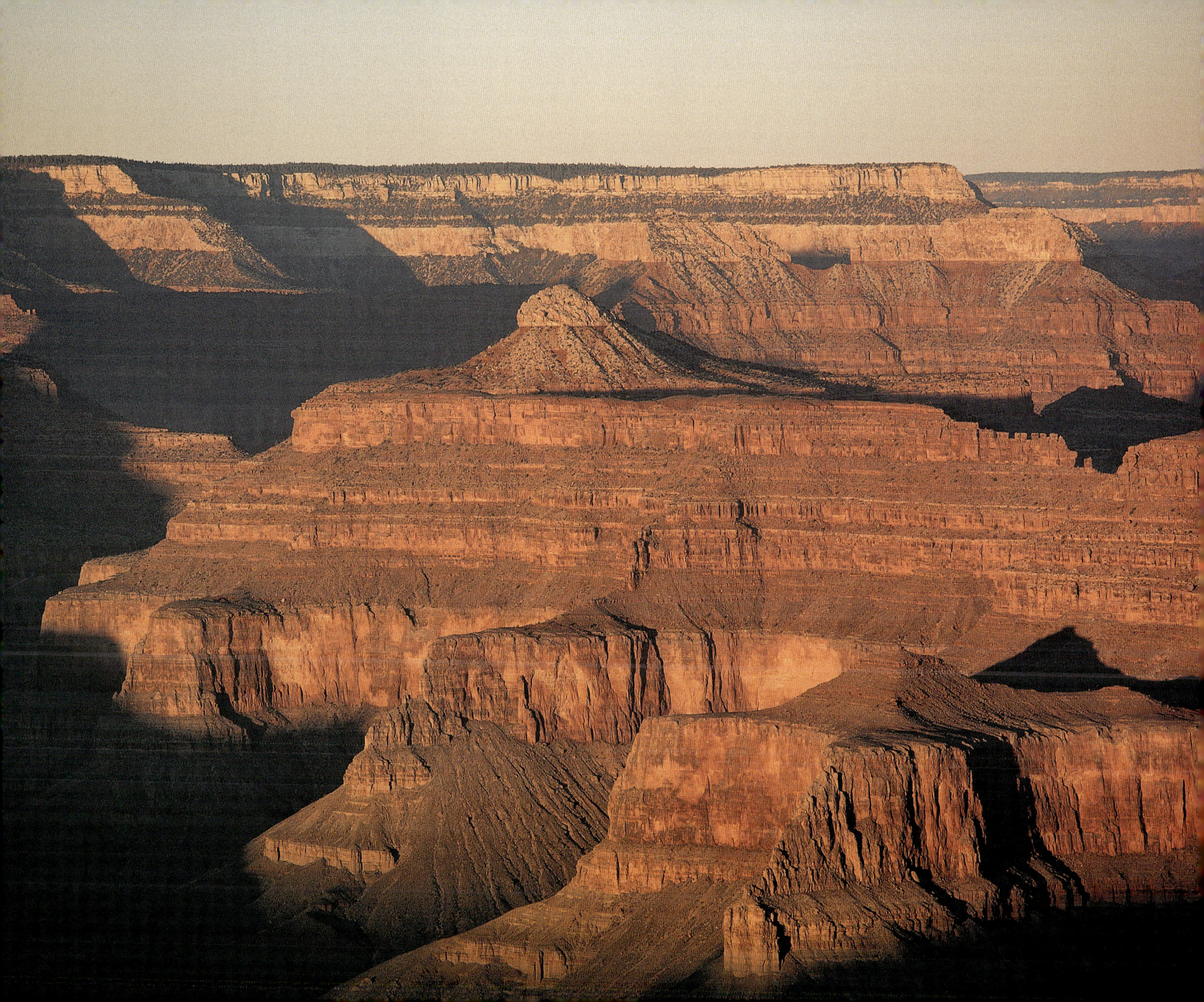

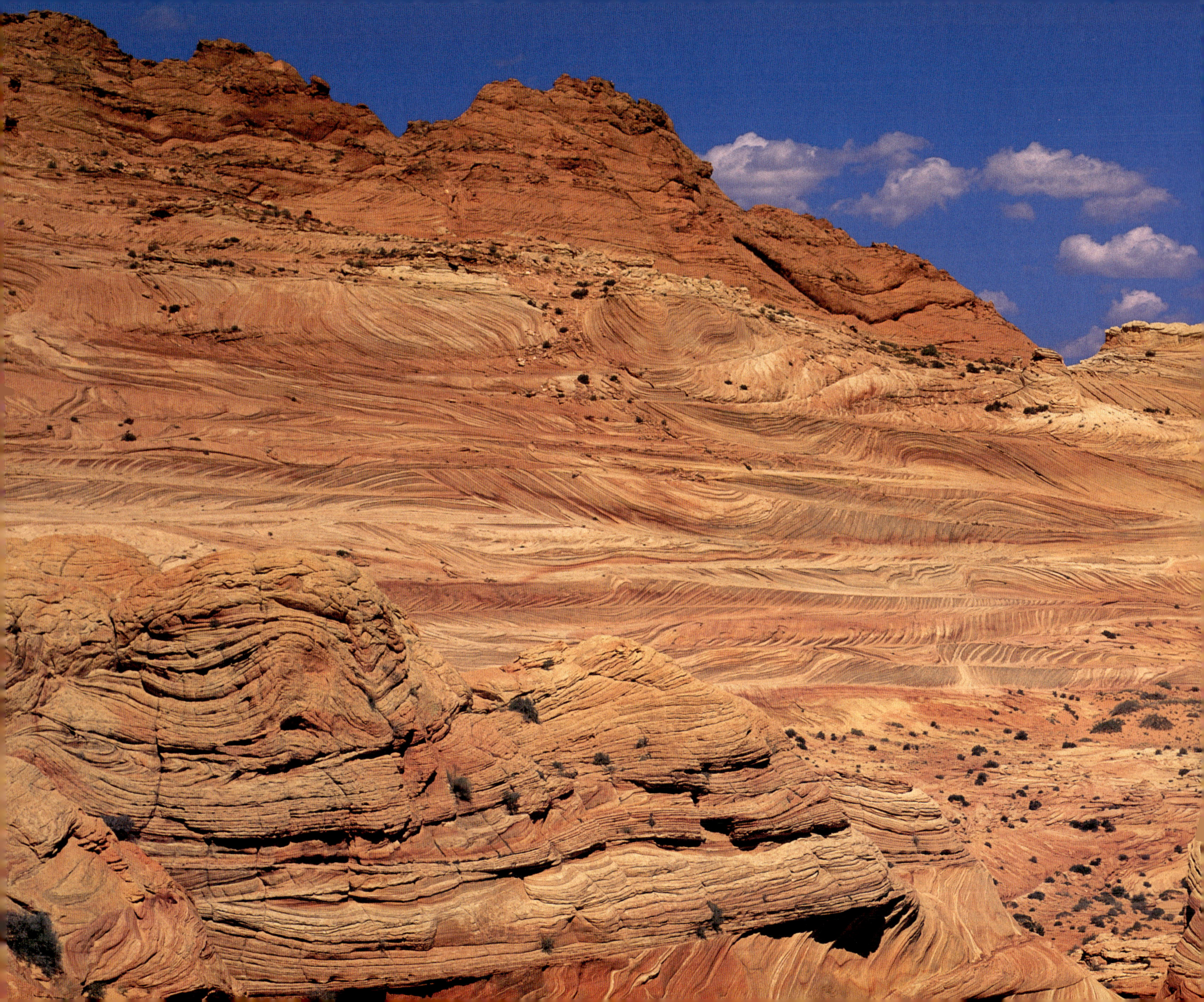

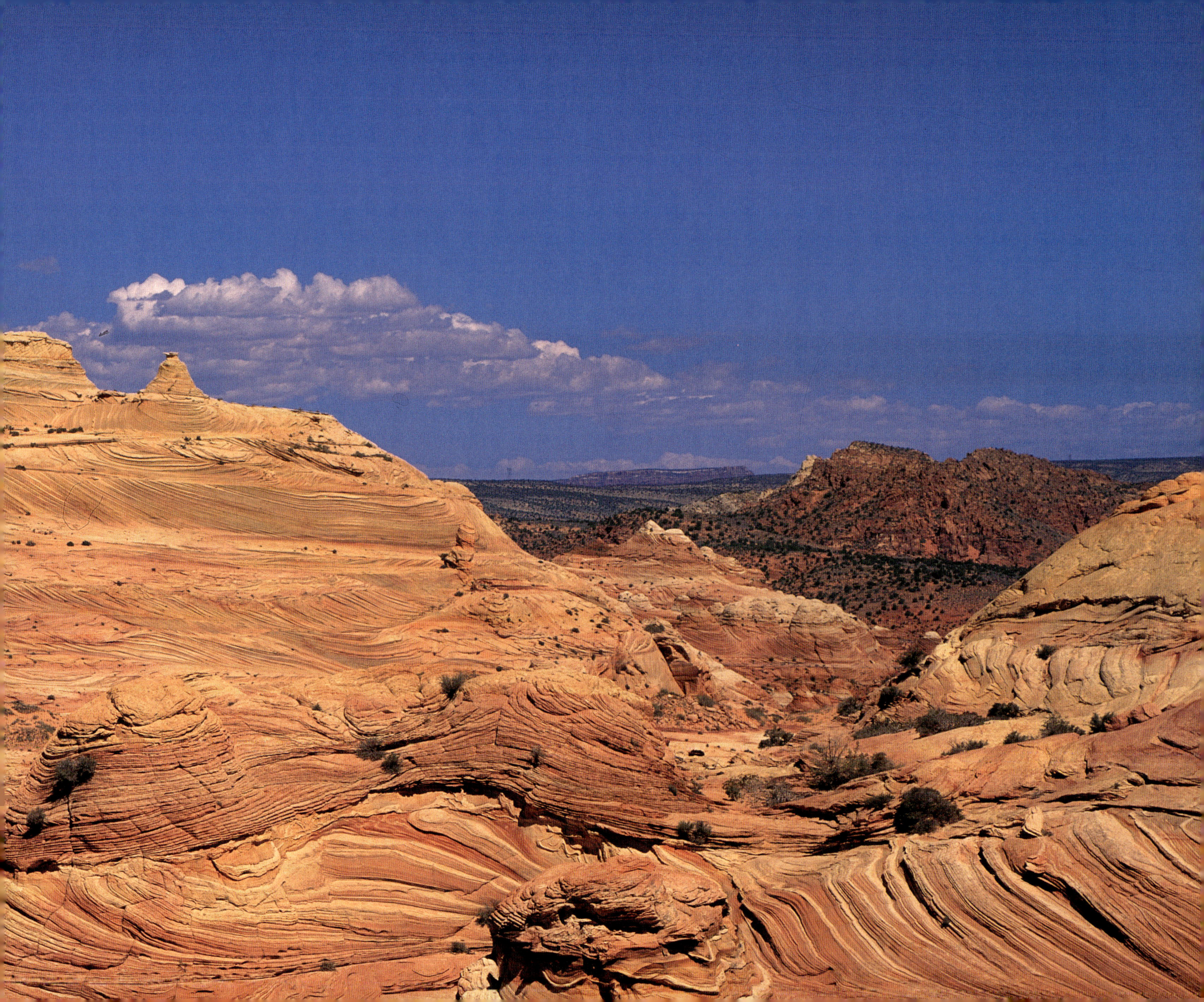

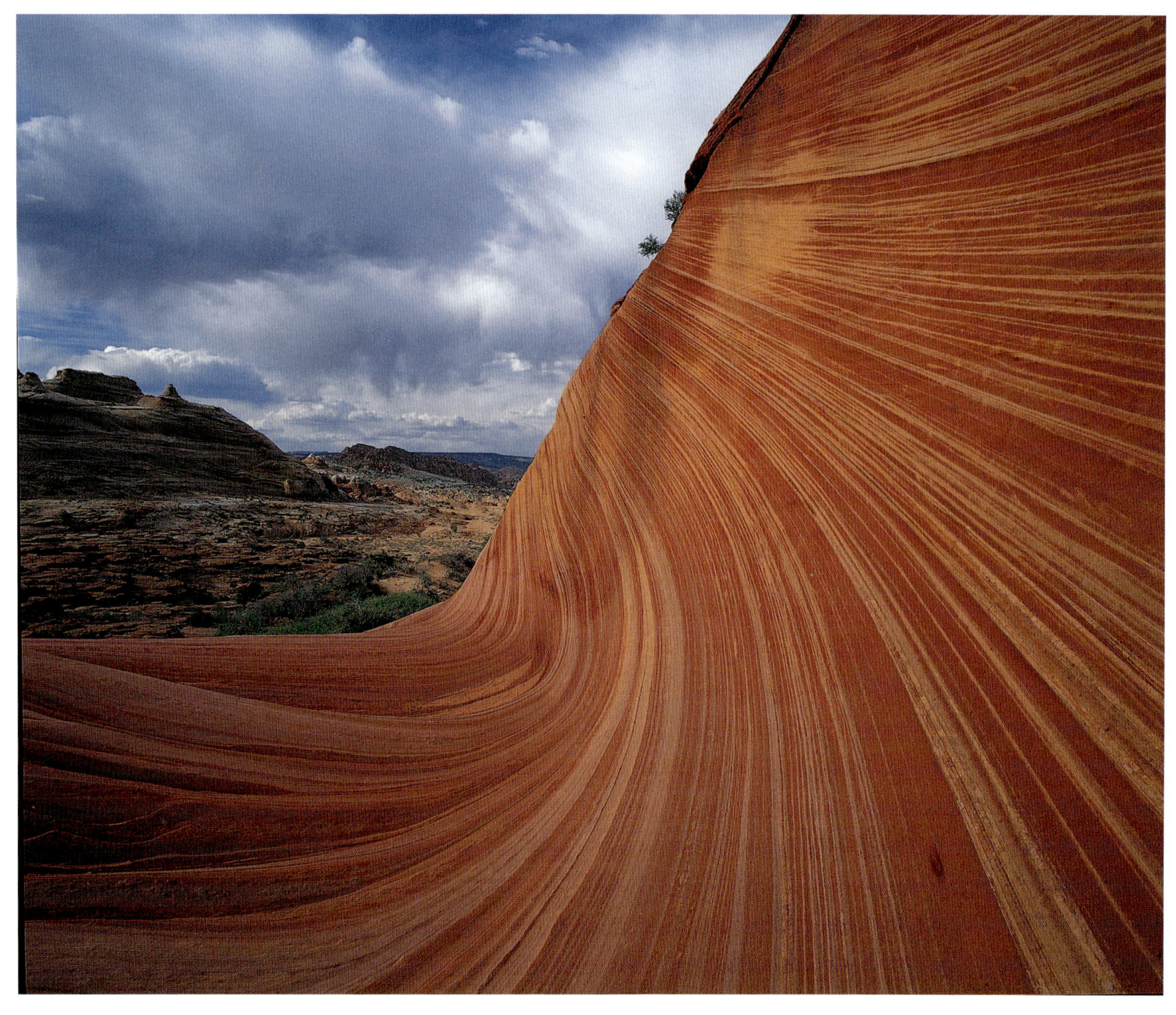

↑→↓ Vermilion Cliffs National Monument, Paria Canyon-Vermilion Cliffs Wilderness

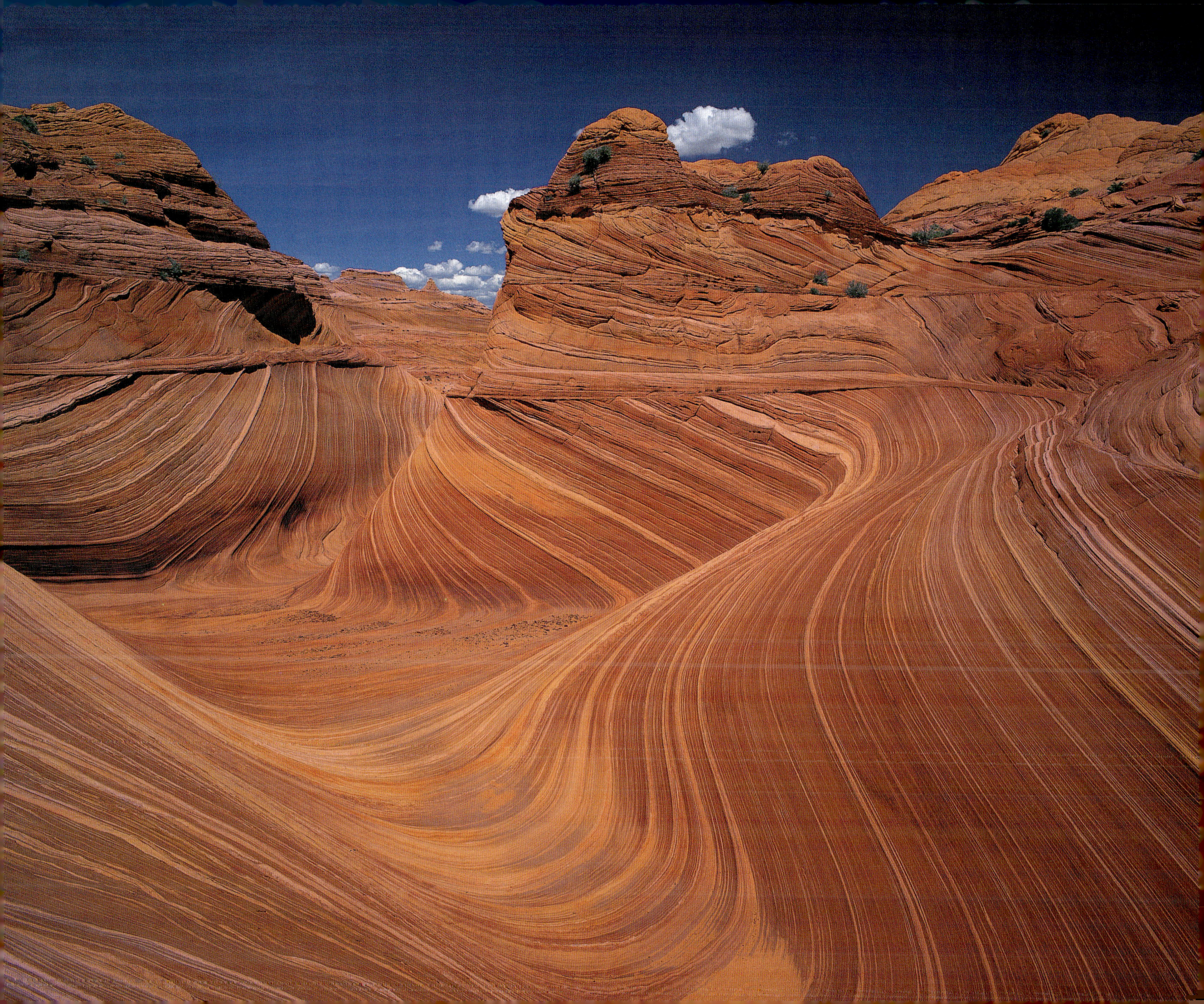

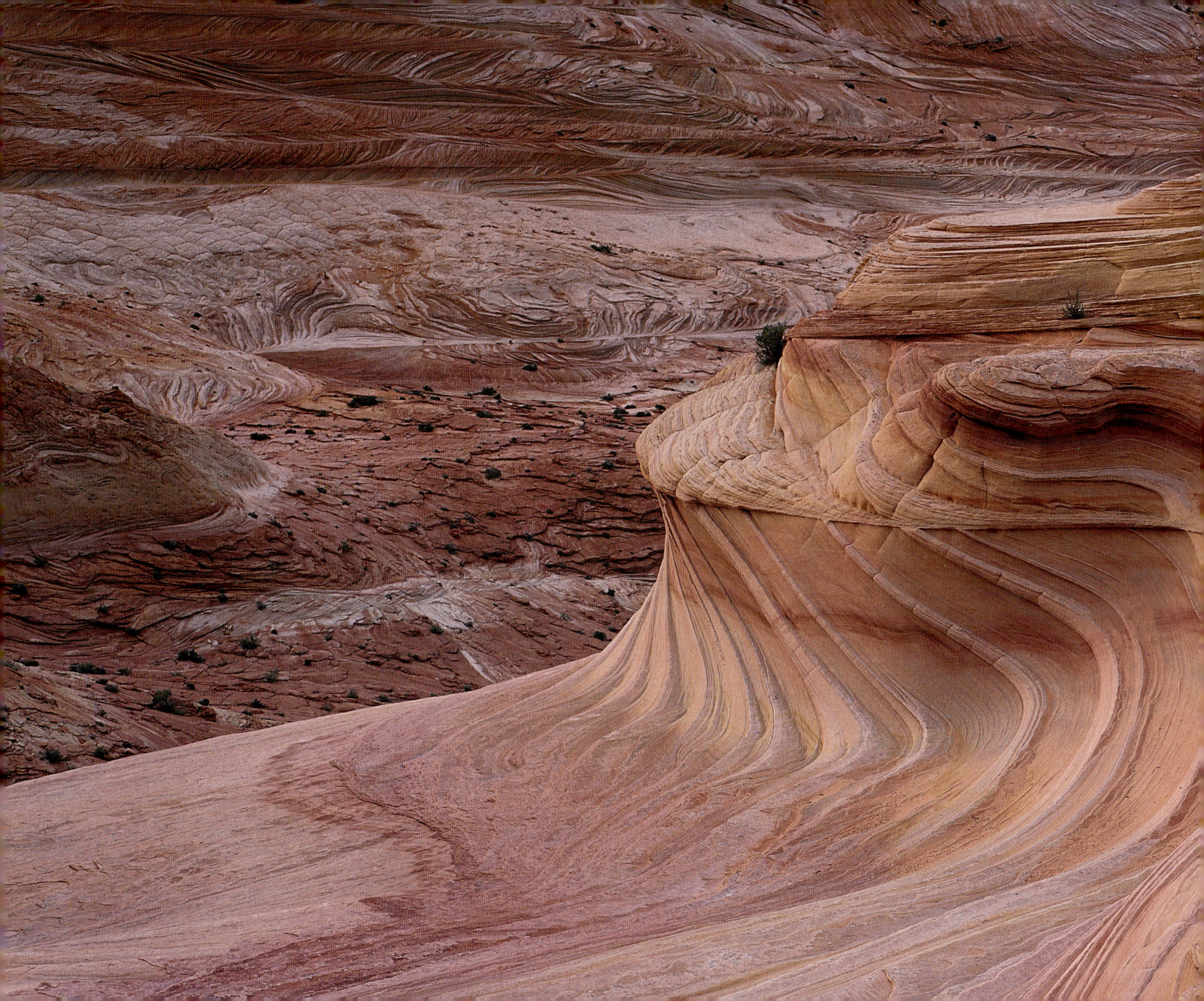

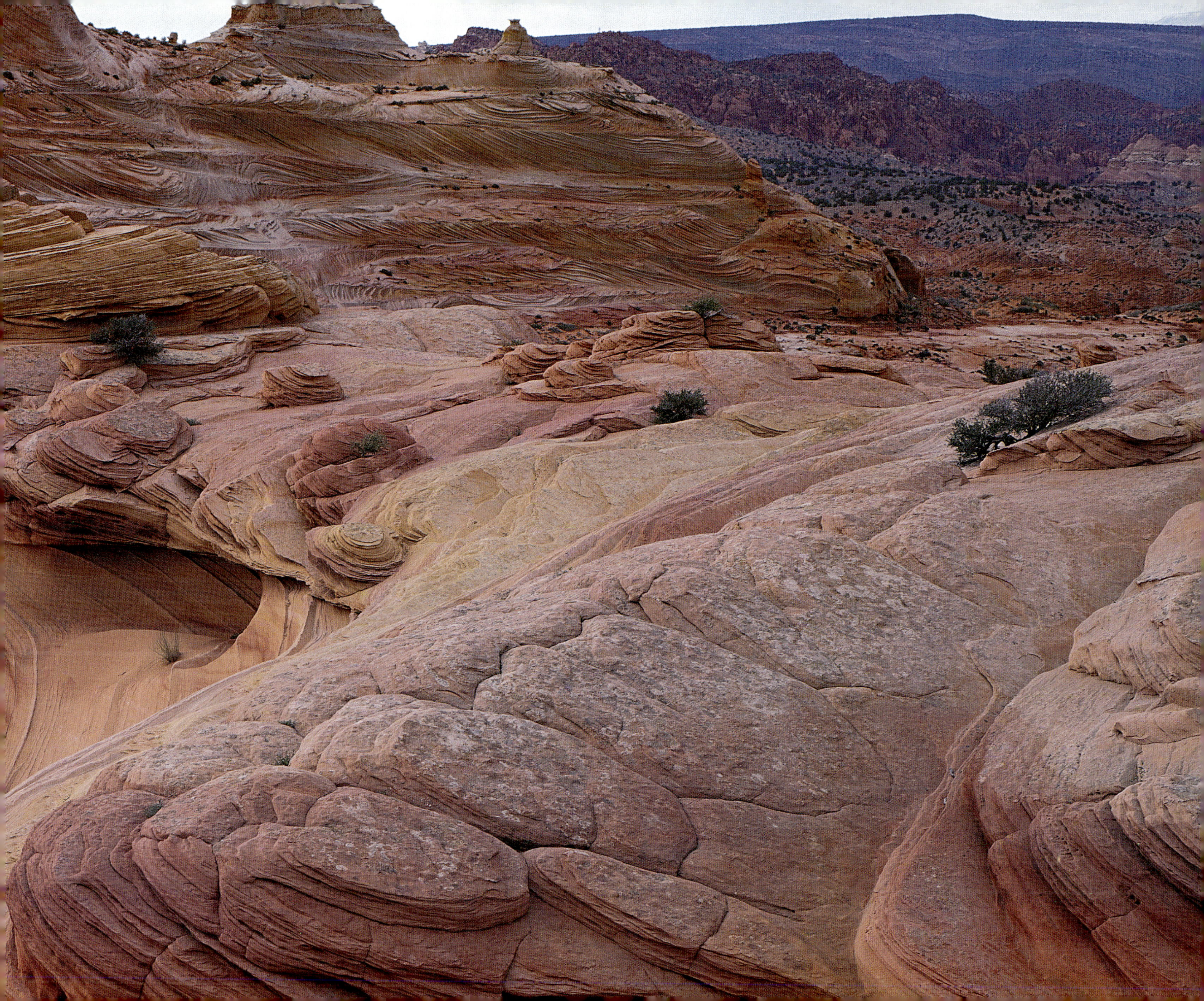

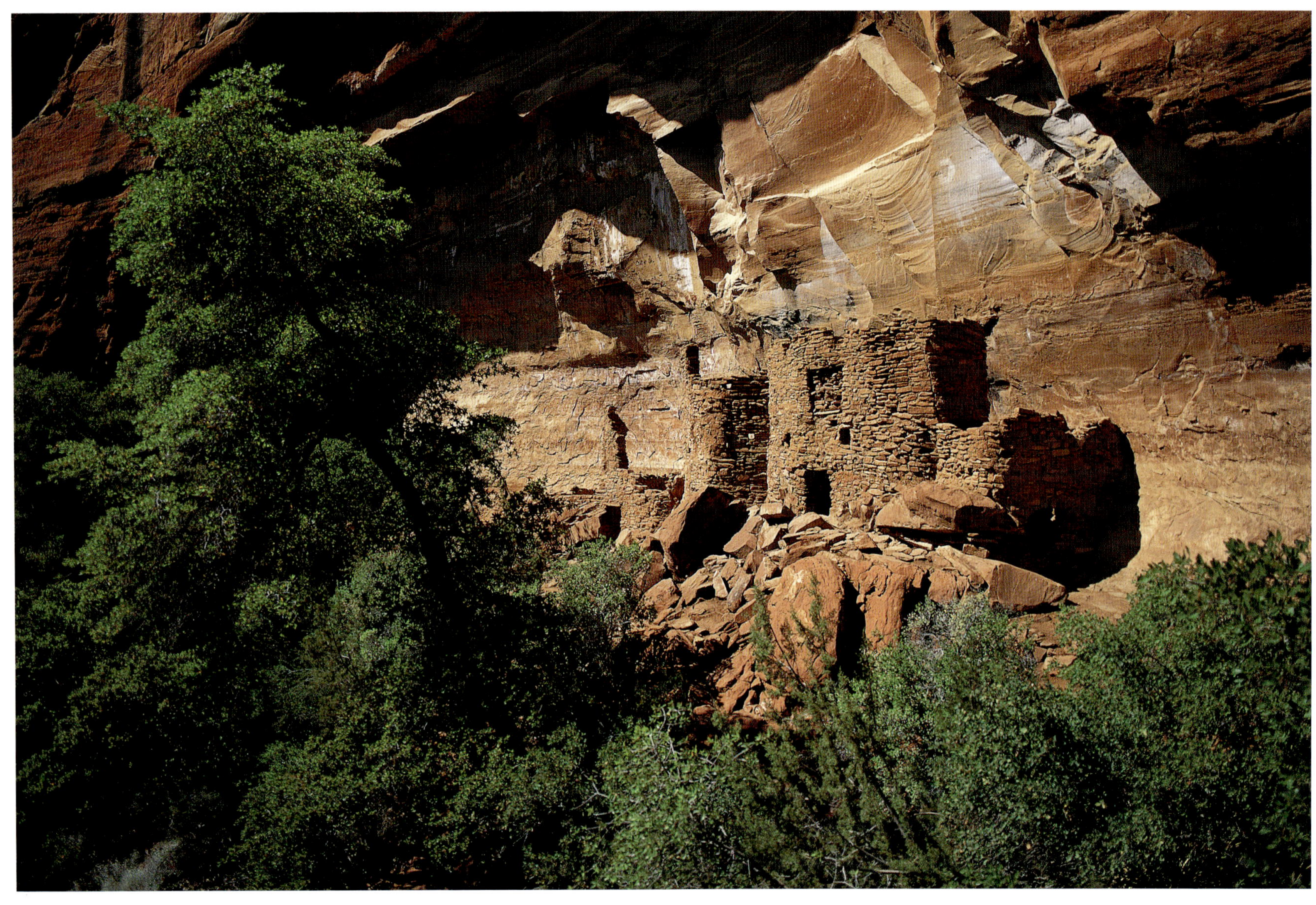

↑→ Palatki Heritage Site, Cocomino National Forest ↓Granite Dells, Prescott

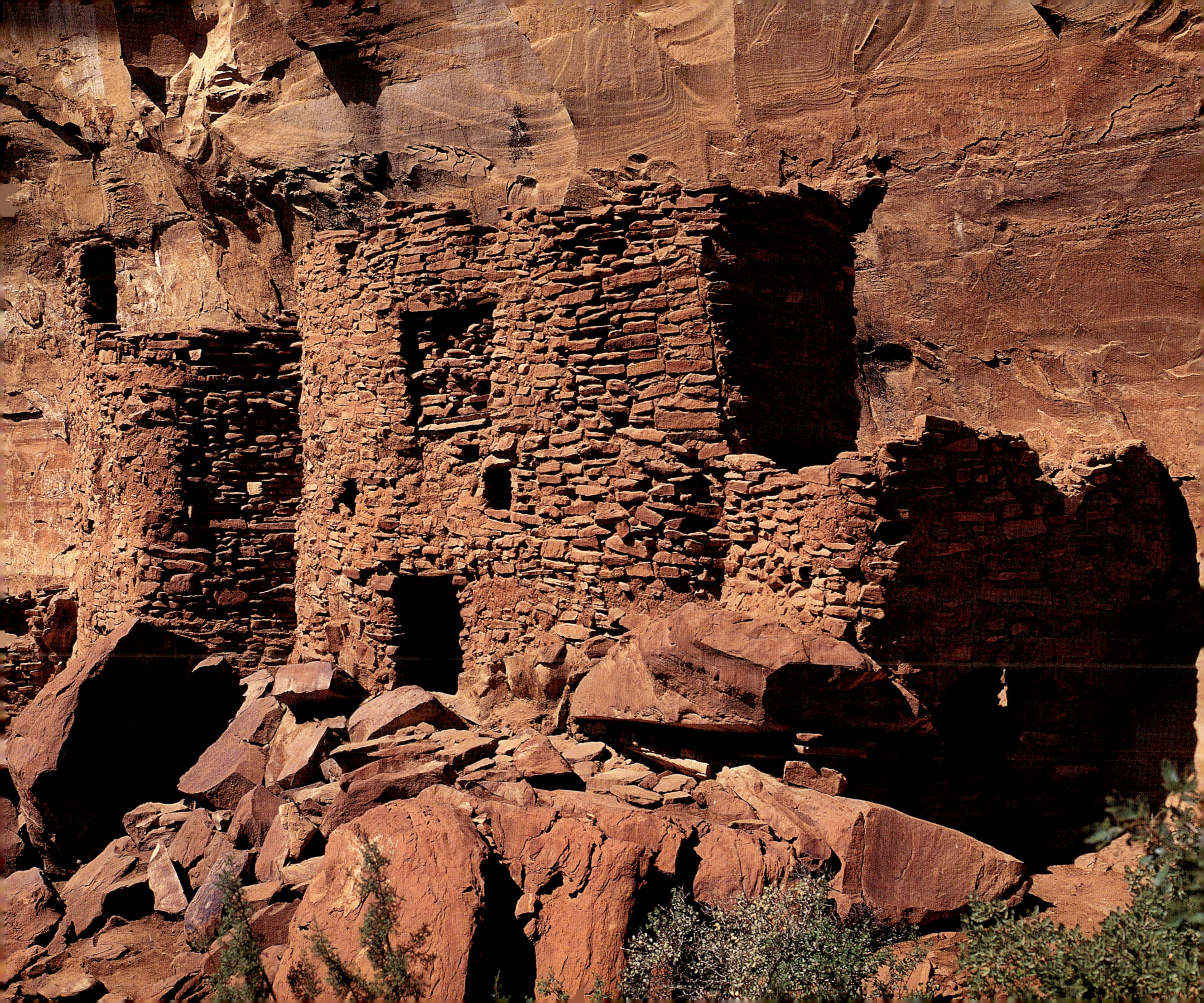

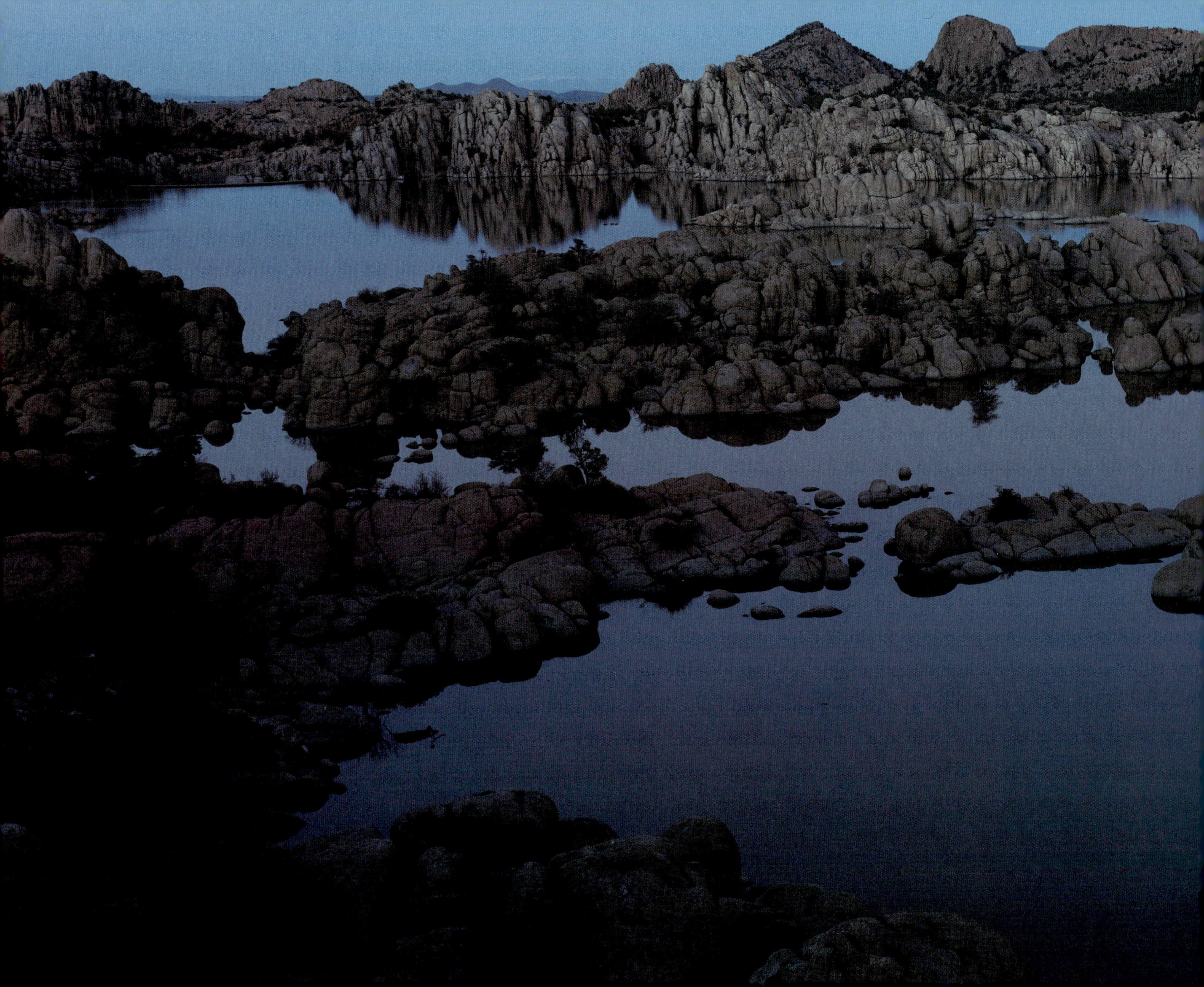

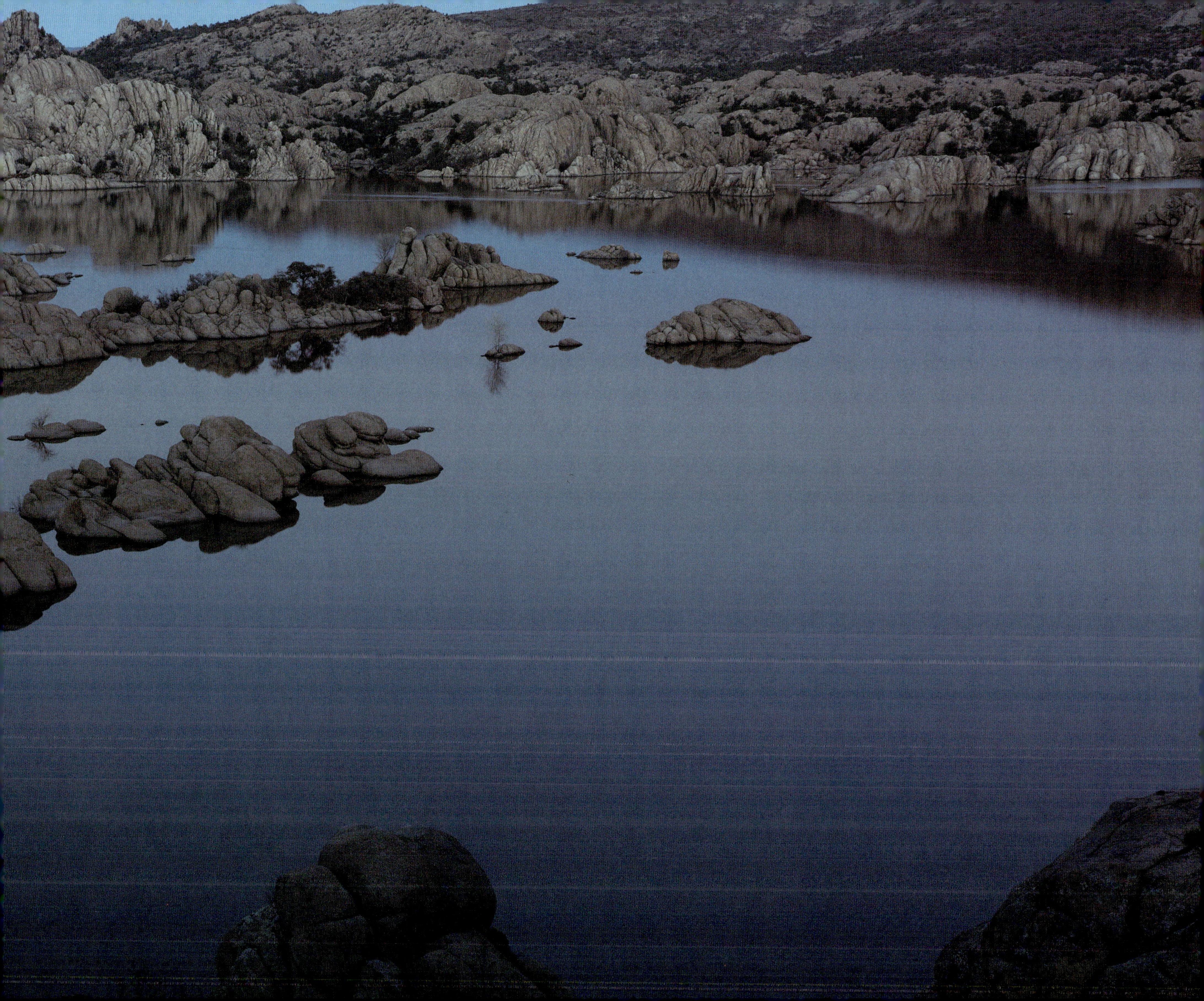

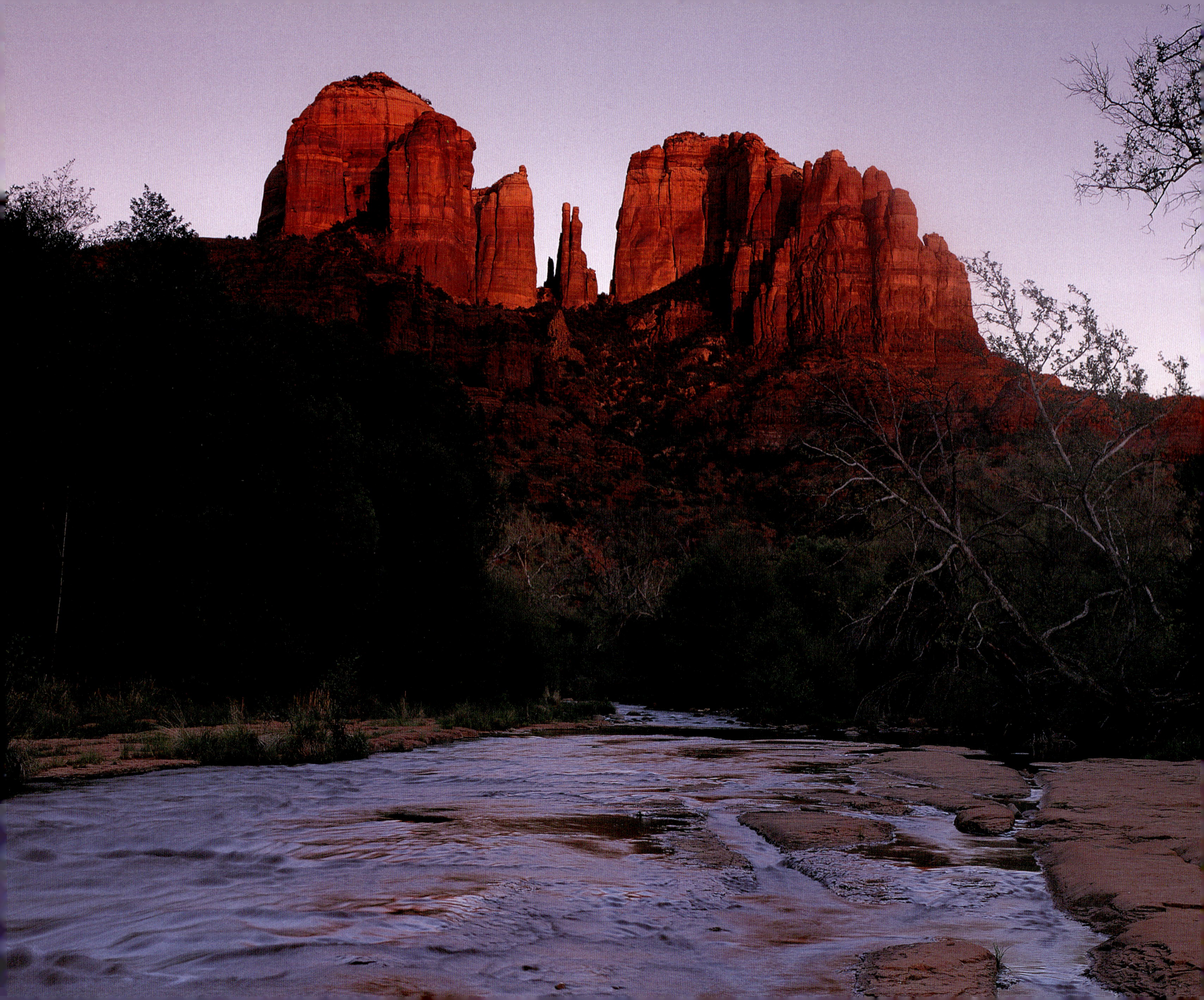

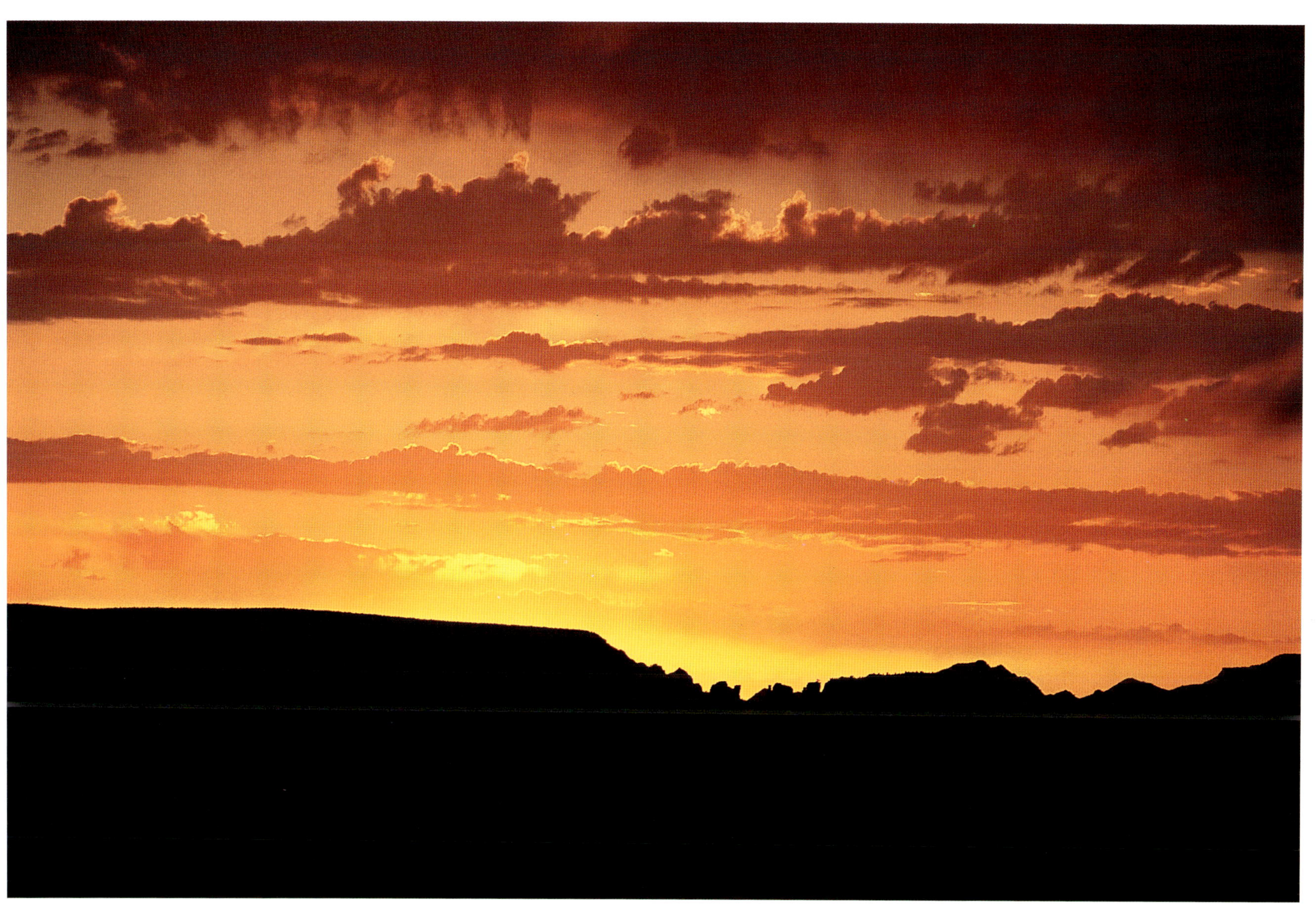

← Cathedral Rock reflected in Oak Creek, Red Creek Crossing, Sedona ↑ Sedona Sunset ↓ Wukoki Pueblo, Wupatki National Monument

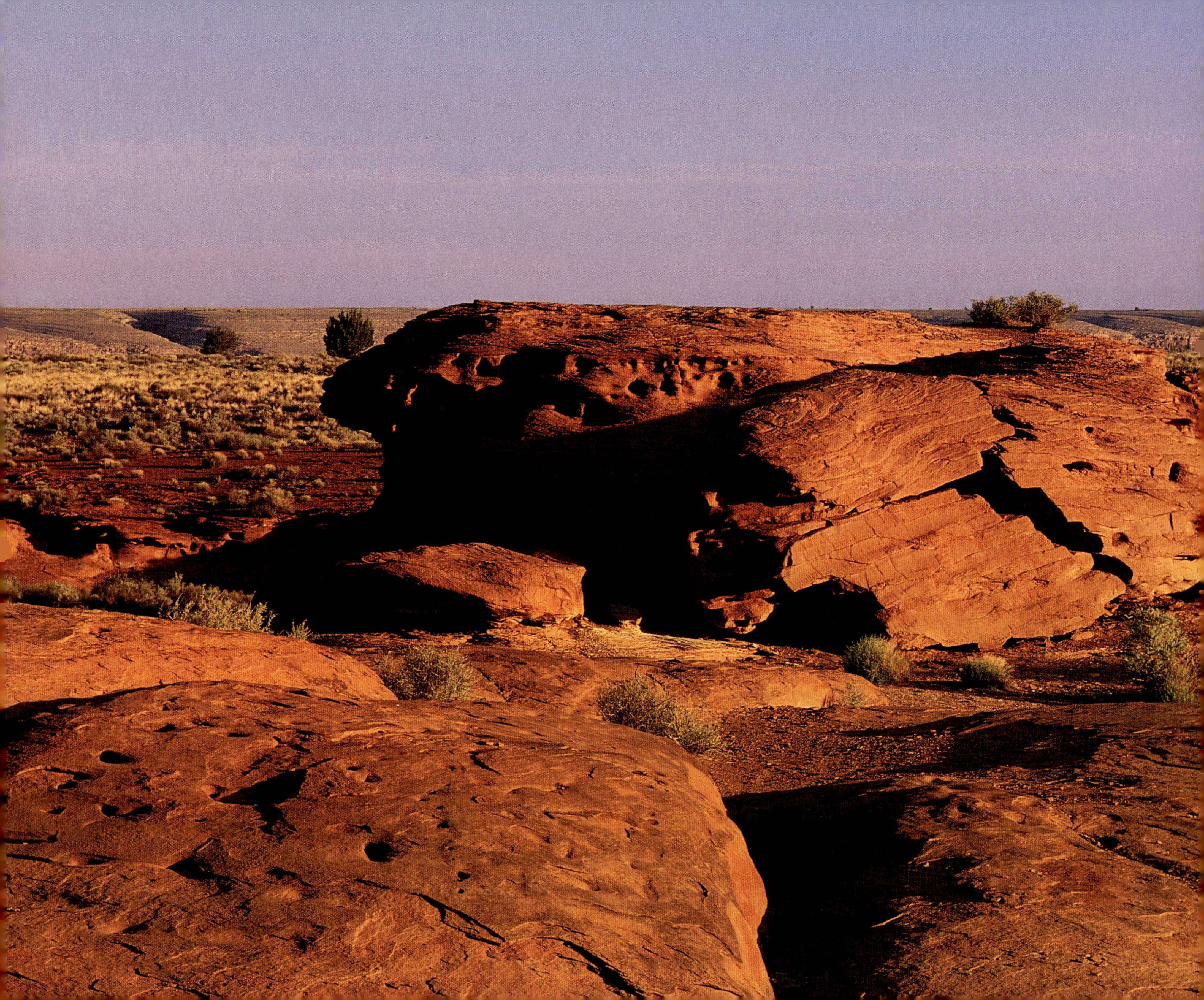

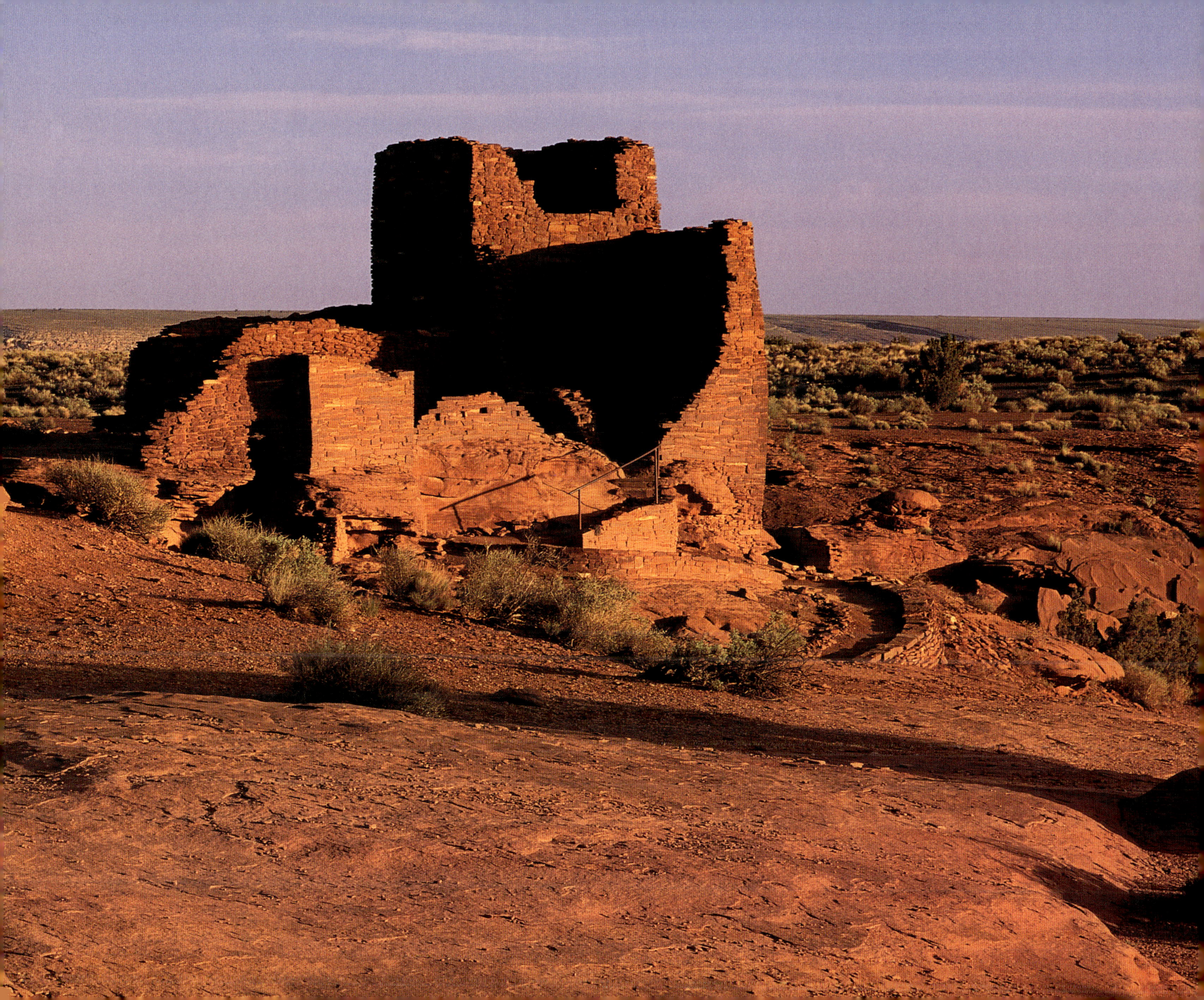

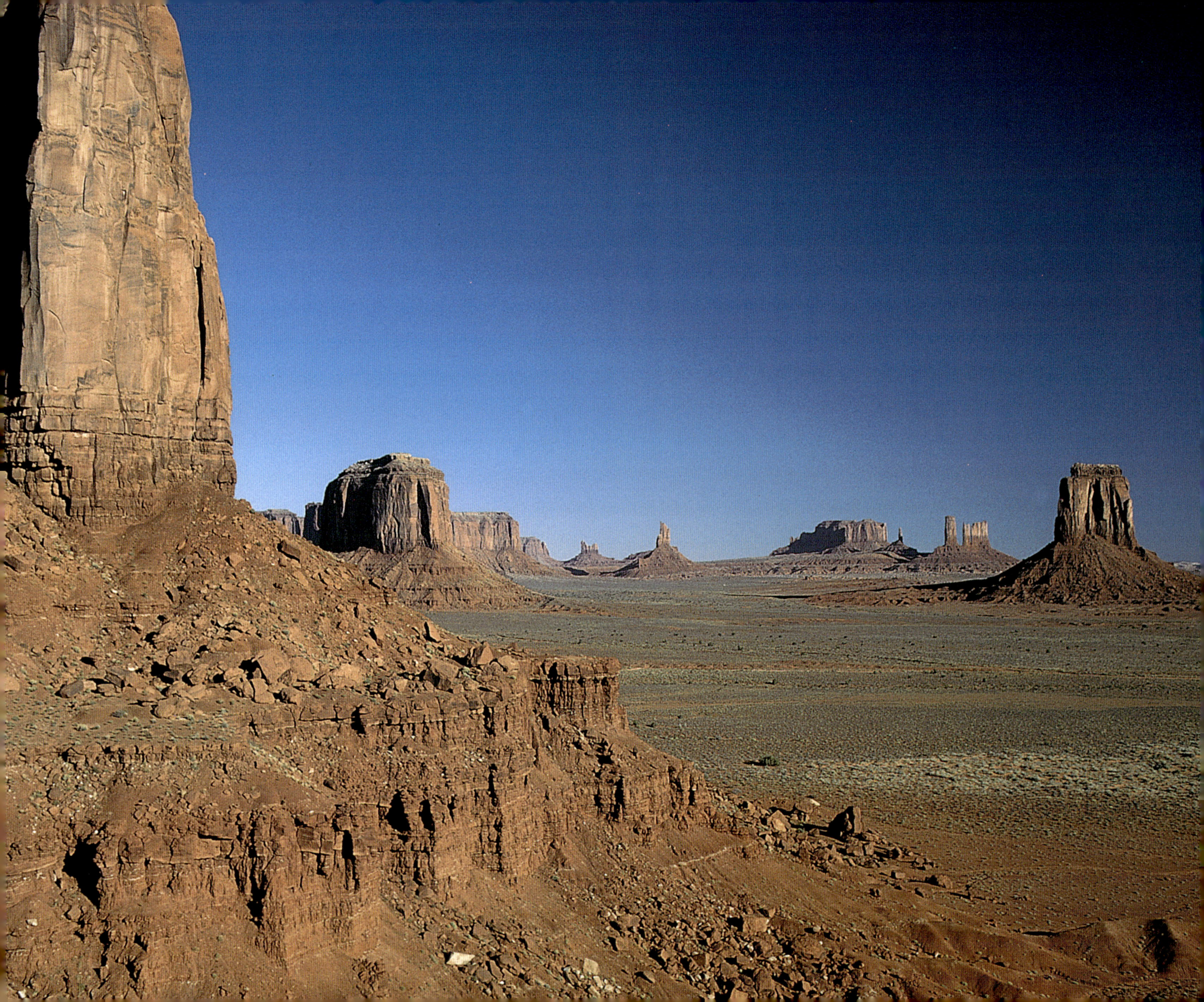

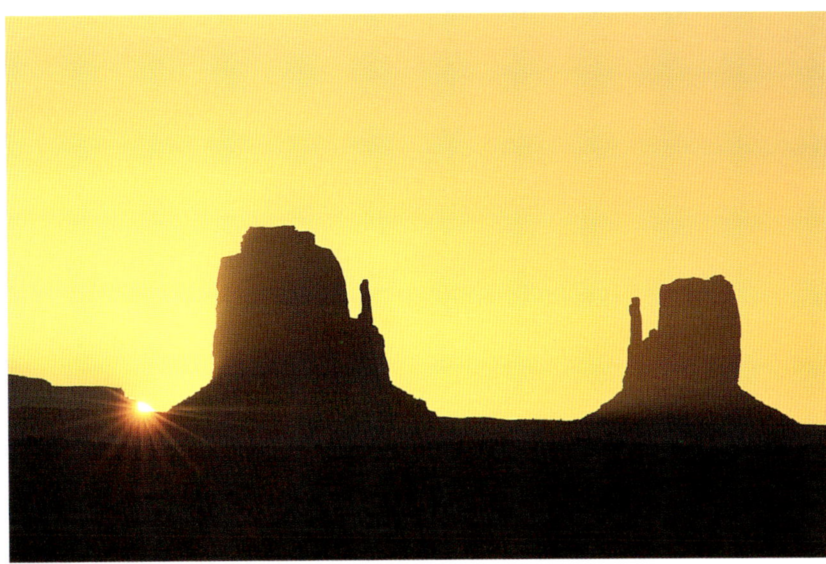

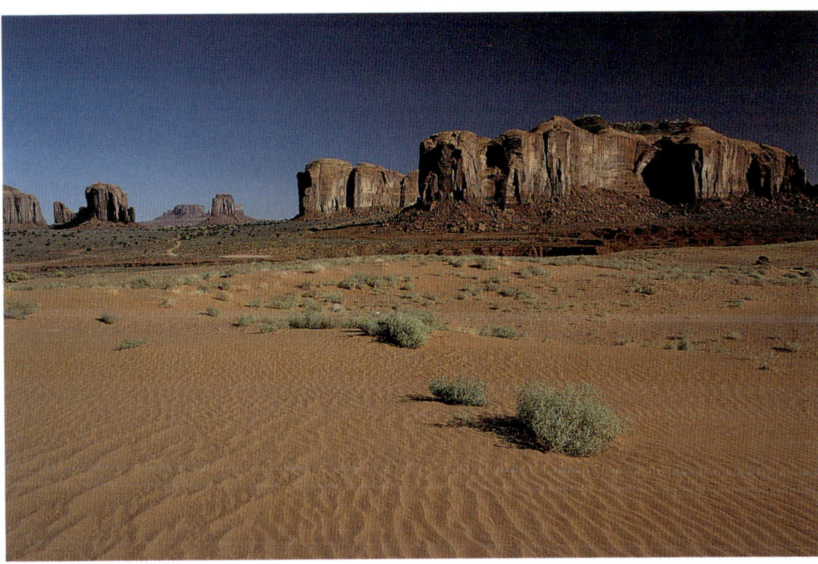

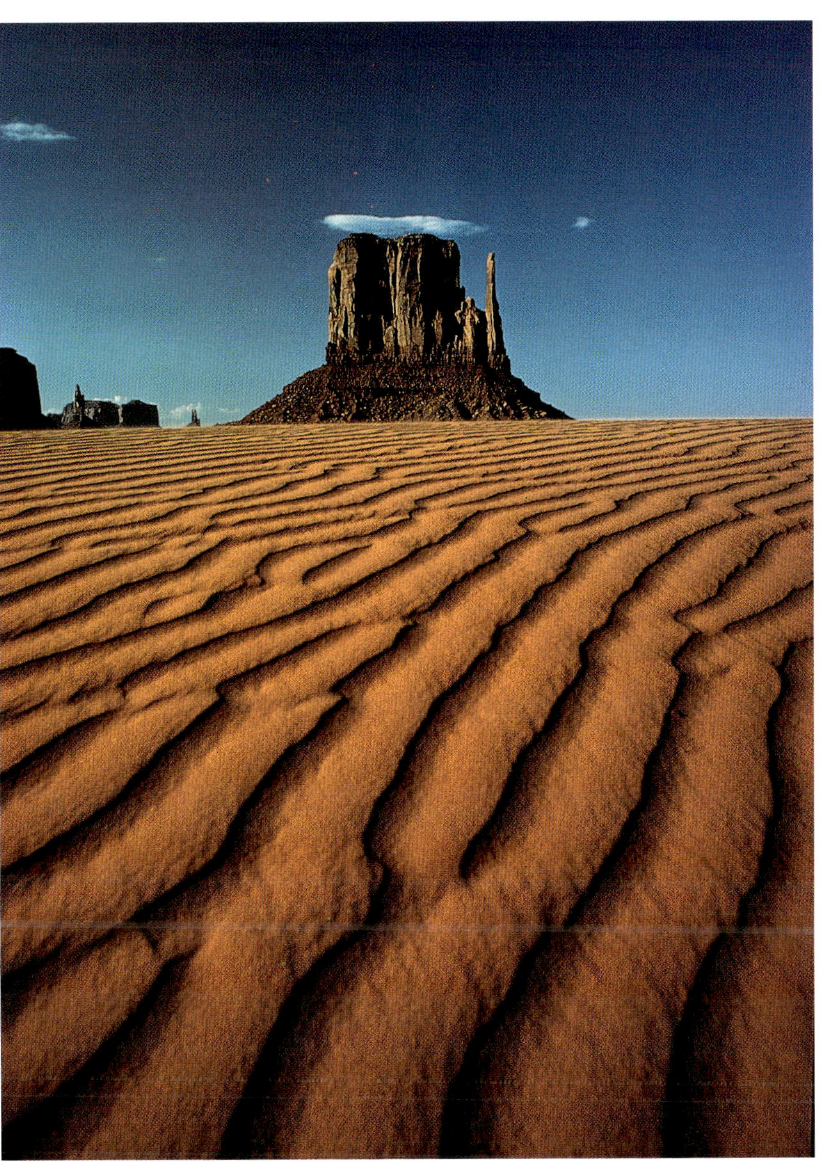

←↑↓ Monument Valley

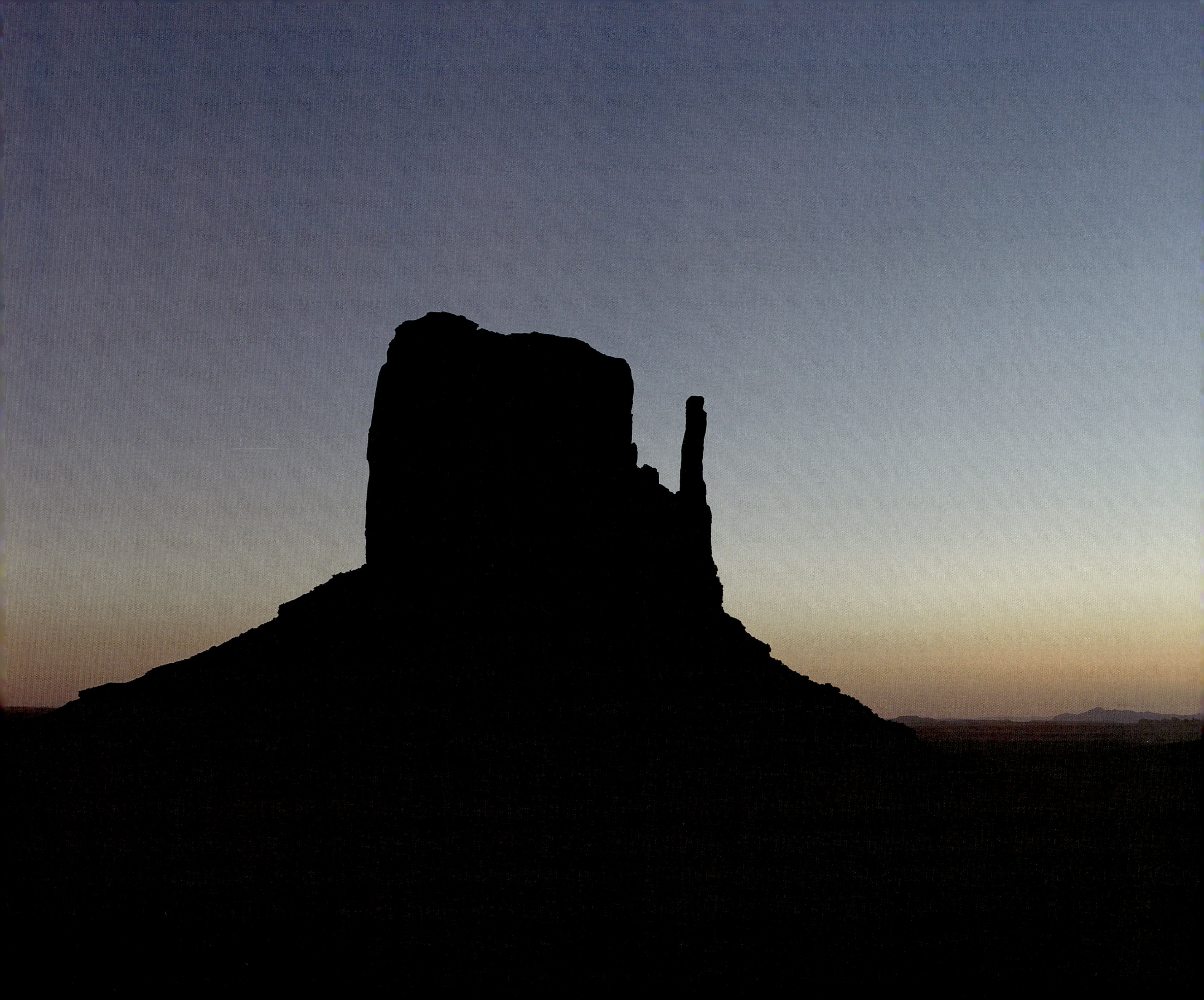

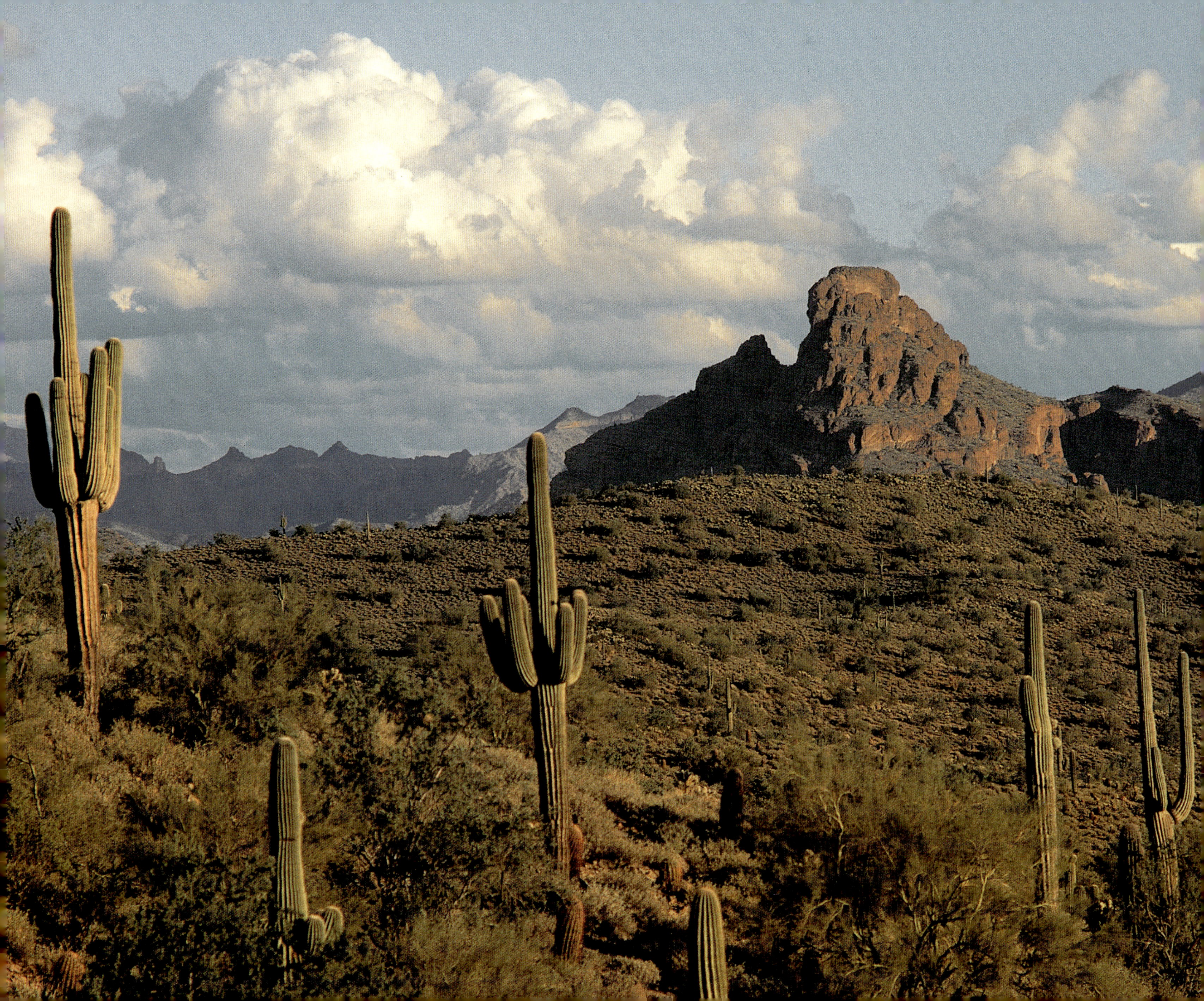

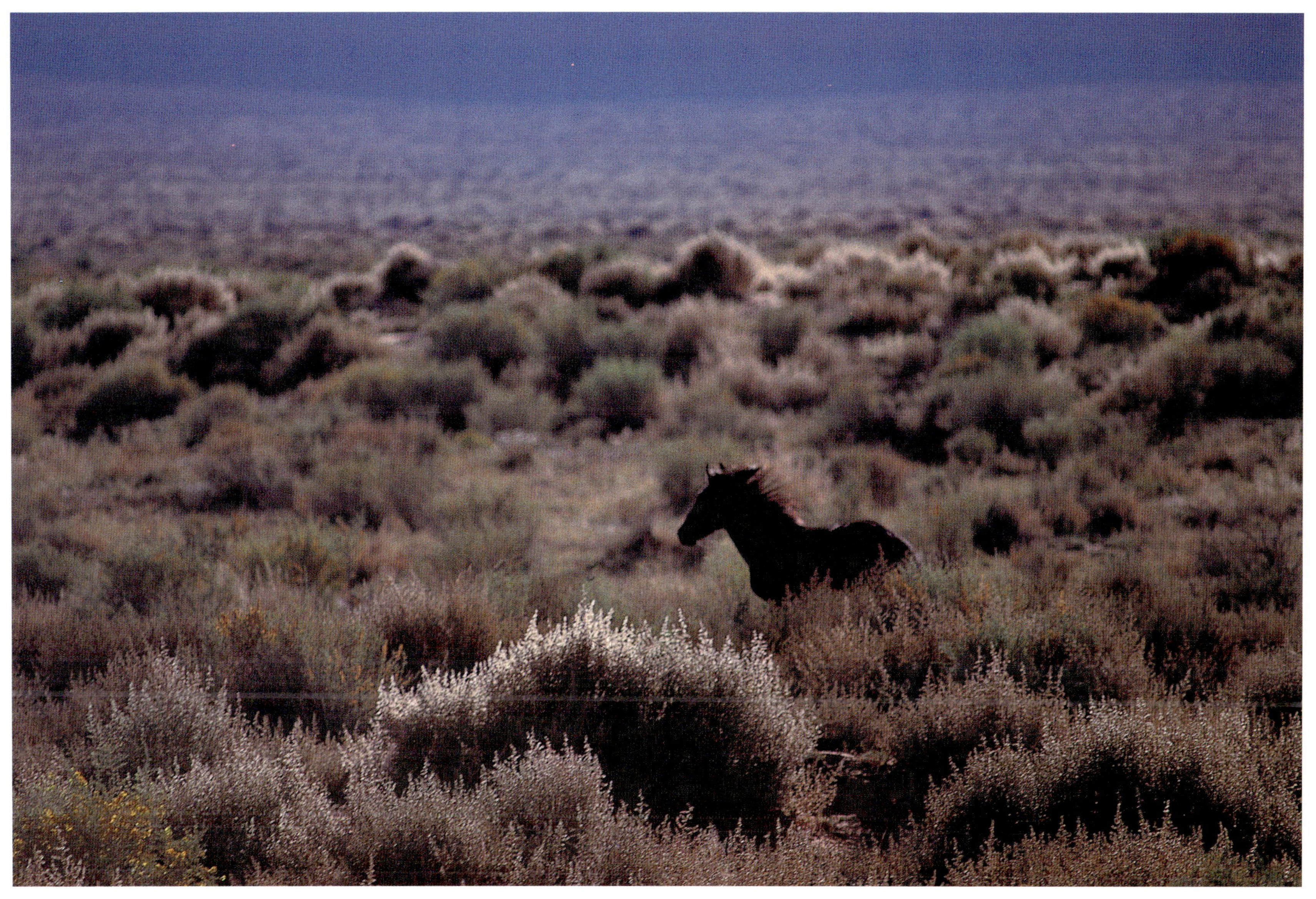

↑ Monument Valley ← Outside of Phoenix

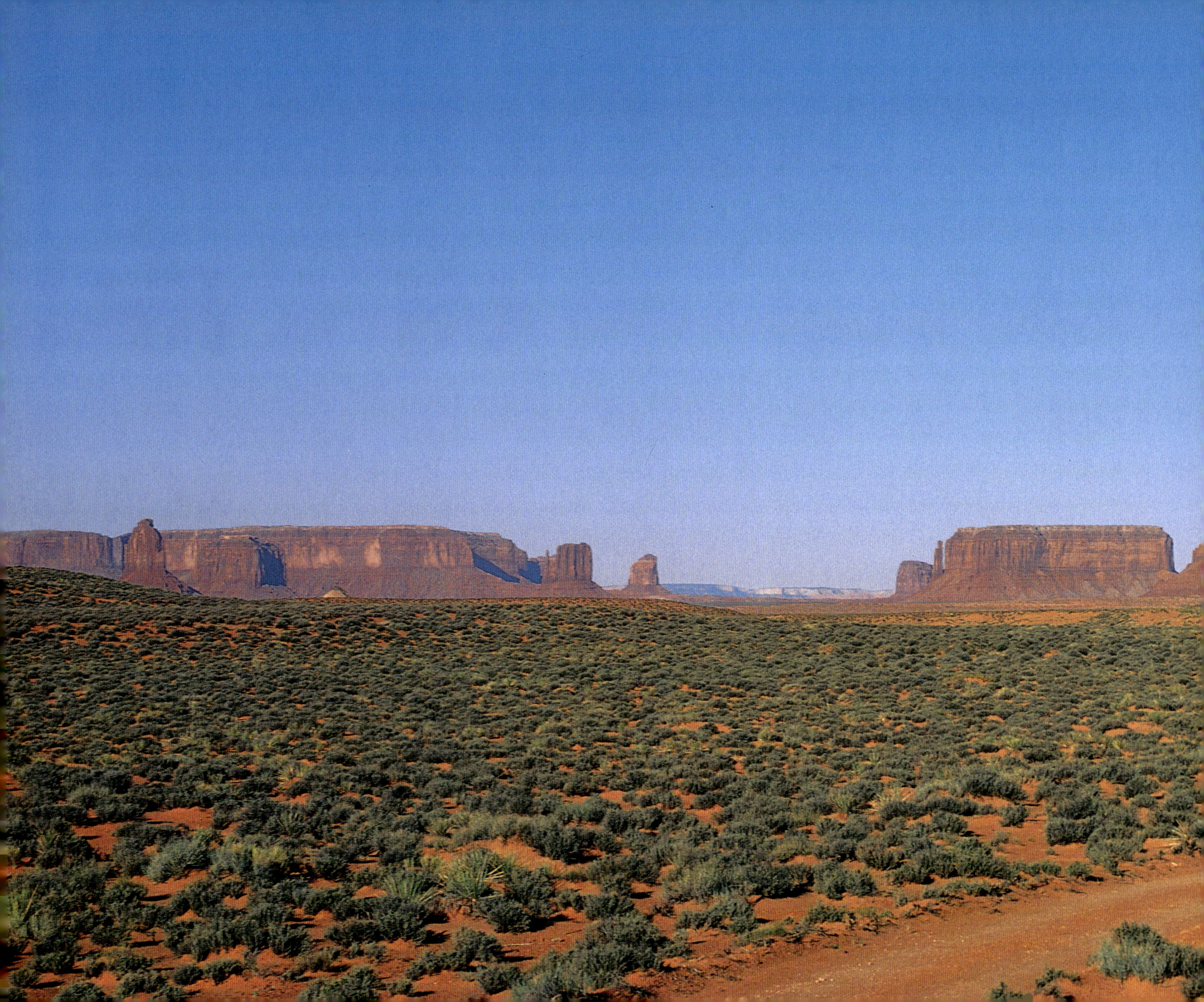

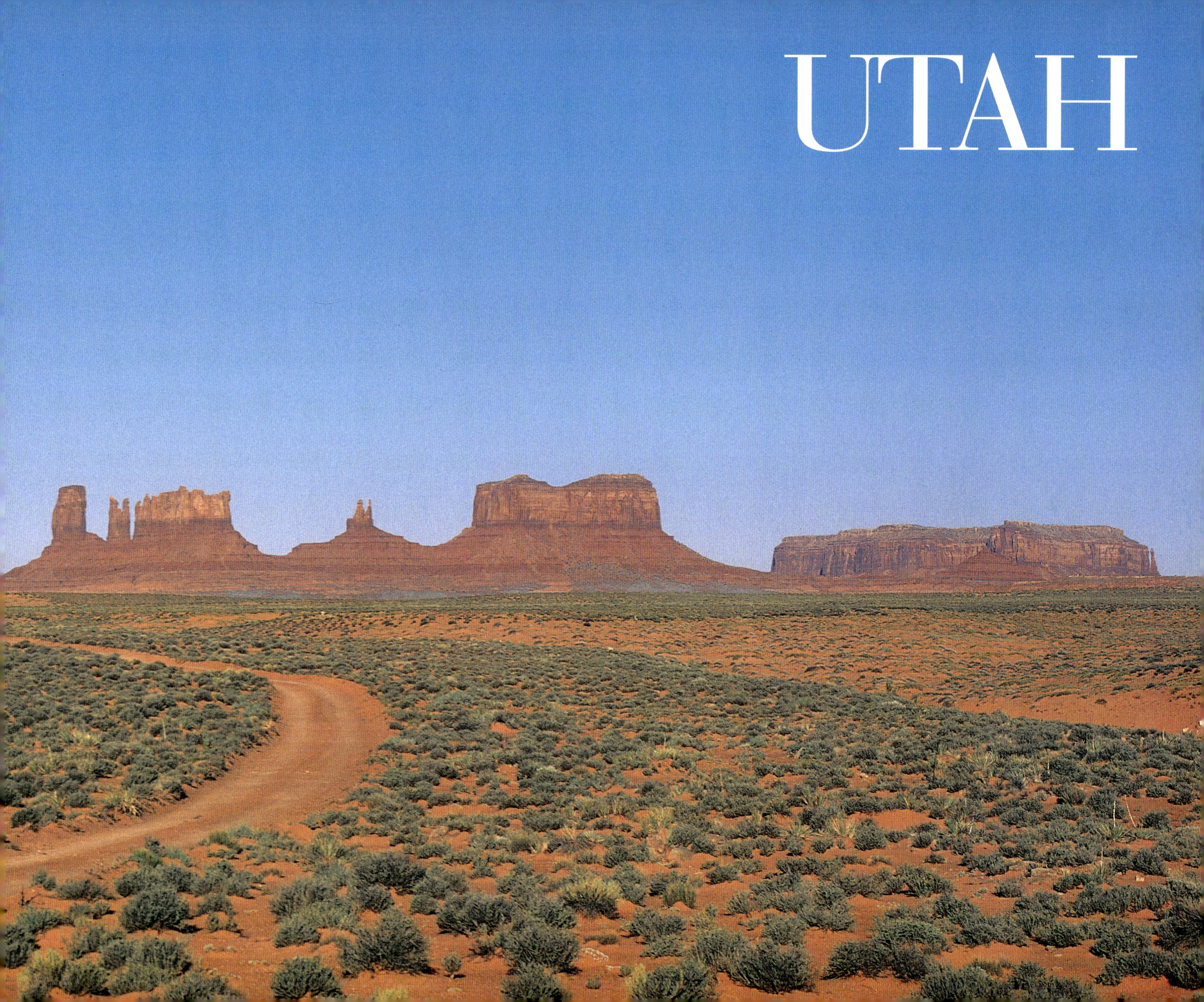
UTAH

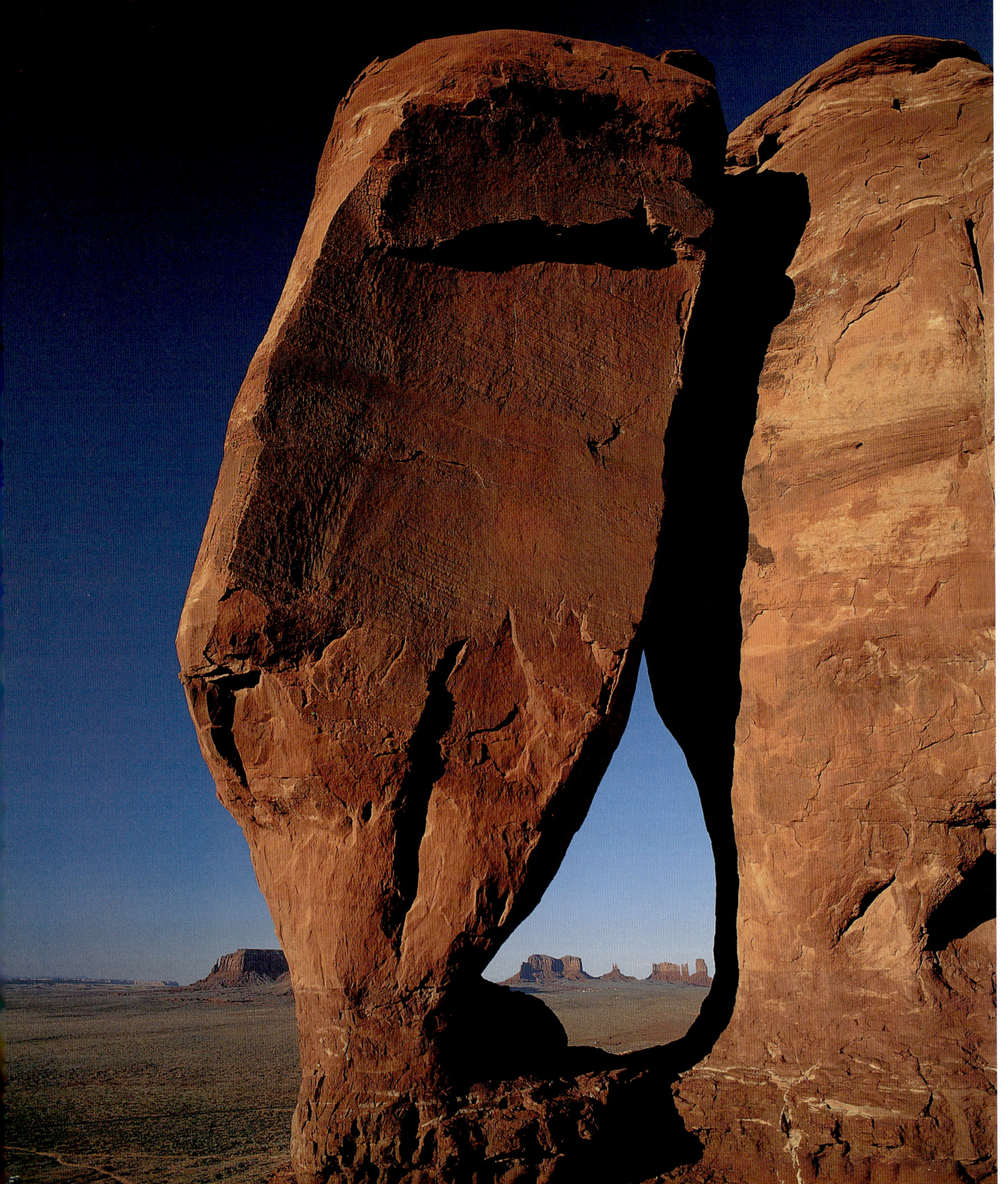

←→ Tear Drop Arch, Monument Valley
↓ Cathedral Valley, Capitol Reef National Park

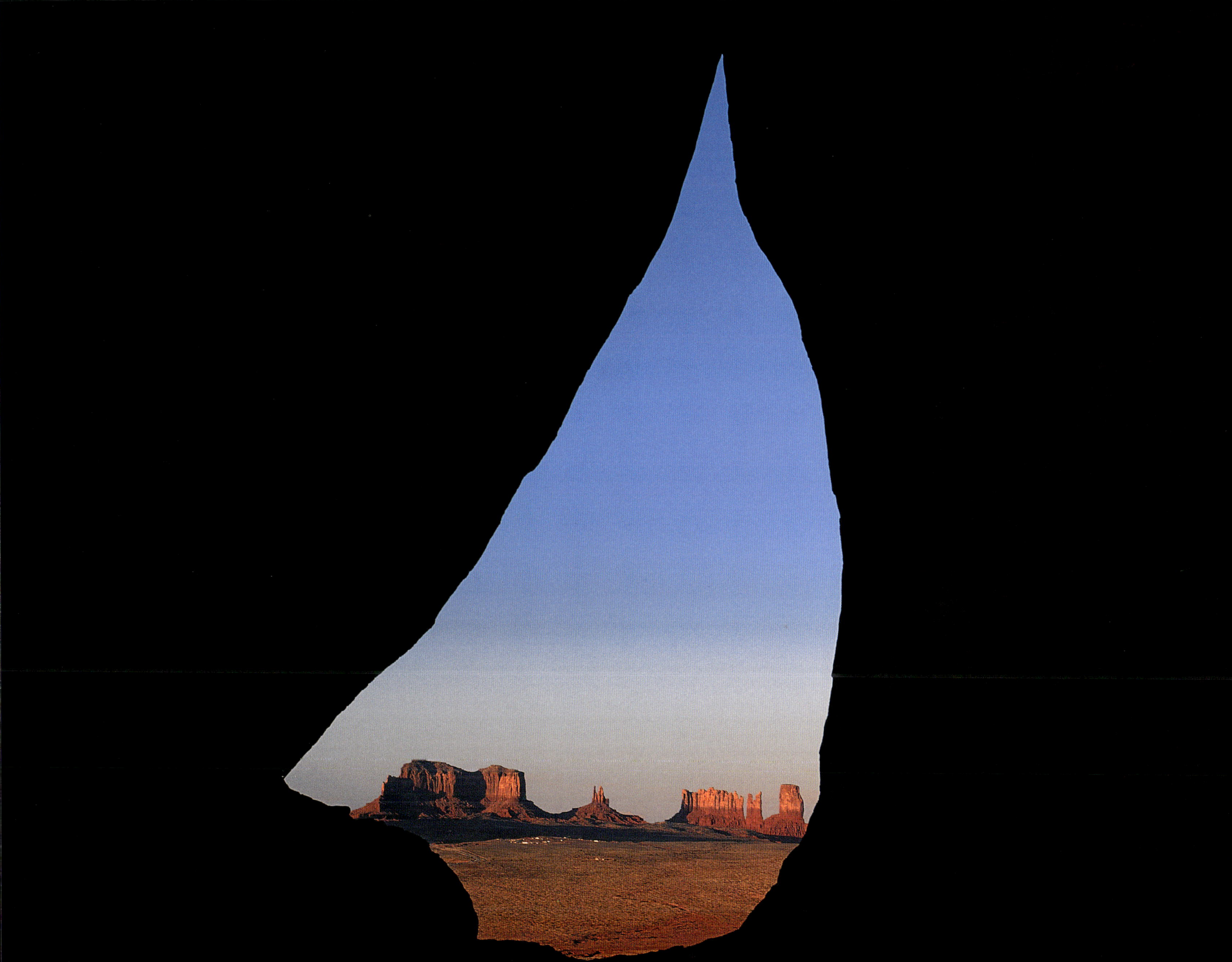

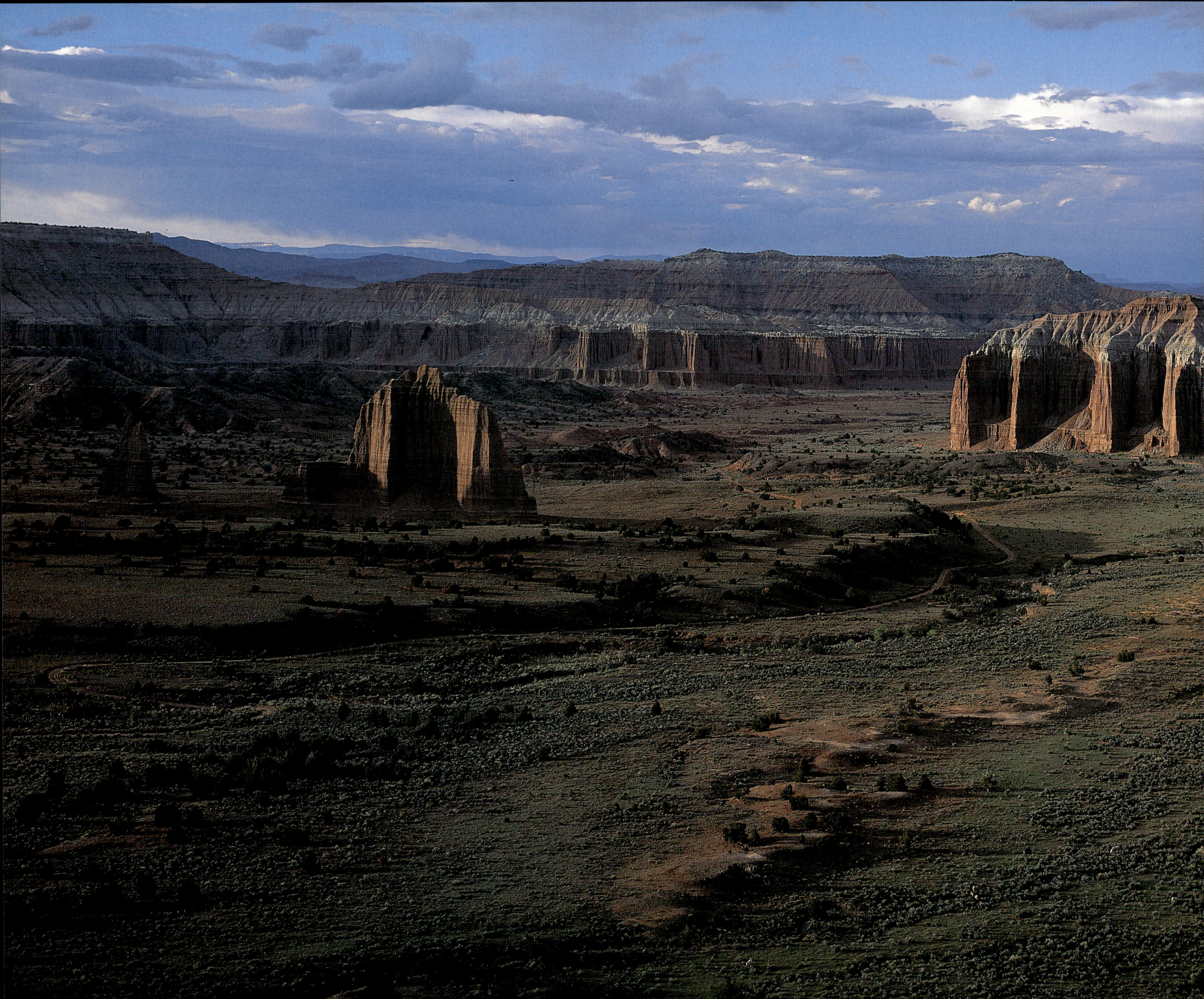

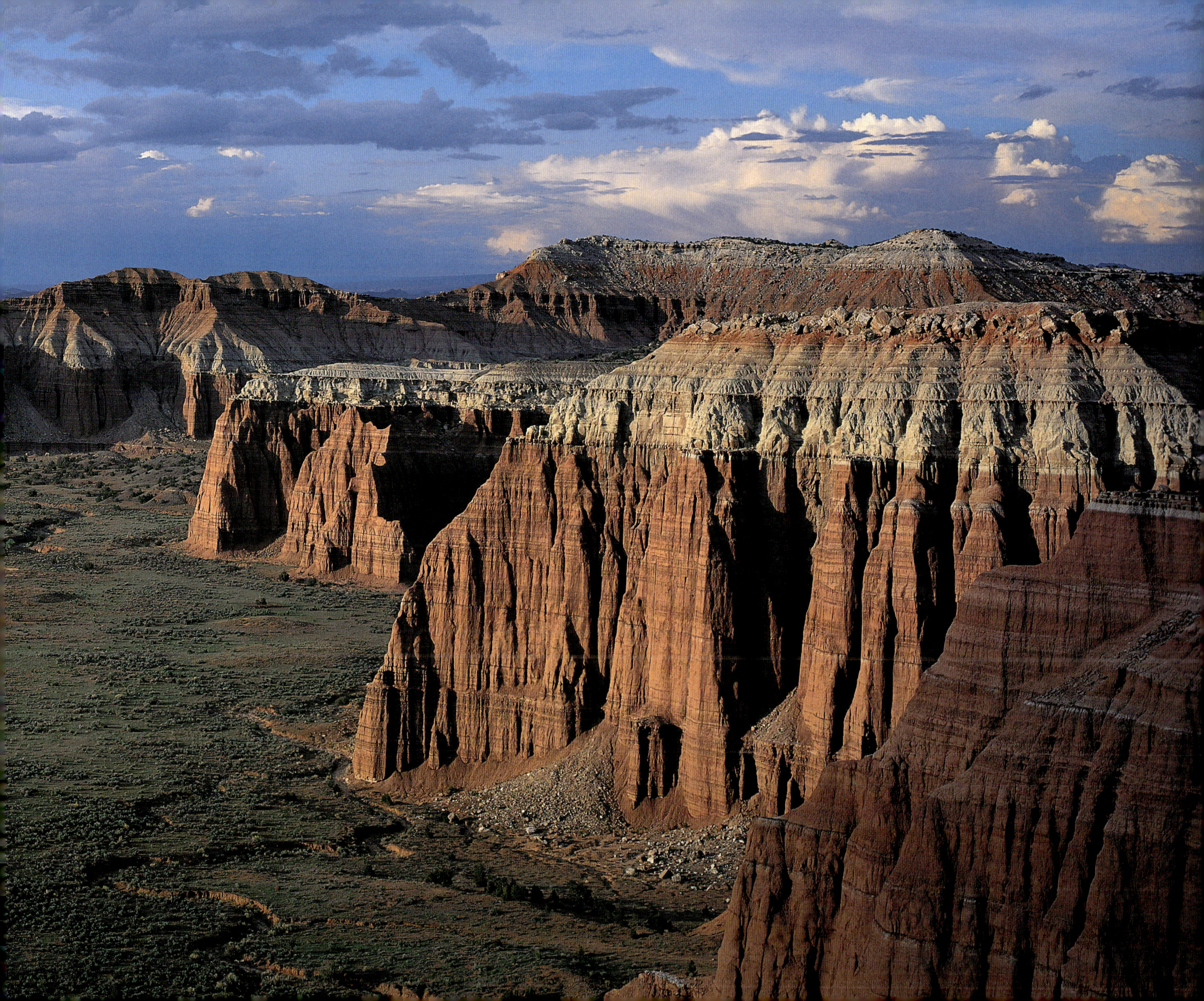

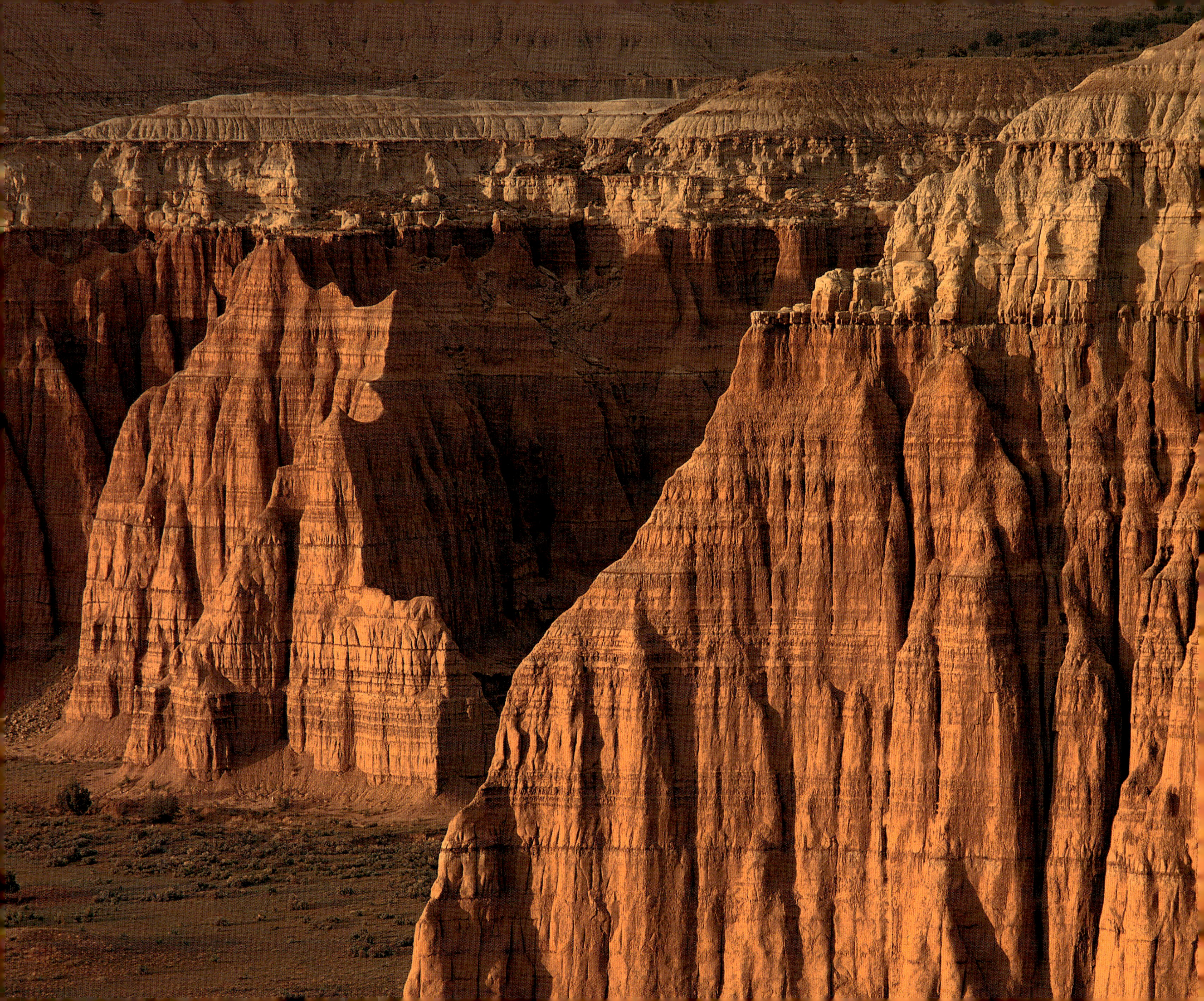

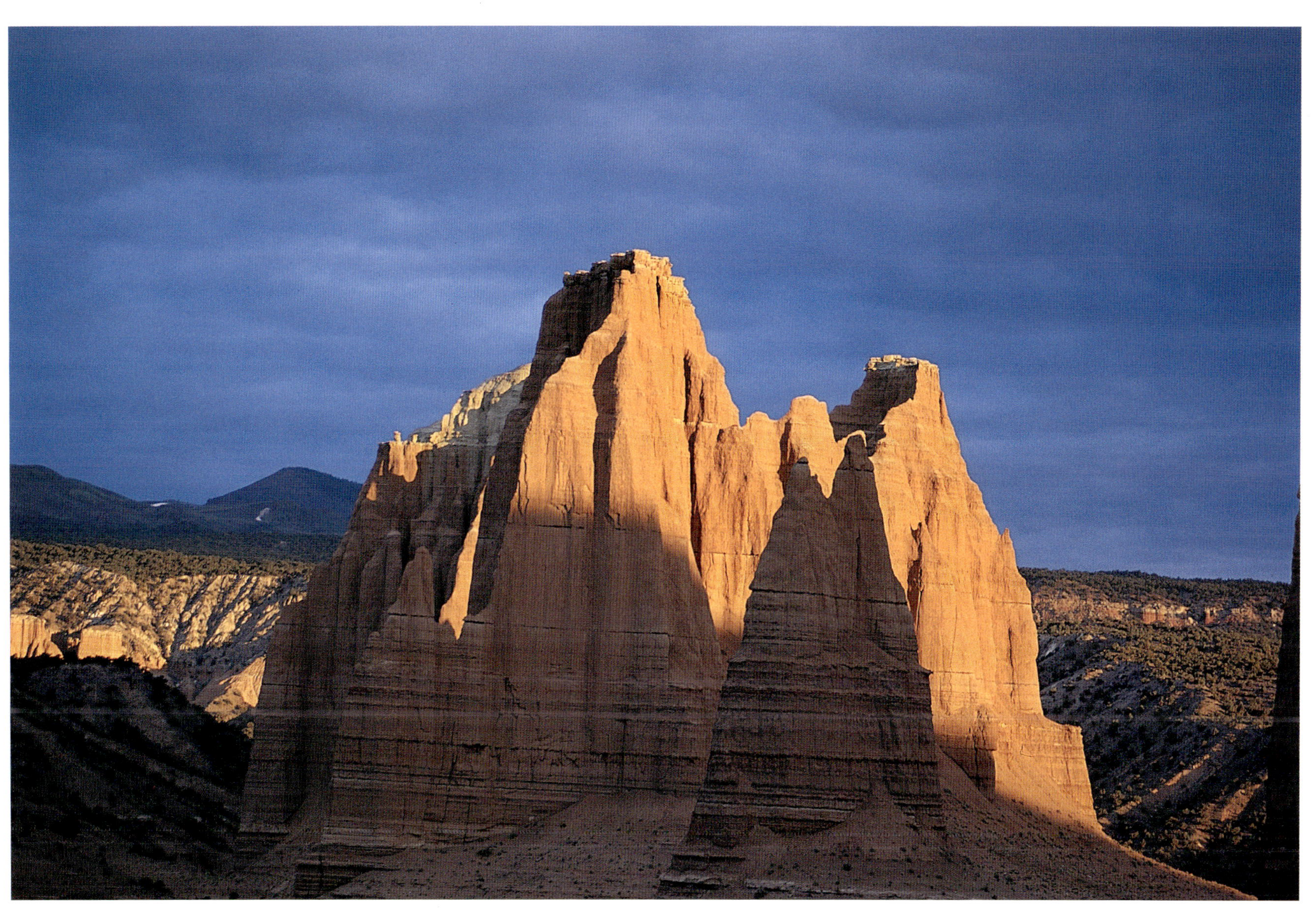

↑← Cathedral Valley, Capitol Reef National Park

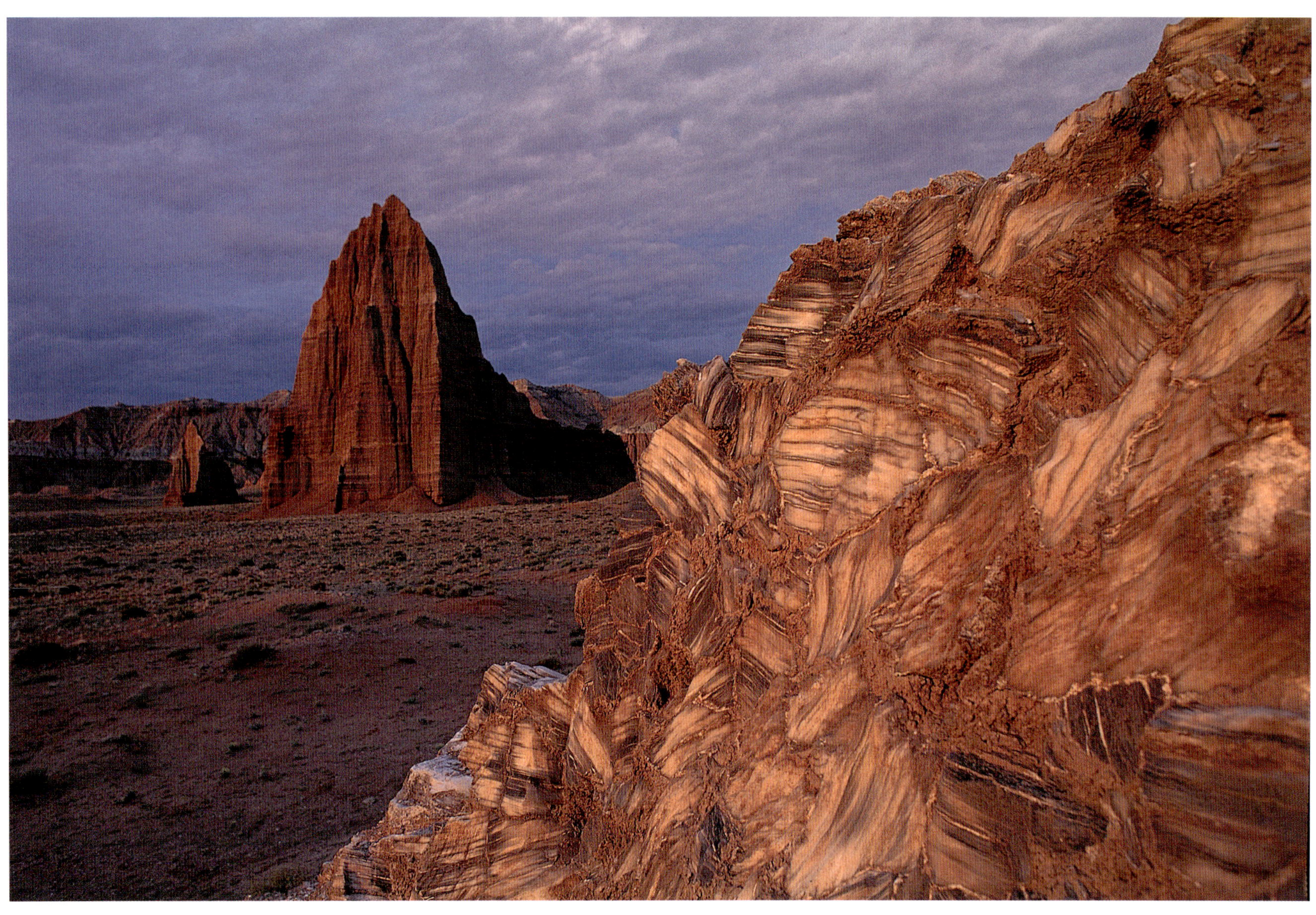

↑→Glass Mountain and Temples of the Sun and Moon, Cathedral Valley, Capitol Reef National Park ↓ Glen Canyon National Recreation Area

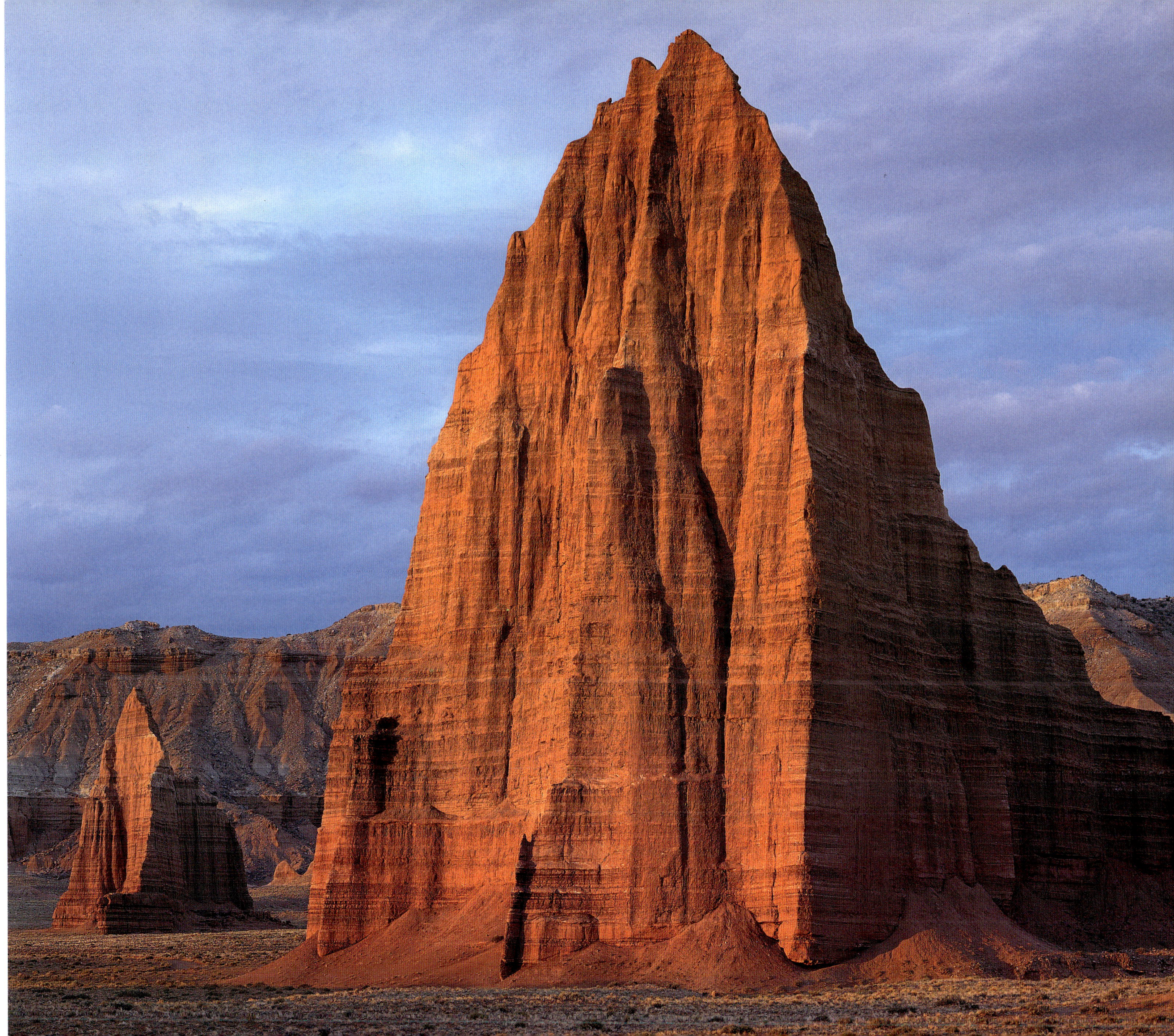

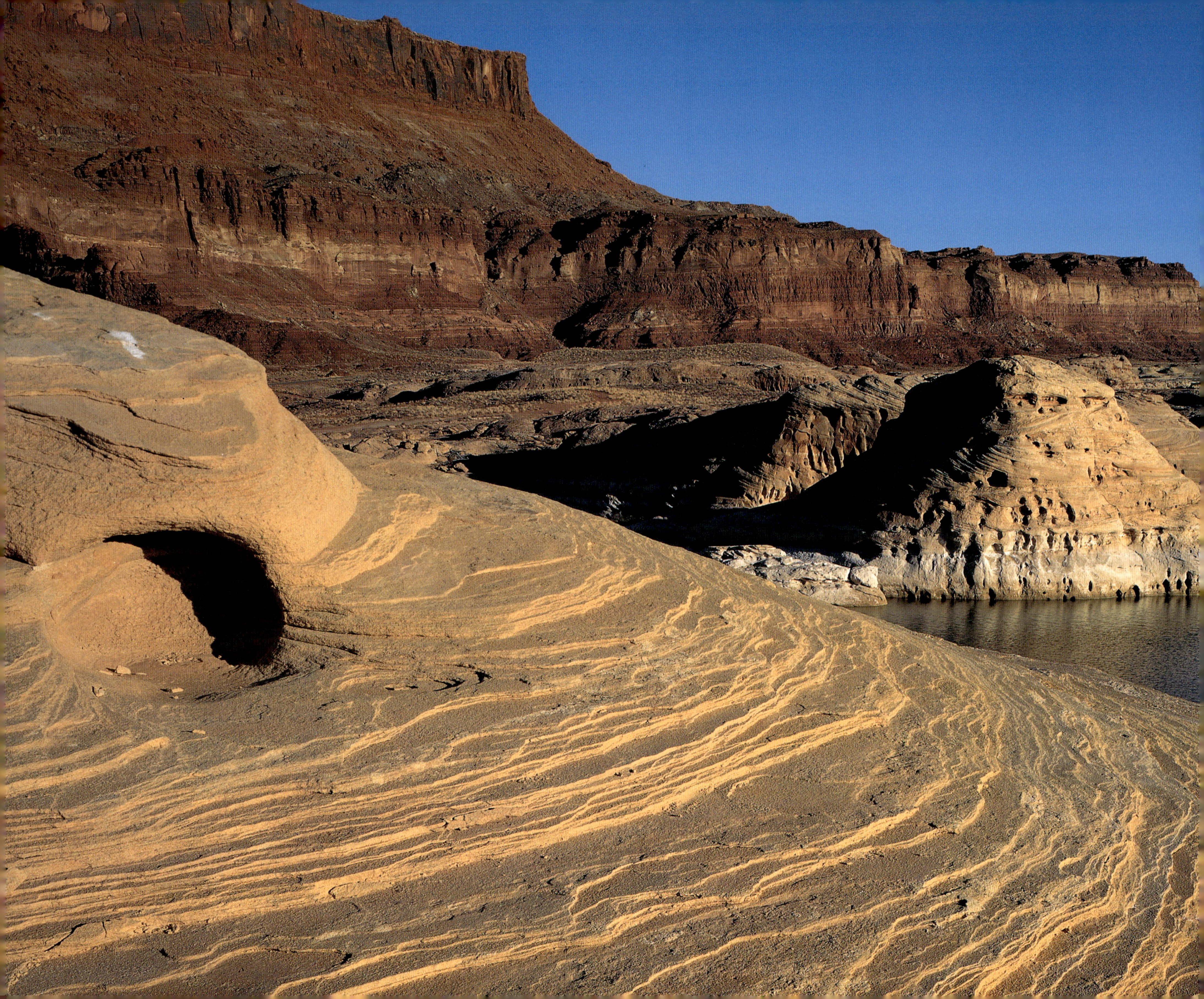

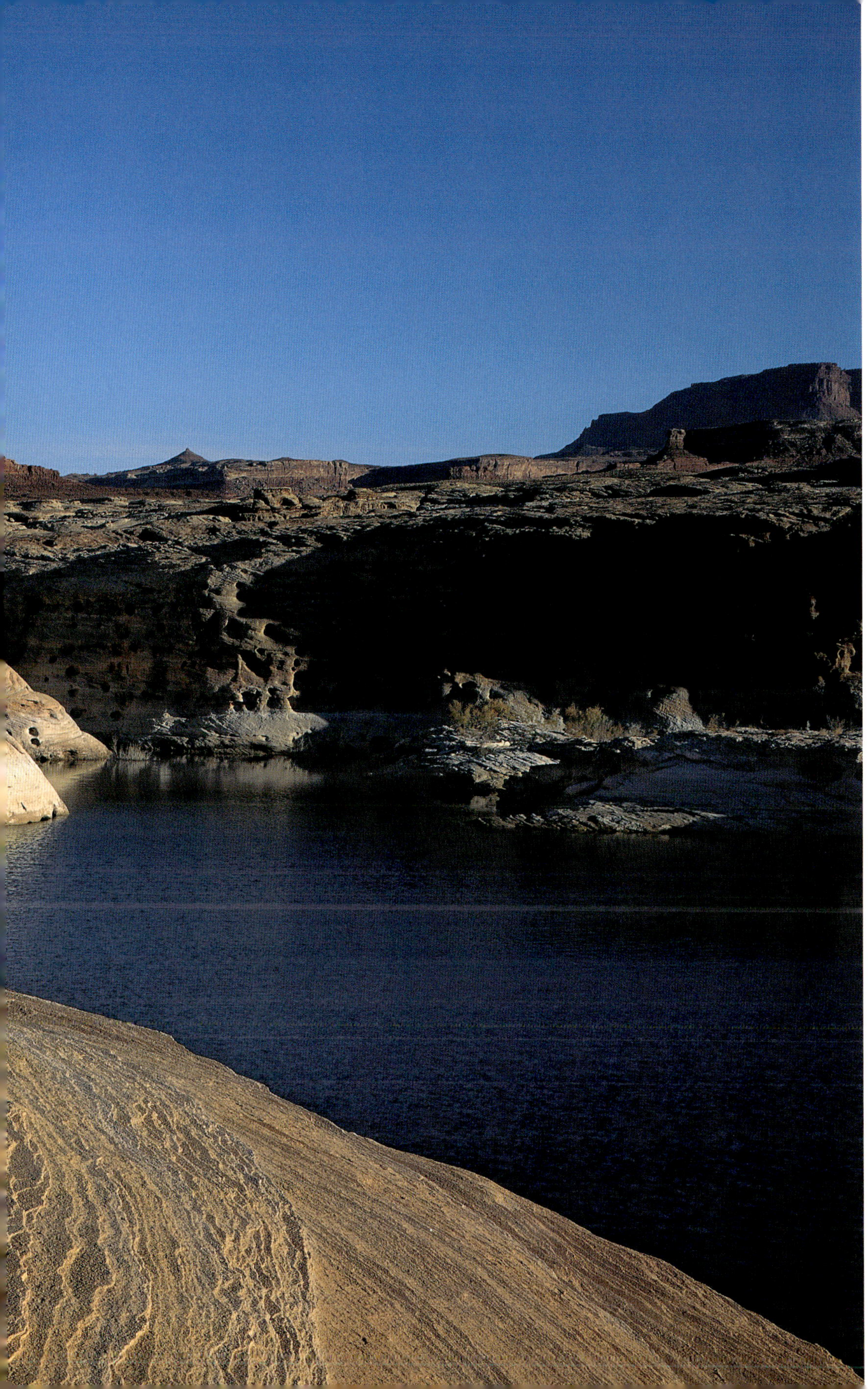

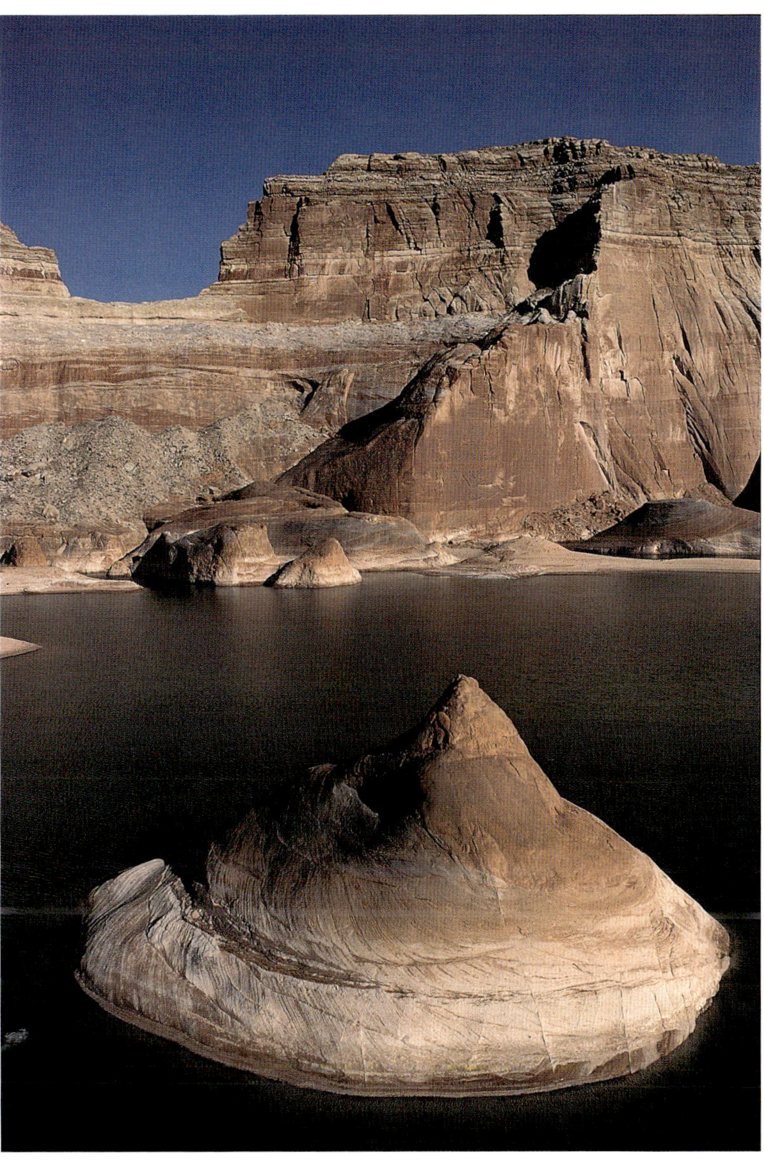

↑←Lake Powell, Glen Canyon National Recreation Area

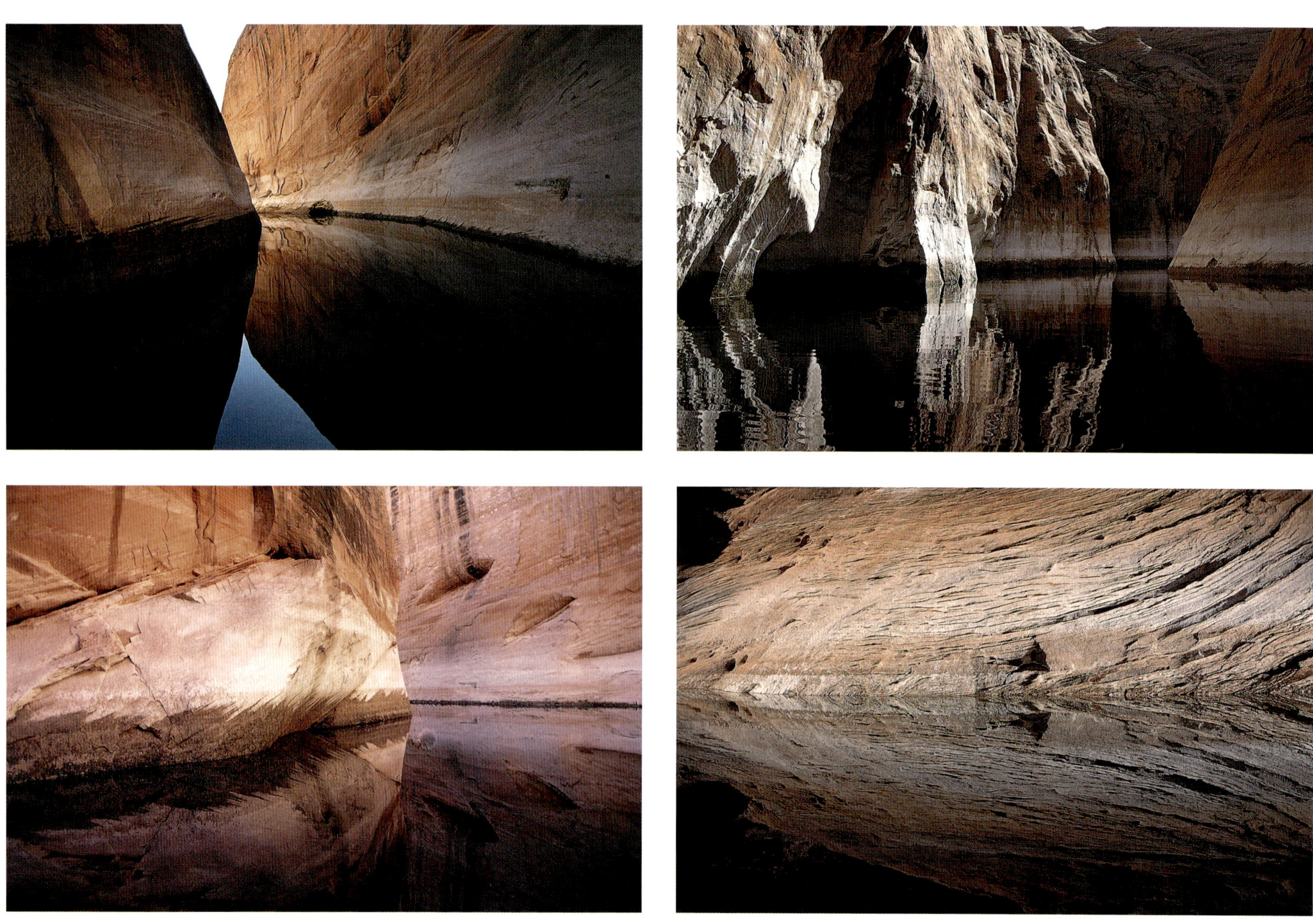

↑→↓ Lake Powell, Glen Canyon National Recreation Area

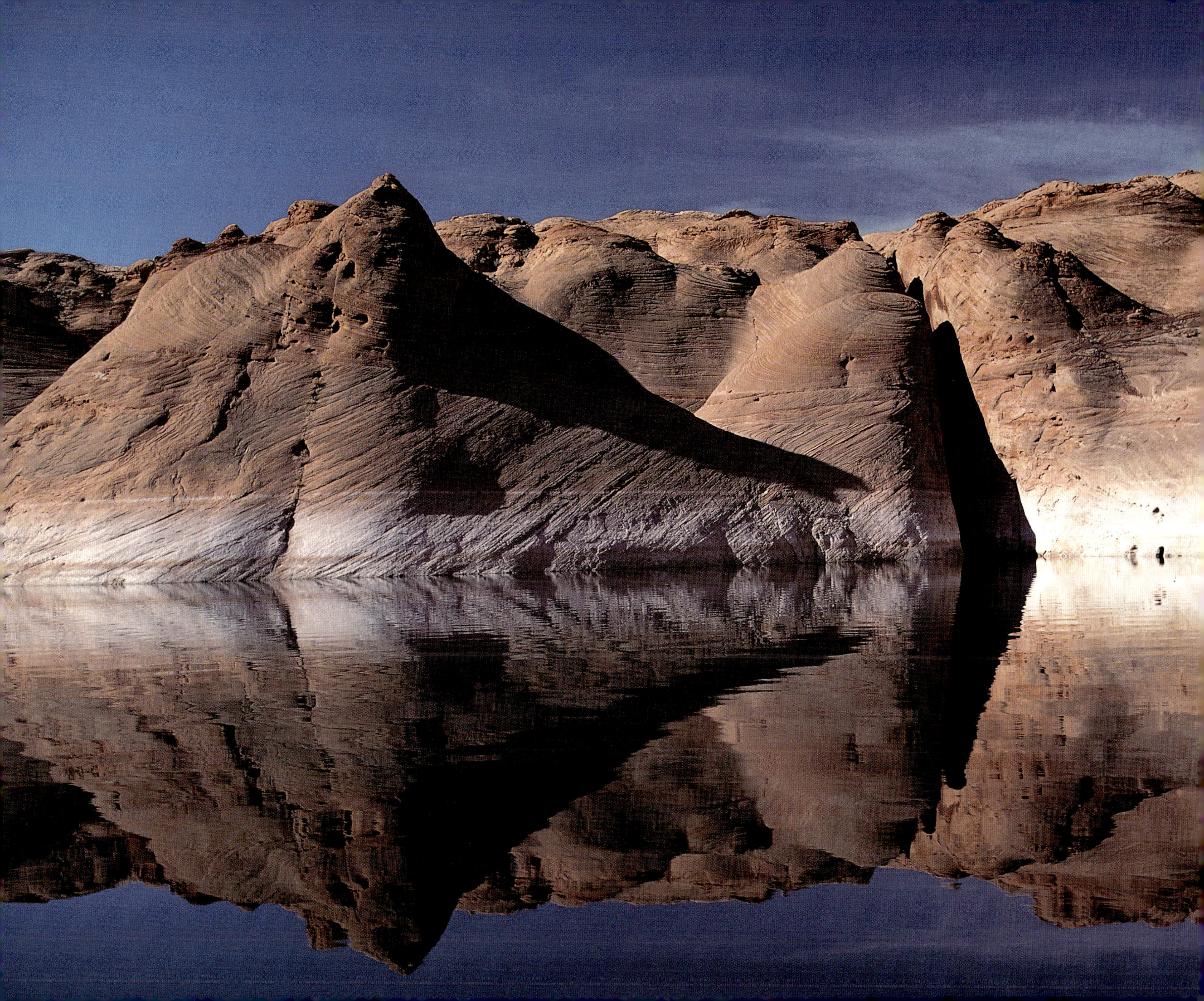

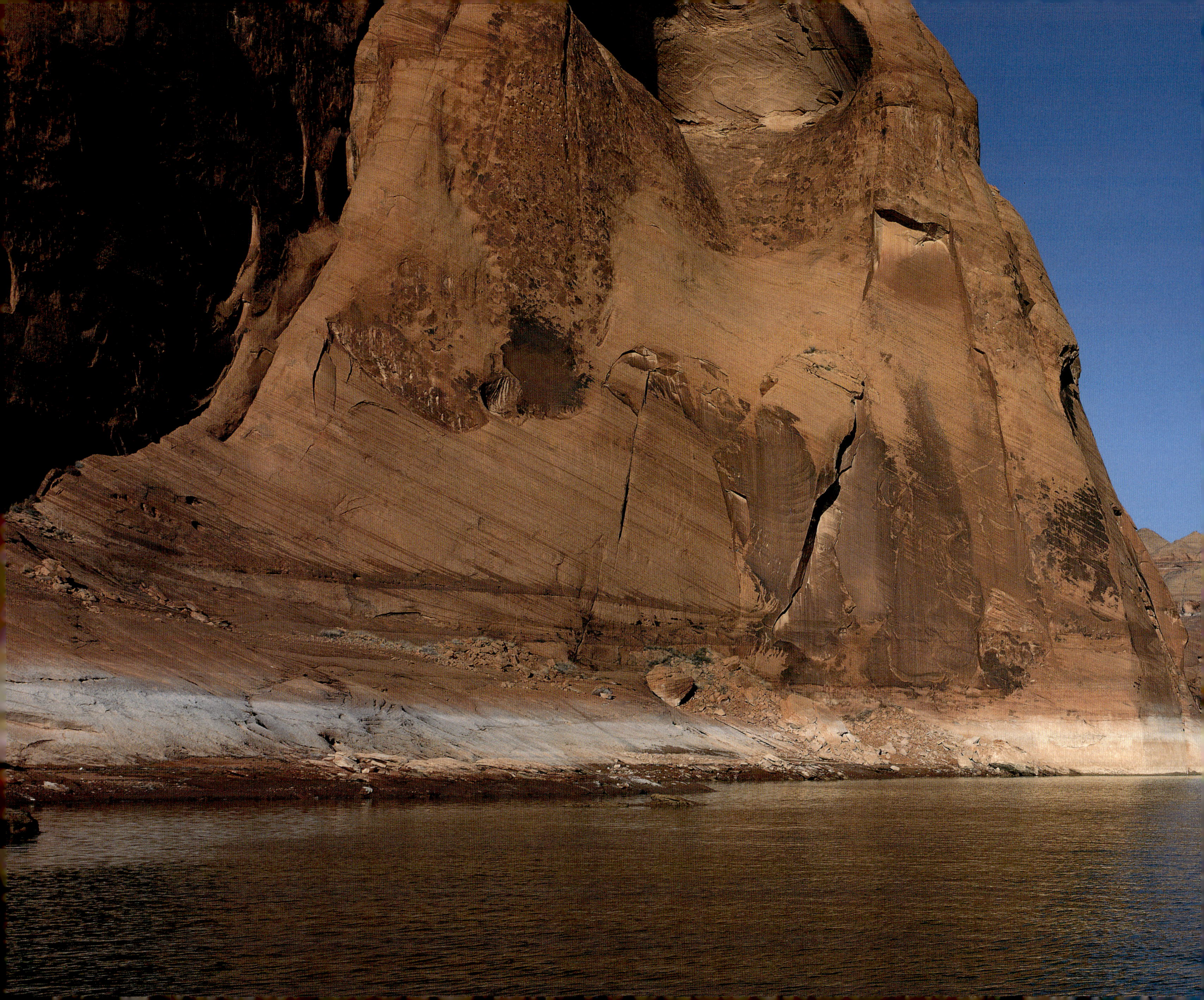

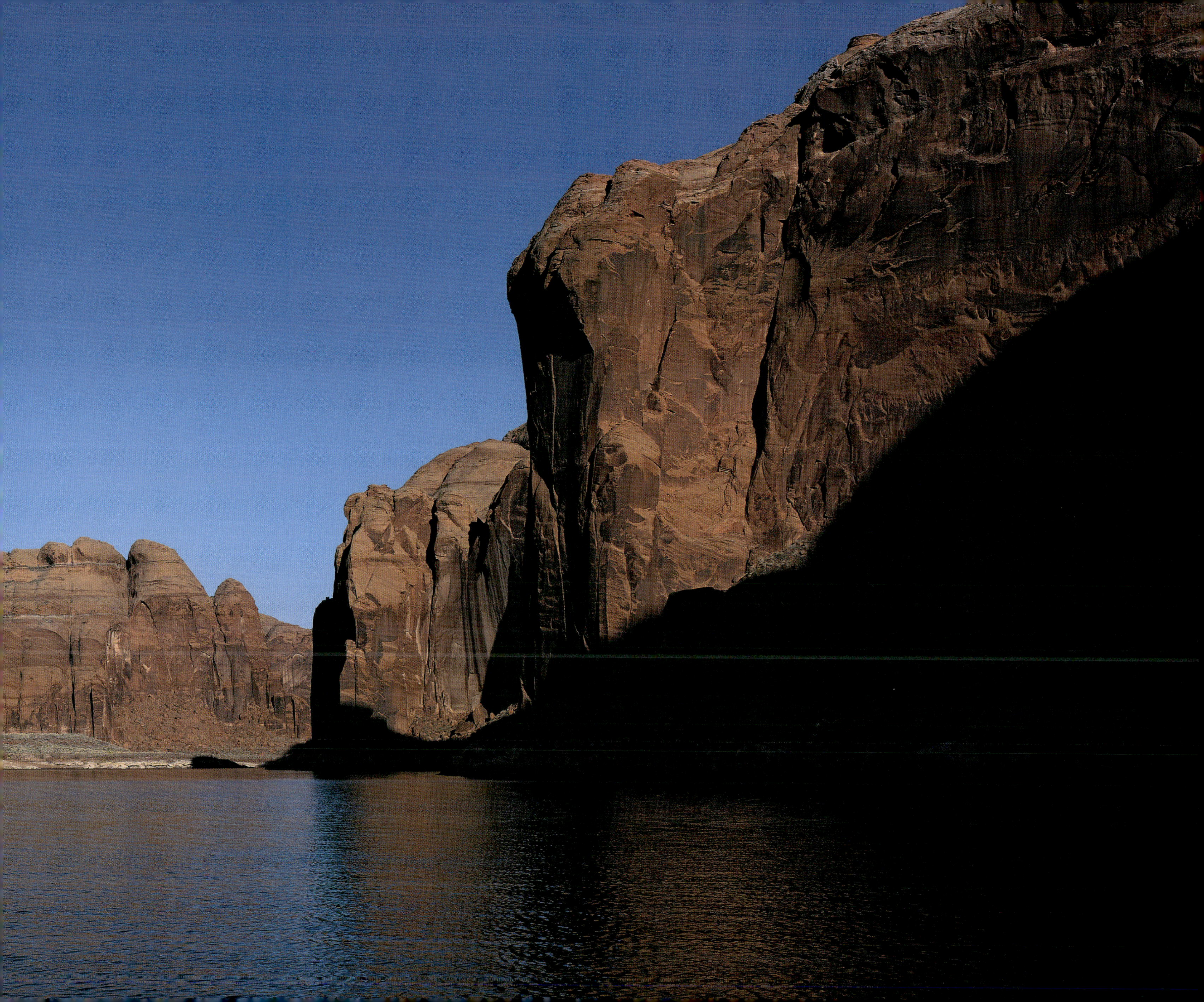

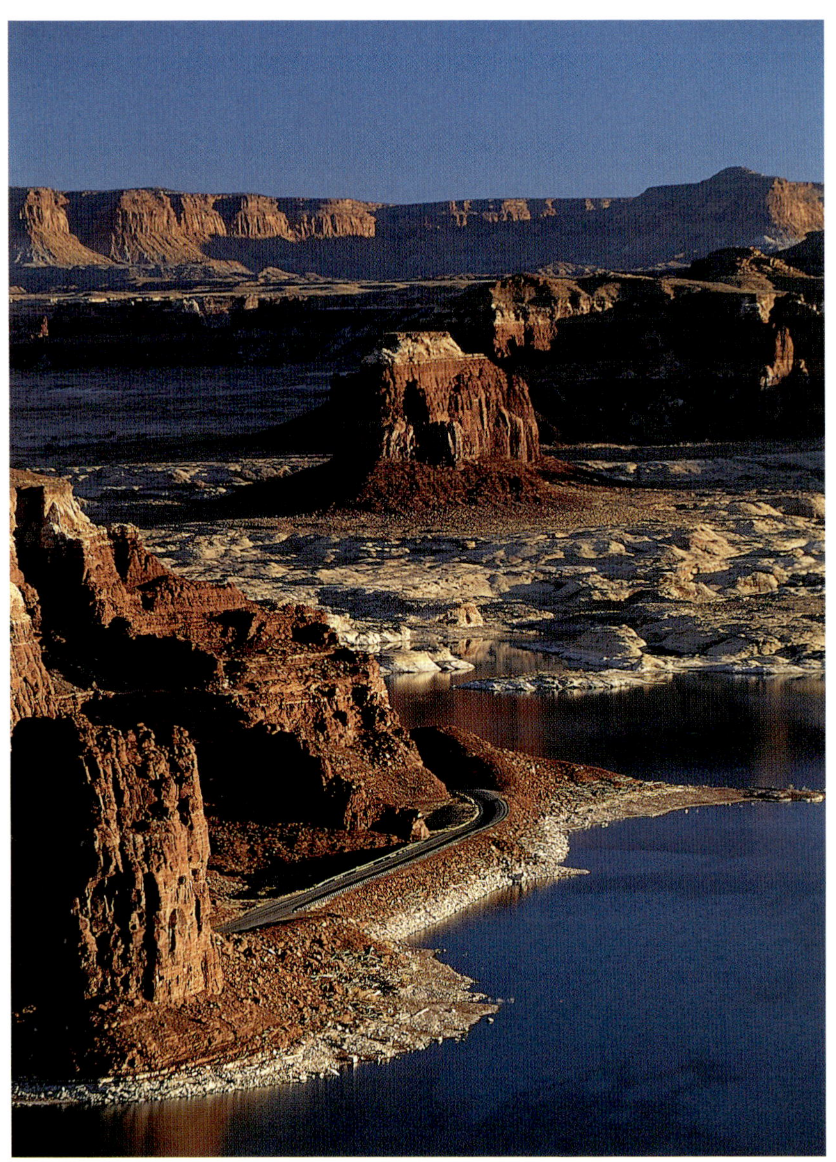

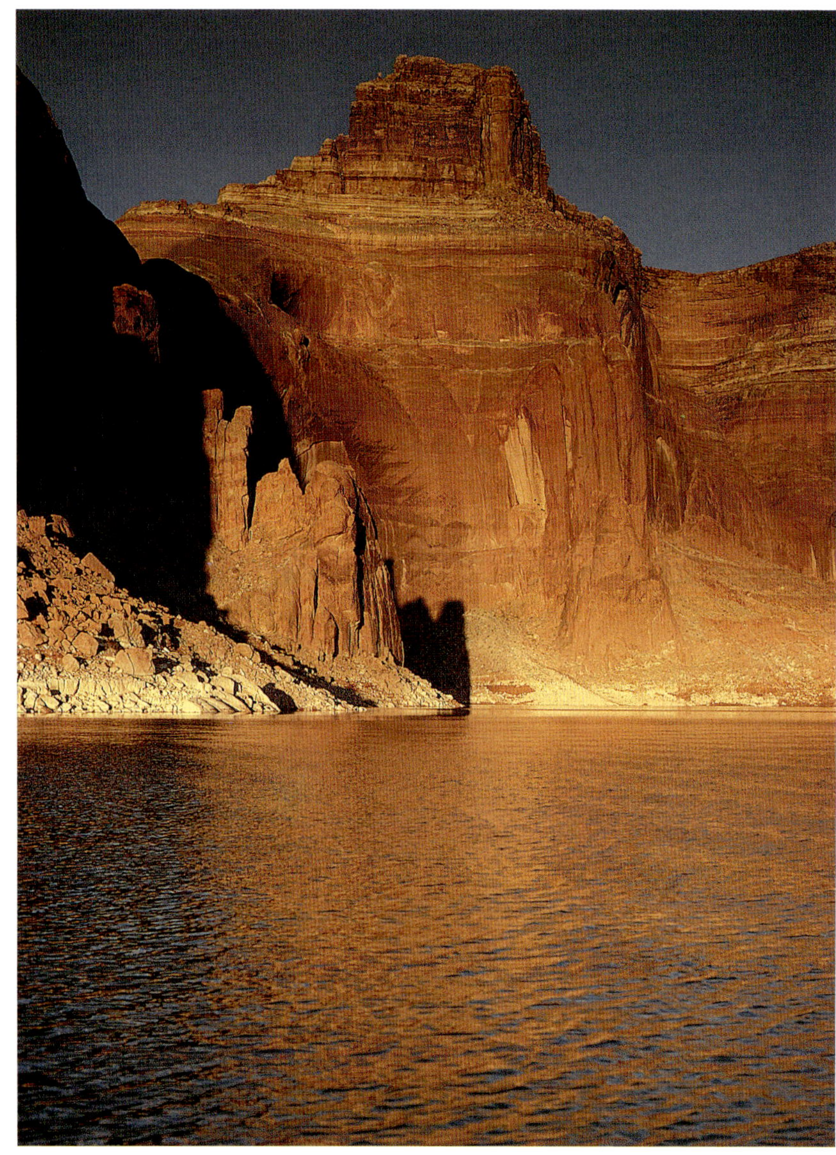

↑→↓ Lake Powell, Glen Canyon National Recreation Area

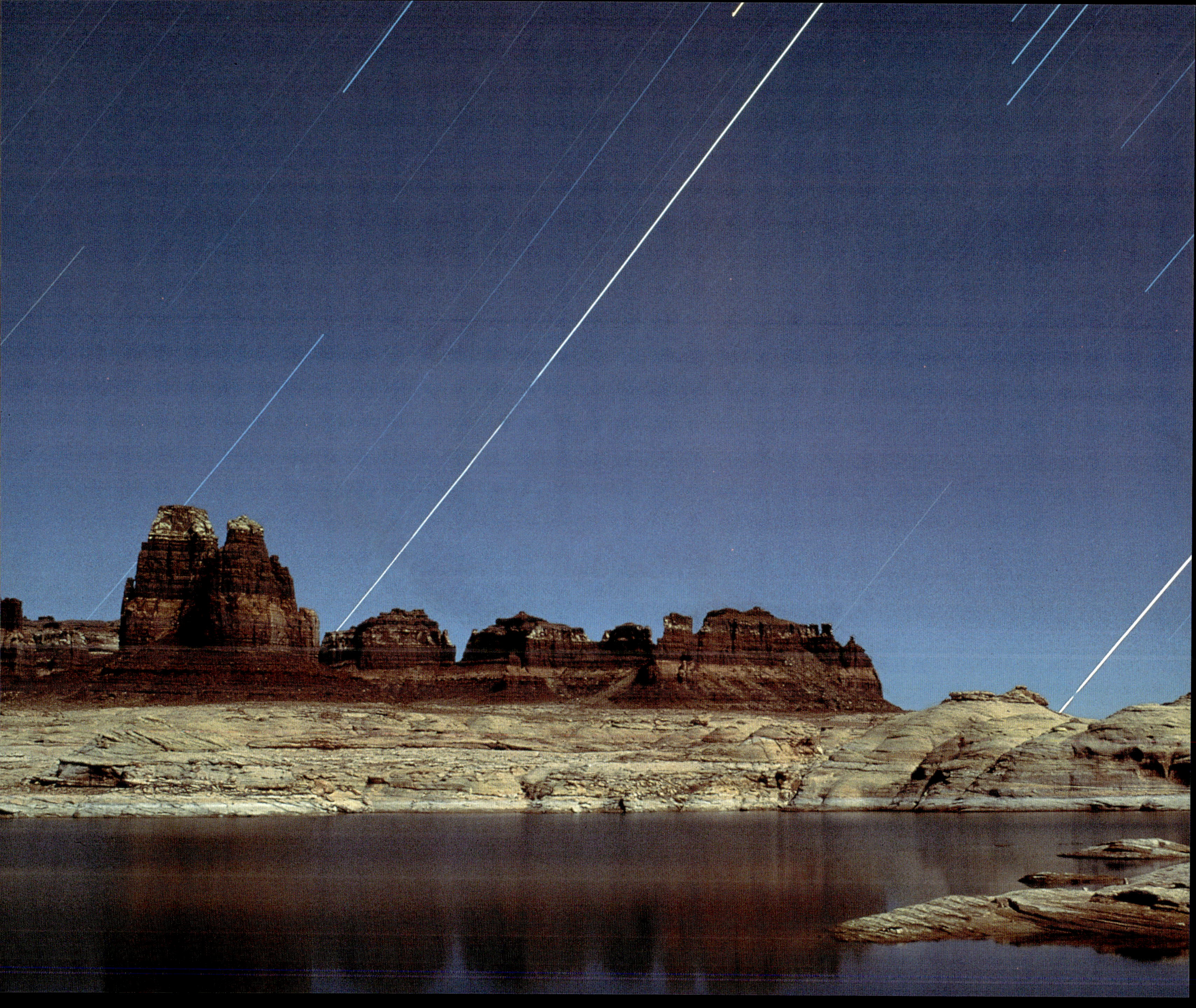

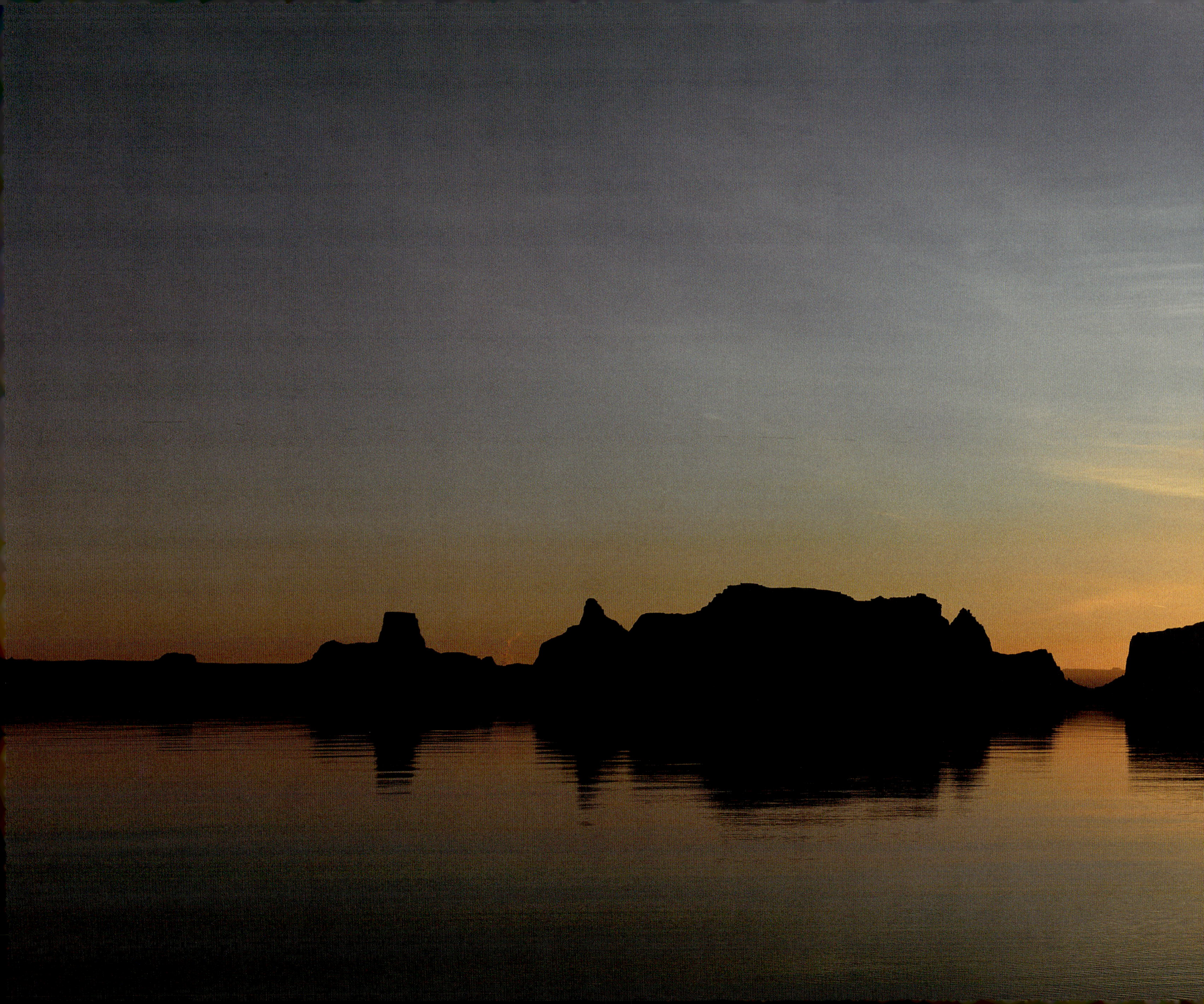

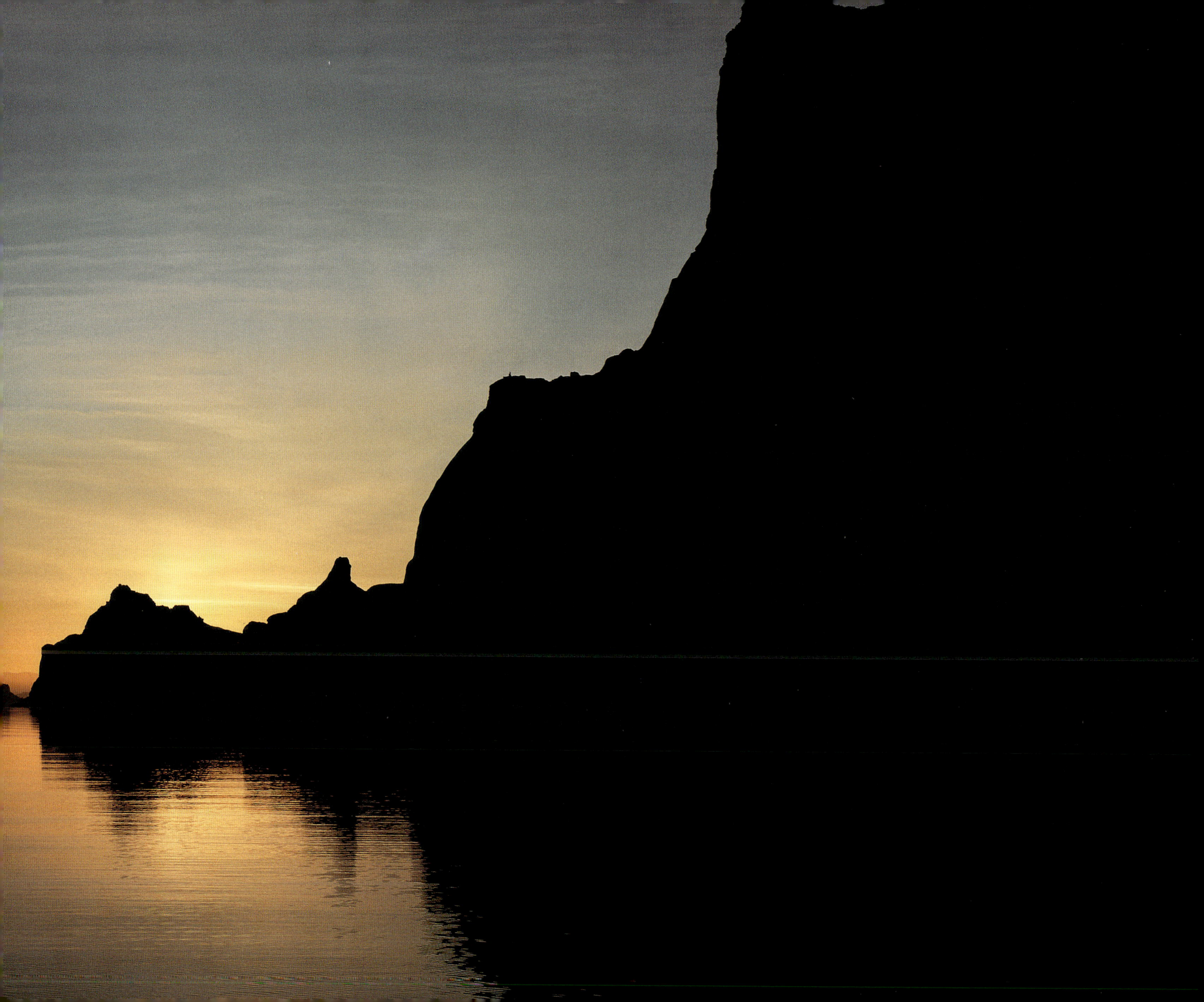

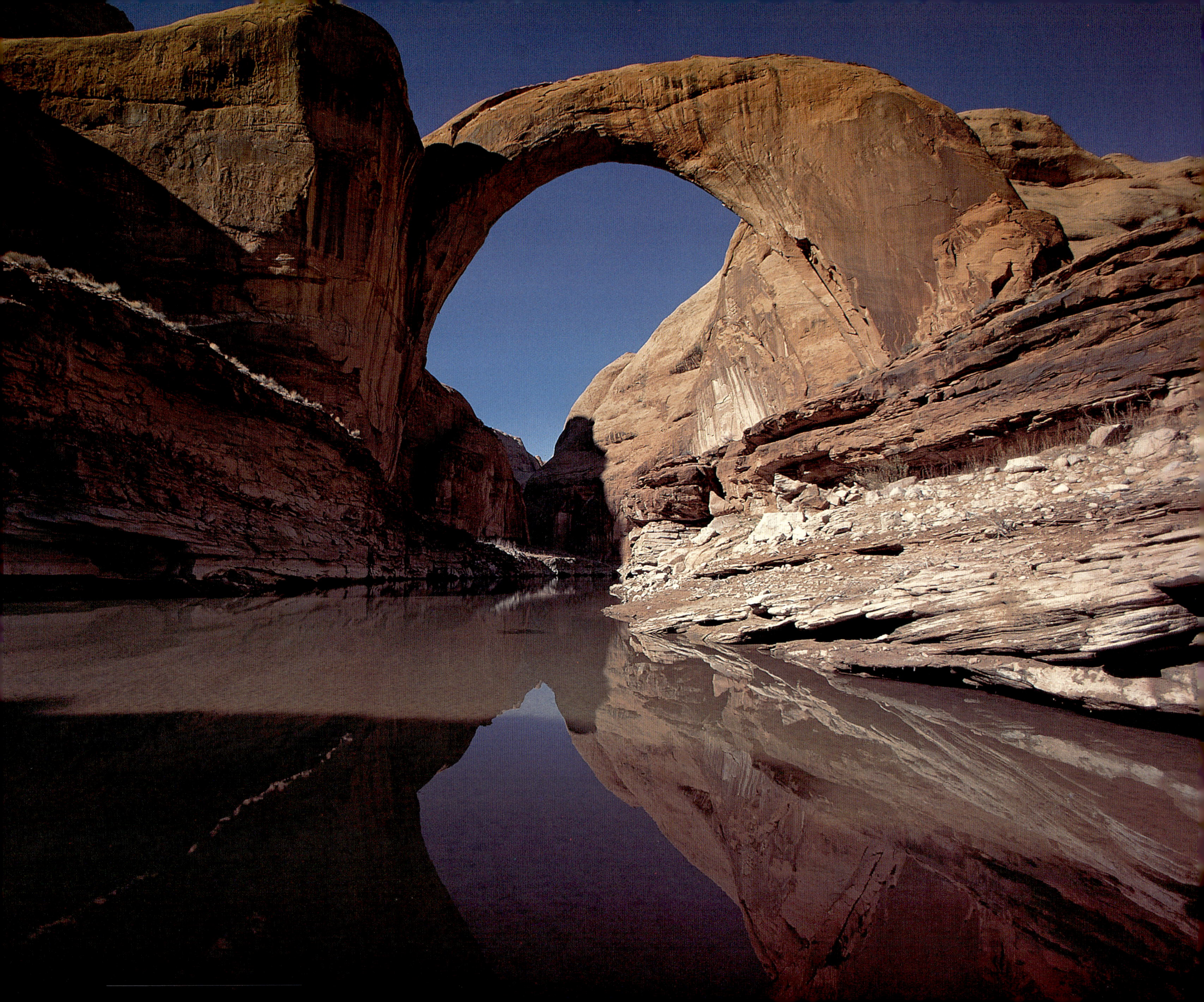

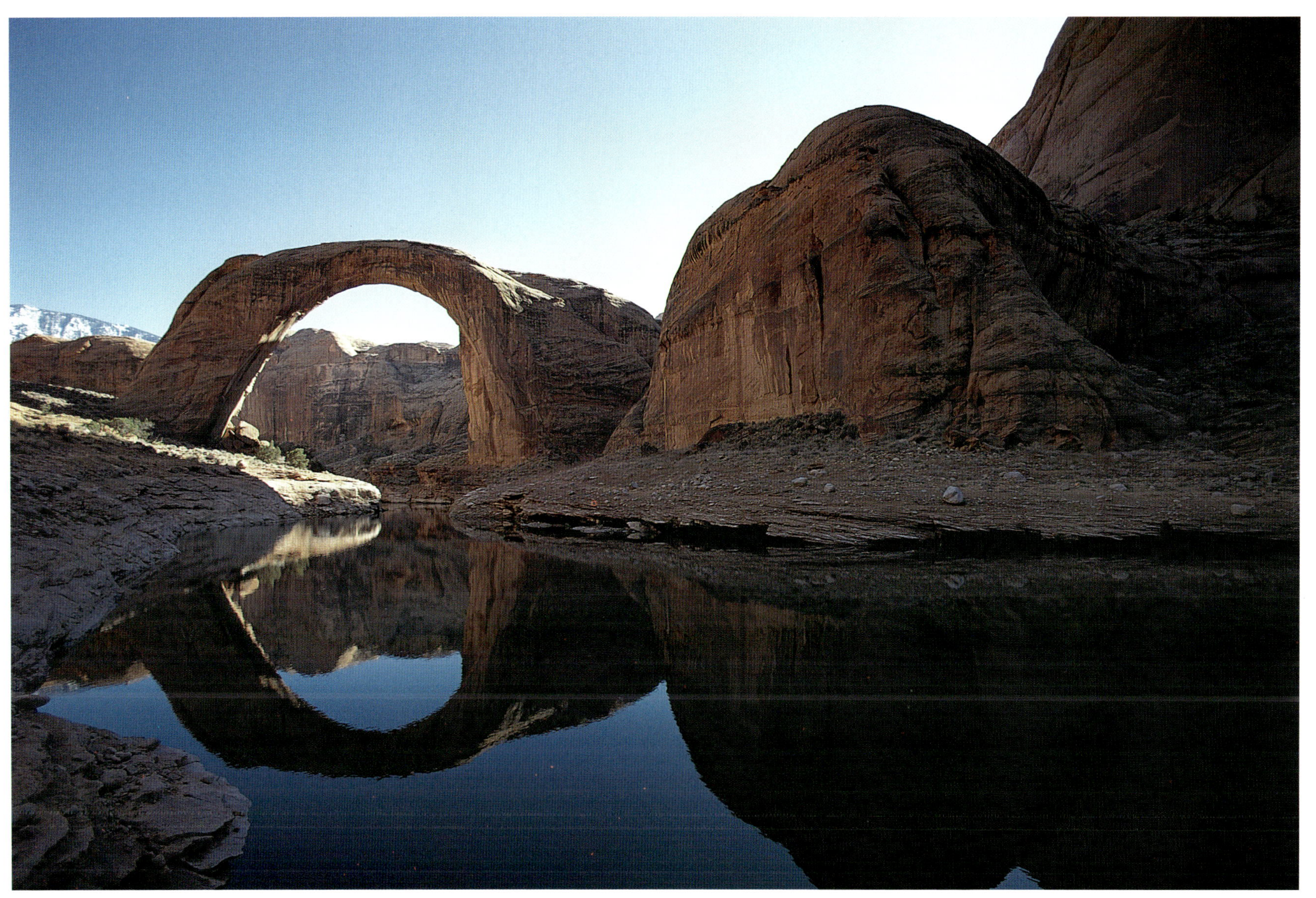

↑← Rainbow Bridge National Monument, Lake Powell, Glen Canyon National Recreation Area

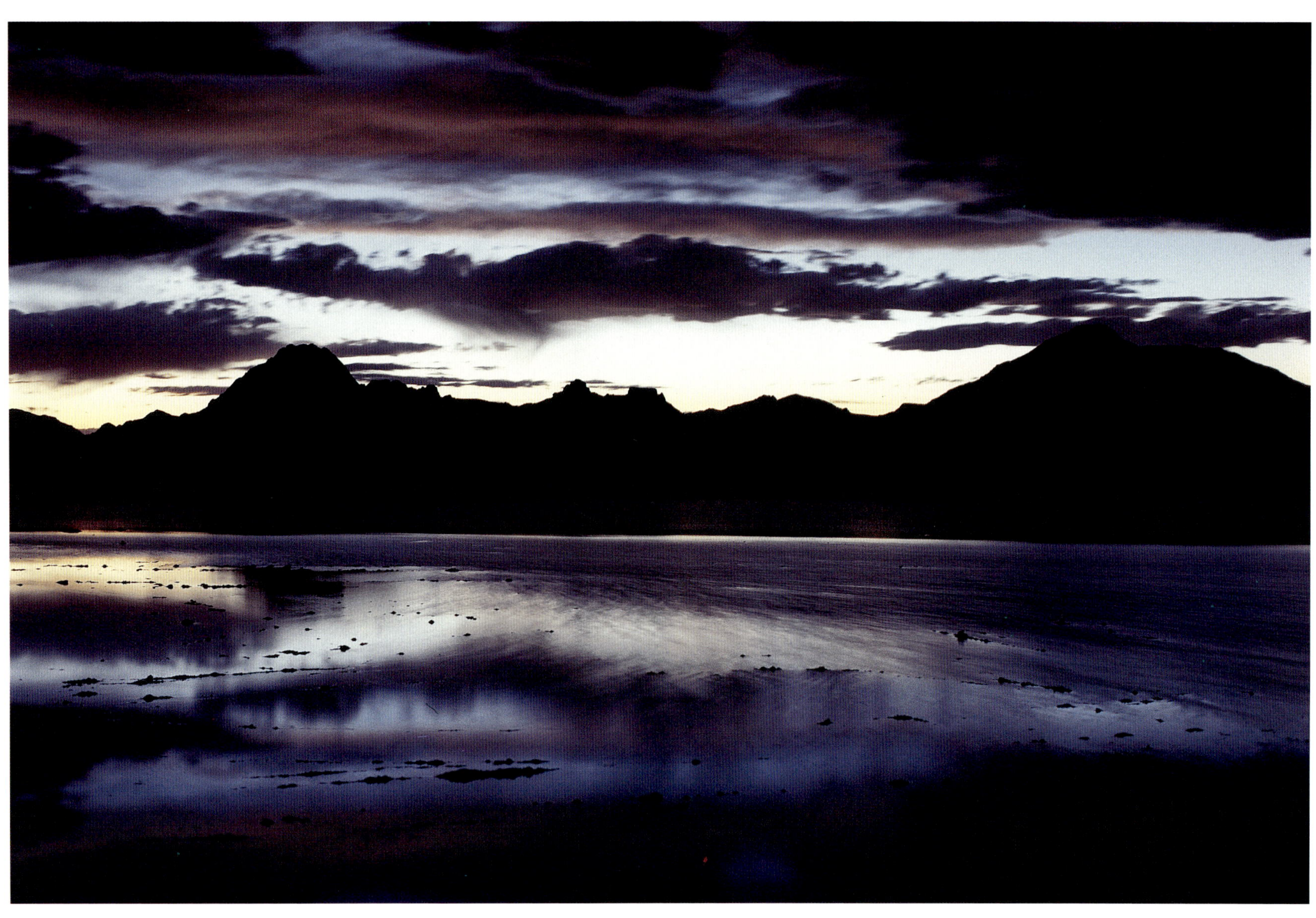

↑→ Bonneville Salt Flats, Great Salt Lake Desert ↓ Bryce Canyon National Park

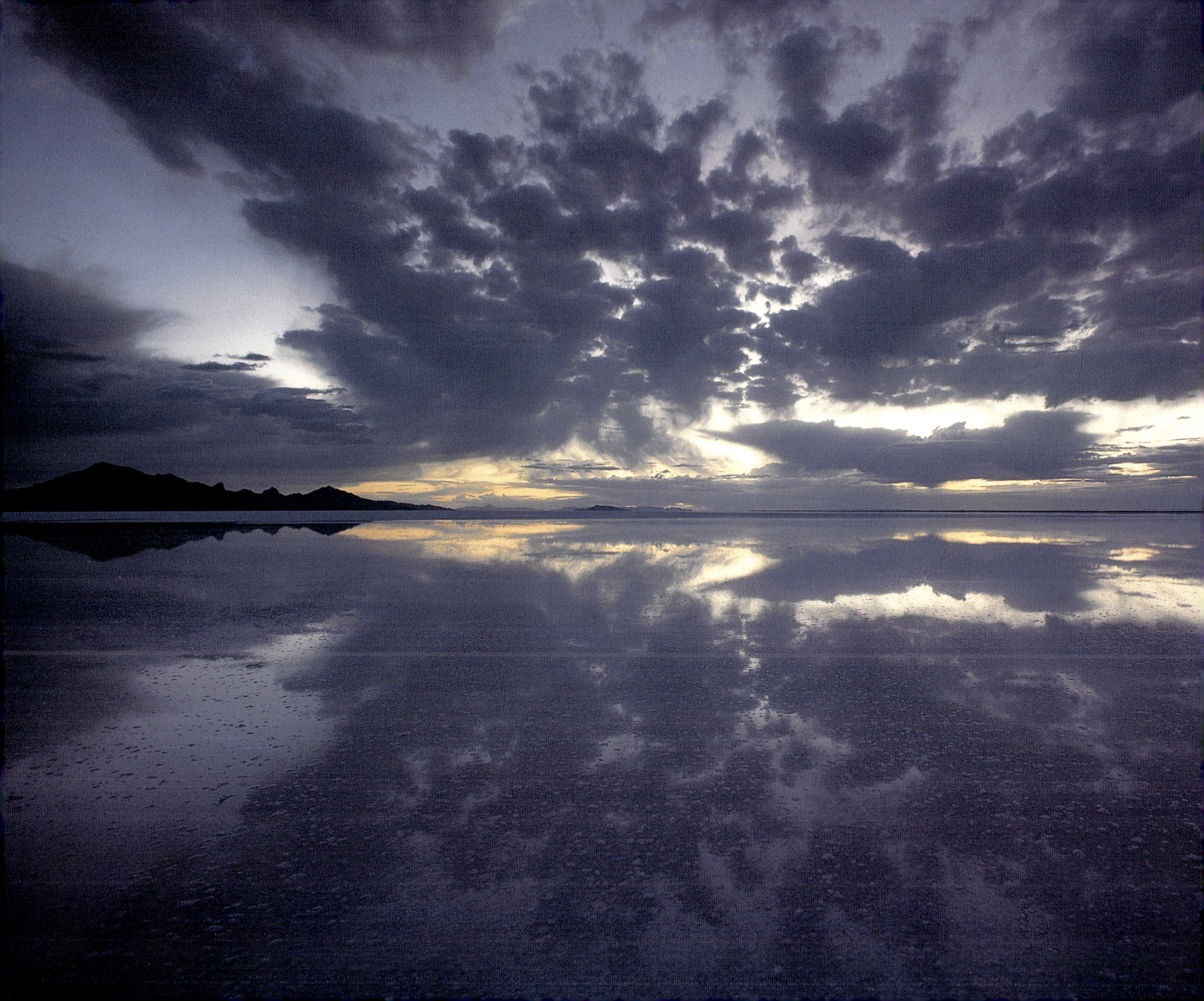

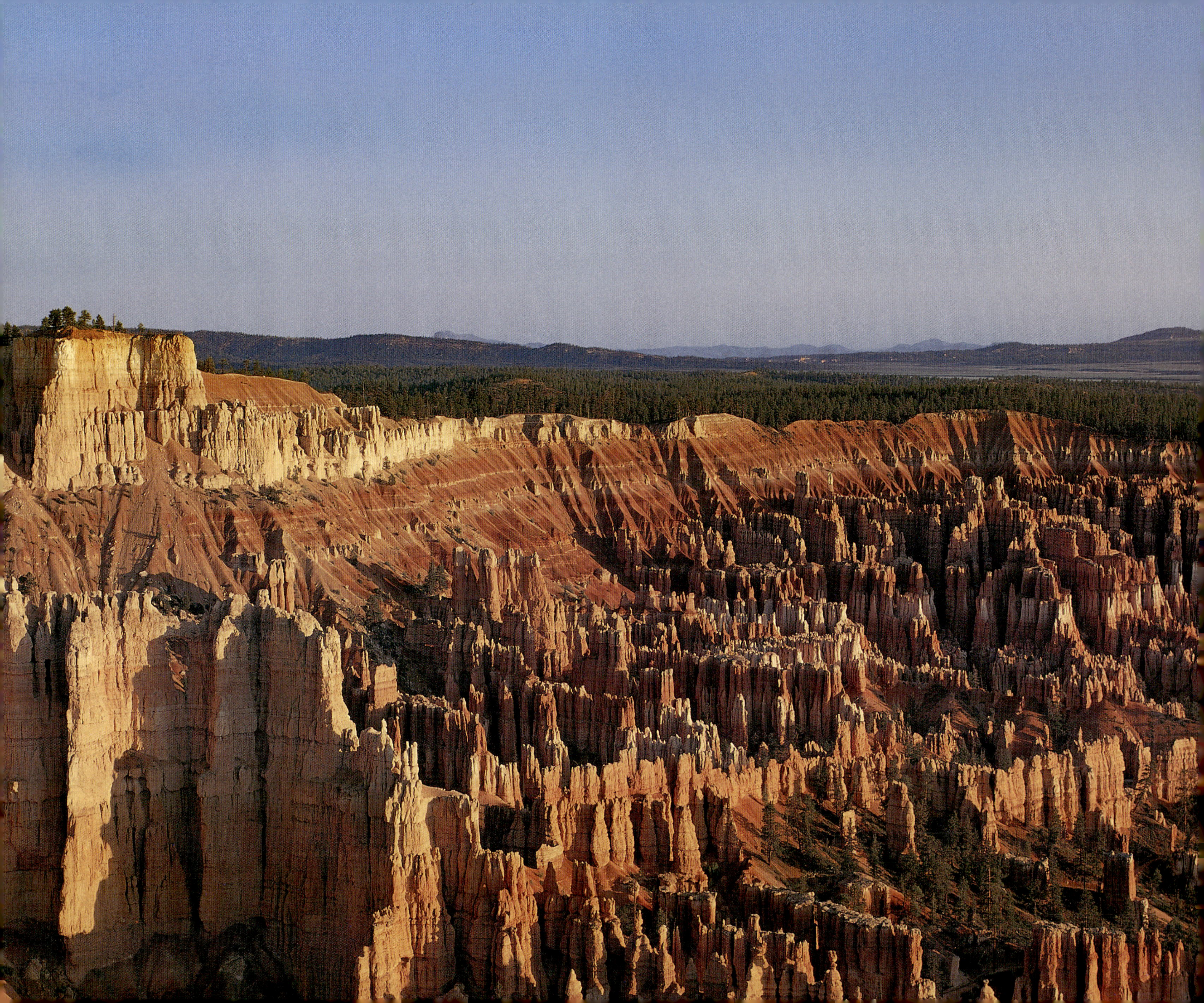

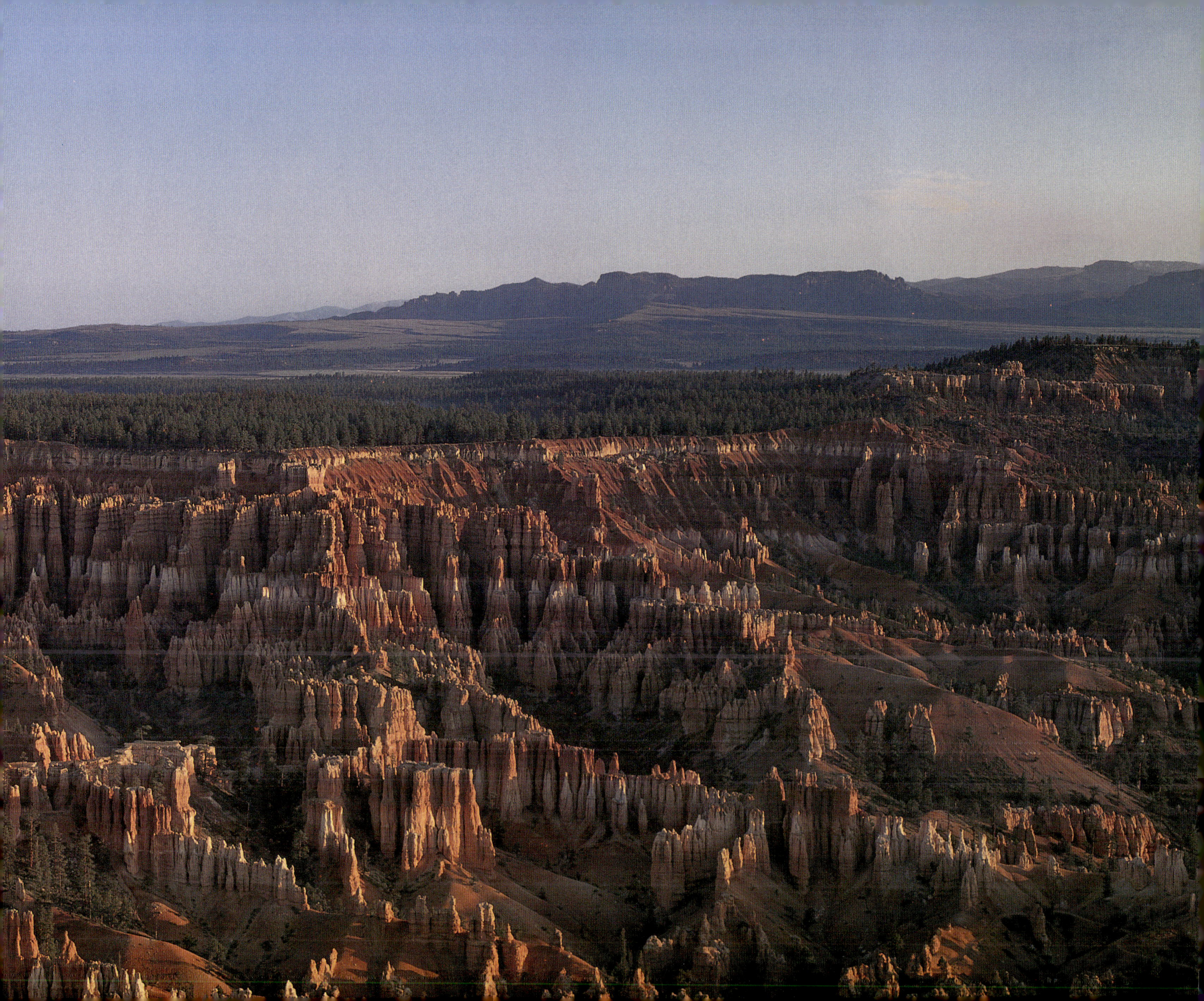

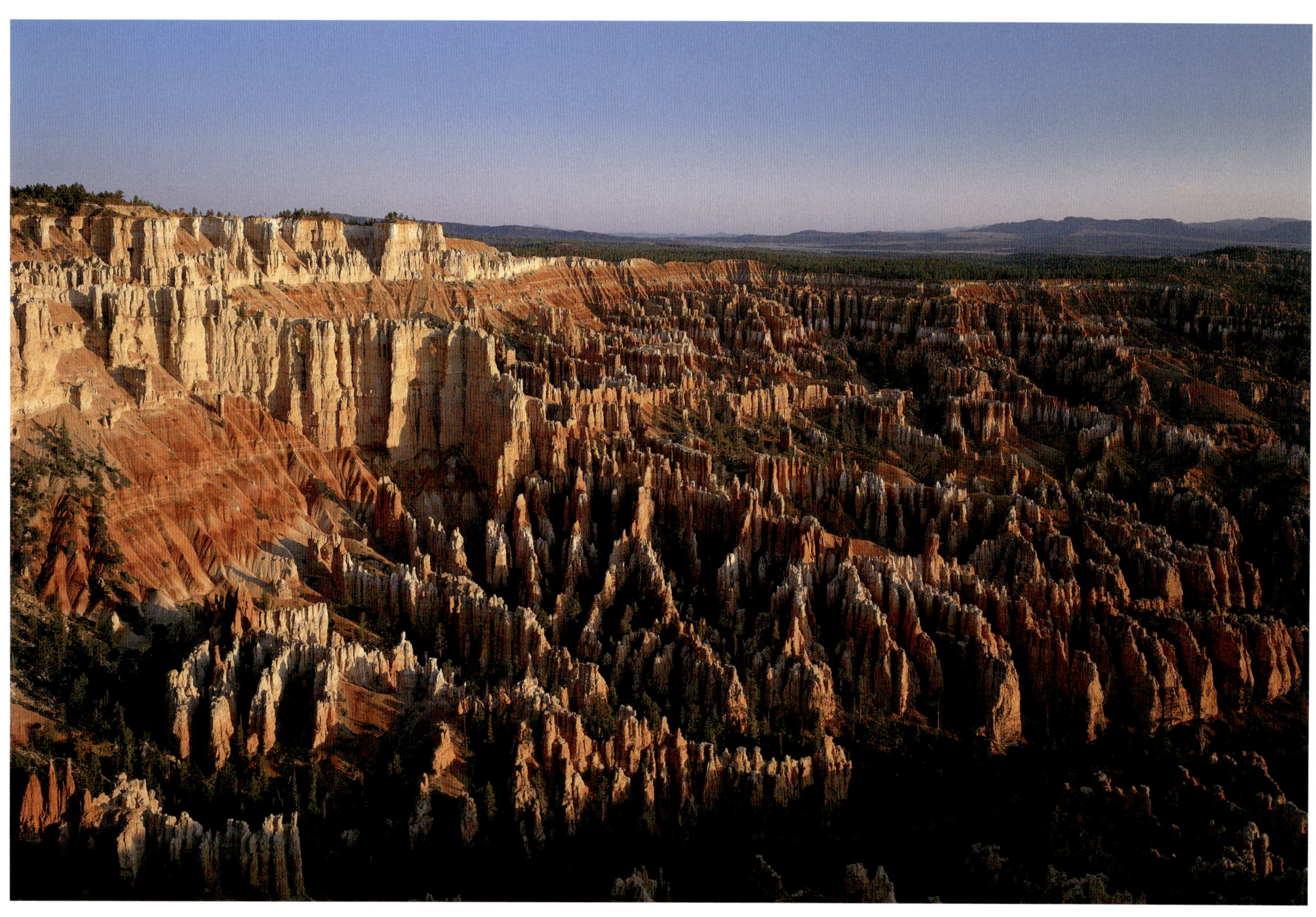

↑→ Bryce Canyon National Park

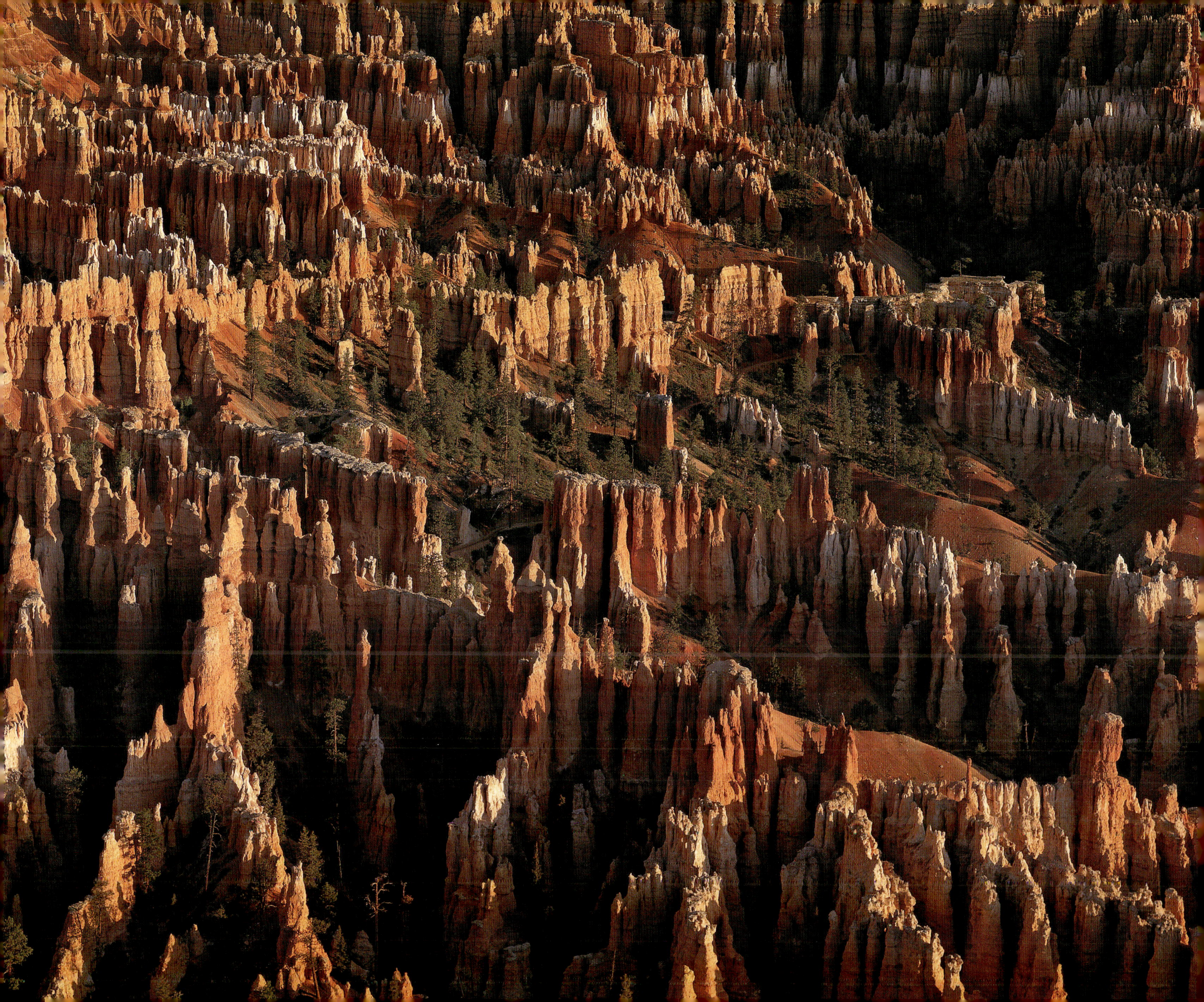

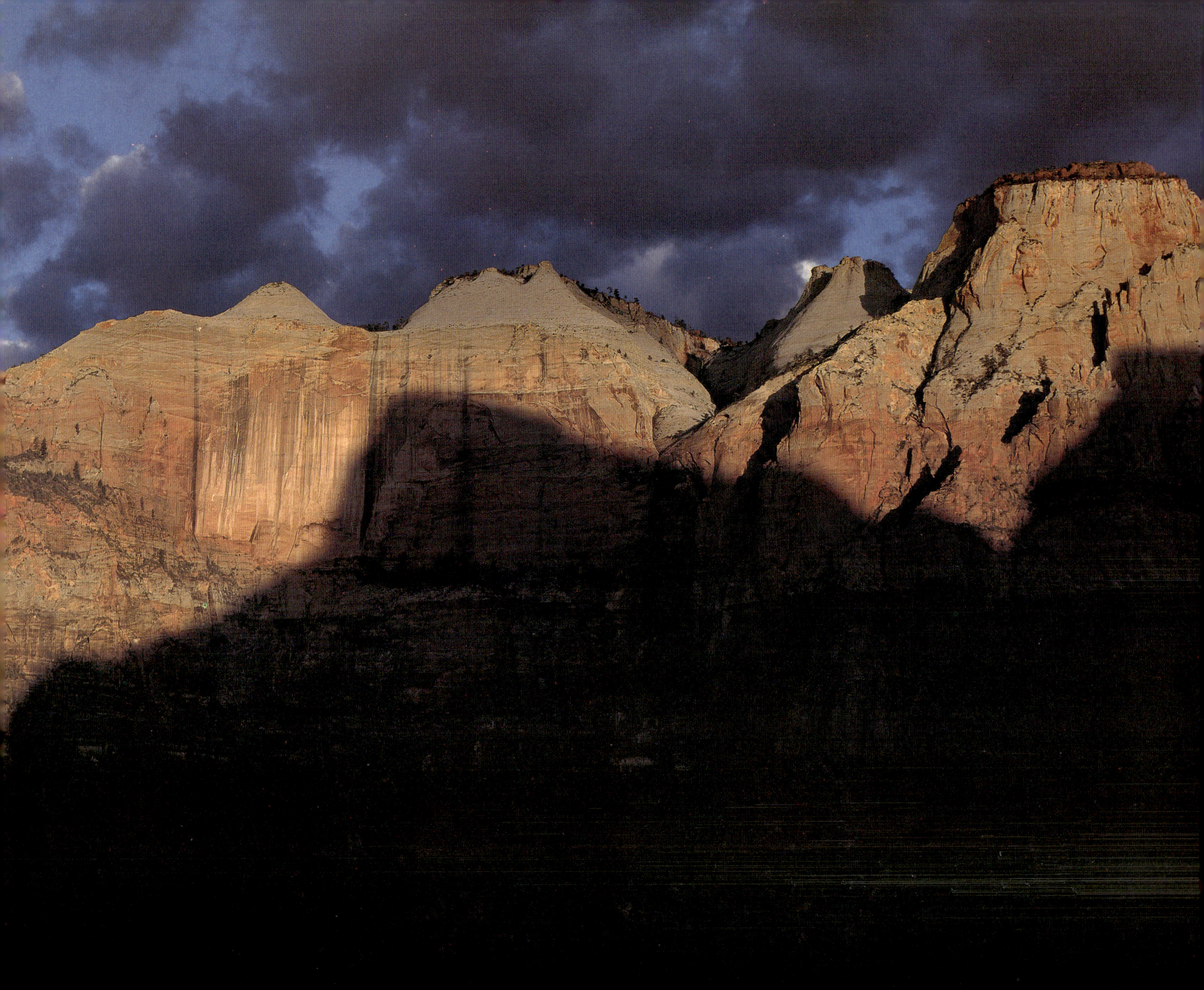

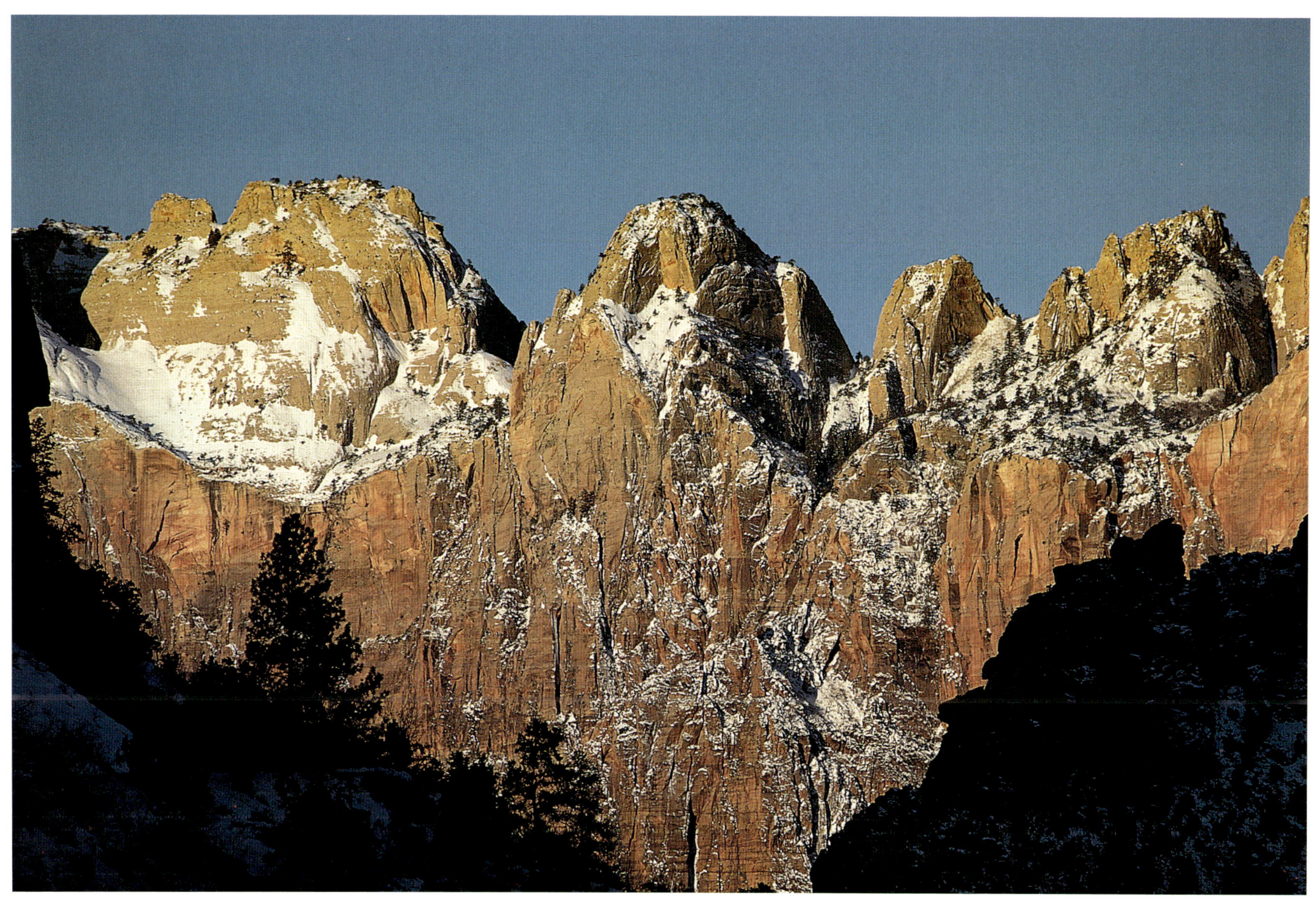

↑← Zion National Park

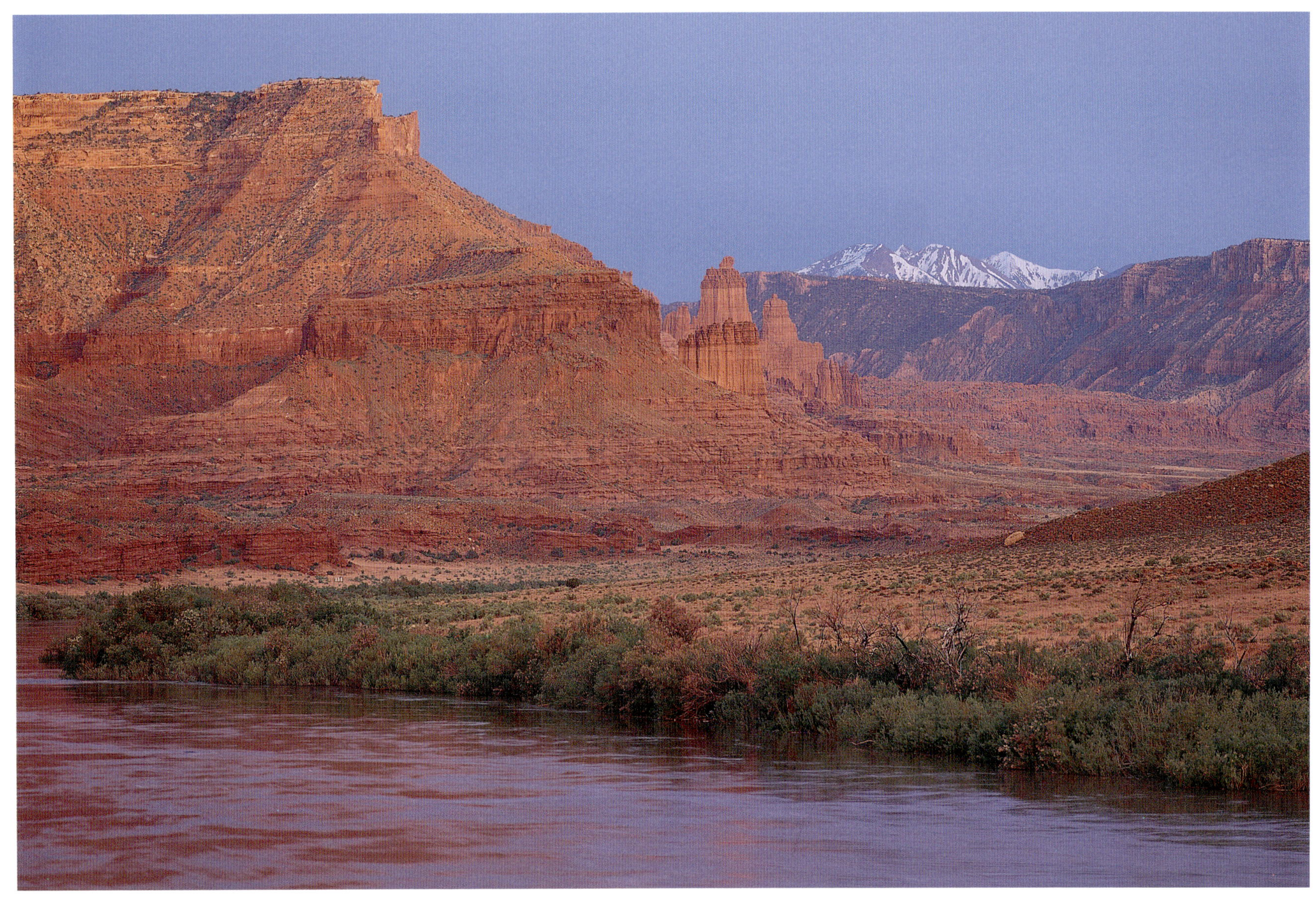

↑→ La Sal Mountains and Fisher Towers, Colorado River ↓ San Juan River, Goosenecks State Park

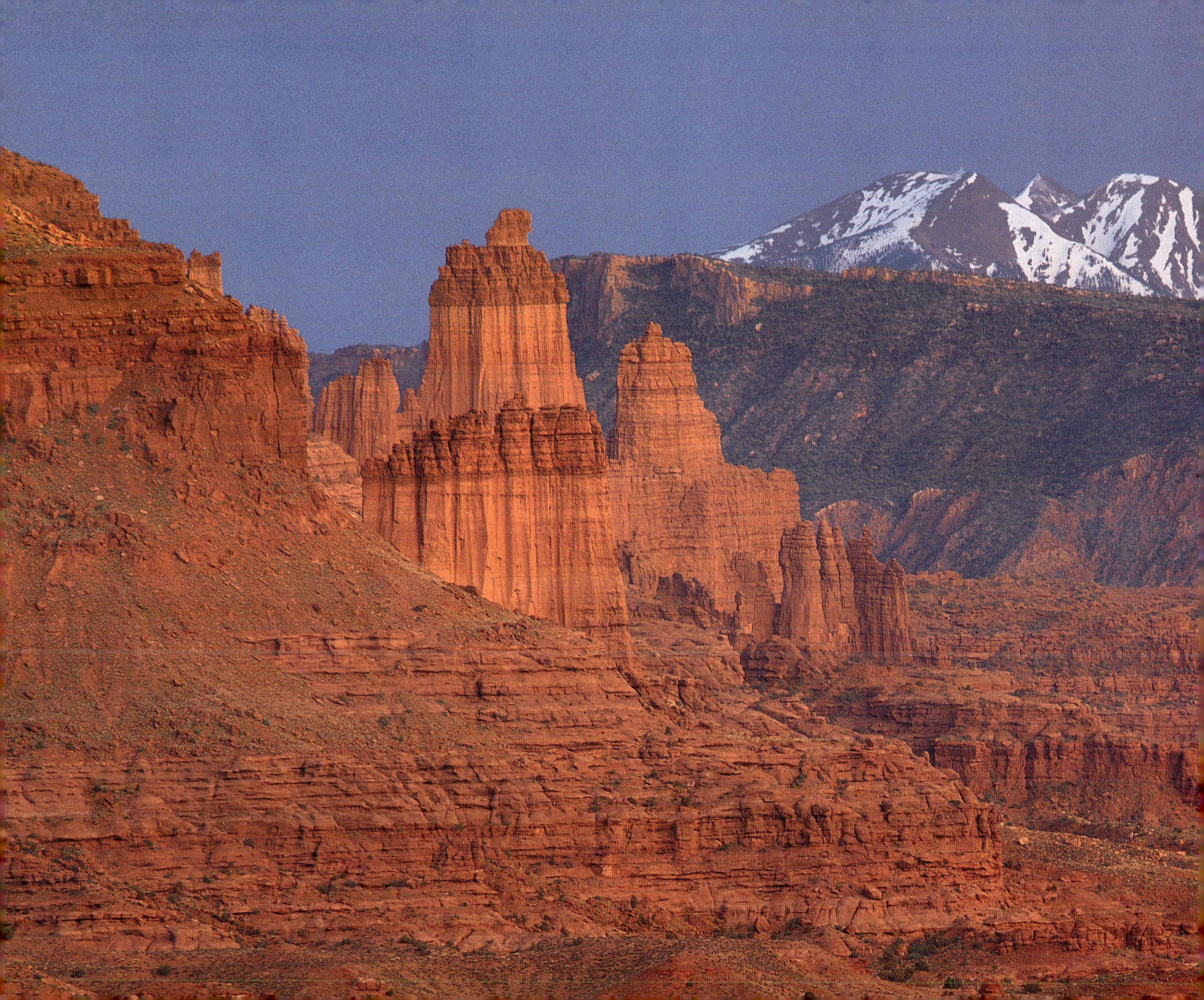

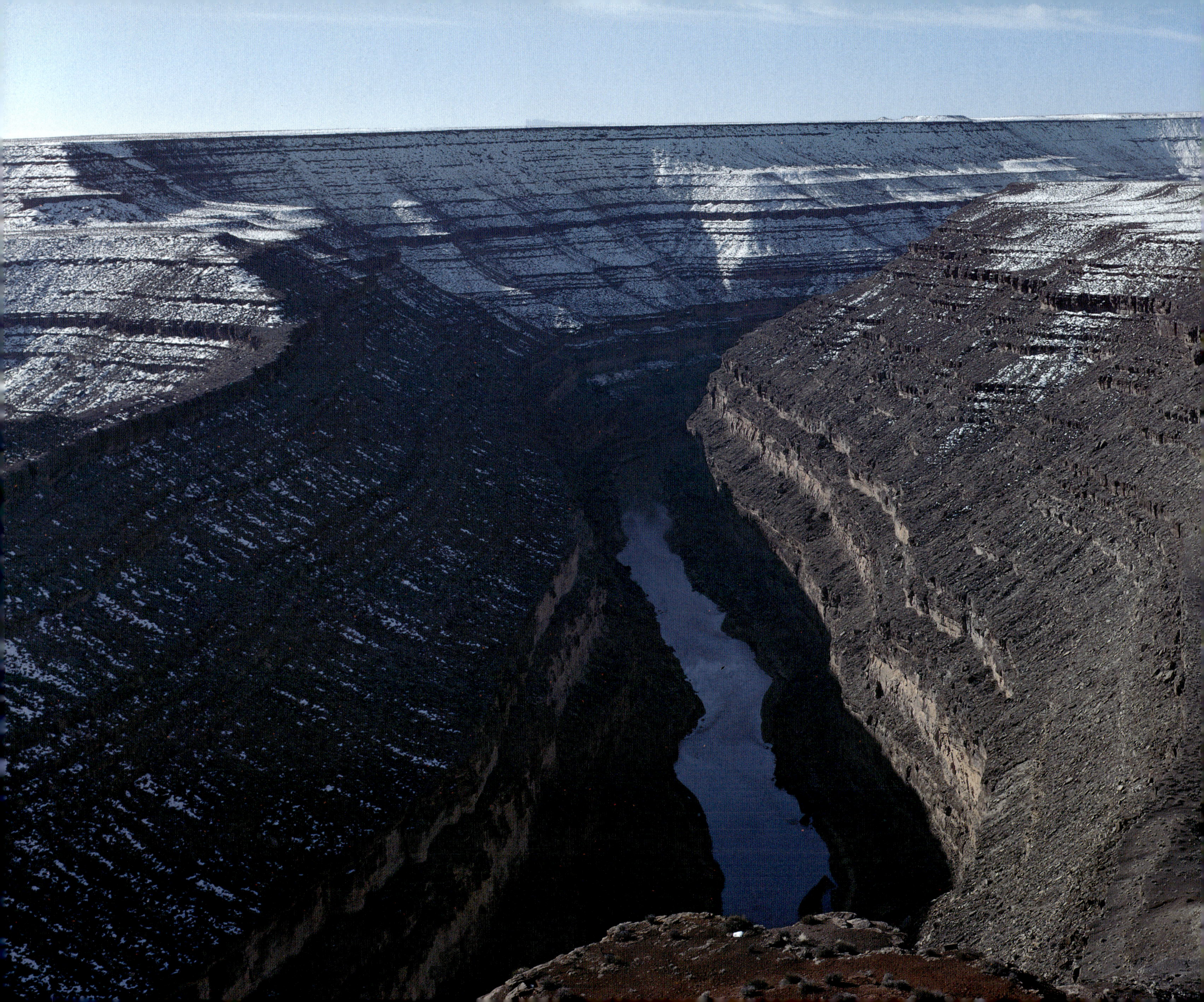

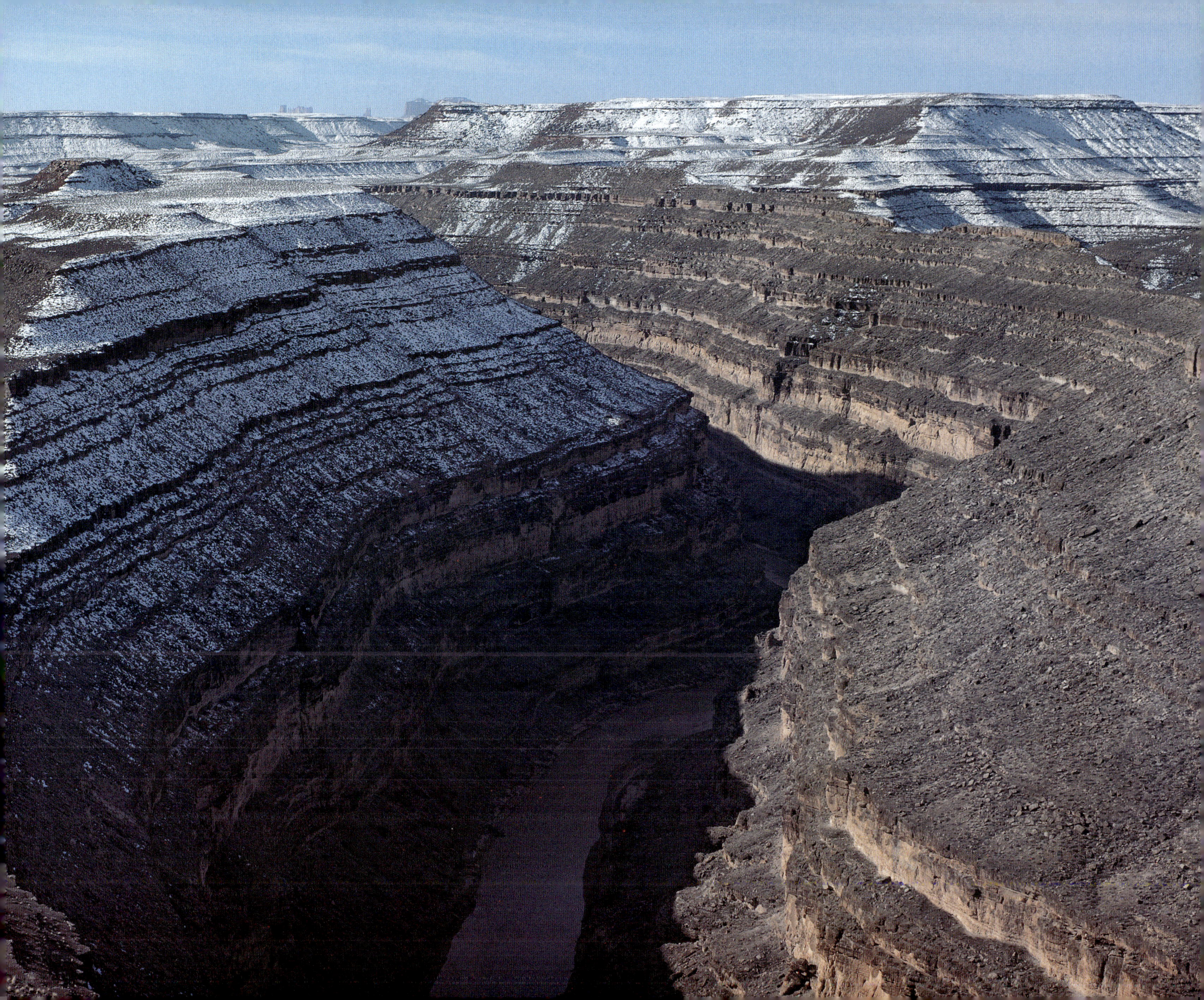

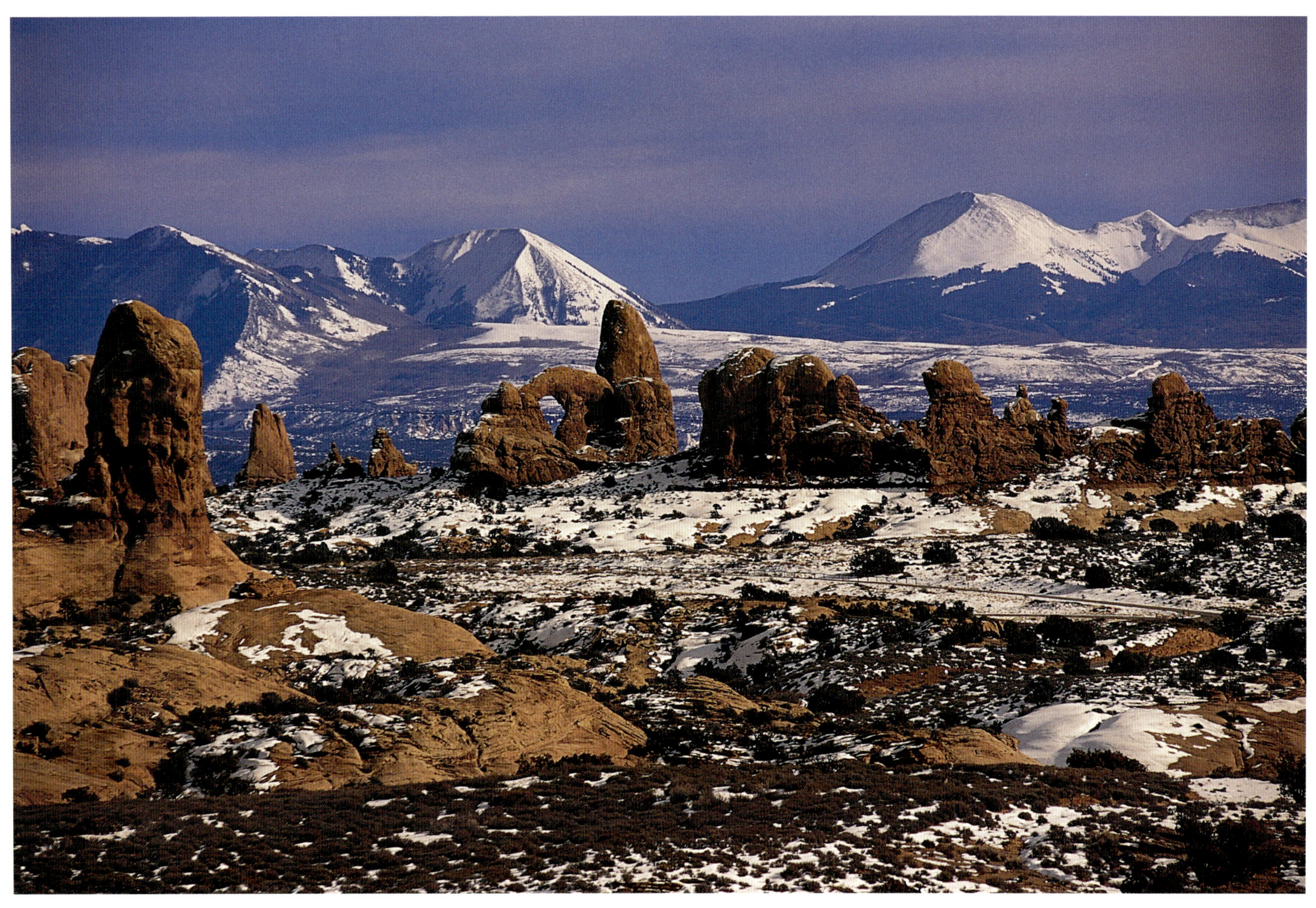

↑ Turret Arch, Arches National Park → Delicate Arch, Arches National Park

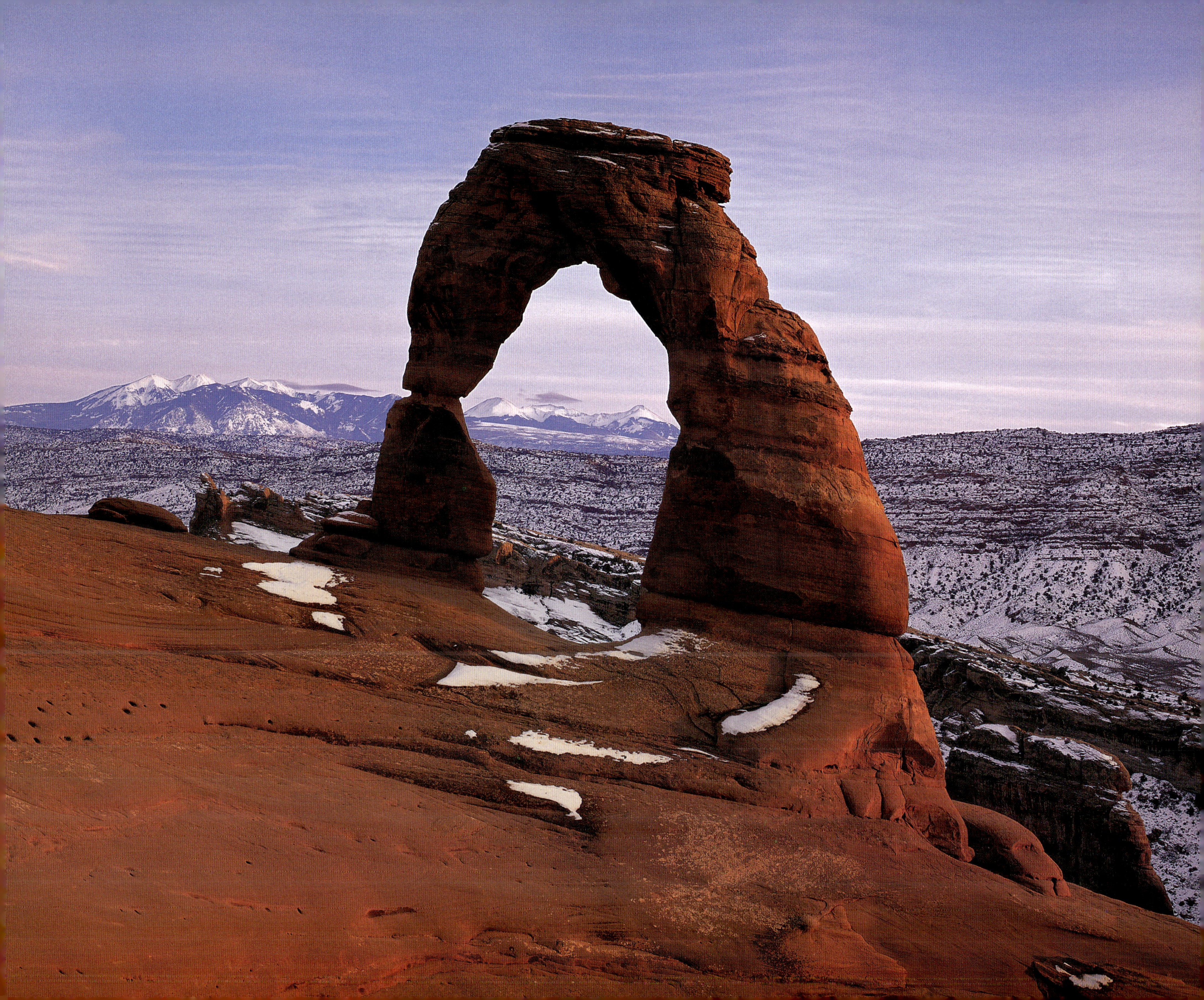

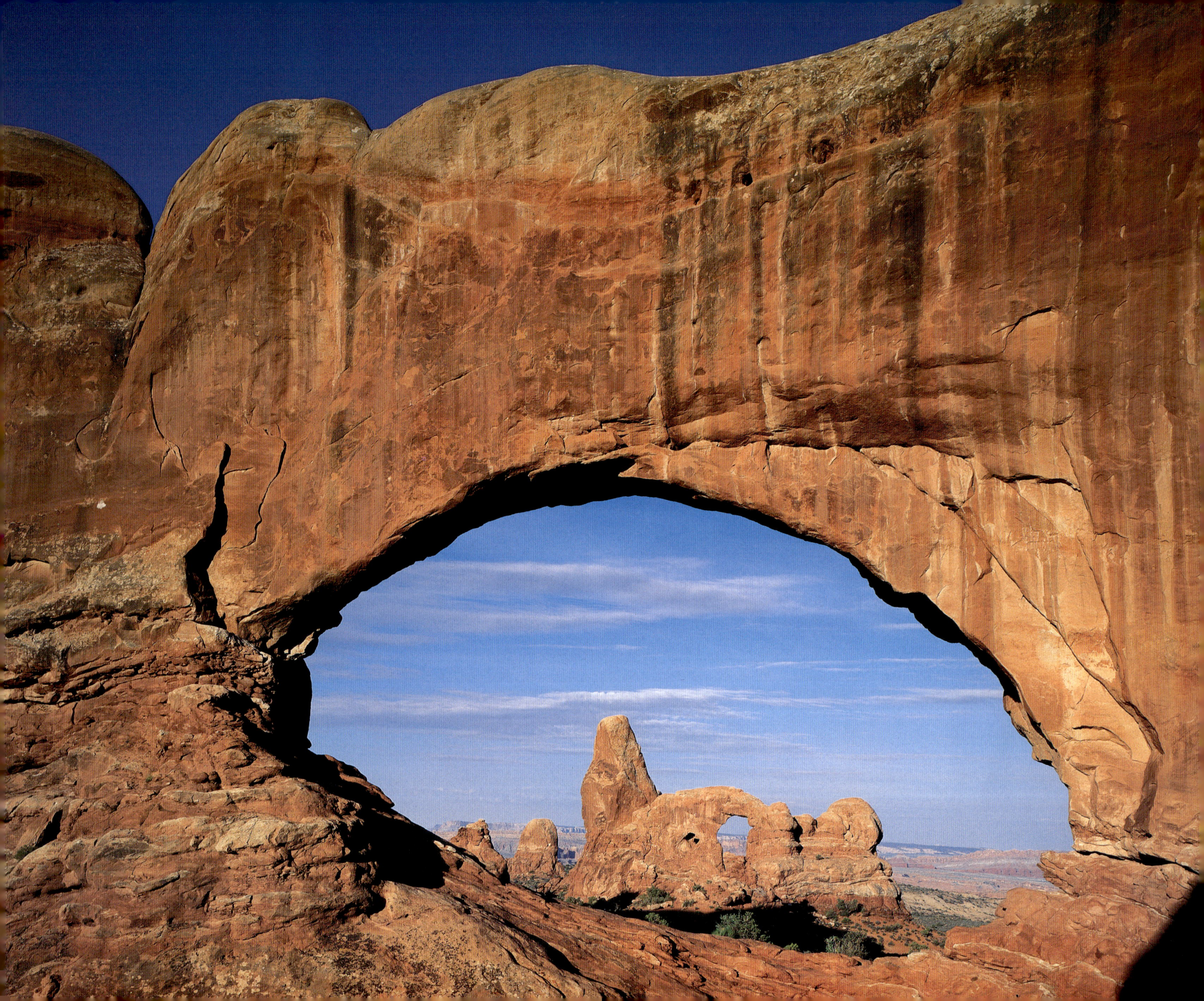

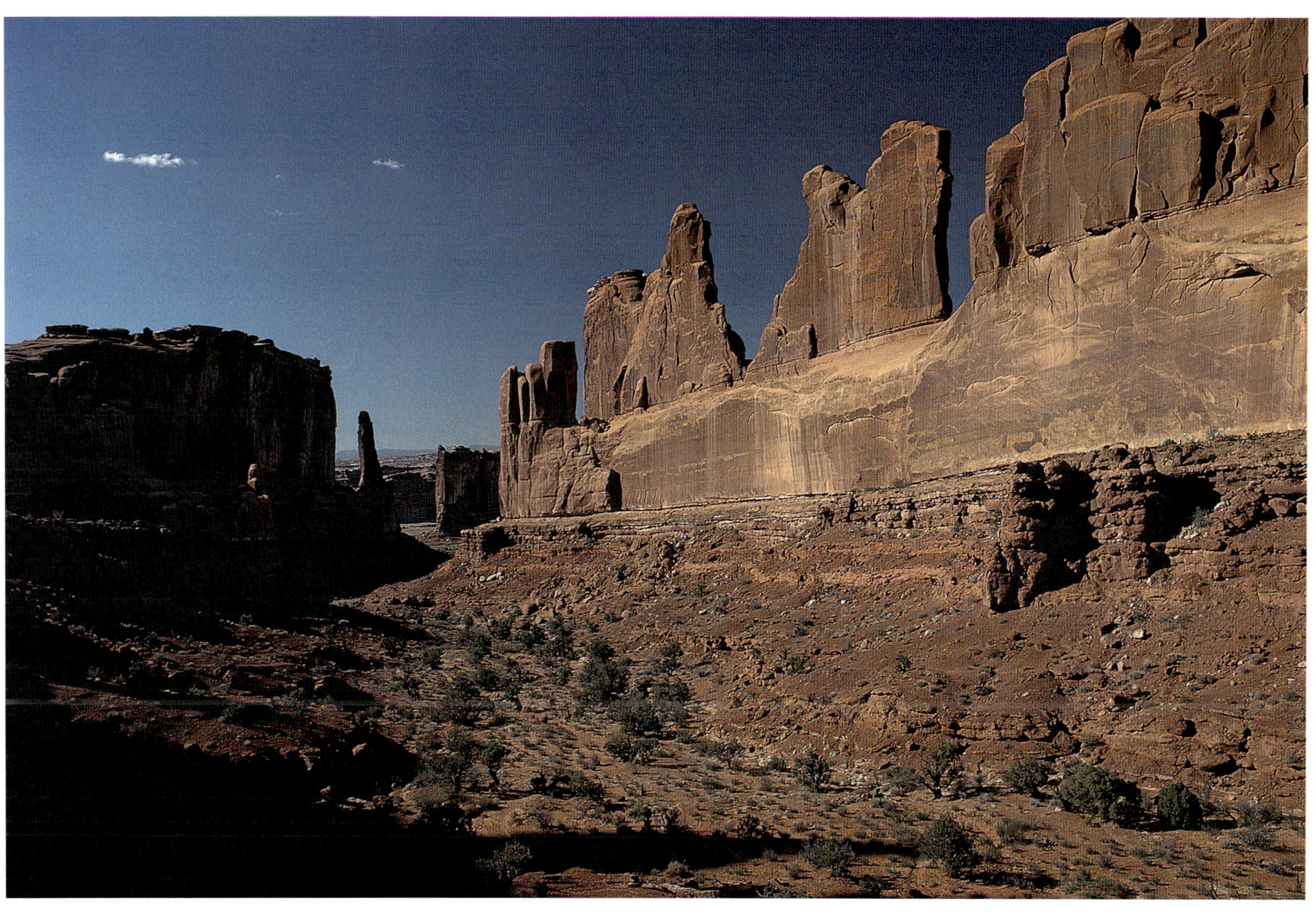

↑←Arches National Park

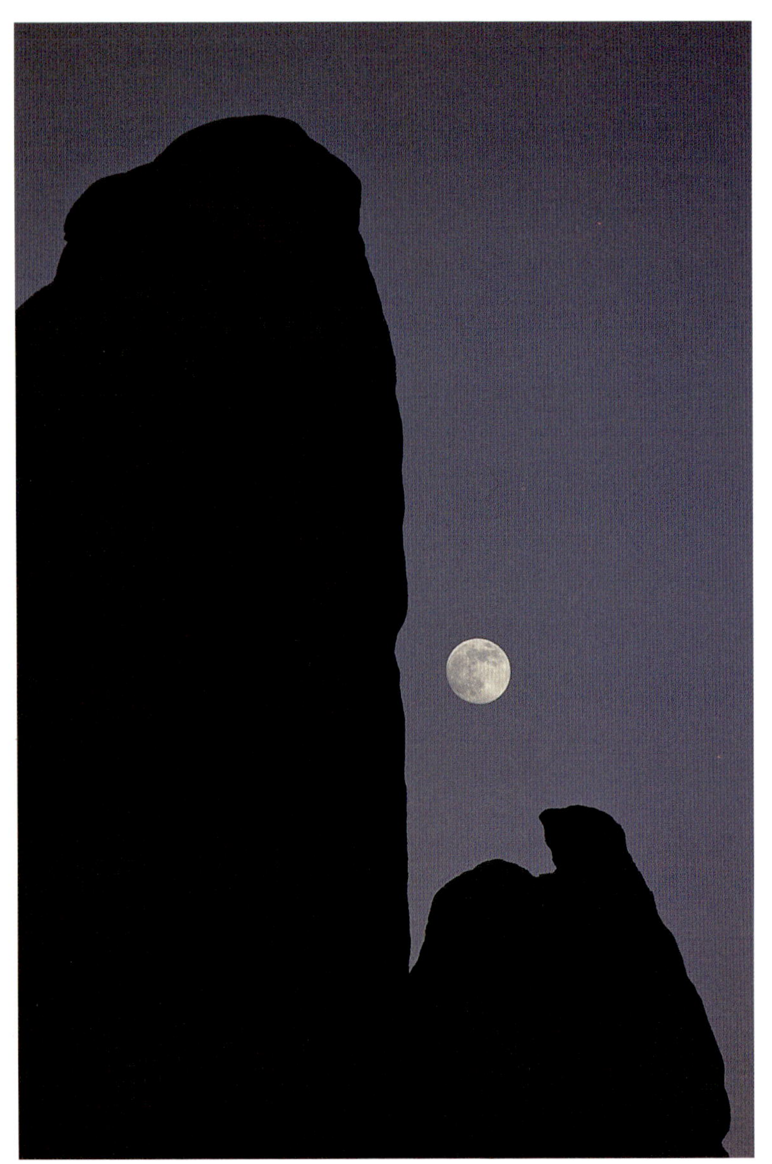

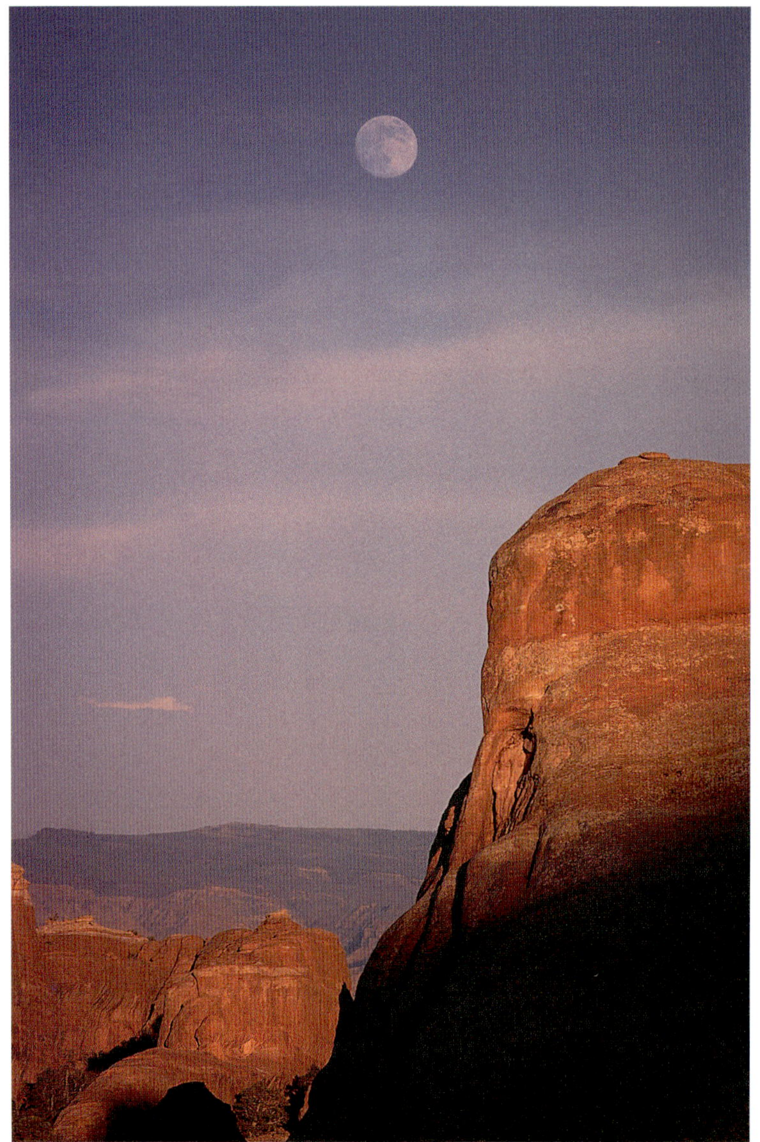

↑ Arches National Park → Mesa Arch, Canyonlands National Park

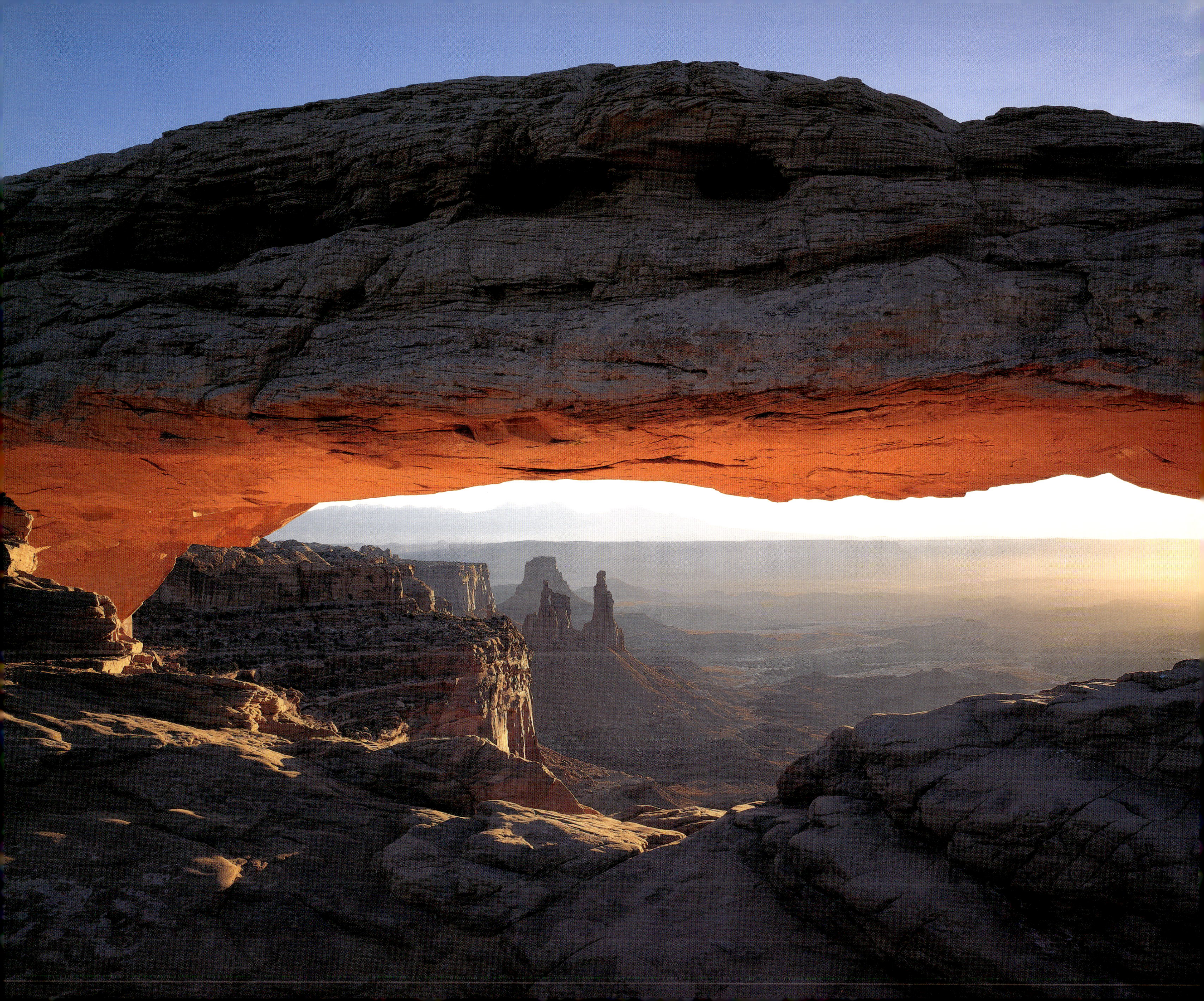

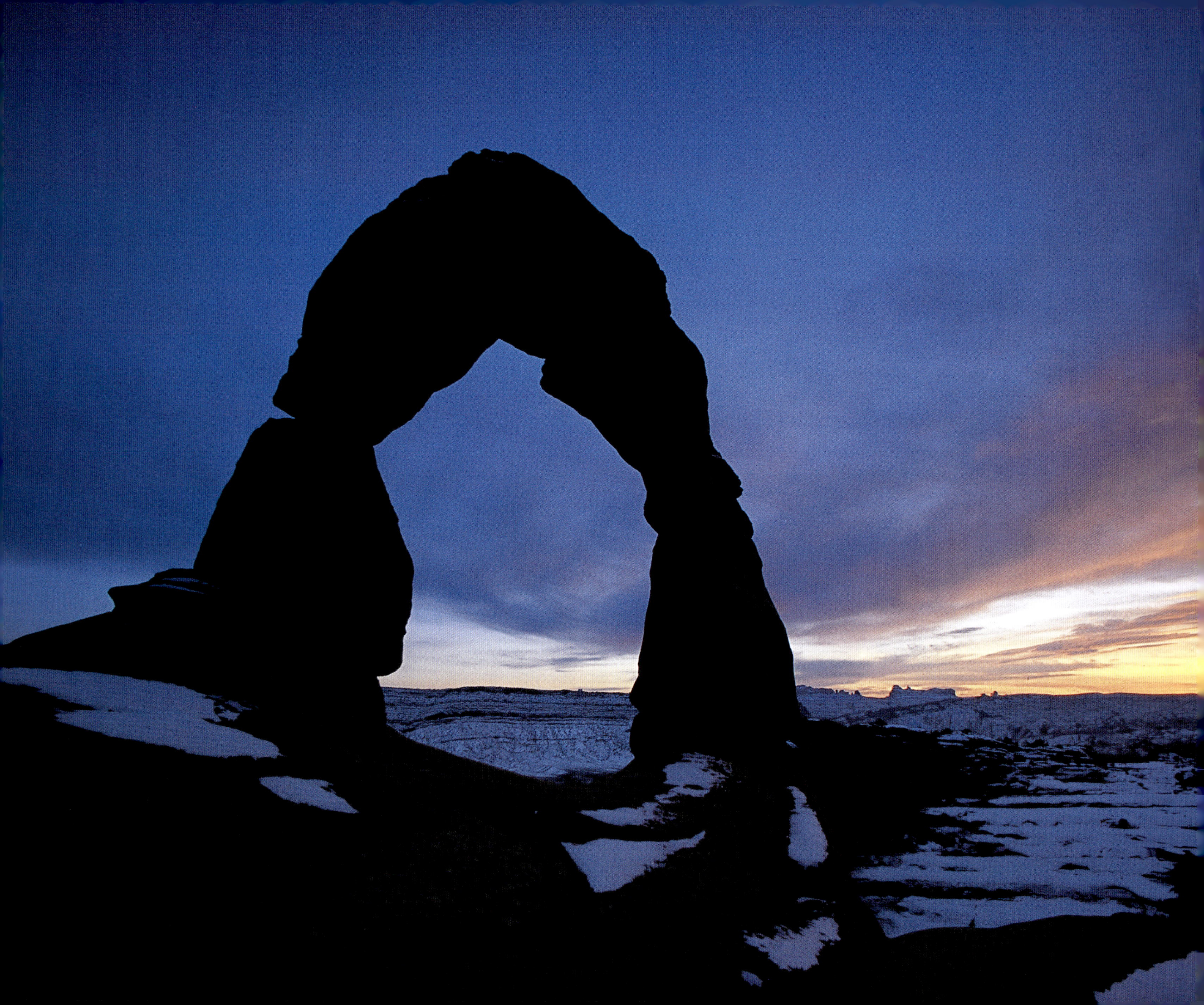

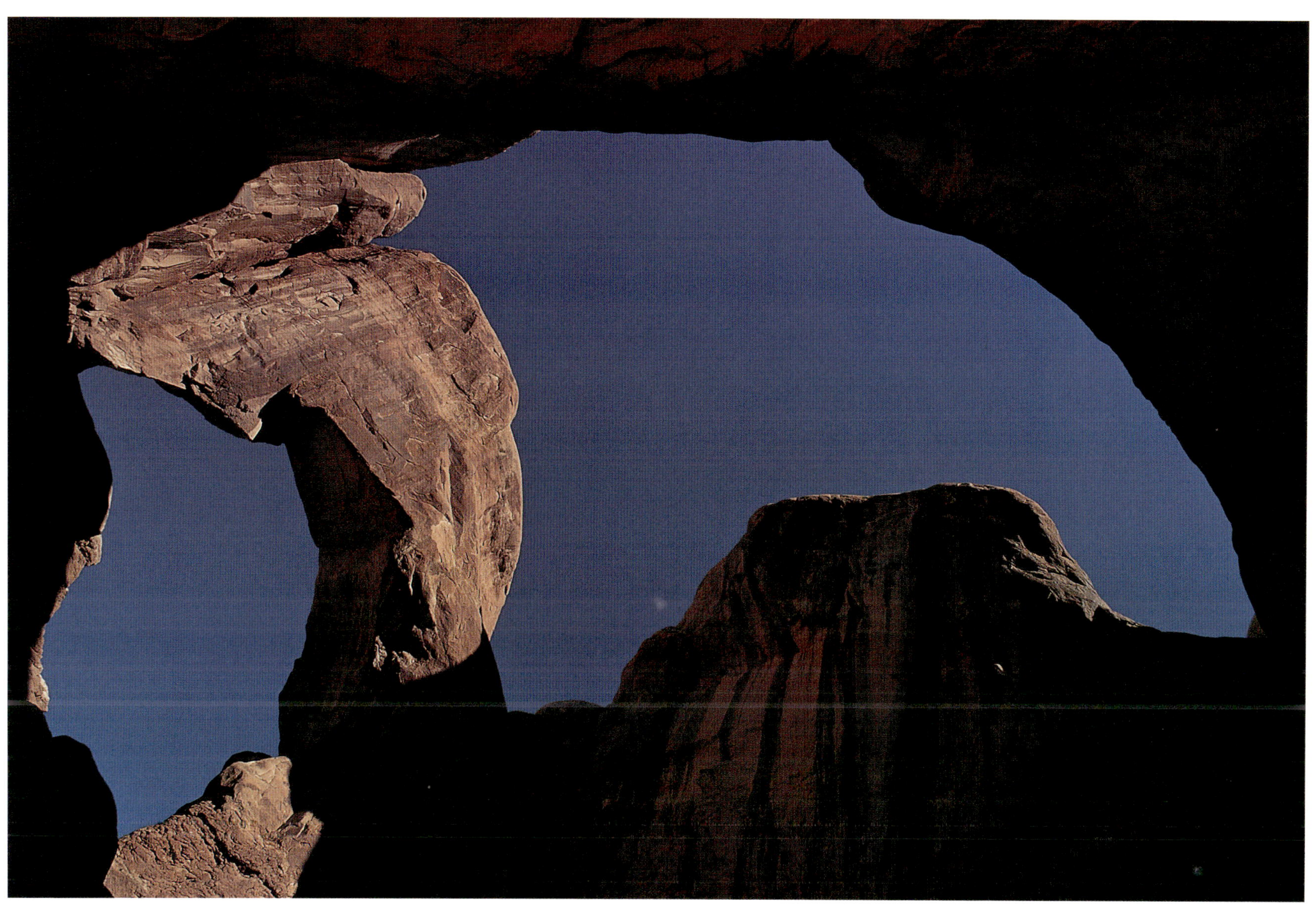

↑ Double Arch, Arches National Park ← Delicate Arch, Arches National Park ↓ Nine Mile Canyon

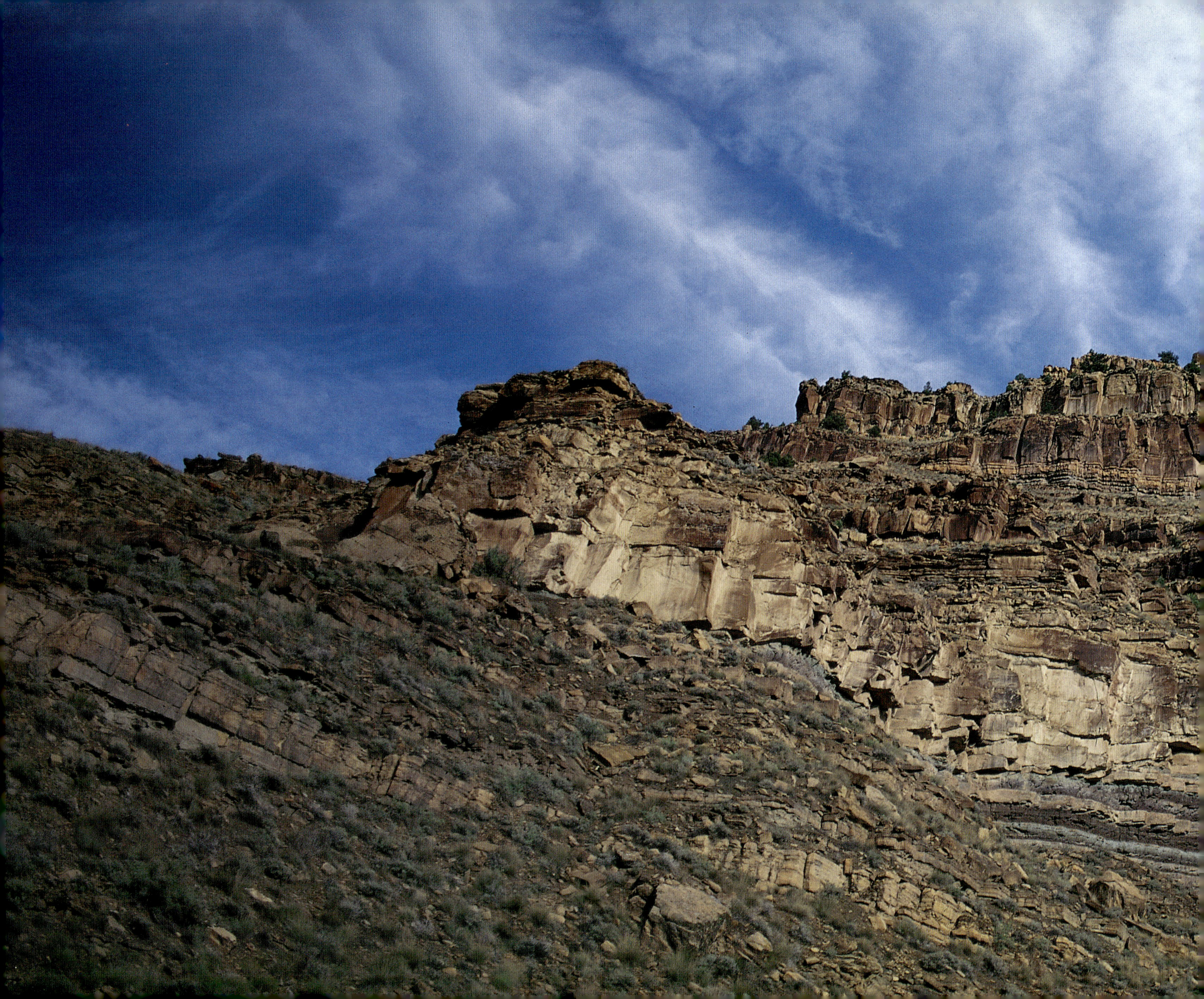

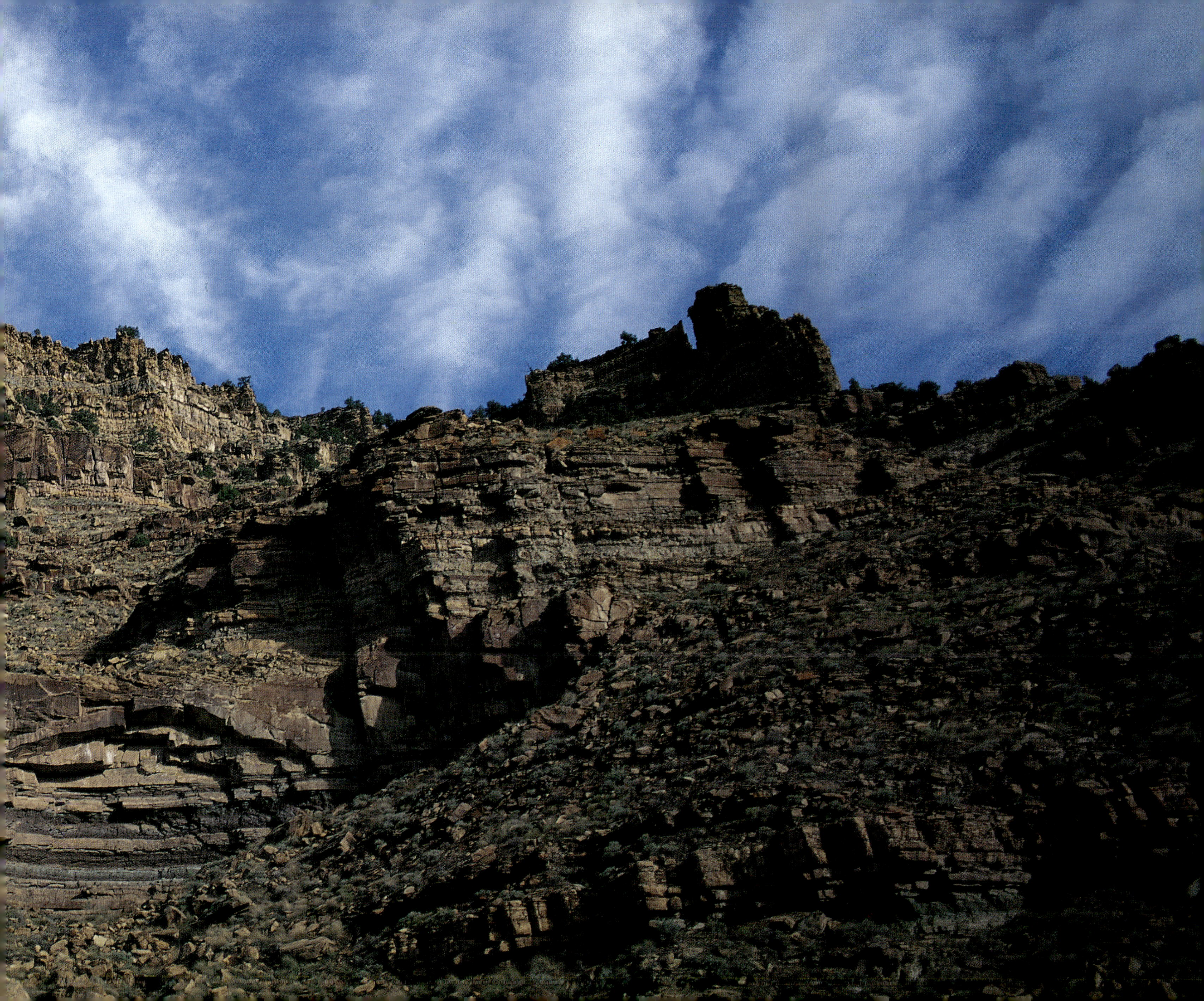

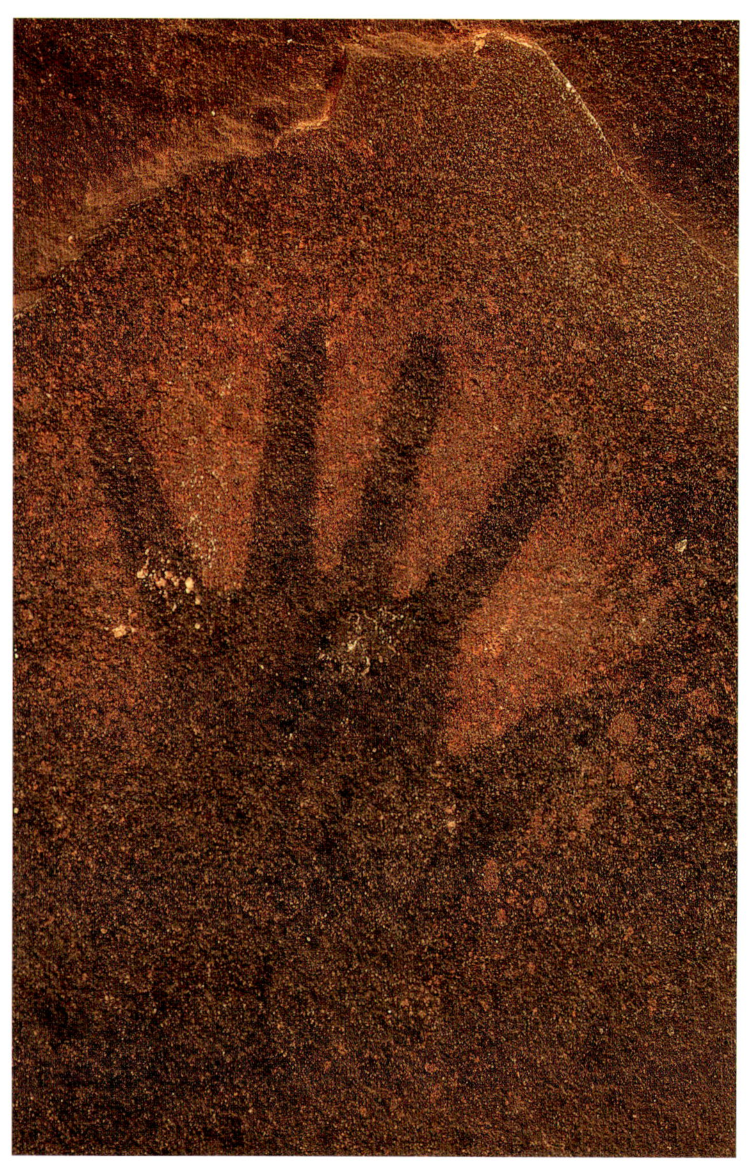

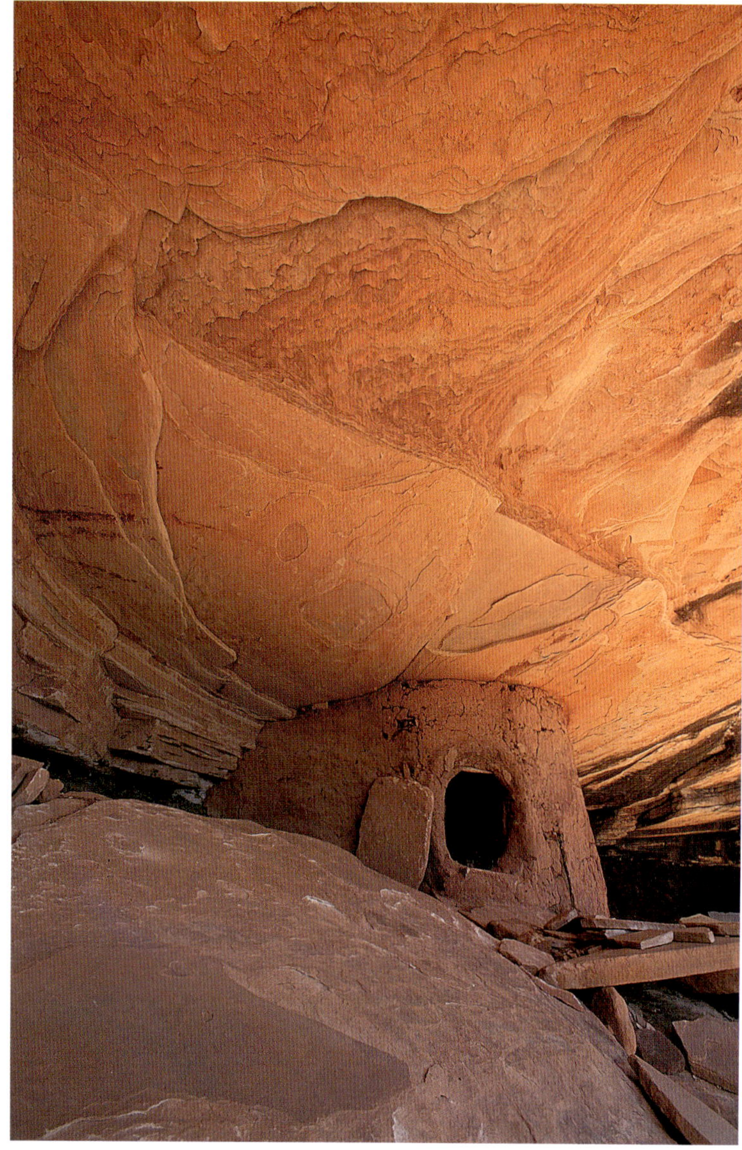

↑→ Cedar Mesa

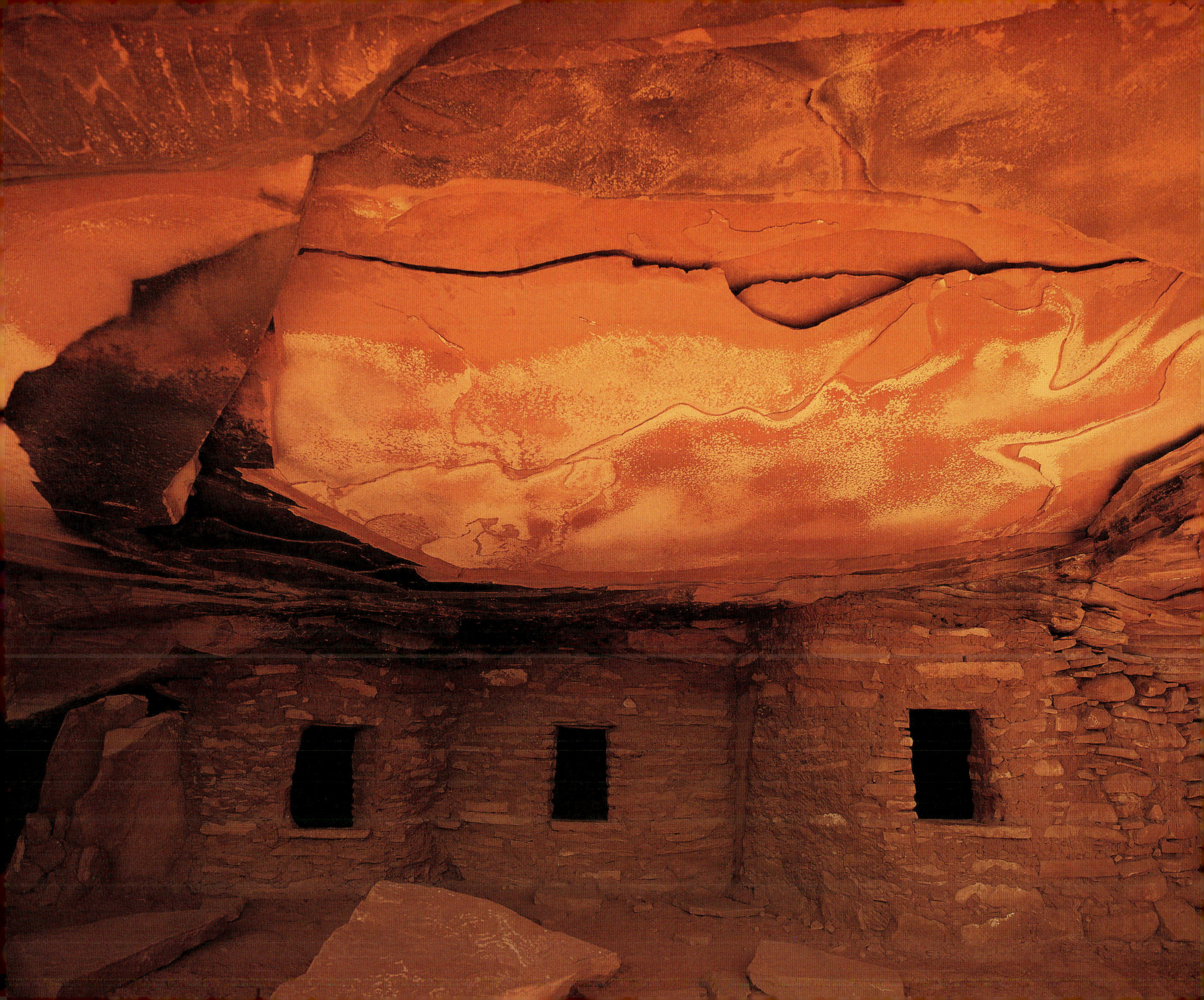

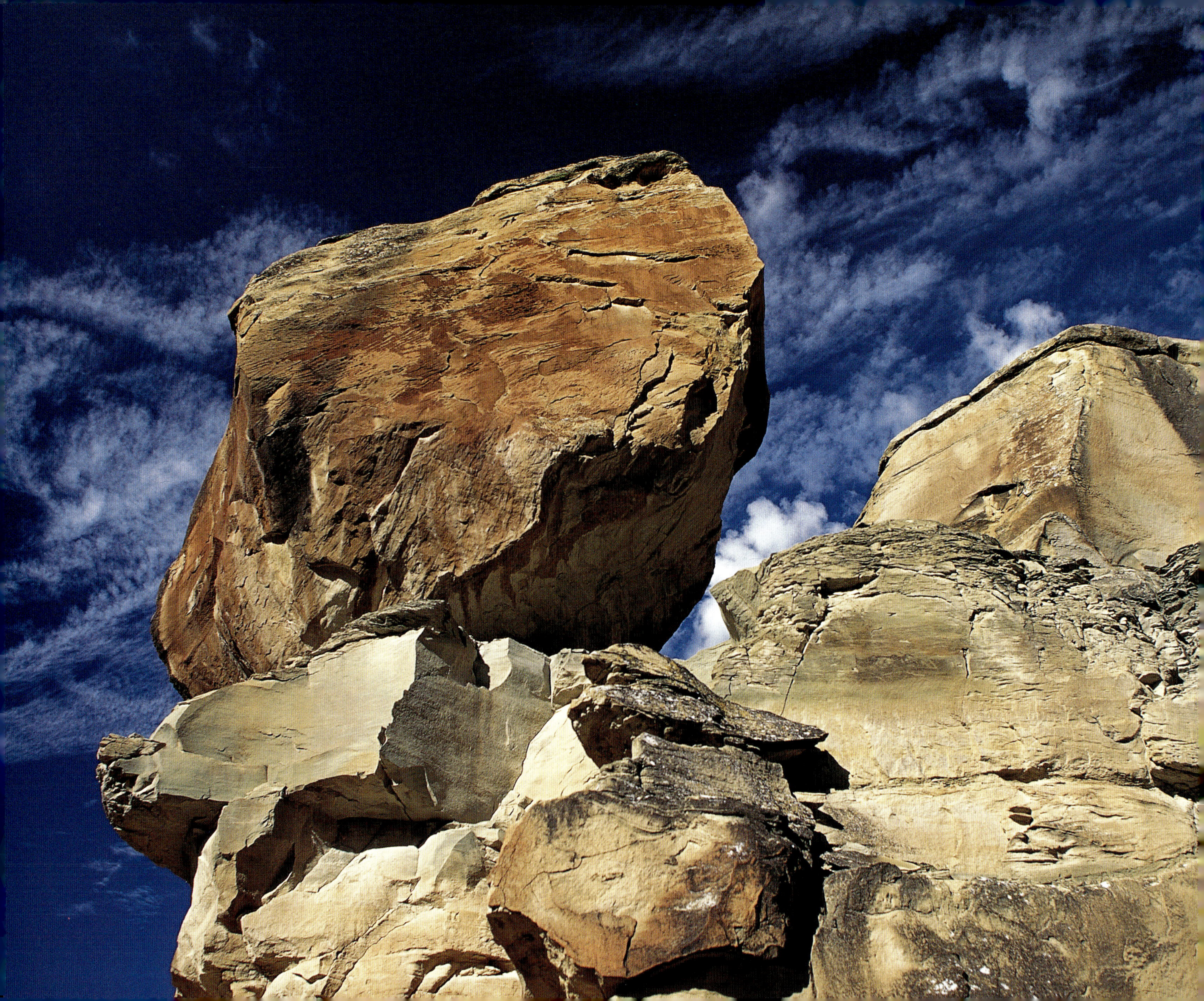

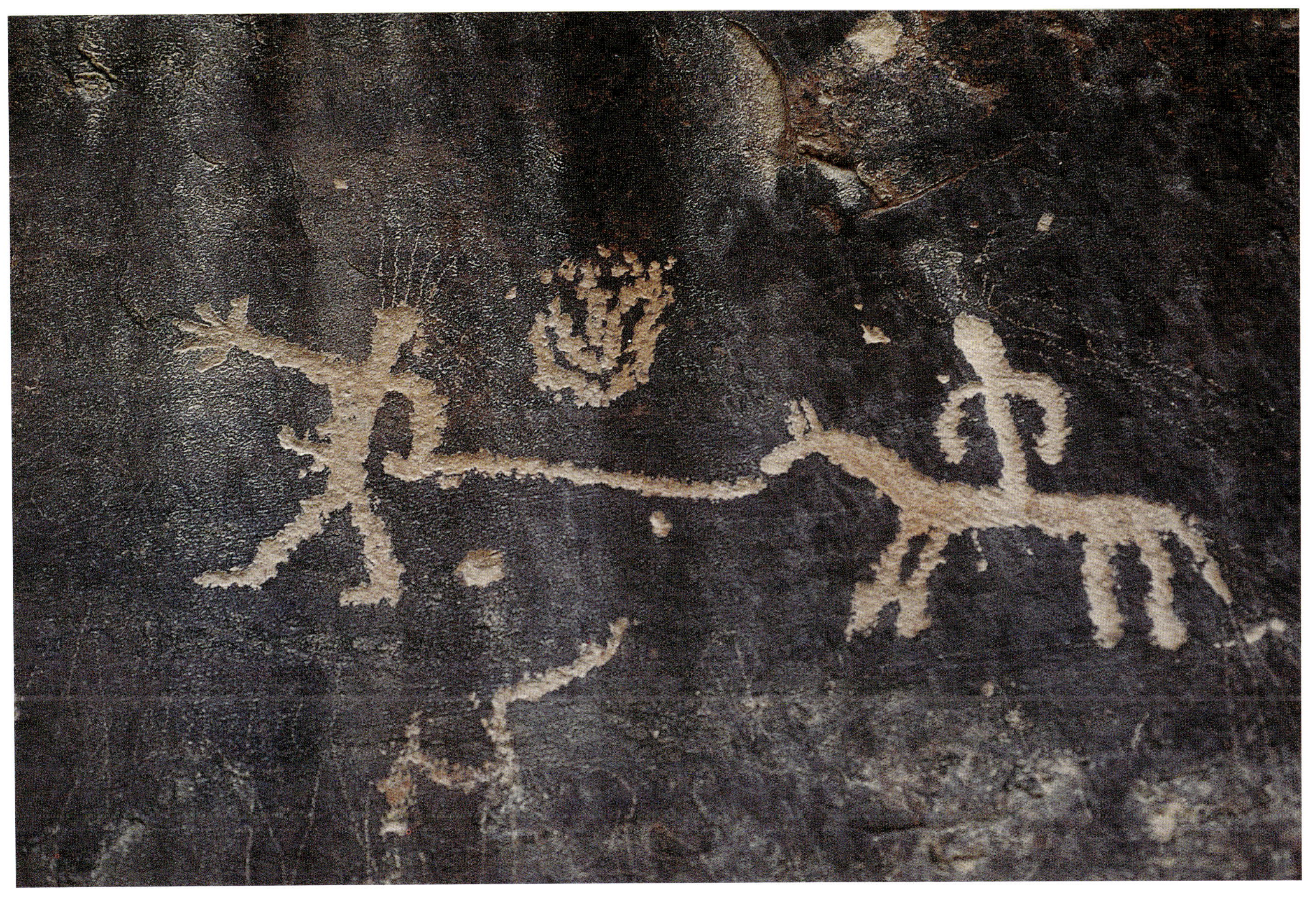

↑←Nine Mile Canyon

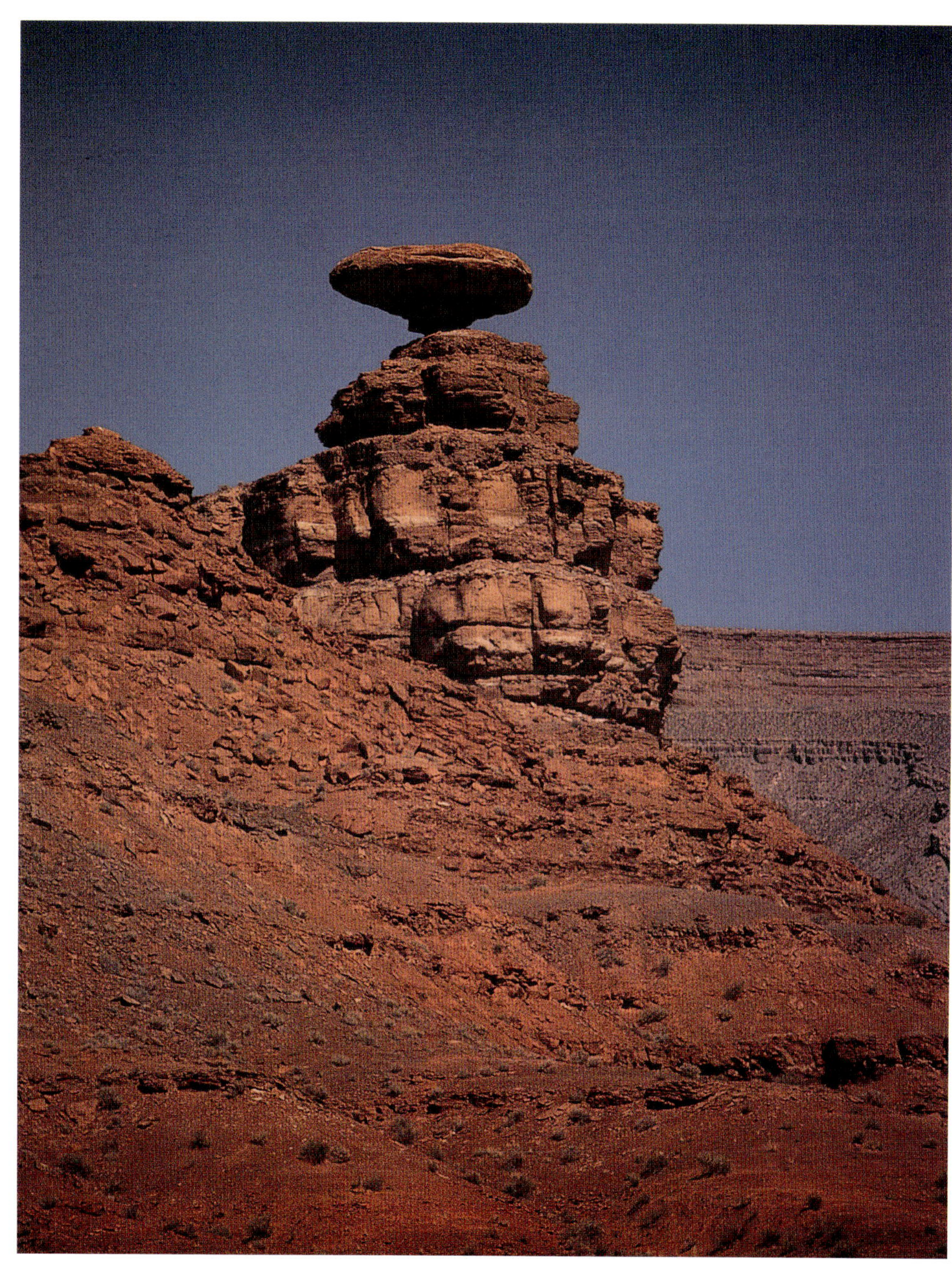

↑ Mexican Hat → Valley of the Gods ↓ Green River, Dinosaur National Monument

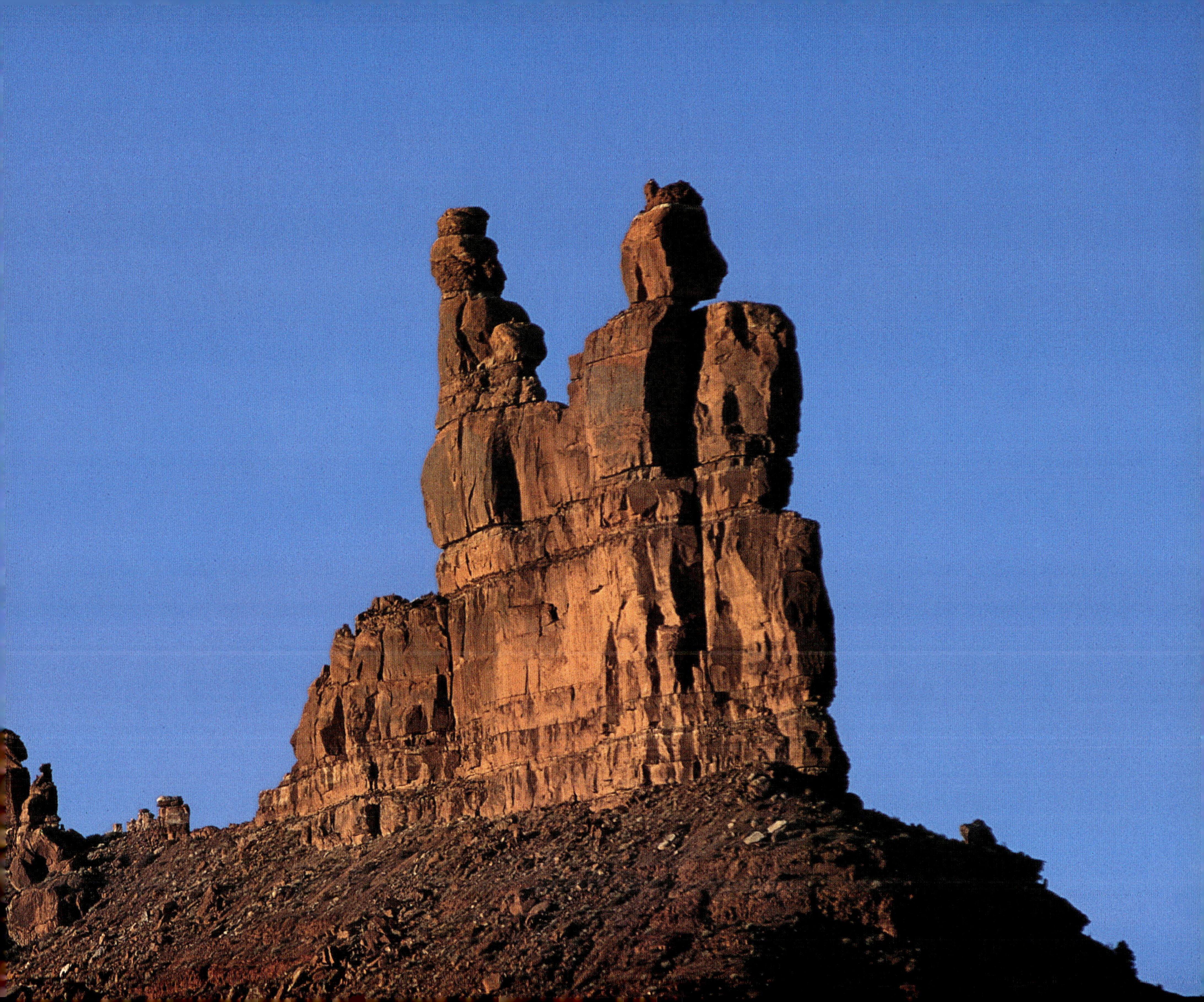

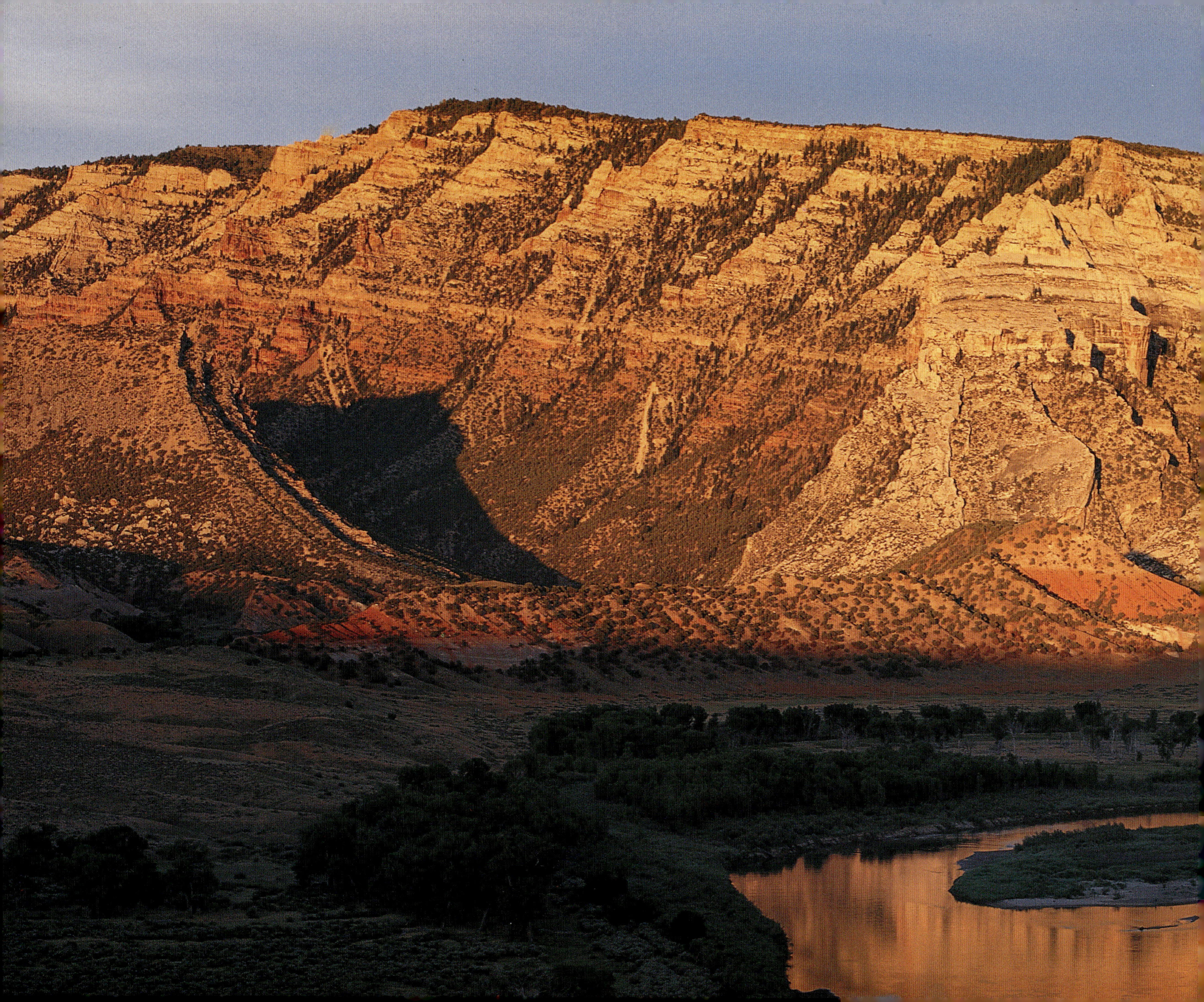

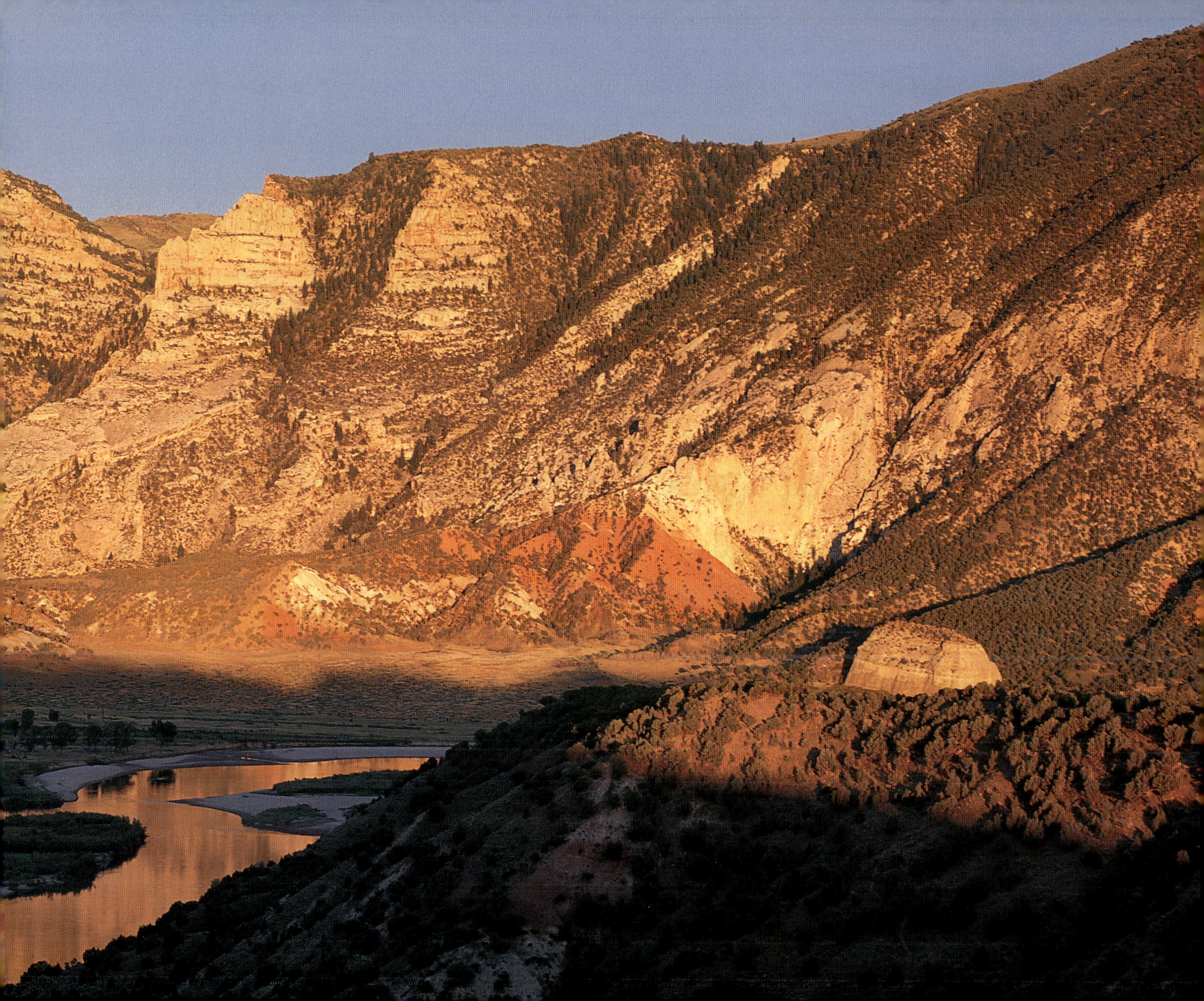

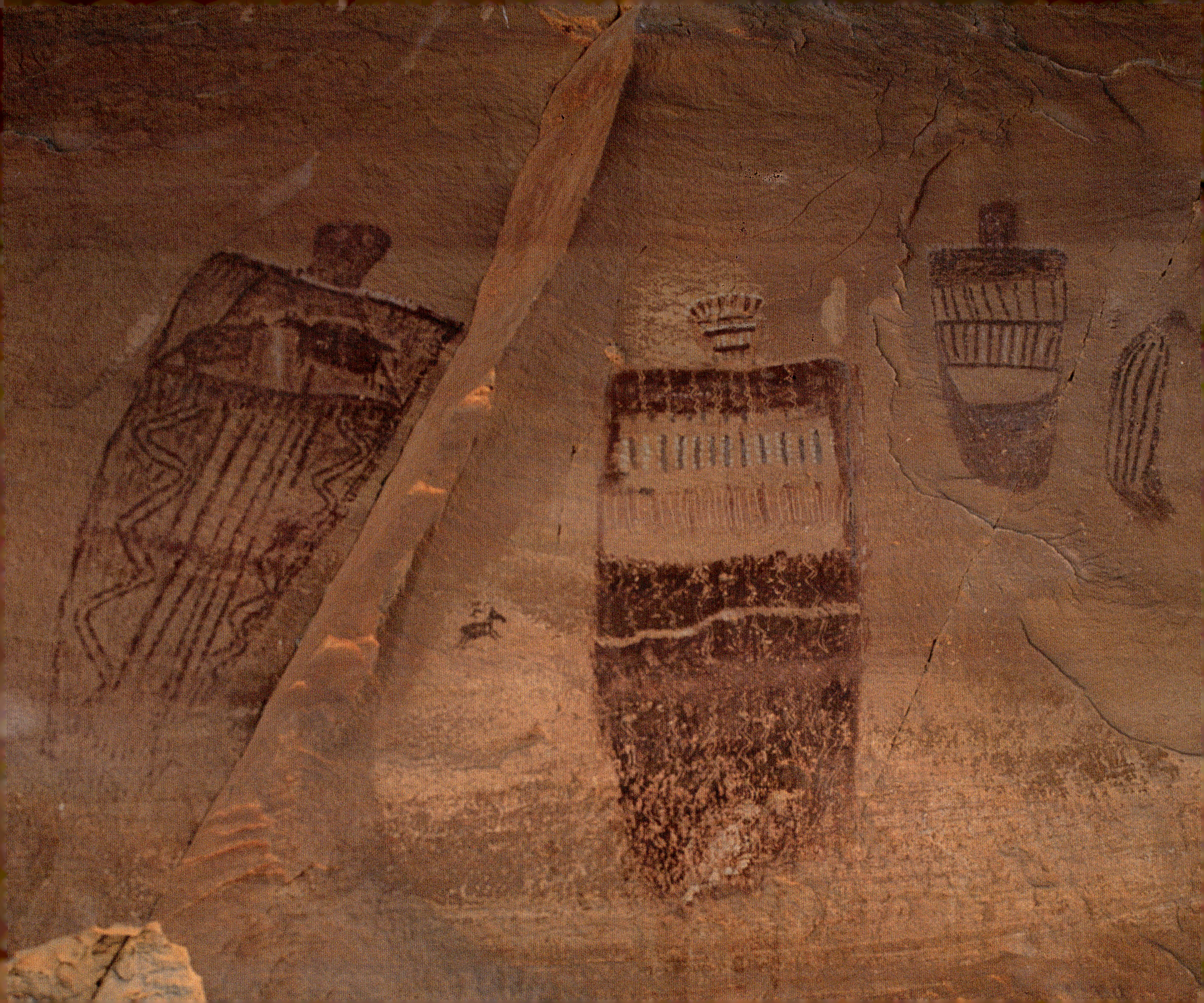

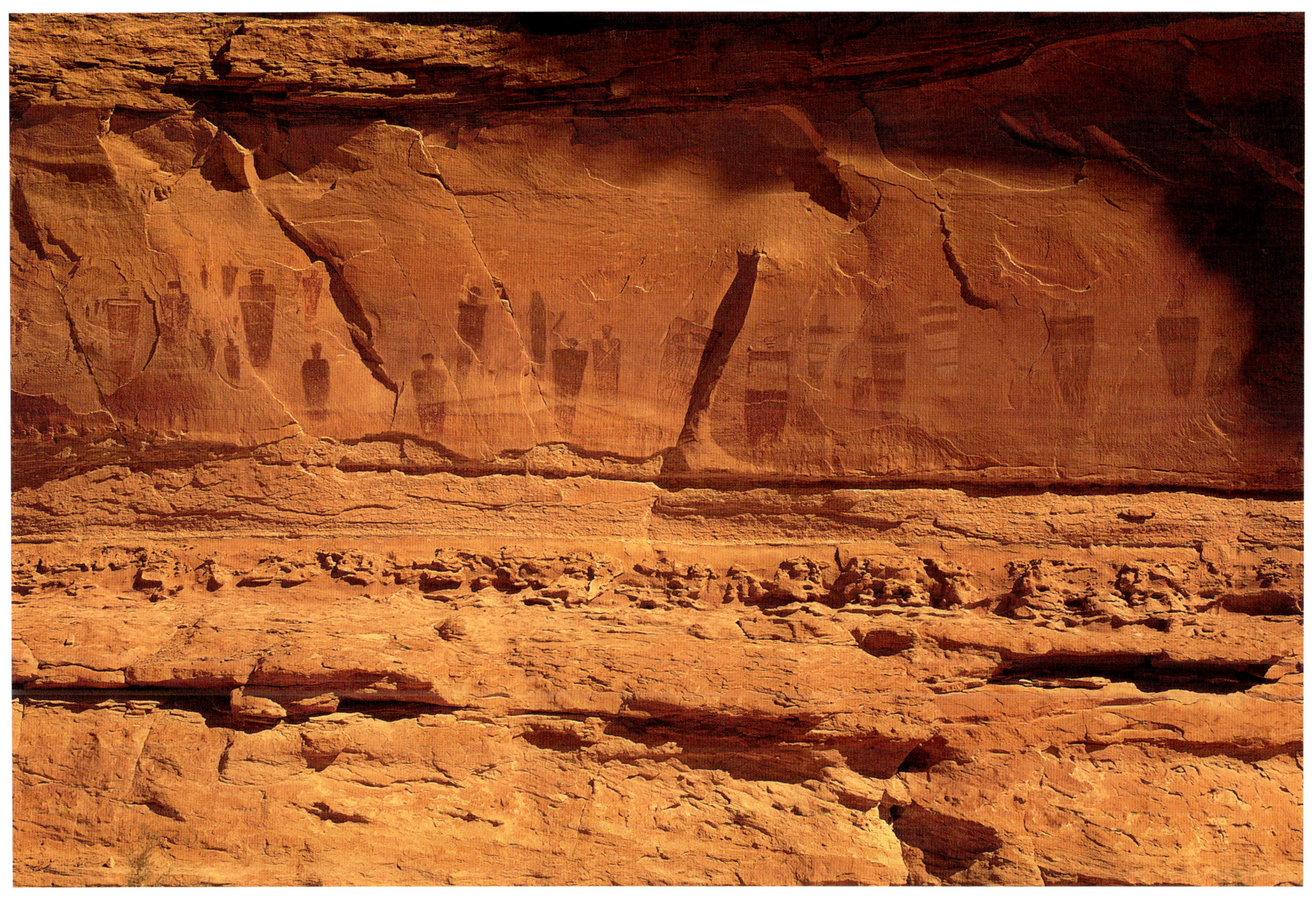

↑←Horseshoe Canyon, Canyonlands National Park

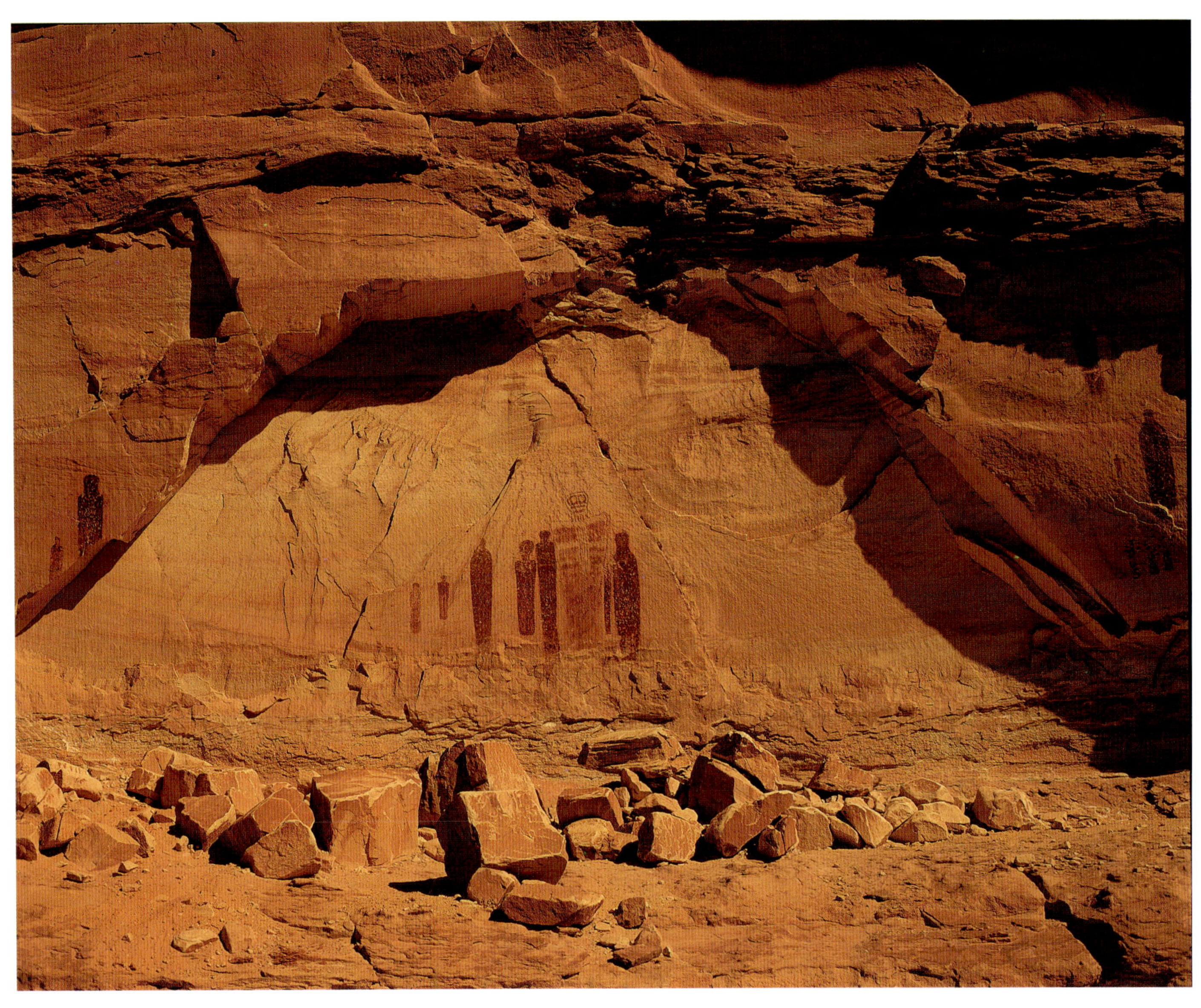

↱ Horseshoe Canyon, Canyonlands National Park

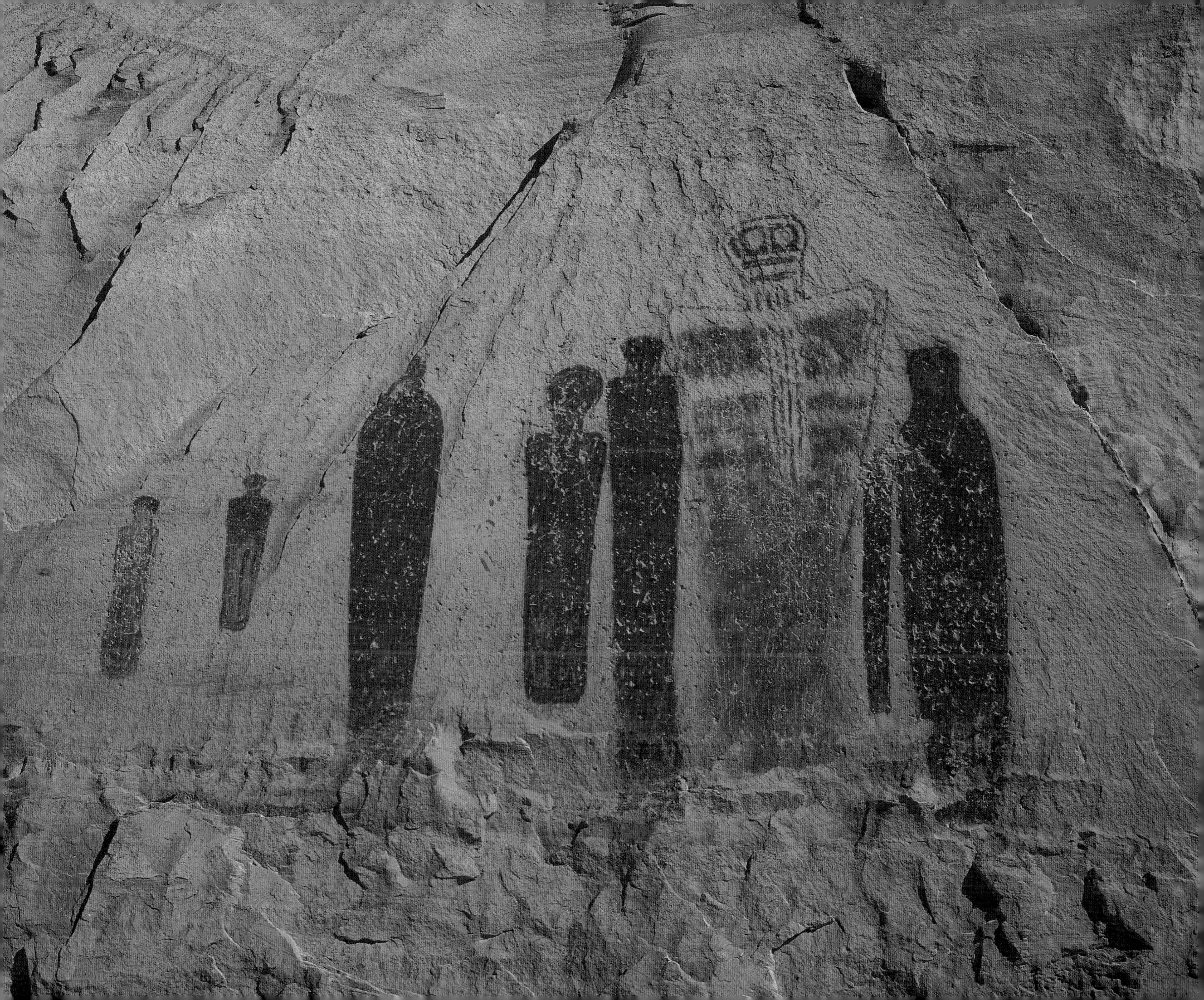

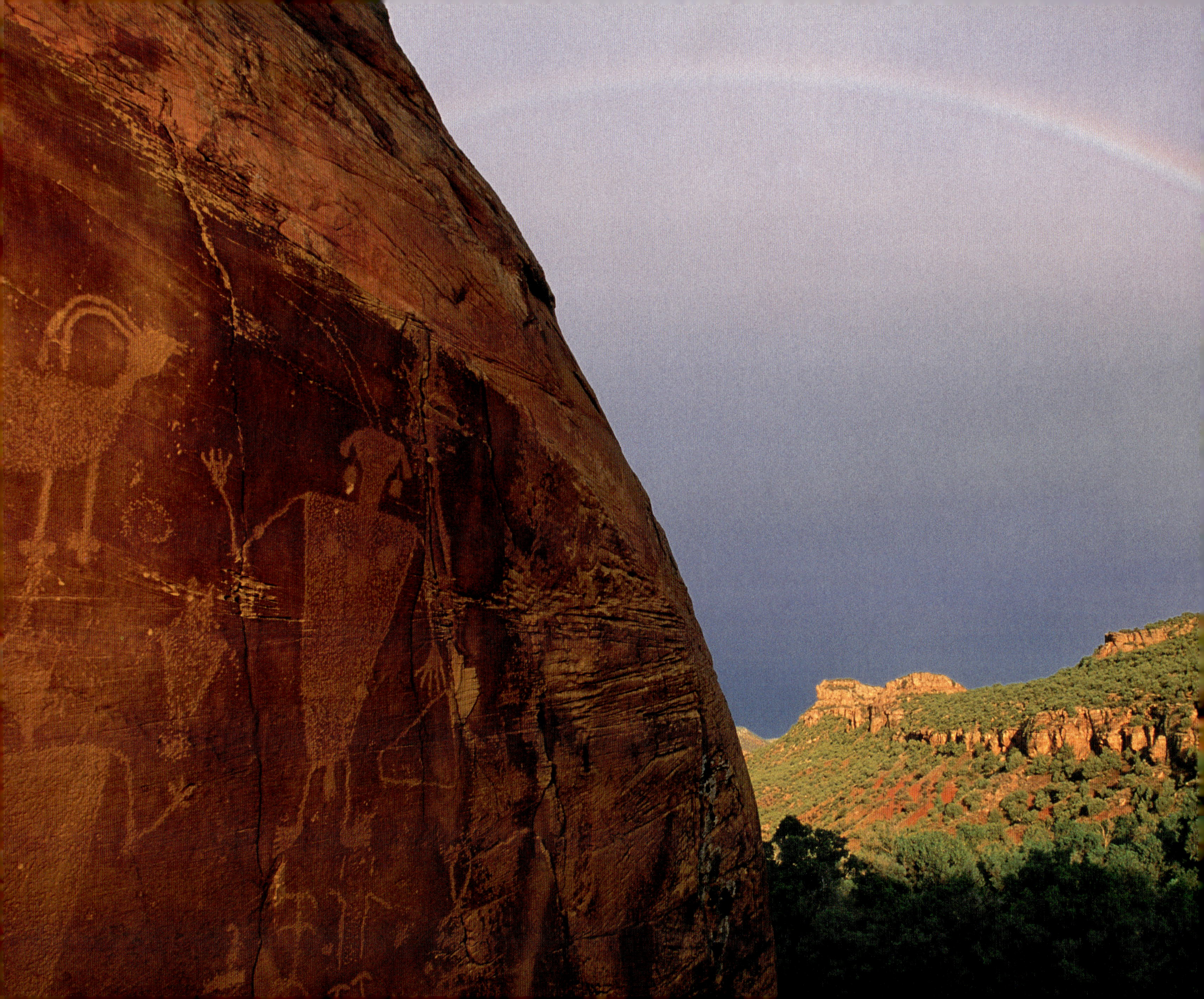

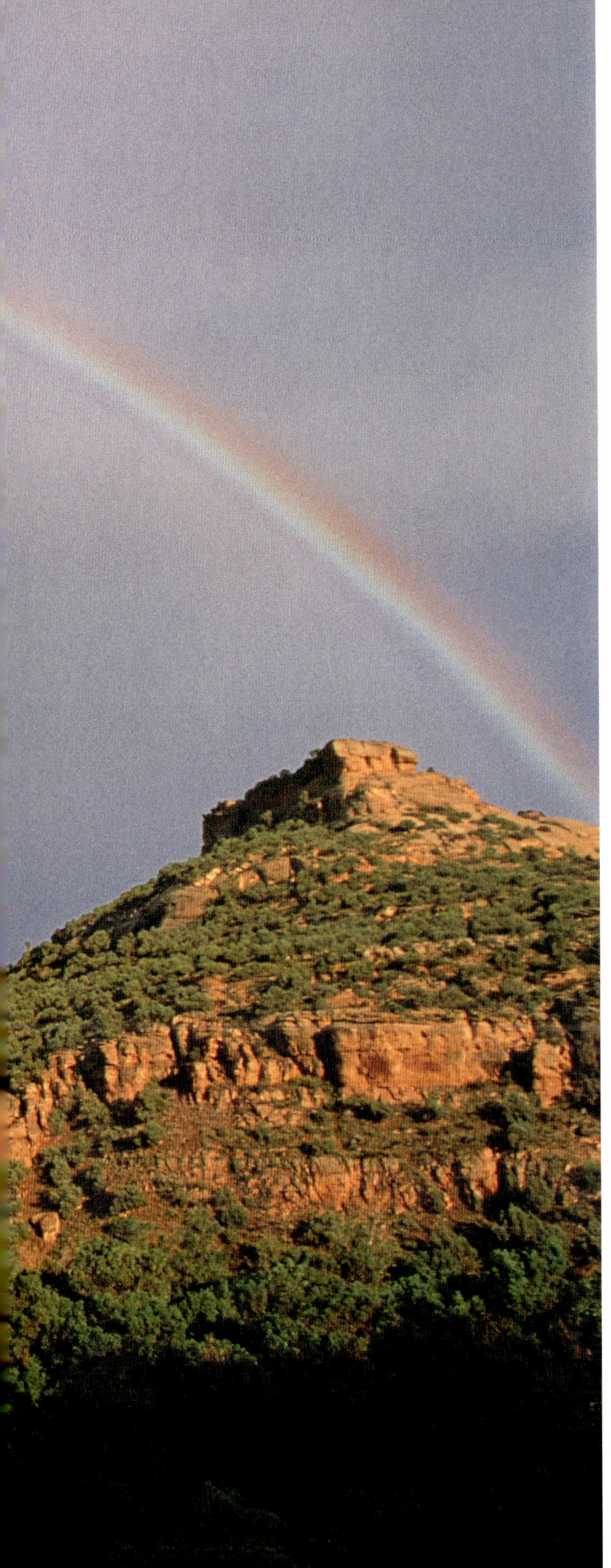

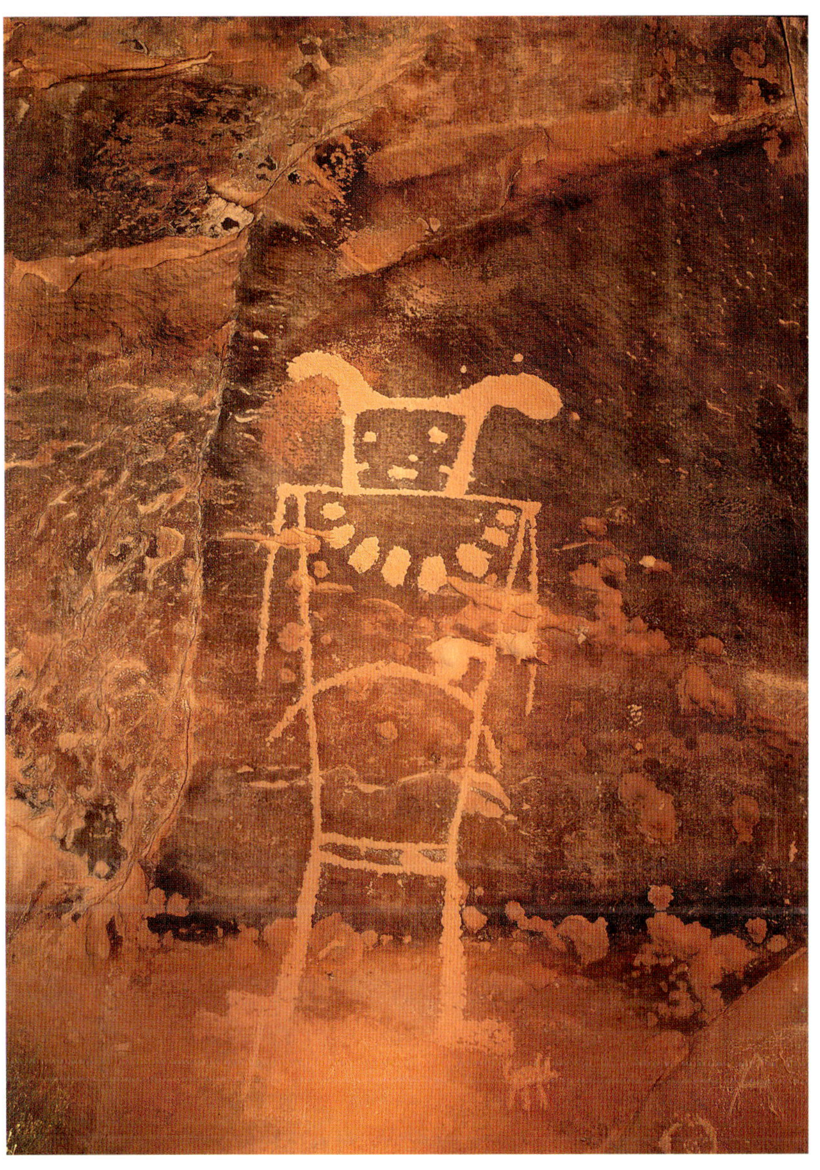

↑←Dinosaur National Monument

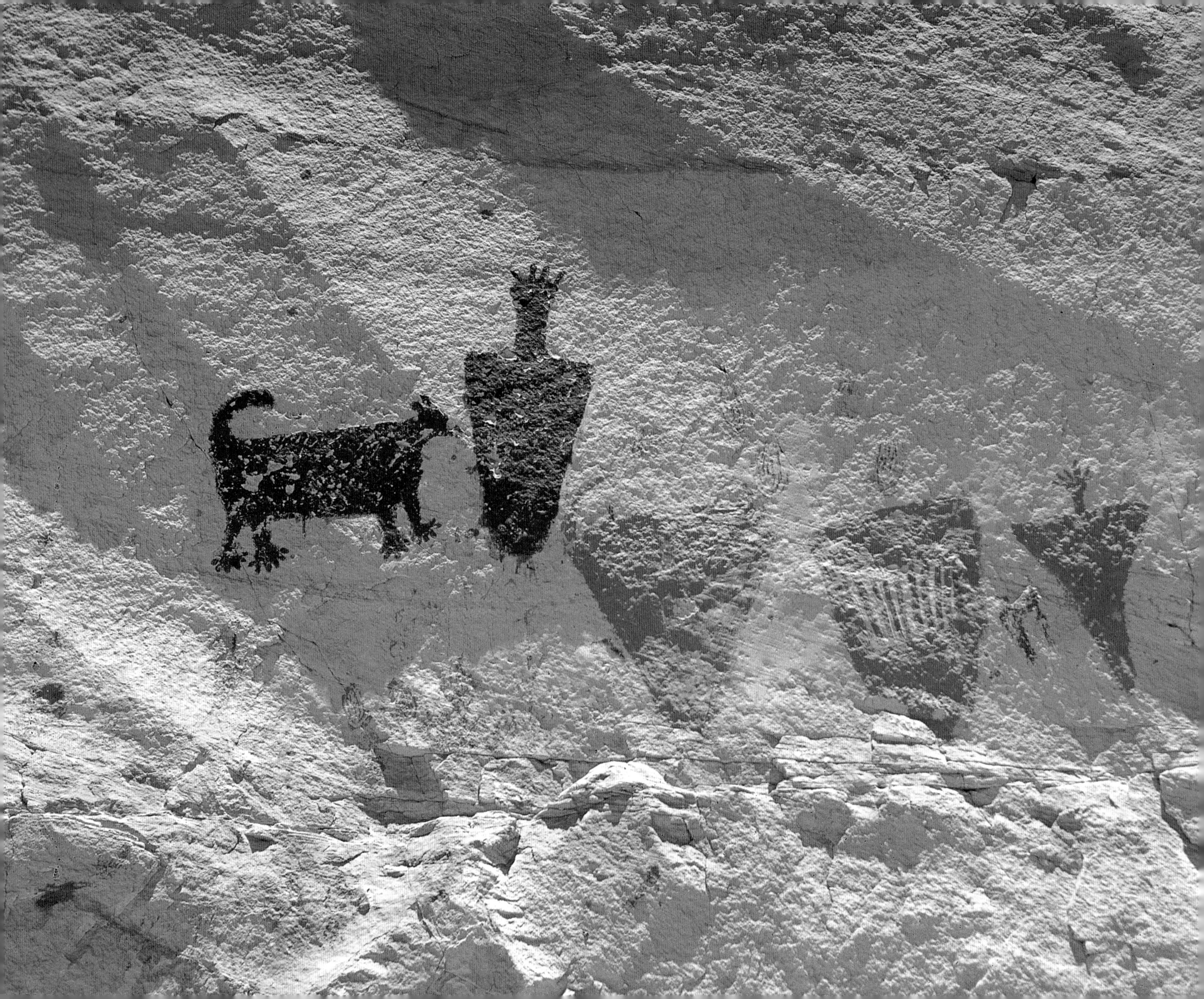

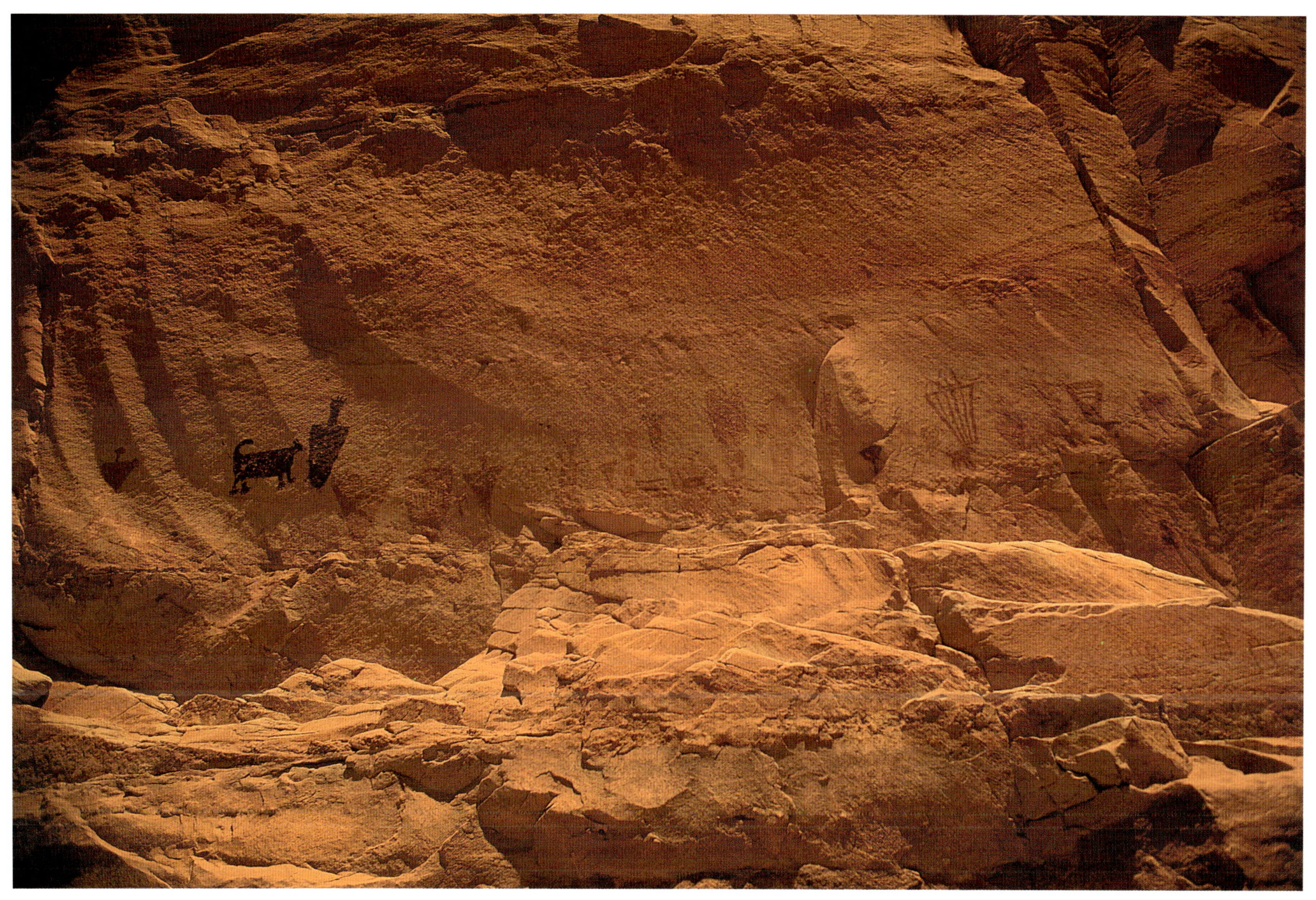

↑←Horseshoe Canyon, Canyonlands National Park

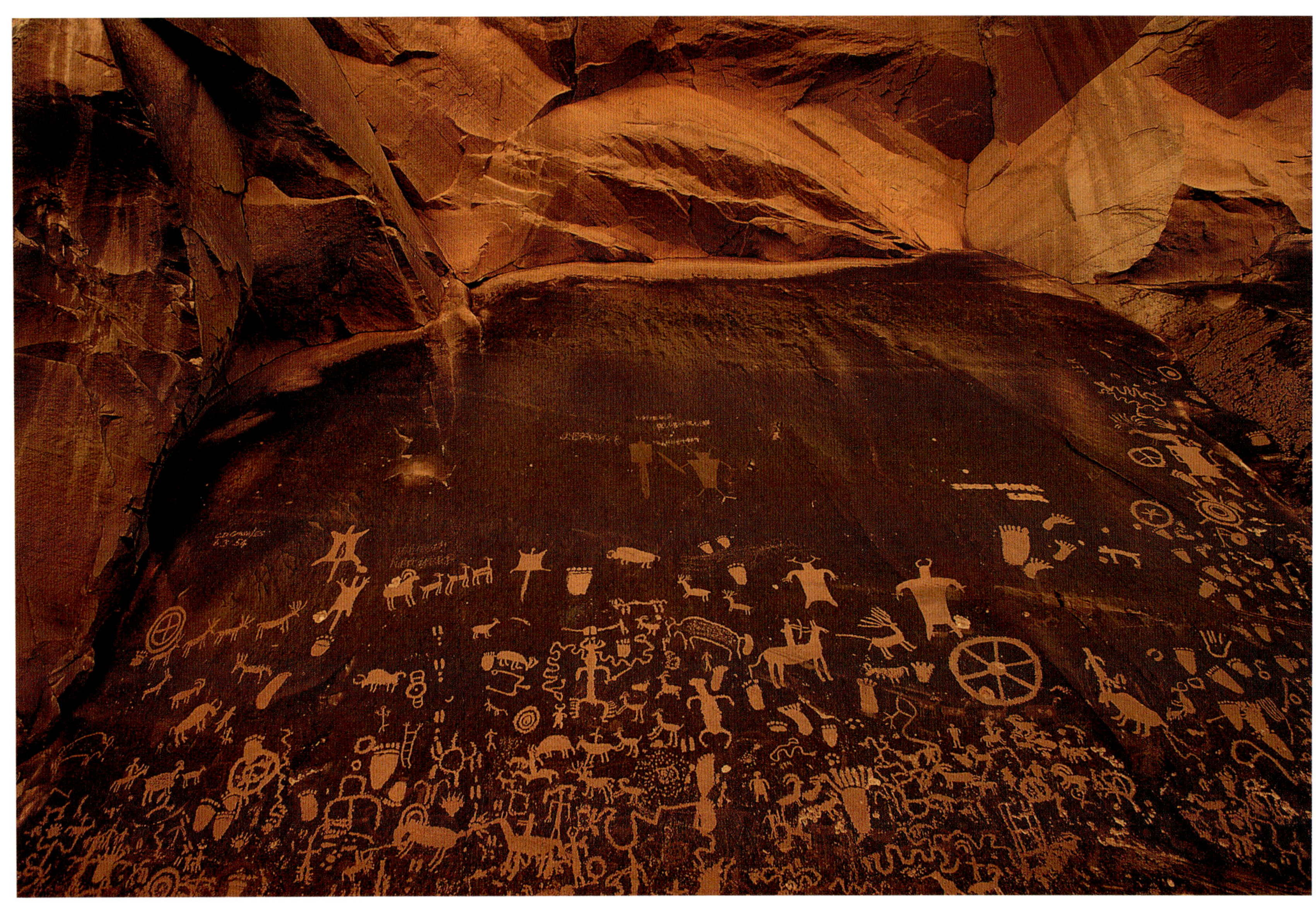

↑ Newspaper Rock State Historical Monument → Canyonlands National Park

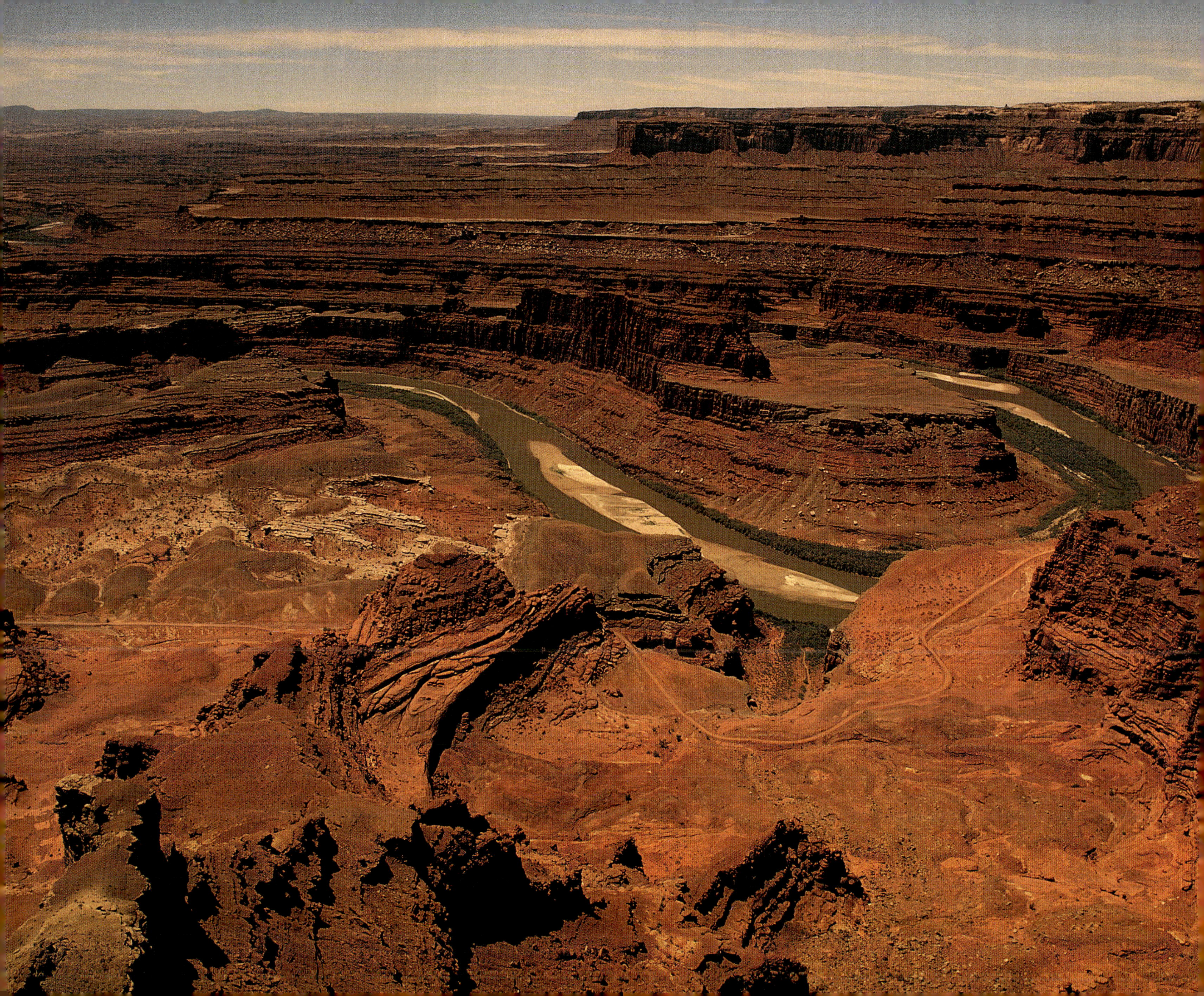

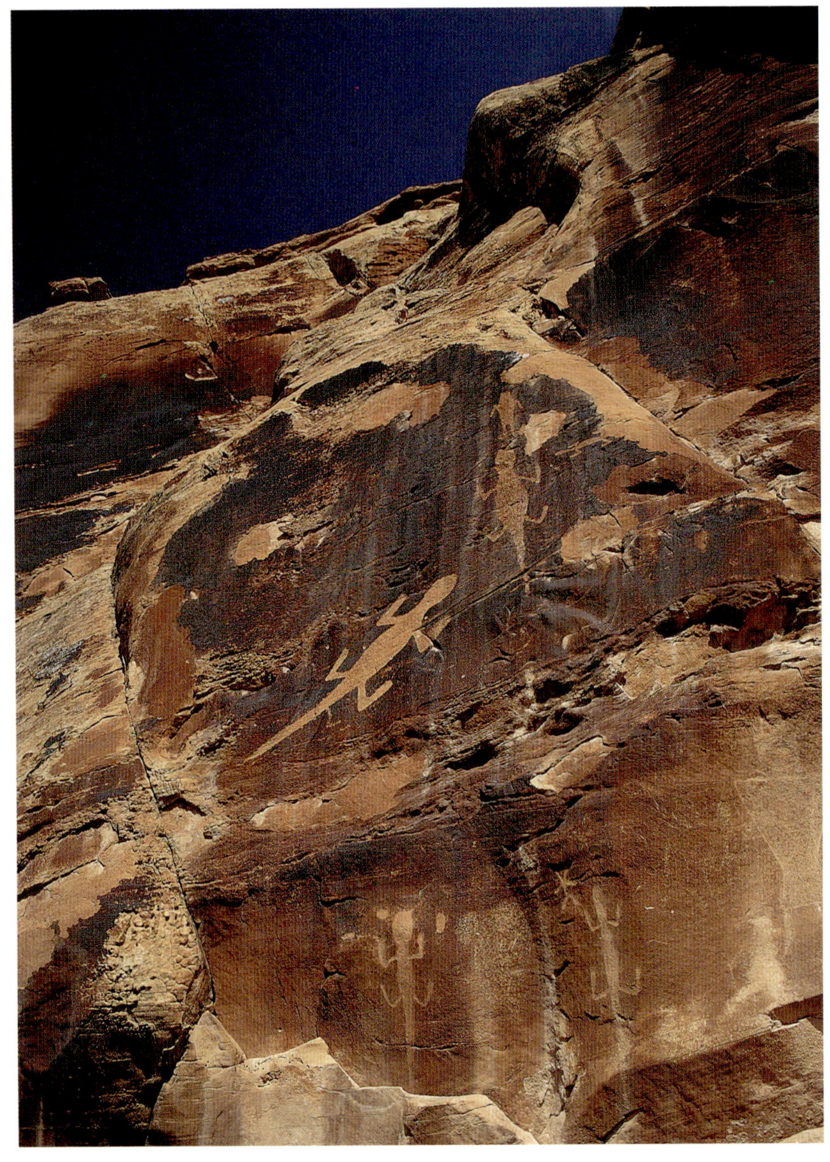

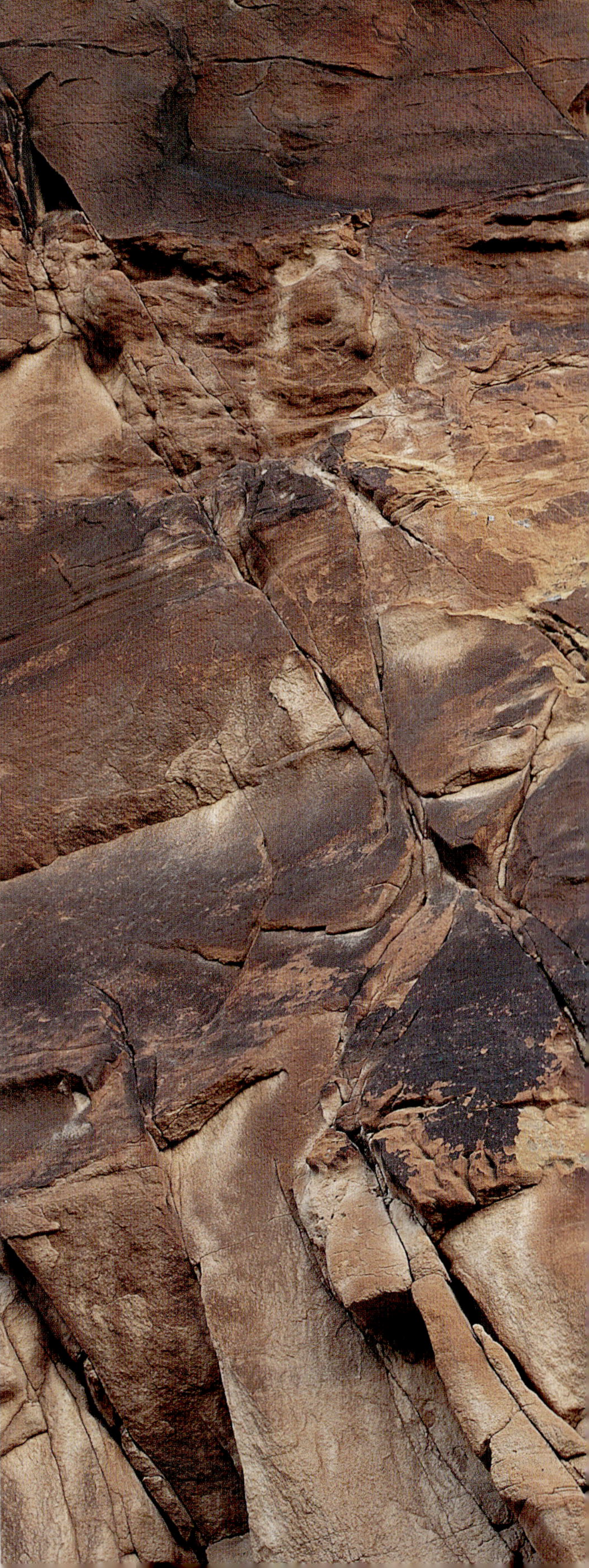

↬ Dinosaur National Monument

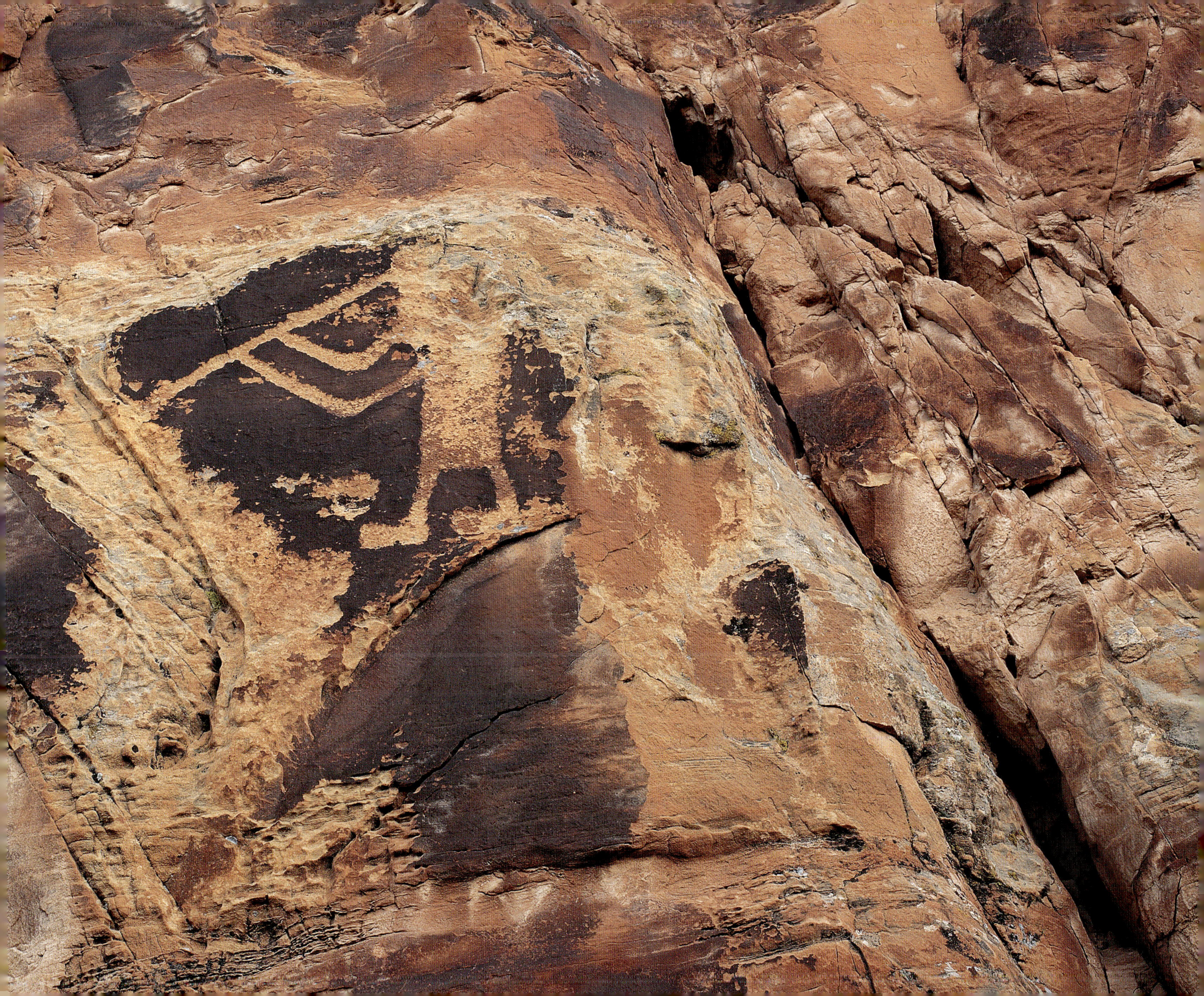

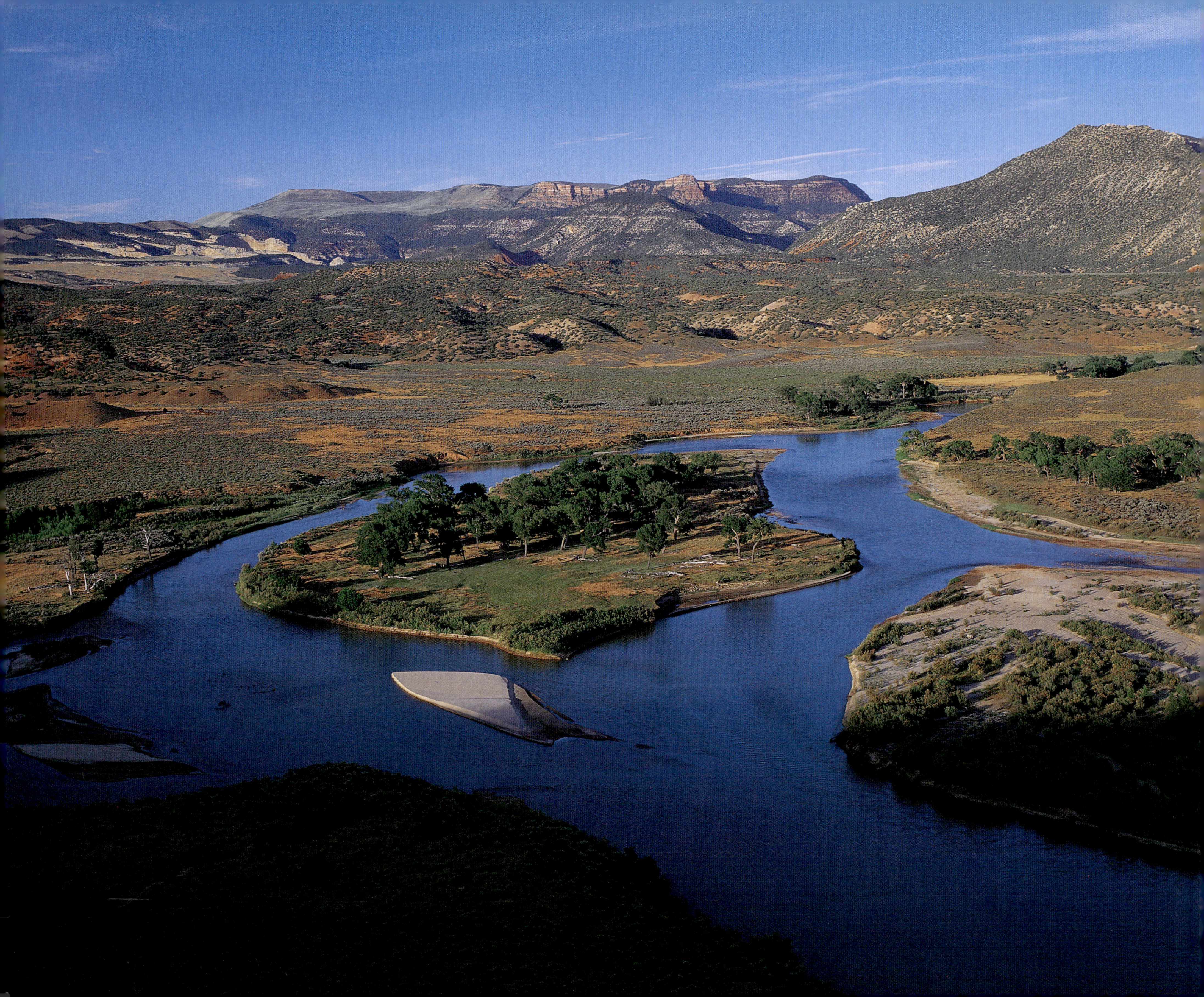

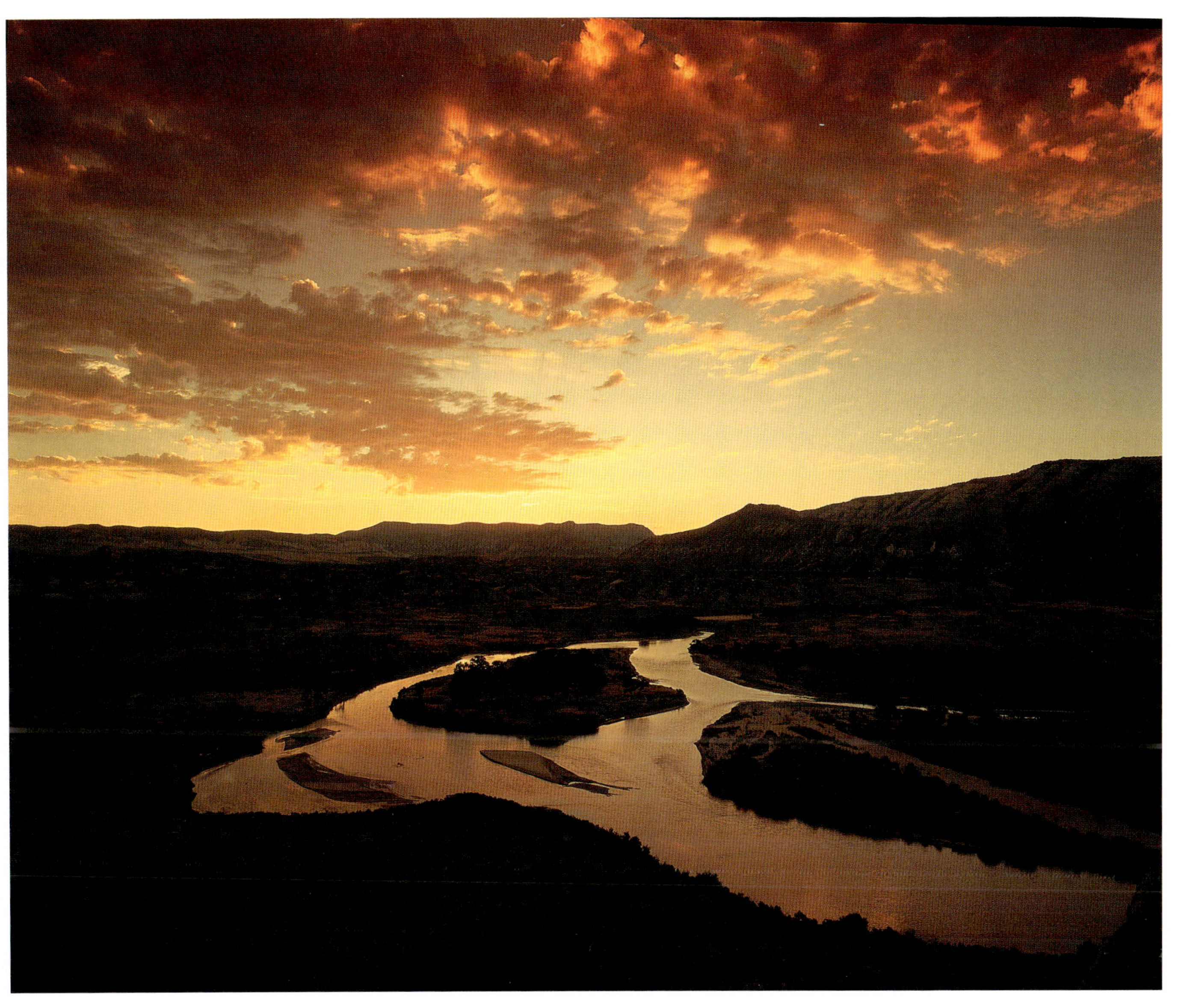

↑← Green River, Dinosaur National Monument

To my daughter Chloe with great affection and love.
I never realized how quickly you would grow.
You are precious to me.

I would like to thank the following people and institutions for their kindness and assistance in helping to make this book possible:
Gil and Tama Alfring, Steve Dailey, Alice Friedman, Jim Good, Joseph Guglietti, Havasupai Tribe, Jill and Das Markus, Gianfranco Monacelli, National Park Service. Navajo Nation, Grant Parish, Jonathan Pite, Janina and Julius Rajs, Jules Solo, Mark Speed, Hampton Sides, Catrine Turillon, Frances, Tim, Benjamin and Guiliana Wagner, Jimmy Winstead, Elizabeth White.

And to my wonderful family:
Amy, Chloe, Jack, Olivia, Sean, and Grace.